OXFORD MATHEMATICS

INTERMEDIATE
GCSE

D1347929

Authors

Sue Briggs

Peter McGuire

Derek Philpott

Susan Shilton

Ken Smith

Course Editors

Peter McGuire

Ken Smith

Oxford University Press

Acknowledgements

The publisher and authors are grateful to the following for permission to reproduce material.

Illustrators Gecko, Oxford Illustrators

Photographers Mike Dudley, Martin Sookias, Andrew Ward

Photographic Libraries Ancient Art & Architecture Collection Ltd, Architectural Association, Mary Evans Picture Library, The Science Photographic Library (cover)

Suppliers Cornish Seal Sanctuary, Eurostar

Every reasonable effort has been made to contact copyright owners, but we apologise for any unknown errors or omissions.

Oxford University Press, Great Clarendon Street, Oxford OX2 6DP

Oxford New York
Athens Auckland Bangkok Bogota Bombay
Buenos Aires Calcutta Cape Town Dar es Salaam
Delhi Florence Hong Kong Istanbul Karachi
Kuala Lumpur Madras Madrid Melbourne
Mexico City Nairobi Paris Singapore
Taipei Tokyo Toronto Warsaw

and associated companies in
Berlin Ibadan

Oxford is a trade mark of Oxford University Press

© Oxford University Press 1997

First published 1997

ISBN 0 19 914694 2

Printed in Spain by Graficas Estella S.A.

About this book

This book is designed to help you understand and learn the mathematics needed for GCSE. You will also be able to use the book for pre-examination revision, and practice of skills and techniques. Colour is used to help with the organisation of the different parts of the book. In this book you will find:

Contents This includes a listing of the mathematics in each of the 24 Sections.

Wordfinder This lists alphabetically, words and mathematical terms that will enable you to refer to specific aspects of mathematics quickly and easily. The colours will help you to decide whether you want to refer to:
- Starting points
- Section
- In Focus
- Exam-style questions

Starting points This introduces the mathematics you need to be familiar with, before starting on a particular section. There are some questions for you to try out so that you can test what you know already. See page 158 as an example of Starting points.

If you are confident about your grasp of the starting points, you should be able to begin work on the mathematics in the section.

Sections As you work through each section you will find information in yellow panels. In these panels are:
- explanations of new mathematical ideas, skills and procedures
- worked examples on specific aspects of the mathematics
- methods to help you to use and apply your mathematics

There are many questions for you to answer to consolidate your learning. More difficult questions are numbered in blue – for example, on page 194:

5 Which of these expressions is equivalent to $12a^2 + 5ab - 2b^2$?

You will also see that blue text is used at times to stress important points. For example, on page 104: The number 0.00403 has the digits 4 and 0 emphasised.

Within a section the margins of a page give you additional information such as the definitions of mathematical terms.

Words in the margin that link with the main text are coloured red. For example, on page 261: regular tetrahedron links the definition in the margin and its reference in the main text.

Thinking ahead This provides an opportunity to try out some questions and discuss ideas that will be introduced in the next subsection.

End points This is where the work of the section is listed for you. It is one way to check that you have understood the mathematical ideas, skills and techniques which have been taught in that section. See page 170 as an example of End points.

Skills breaks These provide a variety of questions all linked to the same data. They are one way to revise the mathematics you have learned and already know. You will have to decide on the mathematical skills and techniques you need to answer each of the questions.

In focus pages Each In focus page offers a set of questions for you to practice and revise individual mathematical skills and techniques.

Exam-style questions These questions will allow you to become familiar with the style and difficulty you can expect at the Intermediate level of entry.

Answers You will find the numerical answers to questions at the end of the book.

This is more than just a book of questions: it is a learning package that will help you to make the most of your mathematical talents and expertise. You can be confident that you will be well prepared for your GCSE examination.

Ⓧ CONTENTS

A note on accuracy

Make sure your answer is given to any degree of accuracy stated in the question, for example 2 dp or 1 sf. Where it is not stated, choose a sensible degree of accuracy for your answer, and make sure you work to a greater degree of accuracy through the problem. For example, if you choose to give an answer to 3 sf, work to at least 4 sf through the problem, then round your final answer to 3 sf.

Examination groups differ in their approach to accuracy. Some say that you should not give your final answer to a greater degree of accuracy than that used for the data in the question, but others state answers should be given to 3 sf.

If you are in any doubt, check with your examination group.

Metric and imperial units

	Metric	**Imperial**	**Some approximate conversions**
Length	millimetres (mm) centimetres (cm) metres (m) kilometres (km) 1 cm = 10 mm 1 m = 100 cm 1 km = 1000 m	inches (in) feet (ft) yards (yd) miles 1 ft = 12 in 1 yd = 3 ft 1 mile = 1760 yd	1 inch = 2.54 cm 1 foot ≈ 30.5 cm 1 metre ≈ 39.4 in 1 mile ≈ 1.61 km
Mass	grams (g) kilograms (kg) tonnes 1 kg = 1000 g 1 tonne = 1000 kg	ounces (oz) pounds (lb) stones 1 lb = 16 oz 1 stone = 14 lb	1 pound ≈ 454 g 1 kilogram ≈ 2.2 lb
Capacity	millilitres (ml) centilitres (cl) litres 1 cl = 10 ml 1 litre = 100 cl = 1000 ml	pints (pt) gallons 1 gallon = 8 pt	1 gallon ≈ 4.55 litres 1 litre ≈ 1.76 pints ≈ 0.22 gallons

		Starting points	Section	Focus	Exam-style
Accuracy and limits			109, 204	311	331
Angles	between lines	33	36	306	357
	elevation and depression		295	327	368
	in polygons		42	306	356
	in triangles	33	35	306	356
Area	composite shapes	72	76	309	360
	quadrilaterals	71, 259	73	309	360
	triangles	71, 259		309	360
Averages		59			381, 383, 384
Bar chart (including comparative and split-bar chart)		58, 60			377, 384
Bar-line graph		58			384
Bearings		291	296	327	365, 369
Bisecting (angles and lines)			135	314	
Box-and-whisker plot			69	308	
Brackets		86, 120, 270	31, 88, 123, 193	305, 313	350
Capacity			262, 266	324	361
Circle	area and circumference	71, 259	79	309	360
	parts and properties	131	79, 137, 140		358
Class and class interval		198			382, 385
Collecting like terms		86, 120, 186	87, 126	310, 313	
Compound measures			169	316	330
Congruent		131, 221			372
Construction	triangles		133	314	364
	perpendiculars		136	314	
Coordinates (including 3–D)		45, 220			359
Conversion graph		158			
Correlation			286	326	378
Cube numbers and cube root			13	304	332
Cubic equation			278	325	345
Cumulative frequency		197	66, 205	308, 319	383
Data collection		282	285	326	375
Decimal places (dp)		100		311	331
Decimals	adding and subtracting	100			333
Density (including population density)			105, 266		
Dimensions in formulas			268	324	362
Distance			160	316	339
Enlargement		144, 221	149, 229	315, 321	371
Equations	forming	186	88, 98, 125	310	342
	linear	86, 120, 186	51, 88, 224	307, 310	342
	quadratic		271	325	345
Errors in calculations			109		
Estimation and approximation			101	311	331, 336
Expressions	forming		88, 122	310, 313	342, 353
Exterior angles			42	306	357
Factor		10	128		332
Factorising		270	127, 195, 271	313, 318, 325	350
Fibonacci sequence		21, 143	148		
Flow chart		186	187		351
Formulas (including rearranging)		186	187, 268	318	341, 350, 352
Fractions		11, 111, 209	18	304	333
Frequency	diagram	58, 198			384
	distribution	197	62, 199	308, 319	381
	polygon		199	319	378
	table	58	62		382
Gradient			47	307	346
Graphs	distance–time (travel)		162	316	339
	linear (straight-line)	86, 220		307, 310	346
	quadratic		273	325	346
Highest common factor			19	304	
Histogram			199	319	
Hypothesis testing		282	203, 285	326	375, 383
Indices (including rules)		10, 120	15, 17	304, 313	336
Inequalities (including regions)		248	249	323	349
Interest	simple and compound		215	320	335
Interior angles		34	38	306	356
Interquartile range		198	65, 206	308, 319	383
Line graph		60			

Starting points

You need to know about ...

... so try these questions.

A Negative numbers

... ⁻5 ⁻4 ⁻3 ⁻2 ⁻1 0 1 2 3 4 5 6 ...

Negative   Positive

- ◆ To **add** a negative number:
  - ❖ subtract the corresponding positive number.

$7 + {}^-4$	$2 + {}^-5$	${}^-4 + {}^-3$
$= 7 - 4$	$= 2 - 5$	$= {}^-4 - 3$
$= 3$	$= {}^-3$	$= {}^-7$

- ◆ To **subtract** a negative number:
  - ❖ add the corresponding positive number.

$7 - {}^-4$	$2 - {}^-5$	${}^-4 - {}^-3$
$= 7 + 4$	$= 2 + 5$	$= {}^-4 + 3$
$= 11$	$= 7$	$= {}^-1$

A1 Calculate these missing numbers.
- **a** $1 + {}^-3 = \square$ **b** ${}^-5 + {}^-2 = \square$
- **c** $9 + {}^-5 = \square$ **d** $4 - 6 = \square$
- **e** ${}^-7 - {}^-3 = \square$ **f** ${}^-2 - {}^-7 = \square$

A2 Calculate these missing numbers.
- **a** $3 + {}^-5 = \square$ **b** ${}^-5 + 3 = \square$
- **c** $7 - {}^-2 = \square$ **d** ${}^-2 - 7 = \square$
- **e** $6 + \square = 3$ **f** $7 - \square = 5$
- **g** ${}^-3 - \square = 1$ **h** ${}^-4 + \square = {}^-9$
- **i** ${}^-5 + \square = {}^-1$ **j** ${}^-6 - \square = 0$

B Multiples, factors and primes

- ◆ The **multiples** of a number can be divided by the number without leaving a remainder.
- ◆ The **common multiples** of two numbers are numbers that are multiples of both the numbers.

Multiples of 4:
4, 8, 12, 16, 20, 24, 28, 32, ...
Multiples of 6:
6, 12, 18, 24, 30, 36, 42, ...
Common multiples of 4 and 6:
12, 24, 36, ...

- ◆ The **factors** of a number are whole numbers that divide into it without leaving a remainder.
- ◆ The **common factors** of two numbers are numbers that are factors of both the numbers.

Factors of 18:
1, 2, 3, 6, 9, 18
Factors of 42:
1, 2, 3, 6, 7, 14, 21, 42
Common factors of 18 and 42:
1, 2, 3, 6

- ◆ A number is **prime** if it has only two different factors.

5 is a prime number:
it has factors
1 and 5.

9 is not prime:
it has factors
1, 3 and 9.

B1 Give seven multiples of:
- **a** 5   **b** 8   **c** 12

B2 Give three common multiples of:
- **a** 5 and 8   **b** 8 and 12

B3 Give all the factors of:
- **a** 24   **b** 30
- **c** 25   **d** 17

B4 Give the common factors of:
- **a** 24 and 30   **b** 25 and 30

B5 Explain why 1 is not prime.

B6 Give all the prime numbers less than 20.

C Writing powers using index notation

$3 \times 3 \times 3 \times 3 = 3^4$
$1.6 \times 1.6 = 1.6^2$

4 is the **index**.
4 and 2 are **indices**.

We say 3^4 is:
3 **to the power** 4, or
3 **raised to the power** 4.

C1 Write in index notation:
- **a** 5×5 **b** $2 \times 2 \times 2 \times 2 \times 2$

C2 Evaluate:
- **a** 4^3 **b** 3^4 **c** 1.5^2 **d** 1.1^5

D Writing a number as a product of primes

- ◆ The factors of a number which are prime are called **prime factors**.
- ◆ A multiplication of prime factors is called a **product of primes**.
- ◆ To write a number as a product of primes:
  - ❖ break the number down into pairs of factors until all the factors are prime
  - ❖ use index notation to write the powers of each prime.

126
2 × 63
2 × 9 × 7
2 × 3 × 3 × 7
$2 \times 3^2 \times 7$

180
10 × 18
2 × 5 × 3 × 6
2 × 5 × 3 × 2 × 3
2 × 2 × 3 × 3 × 5
$2^2 \times 3^2 \times 5$

D1 Give the prime factors of:
- **a** 84   **b** 154

D2 Write these as a product of primes.
- **a** 120   **b** 350

E Types of fraction

◆ There are several ways to think of a fraction such as $\frac{3}{5}$.

This shows that **multiplying by $\frac{1}{5}$** has the same effect as **dividing by 5.**

$\frac{3}{5}$

$3 \times \frac{1}{5}$

$3 \div 5$

◆ An **improper fraction** is one where the numerator is larger than the denominator.

$\frac{9}{7}$

◆ An improper fraction is greater than 1, so it can be written as a **mixed number**.

$\frac{9}{7} = \frac{7}{7} + \frac{2}{7} = 1\frac{2}{7}$

◆ A **whole number** can be written as an improper fraction.

$3 = \frac{3}{1}$

F Equivalent fractions

◆ To write an equivalent fraction:
  ❖ multiply or divide the numerator or denominator by the same number.

$\overset{\times 5}{\frac{3}{4}} = \underset{\times 5}{\frac{15}{20}}$ $\overset{\div 3}{\frac{27}{42}} = \underset{\div 3}{\frac{9}{14}}$

G Writing fractions as decimals

◆ To write a fraction as a decimal:
  ❖ divide the numerator by the denominator.

$\frac{3}{8} = 3 \div 8 = 0.375$

Some fractions give **recurring decimals**.

$\frac{2}{3} = 0.\dot{6}$ $\frac{5}{6} = 0.8\dot{3}$ $\frac{59}{270} = 0.2\dot{1}8\dot{5}$

H Calculating with fractions

◆ Multiplying by a fraction less than 1 gives a smaller amount.

◆ To calculate a fraction of an amount: either
  ❖ divide the amount by the denominator and multiply by the numerator
  or
  ❖ write the fraction as a decimal and multiply by the amount.

$\frac{3}{8}$ of **£1760**

$1760 \div 8 \times 3 = £660$

$0.375 \times 1760 = £660$

◆ Dividing by a fraction less than 1 gives a larger amount.

$6 \div \frac{2}{3} = 9$

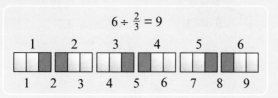

E1 Draw a diagram to show that $\frac{2}{3}$ is the same as $2 \times \frac{1}{3}$ and $2 \div 3$.

E2 Write as a mixed number:
a $\frac{4}{3}$ **b** $\frac{13}{6}$ **c** $\frac{23}{4}$

E3 Write as an improper fraction:
a $1\frac{2}{5}$ **b** $3\frac{1}{3}$ **c** 5
d $2\frac{11}{13}$ **e** 11

F1 Write three equivalent fractions for:
a $\frac{2}{5}$ **b** $\frac{4}{12}$ **c** $\frac{20}{30}$

G1 Write these fractions as decimals.
a $\frac{7}{16}$ **b** $\frac{5}{9}$
c $\frac{7}{11}$ **d** $\frac{23}{54}$

H1 Calculate:
a $\frac{5}{8}$ of £1760
b $\frac{2}{7}$ of 322 litres
c $\frac{9}{14}$ of 175 m

H2 Draw a diagram to show that $6 \div \frac{3}{4} = 8$

Multiplying and dividing negative numbers

♦ Multiplying or dividing numbers give either a negative or a positive answer.

Negative answer	Positive answer
Positive × Negative	Positive × Positive
Negative × Positive	Negative × Negative
Positive ÷ Negative	Positive ÷ Positive
Negative ÷ Positive	Negative ÷ Negative

Exercise 1.1
Multiplying and dividing negative numbers

Do not use a calculator for Exercise 1.1.

1 Which of these calculations give a negative answer?

$$\boxed{A\ \ 4 \times {}^-5} \quad \boxed{B\ \ {}^-2.5 \times 6} \quad \boxed{C\ \ {}^-3 \div {}^-2.8} \quad \boxed{D\ \ {}^-7.1 \div 4.6} \quad \boxed{E\ \ {}^-6.9 \times {}^-5}$$

$$\boxed{F\ \ {}^-3.7 \times 4.2} \quad \boxed{G\ \ {}^-3 \div {}^-4} \quad \boxed{H\ \ 1.8 \times 6} \quad \boxed{I\ \ 6.2 \div {}^-3.9} \quad \boxed{J\ \ 12.5 \div 3}$$

2 Copy and complete these calculations.

a $3 \times {}^-5 = \square$ **b** ${}^-2 \times 6 = \square$ **c** $5 \times {}^-4 = \square$ **d** ${}^-3 \times {}^-6 = \square$

e ${}^-12 \div {}^-3 = \square$ **f** ${}^-8 \div 4 = \square$ **g** $24 \div {}^-6 = \square$ **h** ${}^-40 \div 5 = \square$

3 Copy and complete these calculations.

a $4 \times \square = {}^-28$ **b** ${}^-15 \div \square = 3$ **c** ${}^-4 \times \square = {}^-32$ **d** $\square \times {}^-6 = 18$

e $\square \div {}^-7 = 5$ **f** $\square \div {}^-6 = {}^-6$ **g** ${}^-3 \times \square = 36$ **h** $\square \div 7 = 2$

4 $\boxed{{}^-2.3 \times 4.1 = {}^-9.43} \quad \boxed{{}^-12.6 \div {}^-1.75 = 7.2}$

Use these two calculations to answer:

a 2.3×4.1 **b** ${}^-2.3 \times {}^-4.1$ **c** ${}^-4.1 \times 2.3$

d ${}^-12.6 \div 1.75$ **e** $12.6 \div 1.75$ **f** $12.6 \div {}^-1.75$

5 $\boxed{{}^-1.9 \times 7.4 \times {}^-5.8} \quad \boxed{3.4 \times 5.7 \times 1.2 \times {}^-5.3 \times {}^-2.6}$

Can you predict if these calculations have a negative or a positive answer? If so, explain how.

Squares and square roots

♦ To **square** a number is to multiply the number by itself.

$3 \times 3 = 9$	9 is the **square** of 3	$3^2 = 9$
3 rows of 3 dots gives 9 dots.	3 is a **square root** of 9	$\sqrt{9} = 3$

♦ You can also square negative numbers and decimal numbers.

${}^-3 \times {}^-3 = 9$	$2.7 \times 2.7 = 7.29$	${}^-2.7 \times {}^-2.7 = 7.29$
${}^-3^2 = 9$	$2.7^2 = 7.29$	${}^-2.7^2 = 7.29$
$\sqrt{9} = {}^-3$	$\sqrt{7.29} = 2.7$	$\sqrt{7.29} = {}^-2.7$
${}^-3$ is a square root of 9	2.7 is a square root of 7.29	${}^-2.7$ is a square root of 7.29

This type of curve is called a **parabola**.

♦ The square roots of 9 are **3** and **¯3**.

♦ The square roots of 7.29 are **2.7** and **¯2.7**.

♦ Each positive number has two square roots:
  ❖ a **positive** one
  ❖ a **negative** one.

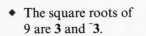

Square roots graph: numbers 0 to 100

The square roots of ¯45 are about **¯6.7** and **6.7**.

Exercise 1.2
Square roots

1　Draw the square roots graph above.

2　**a**　Explain how to use your graph to estimate the square roots of a number.
　　b　Use your graph to check the estimates of √45.

3　Use your graph to estimate the values of each of these square roots.
　　a　√30　　**b**　√74　　**c**　√12

Using the square root key on a calculator only gives the positive square root.

4　Use your calculator to find the values to 2 dp of each of these square roots.
　　a　√48　　**b**　√72　　**c**　√39.1　　**d**　√26.82　　**e**　√900
　　f　√0.01

Cubes and cube roots

♦ To **cube** a number is to multiply the number by itself twice.

The symbol for a cube root is $\sqrt[3]{}$.

$4 \times 4 \times 4 = 64$
4 layers of 4 rows of 4 cubes gives 64 cubes.

64 is the cube of 4
4 is the cube root of 64

$4^3 = 64$
$\sqrt[3]{64} = 4$

♦ You can also cube negative numbers and decimal numbers.

$¯4 \times ¯4 \times ¯4 = 64$
$¯4^3 = ¯64$
$\sqrt[3]{¯64} = ¯4$

$2.7 \times 2.7 \times 2.7 = 19.683$
$2.7^3 = 19.683$
$\sqrt[3]{19.683} = 2.7$

$¯2.7 \times ¯2.7 \times ¯2.7 = 19.683$
$¯2.7^3 = 19.683$
$\sqrt[3]{¯19.683} = ¯2.7$

♦ All numbers, positive and negative, have only one cube root.

Exercise 1.3
Cubes and cube roots

1　List the key presses on your calculator to find 6^3.

2　Find:
　　a　9^3　　**b**　30^3　　**c**　3.5^3　　**d**　$¯9^3$　　**e**　$¯1.1^3$　　**f**　0.4^3

3　List the key presses on your calculator to find $\sqrt[3]{68.921}$.

4　Find:
　　a　$\sqrt[3]{343}$　　**b**　$\sqrt[3]{15.625}$　　**c**　$\sqrt[3]{8000}$　　**d**　$\sqrt[3]{¯125}$　　**e**　$\sqrt[3]{0.343}$

An integer is a positive or negative whole number. 0 is also an integer.

5　**a**　Find the cube of each integer from ¯5 to 5.
　　b　Draw a graph to show these integers and their cubes.

6　**a**　What do you think the symbol $\sqrt[4]{}$ stands for?　　**b**　Find $\sqrt[4]{81}$.

Reciprocals

◆ Two numbers which multiply together to equal 1 are **reciprocals** of each other.

$$0.8 \times 1.25 = 1$$

0.8 is the reciprocal of 1.25.
1.25 is the reciprocal of 0.8.

◆ The reciprocal of any number **n** is: $\dfrac{1}{n}$ or $1 \div n$.

$$\dfrac{1}{0.8} = 1.25$$ $$\dfrac{1}{1.25} = 0.8$$

◆ The reciprocal of any fraction $\dfrac{p}{q}$ is: $\dfrac{q}{p}$.

Writing 0.8 and 1.25 as fractions gives:

$$\dfrac{4}{5} \times \dfrac{5}{4} = 1$$

$\dfrac{4}{5}$ is the reciprocal of $\dfrac{5}{4}$.
$\dfrac{5}{4}$ is the reciprocal of $\dfrac{4}{5}$.

Exercise 1.4
Reciprocals

1   Find the reciprocal of:

   a 4   **b** 0.1   **c** 2.5   **d** 3   **e** $0.\dot{6}$ **f** $0.8\dot{3}$

2   Write as a fraction the reciprocal of:

   a $\dfrac{3}{5}$ **b** $\dfrac{7}{4}$ **c** $1\dfrac{1}{2}$ **d** $3\dfrac{1}{3}$ **e** 1.2

3   **a** Copy these axes.
   b Draw a graph to show the relationship between positive numbers and their reciprocals.

4   Investigate the relationship between negative numbers and their reciprocals.

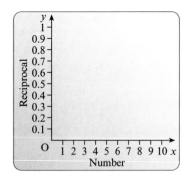

Thinking ahead to ...
zero and negative indices

A   This diagram shows that: $1 \div 3 = \frac{1}{3}$
                                  $\frac{1}{3} \div 3 = \frac{1}{9}$

   Draw a diagram to show that:

   a $1 \div 2 = \frac{1}{2}$, and $\frac{1}{2} \div 2 = \frac{1}{4}$

   b $1 \div 5 = \frac{1}{5}$, and $\frac{1}{5} \div 5 = \frac{1}{25}$

B   This diagram shows that:

   $$1 \div 3 = \tfrac{1}{3}, \ \tfrac{1}{3} \div 3 = \tfrac{1}{9}$$
   $$\tfrac{1}{9} \div 3 = \tfrac{1}{27}, \ \tfrac{1}{27} \div 3 = \tfrac{1}{81}$$

   Draw a diagram to show that:

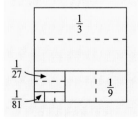

   $$1 \div 2 = \tfrac{1}{2}, \ \tfrac{1}{2} \div 2 = \tfrac{1}{4}, \ \tfrac{1}{4} \div 2 = \tfrac{1}{8}, \text{ and } \tfrac{1}{8} \div 2 = \tfrac{1}{16}$$

Zero and negative indices

♦ These powers of 3 have positive indices.

3^1	3^2	3^3	3^4	3^5
3	9	27	81	243

×3 ×3 ×3 ×3 ×3

For 3^{-1} we say '3 to the power negative 1'.

♦ The sequence of powers can be continued using zero and negative indices.

3^{-4}	3^{-3}	3^{-2}	3^{-1}	3^0	3^1	3^2	3^3	3^4	3^5
$\frac{1}{81}$	$\frac{1}{27}$	$\frac{1}{9}$	$\frac{1}{3}$	1	3	9	27	81	243

÷3 ÷3 ÷3 ÷3 ÷3 ÷3 ÷3 ÷3 ÷3 ÷3 ÷3

♦ A number to a negative power is a fraction. The fraction is the reciprocal of the number to the corresponding positive power.

$3^{-1} = \frac{1}{3^1} = \frac{1}{3}$ $3^{-4} = \frac{1}{3^4} = \frac{1}{81}$

Exercise 1.5
Zero and negative indices

1 Copy this powers of 2 table and fill in the missing numbers.

2^{-4}		2^{-2}	2^{-1}	2^0		2^2	2^3
	$\frac{1}{8}$				2		16

2 Make a powers of 4 table from 4^{-3} to 4^3.

3 Write these as fractions.

  a 5^{-1} **b** 3^{-5} **c** 2^{-6} **d** 7^{-2} **e** 10^{-2} **f** 5^0

4 **a** Explain why $6^0 = 1$.
   b Explain why any number to the power 0 is 1.

Using negative indices

♦ To multiply by a number to a negative power:

  ❖ divide by the number to the corresponding positive power.

1296×3^{-2}
$= 1296 \div 3^2$
$= 1296 \div 9$
$= 144$

♦ To divide by a number to a negative power:

  ❖ multiply by the number to the corresponding positive power.

$54 \div 3^{-2}$
$= 54 \times 3^2$
$= 54 \times 9$
$= 486$

Exercise 1.6
Using negative indices

1 Calculate:

  a 336×2^{-3} **b** 65×4^{-1} **c** 156×5^{-2} **d** 1.32×10^{-2}
  e $28 \div 3^{-3}$ **f** $12.7 \div 5^{-3}$ **g** $0.34 \div 6^{-2}$ **h** $47 \div 10^{-1}$

$2^{-3} = \frac{1}{2^3} = \frac{1}{8}$

2 Write these as decimals.

  a 2^{-3} **b** 4^{-1} **c** 5^{-2} **d** 10^{-2}

3 Use your answers to Question **2** to calculate:

  a 336×2^{-3} **b** 65×4^{-1} **c** 156×5^{-2} **d** 1.32×10^{-2}

4 Write these as decimals.

  a 10^{-1} **b** 10^{-3} **c** 10^{-4} **d** 10^{-5}

Standard form

♦ A number can be written in several ways using powers of 10. For example:

10^{-3}	10^{-2}	10^{-1}	10^0	10^1	10^2	10^3	10^4
0.001	0.01	0.1	1	10	100	1000	10 000

3600

$0.36 \times 10\,000$
3.6×1000
36×100
360×10
3600×1
$36\,000 \times 0.1$
$360\,000 \times 0.01$
$3\,600\,000 \times 0.001$

0.729

$0.000\,729 \times 1000$
$0.007\,29 \times 100$
0.0729×10
0.729×1
7.29×0.1
72.9×0.01
729×0.001
7290×0.0001

> Standard form is also called standard index form.

♦ One way of writing a number is called standard form. 3600 and 0.729 in standard form are:

- ❖ the first part is a number greater than or equal to 1 and less than 10

  3.6×10^3
  7.29×10^{-1}

- ❖ the second part is a power of 10 written in index notation.

> Include any zeros between non-zero digits.
> For example: 40 900 000

♦ To write a number in standard form:

- ❖ use all the non-zero digits for the first part

  43 900 000
  4.39

  0.000 58
  5.8

- ❖ decide what power of 10 the first part must be multiplied by to give the number

  43 900 000
  $= 4.39 \times 10\,000\,000$

  0.000 58
  $= 5.8 \times 0.0001$

- ❖ write the power of 10 in index notation.

  43 900 000
  $= 4.39 \times 10^7$

  0.000 58
  $= 5.8 \times 10^{-4}$

♦ To rewrite a number in standard form as an ordinary number:

- ❖ write the power of 10 in full and multiply by the first part.

  2.4×10^6
  $= 2.4 \times 1\,000\,000$
  $=\qquad 2\,400\,000$

  3.152×10^{-3}
  $= 3.152 \times 0.001$
  $=\qquad 0.003\,152$

Exercise 1.7
Standard form

1 Write these numbers in standard form.
  a 380 000   **b** 45 100 000   **c** 0.000 92   **d** 0.000 0262

2 Write these as ordinary numbers.
  a 9.42×10^4 **b** 2.5×10^{-3} **c** 7.414×10^8 **d** 6.27×10^{-7}

3
  | P 13×10^4 | Q 5.7×1000 | R $6.42 \div 10^3$ | S 0.58×10^{-4} |

  a Explain why each of these numbers is not written in standard form.
  b Write each number in standard form.

4 List the key presses on your calculator to find $60 \times (6.19 \times 10^{-11})$.

5 Use your calculator to find:

a $365 \times (2.4 \times 10^4)$ b $(8.84 \times 10^6) \div 52$

c $(5.5 \times 10^{-4}) \times (3.6 \times 10^7)$ d $(8.2 \times 10^8) \div (1.04 \times 10^{-5})$

e $(6.8 \times 10^{-16}) + (7 \times 10^{-15})$ f $(4 \times 10^4) - (2.8 \times 10^2)$

Give your answers in standard form.

Rules of indices

♦ To multiply powers of the same number:
  ❖ add the indices.

$3^2 \times 3^3$
$= 3^{2+3}$
$= 3^5$

$(3 \times 3) \times (3 \times 3 \times 3)$
$= 3 \times 3 \times 3 \times 3 \times 3$
$= 243$

♦ To divide powers of the same number:
  ❖ subtract the indices.

$3^5 \div 3^2$
$= 3^{5-2}$
$= 3^3$

$(3 \times 3 \times 3 \times 3 \times 3) \div (3 \times 3)$
$= 243 \div 9$
$= 27$

♦ To raise a power of a number to another power:
  ❖ multiply the indices.

$(3^4)^2$
$= 3^{4 \times 2}$
$= 3^8$

$(3 \times 3 \times 3 \times 3) \times (3 \times 3 \times 3 \times 3)$
$= 81 \times 81$
$= 6561$

Exercise 1.8
Rules of indices

1 Give the answer to these using index notation.

a $3^2 \times 3^5$ b $4^{-3} \times 4^5$ c $2^7 \div 2^4$ d $7^{-4} \times 7^{-2}$ e $6^3 \div 6^5$

f $7^{-4} \div 7^2$ g $5^{-1} \times 5^1$ h $2^4 \div 2^{-1}$ i $6^{-3} \div 6^{-2}$ j $7^{-3} \times 7^0$

2 Copy and complete these calculations.

a $2^3 \times 2^\square = 2^7$ b $4^5 \times 4^\square = 4^3$ c $3^5 \div 3^\square = 3^2$ d $7^\square \times 7^{-3} = 7^4$

e $8^4 \div 8^\square = 8^{-2}$ f $5^\square \div 5^2 = 5^2$ g $2^\square \times 2^5 = 2^{-1}$ h $3^4 \div 3^\square = 3^3$

3 Give the answer to these using index notation.

a $(3^2)^4$ b $(5^3)^3$ c $(4^5)^{-2}$ d $(4^{-2})^5$ e $(2^4)^{-4}$ f $(7^3)^0$

4 Copy and complete these calculations.

a $2^\square \times 2^2 = 32$ b $3^6 \times 3^{-3} = \bigcirc$ c $2^8 \div 2^\square = 64$ d $4^2 \div 4^{-1} = \bigcirc$

e $(3^2)^\square = 81$ f $(5^3)^\square = 125$ g $(2^{-3})^\square = 0.125$ h $(5^\square)^2 = 0.04$

Standard form without a calculator

♦ To multiply: $(6 \times 10^7) \times (3 \times 10^{-2})$
  ❖ multiply the first parts
  ❖ multiply the second parts
  ❖ combine the two answers
  ❖ write in standard form.

$6 \times 3 = 18$
$10^7 \times 10^{-2} = 10^5$
18×10^5
1.8×10^6

♦ To divide: $(4 \times 10^{-3}) \div (8 \times 10^5)$
  ❖ divide the first parts
  ❖ divide the second parts
  ❖ combine the two answers
  ❖ write in standard form.

$4 \div 8 = 0.5$
$10^{-3} \div 10^5 = 10^{-8}$
0.5×10^{-8}
5×10^{-9}

Exercise 1.9
Standard form
without a calculator

1 Give the answer to these in standard form.

a $(6 \times 10^{-4}) \times (4 \times 10^7)$ b $(6 \times 10^{-2}) \div (3 \times 10^4)$

c $(5 \times 10^{-9}) \div (2.5 \times 10^{-12})$ d $(4 \times 10^{-3}) \times (1.5 \times 10^{-8})$

Lowest common multiples

♦ To find the lowest common multiple (LCM) of 24 and 45:

♦ write each number as a product of primes

$$24 = 2^3 \times 3$$
$$45 = 3^2 \times 5$$

♦ take the highest power of each prime factor to give a new product of primes

$$2^3 \times 3^2 \times 5$$

♦ evaluate the new product of primes.

$$8 \times 9 \times 5 = \mathbf{360}$$

Exercise 1.10
Lowest common multiples

1   Find the LCM of:

a 12 and 18   **b** 20 and 42   **c** 28 and 30   **d** 150 and 315
e 10, 18 and 35   **f** 15, 27 and 70   **g** 66, 135 and 275

2   The LCM of two numbers is 630. One number is 42.
Give the numbers the other one could be.

Adding and subtracting fractions

♦ You can only add or subtract fractions when the denominators are the same.

♦ To add or subtract fractions:

$$\frac{3}{4} + \frac{1}{6} \qquad \frac{7}{8} - \frac{1}{3}$$

♦ find the LCM of the denominators

12   24

♦ find equivalent fractions with the LCM as the new denominator

$$\frac{9}{12} + \frac{2}{12} \qquad \frac{21}{24} - \frac{8}{24}$$

♦ add or subtract the numerators.

$$\frac{11}{12} \qquad \frac{13}{24}$$

Any common multiple can be used as the new denominator.

Using the LCM will usually give an answer in its lowest terms.

Exercise 1.11
Adding and subtracting fractions

1   Evaluate:

a $\frac{1}{2} + \frac{1}{3}$ **b** $\frac{2}{5} + \frac{1}{4}$ **c** $\frac{1}{2} - \frac{1}{3}$ **d** $\frac{3}{4} - \frac{1}{5}$

e $\frac{2}{5} + \frac{3}{7}$ **f** $\frac{1}{3} + \frac{1}{4} + \frac{1}{6}$ **g** $\frac{2}{3} - \frac{1}{6}$

2   Write the answer to each of these as a mixed number.

a $\frac{2}{3} + \frac{1}{2}$ **b** $\frac{1}{4} + \frac{4}{5}$ **c** $\frac{1}{2} + \frac{1}{3} + \frac{1}{4}$

3   Evaluate:

a $1\frac{1}{2} + \frac{4}{5}$ **b** $1\frac{4}{5} - \frac{1}{2}$ **c** $1\frac{1}{3} + 2\frac{1}{2}$

d $2\frac{2}{5} - 1\frac{1}{2}$ **e** $2\frac{5}{8} + 1\frac{1}{3}$ **f** $2\frac{1}{4} - 1\frac{3}{7}$

Write any mixed numbers as improper fractions before adding or subtracting.

4   Fractions with a numerator of 1 are called **unit fractions**.

Investigate fractions like this which can be written as the sum of two unit fractions.

$$\frac{2}{5} = \frac{1}{3} + \frac{1}{15}$$

Thinking ahead to ...
multiplying and
dividing fractions

A   Calculate:

     a $10 \div 1.25$ **b** 10×0.8

     c $16 \div 1.25$ **d** 16×0.8

$$1.25 = \frac{5}{4} \qquad 0.8 = \frac{4}{5}$$

B   What do your answers to Question **A** tell you about dividing by a fraction?

Multiplying and dividing fractions

> The answer may already be in its lowest terms.

- ◆ To multiply fractions:
  - ❖ multiply the numerators
  - ❖ multiply the denominators
  - ❖ write the answer in its lowest terms.

$$\frac{4}{5} \times \frac{3}{8} = \frac{12}{40} = \frac{3}{10}$$

- ◆ Dividing by a fraction has the same effect as multiplying by its reciprocal.
- ◆ To divide fractions:
  - ❖ write the division as a multiplication
  - ❖ multiply the fractions.

$$\frac{1}{6} \div \frac{2}{3}$$
$$= \frac{1}{6} \times \frac{3}{2} = \frac{3}{12} = \frac{1}{4}$$

Exercise 1.12
Multiplying and
dividing fractions

1 Evaluate:

   a $\frac{2}{3} \times \frac{5}{8}$ **b** $\frac{3}{5} \times \frac{5}{6}$ **c** $\frac{4}{7} \times \frac{3}{5}$ **d** $\frac{9}{14} \times \frac{2}{3}$

   e $\frac{1}{4} \div \frac{5}{8}$ **f** $\frac{2}{3} \div \frac{6}{7}$ **g** $\frac{2}{5} \div \frac{3}{4}$ **h** $\frac{1}{4} \div \frac{3}{5}$

> Write any mixed numbers or whole numbers as improper fractions before multiplying or dividing.

2 Write the answer to each of these as a mixed number or a whole number.

   a $6 \times \frac{2}{5}$ **b** $8 \times \frac{3}{4}$ **c** $10 \div \frac{5}{6}$ **d** $7 \div \frac{2}{3}$

   e $12 \times 1\frac{3}{4}$ **f** $9 \times 3\frac{1}{2}$ **g** $5 \div 1\frac{1}{6}$ **h** $11 \div 2\frac{3}{5}$

3 Evaluate:

   a $2\frac{1}{2} \times 1\frac{4}{5}$ **b** $1\frac{1}{6} \div \frac{2}{5}$ **c** $4\frac{1}{2} \div 1\frac{3}{4}$ **d** $2\frac{3}{4} \times 2\frac{2}{3}$

   e $\frac{4}{5} \times 1\frac{1}{4}$ **f** $2\frac{1}{2} \div 2\frac{1}{4}$ **g** $1\frac{3}{5} \times 3\frac{3}{4}$ **h** $\frac{5}{6} \div 1\frac{3}{8}$

Highest common factors

- ◆ To find the highest common factor (HCF) of 120 and 252:
  - ❖ write each number as a product of primes

    $$120 = 2^3 \times 3 \times 5$$

    $$252 = 2^2 \times 3^2 \times 7$$

  - ❖ take the lowest power of each common prime factor to give a new product of primes

    $$2^2 \times 3$$

  - ❖ evaluate the new product of primes.

    $$4 \times 3$$
    $$= 12$$

Exercise 1.13
Highest common factors

1 Use products of primes to find the HCF of:

   a 252 and 360   **b** 120 and 315   **c** 693 and 1078

   d 48, 66 and 225

End points

You should be able to ...   ... so try these questions.

A   Multiply and divide negative numbers

A1   Copy and complete these calculations.
a $7 \times {}^-2 = \square$ b ${}^-3 \times {}^-5 = \square$ c ${}^-12 \div 4 = \square$
d $20 \div {}^-5 = \square$ e $\square \times {}^-3 = {}^-18$ f $\square \div {}^-2 = 8$
g ${}^-4 \times \square = 36$ h $\square \div 7 = {}^-3$

B   Find roots, cubes and reciprocals

B1   Use your calculator to find:
a $\sqrt{1.44}$ b 3.3^3 c $\sqrt[3]{216}$ d $\sqrt[3]{3.375}$

B2   Find the reciprocal of:
a   8   b   0.2   c $0.\dot{5}$ d $\frac{2}{5}$ e $1\frac{1}{4}$

C   Understand and use zero and negative indices

C1   Copy this powers of 3 table and fill in the missing numbers.

3^{-4}		3^{-2}	3^{-1}	3^0		3^2	3^3
	$\frac{1}{27}$				3		81

C2   Write these as fractions.
a 6^{-1} b 2^{-4} c 10^{-1} d 4^0

C3   Calculate:
a 153×3^{-2} b $37 \div 2^{-5}$ c 6.4×4^{-3} d $0.45 \div 5^{-3}$

D   Understand and use standard form

D1   Write these numbers in standard form.
a $70\,620\,000$ b $0.000\,003\,75$

D2   Write these as ordinary numbers.
a 6.9×10^{-8} b 1.03×10^{10}

D3   Use your calculator to find:
a $52 \times (1.92 \times 10^{13})$ b $(6.58 \times 10^{-7}) \div 7$ c $(4.1 \times 10^{27}) + (7 \times 10^{26})$

D4   Without using a calculator, give the answer to these in standard form.
a $(7 \times 10^5) \times (6 \times 10^{-9})$ b $(8 \times 10^{-2}) \div (4 \times 10^{-6})$

E   Use rules of indices

E1   Give the answer to these using index notation.
a $2^5 \times 2^{-3}$ b $3^{-2} \div 3^7$ c $(5^2)^5$ d $(4^{-2})^3$

E2   Copy and complete these calculations.
a $3^4 \times 3^{\square} = 3^{10}$ b $4^3 \div 4^{\square} = 4^7$
c $7^{\square} \times 7^7 = 7^5$ d $(6^{-2})^0 = 6^{\square}$

F   Calculate with fractions

F1   Evaluate:
a $\frac{2}{3} + \frac{1}{5}$ b $\frac{5}{6} - \frac{2}{5}$ c $2\frac{3}{8} - 1\frac{3}{4}$ d $1\frac{5}{7} + 2\frac{1}{6}$

F2   Evaluate:
a $\frac{3}{4} \times \frac{2}{5}$ b $\frac{1}{6} \div \frac{2}{3}$ c $3\frac{1}{3} \times 1\frac{4}{5}$ d $2\frac{1}{2} \div 1\frac{3}{4}$

G   Find lowest common multiples and highest common factors

G1   Find the LCM of:
a   12 and 21   b   24 and 90

G2   Find the HCF of:
a   14 and 35   b   105 and 350

Some points to remember

- ◆ Each positive number has two square roots: a positive one and a negative one.
- ◆ All numbers, positive and negative, have only one cube root.
- ◆ A number to a negative power is a fraction.
- ◆ Fractions can only be added or subtracted when the denominators are the same.

Starting points
You need to know about ...

... so try these questions.

A Finding the value of an expression

◆ Examples of expressions are:

$$3n + 1 = (3 \times n) + 1 \qquad 9 - 4n = 9 - (4 \times n) \qquad 2a - b = (2 \times a) - b$$

$$k^2 + 1 = (k \times k) + 1 \qquad 2y^2 = 2 \times y \times y \qquad g(g + 1) = g \times (g + 1)$$

◆ The value of an expression depends on the value of the letters.

For example: ❖ when $n = 5$, $\quad 3n + 1 = (3 \times n) + 1$
$$= (3 \times 5) + 1$$
$$= 16$$

❖ when $y = 3$, $\quad 2y^2 = 2 \times y \times y$
$$= 2 \times 3 \times 3$$
$$= 18$$

B Some types of number sequences

◆ Even numbers: 2, 4, 6, 8, 10, ...

◆ Odd numbers: 1, 3, 5, 7, 9, ...

◆ Square numbers: 1,   4,   9,   16, ...

◆ Triangle numbers: 1,   3,   6,   10, ...

◆ Powers of 2: 2, 4, 8, 16, 32, ...

◆ Powers of 3: 3, 9, 27, 81, 243, ...

◆ Fibonacci numbers: 1, 1, 2, 3, 5, 8, 13, ...

The sequence of Fibonacci numbers begins 1, 1, ...
Further numbers in the sequence are found by adding the previous two numbers together. For example, the next Fibonacci number is $8 + 13 = 21$.

Start with two different numbers to find other sequences like this, for example: 3, 6, 9, 15, 24, ...

A1 Find the value of these expressions when $n = 4$.
  a $5n + 1$ **b** $7 - n$
  c $2n - 8$ **d** $3(2 + n)$

A2 Find the value of these expressions when $a = 3$.
  a $a^2 + 10$ **b** $4a^2$
  c $a^2 - 5$ **d** $a(a + 1)$

B1 Draw a pattern of dots to show that 25 is a square number.

B2 Find four odd square numbers.

B3 Write down the first six triangle numbers.

B4 List the first four powers of 5.

B5 Which of these are Fibonacci numbers:
    30   34   62   90?

B6 Each number in this sequence is found by adding the previous two numbers together.

  1, 3, 4, 7, 11, 18, ...

Find the next four numbers in this sequence.

C Continuing a sequence

- ◆ A **sequence** of numbers usually follows a pattern or rule.

- ◆ Each number in a sequence is called a **term**.

  For example,
  in the sequence: 3, 5, 7, 9, 11, ...   the 1st term is 3
                                          the 2nd term is 5
                                          the 3rd term is 7.

- ◆ A sequence can often be continued by finding a pattern in the **differences**.

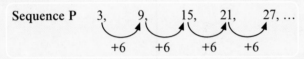

- ❖ In Sequence P, the **first difference** is 6 each time.
  So continue the sequence by adding 6.

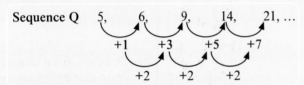

- ❖ In Sequence Q, the **second difference** is 2 each time.
  So continue the sequence by adding 9, then 11, and so on.

D A rule for a sequence

These are the first three matchstick patterns in a sequence.

Pattern 1   Pattern 2   Pattern 3

- ◆ The number of matches in each pattern can be shown in a table.

Pattern number (n)	Number of matches (m)
1	9
2	16
3	23
4	30

- ❖ The pattern number goes up by 1 each time.
- ❖ The number of matches goes up by 7 each time.
- ❖ So a rule that links the number of matches (m) with the pattern number (n) begins $m = 7n$ ...
- ❖ A rule that fits all the results in the table is $m = 7n + 2$

- ◆ This rule can be used to calculate the number of matches in any pattern,
  for example: in Pattern 10 there are $(7 \times 10) + 2 = 72$ matches.

C1 Find the 6th and 7th term in:
   a sequence P
   b sequence Q.

C2 What is the 10th term in this sequence?

   4, 7, 10, 13, 16, ...

C3 For each sequence, find the next three terms.
   a 6, 7, 10, 15, 22, ...
   b 2, 8, 14, 20, 26, ...
   c 2, 5, 11, 20, 32, ...
   d 2, 3, 9, 20, 36, ...

D1 These are the first three matchstick patterns in a sequence.

   Pattern 1

   Pattern 2

   Pattern 3

   a Draw pattern 4 and pattern 5 in this sequence.

   b How many matches are in:
      i pattern 3   **ii** pattern 5?

   c Make a table for the first five patterns in this sequence.

   d Which of these rules fits the results in your table?

   $m = 4n + 2$ $m = 5n + 1$

   $m = 6n - 1$

Sequences and mappings

These equilateral triangles are the first three in a sequence of shapes.

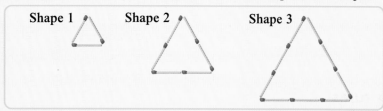

♦ Data for this sequence can be shown in a table.

Shape number	1	2	3	4
Number of matches	3	6	9	12

♦ The data can also be shown in a **mapping diagram** like this.

Shape number	Number of matches
1	⟶ 3
2	⟶ 6
3	⟶ 9
4	⟶ 12 ...

> You can choose any letter to stand for the shape number.
>
> For example:
> the rule
> $n \longrightarrow 3n$
> can be written as
> $s \longrightarrow 3s$
> or
> $p \longrightarrow 3p$
> or ...

♦ The total number of matches is 3 times the shape number.
For example, the 50th shape in the sequence uses 150 matches.

Using n to stand for the shape number,
the rule for the mapping diagram can be written: $n \longrightarrow 3n$

Exercise 2.1
Sequences and mappings

1 These are the first three patterns in a sequence.

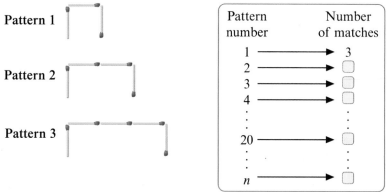

Pattern 1

Pattern 2

Pattern 3

Pattern number	Number of matches
1	⟶ 3
2	⟶ ☐
3	⟶ ☐
4	⟶ ☐
⋮	⋮
20	⟶ ☐
⋮	⋮
n	⟶ ☐

Copy and complete the mapping diagram for the sequence.

2 These patterns of touching squares are the first four in a sequence.

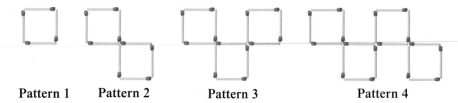

Pattern 1   Pattern 2   Pattern 3   Pattern 4

a Draw a mapping diagram for the first six patterns of touching squares.
b Find a rule for the sequence in the form $n \longrightarrow$ .... , where n is the pattern number.
c Use your rule to calculate the number of matches in the 100th pattern.

23

Thinking ahead to ...
finding rules

A   These are the first three patterns in sequence A.

Sequence A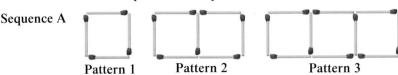

Pattern 1   Pattern 2   Pattern 3

How many matchsticks are in the 100th pattern?
Explain how you worked it out.

Finding rules

To find a rule for the number of matches (*m*) in the *n*th pattern in sequence A above

- ◆ **Method 1** Look at how the patterns are made.

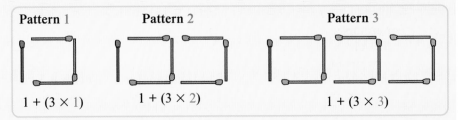

Pattern 1   Pattern 2   Pattern 3

$1 + (3 \times 1)$ $1 + (3 \times 2)$ $1 + (3 \times 3)$

- ❖ So a rule for the number of matches (*m*) in the *n*th pattern is **_m_ = 1 + 3_n_**

- ◆ **Method 2** Look at differences.

Pattern number (*n*)	3*n*	Number of matches (*m*)
1	3	4
2	6	7
3	9	10
4	12	13
5	15	16

+3
+3
+3
+3

- ❖ The pattern number goes up by 1 each time.

- ❖ The number of matches goes up by 3 each time so there is a linear rule that begins $m = 3n \dots$.

Examples of linear rules are:

$$m = 4n + 3$$
$$y = 2 - 5x$$
$$a = 3b - 1$$

Rules such as $m = n^2 + 1$ and $y = \dfrac{5}{x} - 6$ are non-linear.

- ❖ Compare 3*n* with the number of matches.

- ❖ The number of matches is 1 more than 3*n* each time.

- ❖ So a rule for the number of matches (*m*) in the *n*th pattern is **_m_ = 3_n_ + 1**.

Exercise 2.2
Finding rules

1   These triangle patterns are the first three in sequence B.

Sequence B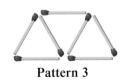

Pattern 1   Pattern 2   Pattern 3

a   Find a rule for the number of matches (*m*) in the *n*th triangle pattern. Explain your method.

b   Use your rule to find the number of matches in the 8th pattern.

c   Check your answer by drawing the 8th pattern and counting the matches.

2 Sequence C

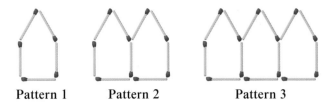

Pattern 1   Pattern 2   Pattern 3

  a For sequence C, find a rule for the number of matches (*m*) in the *n*th pattern.
Explain your method.

  b Calculate the number of matches in the 40th pattern.

  c Which pattern uses exactly 129 matches?

3 Sequence D

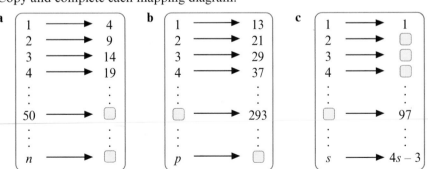

Pattern 1   Pattern 2   Pattern 3

  a For sequence D, find a rule for the number of matches (*m*) in the *n*th pattern.
Explain your method.

  b How many of matches are in the 100th pattern?

4 This mapping diagram fits a sequence of matchstick patterns.

Pattern number (*n*)	Number of matches (*m*)
1	6
2	10
3	14
4	18
5	22

  a Draw a sequence of matchstick patterns that fits this mapping diagram.

  b Find a rule for the number of matches (*m*) in the *n*th pattern.

5 Copy and complete each mapping diagram.

  a

1	→	4
2	→	9
3	→	14
4	→	19
⋮		⋮
50	→	☐
⋮		⋮
n	→	☐

  b

1	→	13
2	→	21
3	→	29
4	→	37
⋮		⋮
☐	→	293
⋮		⋮
p	→	☐

  c

1	→	1
2	→	☐
3	→	☐
4	→	☐
⋮		⋮
☐	→	97
⋮		⋮
s	→	4*s* − 3

Thinking ahead to ...
finding the *n*th term

A
> 7, 9, 11, 13, 15, 17, ...

    a Write the next two terms in this sequence.
    b Find the 12th term.
    c What is the 50th term?

The *n*th term of a sequence

To find an expression for the *n*th term in the sequence 7, 9, 11, 13, 15, ...

The 1st term is 7
The 2nd term is 9
The 3rd term is 11
The 4th term is 13
The 5th term is 15
. . .

* These results can
  be shown in
  a mapping diagram.

Term number (n)	$2n$	Term
1	2	7
2	4	9
3	6	11
4	8	13
5	10	15

❖ The first difference for the terms is 2 each time.
   So there is a linear expression for the *n*th term that begins $2n$ ... .

❖ Each term is 5 more than $2n$.
   So an expression for the *n*th term is $2n + 5$.

Exercise 2.3
Finding the *n*th term

1   A   6, 9, 12, 15, 18, ...   B   1, 6, 11, 16, 21, ...
       C   13, 23, 33, 43, 53, ...   D   2, 10, 18, 26, 34, ...

For each of the sequences A to D:
a find an expression for the *n*th term
b use your expression to calculate the 50th term.

2 A student has tried to find the *n*th term of this sequence.

> 5, 8, 11, 14, 17, ...
>
> *n*th term is $n + 3$ ✗

a Explain the mistake you think he has made.
b Find a correct expression for the *n*th term of this sequence.

3 The 2nd term of a sequence is 7.
Which of these could not be an expression for the *n*th term?

> $3n + 1$ $11 - 2n$ $n + 5$ $n + 7$ $5n - 3$

4 Find an expression for the *n*th term of the sequence: 20, 18, 16, 14, 12, ...

Thinking ahead to ...
non-linear rules

A These are the first three shapes in a sequence.

Shape 1 ▭   Shape 2 ▭   Shape 3 ▭

a Draw the next shape in the sequence.
b How many small squares ▭ are in shape 20?

Sequences with non-linear rules

To find an expression for the number of squares in the *n*th shape

Shape number (*n*)	Number of squares
1	2
2	8
3	18
4	32

$\}$ + 6
$\}$ +10
$\}$ +14

♦ Look at the differences.

   ❖ The first differences are not the same each time so there is no linear expression.

♦ Try looking at how the shapes can be made.

   ❖ Each shape can be cut into two square shapes.

   Shape 1: $2 \times (1 \times 1) = 2$ squares

   Shape 2: $2 \times (2 \times 2) = 8$ squares

   Shape 3: $2 \times (3 \times 3) = 18$ squares

   Shape *n*: $2 \times (n \times n) = 2n^2$ squares

   ❖ So an expression for the number of squares in the *n*th shape is $2n^2$.

Exercise 2.4
Looking at how
shapes can be made

1 For each sequence, find an expression for the number of small squares in the *n*th shape.

a Shape 1 ▭   Shape 2 ▭   Shape 3 ▭

b Shape 1 ▭   Shape 2 ▭   Shape 3 ▭

c Shape 1 ▭   Shape 2 ▭   Shape 3 ▭

2 How many squares are in the *n*th shape for this sequence?

Shape 1 ▭   Shape 2 ▭   Shape 3 ▭

Thinking ahead to ...
looking at differences

A   These patterns are the first four in a sequence.

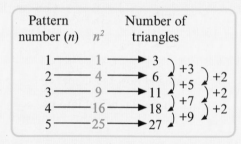

Pattern 1

Pattern 2

Pattern 3

Pattern 4

How many triangles or are in pattern 20?

Looking at differences

It is not easy to find an expression for the number of triangles in the nth triangle pattern by looking at how the patterns can be made.

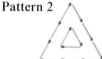

Pattern number (n)	n^2	Number of triangles		
1	1	3		
2	4	6	+3	+2
3	9	11	+5	+2
4	16	18	+7	+2
5	25	27	+9	

◆ Look at first and second differences.

❖ The second differences are the same each time so there is an expression that involves n^2.

❖ Compare n^2 with the number of triangles.

❖ The number of triangles is 2 more than n^2 each time.

❖ So an expression for the number of triangles in the nth pattern is **$n^2 + 2$**

Exercise 2.5
Looking at differences

1   These matchstick patterns are the first three in a sequence.

Pattern 1   Pattern 2   Pattern 3

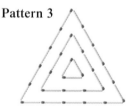

a   Find an expression for the number of matches in the nth pattern.
b   Use your expression to calculate the number of matches in pattern 20.

2   Here is a sequence of numbers:

$$0, 3, 8, 15, 24, ...$$

a   What is the next term in this sequence?
b   Copy and complete this mapping diagram for the first six terms.
c   Find an expression for the nth term in this sequence.

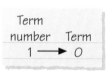

Term
number   Term
1 ⟶ 0

3   A 4, 7, 12, 19, 28, ...   B 4, 16, 36, 64, 100, ...
        C 6, 13, 20, 27, 34, ...   D 6, 9, 14, 21, 30, ...

For each of the sequences A to D:
a   write down the next two terms
b   find an expression for the nth term.

Extending number patterns

Exercise 2.6
Extending patterns

1 Morag finds an expression for the *n*th number in this sequence.

> 4, 10, 18, 28, 40, ...

This is her working:

1st number	4	= 1 × 4
2nd number	10	= 2 × 5
3rd number	18	= 3 × 6
4th number	28	= 4 × 7 ...
So *n*th number		= *n* × (*n* + 3)

a Show Morag's line of working for the 5th number.
b Find the 10th number in this sequence.
c Explain how Morag's working helps to find an expression for the *n*th number in this sequence.

2 These are the first five triangle numbers:

> 1, 3, 6, 10, 15, ...

The triangle numbers follow this pattern:

1st triangle number	$1 = \dfrac{1 \times 2}{2}$
2nd triangle number	$3 = \dfrac{2 \times 3}{2}$
3rd triangle number	$6 = \dfrac{3 \times 4}{2}$
4th triangle number	$10 = \dfrac{4 \times 5}{2}$

a What is the next line in this pattern?
b Use the pattern to find the 12th triangle number.
c Find an expression for the *n*th triangle number.

3 These are the first five powers of 2:

> 2, 4, 8, 16, 32, ...

Powers of 2 follow this pattern:

1st power	2	$= 2^1$
2nd power	4 = 2 × 2	$= 2^2$
3rd power	8 = 2 × 2 × 2	$= 2^3$
4th power	16 = 2 × 2 × 2 × 2	$= 2^4$

a What is the next line in this pattern?
b Use the pattern to find the 8th power of 2.
c Write an expression for the *n*th power of 2.

Writing rules in different ways

Exercise 2.7
Different ways
to write rules

1 These hollow square tile designs are the first three in a sequence.

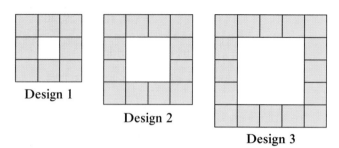

Design 1

Design 2

Design 3

Three students find a rule for the number of tiles in the *n*th design.
All three students are correct.

Andrew	**Aisha**	**Fiona**
Number of tiles	Number of tiles	Number of tiles
$= 4(n + 1)$	$= 4n + 4$	$= 2(n + 2) + 2n$

The way each student wrote their rule shows how they found it.

Andrew drew this diagram to
show how he found his rule.

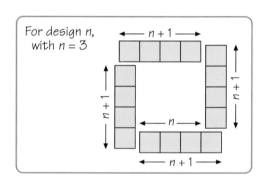

For design *n*,
with *n* = 3

Fiona's rule is not as easy to
use as the other two rules.

Using Fiona's rule to find
the number of tiles in the
10th design gives:

Number of tiles

$= 2 \times (10 + 2) + (2 \times 10)$
$= 24 + 20$
$= 44$

a Draw a diagram for Aisha's rule.
b Draw a diagram for Fiona's rule.
c Show how you can calculate the number of tiles in the 50th design using:
   i Andrew's rule   **ii** Aisha's rule   **iii** Fiona's rule
d Which design has 324 tiles?
   Explain how you found your result.

2 These designs are the first three in a sequence.

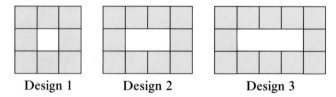

Design 1   Design 2   Design 3

a Find two different ways of writing a rule for the number of tiles in
the *n*th design.
b Explain how you found your results.

Thinking ahead to ...
using brackets

A Sort these calculations into pairs with the same value.

| $\boxed{A}$ $200 - 30$ | $\boxed{B}$ $5 \times (100 + 6)$ | $\boxed{C}$ $5 \times (100 + 30)$ |

| $\boxed{D}$ $5 \times (100 - 30)$ | $\boxed{E}$ $500 + 30$ | $\boxed{F}$ $2 \times (100 - 15)$ |

| $\boxed{G}$ $(5 \times 100) + (5 \times 30)$ | $\boxed{H}$ $(5 \times 100) - (5 \times 30)$ |

Using brackets in linear expressions

> **To multiply out brackets:**
>
> ◆ Multiply **every** term inside the brackets.
>
> **Examples**
>
> | $2(n + 3) = 2 \times (n + 3)$ | $5(3n - 2) = 5 \times (3n - 2)$ |
> | $\quad\quad\quad = (2 \times n) + (2 \times 3)$ | $\quad\quad\quad = (5 \times 3n) - (5 \times 2)$ |
> | $\quad\quad\quad = 2n + 6$ | $\quad\quad\quad = 15n - 10$ |
>
> $2(n + 3)$ and $2n + 6$ are $5(3n - 2)$ and $15n - 10$ are
> **equivalent expressions**   equivalent expressions

Exercise 2.8
Using brackets

1 For $n = 5$, find the value of $2(n + 3)$ and $2n + 6$.

2 For $n = 2$, find the value of $5(n - 2)$ and $5n - 10$.

3 Sort these into pairs of equivalent expressions.

| $2(a + 4)$ | $8a - 12$ | $2(a + 2)$ | $2a + 8$ |

| $4(2a - 3)$ | $2a - 12$ | $2a + 4$ | $2(a - 6)$ |

4 A student has tried to multiply out the brackets from $3(4 + x)$.

$3(4 + x) = 4 + 3x$ ✗

  a Explain the mistake you think she has made.
  b Multiply out the brackets from $3(4 + x)$.

5 Two students find expressions for the nth term in a sequence.

Sue: nth term $= 5(2n - 1)$ **Ahmet:** nth term $= 10n - 5$

Show that the two expressions are equivalent.

6 Multiply out the brackets from:

  a $4(n + 1)$ **b** $5(m - 3)$ **c** $6(c - 9)$
  d $2(3p + 2)$ **e** $8(2s - 5)$ **f** $4(3 + t)$
  g $3(5 - k)$ **h** $2(7n - 5)$ **i** $30(2f - 13)$
  j $180(5 + 3h)$ **k** $10(3 - 7q)$ **l** $5(2y + 3z)$

7 Show that $2(n + 2) + 2n$ and $4n + 4$ are equivalent expressions.

8 Multiply out the brackets from:

  a $5(p + 2) + 3p$ **b** $4(2q - 1) - 3q$
  c $4r + 10(3 + 5r)$ **d** $3(2s - t) + 5t$

End points

You should be able to ...   **... so try these questions**

A Find a rule that fits a sequence of patterns

A1 These are the first three matchstick patterns in a sequence.

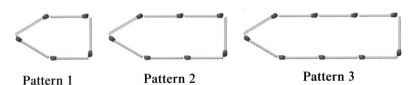

Pattern 1   Pattern 2   Pattern 3

a Find a rule for the number of matches (m) in the nth pattern. Explain your method.

b Use your rule to find the number of matches in the 100th pattern.

B Find rules for mapping diagrams

B1 Copy and complete these mapping diagrams.

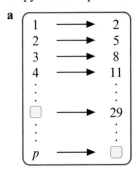

a

```
1  ⟶  2
2  ⟶  5
3  ⟶  8
4  ⟶  11
⋮      ⋮
☐  ⟶  29
⋮
p  ⟶  ☐
```

b

```
1  ⟶  7
2  ⟶  10
3  ⟶  15
4  ⟶  22
⋮      ⋮
20 ⟶  ☐
⋮
n  ⟶  ☐
```

C Find an expression for the nth term in a sequence

C1 A 7, 10, 13, 16, 19, ...   B 2, 7, 12, 17, 22, ...
C 2, 5, 10, 17, 26, ...   D 6, 7, 8, 9, 10, ...
E 9, 12, 15, 18, 21, ...   F 5, 20, 45, 80, 125, ...

For each of the sequences A to F:

a find an expression for the nth term

b use your expression to calculate the 20th term.

D Multiply out brackets from linear expressions

D1 Multiply out the brackets from:

a $4(n + 5)$ **b** $7(x - 2)$
c $5(3k - 1)$ **d** $6(2 + 5t)$

Some points to remember

- ◆ It is often possible to find a rule for the nth pattern in a sequence of patterns by looking at how each pattern can be made.

- ◆ In a sequence: ❖ If the first differences are k each time, there is a simple linear expression for the nth term that begins kn ... .

  ❖ If the second differences are the same non-zero number each time, there is an expression for the nth term that involves n^2.

Starting points
You need to know about ...

... so try these questions

A Naming angles and triangles

- Any angle less than 90° is an **acute angle**.
- Any angle equal to 90° is a **right angle**.
- Any angle between 90° and 180° is an **obtuse angle**.
- Any angle between 180° and 360° is a **reflex angle**.

- Any triangle which has:
  - three sides of equal length
  - three equal angles (60°)

  is an **equilateral triangle**.

- Any triangle which has:
  - two sides of equal length
  - two equal angles

  is an **isosceles triangle**.

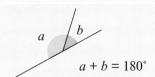

- Any triangle which has no sides of equal length and no equal angles is a **scalene triangle**.
- Any triangle which has one right angle is a **right-angled triangle**.

B Angle sums

- Angles at a point on a straight line add up to 180°.

- Angles round a point add up to 360°.

$a + b = 180°$

$c + d + e = 360°$

- Vertically opposite angles are equal.

- Angles in a triangle add up to 180°.

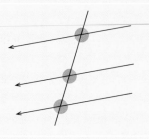

$x + y + z = 180°$

C Parallel lines

At each point where a straight line crosses a set of parallel lines there are two pairs of vertically opposite angles.

Parallel lines are marked with arrows.

Here equal angles are marked with the same colour.

A1

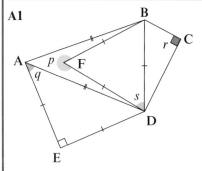

a What type of angle is:
  i p ii q iii r?
b What type of triangle is:
  i BFD   ii BCD?
c Which triangles are isosceles?

B1 In the diagram above calculate:
  a the size of angle s
  b angle p
  c angle $\hat{\text{ADE}}$.

B2 On this diagram, angles marked with the same letter are equal in size.

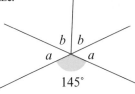

a Work out angles a and b.
b Explain why a triangle can only have one obtuse angle.

C1

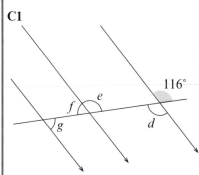

Work out the angles d to g in this diagram.

D Quadrilaterals

/ = line of symmetry

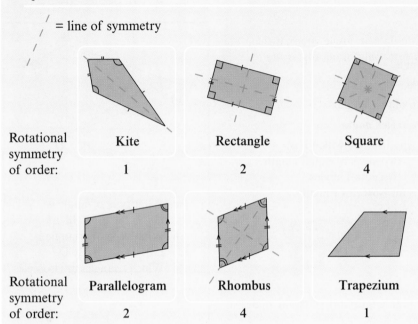

	Kite	Rectangle	Square
Rotational symmetry of order:	1	2	4

	Parallelogram	Rhombus	Trapezium
Rotational symmetry of order:	2	4	1

E Polygons

- In ABCDE:
  - the **interior angles** are marked in red
  - the angles marked in blue are not interior angles.

- The **sum of the interior angles** of a polygon with n sides is: $(n - 2) \times 180°$
  So for ABCDE the sum of interior angles is: $(5 - 2) \times 180°$
  $= 3 \times 180°$
  $= 540°$

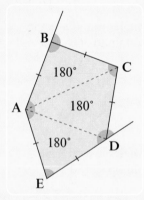

- In a **regular polygon** all the sides are equal and the interior angles are equal.

- ABCDE is an **irregular polygon** The sides are all equal but the interior angles are not.

Name of polygon	Number of sides	Sum of interior angles	Interior angle of a regular polygon
Triangle	3	180° ——÷3—▶	60°
Quadrilateral	4	360° ——÷4—▶	90°
Pentagon	5	540° ——÷5—▶	108°
Hexagon	6	720° ——÷6—▶	120°
Heptagon	7		
Octagon	8		
Nonagon	9		
Decagon	10		

Another expression for the **sum of the interior angles** of a polygon with n sides is: $(180° \times n) - 360°$

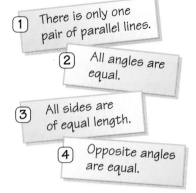

D1 Name all the quadrilaterals that fit each of these labels.

(1) There is only one pair of parallel lines.

(2) All angles are equal.

(3) All sides are of equal length.

(4) Opposite angles are equal.

D2 Draw a trapezium with one line of symmetry.

E1 What is the sum of the interior angles of an octagon?

E2 Calculate the angle a in this pentagon.

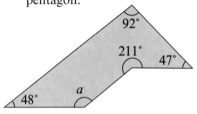

E3 Calculate the interior angle of a regular heptagon to the nearest degree.

E4 A dodecagon has 12 sides.
  a What is the sum of the interior angles of a dodecagon?
  b Calculate the interior angle of a regular dodecagon.

Angles in triangles

To calculate an angle you may need to work out some other angles first.

Example

Calculate the angle $\hat{EGF}$.

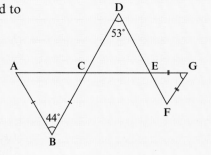

♦ You should sketch a diagram and label each angle that you calculate.

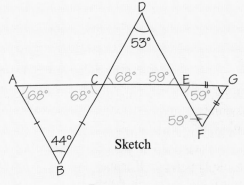

Sketch

△ stands for triangle

An angle can be written in different ways.

For example:

$\hat{DCE}$ is the same angle as $\hat{DCG}$ and $\hat{ECD}$

$\hat{DEC}$ is the same angle as $\hat{DEA}$ and $\hat{CED}$.

You may not need to calculate all the intermediate angles.

To calculate $\hat{EGF}$

Calculation …	**… Reason**
$\hat{ACB} = \hat{CAB}…$	…ABC is an isosceles △
$\quad = (180° - 44°) \div 2$	
$\quad = 68°$	
$\hat{DCE} = 68°…$	…Vertically opposite ACB
$\hat{DEC} = 180° - (68° + 53°)…$	…Angle sum of △
$\quad = 59°$	
$\hat{FEG} = 59°…$	…Vertically opposite DEC
$\hat{GEF} = \hat{EFG}…$	…EFG is an isosceles △
$\hat{EGF} = 180° - (59° \times 2)…$	…Angle sum of △

So the angle $\hat{EGF} = 62°$

Exercise 3.1
Angles in triangles

1 a Which is the easiest angle to calculate in this diagram?

   b Calculate the angles *a* to *f* in this diagram.

   c In what order did you calculate the angles? Explain why.

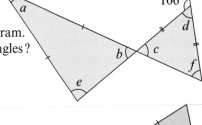

2

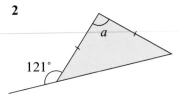

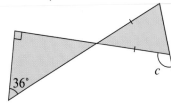

You will need to work out some other angles first.

Calculate the angles *a*, *b* and *c* in these diagrams.
Give a reason for each calculation that you do.

Parallel lines

In each of these diagrams a straight line crosses two parallel lines.

♦ In each diagram a pair of **corresponding angles** is labelled. Corresponding angles are equal.

♦ In each diagram a pair of **alternate angles** is labelled. Alternate angles are equal.

Exercise 3.2
Angles in parallel lines

1 a List five pairs of corresponding angles in this diagram.
  b List three pairs of alternate angles.

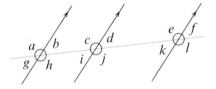

> To find corresponding angles in a diagram you could look for an F shape which may be upside down and/or back to front.
>
> To find alternate angles in a diagram you could look for a Z shape which may be back to front.

2 Sketch these diagrams. Work out the angles a, b and c. You may need to calculate some other angles first.

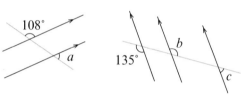

3 In this diagram AS, BR and NQ intersect to make the triangle DPO. CE, FI, JM and NQ are parallel.

  a List three pairs of corresponding angles along the line:
    i AS   **ii** BR

  b Explain why DĜH and DĤI are not corresponding angles.

  c List three pairs of alternate angles in this diagram.

  d Calculate each of these angles.

    i HD̂G   **ii** AD̂C
    iii GK̂L   **iv** HL̂K
    v QP̂L   **vi** NÔR

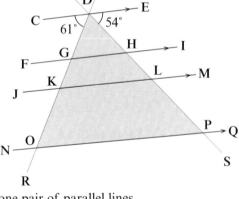

> Give a reason for each calculation that you do.

4 In each of these diagrams there is one pair of parallel lines.

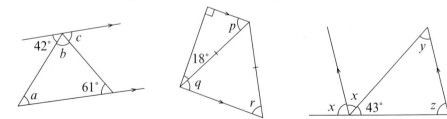

Sketch these diagrams and calculate each of the angles marked with a letter.

5 a Work out each of these angles in ABCD.

i AB̂D   ii AD̂B

iii BD̂C   iv BĈD

b Which two lines are parallel?

c What is the mathematical name for ABCD?

d Explain why ABCD is not a rhombus.

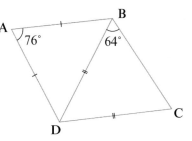

Properties of polygons

Exercise 3.3
Properties of quadrilaterals

1 AB and CD are plastic strips joined by red and yellow elastic bands.
ABCD is a parallelogram; its diagonals intersect at M.
You can stretch the parallelogram if you fix AB and pull CD sideways.

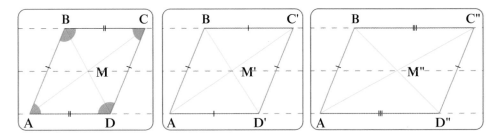

Below are some diagrams of the parallelogram as it is stretched.
ABC′D′ is a rhombus.

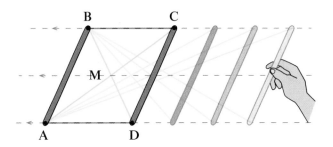

a Trace the angles AB̂C, AB̂D and CB̂D.

b Use your tracings to find out what happens to each of these angles as the parallelogram is stretched.

i AB̂C   ii AB̂D   ii CB̂D

c What happens to AM̂B as the parallelogram is stretched?

d What type of angle is each of these?

i AM̂B   ii AM̂′B   ii AM̂″B

> The interior angles of ABCD are marked in green.

> If you bisect a line or angle, you cut it into 2 equal parts.

> If two lines bisect each other, they are both cut into two equal lengths.

2

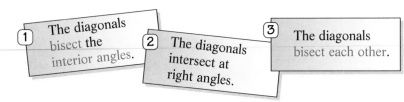

Which of these statements do you think is always true:

a for a parallelogram   b for a rhombus?

On an isometric grid the lines intersect to form equilateral triangles.

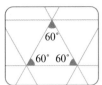

3 This kite is drawn on an isometric grid.
The interior angles of ABCD are marked in green.
The diagonals are marked in red and intersect at M.

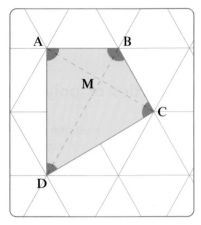

a Calculate the interior angles of ABCD.
b Which angle is equal to:
   i $\hat{BAC}$ **ii** $\hat{CAD}$?
c What type of angle is $\hat{AMB}$?
d List three pairs of equal lengths in ABCD.
e Do the diagonals of ABCD bisect each other?
f Which is the line of symmetry for ABCD?

Exercise 3.4
Properties of polygons

1 These polygons are drawn on a seven-dot isometric grid.

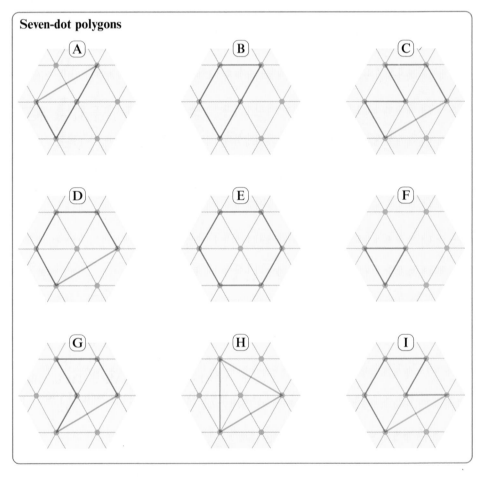

Seven-dot polygons

A   B   C
D   E   F
G   H   I

a On an isometric grid draw each of the polygons A to I.
b Give a mathematical name for each polygon.
c **i** List all the interior angles of each polygon.
    ii Check that the sum of the interior angles is correct for each polygon.

The sum of the interior angles for a polygon with *n* sides is

$$(n - 2) \times 180°$$

2 Each of these cards matches some of the seven-dot polygons A to I.

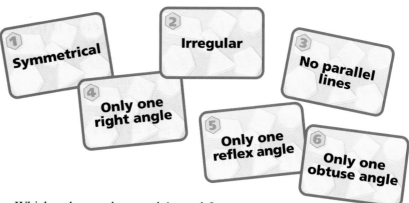

1 Symmetrical

2 Irregular

3 No parallel lines

4 Only one right angle

5 Only one reflex angle

6 Only one obtuse angle

a Which polygons does card 4 match?
b Which cards match polygon C?
c Which card matches:
   i the highest number of polygons
   ii the lowest number of polygons?
d Draw another seven-dot polygon to match each card.
   Some polygons may match more than one card.
e Which of the cards would match a regular pentagon?

> Do not count any that are a rotation or reflection of another polygon.

3 How many different seven-dot polygons is it possible to draw?

Exercise 3.5
Property puzzle

1

Property puzzle	No reflex angles	More than one obtuse angle	No line of symmetry
Only one pair of parallel lines	a	b	c
Regular	d	e	f
More than one acute angle	g	h	i

You can put polygon A in cell i
because it has
no line of symmetry
and two acute angles.
You can also put it in cell g.

Use the polygons A to I.

You can:
● only use each polygon once
● put one polygon in each cell.

Fill as many cells as possible.

a **i** Which polygons can you put in cell h?
   ii In which cells can you put polygon F?
b **i** Solve the puzzle
   ii How many cells can you fill?
   iii Which cell can you never fill? Explain why.
c Rearrange the labels in the table so that you can fill all the cells.

Tessellations

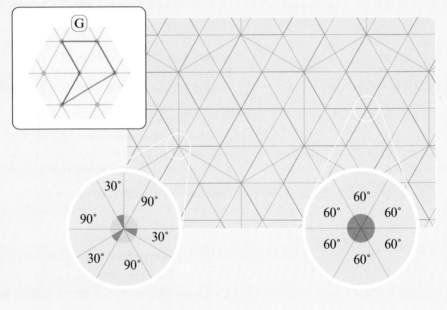

♦ Shapes tessellate if they fit together with no gaps and no overlaps. A tessellation can be continued in any direction.

You can use translations, reflection and rotations of shapes in a tessellation Using polygon G you can:

❖ fit 6 polygons together to make a hexagon

❖ repeat the hexagon to make this tessellation.

♦ At each vertex of the tessellation the angles add up to 360°.

Exercise 3.6
Tessellations

1 These are three seven-dot polygons on an isometric grid.

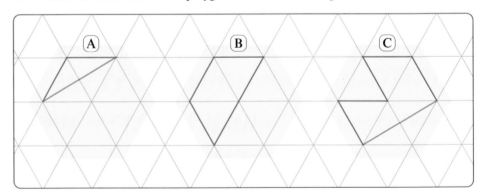

a **i** Draw a tessellation of polygon A.
  ii Check that the total of the angles at each vertex is 360°.
b Draw two different tessellations of polygon B.
c Draw a tessellation of polygon C.

You need to use equilateral grid paper.

2 **a** Calculate the interior angle of a regular decagon.
  b Will regular decagons tessellate on their own?
    Explain your answer.

3 Explain why regular octagons will not tessellate on their own.

4 Decide whether each of these will tessellate on their own.

  a regular hexagons   **b** regular heptagons

  Explain your answers.

5 Explain why it is possible to draw a tessellation using:

  a any triangle   **b** any quadrilateral.

Exercise 3.7
Combined tessellations

1 This is a tessellation using three different polygons J, K and L.

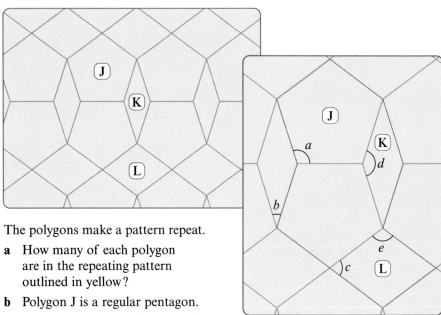

  The polygons make a pattern repeat.

  a How many of each polygon are in the repeating pattern outlined in yellow?

  b Polygon J is a regular pentagon.

   i Give a mathematical name for polygons K and L.

   ii Calculate the angles *a* to *e*.

2 Each of these tessellations uses two different polygons.

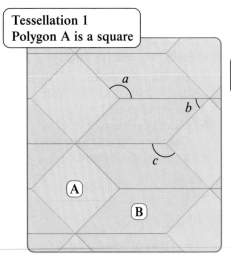

Tessellation 1
Polygon A is a square

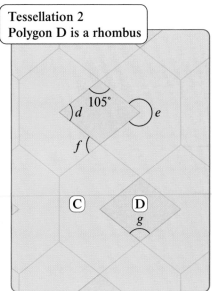

Tessellation 2
Polygon D is a rhombus

  a Give a mathematical name for:

   i polygon B

   ii polygon C.

  b Calculate the angles *a* to *g*.

Angles in polygons

◆ At each vertex of a polygon the angle between an extended side and the adjacent side is called **an exterior angle**.

In ABCDE:

❖ the exterior angles are marked in orange
❖ the interior angles are marked in blue.

◆ The sum of the exterior angles of any polygon is 360°.

In ABCDE:
$a + b + c + d + e = 360°$

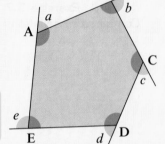

You can show this by tracing the angles and fitting them together round a point.

◆ At each vertex the sum of the interior angle and exterior angle is 180°.

Exercise 3.8
Exterior angles of polygons

1 For this polygon:

  a calculate each exterior angle
  b check that the total of the exterior angles is 360°.

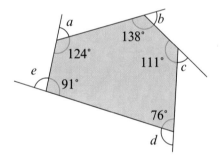

2 A dodecagon has 12 sides. In this regular dodecagon one side is extended to form the angle p.

  a Explain why the exterior angles of a regular dodecagon are all equal to 360° ÷ 12.
  b Calculate the angle p.
  c Calculate the interior angle of a regular dodecagon.

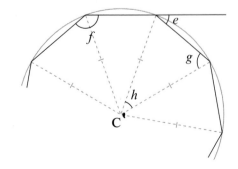

3 This is part of regular nonagon drawn inside a circle with centre C. One side of the nonagon is extended to form the angle e. Calculate the angles e to h.

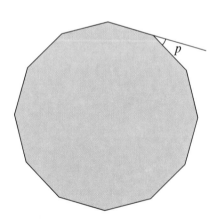

Exercise 3.9
Triangles investigation

You can mark eight points that are equally spaced on the circumference of a circle if you:
◆ draw a circle on square grid paper
◆ mark in lines that are vertical, horizontal and at 45° to the horizontal.

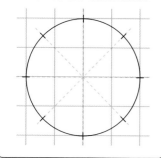

1 This eight-point circle has the points A to H equally spaced on the circumference.
Δ ABD is drawn by joining three of the points.

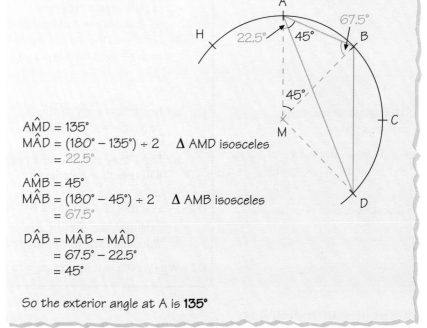

This is how a student calculated the exterior angle at A for Δ ABD.

To find the exterior angle at A

$A\hat{M}D = 135°$
$M\hat{A}D = (180° - 135°) \div 2$ Δ AMD isosceles
   $= 22.5°$

$A\hat{M}B = 45°$
$M\hat{A}B = (180° - 45°) \div 2$ Δ AMB isosceles
   $= 67.5°$

$D\hat{A}B = M\hat{A}B - M\hat{A}D$
   $= 67.5° - 22.5°$
   $= 45°$

So the exterior angle at A is **135°**

a Explain why $A\hat{M}D$ is 135°.
b For triangle ABD:
   i explain why the exterior angle at A is 135°
   ii calculate the exterior angles at B and D
   iii check that the total of the exterior angles is 360°.

2 Triangle ACF is also drawn on an eight-point circle.

a For triangle ACF:
   i calculate each interior angle
   ii calculate each exterior angle.
b How many different triangles is it possible to draw in an eight-point circle?
c What different exterior angles are possible for triangles drawn on an eight-point circle?

Do not count any that are reflections or rotations of another polygon.

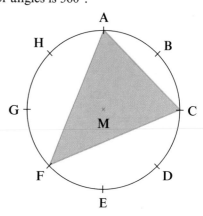

End points

You should be able to ...   ... so try these questions

A Calculate angles in parallel lines

A1 Calculate the angles *a*, *b* and *c* in this diagram.

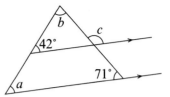

B Use the properties of polygons

B1 Polygons A to E are drawn on an equilateral grid.

    a Which of these polygons:
      i is a regular polygon
      ii has only one obtuse angle?
    b Give a mathematical name for each of the polygons A to E.

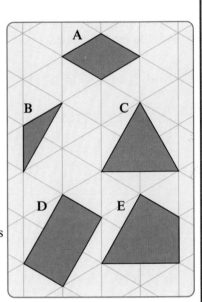

C Decide whether shapes will tessellate

C1 **a** Show how each of these polygons will tessellate on their own.
    b Show how two of these polygons will tessellate together.

D Calculate angles in polygons

D1 For each of the polygons B and E:
    a calculate the interior angles
    b calculate the exterior angles.

D2 What is the exterior angle of a regular octagon?

Some points to remember

- For a polygon with *n* sides:
  - the sum of the interior angles is $(n - 2) \times 180°$
  - the sum of the exterior angles is 360°
  - each exterior angle of a regular polygon is $360° \div n$.

- Examples of quadrilaterals

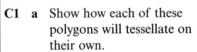

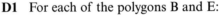

	Square	Rectangle	Kite	Rhombus	Parallelogram
The diagonals: • bisect the interior angles • bisect each other • intersect at 90°.	✓ ✓ ✓	✓ ✓ ✓	✗ ✗ ✓	✓ ✓ ✓	✗ ✓ ✗
Number of lines of symmetry	4	2	1	2	0
Order of rotational symmetry	4	2	1	4	2

Starting points
You need to know about ...

... so try these questions

A Graphs of vertical and horizontal lines

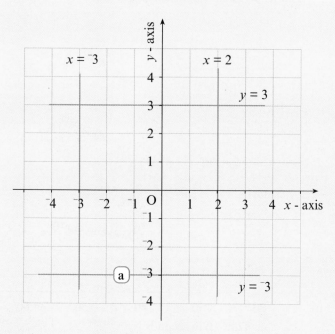

The equation of **line a** is $y = ^-3$ as:
all points on **line a** have a y-coordinate of $^-3$.
The equation of the x-axis is $y = 0$ and
the equation of the y-axis is $x = 0$.

A1 a Draw a pair of axes.
  b Label the x-axis.
  c Label the y-axis.
  d Draw and label the line $y = 2$ and the line $x = ^-1$
  e Give the coordinates of where lines $y = 2$ and $x = ^-1$ cross.

A2 a Give the coordinates of where the lines $x = 0$ and $y = 2$ cross.
  b Will the line $y = 2$ cross the line $y = ^-2$? Explain your answer.
  c What can you say about all the points on the line $x = 0$?

A3 Will each of these lines be vertical or horizontal?

  a $y = 4$ **b** $x = ^-2$
  c $x = 3$ **d** $y = ^-8$
  e $y = 0$ **f** $x = 0$

B A graph from a table of values

This table of values shows how values of x and y are linked by the equation $y = x + 1$

x	$^-1$	0	1	1.5	2
y	0	1	2	2.5	3

From the table of values:
the points

  $(^-1, 0)$
  $(0, 1)$
  $(1, 2)$
  $(1.5, 2.5)$
  $(2, 3)$

can be plotted and
joined for the graph.

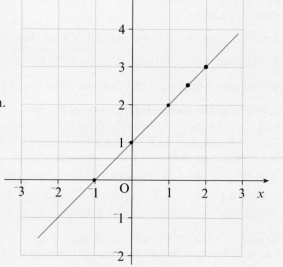

B1

x	$^-2$	$^-1$	0	1	2	3
y						

Copy and complete this table of values for each equation.

  a $y = 3x - 1$
  b $y = x + 2$
  c $y = x$
  d $y + 3 = x$
  e $y = 1.5x + 1$

B2 For each equation in **B1** draw and label a graph.

B3 Do not draw a graph.
Which of these points lie on the line $y = 2x - 3$?

  a $(^-2, ^-7)$ **b** $(0, 3)$
  c $(2, 1)$ **d** $(3, 3)$
  e $(0, 1.5)$ **f** $(^-15, ^-27)$
  g $(^-0.25, ^-3.5)$ **h** $(4, 4)$

Linear graphs

Exercise 4.1
Interpreting linear graphs

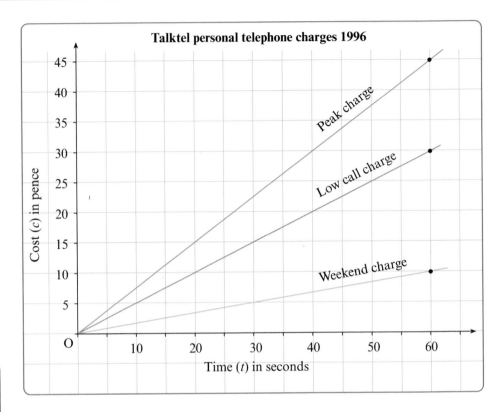

Talktel personal telephone charges 1996

> Linear is another word for straight.
>
> A linear graph is a straight line graph

Each linear graph shows a different charge made by Talktel.
Each call is timed (in seconds), and the cost is calculated for the customer bill.

1   Talktel's peak charge is 45 pence per minute.
    a   From the graph, what is the low call charge per minute?
    b   What is the weekend charge per minute?

2   **a**   Does a 35 second call at peak charge cost more or less than 25 pence?
    b   Estimate the cost of this call.

3   Estimate the cost of a 45 second call at peak charge.

4   Which is cheaper: 15 seconds at peak or 20 seconds at low call charge?
    Explain your answer.

5   Jess paid 7.5 pence for a 15 second call. Which charge was used for this?

6   At the weekend charge, estimate the cost of a 2 minute 35 second call.

7   At peak charge, how long a call can you make for 75 pence?

8   **a**   Copy the graph for the Talktel charges in 1996.
    b   Add a line to show the Infotel charge of 32 pence per minute.
    c   The line graph for which charge is the steepest?
    d   List the charges in order of the steepness of their line graphs.
    e   Describe any link you can spot between charge rates and steepness.

> In the formula $c = t \div 6$:
>
> c is the cost in pence
>
> t is the time in seconds.

9   Talktel use the formula $c = t \div 6$ for their weekend charge.
    Use the formula to find the cost of a 96 second call at weekend charge.

10   **a**   Write a formula for the low call charge.
    b   Use your formula to find the cost of $1\frac{1}{2}$ minutes at low call charge.

The gradient of a linear graph

◆ The gradient of a linear graph is a measure of how steep the line is.

◆ The gradient of a linear graph is the same for any part of the line.

◆ The gradient of a linear graph is given by:

$$\frac{\text{Change along the } y\text{-axis}}{\text{Change along the } x\text{-axis}}$$

The change along an axis can be an **increase** or a **decrease**.

For a gradient we need to look at what happens for an **increase** along the x-axis.

When:
an **increase** along the x-axis gives
an **increase** along the y-axis

We say the gradient of the line is **positive**.

For example:
To find the gradient of this linear graph:

◆ choose two points on the line, e.g. A and B

◆ along the y-axis the change is 6 units (from 8 to 14)

◆ along the x-axis the change is 2 units (from 2 to 4).

The gradient is given by:

$$\frac{6}{2} = 3$$

The gradient of the line is 3.

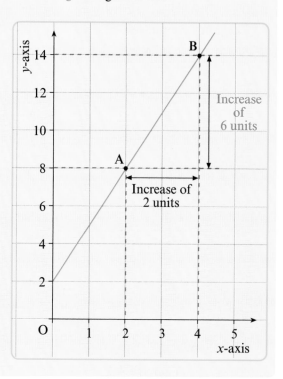

Exercise 4.2
Gradients of linear graphs

1   Calculate the gradients of lines **a** to **h**.

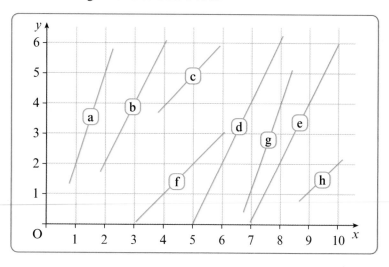

2   **a**   Draw a pair of axes: x-axis from 0 to 10, y-axis from 0 to 10.
     b   On your axes draw and label lines with each of these gradients:
              5   6   4   1   2   0.5

3   How are the gradient of a linear graph and its steepness linked?

The gradient of a linear graph has a value that can be given:

or

or

  ◆ as a whole number
  ◆ as a fraction (in its lowest terms)
  ◆ as a decimal.

For example:

> The gradient of a linear graph is given by:
>
> $$\frac{\text{Change in } y\text{-coordinates}}{\text{Change in } x\text{-coordinates}}$$

The linear graph **a** has a gradient given by:

$$\frac{3}{1} \quad \begin{array}{l}\text{(increase of 3)}\\ \text{(increase of 1)}\end{array}$$

$$= \quad 3 \text{ (whole number)}$$

The linear graph **b** has a gradient given by:

$$\frac{5}{2}$$

$\frac{5}{2}$ is a fraction in its lowest terms

but $\frac{5}{2} = 2\frac{1}{2}$

The linear graph **c** has a gradient given by:

$$\frac{1}{4} \quad \text{or} \quad 0.25 \text{ (decimal)}$$

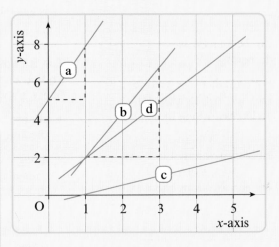

The linear graph **d** has a gradient of:

$$\frac{6}{4} = \frac{3}{2} \text{ (in its lowest terms)}$$

Exercise 4.3
Calculating gradients

1

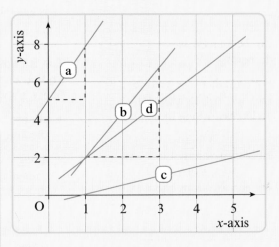

a   Give the gradient of each linear graph *a* to *g*, as:
  i   a fraction in its lowest terms
  ii a decimal value.

b   List the lines with their gradients in order of steepness.
    Start with the steepest.

2   What can you say about the gradients of lines which are parallel?
    Explain your answer with an example and a diagram.

The line CD slopes:
downwards from left to right.

To find the gradient of line CD, use the points C and D:

- the change along the y-axis is
  5 units   (decrease)

- the change along the x-axis is
  2 units   (increase)

The gradient of CD is $\frac{-5}{2}$ or $^-2.5$

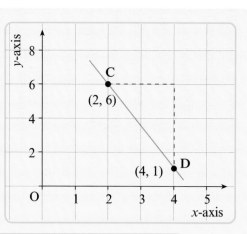

When:
an **increase** along the x-axis gives
a **decrease** along the y-axis

we say the gradient of the line is **negative**.

A negative sign is used to show a negative gradient. For example a gradient of $\frac{-3}{4}$

Gradients of straight lines can be described in this way:

A line which slopes   **upwards from left to right** (╱)
            has   **a positive gradient**.

A line which slopes   **downwards from left to right** (╲)
            has   **a negative gradient**.

Exercise 4.4
Gradients:
positive and negative

1

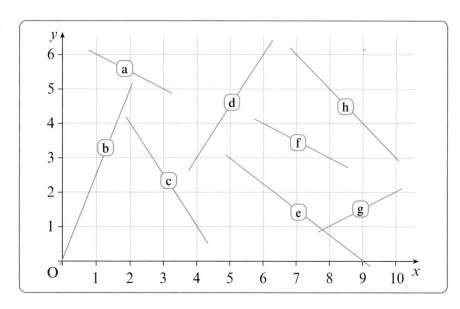

a   Which of the lines, **a** to **h**, has a negative gradient?
b   For each of the lines **a** to **h**, give its gradient as:
   i   a fraction in its lowest terms
   ii a decimal value.

2 a   Draw a pair of axes: the x-axis from 0 to 10 and the y-axis from 0 to 6.
    b   For each of these gradients, draw and label a line:
       gradient of 3, gradient of $^-2$, gradient of $\frac{2}{3}$, gradient of $\frac{-3}{4}$.

3 A line slopes downwards from right to left. Describe its gradient.

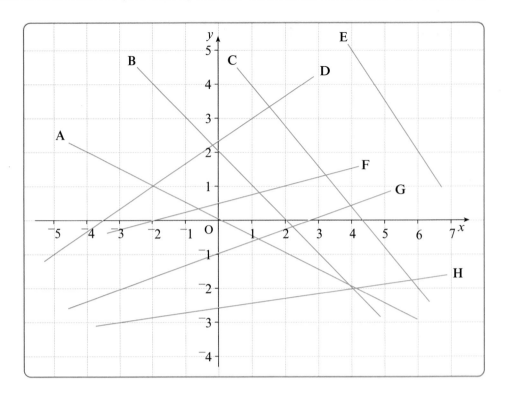

4 Which of these lines has a gradient of $\frac{-1}{2}$?

5 Which line has a gradient of $\frac{1}{3}$?

6 Which is steeper: line F or line H?
   Explain your answer using gradients.

7 Give the gradient of line B.

8 Which line has a gradient of $^-1.2$?
   Explain your answer.

9 Asa gave the gradient of line E as $\frac{2}{3}$.
   Do you agree? Explain your answer.

10 Mina gave the gradient of line D as $\frac{3}{2}$.
    Do you agree? Explain your answer.

11 a Draw a pair of axes with:
       values of x from $^-5$ to $^+5$, and values of y from $^-5$ to $^+5$
    b Plot the point ($^-3$, $^-5$) and label it P, and label ($^-5$, 5) as R.
    c Line T has a gradient of $\frac{4}{3}$, and it passes throught point P.
       On your axes draw and label line T.
    d Line V has a gradient of $\frac{-1}{4}$, and it passes through point R.
       On your axes draw and label line V.
    e Give the coordinates of where line T and line V cross.
    f Line W joins points R and P.
       What is the gradient of line W?
    g Line Z has a gradient of $\frac{9}{2}$, and passes through point P.
       Give the coordinates of where line Z and line V cross.

Drawing linear graphs from a table of values

A linear graph has a rule that links the x-coordinates and the y-coordinates. We call this rule the **equation** of the line, and we can use it to find the coordinates of points on the line.

Example Find the coordinates of a point on the line $y = 2x + 3$.

To find the y-coordinate you multiply the x-coordinate by 2, then add 3
When $x = {}^-2$, $y = (2 \times {}^-2) + 3$, which gives $y = {}^-4 + 3$: so $y = {}^-1$

For any x-coordinate you choose, you can calculate the value of the y-coordinate that goes with it.

To draw the graph of $y = 2x + 3$:

♦ choose values for x
(say $^-2$, $^-1$, 0, 1 and 2)

♦ draw up a table and calculate values for y

x	$^-2$	$^-1$	0	1	2
y	$^-1$	1	3	5	7

♦ from the table, list points on the line
$(^-2, {}^-1)$, $(^-1, 1)$, $(0, 3)$, $(1, 5)$, $(2, 7)$

♦ on a pair of axes, plot the points

♦ draw the line through the points for the graph of $y = 2x + 3$.

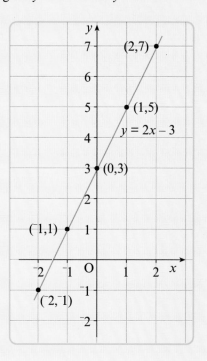

From the table of values you can decide how to label your axes.

Here:

the x-axis shows from $^-2$ to 2

and

the y-axis shows from $^-1$ to 7

Exercise 4.5
Drawing graphs from tables of values

1 For the equation $y = 3x + 2$:
   a Explain in words how to calculate values for y.
   b Draw up a table of values with these values of x: $^-2$, $^-1$, 0, 1, 2 and 3.
      For each value of x calculate a value for y.
   c From the table list points on the line.
   d Draw a pair of axes. Plot and label each point with its coordinates.
   e Draw a line to show the graph of $y = 3x + 2$.

2 For the equation $y = 2x - 3$:
   a Explain in words how to calculate values for y.
   b Draw up a table of values. Use values of x from $^-1$ to 3.
   c Draw the graph of $y = 2x - 3$.

3 a Draw up a table of values for $y = 2x + 1$. Use values of x from $^-2$ to 3.
   b Draw the graph of $y = 2x + 1$.

4 Draw the graph of $y = 4x - 1$.
   Use values of x from $^-2$ to 2.

5 a On the same pair of axes draw graphs of $y = 3x - 3$ and $y = 2x - 1$.
   b Give the coordinates of the point where the two graphs cross.

Linear graphs and their equations

For equations to be the same they do not have to be written in the same order.

For example:

$y = 2x + 1$ is the same as:
$$y = 1 + 2x$$
$$2x + 1 = y$$
$$1 + 2x = y$$

and

$y = 3x - 2$ is the same as: $y = {}^-2 + 3x$

Three linear graphs are shown here, and their equations.

We can list the gradient of each line:
$y = 2x - 2$ has a gradient of 2
$y = 2x + 1$ has a gradient of 2
$y = 2x + 4$ has a gradient of 2.

We can list where each line crosses the y-axis:
$y = 2x - 2$ crosses the y-axis at $^-2$
$y = 2x + 1$ crosses the y-axis at $^+1$
$y = 2x + 4$ crosses the y-axis at $^+4$.

So we have:

$y = 2x - 2$ has a gradient of 2 it crosses the y-axis at $^-2$

$y = 2x + 1$ has a gradient of 2 it crosses the y-axis at $^+1$

$y = 2x + 4$ has a gradient of 2 it crosses the y-axis at $^+4$.

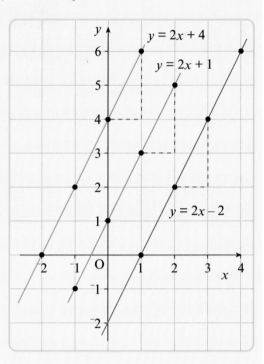

From the equation of a line we can tell:
♦ the gradient of the line
♦ where the line crosses the y-axis.

Exercise 4.6
Using equations of linear graphs

1 For the graph of $y = 2x - 5$
  a give the gradient of the line   **b** where does the line cross the y-axis?

2 For the line $y = 3x - 1$
  a what is the gradient of the line?   **b** where does the line cross the y-axis?

Where a line crosses the y-axis is called the y-intercept.

3 Which of these lines has a gradient of 4 and crosses the y-axis at $^+2$?
  a $y = 2x + 4$ **b** $y = 4x + 2$ **c** $y = 2 + 4x$

4 For each of these lines give the gradient and the y-intercept.
  a $y = 3x - 2$ **b** $y = x + 2$ **c** $y = 4x$ **d** $y = 5x - 4$
  e $y = 3 + 2x$ **f** $y = 3x - \frac{1}{2}$ **g** $5x + 1 = y$ **h** $\frac{1}{2}x = y$
  i $y = 5 - 5x$ **j** $y = x$ **k** $x - 2 = y$ **l** $y = {}^-4x$

5 Here is a description of five different linear graphs.
  Line K has a gradient of 3 and a y-intercept at $^+5$
  Line M has a gradient of $\frac{1}{2}$ and a y-intercept at $^-1$
  Line P has a y-intercept at 1.5 and a gradient of 2
  Line R has a y-intercept at $^+2$ and a gradient of $^-3$
  Line T has a gradient of 1 and a y-intercept at 0.
  Give an equation for each of these lines.

Drawing linear graphs from their equation

As the equation of a line tells us about:
- the gradient of the line
- the y-intercept

it is possible to draw a linear graph just by using the data in the equation.

Example

To draw a linear graph of the equation $y = 3x - 4$

We can tell that the gradient of the line is 3 and the y-intercept is $^-4$.

To draw the graph of $y = 3x - 4$:

- Draw a pair of axes.

- **Step 1**
  Mark the
  y-intercept, $^-4$.

- **Step 2**
  From the y-intercept
  draw in the gradient 3.

- **Step 3**
  Join the points with
  a line and label.

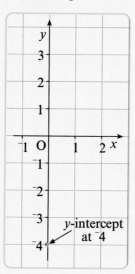
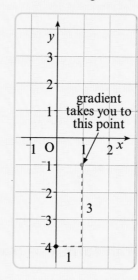
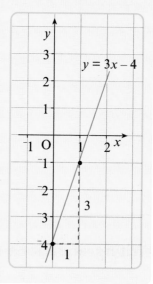

Exercise 4.7
Drawing linear graphs
from equations

1   **a**   Draw a pair of axes. Use x from $^-1$ to 2, and y from $^-5$ to 5.
    b   On your axes draw and label graphs of these lines:
      $y = 4x - 3$ $y = 2x + 1$ $y = x - 1$

2   **a**   Draw a pair of axes. Use x from $^-1$ to 4, and y from $^-4$ to 6.
    b   On your axes draw graphs of these lines:
      $y = 3x - 3$ $y = x + 2$ $y = 3x$
    c   Which two of these lines go through the point (1, 3)?
    d   Which of these lines go through the point (3, 5)?

3   **a**   What is the gradient of the line $y = 2 - 3x$? What is the y-intercept?
    b   Draw the graph of $y = 2 - 3x$.

Exercise 4.8
Building equations
from graphs

1

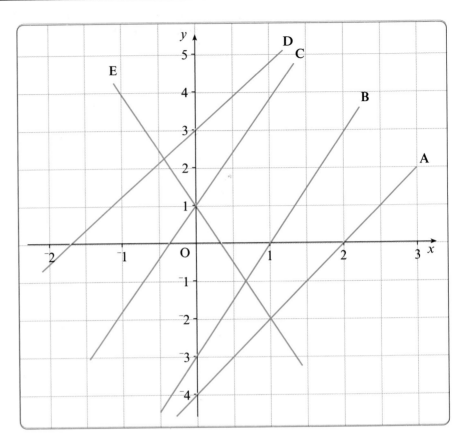

a What is the gradient of line A?
b What is the y-intercept for line A?
c Write an equation for line A.

2 a What is the y-intercept for line B?
b Write an equation for line B.

3 Write an equation for each of the lines C, D, and E.

Writing equations in the form $y = mx + c$

'Rewrite an equation' is not the same as 'change an equation'.

An equation, and its rewritten form give the same data, we say they are equivalent.

When the equation of a linear graph starts $y = ...$, it is easy to draw a graph.
Sometimes you will have to rewrite an equation to make it read $y = ...$
One way to rewrite an equation is to divide each term by the same number.

Examples

To rewrite the equation: $3y = 6x - 3$ To rewrite the equation: $5y = 3x + 10$

divide each term by 3   divide each term by 5

$$y = 2x - 1$$ $$y = \tfrac{3}{5}x + 2$$

as $3y \div 3 = y$, $6x \div 3 = 2x$ as $5y \div 5 = y$, $3x \div 5 = \tfrac{3}{5}x$
and $^-3 \div 3 = ^-1$ and $10 \div 5 = 2$

Exercise 4.9
Rewriting equations

1 a To rewrite the equation $4y = 8x - 20$, to make it read $y = ...$,
      what number will you divide each term by?
  b Rewrite $4y = 8x - 20$, to make it read $y = ...$.

2   **a**   To rewrite $2y = 3x + 4$ in the form $y = \ldots$,
what will you divide each term by?

   b   Rewrite $2y = 3x + 4$ in the form $y = \ldots$.

3   Rewrite each of these equations in the form $y = \ldots$.

   a $2y = 4x + 8$ **b** $3y = 4x - 9$ **c** $3y = 3x - 6$ **d** $5y = 3x$
   e $5y = 2x + 5$ **f** $2y = 6x - 4$ **g** $2y = 3 - 4x$ **h** $4y = x$
   i $4y = 4 - 4x$ **j** $6y = 12 + 12x$ **k** $5y = x + 1$ **l** $2x = 3y$

4   Which of these equations can be rewritten as $y = 2x - 3$?

   a $2y = 3x - 6$ **b** $4y = 8x - 16$ **c** $3y = 6x - 9$ **d** $2y = 4x$

5   Write three different equations that can be rewritten as $y = 3x - 1$.

Rewriting equations and drawing graphs

Example

Draw the graph of $3y = 4x - 6$
One way is with the equation in
the form $y = \ldots$.

♦ Rewrite the equation

$3y = 4x - 6$

Divide each term by 3

$y = \frac{4}{3}x - 2$

♦ Draw the graph from the equation:

gradient $\frac{4}{3}$

y-intercept, $^-2$

♦ Label the graph with
its equation $3y = 4x - 6$.

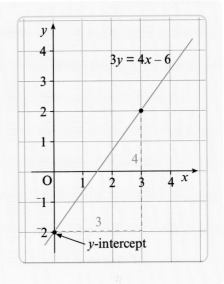

When you divide your
equation, the gradient can
work out as a fraction.

A fraction is easier to work
with for the gradient than a
decimal value.

Exercise 4.10
Drawing graphs

1   For the graph of $2y = 3x + 2$:

   a   Rewrite the equation in the form $y = \ldots$.
   b   What is the gradient of the line?
   c   What is the y-intercept?
   d   Draw a pair of axes: use x from $^-1$ to 3 and y from $^-1$ to 5.
   e   Draw the graph of $2y = 3x + 2$.

2   For the graph of $3y = 2x - 3$:

   a   What is the gradient of the line?
   b   What is the y-intercept?
   c   Draw a graph of $3y = 2x - 3$.

3   Draw a graph of $4y = 8x - 12$.

4   **a**   Draw a pair of axes, use x from $^-1$ to 5 and y from $^-4$ to 4.
   b   On your axes draw a graph for each of these:
            $2y = x$ $4y = x + 4$ $4y = 5x - 12$
   c   Give the coordinates of a point where all three lines cross.

5   Draw a graph of $3y = 4x - 2$.

6   Is the point (2, 3) on the graph of $2y = 5x - 4$?
Explain your answer.

Linear graphs that cross

Any linear graph is part of a straight line drawn through every point that fits its equation.

Where two graphs cross, the point must be on both lines.

For example, at A the graphs of:
$$y = 2x - 2$$
$$\text{and} \quad 2y = x + 2$$

both have a point of (2, 2)

We can say that at (2, 2) the equations must both be true for these values of x and y.

You can test this by using the values of the x- and y-coordinates in each equation.

At A: $x = 2$ and $y = 2$
$y = 2x - 2$ is true as:
$\qquad y = 2$ and $2x - 2 = 2$
$2y = x + 2$ is true as
$\qquad 2y = 4$ and $x + 2 = 4$

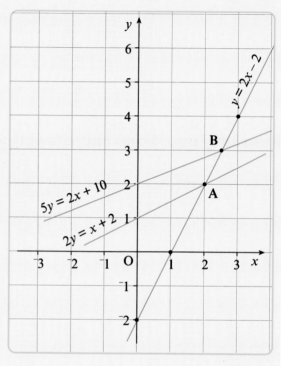

Exercise 4.11
Crossing points

1　a　Give the coordinates of point B.
　　b　Give the equations of two lines that go through B.
　　c　Test that the values for x and y at B are true for the equations.

2　a　On a pair of axes draw the graphs of:
　　　　$y = x + 1$　and　$y = 2x - 1$
　　b　Give the coordinates of a point that both lines are drawn through.
　　c　Test that the equations are true at this point.

3　As lines C and D cross, they must have one point that is the same.

　　a　Estimate the coordinates where lines C and D cross.
　　b　Test these values on each equation.
　　c　Try other estimates to see if you can find the exact coordinates.

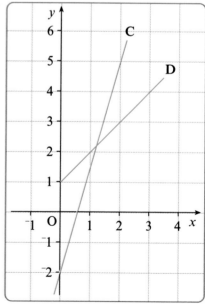

End points

You should be able to ...   **... so try these questions**

A Explain gradients of linear graphs

A1 a In words, and with a diagram, describe a positive gradient.
  b In words, and with a diagram, describe a negative gradient.
  c What does the gradient of a line tell you:
- the length of the line
- the colour of the line
- something else?

Explain your answer.

B Give the value of the gradient of a linear graph

B1 Give the gradient of line D.

B2 Give the gradient of line A
  a as a fraction
  b as a decimal.

B3 Give the gradients of lines B and C.

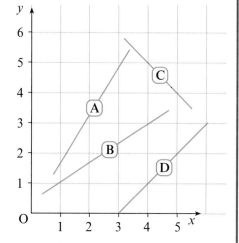

C Use a table of values

C1 Draw up a table of values for the graph of $y = 3x - 4$
Use values of x from $^-1$ to 3.

C2 Draw the graph of $y = 3x - 4$.

D Rewrite equations to read $y =$

D1 Change the equation $4y = 3x + 6$ to read $y = \dots$.

E Use $y = mx + c$

E1 For this line, give the gradient and the y-intercept.
$$y = 2x - 5$$

E2 Draw the graph of $y = \frac{1}{2}x + 1$.

E3 Draw a graph of $3y = 5x - 6$.

F Test to see if a line goes through a point

F1 Which of these lines pass through the point (3, 4)?
$$3y = 2x + 6 \qquad y = 2x - 2 \qquad 3y = 4x + 1$$

Some points to remember

- $y = mx + c$ is the general form of a linear equation where, m is the gradient and c the y-intercept.
- Rewriting a linear equation is not the same as changing the equation.

Starting points
You need to know about ...

... so try these questions

A Types of data

- There are two main types of data:

  - data that is divided into **categories**, such as:
    make of car,
    colour of car.
  - data that is **numerical**, such as:
    number of people in car,
    length of car.

TRAFFIC SURVEY

Car	Make of car	Number of people in car
A	Peugeot	1
B	Ford	3
C	Vauxhall	1
D	Ford	2
E	Rover	2

B Presenting data in frequency tables

Make of car	Tally	Number of cars
Ford	̶H̶H̶ ////	9
Rover	̶H̶H̶ /	6
Vauxhall	//	2
Others	̶H̶H̶ //	7

Number of people in car	Frequency
1	3
2	10
3	6
4	3
5	2

NUMBER OF CHILDREN IN CAR

```
1  0  1  2  1  1  0  0
4  1  0  1  0  0  2  0
2  0  3  0  0  2  0  1
```

COLOUR OF CAR

Red	Blue	Green	White
Silver	Red	White	Black
Black	Green	Red	Blue
Black	Blue	Blue	Silver
Red	White	Blue	Brown
Blue	Black	Brown	Red

B1 Use a tally to present the number-of-children-in-car data in a frequency table.

B2 Present the colour-of-car data in a frequency table.

C Diagrams that present one set of data

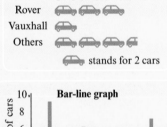

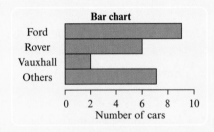

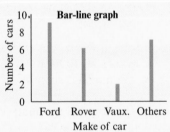

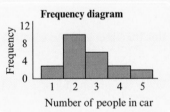

C1 Draw a bar-line graph to show the colour-of-car data.

C2 Draw a frequency diagram to show the number-of-children-in-car data.

C3 Draw a pictogram to show the colour-of-car data.

C4 Draw a bar chart to show the colour-of-car data.

D Constructing a percentage pie chart

- To calculate the percentage for each category.
  For Vauxhall, there are 2 cars out of 24 so
  $100 \div 24 \times 2 = 8.3\%$ (to 1 dp).

	No. of cars	%
Ford	9	37.5
Rover	6	25
Vauxhall	2	8.3
Others	7	29.2
Totals	24	100

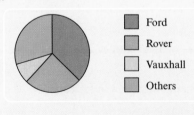

Ford
Rover
Vauxhall
Others

D1 For the colour-of-car data, calculate the percentage for each colour.

D2 Draw a pie chart to show the colour-of-car data.

E Finding averages and the range

♦ For data in categories, you can only find one average:
  ❖ the **mode** (the **modal** category is the most common)

| Red | Blue | Yellow | Blue | Green | Black | Red | Blue |

The modal colour is **Blue**.

♦ For numerical data, you can find several averages:
  ❖ the **mode** is the most common value (or values)
  ❖ the **median** is the middle value when the data is in order
    (for an **even** number of values, take the median as halfway
    between the middle pair of values)
  ❖ the **mean** is the total of all the values divided by the number
    of values.

♦ A measure of how spread out the data is can also be found:
  ❖ the **range** is the difference between the highest and lowest values.

| 46 | 27 | 82 | 46 | 102 | 27 | 60 |

Mode = **27** and **46**
Median = **46**   (27 27 46 46 60 82 102)
Mean = **55.7** $\left(\dfrac{46 + 27 + 82 + 46 + 102 + 27 + 60}{7}\right)$
   (to 1 dp)
Range = **75**   (102 − 27)

| 87 | 43 | 101 | 56 | 87 | 67 |

Mode = **87**
Median = **77**   (43 56 67 87 87 101)
Mean = **73.5**   (441 ÷ 6)
Range = **58**   (101 − 43)

F Finding the mode and the range from a frequency table

♦ For data in categories:
  ❖ the **mode** is the category with the highest frequency.

Make of car	Ford	Rover	Vaux.	Other
Number of cars	9	2	6	7

The modal make of car is **Ford**.

♦ For numerical data:
  ❖ the **mode** is the value (or values) with the highest frequency
  ❖ the **range** is the difference between the highest and lowest values.

Number of people in car	Frequency
1	3
2	10
3	6
4	3
5	2

The mode is **2** people.
The range is **4** people (5 − 1).

E1

| 15 | 42 | 33 | 37 | 84 | 42 | 50 |
| 81 | 29 | 26 | 67 | 15 | 19 | 55 |

For this set of data, find:
a the mode
b the median
c the mean
d the range.

E2

| 38 | 25 | 106 | 78 | 44 | 62 |
| 13 | 90 | 25 | 31 | 25 | |

For this set of data, find:
a the mode
b the median
c the mean
d the range.

E3

Mode 3 and 7
Median 6
Mean 6

These are averages for a set of
data with 8 values.
List what the values might be.

F1 Use your frequency table from
Question **B2** to find the modal
colour of car.

F2 Use your frequency table from
Question **B1** to find:
a the modal number of
children in car
b the range of the number
of children in car.

G Deciding which average to use

◆ The **mean** is the most widely used average.
It is not a sensible average to use for data with **extreme values**, values which are much smaller or much greater than the others.

G.T. Small & Son – Monthly Salaries (£)					
870	870	870	870	1050	1050
1050	1210	1210	1210	**2080**	**2330**

Mean = £1222.50
Median = £1050
Mode = £870

10 of the 12 salaries are smaller than the mean, so the **median** is the more sensible average to use.

◆ The **mode** can also be a poor choice of average.
For this data, it is a poor choice because it is the lowest salary.

H Diagrams that present two or more sets of data

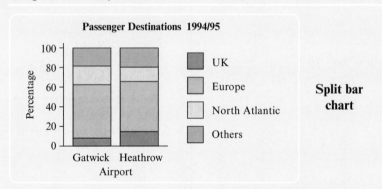

Split bar chart

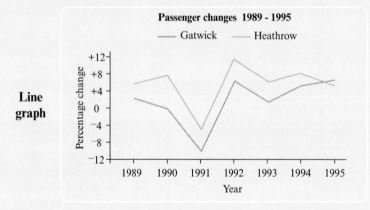

Line graph

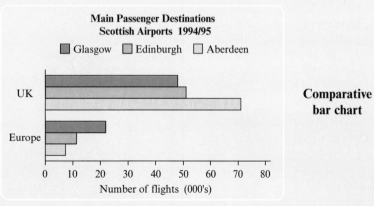

Comparative bar chart

G1

S. Fry & Partners – Weekly Wages (£)
112 285 285 340 340
340 372 372 388

Find
a the modal wage
b the median wage
c the mean wage
d For each average wage:
  i decide whether it is sensible to use or not
  ii if you think it is not sensible, explain why.

H1

Southampton to Channel Islands 1994/95		
	Number of passengers (000's)	Number of flights (000's)
Jersey	156	4.0
Guernsey	100	3.4
Alderney	31	2.9
Totals	287	10.3

Calculate the percentage of passengers going to:
a Jersey   **b** Guernsey
c Alderney

H2 Calculate the percentage of flights going to each of the three islands.

H3 Draw a split bar chart to show the two sets of data.

H4

% change in no. of passengers					
	1990	1991	1992	1993	1994
Glasgow	11.0	⁻3.1	12.4	7.4	8.8
Edinburgh	5.3	⁻6.1	8.4	7.2	10.3

Draw a line graph to show this data for Glasgow and Edinburgh.

H5

NUMBER OF FLIGHTS 1994/95 (000's)		
	Heathrow	Gatwick
UK	75	33
Europe	252	111
North Atlantic	40	19
Others	47	21

Draw a comparative bar chart to show this data.

Constructing a pie chart using degrees

> £m stands for millions of pounds.

* A set of data in categories can be shown on a pie chart.

* To construct a pie chart using degrees:

CHILD CONCERN	£m		£m
Expenditure	Child care 18.8	Administration	2.8
(1994/95)	Fundraising 6.0	Other costs	1.2

❖ add the amounts to find the total

> 18.8 + 6.0 + 2.8 + 1.2 = **28.8**

£28.8m is shared between the 360° in a circle: each £1m is given 12.5°

> There are 360° at the centre of a circle.

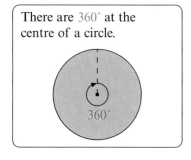

❖ divide 360° by the total

> 360° ÷ 28.8 = **12.5°**

❖ work out the angle for each category

Child care	18.8 × 12.5° = 235°
Fundraising	6.0 × 12.5° = 75°
Administration	2.8 × 12.5° = 35°
Other costs	1.2 × 12.5° = 15°

Multiply each number of millions by 12.5°

❖ use the angles to draw a pie chart.

Child Concern Expenditure (1994/95)
- ▮ Child Care
- ▯ Fundraising
- ▯ Administration
- ▮ Other costs

> **Exercise 5.1**
> Presenting data divided into categories

1 These tables show what three different charities spent in 1994–95.

> Use the same method for data given in %:
> divide 360° by 100.

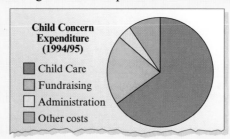

CARING FOR CHILDREN	
Expenditure (1994–95)	
	£m
Child Care	61.2
Fundraising	6.4
Administration	1.6
Other costs	2.8

CHILD ACTION	
Expenditure (1994–95)	
	£m
Child Care	33.6
Fundraising	8.8
Administration	2.4
Other costs	3.2

Children in Crisis	
Expenditure (1994–95)	
	%
Child Care	70
Fundraising	15
Administration	10
Other costs	5

For each charity:

a add the amounts to find the total
b divide 360° by the total
c work out the angle for each category
d draw a pie chart.

> A split bar chart can show differences between data more clearly than pie charts.

2 a Convert the expenditures for two of the charities into percentages.
b Draw a split bar chart to show the three sets of data.

3 Write a short report which compares how these charities spend money.

Thinking ahead to ...
finding the median

A Archers use a 10-ring target.
Give the ring score for:

a the outer red ring
b the inner black ring.

Finding the median of a frequency distribution

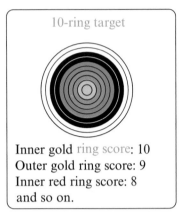

10-ring target

Inner gold ring score: 10
Outer gold ring score: 9
Inner red ring score: 8
and so on.

The frequency here is
the number of arrows.

♦ A set of data presented in a frequency table is called a **frequency distribution**.

♦ To find the median by listing the data:

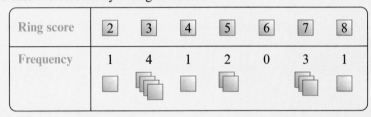

Ring score	2	3	4	5	6	7	8
Frequency	1	4	1	2	0	3	1

❖ list the data in order

2 3 3 3 3 4 5 5 7 7 7 8

❖ find the middle value.

2 3 3 3 3 4 5 5 7 7 7 8
Median score = **4.5**

Exercise 5.2
Finding the median
by listing the data

1

Ring score	5	6	7	8	9
Frequency	4	2	1	2	1

Ravi

a How many of Ravi's arrows hit the 8 ring?
b List Ravi's scores for his ten arrows.
c Find Ravi's median score.

2

Ring score	5	6	7	8	9	10
Frequency	3	2	4	0	3	3

Sally

a How many arrows did Sally fire in total?
b List all Sally's scores.
c Find Sally's median score.

3

Ring score	3	4	5	6	7	8	9
Frequency	1	5	6	2	1	1	2

Peta

Peta hit seven different rings: 3 4 5 6 7 8 9
The middle ring of these is the 6 ring.
a Explain why 6 is not Peta's median score.
b Find Peta's median score.

4 Karl fires 14 arrows: his lowest score is 2,
his highest score is 10,
his median score is 6.5
Write a possible frequency distribution for Karl's scores.

Thinking ahead to ...
calculating the mean of a
frequency distribution

A

Ring score	1	2	3	4	5	6	7	Saul
Frequency	1	0	1	3	5	4	3	

What is the total score for Saul's arrows that hit the 6 ring?

Calculating the mean of a frequency distribution

♦ To calculate the mean of a frequency distribution:

Ring score	2	3	4	5	6	7	8
Frequency	1	4	1	2	0	3	1

❖ calculate the total of all the values

Ring score	Frequency	Total score in ring	
2	1	2×1	2
3	4	3×4	12
4	1	4×1	4
5	2	5×2	10
6	0	6×0	0
7	3	7×3	21
8	1	8×1	8
Totals	12		57

1 arrow hit the 2 ring:
a total score of 2.

2 arrows hit the 5 ring:
a total score of 10.

12 arrows scored
57 in total.

❖ divide the total of all the values by the **total frequency**.

Mean score = $\frac{57}{12}$ = **4.8** (to 1 dp)

Exercise 5.3
Calculating the mean

1

Ring score	3	4	5	6	7	8	Jodie
Frequency	2	5	2	2	4	1	

Geeta	
Ring score	Frequency
6	2
7	6
8	7
9	4
10	1

For each archer:

a calculate the total of all their scores
b calculate the total frequency
c calculate their mean score.

Give your answers to 1 dp.

2

Ring score	6	7	8	9	10
Frequency	4	2	1	2	1

The calculation at the side is wrong.

a Explain the mistake.
b Calculate the correct mean score.

Mean score = $\frac{6 + 7 + 8 + 9 + 10}{5}$

$= \frac{40}{5}$

$= 8$ ✗

Comparing sets of data

A measure of spread measures how spread out data is.

The simplest measure of spread is the range.

◆ One way to compare sets of data is to compare two types of value:
    A – an average
    B – a measure of spread.

Example

Compare Kate's and Bob's scores using the median and the range.

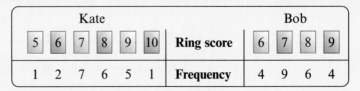

Kate						Ring score	Bob			
5	6	7	8	9	10	**Ring score**	6	7	8	9
1	2	7	6	5	1	**Frequency**	4	9	6	4

Kate   5 6 6 7 7 7 7 7 7 7 8 8 8 8 8 8 9 9 9 9 9 10

Median = **8**
Range = 10 – 5 = **5**

Bob   6 6 6 6 7 7 7 7 7 7 7 7 7 8 8 8 8 8 8 9 9 9 9

Median = **7**
Range = 9 – 6 = **3**

A – Kate's scores are higher on average.
B – Bob is more consistent because his scores are less spread out.

Exercise 5.4
Comparing sets
of data

1

Ring score	3	4	5	6	7	8	9	Total
Frequency	3	2	6	5	5	3	1	25

Javed

Lisa

Ring score	4	5	6	7	Total
Frequency	4	8	9	3	24

    a Find the median score for each frequency distribution.
    b Calculate the range of the scores for each distribution.
    c Use the median and range to compare Javed's and Lisa's scores.

2

Ring score	4	5	6	7	8	Total
Frequency	3	5	4	3	2	17

Amy

Paul

Ring score	3	4	5	6	7	8	Total
Frequency	4	2	0	7	5	2	20

    a Calculate the mean and the range of each distribution.
    b Compare Amy's and Paul's scores using the mean and the range.

3

Ring score	1	2	3	4	5	6	7	8	9	Total
Frequency	1	1	1	2	3	2	1	2	2	15

Imran

Ring score	1	2	3	4	5	6	7	8	9	Total
Frequency	1	0	0	2	1	3	4	0	1	12

Viv

    a Compare Imran's and Viv's scores using the mode and the range.
    b Explain why the range is not a sensible measure of spread for Viv's scores.

Calculating the interquartile range

* The **interquartile range** of a set of data measures how spread out the middle 50% of the data is.

* To calculate the interquartile range:

Ring score	1	2	3	4	5	6	7	8	9
Frequency	1	0	0	2	1	3	4	0	1

* list the data in order

1	4	4	5	6	6	6	7	7	7	7	9

> You can divide the data into four quarters by first dividing it into two halves.
>
> The end values are the medians of the two halves.

* divide the data into four quarters

1 4 4 ¦ 5 6 6 ¦ 6 7 7 ¦ 7 7 9

* find the end values of the middle 50% of the data

1 4 4 ¦ 5 6 6 ¦ 6 7 7 ¦ 7 7 9
　　　　　4.5　　　　　　　**7**
　　　Lower quartile　　**Upper quartile**

* calculate the difference between the upper and lower quartiles.

Interquartile range = 7 − 4.5
= 2.5

Exercise 5.5
Calculating the interquartile range

1

Ring score	2	3	4	5	6	7	8	Total
Frequency	1	0	3	2	5	3	2	16

William

Ring score	4	5	6	7	8	9	Total
Frequency	2	4	3	3	0	2	14

Bryony

Ring score	2	3	4	5	6	7	8	9	10	Total
Frequency	1	1	2	3	5	3	0	3	2	20

Daniel

For each archer:
a list the data
b find the upper and lower quartiles
c calculate the interquartile range of their scores.

2

Ring score	1	2	3	4	5	6	7	8	9	Total
Frequency	1	2	5	4	2	1	0	2	1	18

Sheera

Ring score	1	2	3	4	5	6	7	Total
Frequency	2	4	4	3	4	5	2	24

Dave

> Calculate some figures to support your explanation.

Is Sheera or Dave the more consistent archer?
Give reasons for your answer.

Thinking ahead to ...
constructing a cumulative
frequency table

A

Ring score	2	3	4	5	6	7	8	Total
Frequency	1	4	1	2	0	3	1	12

Calculate how many arrows in total scored:

a 2 or 3

b less than or equal to 5

c less than or equal to 6.

Constructing a cumulative frequency table

♦ The total of frequencies up to a particular value in a set of data is called the **cumulative frequency**.

♦ To construct a cumulative frequency table from a frequency table.

Frequency table

Ring score	2	3	4	5	6	7	8	Total
Frequency	1	4	1	2	0	3	1	12

≤ stands for 'is less than or equal to'

Cumulative frequency table

Ring score	Cumulative Frequency
≤2	1
≤3	5
≤4	6
≤5	8
≤6	8
≤7	11
≤8	12

6 arrows hit the 2, 3 or 4 rings:
1 + 4 + 1

11 arrows hit the 2, 3, 4, 5, 6 or 7 rings:
1 + 4 + 1 + 2 + 0 + 3

♦ You can find the cumulative frequency for each score by adding its frequency to the cumulative frequency for the previous score.

Ring score	2	3	4	5	6	7	8
Frequency	1	4	1	2	0	3	1
Cumulative frequency	1	5	6	8	8	11	12

Exercise 5.6
Constructing cumulative frequency tables

1

Ring score	5	6	7	8	9	Total
Frequency	2	5	12	7	5	31

André

Ring score	Cumulative Frequency
≤5	
≤6	
≤7	
≤8	
≤9	

a Copy this cumulative frequency table.

b Calculate the cumulative frequencies for André's scores.

2

Ring score	2	3	4	5	6	7	8	
Frequency	3	7	12	19	13	9	4	Simone
Cumulative frequency								

    a Copy this table.
    b Calculate the cumulative frequencies for Simone's scores.

3 This distribution shows the ages of archers at a junior event.

Age	10	11	12	13	14	15	16	Total
Number of archers	8	7	10	11	8	9	11	64

    How many archers can enter these age group competitions?
    a 11 and under   **b** 13 and under   **c** 16 and under.

4 **a** Copy this cumulative frequency table.
    b Calculate the cumulative frequency for each age group.

Age	Cumulative frequency
10 and under	
11 and under	
12 and under	
13 and under	
14 and under	
15 and under	
16 and under	

5 Dani fired 20 arrows at the target from each of seven different distances.

Distance to target in metres	10	15	20	25	30	35	40
Number of arrows hitting target	20	19	17	16	15	13	11

    Construct a cumulative frequency table for this distribution.

6 This table shows Jade's scores in the April, May and June competitions.

	Ring score										Total
	1	2	3	4	5	6	7	8	9	10	
April	4	7	7	8	5	6	2	3	5	1	48
May	6	5	4	9	5	3	8	2	2	4	48
June	3	6	6	4	5	4	8	4	2	6	48

Construct a cumulative frequency table like this.

7 Do you think Jade is improving as an archer or getting worse? Explain why.

	Ring score			
	≤1	≤2	≤3	≤4
April	4	11	18	
May	6	11	1	
June	3			

Thinking ahead to ...
finding the median

A

Ring score	5	6	7	8	9	Total
Frequency	7	8	13	18	14	60

Emily

a List all Emily's scores.
b Find Emily's median score.

Using cumulative frequencies to find the median of a frequency distribution

You can find the median for a small set of data by listing it.

This method is quicker for a distribution with a large total frequency.

◆ The median can be found without listing all the data.

◆ To find the median using cumulative frequencies:

❖ construct a cumulative frequency table
❖ use the total frequency to decide where the median is
❖ find the median.

Ring score	Frequency	Cumulative Frequency
5	7	7
6	8	15
7	13	28
8	18	46
9	14	60

The total frequency is 60, so the median score is halfway between the 30th largest and the 31st largest.

The 28th largest score is 7.

All the scores between the 29th and 46th largest are 8.

The 30th and 31st largest scores are both 8, so
Median score = **8**

Exercise 5.7
Finding the median using cumulative frequencies

1

Ring score	3	4	5	6	7	8	Total
Frequency	7	10	5	1	6	11	40

Lee

	4	5	6	7	8	Total
Frequency	11	7	8	9	10	45

Faith

Ring score	1	2	3	4	5	6	7	8	9	Total
Frequency	2	4	2	3	1	4	7	9	7	39

Aqib

Ring score	1	2	3	4	5	6	7	8	9	10	Total
Frequency	6	9	5	4	2	5	6	4	3	4	48

Tegan

For each archer:
a construct a cumulative frequency table
b decide where the median is
d find the median score.

2

Ring score	4	5	6	7	8	9	10
Cumulative Frequency	7	18	31	40	48	62	80

Jake

a Explain why Jake's median score is 7.5.
b Explain why the interquartile range of this distribution is 3.

Thinking ahead to ...
box-and-whisker plots

A A survey of three fast food restaurants recorded the number of chips in a serving. A sample of 80 servings was taken from each restaurant.

Restaurant	Number of chips													Total
	32	33	34	35	36	37	38	39	40	41	42	43	44	
X	1	2	3	5	9	13	14	12	8	5	4	3	1	80
Y	4	6	11	14	13	11	8	6	4	3	0	0	0	80
Z	1	1	2	6	9	13	15	13	10	6	2	1	1	80

a i Which restaurant do you think gives more chips in a serving?
  ii Explain your answer.

b i Find the median number of chips for each restaurant.
  ii Calculate the interquartile range for each distribution.

Drawing box-and-whisker plots

◆ A **box-and-whisker** plot shows a frequency distribution by using:

❖ the lowest and highest values
❖ the median
❖ the lower and upper quartiles.

Example

Draw a box-and-whisker plot for these chips from restaurant W.

Number of chips	34	35	36	37	38	39	40	41	42	43
Frequency	1	2	4	7	12	14	16	15	7	2
Cumulative frequency	1	3	7	14	26	40	56	71	78	80

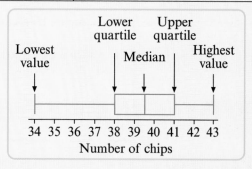

Exercise 5.8
Drawing box-and-whisker plots

1 Copy this box-and-whisker diagram on squared paper. Use the data from Question **A** to draw a box-and-whisker plot for each restaurant.

2 Write a short report that compares the number of chips per serving from the four fast food restaurants.

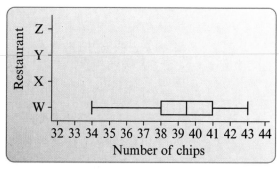

End points

You should be able to ... ... so try these questions.

A Construct a pie chart using degrees

A1

SAVING CHILDREN		£m		£m
Expenditure	Child care	9.2	Administration	1.0
(1994/95)	Fundraising	3.4	Other costs	0.8

Draw a pie chart to show how Saving Children spend their money.

Manoj

Ring score	2	3	4	5	6	7	Total
Frequency	1	0	3	5	7	2	18

Ring score	1	2	3	4	5	6	7	8	Total
Frequency	2	1	5	8	7	5	3	2	33

Pat

B Find the median of a frequency distribution

B1 **a** Find Manoj's median score by listing the data.
  b **i** Construct a cumulative frequency table for Pat's scores.
    ii Find Pat's median score.

C Calculate the mean of a frequency distribution

C1 Calculate the mean of:
  a Manoj's scores   **b** Pat's scores
Give your answers to 1 dp.

D Compare sets of data

D1 Compare Manoj's and Pat's scores using the mean and the range.

Kim

Ring score	2	3	4	5	6	7	8	Total
Frequency	3	2	1	3	4	5	2	20

Ring score	3	4	5	6	7	8	9	10	Total
Frequency	2	0	3	6	5	2	3	1	22

Stuart

D2 Compare Kim's and Stuart's scores using the mode and the range.

E Calculate the interquartile range

E1 Calculate the interquartile range of:
  a Kim's scores   **b** Stuart's scores

F Draw a box-and-whisker plot

F1 Draw box-and-whisker plots on the same diagram to show
  a Kim's scores   **b** Stuart's scores

Some points to remember

- ◆ The median of a frequency distribution can be found by:
    - ❖ listing the data, or
    - ❖ using cumulative frequencies.

- ◆ Sets of data can be compared using:
    - ❖ an average, and
    - ❖ a measure of spread.

- ◆ The range is not a sensible measure of spread to use when there are extreme values in the data.

- ◆ The interquartile range measures how spread out the middle 50% of the data is.

Starting points
You need to know about ...

... so try these questions

A Perimeter and circumference

The perimeter of a shape is the distance around the edges of the shape.

Example

Find the perimeter of ABCDE.

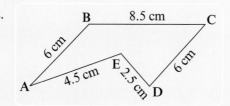

The perimeter (p) of ABCDE
is given by:

$p = 6 + 8.5 + 6 + 2.5 + 4.5$
$ = 27.5$

Perimeter of ABCDE is 27.5 cm.

The perimeter of a circle is called the circumference.
The formula for the circumference (c) of a circle is:

$c = \pi D$ (where D is the diameter of the circle)

Example

The circumference (c) of this circle
is given by:

$c = \pi \times 4.5$
$c = 14.1$ (to 1 dp)

**The circumference of a circle of
diameter 4.5 cm is 14.1 cm (1 dp).**

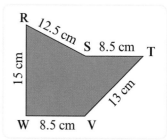

B Area

The area of a rectangle is given by: Base × Height

The area of a parallelogram
is given by: Base × Height

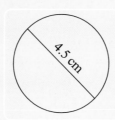

The area of a triangle
is given by: 0.5 × Base × Height

or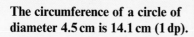

$\dfrac{\text{Base} \times \text{Height}}{2}$

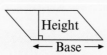
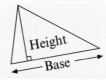

The area of a circle
is given by: πr^2 (where r is the radius)

Example

The area (A) of this circle
is given by:

$A = \pi \times 5.4^2$ ($\pi \times 5.4 \times 5.4$)
$A = 91.6$ (to 1 dp)

The area of a circle of radius 5.4 cm is 91.6 cm² (1 dp).

A1 Calculate the perimeter of a
square of side 5.8 cm.

A2 Find the perimeter of RSTVW.

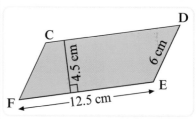

A3 A rectangle has:
long sides of 12.4 cm
and short sides of 9.8 cm
Calculate its perimeter.

A4 Calculate the circumference of
each of these circles (to 1 dp):
  a circle with diameter 5.2 cm
  b circle with diameter 0.7 cm
  c circle with radius 2.4 cm.

B1 A rectangle has:
long sides of 15.2 cm
and short sides of 8 cm.
Calculate its area.

B2 Calculate the area of CDEF.

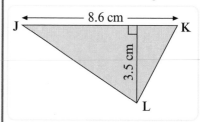

B3 Find the area of triangle JKL.

B4 Find the area of a circle of
radius 4.3 cm.

C Splitting up a shape to find its area

Often you can find the area of a complicated shape by splitting it into simple shapes that you can calculate the area for.

Example

Find the area of the whole shape. One way to split the shape is to make two rectangles and one triangle as shown.

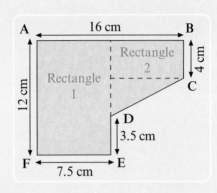

The area (A) of ABCDEF is given by:

A = Area of rectangle 1 + Area of rectangle 2 + Area of triangle

Area Rectangle 1 given by:	Area Rectangle 2 given by:	Area Triangle given by:
7.5×12	8.5×4	$0.5 \times 8.5 \times 4.5$
$= 90$	$= 36$	$= 19.125$

So: $A = 90 + 36 + 19.125 = 145.125$

Area of whole shape = 145.1 cm² (1 dp)

D Pythagoras' rule

Pythagoras' rule is:
In any **right-angled triangle**, the area of the square on the hypotenuse is equal to the sum of the areas of the squares on the other two sides.

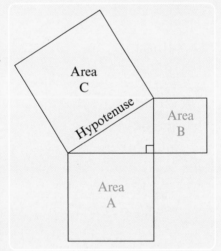

For this triangle:

Area C = **Area A + Area B**

From this we can also say:

Area A = **Area C – Area B**

and

Area B = **Area C – Area A**

For RST: to find the length of RS

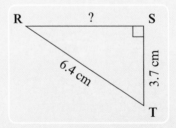

$RS^2 = RT^2 - ST^2$
$RS^2 = 6.4^2 - 3.7^2$
$RS^2 = 40.96 - 13.69 = 27.27$
$RS = 5.2$ (1 dp)

RS is 5.2 cm long (1 dp).

C1 Calculate the area of each shape.

a

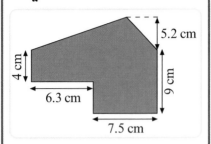

b

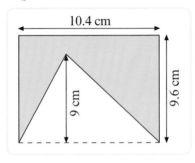

D1 Calculate the length p and the length e.

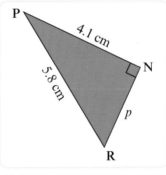

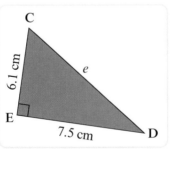

The area of a trapezium

> A quadrilateral is a shape with four straight edges.

A trapezium is a quadrilateral with one pair of opposite sides that are parallel.

ABCD is a trapezium as:
- it is a quadrilateral
- AB and CD are parallel.

One way to find the area of ABCD is to split it into two triangles and a rectangle, then calculate the total area.

Another way to find the area is to use the formula for the area of a trapezium.

Start with ABCD, then add to it a rotation of ABCD to make a parallelogram.

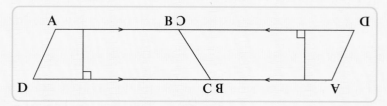

The formula for the area (A) of a parallelogram is: $A = $ Base $\times$ Height

The area of this parallelogram is: (DC + BA) $\times$ Height

Base

The area of the trapezium ABCD is half the area of the parallelogram
So, the area (A) of trapezium ABCD is given by:

$$A = 0.5 \times (AB + CD) \times \textbf{Height}$$

In general, the formula for the area (A) of a trapezium is:

$$A = 0.5 \times (\text{sum of the parallel sides}) \times \textbf{Height}$$

> The sum is the result of adding.
> For example:
> the sum of 3 and 5 is 8.

> In calculations with decimals you should either:
> - give your answer to the degree of accuracy asked for e.g. 1 dp, or 2 sf
>
> or
> - give your answer to the same degree of accuracy as is used in the question.

Example

Calculate the area of STVW.

Area (A) given by
$A = 0.5 \times (ST + VW) \times 6.6$
$= 0.5 \times (12.4 + 7.5) \times 6.6$
$= 0.5 \times 19.9 \times 6.6$
$= 65.7$ (to 1 dp)

Area of STVW is 65.7 cm².

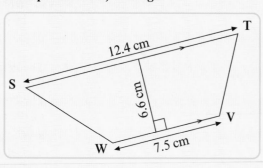

Exercise 6.1
Using the formula for the area of a trapezium

1 Calculate the area of STVW:
  a when ST = 15.2 cm, VW = 9.5 cm, and the height is 8.3 cm.
  b when the height is 1.7 cm, VW = 2.1 cm, and ST = 4.5 cm.

2 This logo uses the same shape trapezium three times.
  a Calculate the area of CDEF.
  b What is the area of the complete logo?

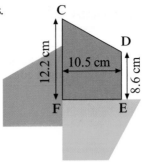

3 The diagram shows the door of a cupboard under some stairs.
One side of the door is shorter than the other by 32.5 cm.
The door is 76.4 cm wide.

  a Draw a diagram of the door and show all the distances you know.
  b What shape is the front of the door?
  c Calculate the area of the front of the door.

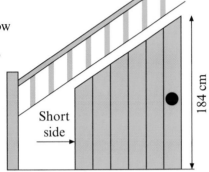

4 The diagram shows the baffles on the front of a spotlight.
All four baffles are the same size.

  a Draw a diagram of one baffle, and label all the dimensions you know.
  b Calculate the area of one baffle.

The front of all four baffles are to be painted black.

  c What is the total area to be painted?

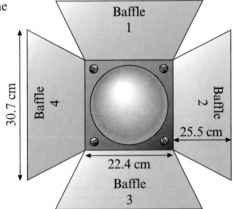

5 The diagram shows the vertical end of a feed bin.
The bin is on a stand, and the total height of the bin and the stand is 82.4 cm.

  a Calculate the height of the feed bin.
  b Calculate the area of the end of the bin.

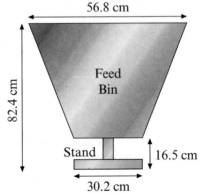

6 The diagram shows how two tables are joined so that six people can eat together.

Measurements are to the nearest 0.5 cm.

a Calculate the area of one table.
b What is the area of the table for six?
c Find the perimeter of one table.
d What is the perimeter of a table for six?

7 The manufacturers claim in their brochure:

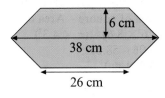

"When tables are joined, six people can eat together. Each person will have about half a square metre of table top."

Do you think this is a fair claim? Explain your answer.

Times in the 24-hour clock system are written using four digits.

8 This display, on a building, shows the time. Each digit is made by lighting up some of the 4 vertical, and 3 horizontal bars. The digit 3 is made by lighting: 3 horizontal and 2 vertical bars.

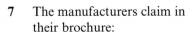

Horizontal bars are this size:

Vertical bars are this size:

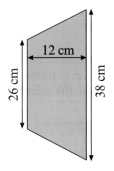

a What is the area lit in a vertical bar?
b What area is lit in a horizontal bar?

9 **a** What area in the display is lit for the digit 3?
b What area is lit to display 03–25?

10 What area is lit to display 17–26?

11 What time has the largest area lit?

12 The diagram shows the pattern piece for a sleeve. The sleeve will be cut from a rectangle of fabric.

Draw a diagram to show how the pattern piece can be divided into two trapeziums.

13 Calculate the area of fabric used for the sleeve.

14 Calculate the area of fabric wasted when the sleeve is cut out.

15 Divide the sleeve into rectangles and triangles. Show how the total area is calculated.

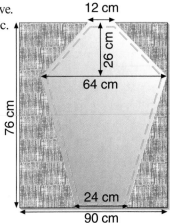

Composite shapes

Composite shapes are made up from more than one shape.
Sometimes you can find the area by adding areas, at other times it is easier to subtract.

Example 1

Find the area of ABCDEF.

The area (A) of ABCDEF can be given by:
$$A = (12.4 \times 4.5) + (4.6 \times 4.8)$$
$$= 55.8 + 22.08$$
$$= 77.9 \text{ (1 dp)}$$

The area of ABCDEF is 77.9 cm^2

or

The area (A) of ABCDEF is given by:
$$A = \text{Area of large rectangle} - \text{Area cut out for L-shape}$$
$$A = (12.4 \times 9.3) - (4.8 \times 7.8)$$
$$A = 115.32 - 37.44$$
$$A = 77.9 \text{ (1 dp)}$$

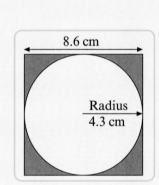

> It can be cut out in this way.

> The answer is rounded at the end of the calculation.

Example 2

Find the shaded area.

The area of the shaded part (A) is given by:
$$A = \text{Area of square} - \text{Area of circle}$$
$$A = (8.6 \times 8.6) - (\pi \times 4.3^2)$$
$$A = 73.96 - 58.09\ldots$$
$$A = 15.9 \text{ (1 dp)}$$

The shaded area is 15.9 cm^2

Exercise 6.2
Working with composite shapes

1 A rectangle of card 7.4 cm by 8.3 cm had a piece cut from it to leave shape R.

   a What shape was cut from the rectangle?
   b What was the area of the rectangle before the cut?

2 Calculate the area of shape R.

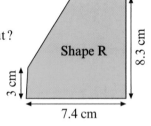

3 This shows how milk bottle tops are cut from a strip of foil.

   a What is the radius of a foil bottle top?
   b Calculate the area of a foil bottle top.

4 How long is this strip of foil?

5 Calculate the area of foil wasted by cutting out these five tops.

6 Tops are cut from a 7.2 m strip of foil. Calculate the area of wasted foil.

7 This card is used to frame photographs.
A circle of radius 4 cm is cut from the card.
Gold lines are printed 1 cm from the edge of
the circle and the card as shown.

Calculate the area of card after the cut out.

8 Is the area of photograph showing more or less
than $\frac{1}{4}$ of the blue card?

Explain your answer.

9 Calculate the length of gold line on the card.

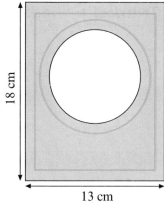

18 cm

13 cm

10 This diagram shows the net of
a box for playing cards.
The net is cut from a
rectangle of card.

For the rectangle of card:
a what is its length?
b how wide is it?

11 Calculate the area of the
glue flap.

12 The box opens at either end.

Find the area of an opening end.

13 Calculate the total area of the net.

14 Calculate the area of waste card.

15 Roughly, what fraction of the card is wasted? Explain how you decided.

16 This logo design uses two parts of a circle in a red square. 36 mm

What is the radius of the circle?

17 What fraction of the circle stands for the
visor (the blue part)?

18 Calculate the area of the visor in the logo.

19 Find the area of the helmet in the logo
(the yellow part).

20 Calculate the area of the logo that is red.

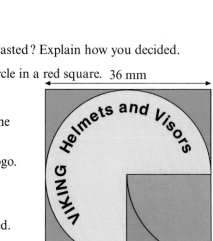

21 These are diagrams of square filters used in spotlights.

A blue and yellow double filter
gives blue, yellow, and green light.

For the double filter:
a Give the area of each colour.
b Roughly what fraction of the
area is green? Explain your answer.

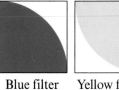 

Blue filter   Yellow filter   Both filters

15 cm

Involving Pythagoras

Sometimes to find the area of a shape you have to calculate a distance before you can calculate the area.

Example

Calculate the area of ABC.

The area of ABC (A) can be given by:

$$A = 0.5 \times AC \times DB$$

but we first have to calculate the length of AC:

$$AC = AD + DC$$

To find AD. In triangle ADB:
$$AD^2 = AB^2 - DB^2$$
$$AD^2 = 3.5^2 - 2.8^2 = 12.25 - 7.84 = 4.41$$
$$AD = \sqrt{4.41} = 2.1$$

To find DC. In triangle DBC:
$$DC^2 = BC^2 - DB^2$$
$$DC^2 = 5.5^2 - 2.8^2 = 30.25 - 7.84 = 22.41$$
$$DC = \sqrt{22.41} = 4.73 \ldots$$

So $AC = 2.1 + 4.73 \ldots = 6.83 \ldots$

Area of ABC (A) = $0.5 \times AC \times DB = 0.5 \times 6.83 \ldots \times 2.8 = 9.6$ (1 dp)

The area of ABC is 9.6 cm²

> The area of ABC is given by:
> $0.5 \times$ Base $\times$ Height
>
> Think of AC as the base
> and
> DB as the height.

> The answer is rounded at the end of the calculation.

Exercise 6.3
Finding areas involving Pythagoras

1

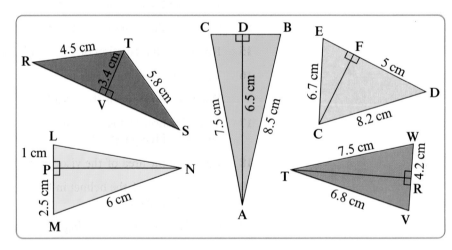

In triangle RST:

  a Calculate the length of RV.
  b Calculate the length of VS.
  c Calculate the area of triangle RST.

2 Calculate the area of triangle ABC.

3 **a** Calculate the height of triangle CDE.
   b Calculate the area of triangle CDE.

4 **a** Calculate the area of LMN.
   b Calculate the area of TVW.

Each face of this box is a triangle. This 3-D shape is a **tetrahedron**.

5 The diagram shows the net for this paperclip box.

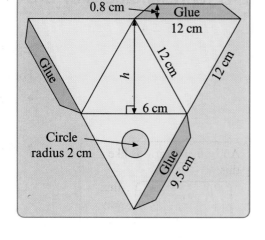

Calculate the length marked *h*.

6 Find the area of the bottom of the box.

7 Calculate the area of a glue tab.

8 Find the area of the face with the circle cut out.

9 Calculate the total area of the net.

10 Find the area wasted, when the net is cut from a 26 cm square of card.

11 Calculate the perimeter of the net (including the glue flaps).

Using circumference

Exercise 6.4
Using circumference

1 The larger of these crop circles has a diameter of 31.5 metres, and the smaller a radius of 5.25 metres.

Calculate the circumference of:
a the larger circle
b the smaller circle.

2 For a circumference of about 300 metres, roughly what is the diameter?

3 This tin of travel sweets is sealed by sticky tape.
The tin has a diameter of 72 mm.
The ends of the tape overlap by 6 mm.

Give the length of tape used for one tin in cm.

4 Rolls of tape are 1450 metres long, and 1 metre is wasted.

How many tins can be sealed with one roll of tape?

A semicircle is half a circle.

When you think about the perimeter of a semicircle you will need to decide if you need to include the length of the diameter.

5 The straights of this running track are 84.4 metres long.
The diameter of each semicircular end is 73 metres.

Show that the distance around this track is about 400 metres.

2-D representations of 3-D shapes

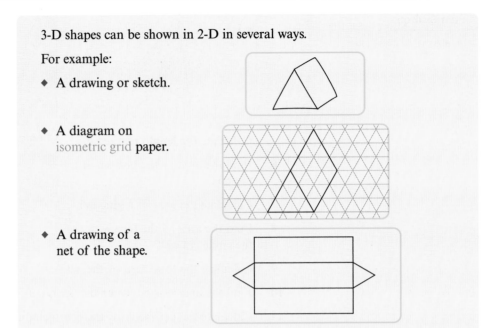

3-D shapes can be shown in 2-D in several ways.

For example:

♦ A drawing or sketch.

♦ A diagram on isometric grid **paper**.

♦ A drawing of a net of the shape.

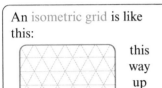

An isometric grid is like this:

this way up

Exercise 6.5
2-D/3-D representation

1 This is a drawing of a box for a double CD.

Draw a diagram of a box like this on isometric paper.

2 Draw a net for a box of this shape. (Do not include glue flaps.)

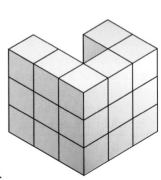

3 This drawing is of a symmetrical box for sweets.

What shape is:

a an end of the box
b a side of the box
c the bottom of the box?

50 mm

top

side

15 mm   end

60 mm

90 mm

4 Make an accurate drawing of one end of the box.

5 One dimension of a side of the box is 60 mm.
Calculate the other dimension and the area of one side of the box.

6 Draw an accurate net for the box.

7 This a sketch of a stack of blank dice.

Draw this stack on isometric paper.

8 **a** What is the smallest number of dice that could be in this stack?
b What is the largest number?

9 A stack of fifteen 3 cm dice is packed in a box.

a Sketch the smallest box you think can be used.
b Draw an accurate net for your box.

End points

You should be able to ...   ... so try these questions

A Use the formula for the area of a trapezium

A1

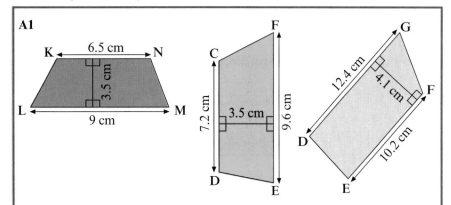

Calculate the area of each shape.

A2 Explain, with a diagram, what is meant by a composite shape.

B Work with composite shapes

B1 **a** Calculate the area of shape P.

Shape P is cut from a 16 cm square of card.

b Calculate the area of waste card.

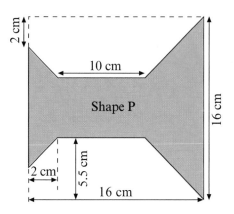

B2 Calculate the area of RST.

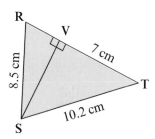

C Calculate perimeters

C1 This hoax crop circle was made by two people with a piece of rope 3.2 metres long.
They simply made two half-circles.

Calculate the perimeter of the crop circle.

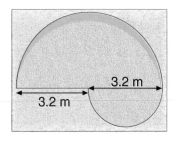

D Work with 2-D representations of 3-D objects

D1 **a** Make a sketch of the two parts of a matchbox.
b Draw the two parts of a matchbox on isometric grid paper.

About the Cornish Seal Sanctuary

It was founded in 1957.

In 1975, it moved to a site of about 40 acres in Gweek.

It has a fully equipped seal hospital and 10 outdoor pools.

Opening hours
Open every day except Christmas
09 00 to 18 30

Feeding times
11 00 • 13 30 • 16 00

Cafe prices

Coffee		60p
Tea		40p
Cola		50p
Rolls:	Bacon	£1.50
	Sausage	£1.25
	Egg	£1.10
Chips		70p
Beans		40p
Salad		55p

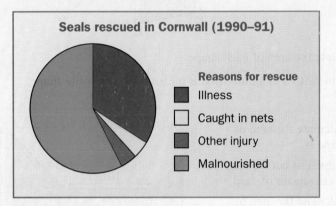

Seals rescued in Cornwall (1990–91)

Reasons for rescue
- Illness
- Caught in nets
- Other injury
- Malnourished

Ratio of male: female seals rescued between Land's End and Porthleven

Year	Ratio
1992–93	1:1
1993–94	1:2
1994–95	2:1

About the grey seals

Weights of pups rescued in December 1992

Name	Weight at rescue (kg)	Weight at release (kg)
Bill	23.4	65.0
Ben	16.8	56.0
Mandy	12.3	66.0
Tony	24.0	98.0
Rory	18.5	85.0

Seals are usually released when they weigh about 60 kg.

Seals at the sanctuary eat over a tonne of fish per week.

Food weight chart (hospital)

Weight of food per day (kg) vs Weight of seal (kg)

Major breeding areas for grey seals

Location	Pups born (1989)	Pups born (1990)	Total population in 1990 (to nearest 100)
Inner Hebrides	2051	2256	7800
Outer Hebrides	9537	9823	34000
Orkney	7038	7319	25400
Isle of May	933	1185	4100
Farne Islands	892	1004	3500

The world population of grey seals is estimated at 120000.

About two thirds of them live around the British coastline.

In water, seals can reach speeds of up to 20 km per hour.

1. How many years is it since the Seal Sanctuary was founded?

2. How long is it open each day?

3. In the cafe, Pritpal orders a cola, bacon roll and chips.
   How much does this cost?

4. What was the most common reason for a seal being rescued in Cornwall in 1990–91?

5. What was the weight of the lightest pup rescued in December 1992?

6. About how many kilograms of fish do the seals at the Sanctuary eat each week?

7. What weight of food will be given to a 10 kg seal pup during a day in hospital?

8. What percentage of seals rescued between Land's End and Porthleven in 1992–93 were male?

9. How many pups were born in Orkney in 1990?

10. How long has the Seal Sanctuary been at Gweek?

11. Pritpal gets there at 8.25 am. How many minutes is it till the Sanctuary opens?

12. About what fraction of the seals rescued in 1990–91 were ill?

13. About what percentage of the seals rescued in 1990–91 were malnourished?

14. 24 seals were rescued in Cornwall in 1990–91. About how many of them were ill?

15. What fraction of the seals rescued between Land's End and Porthleven in 1994–95 were female?

16. About what percentage of the seals rescued in Cornwall in 1990–91 were caught in nets?

17. 4 seals were rescued between Land's End and Porthleven in 1992–93.
    How many were male?

18. 3 seals were rescued between Land's End and Porthleven in 1993–94.
    How many were female?

19. In 24 hours in hospital, what weight of food is given to a 15 kg seal pup?

20. In a day, what weight of food in grams will be given to a pup that weighs 14 kg?

21. In a day, a pup in hospital is given 800 grams of food. Give the weight of this pup in kilograms.

22. Which of the pups rescued in December 1992 gained the most weight before being released?

23. Write Tony's rescue weight as a percentage of his release weight.

24. For the rescue weights, find:
    a the mean   b the median
    c the range

25. Write each rescue weight rounded to the nearest kilogram.

26. Write each release weight in grams.

27. About how many kilograms of fish do the seals at the Sanctuary eat each day?

28. Out of the major breeding areas, which location had the highest total population of grey seals in 1990?

29. For each location in 1989, write down how many pups were born, to the nearest hundred.

30. For each location in 1990, write down how many pups were born, to the nearest thousand.

31. Draw a graph to show the number of pups born in 1989 and 1990 for these locations.

32. About how many grey seals live around the British coastline?

33. At 20 km per hour:
    a How far could a seal travel in 2 hours?
    b How long would it take to travel 35 km?
    c How long would it take to travel 1 km?
    d How far could a seal travel in 1 minute?

34. In June about 800 people visit the Seal Sanctuary each day.
    About how many people visit in June?

35. Susan arrives at the Sanctuary at 3.15 pm.
    How long has she to wait for feeding time?

36. In the cafe, Susan asks her aunt for a hot drink and a roll.
    If her aunt chooses a hot drink and roll at random, what is the probability of her choosing:
    a a coffee and an egg roll?
    b a tea and a bacon roll?

37. If cafe prices are increased by 15%, what is the new price of:
    a a tea?   b a sausage roll?
    c chips?

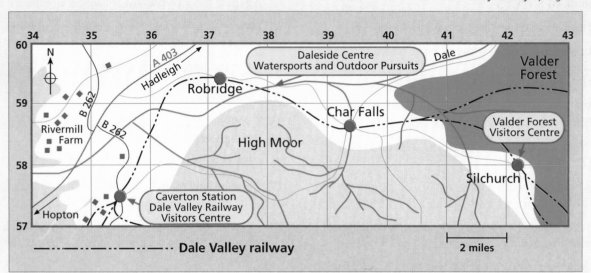

Dale Valley Railway Spring 1997

Dale Valley railway

2 miles

Dale Valley Railway

Timetable 1 May to 30 September

	Depart	Depart	Depart
Caverton Station	1000	1200	1430
Robridge	1012	1212	1445
Char Falls	1025	1225	1505
Silchurch	a 1040	a 1240	a 1520

	Depart	Depart	Depart
Silchurch	1105	1330	1610
Char Falls	1120	1345	1628
Robridge	1135	1400	1645
Caverton Station	a 1145	a 1410	a 1700

a – arrival time

** Note – in May and September there is no 1200 departure

Fares

Adult	£5.50
Child (under 14 years)	£3.00
Senior Citizen	£3.50

* Note all fares are return
  no single tickets are for sale

Festival Special

Adult	£12.50
Child (under 14 years)	£6.50
Senior Citizen	£9.50

* Note all fares include lunch
  at the Railway Arms in Silchurch

Information card

Weights and Measures

Locomotive	55 tons
Type A coach	27 tons
Type B coach	37 tons
Coal	1.5 tons
Water	500 gallons

1 gallon of water weighs 10 lb
1 ton = 2240 lb

Tally for Festival Special

Adult	///////////////////////////// ///////////////////////
Child	/////////////////
Senior Citizen	///////////////////////////// ///////////////////////////// ////////////////////

1   Estimate how far it is by rail from Caverton Station to Silchurch.

2   What area is shown by one square on the map?

3   Estimate the area of High Moor on the map.

4   Estimate the area of Valder Forest on the map.

5   When you travel from Robridge to Char Falls by road, is the railway on your left or right?

6   Which station is at the eastern end of the Dale Valley railway?

7   a   Which station is roughly north-east of Caverton?
    b   Give the bearing of Robridge from Silchurch.

8   Give a 6-figure grid reference for:
    a   the Daleside Centre
    b   Rivermill Farm
    c   places where the railway crosses the River Dale
    d   where the B262 crosses the River Dale
    e   the Valder Forest Visitors Centre.

9   As a very good guide:
    100 miles is equivalent to 160 kilometres.
    Draw a conversion graph for miles to kilometres.

10 Estimate these distances in kilometres:
    a   30 miles   b   55 miles   c   80 miles
    d   25 miles   e   130 miles   f   285 miles

11 Estimate these distances in miles:
    a   55 km   b   96 km   c   40 km
    d   120 km   e   235 km   f   375 km

12 1 km is roughly what fraction of a mile?
    Explain your answer.

13 In kilometres, roughly how far is it by rail from Char Falls to Caverton Station?

14 What is the mean journey time for a journey between Caverton and Silchurch stations.
    Give your answer to the nearest minute.

15 For a return journey, the same day, what is:
    a   the shortest time between departure and return?
    b   the longest time?

16 Between 10 00 and 17 00, how long in total does the train spend in Silchurch?

17 Calculate the shortest journey time between Robridge and Char Falls.

18 a   For how many days does the timetable run?
    b   How many return trips will the train make during the season?

19 Next year the Dale Valley Railway estimate that they will carry 25 000 passengers.
    They expect the ratio of adults to children to be 5 : 3.
    a   How many adults do they expect to carry?
    b   How many children?

20 Will £120 000 be a good estimate of ticket sales? Explain your answer.

21 Calculate the mean number of passengers expected per day (1 May – 30 Sept).

22 DVR expect about 35% of the adults to be Senior Citizens.

    How many Senior Citizens are expected?

23 The yearly running costs of the railway are estimated at £7000 per mile between Caverton and Silchurch.

    Do you expect the railway to make a profit next year? Explain your answer.

24 To build a cafe, Dale Valley Railway plan to increase the ticket charges by 6%, then to round the new charge to the nearest 10 pence.

    Give the new charge for each type of ticket.

25 The Festival Special ran on 1 May 1992.
    Draw up a frequency table to show the number of tickets sold.

26 What was the total amount taken in ticket sales for the Festival Special?

27 To the nearest penny, what was the mean price of a ticket on the Festival Special?

28 Draw a pie chart to show the numbers of tickets sold for the Festival Special.

29 What is the weight of 500 gallons of water?

30 Which is heavier:
    500 gallons of water or 1.5 tons of coal?

31 At the start of the day, the locomotive is loaded with 500 gallons of water and 1.5 tons of coal.
    What is the total weight of the locomotive?

32 An eight coach train is made up of:
    p type A coaches, and n type B coaches.
    Write an equation with p and n for the number of coaches in the train.

33 a   Write an expression in p and n, for the weight of the coaches in the train.
    b   Write an equation for the weight of the train.

Starting points

You need to know about ...

... so try these questions

A Finding the value of linear expressions

- Examples of linear expressions are: $2m + 4$ $6p - 4t$
- The value of an expression depends on the value of the letters.

When $p = 2$ and $t = 1$, $6p - 4t = (6 \times p) - (4 \times t)$
$$= (6 \times 2) - (4 \times 1)$$
$$= 12 - 4 = 8$$

B Adding like terms

- In the expression $2x + 4y + 3x + 5y$:

  - $2x$, $4y$, $3x$ and $5y$ are called **terms**.
  - $2x$ and $3x$ are called **like terms** as both give the number of x's.

- The expression can be simplified by adding like terms:

$$2x + 4y + 3x + 5y$$
$$= 2x + 3x + 4y + 5y$$
$$= 5x + 9y$$

$2x + 4y + 3x + 5y$ and $5x + 9y$ are **equivalent expressions**.

C Multiplying out brackets

- To multiply out brackets, multiply **every** term inside the brackets.

$$7(2n - 5) = 7 \times (2n - 5)$$
$$= (7 \times 2n) - (7 \times 5)$$
$$= 14n - 35$$

D Solving linear equations

- Solving an equation is finding the possible values for each letter.
- With the value of one letter to find, add, subtract, multiply or divide **both** sides of the equation by equal amounts.

Example

Solve $6n - 2 = 2n + 8$

$+ 2 \Big($ $6n - 2 = 2n + 8$ $\Big) + 2$
$- 2n \Big($ $6n = 2n + 10$ $\Big) - 2n$
$\div 4 \Big($ $4n = 10$ $\Big) \div 4$
   $n = 2.5$

The **solution** of this equation is $n = 2.5$.

E Linear graphs

- An example of an equation of a straight line is $y = 3x + 5$.
- For any x-coordinate, you can calculate the y-coordinate.

When $x = {}^-1$, $y = (3 \times {}^-1) + 5$
$$= {}^-3 + 5 = 2$$

So the line $y = 3x + 5$ goes through the point $({}^-1, 2)$.

A1 Find the value of these expressions when $t = 5$.
 a $5t - 8$ b $11 - t$
 c $2(t + 7)$ d $3(t - 6)$

A2 Evaluate these expressions when $a = 2$ and $b = 5$.
 a $4a + b$ b $3b - 4a$
 c $7(a + b)$ d $2a - 3b$

B1 Which of these is equivalent to $5x + 2y + 3x + y$?
 A $15x + 2y$ B $8x + 2y$
 C $8x + 3y$ D $15x + 3y$

B2 Simplify each of these by adding like terms.
 a $5t + 3t + t$
 b $7s + 3s + 5k + 4k$
 c $2c + 6b + c + 2b$
 d $6x + 2 + 5x$
 e $5v + 6 + 2v + 10$

C1 Multiply out the brackets from:
 a $6(x + 5)$ b $3(1 + n)$
 c $4(b - 5)$ d $7(10 - t)$
 e $4(2n + 3)$ f $3(5 + 4y)$
 g $2(4p - 11)$ h $9(1 - 3w)$

D1 Which of these is the solution of: $4x - 5 = 2x + 7$?
 A $x = 1$ B $x = 2$ C $x = 6$

D2 Solve:
 a $6z + 1 = 10$
 b $5y - 2 = 13$
 c $3x + 14 = 8$
 d $2w + 5 = 3w + 1$
 e $5 + v = 2v - 3$
 f $6t + 8 = t + 3$
 g $5s - 1 = 7s - 5$

E1 Which of these points is on the line $y = 5x - 1$?
 A $(1, 4)$ B $(2, 11)$ C $({}^-1, {}^-6)$

E2

x	$^-2$	$^-1$	0	1	2
y					

Copy and fill this table for:
 a $y = 2x + 5$ b $y + x = 6$

Thinking ahead to ...
simplifying linear
expressions

P $10 + (1 \times 0.6)$ Q $10 + (2 \times 0.6) - (3 \times 0.6)$ R $10 - (5 \times 0.6)$

S $10 - (1 \times 0.6)$ T $10 - (2 \times 0.6) - (3 \times 0.6)$

U $10 - (2 \times 0.6) + (3 \times 0.6)$

A   Sort these calculations into pairs with the same value.

Simplifying linear expressions

To simplify an expression   ◆ reorder the terms if you need to
                             ◆ add or subtract like terms

Examples

$6y - x - 3x$ $= 6y - 4x$	$5p + 6 - 3p - 1$ $= 5p - 3p + 6 - 1$ $= 2p + 5$	$7a - 3b - 4a + 2b - a$ $= 7a - 4a - a - 3b + 2b$ $= 2a - b$

Exercise 7.1
Adding and subtracting
like terms

1

A $6q - 3p$ B $8q - 7p + 4q$ C $4q - 7p$

D $12q - 7p$ E $2p - 5q$ F $9q - 7p - 3q$

G $6q - 3p - 4p - 2q$ H $6q - 5p + 2p$ I $6q - 7p$

a   From A to H, find four pairs of equivalent expressions.
b   Find the value of each expression when $q = 10$ and $p = 2$.

2   Simplify each of these expressions:
   a $4t + 7t - 3t$ **b** $6x - 5 - x + 5$ **c** $6 + 4h - 3 + h$
   d $3a - 2b + 2b - 2a$ **e** $2 - y + 6 - 4y - 7$ **f** $10 - 5f - 4 + 2f$

3   Some expressions are arranged in a square.

$3x - y$	$x - 2y$	$2x$
x	$2x - y$	$3x - 2y$
$2x - 2y$	$3x$	$x - y$

In a magic square, the
numbers in each row, each
column and each diagonal
add to give the same total.

   a   Find the value of each expression in the
         square when $x = 5$ and $y = 2$.
   b   Draw the square with these values.
         Is it a magic square?
   c   For each row, column and diagonal, find the total of the
         three expressions.
   d   Explain why your totals show that any values for x and y will give a
         magic square.

Solving linear equations

For linear equations with brackets you can start by multiplying out the brackets.

Examples

- Solve $2(p + 4) = 8p - 1$

$$2(p + 4) = 8p - 1$$
$$2p + 8 = 8p - 1$$
$$8 = 6p - 1 \qquad -2p$$
$$9 = 6p \qquad +1$$
$$1.5 = p \qquad \div 6$$

with $-2p$, $+1$, $\div 6$ applied to both sides.

- Solve $3(4 - t) + 5 = 13 - 5t$

$$3(4 - t) + 5 = 13 - 5t$$
$$12 - 3t + 5 = 13 - 5t$$
$$17 - 3t = 13 - 5t$$
$$17 + 2t = 13 \qquad +5t$$
$$2t = {}^-4 \qquad -17$$
$$t = {}^-2 \qquad \div 2$$

> You can check by finding the value of both sides of the equation for your solution. The values should be equal.

Exercise 7.2
Solving linear equations

1 Solve these equations.

  a $6z + 5 = 2z + 9$ **b** $4y - 1 = y + 8$ **c** $5(x - 2) = 35$
  d $2(w + 8) + 11 = 51$ **e** $3(2v - 1) = 21$ **f** $6(3 + 5u) = 54$
  g $4(t + 1) = 3(t + 3)$ **h** $4(3s - 1) = 4(2s + 7)$ **i** $5(2r + 3) = 7(3r - 1)$
  j $2(q - 3) + 3q = 3$ **k** $10 - p = 4p$ **l** $14 - 4n = 2(1 + 2n)$
  m $3m - 5 = 11 - m$ **n** $2(5l - 3) = 48 - 5l$ **o** $5(2k - 3) = 15 - 2k$
  p $4j - 7 = 3(18 - j) + 9$ **q** $17 - 2h = 22 - 3h$ **r** $2(9 - 2g) = 25 - 6g$

> Each equation has a negative number as its solution.

2 Solve these equations.

  a $2z + 12 = 3z + 17$ **b** $4(y + 6) = 20$ **c** $5(2x + 7) = 15$
  d $5(w + 5) = 2(w + 8)$ **e** $v + 17 = 9 - v$ **f** $3u + 35 = 5 - 2u$
  g $2(3 - t) = 4t + 9$ **h** $8 - 5s = 2 - 10s$ **i** $2r + 29 = 1 - 6r$

> $\dfrac{2x + 1}{4}$ stands for $(2x + 1) \div 4$

3 Solve these equations.

  a $4z + 1 = 10z - 1$ **b** $2(3y - 1) = 12y - 7$ **c** $\dfrac{2x + 1}{4} = 2$

  d $\tfrac{1}{4}(3w + 1) = 4$ **e** $\tfrac{1}{3}(2v - 1) = v - 1$ **f** $\dfrac{5u + 6}{2} = 4$

Forming and solving linear equations

For some problems, you can form a linear equation and then solve it.

Example

The lengths of the sides of a triangle are y cm, $2y$ cm and $(y + 3)$ cm.

If the perimeter of the triangle is 63 cm, what is the length of each side?

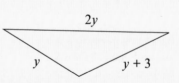

> The perimeter is the total distance around the outside edge of a shape.

- The perimeter, in terms of y, is: $y + 2y + y + 3 = 4y + 3$
- The perimeter is 63 cm so: $4y + 3 = 63$
- Find the value of y: $4y = 60$
                                 $y = 15$
- Find the value of $2y$ and $y + 3$: $2y = 30$ and $y + 3 = 18$
- So the lengths of the sides are: **15 cm, 30 cm and 18 cm.**

Exercise 7.3
Forming and solving
linear equations

1   The lengths of the sides of a triangle
are x cm, $2x$ cm and $(3x - 4)$ cm.

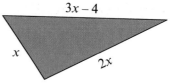

> An expression in terms of
> x does not include any
> letters other than x.

a   List the lengths of the sides when $x = 5$.
b   What is the perimeter when $x = 4$?
c   What is the perimeter of the triangle in terms of x?
d   If the perimeter is 104 cm, form an equation in x and solve it to find the
length of each side.

2   A square has sides of length $2p$ metres.
A rectangle has width p metres and length $(p + 5)$ metres.

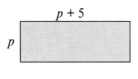

a   What is the perimeter of each shape when $p = 10$?
b   Find the perimeter of the square in terms of p.
c   Find the perimeter of the rectangle in terms of p.
d   If the perimeter of the rectangle is 90 m, how long is each of its sides?
e   Find a value of p so that the perimeters of the square and rectangle
are equal.

3   An equilateral triangle has sides of length $(t + 1)$ cm.
A rectangle has width t cm and length $2t$ cm.

Find a value of t so that the perimeter of the triangle and rectangle are equal.

4   These expressions are arranged
in a magic square.

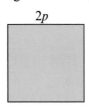

a   What value for x gives 21 at the centre of
the magic square?
b   Draw the complete magic square.
c   Find a value for x that gives a magic square
with a magic total of 117.
d   **i**   Make a magic square where the four numbers in the corner squares
add to give 100.
  ii   Explain how you decided on a value for x.
e   With these expressions, explain why the total of the numbers in the corner
squares will always be four times the number in the centre square.

> The magic total is the total
> of the numbers in each
> row, column or diagonal.

Some number puzzles can be solved using equations.

Example

I think of a number, add 1, and then double. I get the same answer if I subtract my number from 14. What is my number?

> The left-hand side of the equation is for 'add 1 and then double' $2(n + 1)$ is equivalent to $(n + 1) \times 2$.
>
> The right-hand side is for 'subtract ... from 14' $14 - n$ is **not** equivalent to $n - 14$.

- ◆ Choose a letter to stand for the number: n is the number
- ◆ Write an equation for the puzzle: $2(n - 1) = 14 - n$
- ◆ Solve the equation to find the number: $2(n + 1) = 14 - n$

$$+n \left(\begin{array}{c} 2n + 2 = 14 - n \\ 3n + 2 = 14 \\ 3n = 12 \\ n = 4 \end{array} \right) \begin{array}{c} +n \\ -2 \\ \div 3 \end{array}$$

- ◆ So the number is **4**.

Exercise 7.4
Solving number puzzles

1

> I think of a number, subtract 2 and then double. I get the same answer if I multiply my number by 3 and subtract from 21. What is my number?

Which of these equations fits the number puzzle?

A $2(n - 2) = 3n - 21$ **B** $2n - 2 = 21 - 3n$ **C** $2n - 2 = 21 - 3n$

D $2(n - 2) = 21 - 3n$ **E** $n - 4 = 21 - 3n$

> Use n to stand for the number each time.

2 For each puzzle A to E, write an equation and solve it to find the number.

A
> I think of a number, multiply it by 3, and add 5. I get the same answer if I subtract my number from 13. What is my number?

B
> I think of a number, subtract 2, and multiply by 4. I get the same answer if I subtract 3 and multiply by 5. What is my number?

C
> I think of a number, subtract 1, and multiply by 3. I get the same answer if I subtract my number from 8 and multiply by 4. What is my number?

D
> I think of a number, multiply it by 6, and subtract from 10. I get the same answer if I multiply my number by 3 and subtract from 7. What is my number?

E
> I think of a number, double it, and subtract 11. I get the same answer if I double my number and subtract from 15. What is my number?

3 **a** Write a number puzzle for the equation $3(n - 5) = 20 - 2n$
    b Solve the equation to find the value of n.

4 Make up some number puzzles for someone else to solve.

Using graphs to solve problems with two values to find

Exercise 7.5
Using graphs to
solve problems

1 This is part of a receipt from Hetty's Tea Room.

Hetty's
Tea Rooms
2 coffees
4 biscuits
TOTAL £1.72

a If the biscuits cost 15p each, how much is a coffee?
b If the biscuits cost 40p each, how much is a coffee?
c Copy and complete this table to show some possible costs for each item.

Cost of a biscuit	10p	20p	30p	40p
Cost of a coffee	66p			

d Show this data as points on a graph.

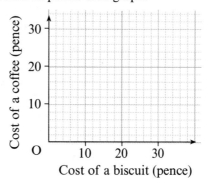

Cost of a coffee (pence)

Cost of a biscuit (pence)

Points on this line with
integer coordinates give
possible costs for each item.

e Join up your points with a straight line.
f From your graph, what is the cost of a coffee, if a biscuit costs 23p?
g Another person in the tea room pays 60p for one biscuit and one coffee.

Hetty's
Tea Rooms
1 coffee
1 biscuit
TOTAL £0.60

i For this information, copy and complete this table.

Cost of a biscuit	10p	20p	30p	40p
Cost of a coffee	50p			

ii Draw the straight line graph for this data on the set of axes used in **d**.
h What are the coordinates of the point that both lines pass through?
i Check that these values give the correct costs for a coffee and a biscuit.

2 At a kiosk: ◆ 3 ice-creams and 2 colas cost £3.68
◆ 2 ice-creams and 1 cola cost £2.24

Find the cost of:

a 1 ice-cream **b** 1 cola.

For some problems, you can form two equations and use graphs to solve them.

Example

Two families visit a funfair.
One family buys 1 adult ticket and 2 child tickets. The total is £10.
The other family buys 2 adult tickets and 1 child ticket. The total is £14.

How much is each type of ticket?

- ◆ Choose letters to stand for each type of ticket:
  Use a to stand for the cost in pounds of an adult ticket.
  Use c to stand for the cost in pounds of a child ticket.

- ◆ Write an equation for each family: $a + 2c = 10$
  $2a + c = 14$

- ◆ Draw up a table of values for each equation:

> Negative values for a and c are not included as the cost of a ticket cannot be negative.

$a + 2c = 10$

a	0	1	2	3	4	5
c	5	4.5	4	3.5	3	2.5

$2a + c = 14$

a	0	1	2	3	4	5
c	14	12	10	8	6	4

- ◆ Draw a graph for each equation, so that the lines cross at a point:

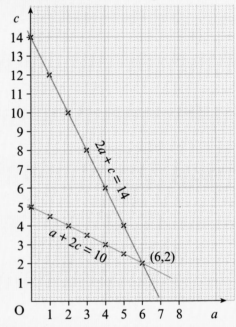

- ◆ Where the lines cross, the values of a and c fit both equations, so they give the cost of each ticket:

  The lines cross when $a = 6$ and $c = 2$,

  So an adult ticket costs £6 and a child ticket costs £2

- ◆ Check your solution:

  When $a = 6$ and $c = 2$,

  $$a + 2c = 6 + (2 \times 2)$$
  $$= 10$$

  $$2a + c = (2 \times 6) + 2$$
  $$= 14$$

- ◆ These are the correct values so the solution is correct.

Exercise 7.6
Using equations and graphs

> £1.30 = 130p

1 Two people visit a cafe.
   Rita pays 70p for 1 tea and 2 biscuits.
   Simon pays £1.30 for 3 teas and 1 biscuit.

   a Write an equation for each person, using t for the cost of a tea in pence and b for the cost of a biscuit in pence.

   b Draw up a table of values like this for each equation for values of t from 0 to 40.

t	0	10	20	30
b				

   c Draw a graph for each equation so that the lines cross.
   d From your graphs, how much does each item cost?

In Questions **2**, **3** and **4** the letters can stand for any type of number, including decimals and negative numbers.

2   Equation 1 $a + b = 6$

Equation 2 $3a + b = 9$

a   For each equation, what is the value of b when $a = 4$?
b   Draw up a table of values for each equation
with these values of a: 0, 1, 2, 3, 4, 5.
c   On one set of axes, draw a graph for each equation.
d   What are the values of a and b at the point where the lines cross?
e   Check that these values fit Equations 1 and 2.

3   Equation 1 $y = x + 4$

Equation 2 $y = 2x + 5$

a   For each equation, what is the value of y when $x = {}^-2$?
b   Draw up a table of values for each equation
with these values of x: $^-4$, $^-2$, 0, 2, 4.
c   On one set of axes, draw a graph for each equation.
d   Use your graphs to find the values of x and y that fit both equations.

4   A $y = x - 5$ B $y = 2x + 6$ C $y = 2x$
             $y = 3x - 11$ $y = 4x + 11$ $y = 7x - 9$

For each pair of equations:

a   Draw up a table of values for each equation
with these values of x: $^-4$, $^-2$, 0, 2, 4.
b   On one set of axes, draw a graph for each equation.
c   Use your graphs to find the values of x and y that fit both equations.

Solving problems without using graphs

Exercise 7.7
Solving problems
without using graphs

1   In a cafe, 2 teas and 4 coffees cost £4.60.
From this information, which of these can you find the cost of?

A   4 teas and 8 coffees   B   1 tea and 4 coffees

C   1 tea and 2 coffees   D   1 coffee   E   6 teas and 8 coffees

2   In a shop:

1 cola and 3 bags of crisps cost £1.52
2 colas and 4 bags of crisps cost £2.48

Find the cost of:

a   2 colas and 6 bags of crisps   b   1 cola and 2 bags of crisps
c   3 colas and 7 bags of crisps   d   1 cola and 1 bag of crisps
e   1 bag of crisps   f   1 cola

3   A woman has twins.
The twins are the same height.
Adding the height of the woman to the height of one twin gives 280 cm.
The total height of the woman and her twins is 400 cm.

a   What is the height of each person?
b   Make up a problem like this for someone else to solve.

4 In this puzzle, each different fruit stands for a number.
The total of the numbers in each row
is shown at the side of the puzzle.

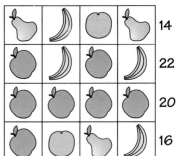

a Find the number each fruit stands for.
b Make up some puzzles like this for
someone else to solve.

Thinking ahead to ...
using algebra

A A value for p and a value for q fit both these equations.

$$3p + 4q = 23$$

$$p + 2q = 11$$

a Copy and complete these equations for p and q.
  i $3p + 6q = \bigcirc$ **ii** $2p + \bigcirc = 22$ **iii** $4p + 6q = \bigcirc$
  iv $2p + 2q = \bigcirc$ **v** $p + q = \bigcirc$

b Find the values of p and q.

Using algebra to solve problems with two values to find

Values that fit two equations can be found using algebra.

Example

Solve these equations to find the values of a and b.

$$2a + b = 19$$
$$3a + 4b = 26$$

- Label the equations (1) and (2):

$$2a + b = 19 \dots (1)$$
$$3a + 4b = 26 \dots (2)$$

- Multiply both sides of
equation (1) by 4 to give
two equations with '+ 4b':

$(1) \times 4 \dots$ $8a + 4b = 76 \dots (3)$
$3a + 4b = 26 \dots (2)$

> Subtract to remove '+ 4b'
> from each equation:
> $4b - 4b = 0$

- Subtract: $(3) - (2) \dots (8a - 3a) + (4b - 4b) = 76 - 26$
  $5a = 50$

- Find the value of a: $a = 10$

> Equation (2) could also be
> used to find the value of b:
>
> $3a + 4b = 26$
> $(3 \times 10) + 4b = 26$
> $30 + 4b = 26$
> $4b = {}^-4$
> $b = {}^-1$

- Substitute the value of a in one
equation to find the value of b:

$2a + b = 19 \dots (1)$
$(2 \times 10) + b = 19$
$20 + b = 19$
$b = {}^-1$

- **So the solution is $a = 10$, $b = {}^-1$.**

Exercise 7.8
Using algebra

1 For each pair of equations, use algebra to find the values of x and y.
  a $x + 4y = 42$ **b** $11x + 3y = 91$ **c** $5x + 7y = 32$
      $2x + 5y = 57$ $3x + y = 25$ $x + 3y = 12$

2 For which pair of equations is it true that $s = 5$ and $t = 2$?

A
$$s + 3t = 11$$
$$5s + t = 32$$

B
$$3s + t = 17$$
$$4s + 5t = 30$$

C
$$3s + 2t = 20$$
$$s + 2t = 9$$

3 A value for m and a value for n fit both these equations.

$$2m + 3n = 28 \ ... \ (1)$$
$$3m + 4n = 37 \ ... \ (2)$$

> Multiply **both** equations to give two equations with '$6m$'.

a Multiply equation (1) by 3.
b Multiply equation (2) by 2.
c Subtract to find the value of n that fits both equations.
d Substitute in one of the equations to find the value of m.

4 For each pair of equations, use algebra to find the values of v and w.

a $2v + 3w = 40$
    $5v + 2w = 34$

b $3v + 2w = 3$
    $6v + 10w = 24$

c $4v + 2w = 9$
    $3v + 7w = 4$

Sometimes it is simpler to **add** the equations.

Example

Solve these equations to find the values of x and y.

$$6x - 2y = 18$$
$$5x + 3y = 1$$

♦ Label the equations (1) and (2):

$$6x - 2y = 18 \quad (1)$$
$$5x + 3y = 1 \quad (2)$$

> This is one way to use algebra to solve this problem. There are other ways.

♦ Multiply equation (1) by 3 and equation (2) by 2 to give '$- 6y$' and '$+ 6y$':

$(1) \times 3$ $18x \ - \ 6y \ = 54 \ (3)$
$(2) \times 2$ $10x \ + \ 6y \ = 2 \ (4)$

> Add to remove '$- 6y$' and '$+ 6y$':
> $-6y + 6y = 0$

♦ Add:

$(3) + (4)$ $(18x + 10x) + (-6y + 6y) = 54 + 2$
$$28x = 56$$

♦ Find the value of x:
$$x = 2$$

♦ Substitute the value of x in one equation to find the value of y:

$$5x + 3y = 1 \quad (2)$$
$$(5 \times 2) + 3y = 1$$
$$10 + 3y = 1$$
$$3y = {}^-9$$
$$y = {}^-3$$

♦ **So the solution is $x = 2$, $y = {}^-3$.**

Exercise 7.9
Using algebra

1 For each pair of equations, use algebra to find the values of a and b.

a $a - b = 8$
    $4a + b = 42$

b $5b + 2a = 29$
    $b - 2a = 1$

c $3a - b = 15$
    $4a + 2b = 25$

d $b + 3a = 2$
    $3b - a = 26$

e $5a + 2b = 17$
    $2a - 3b = 3$

f $7a + 5b = 27$
    $3a - 2b = 24$

2 Two numbers m and n fit both these equations.

$$5m - n = 15$$
$$3m - n = 5$$

> Subtract to remove '$- n$' from each equation:
> $(-n) - (-n) = 0$

a Subtract to find the value of m that fits both equations.
b Substitute in one of the equations to find the value of n.

3   Find the values of p and q that fit: $6p - 2q = 16$
    and $p - 2q = 1$

4   Two numbers m and n fit both these equations:

$5m - 2n = 28$ (1)
$7m - 5n = 37$ (2)

a   Multiply equation (1) by 5.
b   Multiply equation (2) by 2.
c   Subtract to find the value of m that fits both equations.
d   Substitute in one of the equations to find the value of n.

> Here we multiply **both** equations to give two equations with '$- 10n$'.

5   For each pair of equations, use algebra to find the values of x and y.

a $5x - 2y = 16$ b $4y - x = 17$ c $5x - 3y = 7$
    $2x - 3y = 2$ $3y - 4x = 3$ $2x - 4y = 0$

d $5y + 3x = 15$ e $4x + 3y = 17$ f $3x + 2y = 13$
    $5y + 7x = 25$ $5x - 7y = 32$ $5x - 6y = 59$

Magic pentagrams

Exercise 7.10
Magic pentagrams

1   Ten numbers in circles can be linked by straight lines in a star shape like this.

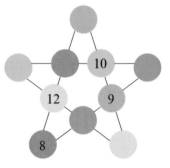

Copy the diagram and place the
numbers 1, 2, 3, 4, 5, and 6 in
the empty circles so that the total of the four numbers along each line is 24.

Ten expressions are used in this pentagram.

> This pentagram is used in Questions **2 – 13**.

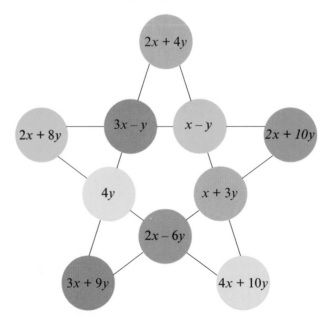

> If the totals of the four numbers along each line are equal, it is a magic pentagram.

2   a   Find the value of each expression in the diagram when $x = 7$ and $y = 2$.
    b   Draw the diagram with these values.
    c   Is it a magic pentagram?

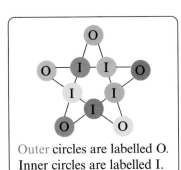

Outer circles are labelled O.
Inner circles are labelled I.

3 **a** Find the value of each expression for your own choice of x and y.
b Draw the diagram with these values.
Is it a magic pentagram?

4 **a** For each line, find the total of the four expressions.
b Explain why your totals show that any values for x and y will give a magic pentagram.

5 Find values of x and y that will give a magic pentagram with a total of 48.

6 Find values for x and y that will give a magic pentagram with 100 in its blue outer circle.

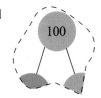

7 A magic pentagram has 12 in its outer blue circle and 18 in its red outer circle.

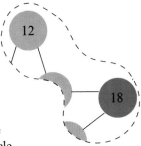

a Complete this equation for the number 18 in the red outer circle.

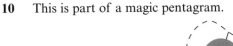

$$2x + 10y = \ldots$$

b Write an equation for the number 12 in the blue outer circle.
c Find values for x and y that fit both equations.
d Use these values to draw the complete pentagram.

8 **a** Write equations for a magic pentagram with 18 in the green outer circle and 10 in the blue outer circle.
b Find values for x and y that fit both equations.

9 Make a magic pentagram with 14 in the blue inner circle and 4 in the red inner circle.

10 This is part of a magic pentagram.

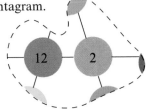

a Draw the complete magic pentagram.
b Write down the total along each line.

11 Make a magic pentagram where the total of the numbers in the red circles is 48 and the total of the numbers in the green circles is 76.

12 Make a magic pentagram where the total of the numbers in the outer circles is 106 and the total of the numbers in the inner circles is 34.

13 Find values of x and y that give a magic pentagram where the total of the numbers in the outer circles is twice the total of those in the inner circles.

Using algebra to solve word problems

Example

A father's age and his son's age add to give 54.
The father is 30 years older than his son.

How old is his son?

- Use f to stand for the father's age and
  s to stand for the son's age:

- The ages add to give 42, so:
- The father is 30 years older than the son, so:

$$f + s = 54 \ldots (1)$$
$$f - s = 30 \ldots (2)$$

- Add: $(1) + (2) \ldots$ $(f + f) + (s + - s) = 54 + 30$

$$2f = 84$$

- Find the value of f: $f = 42$

- Substitute the value of f in one
  equation to find the value of s:

$$f + s = 54 \ldots (1)$$
$$42 + s = 54$$
$$s = 12$$

- **So the son is 12 years old.**

Exercise 7.11
Solving word problems

1 Susan's age and her brother's age add to give 73.
Susan is 3 years older than her brother.
Find the ages of Susan and her brother.

2 A bag contains a mixture of large and small marbles.
Each small marble weighs 2 g.
Each large marble weighs 5 g.
The total weight of the marbles in the bag is 256 g.
Altogether there were 89 marbles in the bag.

Use x to stand for the number of small marbles.
Use y to stand for the number of large marbles.

a Use this information to write two equations in x and y.
b Solve these equations to find the number of each type of marble.

3 Pia's age is quarter the age of her mother, Sonya.
Pia is n years old.

Write down in terms of n:

a Sonya's age b Pia's age 8 years ago
c Sonya's age 8 years ago.

Eight years ago, Sonya was 12 times as old as Pia.
d Use this information to form an equation in n.
e Solve this equation to find Pia's age.

4 A slot machine takes only 10p and 20p coins.
It contains a total of 380 coins.
If the value of the coins is £63.70, find the number of each type of coin.

5 The line $y = mx + c$ passes through (3, 10) and (5, 18).
Find m and c.

End points

You should be able to ...   ... so try these questions

A Add and subtract like terms in linear expressions

A1 Simplify:

    a $6k + 8m - 4k + m$ **b** $5p - 1 - 3p + 9$

B Form and solve linear equations

B1 Solve:

    a $2z - 1 = 12$ **b** $4y + 1 = 2y + 7$

    c $6(x - 1) = 3$ **d** $15 - 3w = w + 11$

    e $3(2v + 7) = v + 6$ **f** $2(t + 3) = 18 - 6t$

B2 The lengths of the sides of a triangle are x cm, $(x + 8)$ cm and $(x - 6)$ cm.

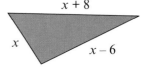

    a What is the perimeter of the triangle in terms of x?

    b The triangle has a perimeter of 26 cm.
       Write down an equation in x, and solve it to find the length of each side of the triangle.

B3

> I think of a number, double it and subtract 1. I get the same answer if I multiply my number by 4 and subtract from 14. What is my number?

Write an equation for this number puzzle and solve it to find the number.

C Solve problems using graphs

C1 Equation 1 $y = 2x - 3$

    Equation 2 $y = 4x - 4$

    a Draw up a table of values for each equation with these values of x: $^-4, ^-2, 0, 2, 4$.

    b On one set of axes, draw a graph for each equation.

    c Use your graphs to find the values of x and y that fit both equations.

D Solve problems using algebra

D1 For each pair of equations, use algebra to find the values of m and n.

    a $3m + 2n = 5$ **b** $2m + 3n = 5$ **c** $2m - n = 22$

        $5m + 2n = 8$ $3m + 4n = 6$ $3m + 2n = 40$

D2 A slot machine takes only 20p and 50p coins.
It contains a total of 140 coins.
The value of the coins is £45.10.

Use x to stand for the number of 20p coins.
Use y to stand for the number of 50p coins.

    a Show that $20x + 50y = 4510$.

    b Write down a different equation in x and y.

    c Use your equations to find the number of each type of coin.

Some points to remember

- ◆ When solving an equation, add, subtract, multiply or divide **both** sides by equal amounts.
- ◆ Problems where two values have to be found can be solved using graphs or algebra.
  The most accurate answer can be found using algebra.

Starting points
You need to know about ...

A Rounding numbers

Rounding is a way to approximate numbers when an exact value is not needed.

Whole numbers are usually rounded to the nearest 10, 100, 1000 and so on.

Example

3837.6 rounded   to the nearest whole number is 3838
to the nearest 10 is 3840
to the nearest 100 is 3800
to the nearest 1000 is 4000
to the nearest 10 000 is 0

Decimals are rounded to a given number of decimal places (dp).

Example

3.6748 rounded   to 1 dp is 3.7
to 2 dp is 3.67
to 3 dp is 3.675

Halfway numbers can be rounded either way but are usually rounded up.

Example

735 to the nearest ten is 740
56.75 to 1 dp is 56.8

A1 Round 2175.6 to the nearest:
  a thousand **b** hundred
  c ten   **d** whole number

A2 Round 45.638 to:
  a 2 dp   **b** 1 dp

A3 Round these numbers.
  a 34.597 to 2 dp
  b 2.501 to the nearest whole number
  c 38.45 to 1 dp
  d 3496 to the nearest ten

A4 Which numbers are not 2.56 when rounded to 2 dp?
  a 2.5555   **b** 2.5648
  c 2.5651   **d** 2.550 99
  e 2.5500   **f** 2.5666

B Adding and subtracting decimals

When you add or subtract decimal numbers you may find it easier to arrange the digits in columns.

Example 1

45.346 + 8.6 + 237

1000	100	10	U		$\frac{1}{10}$	$\frac{1}{100}$	$\frac{1}{100}$	
		4	5	.	3	4	6	
			8	.	6			
	2	3	7	.				+
	2	9	0	.	9	4	6	

Example 2

34.6 − 2.784

```
   3   4  .  6   0   0
       2  .  7   8   4  −
   3   1  .  8   1   6
```

B1 Add these decimal numbers:
  a 45.73 + 8.423 + 123.6
  b 14 + 0.563 + 28.9
  c 0.004 + 0.03 + 0.95 + 3
  d 17.8 + 3425 + 0.0895

B2 Subtract these numbers:
  a 34.78 − 6.8
  b 14 − 2.83
  c 154.36 − 4.5
  d 256 − 23.764

B3 What mistake has been made here?
    34.5 + 2.34 = 57.9

B4 Explain the mistake made in this calculation.
    34.6 − 2.278 = 32.478

Rounding up or down?

People make estimates every day.
They often base an estimate on a calculation they do in their head.

Sometimes it is best to **overestimate** so they **round up** their answer.
At other times it is best to **underestimate** and **round down**.

We should be able to cycle about 78 miles each day so how far apart do we want the hostels to be?

I've worked out that we need 4756 bricks for the extension. How many should I order?

In this case it might be better to **round down** the 78 to say 60 miles a day just in case they felt tired or had an accident.

Here, it would be better to **round up** the number of bricks. An order of say 5000 bricks would allow for breakage or error. Bricks ordered later might not be exactly the same colour.

Exercise 8.1
Rounding up or down?

1   In each of these situations do you think it is better to round up, round down, or not to round at all. Explain why.

  a   You have to draw out some money from the bank.
You work out that you need £8.35 for your trip.

  b   The seat number on your concert ticket is 213.
You must decide where to sit.

  c   You calculate that you need 11 rolls of wallpaper for your room.
You go into the shop to buy the paper.

  d   Don lives at 26 Hayward Road. You decide to pay him a call.

  e   You think you may earn £360 from your holiday job.
You look at hi-fis you think you will be able to afford.

2   Describe a new situation for each of these:

  a   when it would be a good idea to round up

  b   when it would be best to round down

  c   when it would be silly to do any rounding.

3   For each of these situations decide if it is better to round up or down.
Say what number you would use, and explain why.

  a   You calculate that the gap for a desk is 98 cm wide.
You have to decide what width of desk to ask for.

  b   The milometer in your sister's car reads 67 673 miles.
You advertise the car with the mileage it has done.

  c   You expect 74 people for the school-leavers meal.
You have to hire some glasses.

  d   You calculate that you need 15.3 metres of wood for some shelves.
You have to buy the wood.

Significant figures

Exercise 8.2
Rounding

1 In this extract some numbers are given to a greater accuracy than they need to be.

Practical Green Keeping

March edition

Crew measure up while the games are on

THE MAINTENANCE CREW arrived at the stadium at 10:43 while the athletics events were taking place. The 71 934 crowd was already seated when measuring up started. The perimeter railings were measured as 63 479.6 cm long and the supports as 19.6 cm thick. At one point the crowd rose to its feet as Mary Taylor set a new European record of 10.84 sec for the 100 metres sprint. From their calculations the crew estimated the area of grass which needed re-seeding was 1452.56 metres². The measuring was completed in about 56 minutes with little disruption to the 492 or so competitors.

The maintenance contract with the sports committee expires in 2003

'Appropriate' means 'sensible'.

a List the numbers which you think are more accurate than is appropriate. Write what you think each one should be rounded to.

b Which numbers should not be rounded? Explain why.

c In both 63 479.6 and in 19.6 the last digit stands for $\frac{6}{10}$.
   In which of these numbers do you think this 6 is more significant? Explain why.

'Significant' in this case means 'important'.

2 Draw a line on your page.
   Measure its length as accurately as you can.
   How many digits are in the number you have written?

3 Estimate how far it is from Land's End to John O'Groats.
   How many of the digits in your answer are not zero?

4 The digit 4 is in both of these numbers: **24.6   10243**

   a In which number does the 4 have the greater actual value?
   b In which number do you think the 4 is more significant?

5 To what accuracy do you think a 100 metre running track must be measured when it is marked out?

Significant figures means the most important digits in a number.

In 6351.2 the 6 and 3 are the two most significant figures because they show the largest numbers 60 000 and 3000.

Significant figures can be written as **sf**.

Ways of approximating include rounding a number to the nearest ten or to a set number of decimal places.

Another way is to round a number is to a set number of significant figures.

63 479.6   rounded to **2 significant figures** is 63 000

> The three zeros are added to keep the value of the number about the same.

63 479.6   rounded to **3 significant figures** is 63 500

> Note how the 4 has rounded up to 5 because the next digit 7 is above halfway.

63 479.6   rounded to **4 sf** is   63 480

63 479.6   rounded to **5 sf** is   63 480

Exercise 8.3
Rounding using significant figures

1   When 63 479.6 is rounded to 4 sf or 5 sf the answer is the same. Why do you think this is?

2   Round 71 934 to:
   a 1 sf   **b** 2 sf   **c** 3 sf   **d** 4 sf

3   Round each of these numbers to 3 sf:
   a 1452.56   **b** 21 675   **c** 142.51   **d** 2134 518.4   **e** 149 625

4   A number, rounded to 2 sf, is 3200.
   Give three numbers it could be.

5   Copy and complete this table.

Number	45 287	2395	302 604.32	14.823
to 2 sf				
to 3 sf				
to 4 sf				

6   The grass that needed re-seeding in the stadium was a rectangle this size:

54.2 m

Area = 1452.56 m²

26.8 m

In calculations you should either:

♦ give your answer to the degree of accuracy asked for e.g. 1 dp or 2 sf, or

♦ give your answer to the same degree of accuracy as is used in the question.

Why do you think it is not sensible to use all the digits for the area? What would you round the area to?

7   A number, when rounded to 2 sf or to 3 sf is 420 000.
   Give an example of what the number might be.

8   To how many significant figures could a number be rounded to give 164 000?

Numbers less than 1 can also be rounded using significant figures.

0.0753   rounded to **1 significant figure** is   0.08

> The first significant figure is this 7. The zeros at the start do not count as significant.

> The 7 rounds up to 8 because the next digits are above halfway.

0.004 03   rounded to **2 significant figures** is   0.0040

> This zero is significant because it is between two other significant figures.

> This zero must stay to make it clear there are 2 significant figures.

Exercise 8.4
Significant figures

1 The width of a human hair found at the scene of a crime was 0.007 64 cm. Round this number to 1 sf.

2 When 0.000 5246 is rounded to 2 sf it becomes 0.000 52. 0.000 5200 is not really correct. Explain why.

3 For these conversions round the blue numbers.

Metric/Imperial conversions			
	to 1 sf	to 2 sf	to 3 sf
1 inch = 0.0254 metres	0.03	0.025	0.0254
1 yard = 0.009 144 kilometres			
1 millimetre = 0.0394 inches			
1 kilometre = 0.6214 miles			
1 millilitre = 0.001 76 pints			
1 centimetre^3 = 0.061 023 74 inches^3			
1 foot^3 = 0.0283 metres^3			
1 pound = 0.004 535 9237 tonnes			

4 The table shows land areas of some countries.

Which country has a land area of four hundred thousand km^2 when rounded to 1 sf?

5 Why might it not be helpful for a book to give all the areas to 1 sf?

6 Give the following land areas:

   a United Kingdom to 5 sf
   b Andorra to 2 sf
   c Japan to 3 sf
   d China to 4 sf
   e Monaco to 1 sf.

7 For two countries the area stays the same when rounded to 3 sf, 4 sf or 5 sf. Which countries are these?

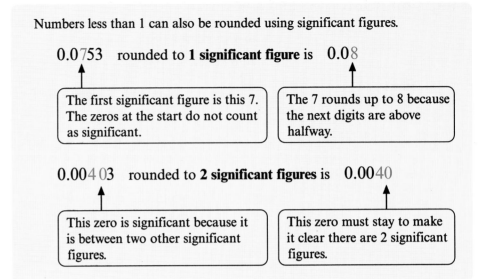

COUNTRY	AREA (km²)
Andorra	464
Argentina	2758 829
Bangladesh	143 998
Cambodia	181 035
Cameroon	475 499
China	9560 948
Congo	348 999
Denmark	43 030
Japan	369 698
Monaco	1.6
United Kingdom	244 019

Using significant figures to estimate answers

One way to check if a calculation gives an answer of about the right size is to round each of the numbers to 1 sf.

For example, to estimate an answer:

> Here are some answers given by four students when they had to calculate the value of **43 183.5 × 184.23** without using a calculator.
>
> **a**   795 569.6   **b**   79 556 962   **c**   7 955 696   **d**   79 557
>
> Which answer is likely to be most accurate?

> A value which is of the correct order of magnitude is about the right size.

To 1 sf these numbers become   40 000 × 200

which is   40 000 × 2 × 100

= 80 000 × 100

= 8 000 000

Answer **c**. 7 955 696 is about the same order of magnitude as 8 000 000 so it is most likely to be most accurate.

Exercise 8.5
Estimating answers

1   Work out estimates of the answers to each of these. Show all the stages you use.

   a   31.2 × 241.45   **b**   5677 × 3.764
   c   54 856 × 83.42   **d**   542 × 52
   e   56 234 ÷ 82.5   **f**   62 381.23 ÷ 578.23
   g   452 ÷ 2.34   **h**   28 536 ÷ 0.9623

2   A theatre sells 562 tickets at £28.50 each.

   a   Roughly what is their income from ticket sales?
   b   Why does rounding both numbers to 1 sf give too large an estimate?

> Population density is the average (mean) number of people to each square kilometre.

3   France has a land area of 549 619 km².
   In 1990 the population was 56 304 000.
   Estimate the population density in people per km².

4   When the numbers in 341.2 × 14.25 are rounded to 1 sf and then multiplied the estimate is much smaller than the true answer.
   For the problem 156 ÷ 34.7 the estimate is much larger.
   Explain why.

5   For each of these problems, say if rounding all numbers to 1 sf makes estimates too large, too small, or about the right size.

   a   56.5 × 1763.2   **b**   184 ÷ 19.6
   c   491.432 × 2061.4   **d**   445 × 84 632
   e   2265 ÷ 27.7   **f**   6834 ÷ 14.23
   g   453 782 + 242 565   **h**   7452.3 − 2837.324

6   For the problem 342 561 + 453, why is rounding to 1 sf not helpful?

7   In problems which only use addition and subtraction, when is rounding to 1 sf useful for finding an estimate?

Thinking ahead to ...
working with numbers
less than 1

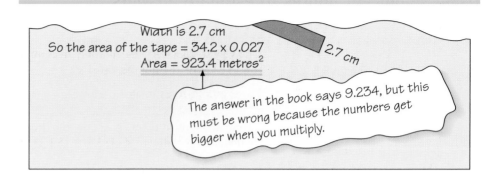

Width is 2.7 cm
So the area of the tape = 34.2 x 0.027
Area = 923.4 metres²
2.7 cm

The answer in the book says 9.234, but this must be wrong because the numbers get bigger when you multiply.

A   Work out 342 × 0.027 with a calculator.
Is the answer larger or smaller than 342?

B   Work out 342 ÷ 0.027. Is this answer larger or smaller than 342?

You may need to do some more calculations to decide this.

C   What can you say about the answer when you:
   a   multiply by a number less than 1
   b   divide by a number less than 1?

Working with numbers less than 1

Example 1   Estimate the value of 342 × 0.052.

Approximating to 1 sf, this becomes 300 × 0.05.

The answer to this estimate will be smaller than 300.
One way to work out the value is to look for patterns.

$$300 \times 5 = 1500$$

$$300 \times 0.5 = 150$$

$$300 \times 0.05 = 15$$ **So the estimate is 15.**

Example 2   Estimate for the value of 26 ÷ 0.0056.

To 1 sf this is 30 ÷ 0.006.

$$30 \div 6 = 5$$

$$30 \div 0.6 = 50$$

$$30 \div 0.06 = 500$$

$$30 \div 0.006 = 5000$$ **So the estimate is 5000.**

Exercise 8.6
Calculating and
estimating answers

1   **a**   Calculate 342 × 52 without a calculator.
   b   Use the example above to help decide what 342 × 0.052 is.

2   Estimate the value of 45 × 0.0023.
Show all the stages you use.
Calculate the exact answer and check it with your estimate.

3   Estimate, then calculate, the exact values of these.
   a   346.3 ÷ 0.04   **b**   26.23 × 0.67   **c**   876.2 × 0.000 23
   d   2.448 ÷ 0.0018   **e**   2567.245 + 6229   **f**   78.4567 − 7.64

4

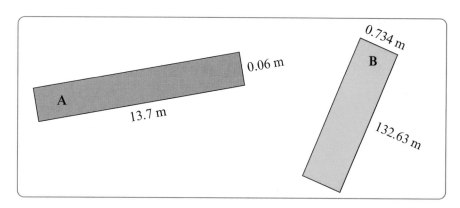

a Estimate the areas of shapes A and B.
   Show the stages in your working.
b Calculate the areas without using a calculator.

5

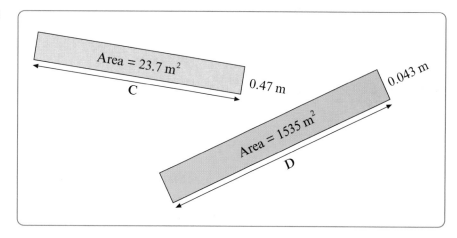

Estimate the dimensions C and D.
Show the stages in your working.

6

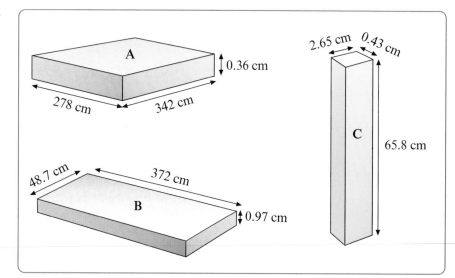

Volume of a cuboid =
Length × Width × Depth

Estimate the volumes of cuboids A to C.
Explain your working.

7 A cuboid is 113.6 cm long, 0.42 cm deep and has a volume of 18.42 cm³.
   Estimate its width.

When should you round?

What is the area of the £20 note? Round your answer to the nearest cm².

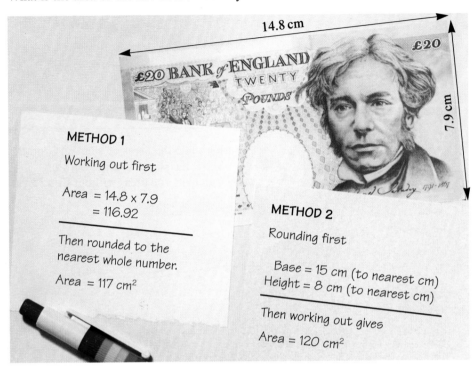

14.8 cm

£20

7.9 cm

METHOD 1

Working out first

Area = 14.8 x 7.9
     = 116.92

Then rounded to the nearest whole number.

Area = 117 cm²

METHOD 2

Rounding first

Base = 15 cm (to nearest cm)
Height = 8 cm (to nearest cm)

Then working out gives

Area = 120 cm²

Alison uses Method 1. She calculates then rounds the answer.
Mark uses Method 2. He rounds all the numbers, then calculates.

Exercise 8.7
The effect of rounding

1   The £5 note has changed in size since 1900.

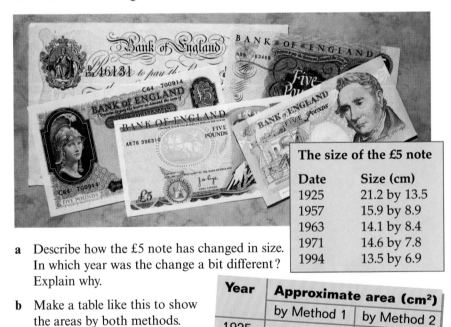

The size of the £5 note

Date	Size (cm)
1925	21.2 by 13.5
1957	15.9 by 8.9
1963	14.1 by 8.4
1971	14.6 by 7.8
1994	13.5 by 6.9

a   Describe how the £5 note has changed in size.
In which year was the change a bit different?
Explain why.

b   Make a table like this to show
the areas by both methods.

Year	Approximate area (cm²)	
	by Method 1	by Method 2
1925		
1957		

c   Which method do you find easier to use?

d   Which method gives the more accurate answer?
Explain why.

Errors in calculations

Rounding at the start of a calculation is fine for a rough check, but for an accurate answer it is better to round at the end.

For example, look what happens when you round at the start of this calculation.

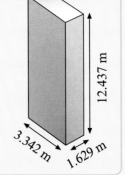

With the values given, the volume $= 3.342 \times 12.437 \times 1.629$
$= 67.708\,495\,57 \, \text{m}^3$

Round all numbers to 1 dp at the start.
Volume $\approx 3.3 \times 12.4 \times 1.6$
$\approx 65.472 \, \text{m}^3$

The error made by rounding to 1 dp is

$67.708\,495\,57 - 65.472$
Error $\approx 2.24 \, \text{m}^3$

12.437 m

3.342 m   1.629 m

$\approx$ means approximately equal to.

In some situations, such as the volume of a fuel tank for a rocket, this error would be much too great.
In others, such as for the size of a compost heap, it would not matter.

Exercise 8.8
Errors in calculations

1 For the cuboid above:

   a Round all the dimensions to 2 dp.
   b Calculate the volume using the rounded dimensions.
   c Calculate the error this gives.

2 Round the dimensions of the cuboid to the nearest whole number and calculate the error this gives in the volume.

3 This cuboid was measured with a ruler as accurately as possible.

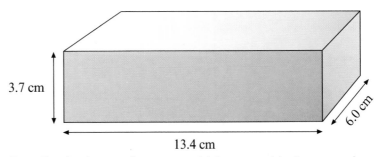

3.7 cm

6.0 cm

13.4 cm

Describe the degree of accuracy which was used in the measuring.

4 The exact base length could lie anywhere between 13.35 and 13.45 cm.

   a What is the minimum possible value for the height of 3.7 cm?
   b What is the maximum value for the height?

In this case the limits are the minimum and maximum values.

5 What are the limits for the depth of 6.0 cm?

6 Since each dimension has a minimum value and a maximum value, there must be a minimum volume and a maximum volume.

   a What is the minimum volume for the cuboid?
   b What is the maximum volume?
   c What is the difference between the maximum and minimum volumes?

End points

You should be able to ...   ... so try these questions

A Decide what rounding is appropriate for the situation

A1

> Alez tuned into her favourite station, Channel 162 on the infrawave. She knew the slot lasted for about 91 minutes so she would need a compulsory meal before the end. She dined on 27 of her favourite food pills with 785 ml of ice-cold isophoric delight. Jeq materialised in 11 minutes raving about some antique maths book with about 416 pages that he'd found and dated as 1997.

Rewrite this extract and round numbers where it is appropriate.

A2 For each of these situations would you round up, down or not at all. Explain why.

a You find the wall area of your bedroom is 330 square feet. You go to buy paint.

b The manual says your car can pull a trailer with a maximum weight of 470 kg. You are loading your camping gear.

B Round a number to a given number of significant figures

B1 Round 345.683 to:

a 3 sf   **b** 5 sf   **c** 1 sf

B2 Round each number to 3 sf.

a 34.673   **b** 1.974   **c** 194 638.2
d 0.003 186   **e** 143.5   **f** 6.987 36

C Estimate then calculate the answers to problems and know when to round

C1 For the cuboid:

a Estimate its volume.
b Calculate the volume and give your answer correct to 2 dp.

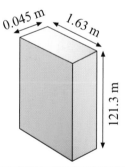

0.045 m   1.63 m   121.3 m

Some points to remember

♦ Give your final answers to an appropriate degree of accuracy for the situation.

♦ In exams, remember to round your answers when you are asked to do so. It is easy to forget.

♦ One way to estimate an answer is to round all the numbers to 1 sf.

♦ It is a good idea to estimate the order of magnitude of your answers before you calculate.

♦ Do not round at the start of, or during, a calculation if you want an accurate answer.

♦ When you multiply a number by a number less than 1, the answer is smaller.

♦ When you divide a number by a number less than 1, the answer is larger.

Starting points
You need to know about...

...so try these questions

A Probability from equally likely outcomes

If outcomes are equally likely, then you can calculate the probability that something will happen by counting the outcomes.

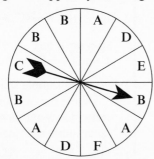

For example: There are twelve sections of equal size.
Four sections have B on them.
So the probability that the spinner stops on B is $\frac{4}{12} = \frac{1}{3}$.

Three sections have A on them and four sections have B.
So the probability that it stops on either A or B is $\frac{7}{12}$.

Probabilities can be shown on a probability scale from 0 to 1.

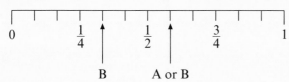

B The probability of a non-event

If you know the probability of something happening, then you can also calculate the probability of it **not** happening.

The probability of **getting B** on the spinner above is $\frac{1}{3}$.

The probability of **not getting B** is $1 - \frac{1}{3} = \frac{2}{3}$.

C Multiplication of fractions

In probability, sometimes you need to multiply fractions.

You can think of $\frac{3}{4} \times \frac{2}{5}$ like this:

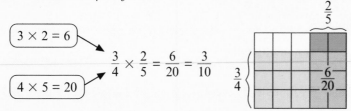

* Multiply the numerators.
* Multiply the denominators.
* Then reduce to the simplest terms if you need to.

A1 What is the probability that the wheel will stop on:
  a A   **b** E   **c** C
  d D   **e** F?

A2 What is the probability that the wheel will stop on:
  a either B or F
  b either E or A
  c either A, B or C
  d a letter after D in the alphabet
  e a letter of the alphabet
  f the letter N?

A3 Draw a probability scale and show the probabilities of the wheel stopping on each of A, B, C, D, E and F.

A4 For a 1 to 6 dice what is the probability that for one roll you will get:
  a the number 5
  b an even number
  c a number less than 3?

B1 The probability of getting a red colour on a spinner is $\frac{4}{5}$.

What is the probability of not getting red?

C1 Multiply these fractions.
  a $\frac{3}{4} \times \frac{1}{4}$
  b $\frac{5}{8} \times \frac{1}{2}$
  c $\frac{2}{3} \times \frac{3}{7}$
  d $\frac{1}{8} \times \frac{3}{4}$

D Sample space diagrams

A sample space diagram can be used to show the outcomes from two events which are not linked (independent events).

For example, when a coin and a dice are spun there are twelve different pairs of outcomes.

Outcome of coin						
H	H1	H2	H3	H4	H5	H6
T	T1	T2	T3	(T4)	(T5)	(T6)
	1	2	3	4	5	6

Outcome of dice

These diagrams can be used to show the probability of two things happening. For example, to find the probability of a tail on the coin and a number more than 3 on the dice.

The three pairs which match have been circled in red **so the probability is $\frac{3}{12} = \frac{1}{4}$.**

E Tree diagrams

A tree diagram has branches showing different events. The probabilities of different events can be shown on the branches. This is a tree diagram for the spin of a coin then Spinner A.

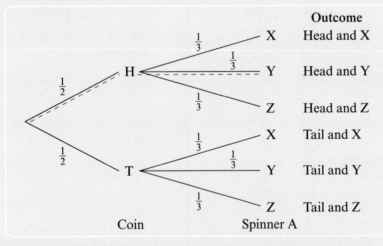

	Outcome
X	Head and X
Y	Head and Y
Z	Head and Z
X	Tail and X
Y	Tail and Y
Z	Tail and Z

Coin   Spinner A

To find the probability of a particular outcome you can multiply the probabilities on the branches that lead to it.

For example, to find the probability of a head and Y you multiply the probabilities along the dotted branches.

Probability of a head and Y is $\frac{1}{2} \times \frac{1}{3} = \frac{1}{6}$.

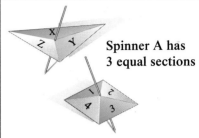

Spinner A has 3 equal sections

Spinner B has 4 equal sections

D1 Draw a sample space diagram to show the outcomes of letters and numbers for the two spinners, A and B.

D2 From your diagram calculate the probability that with a spin of each you get:
a a 4 and a Y
b a number less than 3 and an X.

E1 Draw a tree diagram to show the spinning of spinner B then a coin.

E2 From your tree diagram calculate the probability of a 3 on the spinner and a head on the coin.

Counting outcomes

The outcomes from rolling two dice can be shown by a sample space diagram. Each pair of numbers is equally likely.

Sample space diagram

Number on red dice							
6	6, 1	6, 2	6, 3	6, 4	6, 5	6, 6
5	5, 1	5, 2	5, 3	5, 4	5, 5	5, 6
4	4, 1	4, 2	4, 3	4, 4	4, 5	4, 6
3	3, 1	3, 2	3, 3	3, 4	3, 5	3, 6
2	2, 1	2, 2	2, 3	2, 4	2, 5	2, 6
1	1, 1	1, 2	1, 3	1, 4	1, 5	1, 6
	1	**2**	**3**	**4**	**5**	**6**

Number on blue dice

To calculate the probability that something will happen you can count those pairs that match the question.

For example, to find the probability that at least one dice shows a 4.

On the sample space diagram you can find all the outcomes which show 'at least one 4'.

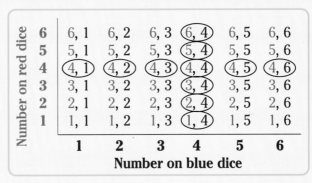

Number on red dice							
6	6, 1	6, 2	6, 3	(6, 4)	6, 5	6, 6
5	5, 1	5, 2	5, 3	(5, 4)	5, 5	5, 6
4	(4, 1)	(4, 2)	(4, 3)	(4, 4)	(4, 5)	(4, 6)
3	3, 1	3, 2	3, 3	(3, 4)	3, 5	3, 6
2	2, 1	2, 2	2, 3	(2, 4)	2, 5	2, 6
1	1, 1	1, 2	1, 3	(1, 4)	1, 5	1, 6
	1	**2**	**3**	**4**	**5**	**6**

Number on blue dice

There are 36 pairs in total and 11 match.

So the probability of 'at least one 4' is $\frac{11}{36}$.

Exercise 9.1
Counting outcomes

1 Copy the sample space diagram and use it to find the probability that when both dice are rolled you get:

  a a 1 and a 5
  b two 6's
  c a total of 7 when the numbers are added
  d the same number on both dice
  e different numbers on each dice
  f a total of 4
  g a total less than 6
  h two prime numbers
  i a total which is a prime number.

2 Draw a sample space diagram for a red 0 to 9 dice and a blue 0 to 9 dice.

A 0 to 9 dice has the numbers 0, 1, 2, 3, 4, 5, 6, 7, 8, 9.

3 Use your sample space diagram to find the probability of getting:

  a two numbers the same
  b a total greater than 13
  c two even numbers.

More than two events

A sample space diagram can be used for two rolls of a dice but it is not suitable for three rolls. Here a tree diagram is better.

Example   A six-sided dice has 2 red faces, 2 blue faces and 2 yellow faces. Each colour, therefore, is equally likely.
This dice is rolled three times.
What is the probability of rolling three faces of the same colour?

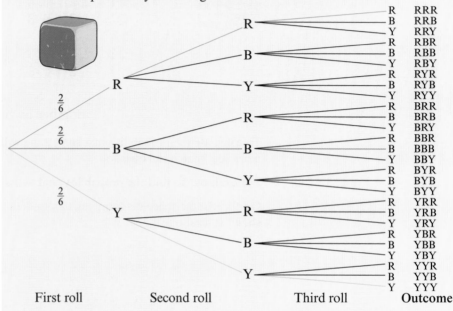

| First roll | Second roll | Third roll | Outcome |

The easiest way to calculate probabilities here is to look at the set of outcomes. There are 27 outcomes and 3 of these have the same colour (RRR, BBB and YYY).

So the probability is $\frac{3}{27} = \frac{1}{9}$.

Exercise 9.2
Three events

1   For three rolls of the dice above what is the probability of:

   a   exactly two blues
   b   at least two reds
   c   all the colours different
   d   only two colours
   e   at least one yellow
   f   all three blues
   g   two blues and a red
   h   exactly two colours the same?

2   An eight-sided dice has four red faces and four blue faces.
     It is rolled three times.
     Draw a tree diagram to show the different outcomes.

3   For three rolls of the eight-sided dice what is the probability that:

   a   all three are blue
   b   all three are the same colour
   c   at least one is blue
   d   exactly two have the same colour
   e   all three are different colours
   f   there are two blues and one red?

Ways of arranging things

Exercise 9.3
Arrangements

There is a saying that, given an enormously long time and a typewriter, a tribe of monkeys would type the complete works of Shakespeare just by hitting the keys at random.

What if ... a typewriter has just 4 keys?

E H N W

What is the probability of typing 'WHEN' by hitting the keys at random if each letter can be typed only once?

When you look at the different arrangements of these four letters you get:

EHNW   EHWN   EWHN   EWNH
EN   HEWN

> Typing at letter at random gives each letter an equal chance of being typed.

1 **a** List all the arrangements which use all the letters E, H, N and W, once only.
 b How can you be sure that you have found all the arrangements?
 c What is the probability of typing WHEN just by chance if each letter can only be typed once?

2 Suppose the typewriter has just the keys N, O and T.
List all the different arrangements possible which use each letter once.

3 How many different ways are there to arrange two letters?

4 **a** Copy this table and fill in the arrangements for up to 4 letters.

No. of letters	1	2	3	4	5	6
No. of arrangements	1					

Multiply by *a*   Multiply by *b*   Multiply by *c*   Multiply by *d*   Multiply by *e*

 b What are the values of *a*, *b*, and *c* for this table?
What pattern can you find in these numbers?
 c Use your pattern to decide how many arrangements there are for 5 different letters and 6 different letters.

5 On a real typewriter it is not actually true that each letter can only be typed once. If you have only the keys N, O and T, you can still type arrangements such as OOT and TNN.
 a With these three letters list the different arrangements of three letters it is possible to make.
 b How many arrangements are there?
 c How could a tree diagram have helped you decide how many arrangements are possible?

Ways of pairing things

Exercise 9.4
Pairing

When people come down to breakfast in France the custom is that each person shakes hands with everyone else.
This can mean a large number of handshakes, but exactly how many depends on the number of people.
Two people shaking hands counts as one handshake.

There are five members of the Leblanc family, Angeline, Bruno, Charles, Danielle and Emmelle.
Here are three of the handshakes that are made: AB, AD, BE.

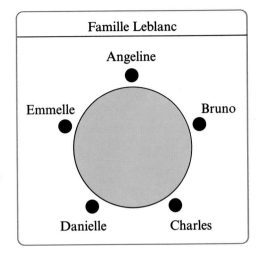

Famille Leblanc

1   **a**   List all the handshakes for the Leblanc family above.
     b   Arrange your list so you can be sure you have every handshake.
     c   How many handshakes in total?

2   A guest, Frederic, stays overnight with the Leblancs.

     a   When they all come down to breakfast list the handshakes made.
     b   How many handshakes are made?

3   **a**   Draw up a table like this.

No. of people	1	2	3	4	5	6
No. of handshakes	0	1				

     b   Describe any patterns you can see in the table.
     c   Use your pattern to predict how many handshakes there will be for seven people. Check your prediction.

4   Emmelle is going on a trip. She wishes to take two books. Her bookshelf has five books she has not read. She picks two books at random.

     a   List all the different pairs of books she might pick.
     b   What is the probability that she picks two books by Sartre?
     c   What is the probability that she picks two books by the same author?
     d   What is the probability that she picks at least one blue book?
     e   Give the probability of picking two books of different colour.

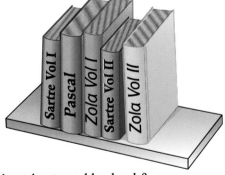

5   Bruno has eight books on his shelf, four of which are by Sartre.
He picks two books at random.
What is the probability that they are both by Sartre?

Relative frequency

A fair dice is one where each of the numbers 1 to 6 is equally likely.

A loaded dice is made so that one number comes up more often. It is how some people cheat when gambling.

When a fair dice is rolled or a coin is spun you can calculate the probability of something happening because outcomes are equally likely. When outcomes are not equally likely you must use other methods to find the probability.

To estimate the probability that Julie will win a tennis match you can look at data to see how well she played in other matches.

Julie Matthews	
Matches played	105
Wins	68

An estimate of the probability that Julie will win her next match is given by:

Probability $= \dfrac{68}{105} = 0.65$

Of her next 12 matches Julie is likely to win about 8 (because $0.65 \times 12 = 7.8$).

To estimate the chance that a loaded dice will give a six you can do an experiment.

No. of rolls	273
No. of 6's	94

An estimate of the probability of a six is given by:

Probability $= \dfrac{94}{273} = 0.34$

This estimate of probability, based on collected data is also called the relative frequency. It is usually given as a decimal.

You do not usually need to give the relative frequency to more than 2 decimal places.

Exercise 9.5
Relative frequency

1   From the data above, in the next 20 rolls of the loaded dice, how many times might you expect a six?

2   Of the 241 trains that arrived at Wayhurst station, 56 were late.
   a   What is the relative frequency of a train being late?
   b   For the next 9 trains, how many would you expect to be late?
   c   What is the relative frequency of trains arriving on time?

Gregor Mendel was an Austrian monk who did experiments on heredity in about 1856. His work led to a breakthrough in our knowledge of how young inherit the characteristics of their parents.

3   Mendel crossed plants from peas with smooth skins with those from peas with wrinkled skins, and planted the seeds.
   He found that out of 7324 new plants 1850 had wrinkled peas.
   a   What is the relative frequency of a plant giving wrinkled peas?
   b   What is the relative frequency of smooth skins?
   c   When 200 of these peas are planted how many would you expect to grow into plants with smooth peas?

4   Mendel also crossed plants with long stems with plants with short stems.
   He found that he got 787 plants with long stems and 277 with short stems.
   What is the relative frequency of getting a plant with a short stem?

Note that the answer is not 0.35.

5   When the relative frequency of male births is 0.51 what is the relative frequency of female births?

6   Calculate the values of **a**, **b** and **c** in these survey results.

Answer given	Number who answered	Relative frequency
YES	**b**	0.56
NO	432	0.40
DON'T KNOW	**c**	**a**

When a drawing pin is dropped it can come to rest either:

point up   or   point down

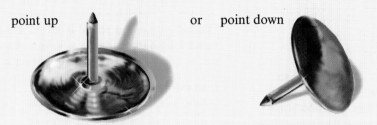

If you want to find an estimate of the probability that it will come to rest point up, you can experiment to find the relative frequency. The more drops you make the more likely it is that your relative frequency is reliable.

Exercise 9.6
Drawing pin experiment

1   Draw up a frequency table like this.

POSITION OF PIN	TALLY	FREQUENCY
Point up		
Point down		
	TOTAL	

> You must decide how many times to drop the pin to give a reliable result.

2   Drop a drawing pin a large number of times and record in the table how it lands, point up, or point down.

3   From your results calculate the relative frequency that a pin will land

   a   point up   **b**   point down.

4   In twenty more drops predict how many times the pin will land point up.
Check your prediction with twenty more drops.
Why might the answer not match your prediction?

5

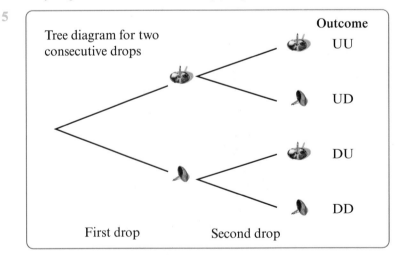

Tree diagram for two consecutive drops

Outcome

UU

UD

DU

DD

First drop   Second drop

   a   Copy the tree diagram for two drops of a pin.
Fill in the probability (relative frequency) on each branch.

   b   Calculate the probability that a pin will land point up in
two consecutive drops.

End points

You should be able to ...

A Calculate probabilities by counting outcomes in sample space, and tree diagrams

B Find how many ways there are to arrange a number of items

C Find how many ways there are to choose two items from a number of items

D Calculate and use relative frequency

... so try these questions

A1 Draw a sample space diagram to show a spin of spinner A then a spin of spinner B.

Spinner A has 3 equal sections

A2 From your sample space diagram find the probability that for a spin of each spinner you get:
  a two of the same colour
  b a blue and a pink
  c two yellows
  d two pinks.

Spinner B has 4 equal sections

A3 Draw a tree diagram to show three consecutive spins of a coin.

A4 Use your tree diagram find the probability that in three spins you get:
  a three heads
  b exactly two coins showing the same
  c all three coins showing the same
  d two heads and one tail.

These four cards are put down in random order.

B1 **a** How many different ways of doing this are there?
  b What is the probability that the red and yellow cards would be next to each other?

C1 How many different ways can any two cards be picked from the four cards?

C2 What is the probability that you will pick two cards where one card is red?

D1 Give the relative frequency of a plane arriving late.

Plane arrivals – Fridays	
Late	On time
183	327

Some points to remember

◆ In most cases when you are asked a question about probability from equally likely outcomes it is best to list all the outcomes and count the ones which match.

◆ You may be asked to find the number of ways to arrange items or to pick from a set of items. It is often a good idea to try it with fewer items and look for patterns.

◆ When you calculate relative frequency make sure you use the total number as the denominator.
(For example, in Question **D1**, add together 183 + 327 for the denominator.)

Starting points
You need to know about ...

... so try these questions

A Multiplying out brackets

- To multiply out brackets, multiply every term inside the bracket by the term outside.

    Example

    $$2(a - 8) = 2 \times (a - 8)$$
    $$= (2 \times a) - (2 \times 8)$$
    $$= 2a - 16$$

B Collecting like terms

- In the expression $7a + 4b - 3a + 6b - 2a$
    - $7a$, $3a$ and $2a$ are like terms as they all give the number of a's
    - $4b$ and $6b$ are like terms as they all give the number of b's.

- The expression can be simplified by collecting like terms.

    $$7a + 4b - 3a + 6b - 2a$$
    $$= 7a - 3a - 2a + 4b + 6b$$
    $$= 2a + 10b$$

C Solving linear equations

- To **solve an equation** find the possible values for each letter.

    Example   Solve $5(2a - 1) = 2(3 + 4a)$

    To solve this equation
    - simplify each expression
    - add, subtract, multiply or divide both sides of the equation by equal amounts.

    $$5(2a - 1) = 2(3 + 4a)$$
    $$+5 \left(\quad 10a - 5 = 6 + 8a \quad \right) +5$$
    $$-8a \left(\quad 10a = 11 + 8a \quad \right) -8a$$
    $$\div 2 \left(\quad 2a = 11 \quad \right) \div 2$$
    $$a = 5.5$$

    The **solution** to this equation is $a = 5.5$.

D Indices

- Indices are used as shorthand for multiplication

    n^2 stands for $\qquad n \times n$

    $2n^2$ stands for $\qquad 2 \times n^2 \qquad$ or $\qquad 2 \times n \times n$

    $2mn^2$ stands for $\qquad 2 \times m \times n^2 \qquad$ or $\qquad 2 \times m \times n \times n$

E Evaluating an expression

- The value of an expression depends on the value of each letter.

    Example   Evaluate $2a^2 + 3ab + 8$ when $a = 6.4$ and $b = 2.1$

    $$2a^2 + 3ab + 8 = (2 \times 6.4^2) + (3 \times 6.4 \times 2.1) + 8$$
    $$= (2 \times 40.96) + (3 \times 6.4 \times 2.1) + 8$$
    $$= 81.92 + 40.32 + 8$$
    $$= 130.24$$

A1 Multiply out the brackets from:
- **a** $3(a + 4)$
- **b** $2(b - 6)$
- **c** $3(2c + 5)$
- **d** $4(2d - 2)$
- **e** $4(8 - 2e)$
- **f** $5(3 + 6f)$

B1 Simplify each of these.
- **a** $8a - 3a + 4b - 6$
- **b** $7p + 2q - 3p + 4q - 10$

B2 Simplify these
- **a** $2(a - 4) + 3(2a + 6)$
- **b** $4(2a + 3) + 2(3a - 1)$

C1 Solve these equations.
- **a** $2p + 5 = 3p + 2$
- **b** $16 + 4q = 6q - 4$
- **c** $10 - 5t = 3t + 4$
- **d** $5(2x - 6) = 6x + 45$
- **e** $2(x - 1) = 2(3x + 8)$

D1 Find 3 pairs of equivalent terms.

- **A** ab^2
- **B** a^2
- **C** a^2b
- **D** $a \times b \times a$
- **E** $a \times b \times b$
- **F** $a \times a$
- **G** $a \times a \times b \times b$

E1 Evaluate these expressions when $p = 3.4$ and $q = 1.8$
- **a** $2p + 4pq$
- **b** $5p + 2q - 8$
- **c** $pq - 2$
- **d** $8p - 3q + pq$
- **e** $p^2 + 3p + 8$
- **f** $2pq + 2p^2 + 3q^2$

Calculating missing dimensions

Exercise 10.1
Missing dimensions

1 This is a plan of a garden. There is a fence round the garden and edging between the lawn and the flower beds.

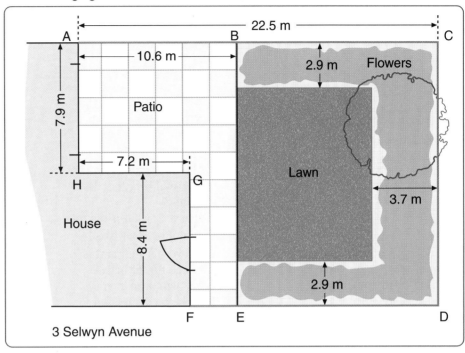

3 Selwyn Avenue

It may help to make a sketch of the garden and mark the lengths on it.

The area of the garden includes the patio.

a Calculate the length of:
   i BE   **ii** EF   **iii** DE
b The fence is shown in orange on the plan.
   Calculate the total length of the fence.
c Calculate the dimensions of the lawn.
d The edging for the lawn is shown in green.
   What is the total length of edging used for the lawn?
e What is the total area of the flower bed?
f Calculate the area of the whole garden.

2 The fence and edging for the lawn are shown in the same way on this plan.

a Calculate the total length of the fence.
b What length of edging is used for the lawn?
c What is the total area of the flower bed?
d Calculate the area of the whole garden.

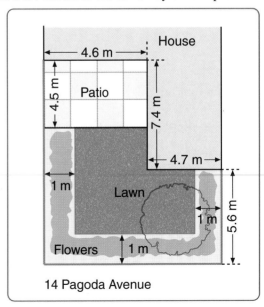

14 Pagoda Avenue

Writing expressions

Exercise 10.2
Writing expressions

On these plans the fence is marked in orange and the edging for the lawn is marked in green.

Simplify each expression by multiplying out any brackets and collecting like terms.

1 On this plan the flower beds are w metres wide.

a Explain why $8.1 + w$ is an expression for the length of BC in metres.

b Write an expression in terms of w for the length of:
  i DF   **ii** HI

c Show that $43 + 2w$ is an expression for the length of the fence in metres.

d **i** Write an expression for the total length of lawn edging.
  ii If $w = 2$, what is the total length of lawn edging?

e **i** Show that the total area of the flower beds is $32.4w$ square metres.
  ii Write an expression for the area of the lawn.

f What is the value of w when the area of the lawn is the same as the total area of the flower bed?

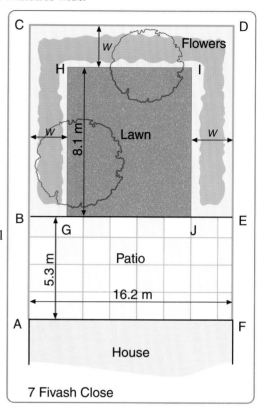

7 Fivash Close

2 On this plan the flower beds are p metres wide.

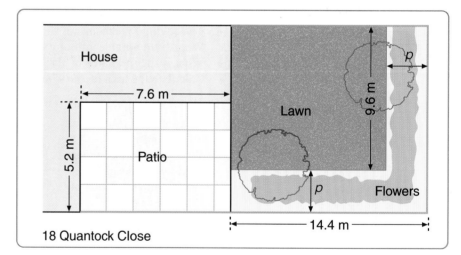

18 Quantock Close

a Write an expression in terms of p for:
  i the total length of the fence
  ii the total length of the lawn edging
  iii the area of the lawn
  iv the total area of the flower bed.

b Calculate the total length of the fence if $p = 2$.

c What value of p makes the area of the lawn twice the total area of the flower bed?

Using brackets

♦ You can use brackets to write an expression for the shaded area in each of these rectangles.

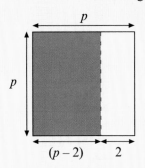

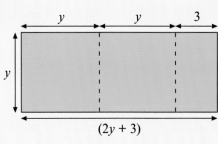

Shaded area = $p(p - 2)$ Shaded area = $y(2y + 3)$

♦ To multiply out a bracket it may help to use a table.

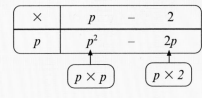

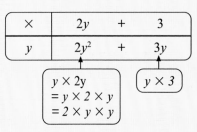

So $p(p - 2) = p^2 - 2p$ So $y(2y + 3) = 2y^2 + 3y$

Exercise 10.3
Using brackets

1   Multiply out each of these.

   a $2(a + 4)$ **b** $3(b - 5)$ **c** $4(2c + 3)$ **d** $d(d + 7)$
   e $e(6 - e)$ **f** $f(4 + f)$ **g** $p(2p + 9)$ **h** $r(4r - 2)$

2   For each of these rectangles write an expression for the shaded area:

   a with brackets   **b** without brackets.

For some of the shaded rectangles you will need to find an expression for the length or the width.

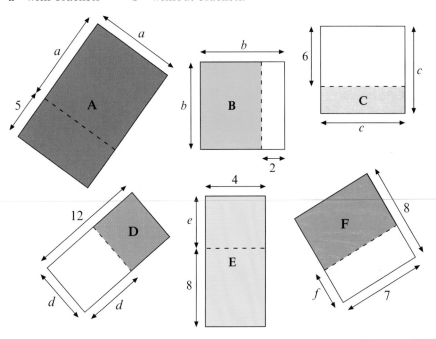

3

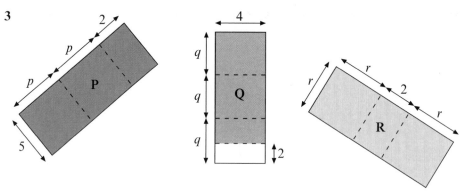

For each of these rectangles P, Q and R write an expression for the shaded area:

a with brackets **b** without brackets.

4

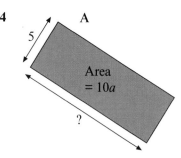

A

Area $= 10a$

B

Area $= b^2$

C

Area $= 3c^2$

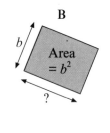
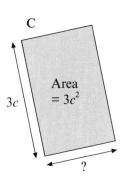

Write down the widths of rectangles A, B and C.

5

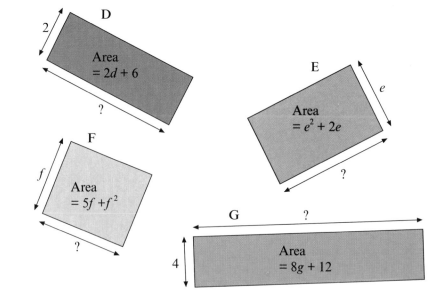

D

Area $= 2d + 6$

E

Area $= e^2 + 2e$

F

Area $= 5f + f^2$

G

Area $= 8g + 12$

Write an expression for the widths of rectangles D to G.

When you complete an expression using brackets check that the two expressions are equivalent.

For example:

$$4a - a^2 = a(\square - \square)$$

$$4a = a \times 4 \quad a^2 = a \times a$$

$\times$	4	$-$	a
a	$4a$	$-$	a^2

So $4a - a^2 = a(4 - a)$

6 Copy and complete these expressions using brackets.

a $4x + 12 = 4(\square + \square)$ **b** $6p - 4 = 2(\square - \square)$

c $2a + 8 = \square(a + \square)$ **d** $10 - 5q = \square(2 - \square)$

e $b^2 - 6b = b(\square - \square)$ **f** $y^2 + 4y = y(\square + \square)$

g $2r^2 + 3r = r(\square + \square)$ **h** $3d^2 - 5d = d(\square - \square)$

i $3t^2 + 4t = \square(\square + \square)$ **j** $6s^2 + 7s = \square(\square + \square)$

Writing expressions to solve problems written in words

Example

The length of a rectangle is 4 m greater than the width.
The perimeter is 36 m. What is the area of the rectangle?

To find the length of this rectangle:

◆ Choose a letter to stand for the width.
> Let the width be w metres.

◆ Write the length in terms of this letter.
> Length = $w + 4$

◆ Draw and label a diagram.

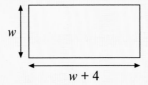

◆ Write and solve an equation for the information given.

Perimeter = $2w + 2(w + 4)$	But Perimeter = 36 metres
$= 2w + 2w + 8$	So $4w + 8 = 36$
$= 4w + 8$	$4w = 28$
	$w = 7$

So Width = 7 metres
Length = 7 + 4 metres
= 11 metres

◆ Answer the problem.
Area = 7×11 m^2
So the area of the rectangle is 77 m^2.

Exercise 10.4
Solving problems
written in words

1 The length of a rectangle is 8 centimetres more than its width.
   a If the width is a centimetres, write an expression for the length of the rectangle.
   b Write an expression for the perimeter of the rectangle in terms of a.
   c If the perimeter of the rectangle is 60 centimetres what is the area of the rectangle?

2 In this triangle AB is twice the length of BC.

   a If BC is d centimetres, write an expression for the perimeter of the triangle in terms of d.
   b If the perimeter is 58 cm, what is the length of AB?

3 The perimeter of a square is 60 metres.
   What is the area of the square?

4 The length of a rectangle is twice its width.
   The perimeter is 39 centimetres.
   What is the area?

Multiplying terms and simplifying

In any term the letters are usually written in alphabetical order.

For example:

$2ba$ is usually written as $2ab$

$4n^2m$ is usually written as $4mn^2$.

♦ You can **multiply any terms** by grouping together the numbers and each of the letters.
For example:

$$2m \times 3n$$
$$= 2 \times m \times 3 \times n$$
$$= 2 \times 3 \times m \times n$$
$$= 6mn$$

$$2ab \times a$$
$$= 2 \times a \times b \times a$$
$$= 2 \times a \times a \times b$$
$$= 2a^2b$$

$$2p \times 3p^2$$
$$= 2 \times p \times 3 \times p \times p$$
$$= 2 \times 3 \times p \times p \times p$$
$$= 6p^3$$

The letters in each term are usually written in alphabetical order.

♦ **Like terms** must have exactly the same letters in them.
For example:

$2p^2q = 2 \times p \times p \times q$
$8p^2q = 8 \times p \times p \times q$
So $2p^2q$ and $8p^2q$ are like terms.

$3pq^2 = 3 \times p \times q \times q$
$2p^2q = 2 \times p \times p \times q$
So $2p^2q$ and $3pq^2$ are not like terms.

♦ To **simplify an expression** collect together any **like terms**.
For example:

These expressions **can be simplified** by collecting together like terms.

$2a^2b + 3ab^2 + 4a^2b = 6a^2b + 3ab^2$
$2x^2 + 2x + 3x^2 - x + 4 = 5x^2 - x + 4$

These expressions **cannot be simplified** because there are no like terms.

$2a^2b + 3ab^2$
$2x^2 + 4x + 3$

Exercise 10.5
Multiplying terms and simplifying

1 Multiply these terms.

a $3a \times 2b$ **b** $p \times 3q$ **c** $4y \times 5x$
d $5q \times 6p$ **e** $x \times 2x$ **f** $ab \times a$
g $2xy \times y$ **h** $2ab \times 3a$ **i** $2p^2 \times 3q$
j $a^3 \times a^2$ **k** $2b^2 \times 3b$ **l** $5c^3 \times 2b$

2 Find four pairs of equivalent terms.

A $(2b^2)^3$ B $6b^5$ C $3b^2 \times 2b^4$

D $5b^5$ E $8b^6$ F $3b^2 \times 2b^3$

G $6(b^4)^2$ H $6b^6$ I $6b^8$

To multiply out each bracket multiply each pair of terms.

$\times$	m	$+$	$3n$
$2n$	$2mn$	$+$	$6n^2$

$2n \times m$
$= 2 \times n \times m$

$2n \times 3n$
$= 2 \times n \times 3 \times n$
$= 2 \times 3 \times n \times n$

So $2n(m + 3n) = 2mn + 6n^2$

3 Multiply out these brackets.

a $a(b + 4)$ **b** $x(y + z)$ **c** $m(2n + 3p)$
d $2x(3y + 2z)$ **e** $c(a + c)$ **f** $p(p - q)$
g $3b(c + b)$ **h** $4a(a - b)$ **i** $p(3p - 4)$
j $a(2b - 4c)$ **k** $2a(3a + 4b)$ **l** $4p(2q - 3p)$
m $2pq(3p + 2q)$ **n** $4xy(x - 2y)$ **o** $3ab(x^2 - y^2)$

4 Simplify these where possible.

a $5a - 3b + 4a + 25b$ **b** $4x^2 + x - 2x^2$
c $5a + 2ab - a + 3ab$ **d** $x^2 + x^3 - 2x$
e $4a - 3b + 7a + 5b$ **f** $7x^2 + xy - x^2 + 3xy$
g $4p^2 - pq + 6q + pq$ **h** $ab + 2a - ab + 4a$

5 Multiply out these brackets and simplify.

  a $2(2a + 3b) + 5(a + 4b)$ **b** $2(2x + 4y) + 3(2x - y)$

  c $x(x - 3) + x(x + 4)$ **d** $2x(3x + 2y) + x(4x - y)$

  e $ab(a + b) + ab(a - b)$ **f** $3a(ab + b) + 2b(ab - b)$

6 Simplify these expressions.

  a $2a(3a - b) + 4b(2a + 3b)$ **b** $5xy(2x + 4y) + 3x(2xy - 2y)$

  c $pq(2p - 3q) + 2p(3pq - 2q^2)$ **d** $2mn(3m - 4n) + 4m^2(2n - 3m)$

Factorising

Exercise 10.6
Common factors

1 In this triangle puzzle:

  ◆ on two sides the numbers in the squares
  are multiplied together to give the
  number in the circle

  ◆ on the bottom the numbers in the
  circles are added to find the total.

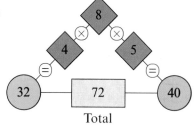

Copy and complete triangles A and B.

Triangle A

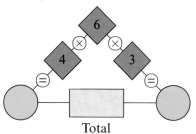

Total

Triangle B

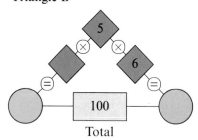

Total

2 For each of the triangles C to F write an expression for the total.

Triangle C **Triangle D**

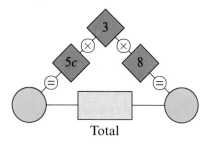

Total

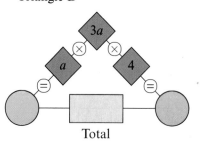

Total

Triangle E **Triangle F**

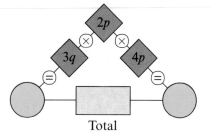

Total

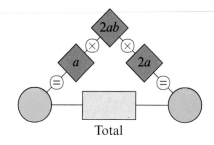

Total

3 Copy and complete these triangle puzzles.

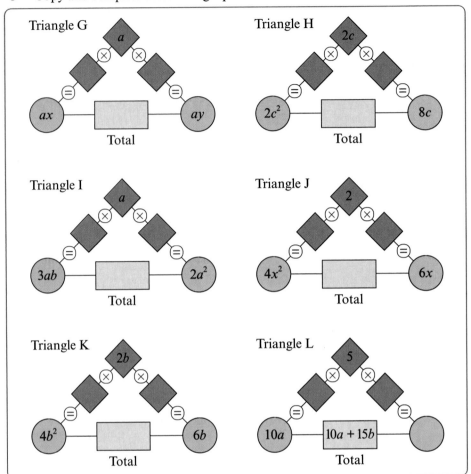

The factors of a number are all **whole numbers**.

♦ A number can be written as a product of factors.
$$48 = 12 \times 4 \qquad\qquad 72 = 12 \times 6$$
$$48 = 3 \times 16 \qquad\qquad 72 = 3 \times 24$$
…   …
12 and 3 are **common factors** of 48 and 72

♦ A term can be written as a product of factors.
$$3a^2 = 3 \times a^2 \qquad\qquad 6ab = 3 \times 2ab$$
$$3a^2 = a \times 3a \qquad\qquad 6ab = a \times 6b$$
…   …
3 and a are **common factors** of $3a^2$ and $6ab$

Look for a **whole number** that is a common factor of both terms.

♦ To **factorise an expression** look for a common factor of the terms and write the expression using brackets.

$$3a^2 + 6ab = 3(a^2 + 2ab) = 3a(a + 2b)$$

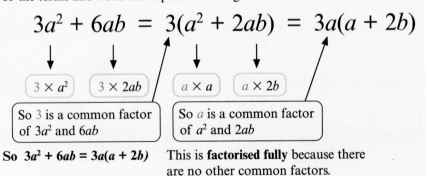

So $3a^2 + 6ab = 3a(a + 2b)$ This is **factorised fully** because there are no other common factors.

Exercise 10.7
Factorising

1 Factorise these fully.

a	$2x + 14$	**b**	$3a + 15$	**c**	$6p - 24$
d	$8x - 10y$	**e**	$5x + xy$	**f**	$pq + 7p$
g	$6d + 4de$	**h**	$5c + ac$	**i**	$6ab + 9a$
j	$2a - 8ab$	**k**	$3a^2 + 12a$	**l**	$15xy + 20yz$
m	$a^2b + ab^2$	**n**	$12c^2d - 15cd$	**o**	$25x^2y + 15yz$

When you have factorised an expression check that the two expressions are equivalent by multiplying out the bracket.

Example

Factorise $3ab^2 + 6a^2$.

$3ab^2 + 6a^2 = 3a(b^2 + 2a)$

Check

$\times$	b^2	$+$	$2a$
$3a$	$3ab^2$	$+$	$6a^2$

$3a \times b^2 = 3ab^2$

$3a \times 2a = 6a^2$

2 Draw a complete solution for triangles M, N, O and P.

Triangle M

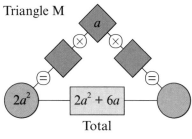
Total

Triangle N

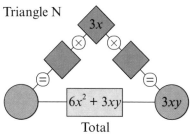
Total

Triangle O

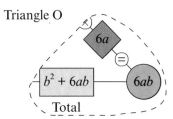
Total

Triangle P

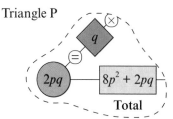
Total

3 **a** In triangle Q what term goes in the top square?
   b Show a complete solution for triangle Q.

Triangle Q

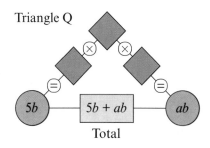
Total

4

Triangle R   Triangle S

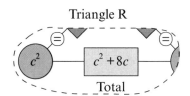
Total

Draw a complete solution for triangles R and S.

5 Draw two different solutions for triangle T.

Triangle T

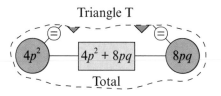
Total

Look for a factor that is common to every term in each expression.

6 Factorise these fully.

a	$5x + 10y + 20$	**b**	$6a - 9b + 12c$	**c**	$2x^2 + 3x + xy$
d	$14x - 28y + 21z$	**e**	$2x^2 + 8xy + 6x$	**f**	$6ab^2 + 2a^2b + 5ab$

End points

You should be able to ...   ... so try these questions

A Simplify expressions

A1 Multiply out the brackets from:

    a $4(5f - 4)$ **b** $m(m + n)$

    c $2p(r - p)$ **d** $ab(a + b)$

    e $mn(2m + 3n)$ **f** $2xy(3y - 5x)$

A2 Simplify these expressions.

    a $2(2b - 4) + 6(4 + 3b)$ **b** $4(2b - 4) + 6(5 + 3b)$

    c $3ab(b - a) + 7ab(b + a)$ **d** $3xy(x - 3) + 7xy(y + 4)$

B Write expressions to solve a problem

B1 The shape ABCDEF is cut from a square. The square is p centimetres wide.

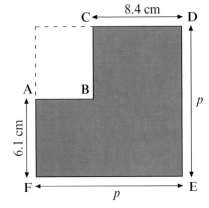

    a Write an expression for the length of:

        i AB   **ii** BC

    b **i** Write an expression for the perimeter of ABCDEF.

        ii What is the value of p if the perimeter is 56 cm?

B2 A rectangle is a centimetres wide.
The length is 5 centimetres more than the width.

    a Write an expression for the length of the rectangle in centimetres.

    b Write an expression for the perimeter of the rectangle in centimetres.

    c Show that $a^2 + 5a$ is an expression for the area of the rectangle in square centimetres.

    d What value of a makes the perimeter 56 cm?

    e If $a = 5.1$, what is the area of the rectangle?

C Factorise expressions

C1 Factorise these fully.

    a $8p + 4q$ **b** $6a - 12b$ **c** $a^2 + ab$

    d $7m + 3mn$ **e** $8xy + 10y$ **f** $4ab + 6a^2$

    g $3xy^2 - 5x^2y$ **h** $4pq - 6p^2q$ **i** $2g^2h - 5h^2$

Some points to remember

    ◆ Like terms must have exactly the same letters in.

    ◆ When simplifying an expression, add and subtract like terms.

    ◆ When factorising an expression check your answer by multiplying out the bracket.

Starting points
You need to know about ...

... so try these questions

A Some mathematical terms

Lines AB and CD are **perpendicular** to line XY because they would meet XY at right angles.

XY is also **perpendicular** to AB and CD.

AB and CD are **parallel**.

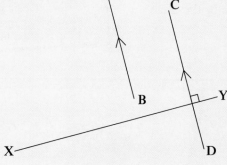

These terms are for parts of a circle.
> Arc
> Chord
> Diameter
> Radius
> Tangent

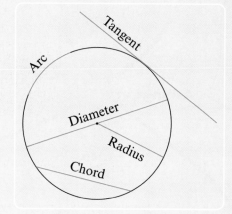

These terms are for different types of triangle.

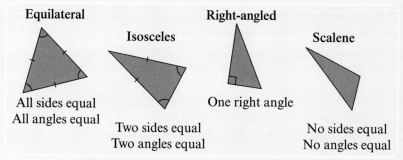

Equilateral	Isosceles	Right-angled	Scalene
All sides equal All angles equal	Two sides equal Two angles equal	One right angle	No sides equal No angles equal

B Congruent triangles

Triangles are said to be **congruent** if they have the same shape or size or if they are reflections of each other.

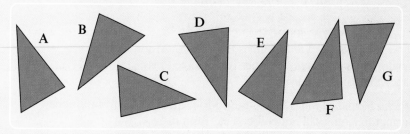

Triangles A and B are **congruent** to each other.

A1 You will need to measure for some of these questions.

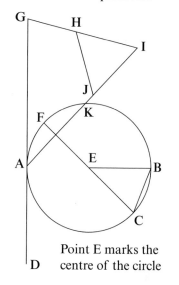

Point E marks the centre of the circle

a Which line is perpendicular to line FC?

b Give a line which is perpendicular to GD.

c Give a line which is a radius of the circle.

d Which triangle is isosceles but not equilateral?

e Which triangle is scalene?

f Which triangle is equilateral?

g Which line is a chord?

h Which line is a tangent?

i Which line is a diameter?

B1 Which of the triangles B to G is not congruent to triangle A?

B2 Draw a different triangle which is congruent to triangle A.

Regions and points on maps

A locus shows where a set of points satisfy a given condition.

The plural of locus is **loci**.

Deliveries are often made up to a certain distance from a town centre.

The locus of all points 6 miles from Pinbury is shown by the circle.

PINBURY PIZZA
Cold pizza? Not any more!
We now deliver up to 6 miles from Pinbury.
Ring 544364 for pizza to your door.

Exercise 11.1
Regions and points
on maps

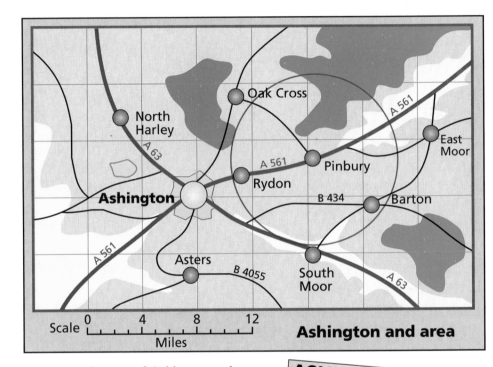

Ashington and area

You will need tracing paper and a pair of compasses for Exercise 11.1.

All distances are given 'as the crow flies' from the town centres.

1   Trace the map of Ashington and area.

2   Which other towns are served by Pinbury Pizza?

ASHINGTON AUTOS
We collect your car for you if you are not more than 5 miles away.

3   Draw the locus of points 5 miles from Ashington.
Which towns are served by Pinbury Pizza **and** Ashington Autos?

4   Shade in the region which is up to 6 miles from Pinbury **and** up to 5 miles from Ashington.

5   The village of Newton is 6 miles from Pinbury and 5 miles from Ashington.
Mark an X on your map for any place where Newton could be.

6
═ South Moor Free Press ═
We deliver up to 8 miles from South Moor

Show the locus of points 8 miles from South Moor.
Newton does not have deliveries of the Free Press.
Label Newton on your map.

7   Brooks Farm is 8 miles from South Moor and 6 miles from Pinbury.
Ashington Autos will not collect a car from there.
How far is Brooks Farm from North Harley?

Constructing triangles

Loci can also be used to construct triangles, when you know all three sides.

Example

Construct a triangle with sides of 4.4 cm, 3.8 cm and 3.2 cm.

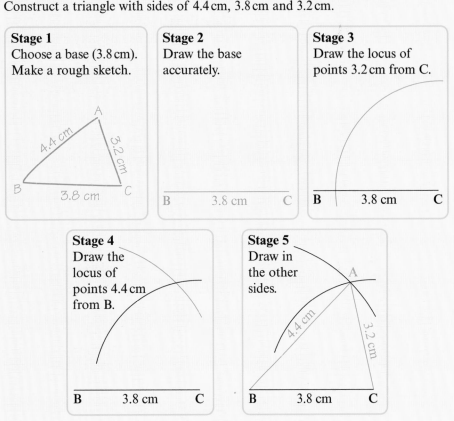

Stage 1
Choose a base (3.8 cm).
Make a rough sketch.

Stage 2
Draw the base
accurately.

Stage 3
Draw the locus of
points 3.2 cm from C.

Stage 4
Draw the
locus of
points 4.4 cm
from B.

Stage 5
Draw in
the other
sides.

> You will need tracing paper
> and a pair of compasses
> for Exercise 11.2.

Exercise 11.2
Constructing triangles

1   Choose one of the other sides for a base of triangle ABC.
    Construct the triangle on this base.
    Check that both triangles are congruent.

2   Construct a triangle with sides of 7 cm, 3 cm and 7 cm.
    What type of triangle is this?

3   Construct triangles with these dimensions.
    In each case state the type of triangle.

    a 4.4 cm, 3.3 cm and 5.5 cm   **b** 5.2 cm, 4 cm and 8 cm
    c 7.5 cm, 7.5 cm and 7.5 cm   **d** 4.3 cm, 9.2 cm and 12.8 cm

4   Construct a triangle with sides of 10 cm, 6 cm and 3 cm.
    What problems did you find? Explain why.

5   A triangular field is 350 metres by 840 metres by 760 metres.
    Use a scale of 1:100 000 to construct a scale drawing of the field.

6   Four ships R, S, T and U have the following distances between them.
    R to S is 60 miles; R to T is 62 miles; S to T is 45 miles; S to U is 76 miles;
    T to U is 43 miles.
    Use a scale of 1 cm to 10 miles to construct a scale drawing of
    their positions.
    From your drawing find the distance between R and U in miles.

> A scale of 1:100 000
> means that 1 cm stands
> for 100 000 cm.
>
> So 1 cm stands for
> 1000 metres.

Constructing triangles from other data

ΔABC means Triangle ABC.

∠B means angle B.

You can construct a triangle when you are not given the length of all three sides. You might be given **one side and two angles**.

Example   Draw ΔABC where AB = 5 cm, ∠B = 55°, and ∠A = 43°.

Stage 1   Make a rough sketch.
   2   Make the side you know (AB) the base and draw it.
   3   At A draw an angle of 43° with a protractor.
   4   At B draw an angle of 55°.

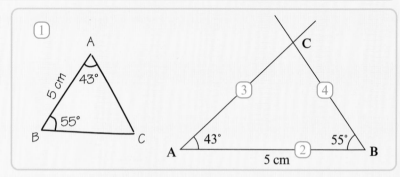

You might be given **two sides and one angle**.

Example   Draw ΔRST where RT = 6.5 cm, RS = 4.5 cm and ∠R = 46°.

Stage 1   Make a rough sketch.
   2   Make the long side (RT) the base, and draw it.
   3   At R draw an angle of 46° and mark S, 4.5 cm from R.
   4   Draw the last side TS.

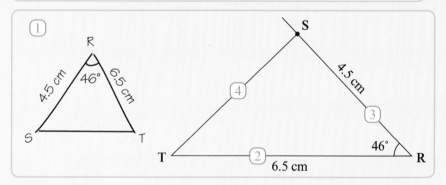

Exercise 11.3
Constructing triangles

1   Construct these triangles.

   a   ΔDEF, where DF = 6 cm, EF = 5 cm and ∠F = 69°
   b   ΔGHI, where GI = 7.2 cm, ∠G = 53° and ∠I = 42°
   c   ΔJKL, where JK = 8 cm, ∠J = 25° and ∠K = 125°
   d   ΔMNP, where NP = 6.3 cm, MP = 5.2 cm and ∠P = 131°

2   Construct ΔQRS, where RQ = 8.3 cm, ∠R = 35° and ∠S = 68°.
   You will need to calculate another angle first.

3   Construct these triangles to decide which two look identical.

   a   ΔIJK, where JK = 5.5 cm, IJ = 8 cm and ∠J = 50°
   b   ΔLMN, where LM = 8 cm, ∠L = 60° and ∠M = 50°
   c   ΔPQR, where PR = 6.5 cm, QR = 7.5 cm and ∠R = 70°

Thinking ahead to ...
bisecting an angle

A pedestrian area is edged by two buildings which meet at an angle of 36°.
The plans say trees must be planted an equal distance from both buildings.

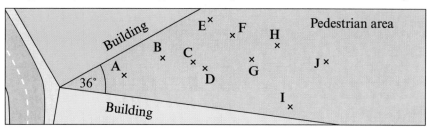

> 'Equidistant from' means
> 'the same distance from'.

A Which crosses on the diagram mark where trees could be planted?

B Draw two lines which meet at an angle of 36°.
Mark the locus of all points which are equidistant from both lines.

Bisecting an angle

> To bisect an angle means
> to draw a line which cuts it
> in two equal parts from its
> vertex.

It is useful to be able to bisect an angle without measuring it.
You can do this using a pair of compasses.

Stage 1
Draw an angle ABC.

Stage 2
With centre B draw an arc so it
cuts AB and BC at D and E.

Stage 3
With centre D, draw an arc.
With centre E, draw an arc.

Stage 4
Draw the bisector BF.

Exercise 11.4
Bisecting an angle

1 Use a protractor to draw each angle then bisect it using compasses.
  a 44°   **b** 100°   **c** 146°   **d** 90°

2 Use compasses to draw an equilateral triangle with sides of 8 cm.
What size is each angle?
Bisect one of the angles. What angle have you made?

Thinking ahead to ...
perpendicular bisectors

> When two lines cross they
> are said to intersect.

A Draw a straight line and
mark two points, A and B,
6 cm apart.

B Draw a circle at A and
another with the same
radius at B.

C Draw larger circles with
equal radii at A and B.
If they intersect, then mark
the points of intersection.

D Continue by drawing
larger circles and marking
the points of intersection.

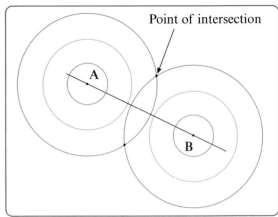

E **a** Draw the locus of all points of intersection of equal circles.
b Describe the link between this locus and the line AB.

Perpendicular bisectors

A line which cuts a straight line exactly in half at right angles is called a
perpendicular bisector.

To construct the perpendicular
bisector of the line EF.

◆ Draw the line EF

◆ With centre E draw an arc
with a radius greater than
half of EF.

◆ With centre F draw another
arc with the same radius.

◆ Join the two points of
intersection.

N marks the midpoint of EF.

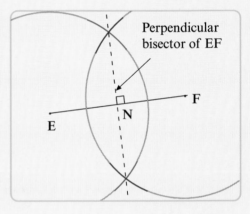

Exercise 11.5
Perpendicular bisectors

1 **a** Draw a line AB, 6 cm long. Construct the perpendicular bisector of AB.
b Mark any point on the bisector and measure its distance to A and to B.
c What can you say about the distance of any point on the
bisector from A and from B?

2 Draw the perpendicular bisectors of lines with these lengths.
Check that both sides are equal in length and that you have right angles.

a 10 cm   **b** 7.7 cm   **c** 4.6 cm

3 **a** Draw this triangle.
b Construct the perpendicular
bisector of each side.
c Where do all three bisectors intersect?
d Does this happen for other triangles?

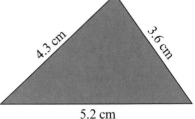

5.2 cm

4 **a** Draw a circle of radius 6 cm and mark its centre C.
  b Draw a chord (AB).
  c Construct the perpendicular bisector
      of the chord.
  d Draw two more chords and bisect them.
  e What do you notice about where the
      bisectors intersect?

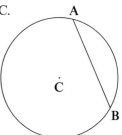

Meeting conditions

Rules that have to be met
such as 'the tap must be the
same distance from A and
B' are known as
conditions.

Constructions such as bisecting angles or lines can be used for making scale
drawings where conditions have to be met.

Example

A water tap is to be put in a large garden but it must meet these conditions:
1 It must be the same distance from the two greenhouses, A and B.
2 It must be the same distance from the grape vine wires as from the hedge.

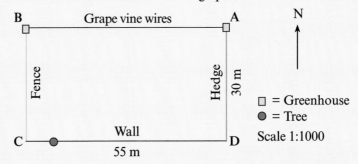

Where must the tap be placed? How far is it from the tree?

To meet condition 1 you
draw the perpendicular
bisector of BA.
This line is the locus of
all points equidistant from
B and A.

To meet condition 2 you
bisect angle BAD.
This line is the locus of all
points equidistant from line
BA and line AD.

Where the two loci intersect
both conditions are met – so
the tap must be at this point.

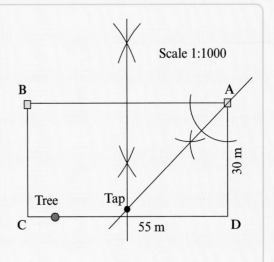

Exercise 11.6
Meeting conditions

1 **a** On the scale diagram above measure the distance in
      centimetres between the tap and the tree.
  b What is this actual distance in the garden?

2 Make a scale drawing to show where the tap will be if:
    condition 1 stays the same
    condition 2 says the tap must be equidistant from the wall and the hedge.

137

3   An Olympic javelin field has lines which make an angle of 29° to each other.
A thrower aims the javelin so that it flies equidistant from both lines.
The thrower hopes to reach the club record of 88 metres.

This diagram only
approximates to how a true
javelin field is marked out.
The throwing point actually
lies on an arc about 2 metres
wide which comes at the end
of a 36 metre run-up.

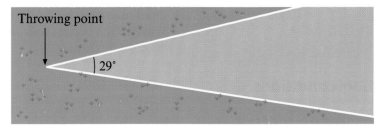

Throwing point

29°

a   Make a scale drawing of the field for throws up to 100 metres.
Use a scale of 1:1000.
b   Mark the locus of all points 88 metres from the throwing point.
c   Construct the locus of points equidistant from the sidelines.
d   Mark where the thrower hopes the javelin will land.

4   Two lighthouses are 3.6 miles apart on a straight coastline.
A ferry sails into port by keeping the same distance from both lighthouses.
A fishing boat sails so that it is always 3 miles from the coast.

a   Make a scale drawing of the coast to show the position
of the lighthouses. Use a scale of 1 cm to 0.5 miles.
b   Show and label the course taken by the fishing boat.
c   Construct and label the course taken by the ferry.
d   Mark the point where there is the greatest risk of a collision.

Loci and regions

Exercise 11.7
Loci and regions

Goats eat almost every type of plant.
They are often tied by a rope to limit their grazing.

Their rope can be fixed to a ring which can slide
along a rail.

Ring

Goat

Rail

For example, a goat is tied in this way to a rail
8 metres long. The rope allows the goat to graze
2 metres from the rail.

When the ring is
halfway along the
rail the goat
can graze the
area inside
the circle
shown.

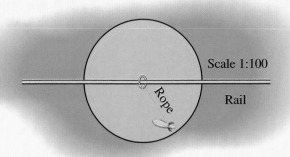

Scale 1:100

Rope

Rail

1   Make a scale drawing of the grazing area shown above.

2   On the same diagram draw the grazing areas for other positions of the
ring along the rail.
Outline in red the shape of the total area the goat can graze.

3 A farmer puts a special rail around a barn to allow the goat's ring to travel right round. The goat can graze 2 metres from the rail.

   a Make a scale drawing of the barn. Use a scale of 1:100.

   b Outline the total area that the goat can graze. This is the locus of points 2 metres from the barn.

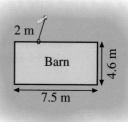

4 This rail which has a right-angled bend in it. The goat can graze up to 11 metres from the rail.

   a Draw the rail to a scale of 1:1000.

   b Outline the total area the goat can graze.

   c Are all the corners of this locus smooth curves? If not, which ones are not?

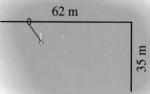

5 Goat A can graze 3 metres from barn A and goat B can graze 2.5 metres from barn B.

   a Make a scale drawing of the barns.

   b Draw the grazing area for each goat.

   c Shade in the area of grass that both goats can graze.

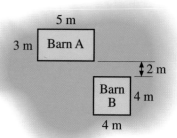

6 For each of these shapes, copy the shape and draw the locus of points 1 cm from the shape.

Copy one shape and draw the locus before you draw the next shape.

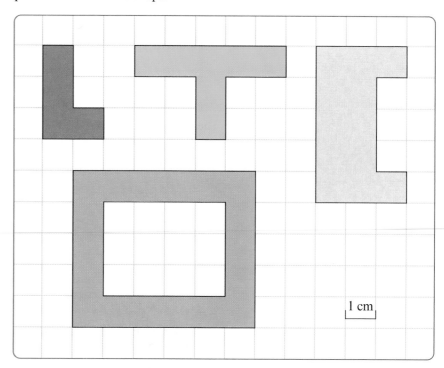

Right angles on the move

Exercise 11.8
Right angles

'Adjacent' means 'next to'.

1 **a** Draw a line AB which is 8 centimetres long.
   b Identify the right angle on a set square.
      Place the set square so that the sides adjacent to the right angle
      touch both points A and B.
      Mark a point P at the right-angled vertex.
   c Rotate the set square to another position so adjacent sides
      touch A and B.
      Mark the new point P.

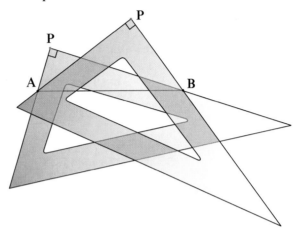

   d Mark the locus of all positions of P as you rotate the set square 360°.
      What shape is this locus?

2 **a** Draw a circle of any size.
   b Draw in a diameter and label it RS.
   c Join point R to any point, C, on the circumference of the circle.
   d Join C to S.
   e Measure angle RCS. What do you notice?
   f For any diameter RS and any point on the circumference C,
      what can you say about the triangle RCS?

3 In this circle point H is the centre and lines
   AG and GC are equal in length.
   Name six angles in the diagram which must
   be right angles.

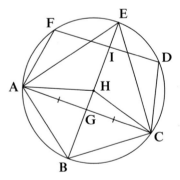

4 The cross-section of a roof is
   semicircular in shape.

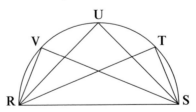

Beam RV is 12 metres long and beam VS is 26 metres.
Beam RU is equal in length to US.
   a Use what you know about the angles in a semicircle to
      calculate the diameter RS to 1 dp.
   b Calculate the length of RU to 1 dp.

End points

You should be able to ...   ... so try these questions

A Construct and draw triangles when you are given their sides or angles

A1 Construct △ ABC where AB = 7 cm, AC = 6 cm and BC = 6 cm.

A2 Draw △ DEF, where ∠EDF = 92°, ∠DFE = 47° and DF = 4.5 cm.

A3 Draw △ PQR, where PQ = 7.4 cm, QR = 4.3 cm and ∠Q = 123°.

B Construct and use perpendicular bisectors

B1

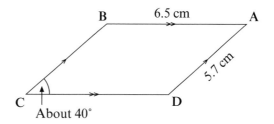

Draw the parallelogram ABCD with B$\hat{C}$D about 40°.
Construct perpendicular bisectors for the sides BC and AD.
What can you say about the gradients of the two bisectors?

B2

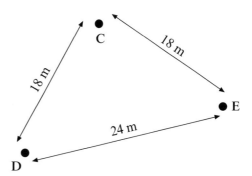

Two dogs are tied at points D and E, 24 metres apart.
A cat at point C wishes to pass between the dogs so that it is always the same distance from each one.
Make a scale drawing and construct the path the cat must take.
Use a scale of 1 cm to 3 metres.

C Construct and use the bisectors of an angle

C1 Draw an angle of 110° with a protractor.
Construct the bisector of the angle.

C2 Construct △ ABC where AB = 4.3 cm, BC = 6.8 cm and AC = 5.9 cm.
Bisect each of the angles.
What do you notice about where the bisectors intersect?

D   Draw loci from some conditions given

D1   This garden is the shape of a trapezium with the dimensions given.

Trees are at the midpoints of sides AD and DC.

A new bush is to be planted:
- equidistant from each fence
- equidistant from each tree.

B ← 8.3 m → A

80°   Fence   Tree

C ← 10 m → D

9.6 m

Fence

Tree

Make a scale drawing of the garden and show by construction the position of the bush. Use a scale of 1 : 100.

Some points to remember

- To construct an angle of 90° draw a line and construct its perpendicular bisector.

- When asked to construct something do not rub out the construction lines when you finish.

- To construct an angle of 60° construct an equilateral triangle.

- The perpendicular bisector of any chord will pass through the centre of the circle.

- All angles in a semicircle which are made by the diameter and a point on the circumference are right angles.

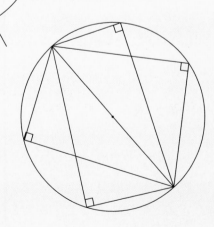

Starting points

You need to know about ...

... so try these questions.

A Writing ratios

- A **ratio** compares the size of two or more quantities.

  $$3:4 \qquad 1:4:2 \qquad 3\tfrac{1}{2}:\tfrac{1}{2}$$

- In the ratio $3:4$, the **number of parts** are 3 and 4.

B Equivalent ratios

- The ratios $3:4$ and $6:8$ are **equivalent ratios**.

$$3:4$$

$$6:8$$

- To write an equivalent ratio:
  - ❖ multiply or divide each number of parts by the same number.

  $$6:8 \overset{\div 2}{\longrightarrow} 3:4 \qquad 2:3:7 \overset{\times 5}{\longrightarrow} 10:15:35$$

- A ratio in its **simplest terms**, or **lowest terms**, is written with the smallest whole numbers possible.

  $$1:\tfrac{1}{4}:3 \overset{\times 4}{\longrightarrow} 4:1:12 \qquad 15:24 \overset{\div 3}{\longrightarrow} 5:8$$

C Writing fractions as decimals and percentages

- To write a fraction as a decimal or a percentage:
  - ❖ divide the numerator by the denominator.

  $$\frac{3}{8} = 3 \div 8 = 0.375 = 37.5\%$$

  $$\frac{5}{6} = 5 \div 6 = 0.8\dot{3} = 83.\dot{3}\%$$

  $$\frac{7}{4} = 7 \div 4 = 1.75 = 175\%$$

  $$\frac{5}{3} = 5 \div 3 = 1.\dot{6} = 166.\dot{6}\%$$

D Fibonacci sequences

- A sequence of numbers is called a **Fibonacci sequence** when:
  - ❖ the first two terms are any numbers
  - ❖ all other terms are the total of the two terms before.

$$1 \quad 4 \quad 5 \quad 9 \quad 14 \quad 23 \quad 37 \quad 60 \ldots$$

- The most common Fibonacci sequence is:

  $$1 \quad 1 \quad 2 \quad 3 \quad 5 \quad 8 \quad 13 \quad 21 \quad 34 \quad 55 \quad 89 \ldots$$

A1 Roughcast is used to cover walls. It is a mix of 3 parts mortar to 1 part gravel.
Write this mix as a ratio of:
a mortar to gravel
b gravel to mortar.

B1 Copy and complete these sets of equivalent ratios.
a $4:1$ **b** $2:5:4$ **c** $9:12$
$\quad 12:?$ $\quad 1:?:2$ $\quad ?:4$
$\quad\qquad\qquad\qquad\qquad\qquad 6:?$

B2
$2:5$	$1:3:2$	$10:20$
$10:25$	$2\tfrac{1}{2}:5$	$1:2:3$
$3:9:6$	$2:1$	$1:2\tfrac{1}{2}$

List the sets of equivalent ratios.

B3 Write each of these ratios in its simplest terms.
a $9:6$ **b** $14:21$
c $4:8:2$ **d** $5:\tfrac{1}{2}$
e $2:1\tfrac{1}{2}:3$

C1 Write each of these fractions as a decimal.
a $\tfrac{5}{8}$ **b** $\tfrac{9}{5}$ **c** $\tfrac{7}{12}$ **d** $\tfrac{15}{11}$

C2 A test has 72 marks.
Write each of these test scores as a percentage.
a $\tfrac{44}{72}$ **b** $\tfrac{36}{72}$ **c** $\tfrac{51}{72}$ **d** $\tfrac{63}{72}$

D1 Copy and complete the first eight terms of each of these Fibonacci sequences.
a $1, 3, \_, \_, \_, \_, \_, \_, \ldots$
b $2, 2, \_, \_, \_, \_, \_, \_, \ldots$
c $\_, 5, \_, 11, 17, \_, \_, \_, \ldots$
d $3, \_, \_, 15, \_, 39, \_, \_, \ldots$

E Naming shapes, sides and angles

- A **vertex** is a point where the edges of a shape meet.
  The plural of vertex is **vertices**.

- If the vertices of a shape are labelled with letters, then
  the shape, the sides and the angles can be named.
  For example:

  - this shape is PQRS

  - the sides of PQRS are
    PQ, QR, SR, PS.

    PQ can also be used for
    the **length** of side PQ.

  - the angles inside PQRS are:
    ∠ QRS (or QR̂S or R̂)
    ∠ PSR (or PŜR or Ŝ)
    ∠ SPQ (or SP̂Q or P̂)
    ∠ PQR (or PQ̂R or Q̂).

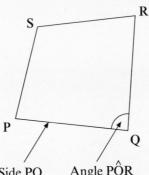

Side PQ   Angle PQ̂R
           ∠ PQR or Q̂

F Enlargement and similar shapes

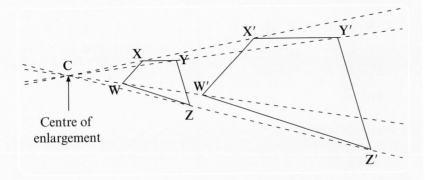

Centre of
enlargement

- Shape W′X′Y′Z′ is an **enlargement** of shape WXYZ so:

  - WXYZ is the **object** and W′X′Y′Z′ is the **image**

  - all **corresponding angles** are equal
    $$\hat{W} = \hat{W}', \ \hat{X} = \hat{X}', \ \hat{Y} = \hat{Y}', \ \hat{Z} = \hat{Z}'$$

  - any length on WXYZ can be multiplied by the **scale factor** of
    the enlargement to give the corresponding length on W′X′Y′Z′

    > 2.5 is the scale factor of this enlargement so,
    > for **corresponding sides**,
    > WX × 2.5 = W′X′   XY × 2.5 = X′Y′
    > YZ × 2.5 = Y′Z′   ZW × 2.5 = Z′W′

- If the scale factor of an enlargement is **less than 1**, then
  the image is **smaller** than the object.

- If one shape is an enlargement of another, then the
  two shapes are **similar**.

E1

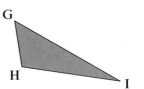

In triangle GHI:
a which side is the longest?
b which angle is the largest?
c which angles are acute?
d which is the shortest side?

F1

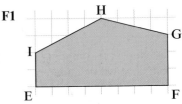

a Copy shape EFGHI on to
   square grid paper.
b Mark a centre of
   enlargement, C.
c Draw an enlargement of
   EFGHI, scale factor 1.5.

F2 Repeat Question **F1** using a
scale factor of 0.5.

F3

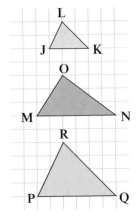

Which of these triangles are
similar?

Multiplying parts of a ratio

◆ The number of parts in a ratio can be multiplied to solve problems.

Example

An orange dye is a mix of red and yellow in the ratio $2:3$.
a What amount of red is mixed with 480 ml of yellow?
b What is the total amount of orange dye produced?

	Red		Yellow	Total
Ratio	2	:	3	
Amounts	?	:	480	?

◆ Find the amount for one part:
480 ml ÷ 3 = 160 ml.

◆ Multiply each number of parts by the amount for one part.

◆ Find the total of the amounts.

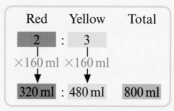

Red		Yellow	Total
2	:	3	
×160 ml		×160 ml	
320 ml	:	480 ml	800 ml

Exercise 12.1
Multiplying parts
of a ratio

For Questions **1** and **2** refer to the panel above.

1 Calculate:

   a the amount of red dye to mix with 720 ml of yellow dye
   b the total amount of orange dye produced.

2 Calculate:

   a the amount of yellow dye to mix with 210 ml of red dye
   b the total amount of orange dye produced.

3 Tropical Fruit Juice is a mix of pineapple and grapefruit in the ratio $5:2$. Calculate:

   a the amount of grapefruit juice to mix with 125 ml of pineapple juice
   b the total amount of Tropical Fruit Juice produced.

4 Walls can be covered with mortar to protect them from the weather.

   a For a clay wall how much cement is mixed with 1500 kg of sand?
   b For a concrete wall:
     i write the mortar mix as a ratio in its simplest terms
     ii calculate how much concrete is produced with 400 kg of cement.

Wall surface	Mortar mix Cement : Lime : Sand
Clay	$1:1:6$
Concrete	$1:\frac{1}{2}:4\frac{1}{2}$

5 A plan is drawn using a scale of $1:200$.

   a What actual distance does 4 cm stand for on the plan?
   b What length on the plan stands for a distance of 18 m?

6 For a plan using a scale of $1:30$, calculate:

   a the length on the plan which stands for a distance of 4.8 m
   b the actual distance shown on the plan as 7.5 cm.

7 On a plan, 4.8 cm stands for a distance of 240 m.

   a What length on the plan stands for a distance of 315 m?
   b What scale is used on the plan?

Ratio and proportion

◆ An amount can be shared in a given ratio.

Example Share £140 in the ratio 2:1:4.

						Total
Ratio	2	:	1	:	4	
Amounts	?	:	?	:	?	£140

◆ Find the total number of parts:
  2 + 1 + 4 = 7

◆ Find the amount for one part:
  £140 ÷ 7 = £20

◆ Multiply each number of parts by the amount for one part.

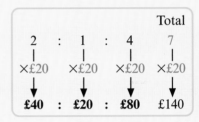

Exercise 12.2
Sharing in a given ratio

1 Sarah and Denzil share 35 conkers in the ratio 4:3.
   Calculate how many conkers each gets.

2 Tim spends his money on sweets, comics and videos in the ratio 1:2:3.
   Calculate how much he spends on each item from £18.

3 Amy, Ben and Zoe are left £150 by their grandmother.
   The money is shared in proportion to their ages: 5, 3 and 2.
   Calculate how much each child gets.

> 'in proportion to'
> means
> 'in the same ratio as'

4 Liz is training for the 100 m hurdles.
   She splits her time between speed work and technique in the ratio 3:5.
   Calculate how long:

   a she spends on technique in two hours of training
   b she spends on speed work in four hours of training.

◆ Some problems need amounts to be kept in proportion.

Example This recipe for Swiss Hot Chocolate serves 2 people.
How much of each ingredient is needed for 5 people?

Swiss Hot Chocolate
• 600 ml milk
• 140 g drinking chocolate
• 80 ml whipped cream

Milk	Chocolate	Cream	Serves
600 ml :	140 g :	80 ml	2
? :	? :	?	5

◆ Find the **multiplier:**
  5 ÷ 2 = 2.5

◆ Multiply each amount by the multiplier.

Milk	Chocolate	Cream	Serves
600 ml :	140 g :	80 ml	2
×2.5	×2.5	×2.5	×2.5
1500 ml :	**350 g :**	**200 ml**	**5**

Exercise 12.3
Keeping in proportion

1 This recipe serves 6 people.
   How much of each ingredient do you need for 9 people?

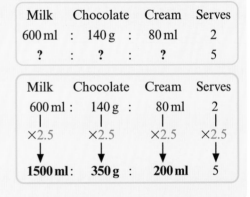

Chilled Chocolate Drink
230 g caster sugar • 300 ml water
50 g cocoa • 1200 ml chilled milk

2 This recipe for chocolate fudge makes 36 pieces.

a How much cocoa is needed to make 72 pieces?
b How much milk is needed to make 18 pieces?
c Calculate how much of each ingredient you need to make 24 pieces.

> **Chocolate Fudge**
> • 450 g white sugar
> • 150 ml milk
> • 150 ml water
> • 75 g butter
> • 30 g cocoa

> The multipliers here are less than 1.

3 This recipe makes 24 sweets.

a Calculate how many drops of peppermint essence are needed to make 42 sweets.
b How many egg whites do you need to make these 42 sweets?

> **Chocolate Peppermint Creams**
> • 230 g icing sugar • 1 egg white
> • 4 drops peppermint essence
> • 100 g plain chocolate

> Discuss your answer.

Ratios as fractions

♦ A ratio that compares two quantities, $p:q$, can be given in the form $\frac{p}{q}$.

Example

3"

4"

The ratio of **width to height** is $4:3$, i.e.

$$\frac{\text{Width}}{\text{Height}} = \frac{4}{3}$$

so the width is $\frac{4}{3}$ of the height.

♦ In some ratios, you can use the **total** number of parts to give other fractions.

Example   The ratio of boys to girls in a class is $1:2$

Boys	:	Girls	Total
1	:	2	3

Ratio of **boys to girls** is $1:2$

$$\frac{\text{Boys}}{\text{Girls}} = \frac{1}{2}$$

Ratio of **boys to total** is $1:3$

$$\frac{\text{Boys}}{\text{Total}} = \frac{1}{3}$$

The number of boys is $\frac{1}{2}$ of the number of girls and $\frac{1}{3}$ of the total.

Exercise 12.4
Ratios as fractions

For Questions **1** and **2** refer to the panel above.

1 Give the ratio of girls to boys in the form:

a Girls : Boys   b $\dfrac{\text{Girls}}{\text{Boys}}$

2 Give the ratio of girls to total in the forms $p:q$ and $\dfrac{p}{q}$.

3 For this photograph, give each of these as a fraction:

a the ratio of width to height
b the ratio of height to width.

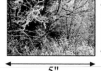

3"

5"

4 The ratio of women to men in a fitness class is $1:4$. Give the fraction of the class which are:

a women   b men.

5 The ratio of height to diameter for this tin is $2:3$.

a What fraction of the diameter is the height?
b Explain why the fraction $\frac{2}{5}$ has no meaning for this tin.

Ratios as decimals

Exercise 12.5
Ratios as decimals

1

$\boxed{P \quad 1:4}$ $\boxed{Q \quad 2:5}$ $\boxed{R \quad 2:3}$ $\boxed{S \quad 3:2}$ $\boxed{T \quad 7:3}$

Write each of these ratios as:

a a fraction **b** a decimal **c** a percentage.

2

> Your cubit is the distance from your elbow to your fingertips.
>
> Your handspan is the distance from the end of your little finger to the end of your thumb when your hand is stretched as wide as possible.

$$\text{Ratio of elegance} = \frac{\text{Length of your cubit}}{\text{Length of your handspan}}$$

a Calculate your ratio of elegance as a decimal to 3 sf.
b Compare your ratio with others in your class.

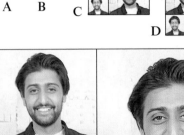

Each of these photographs is made up of smaller square photographs.

The width and height of photograph A are:
1″ by 1″.

3 Make a table like this with space for 15 photographs: A to O.

4 For A to F, write in your table:

> Give each ratio as a decimal to 5 sf.

a the width
b the height
c the width-to-height ratio.

Photo	Width (inches)	Height (inches)	Width/Height
A	1	1	1.0000
B	2		
C			
D			
E			
F			

5 The widths of the photographs are terms of a Fibonacci sequence.

a Calculate the next nine terms in the sequence.
b Write these terms in your table as the widths of photographs G to O.

6 The heights of the photographs give the most common Fibonacci sequence.

a Calculate the next nine terms in the sequence.
b Write these terms in your table as the heights of photographs G to O.

7 Calculate the width-to-height ratios for photographs G to O.

8

> Around the year 1500, the section became known as the golden section, or golden ratio.
> The Greek letter φ is pronounced 'phi'.

The Pythagorean Research News

We have found a special ratio which we shall call the 'section'.

The ratio is equal to $\frac{1}{2}(1+\sqrt{5})$, or roughly 1.618

We shall refer to this ratio using the letter φ.

Write a short report on the Fibonacci sequence and the golden ratio.

Enlargement

> The ratio is calculated by dividing a length in the **image** by the corresponding length in the **object**.

♦ The scale factor of an enlargement is the ratio of corresponding lengths.

Example

Calculate the scale factor of this enlargement, and find the height K′L′.

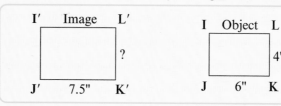

♦ Divide width J′K′ by the corresponding width JK.

$$7.5 : 6 = \frac{7.5}{6} = 1.25$$

♦ Multiply the corresponding height by the scale factor.

	Width	Height
Object	6″ :	4″
	×1.25	×1.25
Image	7.5″ :	5″

Exercise 12.6
Enlargement

1

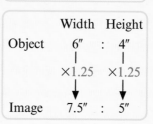

Trapezium A′B′C′D′ is an enlargement of trapezium ABCD.

a Calculate the scale factor of the enlargement.
b Use your scale factor to find the length A′D′.

> If the image is larger than the object, the scale factor is greater than 1.

2

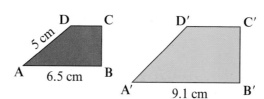

Kite RXYZ is an enlargement of kite RSTU.

a Calculate the scale factor of the enlargement.
b Find the length RY.

3

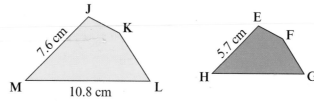

Shape EGFH is an enlargement of shape JKLM.

a Calculate the scale factor of the enlargement.
b Find the length HG.

> If the image is smaller than the object, the scale factor is less than 1.

Similar shapes

* Two shapes are **similar** if:
  * all corresponding angles are equal, **and**
  * all ratios of lengths of corresponding sides are equal.

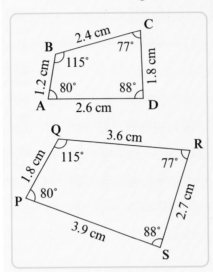

These ratios are greater than 1 because lengths on the larger shape have been divided by lengths in the smaller shape.

A ratio is less than 1 if you divide lengths in the smaller shape by lengths in the larger shape.

$$\frac{AB}{PQ} = \frac{BC}{QR} = \frac{CD}{RS} = \frac{AD}{PS}$$
$$= 0.\dot{6}$$

For shapes ABCD and PQRS:

* corresponding angles are equal:
  $$\hat{A} = \hat{P}, \hat{B} = \hat{Q}, \hat{C} = \hat{R}, \hat{D} = \hat{S}$$

* ratios of lengths of corresponding sides are equal:
  $$\frac{PQ}{AB} = \frac{1.8}{1.2} = 1.5 \quad \frac{RS}{CD} = \frac{2.7}{1.8} = 1.5$$
  $$\frac{QR}{BC} = \frac{3.6}{2.4} = 1.5 \quad \frac{PS}{AD} = \frac{3.9}{2.6} = 1.5$$

So ABCD and PQRS are similar.

Exercise 12.7
Similar shapes

1

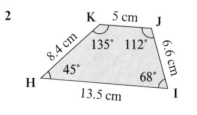

a Calculate each of these ratios.

  i $\dfrac{WX}{DE}$ **ii** $\dfrac{XY}{EF}$ **iii** $\dfrac{YZ}{FG}$ **iv** $\dfrac{ZW}{GD}$

b Do you think DEFG and WXYZ are similar? Explain your answer.

2

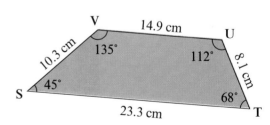

Do you think HIJK and STUV are similar? Explain your answer.

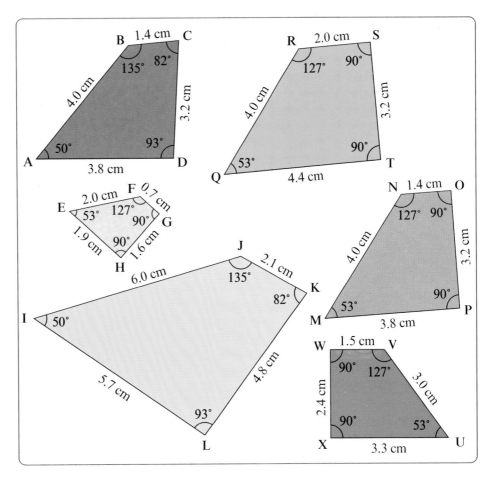

3 Which shape is similar to EFGH?
Explain why.

4 **a** List all the pairs of similar shapes.
   b Give a ratio of the lengths of corresponding sides for each pair.

5 Which shapes have the same angles as MNOP but are not similar to it?

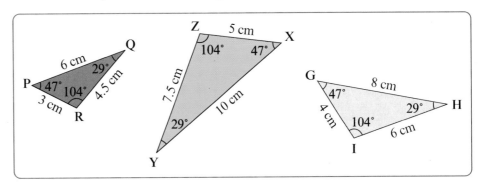

6 **a** Calculate each of these ratios.

   i $\dfrac{PQ}{XY}$ **ii** $\dfrac{QR}{YZ}$ **iii** $\dfrac{RP}{ZX}$

   b Are PQR and XYZ similar?
      Explain your answer.
   c Calculate ratios to explain why PQR and GHI are similar.
   d Show that all triangles with the same angles as PQR are similar to it.
   e Explain why XYZ and GHI are not enlargements of PQR.

Discuss your answer.

Finding lengths in similar shapes

If two triangles have the same three angles, they must be similar.

All ratios of corresponding lengths, therefore, are equal.

♦ You can use a ratio to find a length in the **larger** of two similar shapes.

Example ABC and PQR are similar triangles.
Find the length PQ.

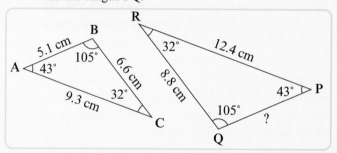

The ratio greater than 1 is found by dividing a length in the **larger** shape by a length in the **smaller** shape.

The ratio less than 1 is found by dividing a length in the **smaller** shape by a length in the **larger** shape.

♦ Calculate the ratio greater than 1 for any two corresponding lengths: $\dfrac{PR}{AC} = \dfrac{12.4}{9.3} = 1.\dot{3}$

♦ Multiply AB, the corresponding length to PQ, by the ratio:

$$\text{AB} \quad \xrightarrow{\times 1.\dot{3}} \quad \text{PQ}$$
$$5.1\,\text{cm} \qquad\qquad \textbf{6.8 cm}$$

♦ To find a length in the **smaller** of two similar shapes:
  ♦ use the same method with the ratio less than 1.

Exercise 12.8
Finding lengths in similar shapes

1

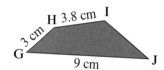

GHIJ and WXYZ are similar.
Find the length:
a YX   **b** IJ.

DE and TU are corresponding sides because they are opposite corresponding angles.

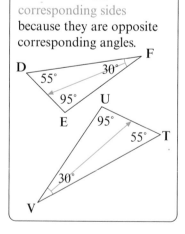

2

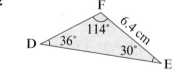

a Give the corresponding side to:
  i DE   **ii** US.
b Explain why this calculation is wrong.

To find DF: $\dfrac{TU}{FE} = \dfrac{8}{6.4} = 1.25$

So DF = US × 1.25 = 7 cm × 1.25
                          = 8.75 cm ✗

3 KLNP and QMNO are similar.
Find the length LN.

4 LMN and LJK are similar triangles.
a Find the length JM.
b Explain why JK and MN are parallel.

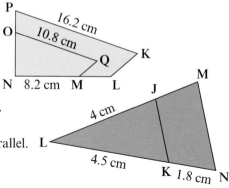

End points

You should be able to ...   ... so try these questions

A Multiply the number of parts
in a ratio

A1 Tropical Fruit Juice is a mix of pineapple and grapefruit in the ratio 5:2.
Calculate:
  a the amount of pineapple juice to mix with 180 ml of grapefruit juice
  b the total amount of Tropical Fruit Juice produced.

B Share an amount in a
given ratio

B1 Amy, Ben and Zoe are left £400 by their grandfather.
The money is shared in proportion to their ages: 10, 8 and 7.
Calculate how much each child gets.

C Keep amounts in the
same proportion

C1 This ice cream recipe serves 8 people.
  a Calculate how much of
each of these ingredients
you need to serve 20 people:
    i caster sugar   **ii** boiling water.
  b How many eggs are needed to serve 6 people?

Chocolate Ice Cream
• 150 g caster sugar
• 20 g cocoa • 4 eggs
• 410 g can evaporated milk
• 4 tablespoons boiling water

D Write ratios as fractions,
decimals and percentages

D1 For this photograph, give the
ratio of height to width:
  a in its simplest terms
  b as a fraction
  c as a decimal
  d as a percentage.

6"

8"

D2 The ratio of girls to boys in a class is 2:3.
What fraction of the class are girls?

E Identify similar shapes

E1
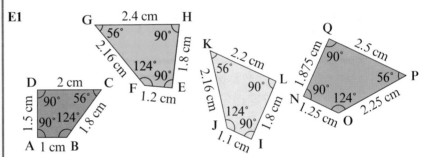

Which of these shapes are similar to ABCD?

F Find lengths in
similar shapes

F1
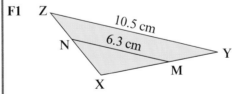

XYZ and XMN are similar triangles.
The length of XY is 7.5 cm.
Find the length XM.

Some points to remember

◆ Write in headings to help you get the ratio the right way round.
For example, a ratio of boys to girls of 1:3 can be written as: **Boys : Girls**
                                                                          1 : 3

SUMMER

NINE ELMS GARDEN CENTRE

Watering cans - plastic			
5 litre	8 litre	10 litre	12 litre
99p	£1.29	£1.69	£1.99

Watering cans - traditional			
1 gallon	1.5 gallon	2 gallon	2.5 gallon
£4. 99	£6.49	£7.99	£9.99

Mower Madness !!! Can you believe this offer ?

- 20% deposit
- 0% interest
- 6 equal monthly payments

Super Hover £179.99	Mowhog £199.99	Mastermow £249.99

LIQUIDGRO
Add one scoop
(15 grams) per gallon
£3.99 1 kg Pack

Superbraid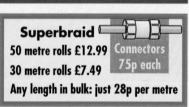
50 metre rolls £12.99
30 metre rolls £7.49
Any length in bulk: just 28p per metre

Connectors
75p each

Rolls of Plastic Sheet

The easy way to stop weeds
15 metres long
and
1650 mm wide

Only £3.75
per roll
while stocks last

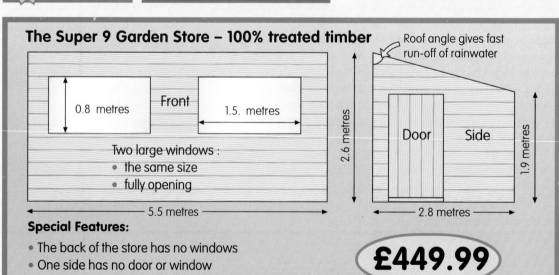

The Super 9 Garden Store – 100% treated timber

Front

0.8 metres

1.5. metres

Two large windows :
- the same size
- fully opening

5.5 metres

Roof angle gives fast
run-off of rainwater

2.6 metres

Door   Side

2.8 metres

1.9 metres

£449.99

Special Features:
- The back of the store has no windows
- One side has no door or window
- The roof has a 10 cm overhang on all sides

1 List the discount price of each size Mulchbag, to the nearest penny.

2 Which plastic watering can do you think is best value for money?
Explain your answer.

3 Which watering can holds most water: the 12 litre or the 2.5 gallon?
Explain your answer.

4 Darren says that a plastic watering can is only about 20% of the cost of a traditional one.
Do you agree? Explain your answer.

5 Which traditional watering can do you think is best value for money?
Explain your answer.

6 A 5 litre plastic watering can weighs 105 grams.
A gallon of water weighs 10 lb.
What do you expect a 5 litre plastic watering can to weigh when it is full?

7 An empty 1.5 gallon traditional can weighs 0.7 lb.
 a Give the weight of this can in kilograms.
 b Do you expect a full 1.5 gallon traditional can to weigh more, or less, than 7.5 kg?
Explain your answer.

8 What does a litre of water weigh:
 a in kilograms
 b in pounds?

9 **a** To the nearest gram, how much Liquidgro is needed for 10 litres of water?
 b To be fairly accurate how many scoops would you put in the 10 litres of water?
Explain your answer.

10 If you measured the Liquidgro accurately:
 a How many gallons will the 1 kg pack treat?
 b How much spare liquidgro is in the pack?
 c What is this spare Liquidgro as:
  i a fraction of the pack?
  ii a decimal of the pack?
  iii a percentage of the pack?

11 The manufacturers of Liquidgro say that a 1 kg pack will treat 300 litres of water.
Is this a fair claim? Explain your answer.

12 Liquidgro costs £285 per tonne to produce.
Packaging costs are 6.8 pence per pack.
Distribution costs are 13.5 pence per pack.

How much profit do the manufacturers make on one tonne of Liquidgro?

13 **a** What is the area of plastic sheet on a roll?
 b To the nearest penny, what is the price per square metre?

14 The sheet is rolled on a tube of radius 4.5 cm.
The tube is made from a rectangle of card, with a 1.5 cm overlap allowed for gluing.

What area of card is used for the tube?

15 Which do you think is better value for money: the 50 metre or the 30 metre roll of hose pipe?
Explain your answer.

16 A hockey club needs a hose 180 metres long.
 a List three different ways to buy 180 metres of hose in the July special offers.
 b What is the cheapest way for the hockey club to buy the hose they need?
Explain your answer.

17 Calculate the total area of glass used for the windows of the Super 9 Garden Store.

18 **a** What shape is the back of the Garden Store?
 b What are the dimensions of the back?

19 Calculate the area of one side of the store (including the door).

20 The front, back and both sides of the store have to be sprayed with timber preservative.
Calculate the total area to be sprayed.

21 Preserver is sprayed at 250 ml per m^2.
Will 5 litres of preserver cover one store?
Explain your answer.

22 Calculate the size of the roof angle.

23 **a** What shape is the roof of the store?

One dimension of the roof is 5.7 metres (including overhangs).
 b What is the other dimension of the roof?
 c Calculate the area of the roof.

The roofing used weighs 4.4 kg per m^2.
 d What is the weight of the roof?

24 Labour charges are 40% of the price of the store which takes $12\frac{1}{2}$ hours to make.
 a What is the labour charge for a store?
 b Calculate the labour charge per hour.

The door takes 45 minutes to make.
 c What is the labour charge for a door?

25 For each mower, give the monthly payment.

Toujours Paris

Ile de la Cité

This boat-shaped island in the River Seine is where Paris was first inhabited by Celtic tribes over 2000 years ago. It is where Notre Dame is situated. This cathedral is a superb example of French medieval architecture and is particularly known for its wonderful stained glass rose windows.

The width of this South Window is 13 metres.

In the Ile de la Cité you will also find Point Zéro. This is a geometer's mark from which all distances in France are measured.

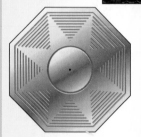

It measures 29 cm across and each side is 12 cm long.

Paris au Quotidien

Arrondissements: Il faut le savoir, Paris est divisé en 20 arrondissements se déroulant en spiraleà partir du 1er (le quartier du Louvre).

Banques: Ouvertes en général du lundi au vendredi de 9h à 16h30, quelques (rares) agences le samedi. Les Caisses d'Epargne ouvrent plus souvent le samedi et ferment le lundi.

Change: On ne peut pas tout prévoir à l'avance; vous pourrez changer vos devises dans les gares, les aéroports, les grandes agences de banque, les points change (ouverts tard le soir), ainsi qu'à notre bureau d'accueil des Champs-Elysées.

Daily Life in Paris

Districts: You should know that Paris is divided into 20 districts numbered in a circular direction, starting with the 1st district (the Louvre area).

Banks: They are generally open from Monday to Friday from 9 am to 4.30 pm, some (rare) branches on Saturday. The savings banks are more often open on Saturday and closed on Monday.

Exchange: You cannot foresee everything; you can therefore change your foreign currency in railway stations, airports, major bank branches, exchange offices (open late in the evening), as well as in the visitors office on the Champs-Elysées.

Eiffel Tower Factfile – 1996

- Built in 1889 for the Universal Exhibition
- Built by Gustave Eiffel (1832–1923)
- Built from pig iron girders
- Total height 320 metres
- The world's tallest building until 1931
- Height to 3rd level is 899 feet
- There are 1652 steps to the third level
- Two and a half million rivets were used
- The tower is 15 cm higher on a hot day.
- Its total weight is 10100 tonnes
- 40 tons of paint are used every 4 years
- On a clear day it is possible to see Chartres Cathedral, 72 km away to the South West.
- The tower is visited by about $5\frac{1}{2}$ million people every year

Admission charge   56 Francs

DAY TRIPS BY EUROSTAR

Waterloo Station (London) to Paris
Celebrate that special occasion in style with a day trip to Paris!

ADULT £
CHILD (4–11 YRS) £

Entry fees in Paris – 1996

Eiffel Tower	56 FF
Louvre	45 FF
Pompidou Centre	35 FF
Picasso Museum	28 FF
Museum of Modern Art	27 FF
Versailles Palace	45 FF
Parc de la Villette	45 FF
Cluny Museum	28 FF

Paris Lucky dip – Superb value !

In the hat are four tickets to the:
Eiffel Tower,
Picasso Museum,
Versailles Palace and
the Museum of Modern Art.
Pick two tickets at random from the four.
Entry fee – only 83 Francs.

83 FF

Datafile

Population of Paris (in 1982)   2 188 918
In 1996, £1 sterling was equivalent to 7.54 French Francs.
1 metre = 3.281 feet
1 kilometre = 0.62 miles

1 How many lines of symmetry has the South Window of Notre Dame?

2 What order of rotational symmetry has the South Window?

3 What is the circumference of the South Window?

4 Calculate the area of the South Window.

5 For Point Zéro in the Ile de la Cité, the outer polygon is regular.
  a What is the name of this polygon?
  b Calculate the size of an exterior angle.
  c Calculate the size of an interior angle.

6 Calculate the total area of Point Zéro.

7 How many planes of symmetry do you think the Eiffel Tower has?

8 How many tons of paint will have been used on the tower from when it was built up to the year 2000?

9 How much higher than the third level is the total height of the tower?
Give your answer to the nearest metre.

10 What is the mean height of a tower step in cm?

11 The ratio of steps to the third level, to steps to the first level is about 9 to 2.
About how many steps are there to the first level?

12 Use standard form to give:
  a the weight of the tower in tonnes
  b the number of rivets used.

13 Round the number of steps to the third level to:
  a the nearest ten
  b the nearest hundred
  c the nearest thousand.

14 Which one of the following gives the approximate percentage that the tower grows on a hot day?
  a 5%   **b** 0.5%   **c** 0.05%   **d** 0.005%

15 What is the approximate bearing of:
  a Chartres from Paris
  b Paris from Chartres?

16 In 1996, what was the Eiffel Tower entry fee equivalent to in £ Sterling?

17 **a** Approximately how much money in Francs was made from entry fees to the Eiffel Tower in 1996?
  b What was this equivalent to in £ Sterling?

18 Give the population of Paris in 1982 to:
  a 2 sf   **b** 3 sf   **c** 4 sf   **d** 5 sf.

19 Compare the French and English texts in the extract on Daily Life in Paris.
What is the relative frequency of a vowel in each language? (Vowels are a, e, i, o, and u.)

20 Compare the French and English extracts. Which language uses the longest words? Describe how you decided.

21 For the Paris Lucky Dip use the following shorthand:
  E – Eiffel Tower
  P – Picasso Museum
  V – Versailles Palace
  M – Museum of Modern Art

  a List each pair of tickets that could be picked at random.
  b What is the probability that a pair of tickets is picked which includes the Versailles Palace?
  c What is the probability of picking P and M?
  d Give the probability of picking a pair of tickets
    i worth more than the entry fee
    ii worth less than the entry fee.
  e Is the seller likely to make a profit or loss on every hundred entries? Give your reasons.

22 These two bills were for Eurostar day trips to Paris.

Paris Special

Enclosed are tickets for:
2 adults and 3 children
Total charge £465

Paris Special

Enclosed are tickets for:
3 adults and 1 child
Total charge £386

Calculate:
a the total cost for these 5 adults and 4 children
b the cost of an adult's ticket
c a child's ticket
d the total cost for 1 adult and 2 children.

Starting points
You need to know about ...

... so try these questions

A Units for measuring distance

- ◆ Kilometres (km), metres (m), centimetres (cm) and millimetres (mm) are **metric** units.

- ◆ Miles, yards, feet and inches are **imperial** units.

Metric	Imperial
1 km = 1000 m	1 mile = 1760 yards
1 m = 100 cm	1 yard = 3 feet
1 cm = 10 mm	1 foot = 12 inches

Some approximate conversions
1 mile ≈ 1.6 km
1 metre ≈ 3.3 feet
1 foot ≈ 30.5 cm
1 inch ≈ 2.5 cm

B Interpreting graphs

- ◆ Graphs that help you change from one unit to another are called **conversion graphs**.

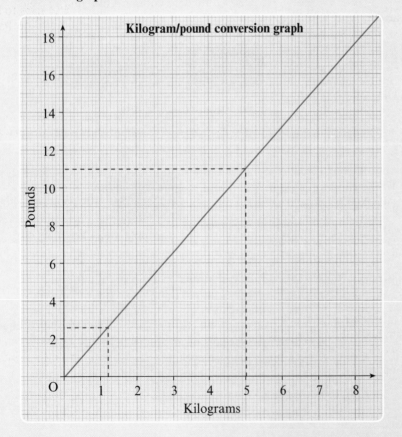

Examples   5 kilograms ≈ 11 pounds
2.6 pounds ≈ 1.2 kilograms

A1 Write these in metres.
  a 5 km   **b** 340 cm

A2 Write these in metres. Choose an appropriate degree of accuracy for each answer.
  a 3 miles   **b** 5 feet
  c 2 yards

A3 Write these in centimetres, correct to the nearest cm.
  a 40 mm   **b** 4 km
  c 3.9 m   **d** 7 inches

A4 Write these in kilometres, correct to 2 dp.
  a 5130 metres   **b** 7.1 miles

A5 Write 20 km in miles, correct to 1 dp.

B1 Use the graph to give an estimate of these in pounds, to 1 dp.
  a 7 kilograms
  b 3.8 kilograms

B2 Use the graph to give an estimate of these in kilograms, to 1 dp.
  a 16 pounds   **b** 5 pounds
  c 7.8 pounds   **d** 4.5 pounds

B3 Use the graph to estimate the number of pounds in 1 kilogram, to 1 dp.

B4 1 gallon ≈ 4.55 litres.
  a Use this approximation to copy and complete this table up to 8 gallons.

Gallons	1	2	3
Litres	4.55	9.1	

  b Make a conversion graph for gallons/litres up to 8 gallons.
  c Use your graph to give an estimate of:
    i 2.5 gallons in litres
    ii 15 litres in gallons.

C Calculating with time

♦ Times can be written:
  ❖ in 12-hour time using am or pm
  ❖ in 24-hour time.

   Examples   6:20 am is 06:20 in 24-hour time.
              6:20 pm is 18:20 in 24-hour time.

♦ Some units for measuring time are hours (h),
  minutes (min) and seconds (s):

> 1 day   = 24 hours
> 1 hour = 60 minutes
> 1 minute = 60 seconds

♦ Times can be written in different ways.

   Examples   250 minutes is 4 hours and 10 minutes.
              3 minutes and 12 seconds is 192 seconds.

D Timetables and time intervals

This shows part of a bus timetable from Paignton to Heathrow.

PAIGNTON	0625	0825	0955	1145	1345	1700
TORQUAY	0640	0840	1010	1205	1400	1715
Newton Abbot	0700	0900	1030	1225	1425	1735
EXETER	0730	0930	1100	1300	1500	1805
Taunton						1855
Calcot Coachway	↓	↓	1345	↓	1745	↓
HEATHROW AIRPORT	1105	1310	1440	1635	1840	2145

♦ Times for each different bus are shown in vertical columns.

   Example   The 0825 bus from Paignton stops at
            0840 in Torquay,
            0900 in Newton Abbot, ...

♦ The arrows show that the bus does not stop.

   Example   The 0825 bus from Paignton does not stop at
            Taunton or Calcot Coachway.

This distance table shows distances in miles between four cities.

London

117	Birmingham		
159	**76**	Sheffield	
397	**292**	**248**	Glasgow

♦ To find the distance
  between two cities, read
  down and across.

Example

The distance from London
to Sheffield is 159 miles.

C1 Write these times using
    am or pm.
    a 09:30   **b** 14:21

C2 Write these in 24-hour time.
    a 2:23 am   **b** 5:25 pm

C3 How many minutes are in
    1 h and 15 min?

C4 Write 400 minutes in hours
    and minutes.

D1 What is the latest time you
    can catch a bus from Exeter
    to reach Heathrow before
    6:00 pm?

D2 In hours and minutes, calculate
    how long each bus takes to go
    from Paignton to Heathrow.

D3 Which bus takes the longest
    time to travel from Torquay
    to Exeter?

D4 After 3:00 pm, what is the time
    of the first bus from Torquay
    to Exeter?

D5 It takes David 8 hours to drive
    from London to Glasgow.
    About how long do you think
    it would take him to drive
    from London to Sheffield?

D6 Suki drives from Glasgow to
    London via Birmingham.
    She leaves at 2.15 pm and
    arrives in Birmingham at
    7.15 pm. She leaves
    Birmingham at 7.45 pm.
    About what time do you think
    she will arrive in London?

Distance, time and constant speed

A **constant speed** is a steady speed.

An object travelling at a constant speed does not slow down or get faster.

At a constant speed of 9 metres per second, how far would a car travel in 20 seconds?

♦ In 1 second the car travels 9 metres.

♦ So in 20 seconds the car would travel $9 \times 20 = 180$ metres.

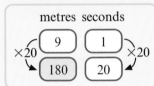

Distance = Speed × Time

At a constant speed, a car travels 8 kilometres in 5 minutes. How fast is it travelling?

♦ In 5 minutes the car travels 8 kilometres.
♦ In 1 minute the car travels $8 \div 5 = 1.6$ kilometres.
♦ So the speed of the car is 1.6 kilometres per minute.

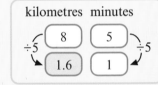

Speed = Distance ÷ Time

To find the formula for speed:

$$\text{Distance} = \text{Speed} \times \text{Time}$$

Now divide both sides by Time:

$$\frac{\text{Distance}}{\text{Time}} = \text{Speed}$$

At a constant speed of 20 miles per hour, how long would it take for a car to travel 50 miles?

♦ To travel 20 miles takes 1 hour.

♦ So to travel 50 miles takes $50 \div 20 = 2.5$ hours.

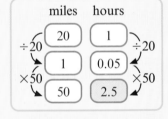

Time = Distance ÷ Speed

To find the formula for time:

$$\text{Distance} = \text{Speed} \times \text{Time}$$

Now divide both sides by Speed:

$$\frac{\text{Distance}}{\text{Speed}} = \text{Time}$$

Exercise 13.1
Calculating with constant speeds

Accuracy
In this exercise, give distances in metres, to 1 dp, and times to the nearest second.

1   At the Cairngorm Ski Area, you can go up and down the ski slopes by chairlift. The chairs on the White Lady Chairlift travel at a constant speed of 2.55 metres per second.

a   How far would you travel on this chairlift in:
   i 2 seconds   ii 10 seconds   iii 4.5 seconds?

b   At this speed, how many metres would a chair travel in:
   i 1 minute   ii 1 hour?

Chairs on the White Lady Chairlift travel 1054 metres to the top of the slope.

c   How long does it take a chair to travel to the top of the slope:
   i in seconds   ii in minutes and seconds?

2 An escalator is a set of stairs that moves at constant speed.

   a Why do you think the speed of an escalator is constant?

This table shows data on some escalators in London Underground stations.

> m/s stands for metres per second.

Station	Normal speed (m/s)	Length (m)	No. of steps
Alperton	0.46	13.7	102
The Angel	0.75	60.0	318
Chancery Lane	0.60	9.1	84
Kentish Town	0.66	44.1	237

   b Calculate how long it takes to travel up each escalator.

> Assume that each person stands still on one step of the escalator.

   c At The Angel, 250 people travel up the escalator.
Each person stands on the step just below the person in front.
If the first person steps onto the escalator at 2.00 pm, when will the last person reach the top of the escalator?

For problems with hours and minutes, it is often easier to work in minutes.

Example

A plane travels 670 miles at a constant speed in 1 hour and 42 minutes.
Calculate its speed in miles per hour.

- Time taken is $60 + 42 = 102$ minutes.
- Speed = Distance ÷ Time
  = $670 ÷ 102$
  = 6.5686 ... miles per minute
- In 60 minutes (1 hour) the plane travels
  $6.5686 ... × 60$
  = 394.1176 ... miles
- So the speed is about 394.1 miles per hour.

Exercise 13.2
Calculating with hours and minutes

1 A plane travels 1310 miles at a constant speed in 2 hours and 10 minutes. Calculate its speed in miles per hour.

2 A student has tried to solve a problem that involves hours and minutes.

> **Accuracy**
> In this exercise, give all answers correct to 1 dp unless stated otherwise.

A plane travels 1115 miles at a constant speed in 1 hour and 50 minutes. Calculate its speed in miles per hour.

> Speed = distance ÷ time
>   = 1115 ÷ 1.50
>   ≈ 743.3 miles per hour. ✗

   a Explain the mistake you think she has made.
   b Solve the student's problem to find the speed of the plane.

3 A Douglas DC-10 jet cruises at a constant speed of 620 miles per hour.

   a Find this speed in miles per minute, correct to 2 dp.
   b At this speed, how many miles would it travel in 10 minutes?

> mph stands for miles per hour.

4 A Boeing 757 jet cruises at a constant speed of 403 mph.

   a Find this speed in miles per minute, correct to 2 dp.
   b How many minutes would it take to travel 120 miles at this speed?

5 Concorde cruises at a constant speed of 1350 mph.

   a At this speed, how long would it take to travel 800 miles?
   b How far would it travel in 2 hours and 35 minutes?

Constant speeds and graphs

These diagrams show the positions of three cars on a road at one-second intervals. Each car is travelling at a constant speed.

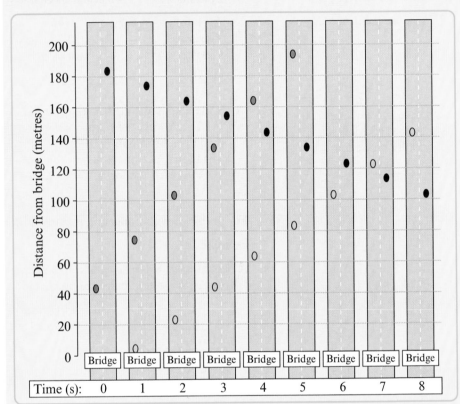

The scale shows the distance along the road from the bridge in metres

This is part of a **distance–time graph** for the red car.

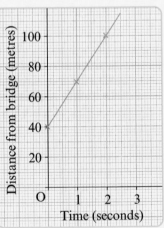

♦ The shortest distance is measured from each car to the bridge.

♦ The red car travels 30 metres every second.

It has a constant speed of 30 metres per second or 30 m/s.

Exercise 13.3
Distance-time graphs

For Question **1** refer to the panel above.

1 a i Draw a set of axes from:
  ♦ 0 to 8 seconds on the horizontal axis
  ♦ 0 to 200 metres on the vertical axis.
  ii Draw the complete distance–time graph for the red car.
  b Use your graph to estimate the distance of the red car from the bridge after 4.5 seconds.
  c After how many seconds was the red car 120 metres from the bridge?
  d How far was the black car from the bridge after 6 seconds?

Title your graph 'Distance–time graph for cars'.

e Draw the graphs for the yellow car and the black car on your axes.
f **i** Find the speeds of the yellow car and black car in metres per second.
   ii Which was travelling fastest: the red, yellow or black car?
   iii How can you tell this from your graph?
g **i** After how many seconds did the red car pass the black car?
   ii Explain how you found your answer.

2 This distance–time graph shows part of the journeys of four cars on a motorway.

> The distances are measured from a speed camera.

> The colour of each line shows the colour of the car.

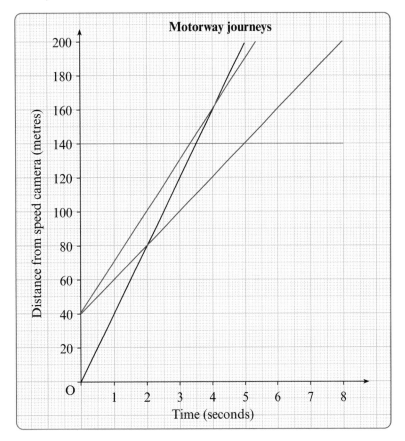

Motorway journeys

> Use tracing paper over the graph if you need to make marks to help you.

a Estimate how far each car was from the speed camera after 2.5 seconds.
b Which car was travelling fastest?
c After how many seconds did:
   i the black car pass the yellow car
   ii the blue car pass the red car?
d Find the speed of each car in m/s.
e What do you think happened to the red car?

3 This diagram shows the position of three cars and their speeds in m/s.
Each car is travelling in the direction of the arrow at a constant speed.

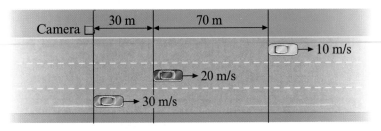

> Use a set of axes from:
> ◆ 0 to 10 seconds on the horizontal axis
> ◆ 0 to 300 metres on the vertical axis.

a Draw a distance–time graph for the next 10 seconds.
b How far is the red car from the camera when it passes the blue car?

Interpreting graphs

Exercise 13.4
Interpreting graphs

1 This is a sketch graph of Geeta's car journey to her workplace one morning.

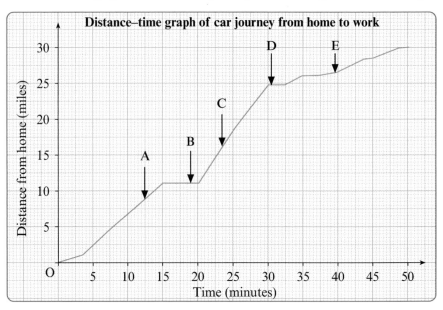

Use tracing paper over the graph if you need to make marks to help you.

a How far from Geeta's home is her workplace?
b How long did it take her to get to work?
c How far had Geeta travelled after 25 minutes?
d How long did it take her to travel:
　i the first 6 miles of her journey
　ii the last 6 miles of her journey?
e She stopped to buy some petrol.
　About how far from home do you think she was when she did this?
f Some points are labelled A to E on the graph.
　The statements 1 to 5 describe Geeta at different times on her journey.

①She is driving in a busy part of town.

②She is paying for her petrol.

③She is travelling at a constant speed and sees her petrol is rather low.

④She is travelling at the fastest speed of her whole journey.

⑤She is waiting at traffic lights.

　Match each statement to a labelled point.

g Sanjay describes points A to E on Geeta's journey.

At points A and C, Geeta was driving uphill. At points B and D, she was driving on level roads. At point E, she was driving on a bumpy road.

　Explain what is wrong with this description.

2 Geeta described her journey to the gym one evening.

The gym is 10 miles away in a town. For the first 5 miles, I cycled at a fairly constant speed along country roads. I stopped for 5 minutes to buy some water and then cycled quickly for 3 miles to the edge of the town.
I went on through the town to the gym. The journey took me 50 minutes.

Compare your sketch graph with someone else's.

Draw a sketch graph that could be for Geeta's journey to the gym.

Average speed

For a journey or part of a journey: **Average speed = Distance ÷ Time**

Example

Find Geeta's average speed for her car journey to work.

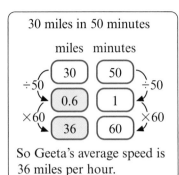

30 miles in 50 minutes

So Geeta's average speed is 36 miles per hour.

- ◆ She travelled 30 miles in 50 minutes.

- ◆ Average speed: Distance ÷ Time = 30 ÷ 50
                                                    = 0.6 miles per minute.

- ◆ Her **average speed** for this journey is 0.6 miles per minute.
  In miles per hour this is: 0.6 × 60 = 36 mph.

Exercise 13.5
Average speed

1 Geeta cycles 10 miles to the gym in 50 minutes.
Calculate her average speed for this journey:

    a in miles per minute   **b** in miles per hour.

2 Jason leaves home at 08.15 and drives 35 miles to his workplace.
He arrives at 08.55.
Calculate his average speed for this journey:

    a in miles per minute   **b** in miles per hour.

3 Geeta drives 373 miles from Bristol to Glasgow in 6 hours and 20 minutes.
What is her average speed for this journey in mph, correct to 1 dp?

4 Jason cycles 50 miles from Perth to Braemar at an average speed of 12 mph.
He leaves Perth at 9.30 am.
When does he arrive at Braemar?

5 On long journeys, Geeta cycles at an average speed of 9 mph.
She begins a long journey at 10.15 am.
To the nearest mile, estimate how far she will have travelled by 12.00 noon.

Accuracy
In Question **6**, give all average speeds correct to the nearest whole number.

6 This is part of a bus timetable.

Taunton	0755	1000	1040	1205
Bridgwater	0815	1020	1100	1225
Burnham-on-Sea........	0845	↓		
Weston-super-Mare ..	0910	1050		
Bristol	1000	1140		1320

    a Each of these buses travels 11 miles from Taunton to Bridgwater.
      i How long do these buses take to travel from Taunton to Bridgwater?
      ii Calculate a bus's average speed between Taunton and Bridgwater.
    b From Taunton to Bristol:
      ◆ the 0755 bus travels 53 miles
      ◆ the 1000 bus travels 49 miles.
      Find the average speed in mph of each of these two buses.
    c The average speed of the 1205 bus between
Taunton and Bristol is 36 mph.
How far does it travel between Taunton and Bristol?
    d The 1040 bus goes to Heathrow Airport by a route 155 miles long.
Between Taunton and Heathrow Airport its average speed is 50 mph.
When does it arrive at Heathrow Airport?

Distance-time graphs and speed

This is a sketch graph for Jay's journey to college one morning.

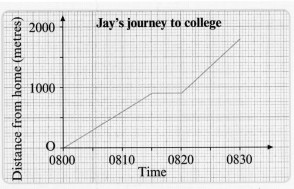

For different parts of Jay's journey, her average speed could be different.

For instance:

> m/min stands for metres per minute.

- ◆ She travels 900 metres in the first 10 minutes.
  So her average speed for the first 10 minutes is 900 ÷ 10 = 90 m/min.

- ◆ In total, she travels 1800 metres in 30 minutes.
  So her average speed for the whole journey is 900 ÷ 15 = 60 m/min.

Exercise 13.6
Graphs and average speed

1   Four students live in a block of flats and go to the same college.
The sketch graph shows each student's journey to college one morning.

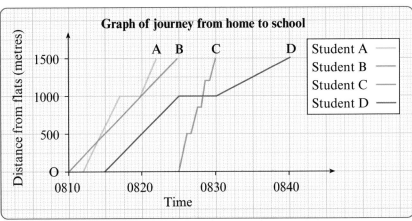

a   How far is the journey from the flats to the college?
b   Which student arrived at college first?
c   How long did student A take to travel to college?
d   The fire alarm was set off at 0822.
    What distance had each student travelled at 0822?
e   Find the average speed for the first 10 minutes of student C's journey.
f   The names of the four students are Jane, Lorna, Jason and Sharon.
    Lorna was buying crisps in the corner shop when she saw Jason go by
    in a car. Jane walked to college. Sharon cycled past Jane on the way.
    i Match each student (A, B, C and D) to Jane, Lorna, Sharon
       and Jason.
       Explain how you decided.
    ii How far is the corner shop from the college?
    iii How do you think Lorna travelled to college?
       Explain your answer.

> m/h stands for metres per hour.
>
> km/h stands for kilometres per hour.

g   Calculate each student's average speed for the whole journey in:
    i m/min   ii m/h   iii km/h.

Accuracy
In Question **2**, give all average speeds correct to the nearest whole number.

2 This sketch graph shows the journey of a car and a motorbike.
The car travelled from Leeds to Doncaster.
The motorbike took the same route to Doncaster but returned to Leeds.

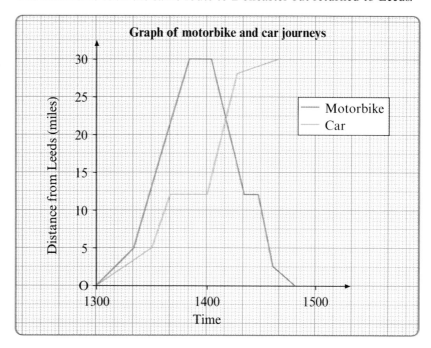

a **i** When did the car stop?
  ii For how many minutes did it stop?
b **i** Between what times was the car travelling fastest?
  ii What was its speed between these times?
c Describe what happened at 1410.
d Describe the motorbike's whole journey as fully as you can.
e **i** What was the total distance travelled by each vehicle on its journey?
  ii Calculate each vehicle's average speed for its whole journey in mph.

Exercise 13.7
Drawing and interpreting graphs

Accuracy
In this exercise, give all average speeds to 1 dp.

1 Ken and his sister Amy go on a cycling holiday.
The graph shows part of Ken's journey for the first day.

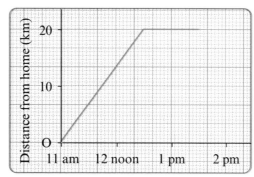

a After 1.30 pm he cycles at 15 km/h to reach a camp-site that is 50 km from home.
  i Copy and complete the graph for Ken's first day.
  ii Find Ken's average speed for his whole journey.
b Amy leaves their home at 1pm and cycles along the same route at 22 km/h.
  i Draw a line on your graph to show Amy's journey.
  ii When did she reach the camp-site?
  iii At about what time did Amy pass Ken on her way to the camp-site?

2 Alice lives in Cupar and Emily lives 10 miles away in St Andrews.
One day Alice cycles to St Andrews.

This graph shows part of her journey.

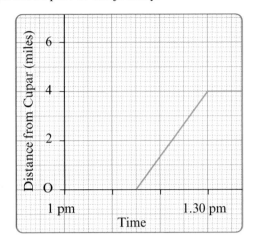

a At 1.30 pm, she stops for 10 minutes to buy cakes and then cycles
at a constant speed to reach Emily's house at 2.20 pm.

  i Copy and complete the graph for Alice's journey.

  ii What is her speed in mph after her stop to buy cakes?

  iii Calculate Alice's average speed in mph for her whole journey.

b On the same day, Emily decides to visit Alice.
She leaves at 1 pm and cycles at a speed of 12 mph for 4 miles.
She stops for five minutes and then carries on at a constant speed
to reach Alice's house at 1.47 pm.

  i How far is Emily from Cupar at the start of her journey?

  ii Show her journey on your graph.

  iii Find Emily's average speed in mph for her journey to Cupar.

  iv Explain why you think Emily did not see Alice on her journey.

c After ringing Alice's door bell for 3 minutes, Emily decides to cycle
home. She reaches St Andrews at the same time as Alice does.

  i Show Emily's journey home to St Andrews on your graph.

  ii How fast does she cycle home?

3 Sharon gave this information about a car journey.

- I travelled on motorways.
- My average speed for the whole journey was 50 mph.
- I set off at 9 am and arrived at 1.45 pm.
- I drove to my destination and did not make a return journey.
- I made two stops: 30 minutes for coffee and 40 minutes for lunch.
- I did not break the motorway speed limit of 70 mph.

a Draw a travel graph that fits this car journey.

b Compare your graph with someone else's graph for this journey.

Compound measures

The rate at which a vehicle uses fuel is called the **fuel consumption**. It is often given in **miles per gallon** (mpg).

Example

What is the fuel consumption of a car that uses 2.5 gallons of petrol to travel 118 miles?

$118 \div 2.5 = 47.2$
So fuel consumption is 47.2 mpg (miles per gallon).

Exercise 13.8
Compound measures

Accuracy
In this exercise, choose an appropriate degree of accuracy for each answer.

1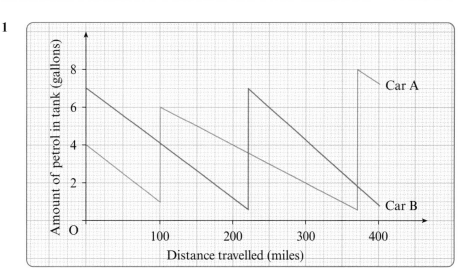

a   How much petrol was in each car's tank after 120 miles?
b   How far did car B travel on its first gallon of petrol?
c   How many times did car A stop for petrol?
d   How much petrol did car B buy on the journey?
e   How much petrol did each car use in the first 100 miles?
f   i   How much petrol did each car use over the whole journey?
    ii   What was the fuel consumption of each car on this journey?

2   Here is some information about Britain in 1993.

Number of households	22 500 000
Number of cars	20 102 000
Total length of motorways in km	3141
Total length of all roads in km	364 477

For these figures:

a   What was the average number of cars per household?
b   If all the cars were on the road at the same time, how many cars would there be per kilometre of road?
c   Would it be possible to fit all the cars on the motorways at the same time? Explain your answer.

A car is about 4 m long. Most motorways have 6 lanes.

3   In 1963 there were 7 479 000 cars and 16 700 000 households.

a   What was the average number of cars per household in 1963?
b   Describe how car ownership changed between 1963 and 1993.

End points

You should be able to ...

A Calculate with distance, speed and time

B Interpret distance–time graphs

... so try these questions

A1 At the Cairngorm Ski Area, chairs on the Car Park Chairlift travel at a constant speed of 2.65 metres per second.
How far would you travel on the chairlift in 1 minute and 25 seconds?

A2 On the Car Park Chairlift, a chair travels 766 metres to the top of the ski-slope.
How long does it take a chair to travel to the top of the slope in minutes and seconds?

A3 Jane drives 76 miles from Birmingham to Sheffield in 1 hour and 40 minutes.
What is her average speed for this journey in mph, correct to 1 dp?

A4 Morag drives 159 miles from London to Sheffield at an average speed of 51 mph.
She leaves London at 13.25.
When does she arrive in Sheffield?

B1 This sketch graph shows the journey of a car and a cycle.
The cyclist travelled from Leeds to York.
The car driver took the same route to York but returned to Leeds.

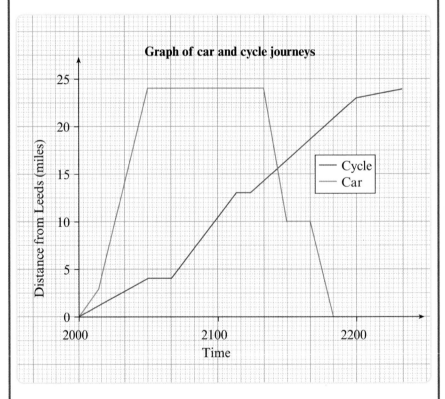

a How far did the cyclist travel in the first 20 minutes?
b How long did it take the car to travel the first 20 miles?
c How many times did the cyclist stop on her journey to York?
d What was the cyclist's average speed for this journey in mph correct to 1 dp?

e i Between which two times was the cyclist travelling fastest?
ii Explain how you can tell from the graph.
f How long did the car driver spend in York?
g What was the speed of the car for the last 10 miles of its return journey?
h i At what time did the car and cycle pass each other?
ii How far were they from Leeds when this happened?

C Draw distance–time graphs

C1 Liz and Pete cycle 17 miles from Keswick to Ambleside.
The graph shows part of Liz's journey.

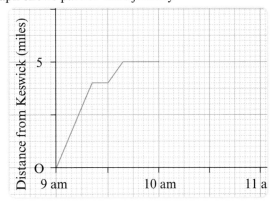

a After 10 am, she cycles at a constant speed of 10 mph to reach Ambleside.
Copy and complete the graph for Liz's journey.

b Find Liz's average speed for her whole journey in mph, correct to 1 dp.
c Pete leaves Keswick at 10 am. Apart from a 10 minute stop at 11 am, he cycles at a speed of 14 mph for the whole journey.
Show Pete's journey on your graph.

D Calculate with compound measures

D1 The White Lady Chairlift can carry 600 people per hour up the ski-slope.
At this rate, how many people would it carry up the slope between 9:30 am and 2:30 pm?

D2 Water flows out of a pipe at a constant rate.
In 30 minutes, 924 litres flow out of the pipe.
In litres per second, correct to 2 dp, at what rate is water flowing out of the pipe?

D3 In 1993, people in the UK spent a total of £113 500 000 on suncare products. The total population was 58 205 000.
Find the amount spent per person on suncare products in 1993.

Some points to remember

♦ Some rules for working with distance, speed and time:

> Distance = Speed × Time
> Time = Distance ÷ Speed
> Speed = Distance ÷ Time

♦ Average speed = Total distance ÷ Total time

♦ For problems involving hours and minutes, it is often easier to work in minutes.

Starting points

You need to know about ...

... so try these questions

A Naming shapes, sides and angles

- ◆ The vertices of a shape can be labelled with letters. The sides and angles can be named using these letters.

  Example

  - ❖ This is ΔPQR (triangle PQR).

  - ❖ The **sides** of PQR are PQ, QR and PR. PQ is also used for the length of the line PQ.

  - ❖ The **angles** in PQR are:
    PQ̂R (or ∠ PQR or Q̂),
    QR̂P (or ∠ QRP or R̂), and
    RP̂Q (or ∠ RPQ or P̂).

  Side PQ   Angle PQ̂R
            ∠ PQR or Q̂

A1

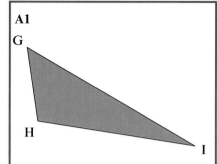

In triangle GHI:
- **a** which side is the longest?
- **b** which angle is the largest?
- **c** which angles are acute?
- **d** which is the shortest side?

B Similar triangles

- ◆ When two shapes are similar:
  - ❖ the corresponding angles are equal
  - ❖ the lengths of the corresponding sides are in the same ratio.

  Two triangles are similar if either:

  - ❖ corresponding angles are equal, or
  - ❖ the lengths of corresponding sides are in the same ratio.

  So to identify similar triangles you only need to check one of these properties.

- ◆ This is one way to identify **corresponding sides** in a pair of similar triangles.

  In triangles ABC and PQR
  AC and PR are
  corresponding sides
  because they are
  opposite equal angles.

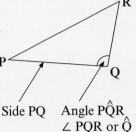

B1

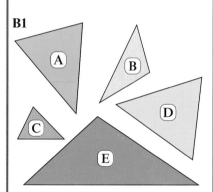

Using triangles A to E find two pairs of similar triangles.

B2 ΔEFG and ΔXYZ are similar.

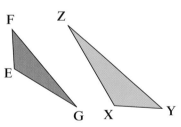

Which side corresponds to:
- **a** EG   **b** ZY?

C Writing ratios as decimals

- ◆ A ratio can be written as a decimal.

  Example

  $\frac{5}{8} = 0.625$ $\frac{5}{6} = 0.8333 ... = 0.8$ to 1 dp

  $\frac{3}{16} = 0.1875 = 0.2$ to 1 dp $\frac{32}{27} = 1.185\,1851 ... = 1.19$ to 2 dp

C1 Write these ratios as decimals correct to 2 dp.

- **a** $\frac{5}{12}$ **b** $\frac{7}{56}$
- **c** $\frac{8}{27}$ **d** $\frac{20}{9}$

Thinking ahead to ...
similar triangles

A Triangles ABC and PQR are similar.

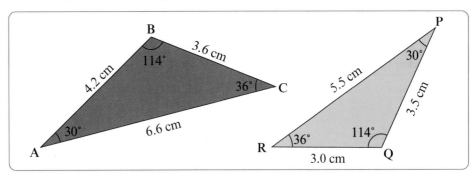

a In triangle ABC, the shortest side is 3.6 cm and the longest side is 6.6 cm.

Check that the ratio $\dfrac{\text{Shortest side}}{\text{Longest side}}$ equals 0.55 (to 2 dp).

b For triangle PQR calculate the ratio $\dfrac{\text{Shortest side}}{\text{Longest side}}$ (to 2 dp).

c What do you notice?

B   **a** Calculate the ratio $\dfrac{\text{Longest side}}{\text{Shortest side}}$ (to 2 dp) for triangles ABC and PQR.

b What do you notice?

Similar triangles

♦ In any triangle you can compare the length of two sides using a ratio.

Example

In triangle KLM:

$$\frac{KL}{ML} = \frac{1.9}{2.0} = 0.85$$

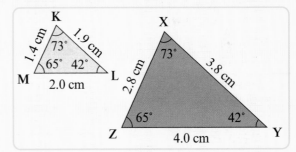

In triangles KLM and XYZ:

KM corresponds to XZ and ML corresponds to ZY.

So $\dfrac{KM}{ML}$ and $\dfrac{XZ}{ZY}$ can be called **corresponding ratios**.

$$\frac{KM}{ML} = \frac{1.4}{2.0} = 0.7 \text{ and } \frac{XZ}{ZY} = \frac{2.8}{4.0} = 0.7 \qquad \text{So } \frac{KM}{ML} = \frac{XZ}{ZY}$$

♦ For two similar triangles, **any** pair of corresponding ratios are equal.

So in triangles KLM and XYZ:

$\dfrac{ML}{KM}$ and $\dfrac{ZY}{XZ}$ are corresponding ratios, so $\dfrac{ML}{KM} = \dfrac{ZY}{XZ}$

$\dfrac{KL}{KM}$ and $\dfrac{XY}{XZ}$ are corresponding ratios, so $\dfrac{KL}{KM} = \dfrac{XY}{XZ}$

Exercise 14.1
Ratios of sides in
similar triangles

Accuracy
For this exercise round
each answer to 2 dp.

It may help if you redraw
the triangles in the same
orientation.

1 Triangles ABC, FDE and IHG are similar.

a i List the ratios that are equal

to $\dfrac{GH}{GI}$

ii Check by calculating the value
of these ratios.

b i List the ratios that are equal

to $\dfrac{GI}{GH}$

ii Check by calculating the value
of these ratios.

c List other sets of corresponding ratios
in triangles ABC, FDE and IHG.
Find the value for each set.

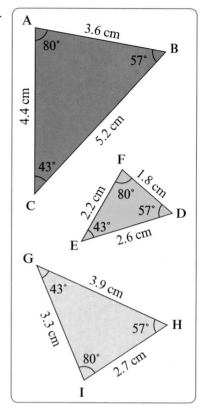

2

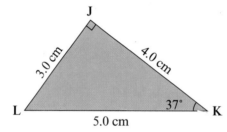

a Explain why triangles JKL and NMO are similar.
b Find the value of all the corresponding ratios in triangles JKL and NMO.

3 For two similar triangles, how many pairs of corresponding ratios are there?

Right-angled triangles

Greek letters are often
used to label angles.
For example: α (alpha),
β (beta) and θ (theta).

◆ The sides of a right-angled triangle can be labelled like this:

the hypotenuse (the longest side)   hyp
the side opposite θ opp
the side adjacent to (next to) θ adj

The **hypotenuse** is the side opposite
the right angle.

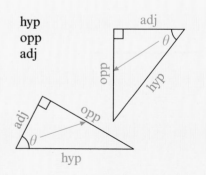

Exercise 14.2
Ratios of sides in
right-angled triangles

1   Triangle A is a 30° right-angled triangle.

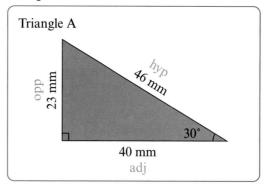

Triangle A

hyp
46 mm

opp
23 mm

40 mm
adj

30°

Make a ratio table like this and fill in the values for triangle A.

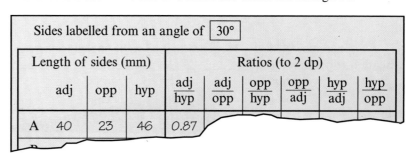

Sides labelled from an angle of	30°							
Length of sides (mm)			Ratios (to 2 dp)					
adj	opp	hyp	$\dfrac{adj}{hyp}$	$\dfrac{adj}{opp}$	$\dfrac{opp}{hyp}$	$\dfrac{opp}{adj}$	$\dfrac{hyp}{adj}$	$\dfrac{hyp}{opp}$
A 40	23	46	0.87					

2   Draw some other 30° right-angled triangles, and for each triangle:

a   label the sides from the 30° angle as hyp, opp or adj
b   measure the length of each side to the nearest millimetre
c   calculate the ratios for each pair of sides and make a ratio table.

Draw your triangles on
squared paper.

3   Describe anything you notice about your ratios.

4   **a**   What do you think will happen to the ratios for
other right-angled triangles?
b   Test your ideas on other right-angled triangles.

Trigonometric ratios

♦ The ratios of the sides in a right-angled triangle are
called **trigonometric ratios**.

In triangle ABC,

sine:	sin 30°	= 0.50
cosine:	cos 30°	= 0.87
tangent:	tan 30°	= 0.58
		(to 2 dp)

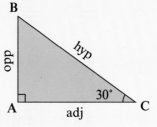

B

opp

hyp

30°

A   adj   C

Exercise 14.3
Trigonometric ratios

1   **a**   Find these keys on your calculator:  sin   cos   tan

Your ratios may not match
the values of sin 30°,
cos 30° and tan 30° exactly.

b   Use them to find the values of sin 30°, cos 30° and tan 30°.
c   Check the values match those given above.
d   Match each value to one of your ratios for the 30° triangles
that you have drawn.

2   **a**   How can you calculate the sine, cosine and tangent of an angle?
b   Check your ideas on the triangles you drew in Exercise 14.2.

Sine, cosine and tangent of an angle

A mnemonic (pronounced *ne-mon-ik*) is a memory aid.

This is a mnemonic used to remember the definitions for the sine, cosine and tangent of an angle:

Skive   off   homework
Cheat   at   homework
Telling   off   after

◆ These are definitions of three trigonometric ratios (or 'trig' ratios):

sine: $\sin \theta = \dfrac{\text{opp}}{\text{hyp}}$

cosine: $\cos \theta = \dfrac{\text{adj}}{\text{hyp}}$

tangent: $\tan \theta = \dfrac{\text{opp}}{\text{adj}}$

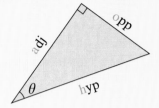

These trig ratios can be used to calculate any side or any angle in **right-angled triangles**.

Exercise 14.4
Calculating trigonometric ratios

Accuracy
For this exercise round each answers to 2 dp.

1   These are all right-angled triangles.

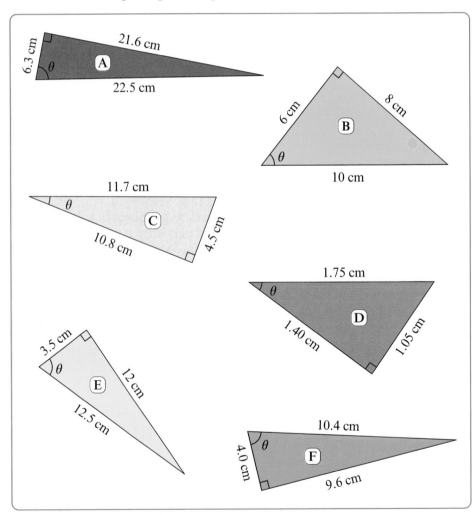

a Sketch each of these triangles and label the sides: opp, adj, hyp.

b For each triangle, find the value of:
   i $\sin \theta$ **ii** $\cos \theta$ **iii** $\tan \theta$.

Finding an angle

These are some pairs of inverse operations:

to add / to subtract
to square / to square-root

On some calculators the inverse button is marked

  or

♦ When you know the value of one trigonometric ratio for an angle, you can use the inverse function on a calculator to find the size of the angle.

Example

Find θ when $\sin \theta = 0.375$
On some calculators, these are the key presses.

$\theta = \mathbf{22°}$ (to the nearest degree)

Exercise 14.5
Calculating angles

1 For your calculator, list the key presses to find θ when $\sin \theta = 0.375$

2 Find the angle α when:

   a $\sin \alpha = 0.3584$ **b** $\tan \alpha = 1.0256$ **c** $\cos \alpha = 0.351$

3 Find the angle β when:

   a $\tan \beta = \dfrac{5}{13}$ **b** $\cos \beta = \dfrac{3.5}{8.16}$ **c** $\tan \beta = \dfrac{8.9}{5.4}$

Do not round the value before using the inverse operation.

Accuracy
For this exercise round each angle to the nearest degree.

When you use trigonometric ratios to solve problems it is useful to write down:

♦ what you know
♦ what you are trying to find
♦ what ratio you need to use.

4 This is part of a calculation to find θ in triangle ABC.

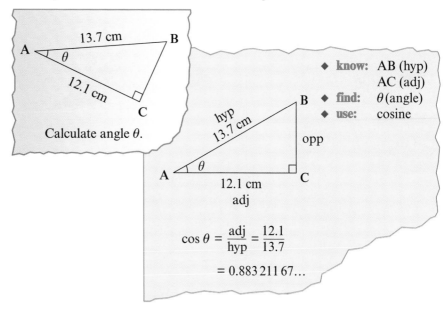

What is the size of angle θ?

5

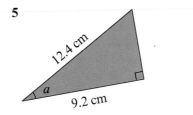 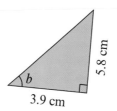 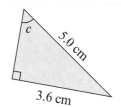

Calculate the size of angles a, b and c.

6 For each triangle, calculate the size of the lettered angle.

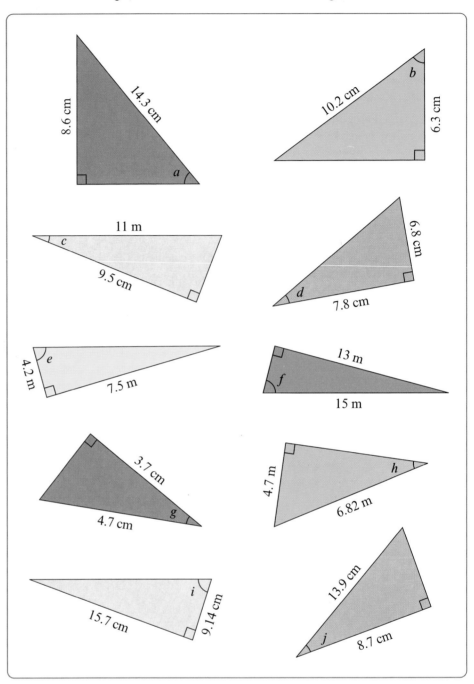

7 Ali and Wayne calculate cos θ for a triangle.
These are their answers:

Ali $\cos \theta = 0.798449612 \dots$

Wayne $\cos \theta = 1.252427184 \dots$

a Which value for cos θ must be incorrect?
b Explain why.

Finding a side

♦ Each trig ratio can be written in different ways.

Starting with the ratio $\sin \theta = \dfrac{\text{opp}}{\text{hyp}}$

we can write: $\dfrac{\text{opp}}{\text{hyp}} = \sin \theta$

Multiply both sides by hyp: $\times \text{hyp} \qquad \times \text{hyp}$

$$\text{opp} = \text{hyp} \times \sin \theta$$

So $\sin \theta = \dfrac{\text{opp}}{\text{hyp}}$ gives: $\text{opp} = \text{hyp} \times \sin \theta$

In the same way, $\cos \theta = \dfrac{\text{adj}}{\text{hyp}}$ gives: $\text{adj} = \text{hyp} \times \cos \theta$

and $\tan \theta = \dfrac{\text{opp}}{\text{adj}}$ gives: $\text{opp} = \text{adj} \times \tan \theta$

♦ The length of any side in a right-angled triangle can be calculated using trigonometry.

Example In △ABC calculate the length of AC.

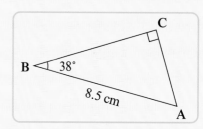

Use the full calculator value for sin 38° and round at the end of the calculation.

On some calculators this set of key presses can be used to calculate $8.5 \times \sin 38°$

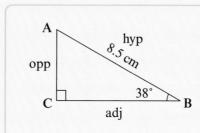

♦ **know:** AB (hyp)
angle
♦ **find:** AC (opp)
♦ **use:** sine

$\text{opp} = \text{hyp} \times \sin \theta$
$\text{opp} = 8.5 \times \sin 38°$
$\text{opp} = 5.2 \text{ (to 1 dp)}$

So the length of AC is 5.2 cm (to 1dp)

Exercise 14.6
Finding lengths in
right-angled triangles

1 List the key presses you use to calculate $8.5 \times \sin 38°$ on your calculator.

2 Sketch each of these triangles and calculate the length of the blue side.

Accuracy
For this exercise round each answer to 1 dp.

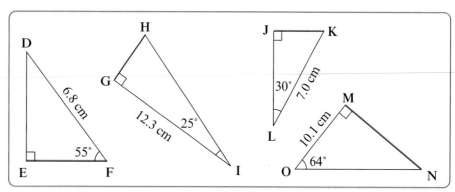

3 This is part of a calculation to find BC in ΔABC.

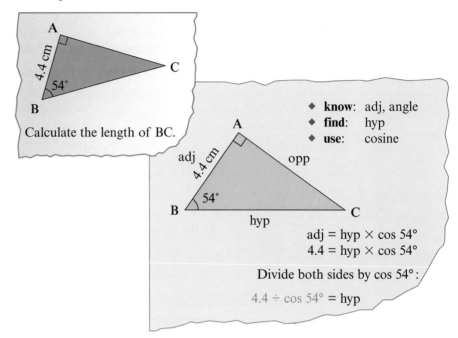

Calculate the length of BC.

- ◆ **know**: adj, angle
- ◆ **find**: hyp
- ◆ **use**: cosine

$$adj = hyp \times \cos 54°$$
$$4.4 = hyp \times \cos 54°$$

Divide both sides by cos 54°:

$$4.4 \div \cos 54° = hyp$$

Use the full calculator value for cos 54° and round at the end of the calculation.

On some calculators this set of key presses can be used to calculate $4.4 \div \cos 54°$

a For **your** calculator, list the key presses to calculate $4.4 \div \cos 54°$.

b What is the length of BC?

4

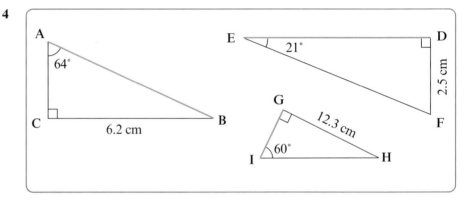

Calculate the length of AB, DE and GI in these triangles.

5

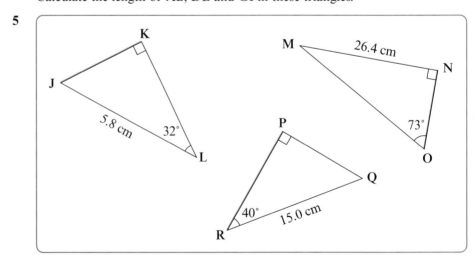

Calculate the length of JK, NO and PR in these triangles.

A In triangle RST:
  a Is RS greater than or less than 5.6 cm?
  b Explain your answer

B Estimate the length of RS.

C Calculate the length of RS to 2 dp.

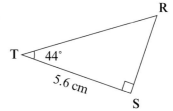

Finding sides and angles

Exercise 14.7
Estimating and calculating
sides and angles

Accuracy
For this exercise round
each answer to 3 sf.

1 The lengths and angles marked in blue on these triangles are incorrect.

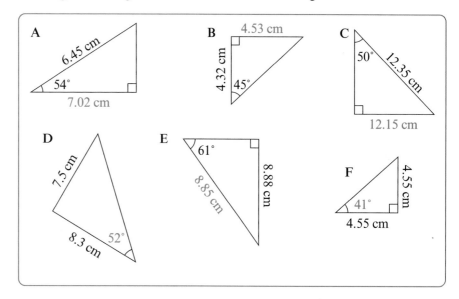

  a For each triangle, without calculating, explain why the length or angle
    marked in blue is wrong.
  b Calculate the correct length or angle for each triangle.

2 Sketch each triangle and calculate the length or angle marked with a letter.

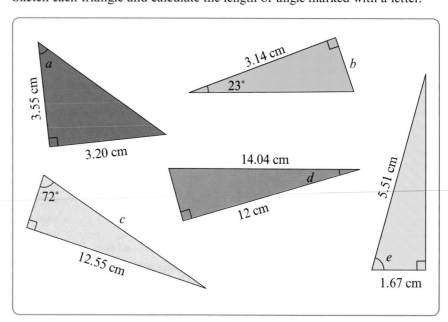

Trigonometry – solving problems

Exercise 14.8
Solving problems

Accuracy
For this exercise:
◆ round each angle to 2 dp
◆ round each distance to
  the nearest cm.

To write a length written
in metres to the nearest
centimetre you can round
it to 2 dp.

Example

 5.3167 m
= 5 metres 31.67 cm
= 5 metres 32 cm
   to the nearest cm
= 5.32 m (to 2 dp)

 25.12906 m
= 25.13 m
   to the nearest cm

1 This ladder is 5 metres long.
The foot of the ladder is 1.25 metres
from the wall.

a The ladder is at an angle θ to the
horizontal. Calculate the angle θ.

b The ladder reaches a height
of h metres up the wall.
Calculate the height h to the
nearest centimetre.

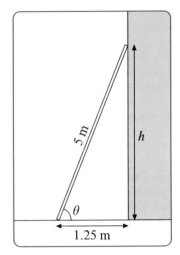

2 The firm Light Ladders recommends that the angle α, between the ladder and
the horizontal, should be between 72° and 76°.

The length of this ladder is 4.5 metres.
The distance from the foot of the ladder
to the wall is d metres.

a **i** What angle α will give the
minimum distance d?

ii Calculate the minimum distance d
for this ladder.

b Calculate the maximum distance d
for this ladder.

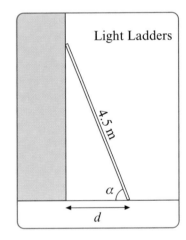

3 This is part of the safety label Light Ladders
put on their extending ladder.

For the minimum distance
you need to round your
answer **up**.

For the maximum distance
you need to round your
answer **down**.

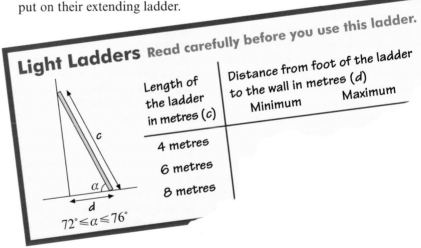

Length of the ladder in metres (c)	Distance from foot of the ladder to the wall in metres (d)	
	Minimum	Maximum
4 metres		
6 metres		
8 metres		

Make a complete safety label for this extending ladder.

4 This diagram shows some steps and a ramp outside a building.

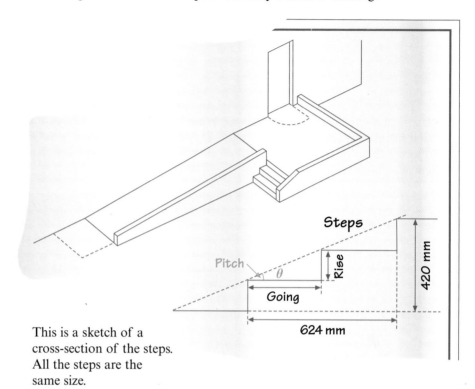

This is a sketch of a
cross-section of the steps.
All the steps are the
same size.

a For each step calculate the length of
   i the rise   **ii** the going.
b The angle θ is the pitch of these stairs.
   Calculate the angle θ.

5 This is a cross-section of the ramp.

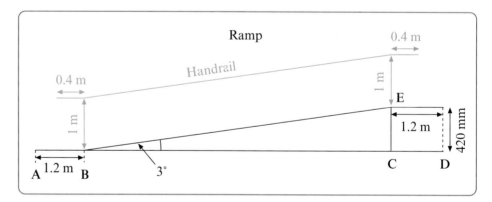

The pitch of the ramp is 3° and the height is 420 millimetres.

a What is the height of the ramp in metres?

b Calculate the length of the ramp, BE, in metres.

c A handrail is fixed to the wall 1 metre above the ramp.
   It extends 0.4 metres beyond each end of the ramp.
   What is the total length of the handrail?

d Calculate the horizontal distance BC.

e At each end of the ramp there must be a landing at least 1.2 metres long.
   Calculate the horizontal distance AD.

> In each calculation you will
> need to use either metres or
> millimetres, not both.

6 For wheelchairs the maximum gradient of a ramp should be 1 in 20.

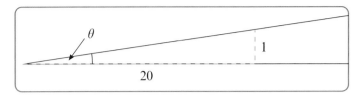

a What is the maximum value of θ for a wheelchair ramp?
b **i** For each of the ramps A to D calculate the angle θ.
   ii Which of these ramps is safe for wheelchair users?

> In each calculation you will need to use either metres or millimetres, not both.

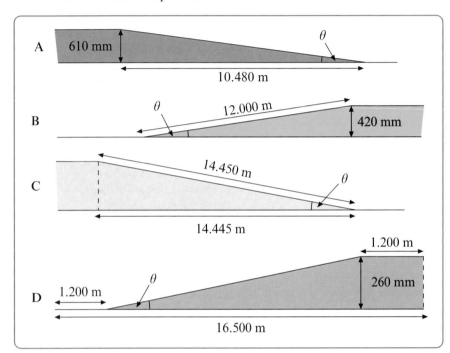

7 The maximum space for a ramp beside this building is 14.260 metres.

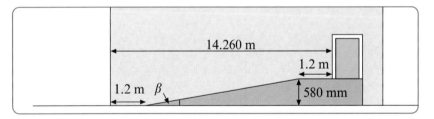

> Think carefully whether you need to round each answer up or down.

If they have to include a landing 1.2 metres long at each end of the ramp, what is the smallest pitch, β, that they can use?

8 These are the regulations for the rise and going on any staircase.

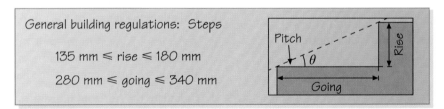

General building regulations: Steps

135 mm ≤ rise ≤ 180 mm

280 mm ≤ going ≤ 340 mm

Calculate the maximum and minimum pitch for a staircase.

End points

You should be able to ...   ... so try these questions

A Recognise similar triangles

A1

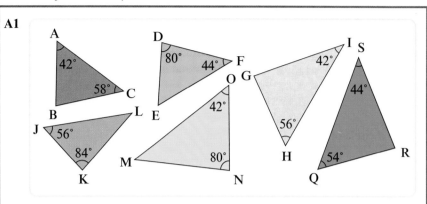

Which pair of triangles is similar?

B Calculate an angle in a right-angled triangle

B1

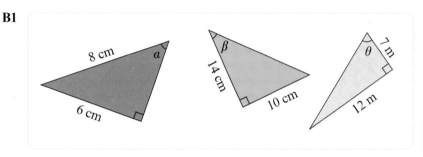

Calculate the angles α, β and θ, each correct to 2 dp.

C Calculate the length of a side in a right-angled triangle

C1

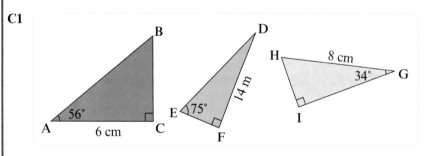

Calculate the lengths AB, EF and GI, each correct to 3 sf.

Some points to remember

♦ For a right-angled triangle, these trigonometric ratios apply:

$$\sin \theta = \frac{\text{opp}}{\text{hyp}} \qquad \cos \theta = \frac{\text{adj}}{\text{hyp}} \qquad \tan \theta = \frac{\text{opp}}{\text{adj}}$$

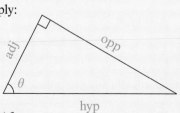

Some mnemonics to remember these by are:

Skive Off Homework, Cheat At Homework, Telling Off After.
Should Old Harry Catch Any Herrings Trawling Off America?

Starting points
You need to know about ...

... so try these questions

A Substituting into simple formulas

Example　A formula for the approximate area (A) of a circle with radius r is: $A = 3r^2$. What is A when $r = 10$?

$$A = 3 \times 10^2 = 3 \times 100 = 300$$

So a circle of radius 10 cm has an approximate area of 300 cm^2.

B Flowcharts

Flowcharts can be used to solve problems.

Example　I think of a number. I subtract 5 and then multiply by 6. My answer is 42. What number was I thinking of?

◆ A flowchart for the problem:

$$\text{Number} \rightarrow \boxed{-5} \rightarrow \boxed{\times 6} \rightarrow 42$$

◆ A reverse flowchart:

$$12 \leftarrow \boxed{+5} \leftarrow \boxed{\div 6} \leftarrow 42$$

So the number I was thinking of is 12.

C Balancing equations

Balancing can be used to solve problems.

Example　I think of a number. I subtract 5 and then multiply by 6. My answer is 42. What number was I thinking of?

◆ An equation for the problem:　$6(n - 5) = 42$

◆ Solve the equation by balancing:

$$6(n - 5) = 42$$
$$6n - 30 = 42 \quad \Big\} +30$$
$$+30 \Big\{ \quad 6n = 72 \quad \Big\} \div 6$$
$$\div 6 \Big\{ \quad n = 12$$

So the number I was thinking of is 12.

D Simplifying expressions

◆ Collect together any like terms.

Example

$$5a^2 + 3a + 10 + 4a - 2$$
$$= 5a^2 + 3a + 4a + 10 - 2$$
$$= 5a^2 + 7a + 8$$

◆ Complete any multiplications as far as possible.

Examples

◆ $p \times p \times 5 = 5p^2$
◆ $3a \times 5b = 15ab$
◆ $3x \times 5x = 15x^2$

A1　What is the approximate area of a circle with radius 4 cm?

A2　For each formula, find the value of A when $x = 5$.
　　a　$A = 4x - 1$　**c**　$A = 7(x + 2)$
　　b　$A = \dfrac{x}{2}$　**d**　$A = 30 - 2x$

B1　Use flowcharts to solve these number puzzles.

　　a　I think of a number. I multiply by 4, then add 5. My answer is 53. What number was I thinking of?

　　b　I think of a number. I subtract 8, then multiply by 3. My answer is 93. What number was I thinking of?

C1　Solve these equations:
　　a　$4(n - 1) = 76$
　　b　$2n + 5 = 5n - 1$

C2　I think of a number. I multiply by 7, then add 9. My answer is 65. What number was I thinking of?

　　a　Write an equation for this puzzle.

　　b　Solve it to find the number.

D1　Simplify these expressions:
　　a　$4x + 3 + x + 5$
　　b　$2a + 3b + 7a - b$
　　c　$2x^2 + 4x + 3x^2 - 2x$
　　d　$2a + 5a^2 + 4a - 7$
　　e　$t \times t \times 3$
　　f　$5c \times 2d$
　　g　$4k \times 3k$
　　h　$w \times 7w$

Thinking ahead to ...
rearranging formulas

A A cook book gives this formula to find the time to cook a piece of lamb.

> Allow 30 minutes per pound and an extra 20 minutes.

  a How long would it take to cook 6 pounds of lamb?
  b What weight of lamb would be cooked in 1 hour and 50 minutes?

Rearranging formulas

The formula that links cooking time (T) with weight (W) can be written as:

$$T = 30W + 20$$

♦ The formula shows how to find T when you know W, but it can be rearranged to show how to find W when you know T.

> Addition 'undoes' subtraction and vice versa. For example:
>
> $10 \longrightarrow \boxed{-8} \longrightarrow 2$
>
> $10 \longleftarrow \boxed{+8} \longleftarrow 2$

> Multiplication 'undoes' division and vice versa. For example:
>
> $10 \longrightarrow \boxed{\div 5} \longrightarrow 2$
>
> $10 \longleftarrow \boxed{\times 5} \longleftarrow 2$

Flowchart method for rearranging formulas

♦ Draw a flowchart for the formula.

$W \longrightarrow \boxed{\times 30} \xrightarrow{30W} \boxed{+20} \xrightarrow{30W + 20} T$

♦ Reverse the flow chart to rearrange the formula.

$W \xrightarrow{\frac{T-20}{30}} \boxed{\div 30} \xrightarrow{T-20} \boxed{-20} \longrightarrow T$

♦ The rearranged formula is: $W = \dfrac{T - 20}{30}$

Balancing method for rearranging formulas

♦ Add, subtract, multiply or divide **both** sides of the formula by equal amounts.

$\begin{array}{l} -20 \\ \div 30 \end{array} \left(\begin{array}{c} T = 30W + 20 \\ T - 20 = 30W \\ \dfrac{T - 20}{30} = W \end{array} \right) \begin{array}{l} -20 \\ \div 30 \end{array}$

♦ The rearranged formula is: $W = \dfrac{T - 20}{30}$

Exercise 15.1
Rearranging linear formulas

> For the formula you need to write £19.85 in pence.

1 The formula that gives the cost in pence (c) of placing an advertisement in a local paper, where n is the number of words is:

$$c = 15n + 50$$

  a Find the cost of a 65-word advert.
  b Rearrange the formula so that it begins, $n = ...$.
  c How many words were used in an advert that cost £19.85?
  d With £10.00, what is the maximum number of words you could use?

2 You can estimate the distance between you and a storm using the formula:

$$d = \frac{t}{5}$$

where d is the distance in miles and t is the number of seconds between the lightning and the thunder.

> When a formula begins, $t = ...$, then t is the subject of the formula.

  a Make t the subject of the formula.
  b For a storm 1.5 miles away, how many seconds will be between the lightning and the thunder?

The interior angles of this polygon are marked in red.

3 The formula for the sum (S) of the interior angles of a polygon is:

$$S = 180(n - 2)$$

where n is the number of sides.

a What is the sum of the interior angles of a hexagon?
b Make n the subject of the formula.
c The sum of the interior angles of a polygon is 3240°.
    How many sides has the polygon?
d Explain why it is not possible to draw a polygon where
    the sum of the interior angles is 600°.

4 The formula for the number of vitamin pills (n) that Jim has left after d days is:

$$n = 100 - 3d$$

a How many vitamin pills would Jim have left after 14 days?
b How many vitamin pills does he take each day?
c Copy and complete this diagram to make d the subject of the formula.

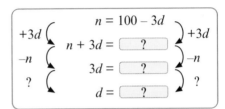

d After how many days does Jim have 10 pills left?

5 In the summer, an ice-cream seller uses this formula to estimate the number of ice-creams (n) she will sell in a day at x pence each.

$$n = 800 - 5x$$

a About how many ice-creams will she sell in a day at 50p each?
b Make x the subject of the formula.
c What price will she need to charge to sell 500 ice-creams?
d Explain why she is unlikely to charge £1.70 for an ice-cream.

6 The formula that links distance (d), speed (s) and time (t) is:

$$d = st$$

a How far will a car travel in 2 hours at a speed of 47 mph?

With s as the subject, the formula $d = st$ can be written:

$$s = \frac{d}{t}$$

To make s the subject of the formula, $d = st$:

$$s \longrightarrow \boxed{\times t} \xrightarrow{st} d$$

$$s \xleftarrow{\frac{d}{t}} \boxed{\div t} \longleftarrow d$$

So $s = \dfrac{d}{t}$

b Calculate the speed of a plane that travels 1800 miles in 3 hours.
c Copy and complete this flow chart for $d = st$:

$$t \longrightarrow \boxed{} \longrightarrow d$$

d Reverse the flow chart and make t the subject of the formula.
e Find the time it takes to travel 125 km at a speed of 50 km/h.

7 Make p the subject of each formula:

a $t = p + 1$ **b** $s = 7p$ **c** $y = 5p - 2$ **d** $v = 10 - p$

e $h = 12 - 9p$ **f** $r = p + q$ **g** $t = pq$ **h** $x = 2p + f$

i $k = lp - m$ **j** $g = \dfrac{p}{9}$ **k** $m = \dfrac{p}{n}$ **l** $s = \dfrac{p}{2} + 1$

A formula for converting kilometres (k) to miles (m) is: $\qquad m = \dfrac{5}{8}k$

♦ Making k the subject gives
a formula for converting miles to kilometres.

$$\times 8 \left(\begin{array}{c} m = \dfrac{5}{8}k \\ 8m = 5k \end{array} \right) \times 8$$

♦ So $k = \dfrac{8m}{5}$

$$\div 5 \left(\begin{array}{c} 8m = 5k \\ \dfrac{8m}{5} = k \end{array} \right) \div 5$$

Exercise 15.2
Rearranging formulas
with fractions

1 A formula for converting kilograms (k) to pounds (p) is:

$$p = \frac{11}{5}k$$

  a How many pounds are in 8 kilograms?
  b Make k the subject of the formula.
  c Convert 3 pounds to kilograms.

2 The formula for the area, (A), of a triangle with base length b and height h is:

$$A = \frac{1}{2}bh$$

  a Make h the subject of the formula.
  b Find the height of a triangle with area $100\,\text{cm}^2$ and base length $2.5\,\text{cm}$.

3 Temperature in °F can be converted to °C using this formula:

$$C = \frac{5(F - 32)}{2}$$

  a Change 68 °F to °C.
  b Copy and complete this flowchart:

$$F \longrightarrow \boxed{-32} \xrightarrow{\;F-32\;} \boxed{} \longrightarrow \boxed{} \longrightarrow C$$

  c Reverse the flowchart to give a formula that converts °C into °F.
  d Change 24 °C to °F.

4 Make y the subject of each formula:

  a $z = \dfrac{3}{4}y$ **b** $m = \dfrac{1}{3}xy$ **c** $d = \dfrac{1}{2}y + 4$ **d** $k = \dfrac{4}{7}y - h$

5 When d metres are travelled in t seconds, a formula for average speed (s) in km/h is:

$$s = \frac{18d}{5t}$$

$$\boxed{\dfrac{18d}{5t} = 18d \div 5t}$$

  a In 1992, Linford Christie ran 100 metres in 9.96 seconds.
    What was his average speed in km/h, correct to 2 dp?
  b Make d the subject of the formula.
  c Make t the subject of the formula.

6 When the temperature at ground level is G°C and the height above the ground in metres is h, the approximate temperature (T°C) is given by:

$$T = G - \frac{h}{300}$$

  a When the temperature at ground level is 26 °C, find the temperature outside a jet flying at 15 000 m above ground.
  b Make h the subject of the formula.
  c Calculate h when $G = 20$ and $T = {}^-30$.

A formula for the total area (A) of glass in this window is:
$$A = 4x^2$$

♦ A flow chart for finding A is:

$$x \longrightarrow \boxed{\text{square}} \xrightarrow{x^2} \boxed{\times 4} \xrightarrow{4x^2} A$$

♦ Reversing the flow chart makes x the subject of the formula:

$$x \xleftarrow{\sqrt{\frac{A}{4}}} \boxed{\begin{array}{c}\text{square} \\ \text{root}\end{array}} \xleftarrow{\frac{A}{4}} \boxed{\div 4} \longleftarrow A$$

♦ So, $x = \sqrt{\dfrac{A}{4}}$

Exercise 15.3
Using roots

Accuracy
In this exercise,
♦ give answers correct to 2 dp
♦ use the π button on your calculator.

1 The formula for the surface area (S) of a cube with an edge length of x is:
$$S = 6x^2$$
   a Find the surface area of a cube with an edge length of $8.2\,$cm.
   b Make x the subject of the formula.
   c What is the edge length of a cube with a surface area of $120\,$cm^2?

2 The formula for the area (A) of a circle with a radius of r is:
$$A = \pi r^2$$
   a Find the area of a circle with a radius of $1.5\,$cm.
   b Which of these is the correct formula for the radius r?

    A $\boxed{r = \sqrt{(A - \pi)}}$ **B** $\boxed{r = \sqrt{\dfrac{A}{\pi}}}$ **C** $\boxed{r = \dfrac{\sqrt{A}}{\pi}}$

   c What is the radius of a circle with an area of $200\,$cm^2?

3 When an object is dropped, a formula for the approximate distance (d) travelled in metres in a time of t seconds is:
$$d = \frac{49}{10}t^2$$
   a A stone is dropped. About how far will it fall in 6.5 seconds?
   b Rearrange the formula to make t the subject.
   c Sears Tower is $443\,$m high.
     About how long will it take an apple to fall from the top to the ground?

4 Make k the subject of:
   a $m = k^2 + 1$ **b** $m = 3k^2 + 1$ **c** $m = k^2 + n$

5 The formulas for the surface area (A) and volume (V) of a sphere with a radius of r are:
$$A = 4\pi r^2 \quad \text{and} \quad V = \tfrac{4}{3}\pi r^3$$
   a Calculate the surface area and volume of a sphere of radius $5\,$cm.
   b Make r the subject of each formula.
   c Find the radius of a sphere with a surface area of $200\,$cm^2.
   d Find the radius of a sphere with a volume of $100\,$cm^3.

$p^3 = p \times p \times p$

If $y = p^3$ then
the **cube root** of y is p.

$\sqrt[3]{y} = p$

6 Make x the subject of:
   a $y = \dfrac{7x^2 - 1}{5}$ **b** $A = \tfrac{2}{3}\pi x^2$ **c** $R^3 = kx^2$

Substitution into non-linear expressions

♦ For the formula, $a = (b + 5)(b - 1)$, find the value of a when $b = 3$.
$$a = (3 + 5) \times (3 - 1)$$
$$= 8 \times 2$$
$$= 16$$

♦ For the formula, $y = x^2 + 4x + 1$, find the value of y when $x = 7$.
$$y = 7^2 + (4 \times 7) + 1$$
$$= 49 + 28 + 1$$
$$= 78$$

Exercise 15.4
Substitution

Accuracy
In this exercise, give each answer correct to 2 dp.

1 The stopping distance is the distance a vehicle travels as it brakes to a halt. A formula that gives the stopping distance of a car on a dry road is:
$$d = \frac{v^2}{200} + \frac{v}{5}$$
where d is the stopping distance in metres and v is the speed in km/h.

Calculate the stopping distance of a car travelling at 110 km/h on a dry road.

2 The net for an open square-based box is made by cutting four square corners from a 12 cm by 12 cm square piece of card as shown.

A formula for the volume, (V cm³), of the box is:
$$V = 4x(x^2 - 12x + 36),$$
where x is the length shown on the diagram.

a When $x = 1.5$, find the volume of the box.
b Calculate V when $x = 4$.
c What value for x gives the box with the greatest volume?

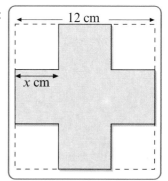

3 A $y = x^2 + 5x - 8$ B $y = x^2 + 3x + 2$

   C $y = (x + 1)(x + 2)$ D $y = (x - 2)(x + 9)$

For each formula find the value of y when:
a i $x = 5$ ii $x = 3$ iii $x = 2$ iv $x = 2.5$
b Comment on any patterns in your results.

4 When an object is dropped, a formula for the approximate speed (v) in m/s after travelling s metres is:
$$v = \sqrt{20s}$$

The Empire State Building is 381 m high.
A coin is dropped from the top. Estimate its speed as it hits the ground.

5 The formula $v = \sqrt{u^2 + 2as}$ gives the speed of an object (v) in m/s, given the speed at the start (u) in m/s, the acceleration (a) in m/s² and the distance (s) travelled in metres.

Find v when:
a $u = 30$, $a = 5$ and $s = 6.8$ b $u = 20$, $a = 9.8$ and $s = 2.4$

Multiplication

The area of this shape is $28 \times 43\,\text{cm}^2$.

One way to calculate the area is as follows.

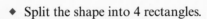

43 cm

28 cm

- Split the shape into 4 rectangles.
- Find the area of each rectangle in cm².

$$20 \times 40 = 800$$
$$20 \times 3 = 60$$
$$8 \times 40 = 320$$
$$8 \times 3 = 24$$

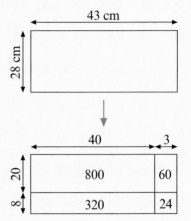

40   3

20   800   60

8   320   24

- Add the areas:

$$800 + 60 + 320 + 24 = 1204$$

- The total area is $1204\,\text{cm}^2$.

> This is one way to multiply without a calculator.

Any multiplication can be calculated in a similar way.

Example $42 \times 19 = (40 + 2) \times (10 + 9)$

- Work in a table.

×	40	+ 2
10	400	20
+ 9	360	18

- The total is:
  $400 + 20 +$
  $360 + 18 = 798$
- So $42 \times 19 = 798$.

Exercise 15.5
Multiplication without a calculator

1 A shape has been split into four rectangles.
   a Calculate the area of each rectangle.
   b Find the total area of the shape.

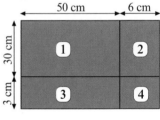

50 cm   6 cm

30 cm

3 cm

1   2

3   4

2   **a** Make a sketch of this diagram and fill in any missing lengths and areas.
   b Find the total area of the shape.

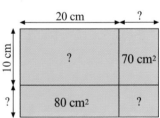

20 cm   ?

10 cm

?   70 cm²

?   80 cm²   ?

3 Copy and complete:

a

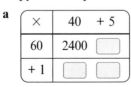

×	40	+ 5
60	2400	☐
+ 1	☐	☐

So $45 \times 61 = $ ☐

b

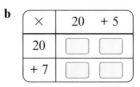

×	20	+ 5
20	☐	☐
+ 7	☐	☐

So $25 \times 27 = $ ☐

c

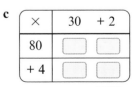

×	30	+ 2
80	☐	☐
+ 4	☐	☐

So $32 \times 84 = $ ☐

Thinking ahead to ...
multiplying out brackets

A This shape is split into four rectangles.

Find an expression for:

a the area of each rectangle
b the total area of the shape.

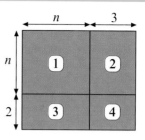

Multiplying out brackets

We can multiply out brackets from $(n + 2)(n + 3)$ like this:

Work in a table:

×	n	$+ 2$
n	n^2	$2n$
$+ 3$	$3n$	6

Example When $n = 4$,

$(n + 2)(n + 3)$
$= (4 + 2)(4 + 3)$
$= 6 \times 7$
$= 42$

$n^2 + 5n + 6$
$= 4^2 + (5 \times 4) + 6$
$= 16 + 20 + 6$
$= 42$

♦ The total is: $n^2 + 2n + 3n + 6$
   which simplifies to: $n^2 + 5n + 6$

♦ This shows that $(n + 2)(n + 3) = n^2 + 5n + 6$ for any value of n so $(n + 2)(n + 3)$ and $n^2 + 5n + 6$ are **equivalent expressions**.

Exercise 15.6
Multiplying out brackets

1 For each of these, multiply out the brackets and simplify.

  a $(a + 1)(a + 3)$ **b** $(b + 2)(b + 4)$ **c** $(c + 8)(c + 5)$
  d $(d + 5)(d + 9)$ **e** $(e + 1)(e + 7)$ **f** $(f + 2)(f + 11)$

$(x + 1)^2$
is shorthand for
$(x + 1)(x + 1)$

2 **a** For each of these, multiply out the brackets and simplify.
     i $(x + 1)^2$ **ii** $(x + 2)^2$ **iii** $(x + 3)^2$
  b Comment on any pattern you see in your results.

3 **a** Which of these expressions gives the area of the rectangle?

   A $n^2 + 10n + 7$ **B** $n^2 + 10n + 10$

   C $n^2 + 7n + 7$ **D** $n^2 + 7n + 10$

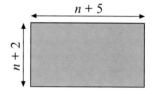

  b Explain your answer.

4 Copy and complete:

×	$2x$	$+ 4$
$3x$	☐	☐
$+ 1$	☐	☐

   So $(2x + 4)(3x + 1) =$ ☐

5 Which of these expressions is equivalent to $(4x + 1)(5x + 2)$?

   A $33x^2 + 2$ **B** $20x^2 + 13x + 2$ **C** $9x^2 + 13x + 3$ **D** $9x + 3$

6 For each of these, multiply out the brackets and simplify.

  a $(2a + 1)(a + 4)$ **b** $(b + 3)(3b + 5)$ **c** $(2c + 7)(3c + 2)$
  d $(4d + 3)(3d + 4)$ **e** $(2e + 3)(2e + 3)$ **f** $(5f + 1)(5f + 1)$

7   Jo and Liz investigate the sequence: 4, 10, 18, 28, 40, ...
     Each finds an expression for the nth term.

     Jo: $n(n + 3)$ Liz: $(n + 1)(n + 2) - 2$

     a   Show that each expression gives 40 for the 5th term in the sequence.
     b   Show that these two expressions are equivalent.

8   Show that these two formulas are equivalent.

     A $y = 4x(x + 2)$ B $y = (2x + 1)(2x + 3) - 3$

Expressions that involve subtraction can also be multiplied using a table.

Example $(2y + 5)(3y - 1) = (2y + 5) \times (3y - 1)$

◆ Work in a table:

$\times$	$2y$	$+ 5$
$3y$	$6y^2$	$15y$
$- 1$	$- 2y$	$- 5$

◆ The total is: $6y^2 + 15y - 2y - 5$
  which simplifies to: $6y^2 + 13y - 5$

◆ So $(2y + 5)(3y - 1) = 6y^2 + 13y - 5$.

Exercise 15.7
Multiplying out brackets

1   Which of these expressions is equivalent to $(n + 5)(n - 2)$?

     A $n^2 + 3n - 10$ B $n^2 + 7n - 10$ C $n^2 + 3n + 10$ D $n^2 + 7n + 10$

2   Find four pairs of equivalent expressions.

     A $(2a + 3)(a - 2)$ B $(2a - 3)(a + 2)$ C $(2a - 1)(a + 6)$

     D $(2a - 1)(a - 6)$ E $2a^2 - 13a - 6$ F $2a^2 + a - 6$

     G $2a^2 - 13a + 6$ H $2a^2 + 11a - 6$ I $2a^2 - a - 6$

3   For each of these, multiply out the brackets and simplify.
     a $(a - 1)(a + 3)$ b $(b + 2)(b - 4)$ c $(c - 8)(c - 5)$
     d $(2d - 5)(d + 9)$ e $(2e + 1)(3e - 7)$ f $(2f - 2)(5f - 11)$

4   Which of these expressions is equivalent to $(2x + y)(5x + y)$?

     A $10x^2 + 7xy + y^2$ B $7x^2 + 10xy + y^2$ C $7x^2 + 7xy + y^2$

5   Which of these expressions is equivalent to $12a^2 + 5ab - 2b^2$?

     A $(6a - 2b)(2a + b)$ B $(12a + b)(a - 2b)$ C $(4a - b)(3a + 2b)$

6   For each of these, multiply out the brackets and simplify.
     a $(z + t)(2z + t)$ b $(3k + m)(2k + 5m)$ c $(2c + 3d)(c + 7d)$
     d $(3p - q)(2p + 5q)$ e $(f - g)(5f - 3g)$ f $(7w - v)(7w + v)$

Thinking ahead to ...
factorising

A   Which pair of expressions multiply to give $x^2 + 8x + 12$?

$x + 1$ $x + 2$ $x + 3$ $x + 4$ $x + 6$ $x + 12$

B   **a**   Draw up this table so that
it gives a total of $p^2 + 5p - 14$.

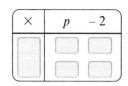

Total: $p^2 + 5p - 14$

b   Copy and complete: $(p - 2)(\ldots) = p^2 + 5p - 14$.

Factorising

> $48 = 12 \times 4$
> so 12 and 4 are factors of 48.
>
> $n^2 + 5n + 6 = (n + 2)(n + 3)$
> so $(n + 2)$ and $(n + 3)$ are
> factors of $n^2 + 5n + 6$.

To **factorise** an expression is to write it as a multiplication of its factors.

Example   Factorise $n^2 + 2n - 8$:

♦ Think about a table that
gives a total of $n^2 + 2n - 8$ and
fill in the parts you are sure about.

$\times$	n
n	n^2
	-8

♦ Try values that give -8 in the correct position.

$\times$	n	-4
n	n^2	$-4n$
-2	$2n$	-8

❖ The total for this table is $n^2 - 2n - 8$
which **is not** what you want.

$\times$	n	$+4$
n	n^2	$4n$
-2	$-2n$	-8

❖ The total for this table is $n^2 + 2n - 8$
which **is** what you want.

♦ So $n^2 + 2n - 8$ factorises to give $(n + 4)(n - 2)$ or $(n - 2)(n + 4)$

Exercise 15.8
Factorising

1   Factorise these expressions.

    a $x^2 + 8x + 7$ **b** $x^2 + 3x + 2$ **c** $x^2 + 4x + 3$
    d $x^2 + 8x + 12$ **e** $x^2 + 6x + 9$ **f** $x^2 + 13x + 36$

2   Copy and complete these statements.

    a $x^2 + 6x + \square = (x + 4)(x + 2)$ **b** $x^2 + 6x + \square = (x + 5)(x + 1)$
    c $x^2 + \square x + 10 = (x + 5)(x + 2)$ **d** $x^2 - \square x + 10 = (x - 1)(x - 10)$
    e $x^2 + 7x + 12 = (x + 4)(\boxed{})$ **f** $x^2 - 10x - 11 = (x + 1)(\boxed{})$

3 $x + 1$ $x - 1$ $x + 2$ $x - 2$ $x + 4$ $x - 4$

    Which pair of expressions multiply to give:

    a $x^2 - 3x - 4$ **b** $x^2 - 6x + 8$?

4   Factorise these expressions.

    a $x^2 + 2x - 3$ **b** $x^2 + 3x - 10$ **c** $x^2 - 4x - 5$
    d $x^2 - 3x - 28$ **e** $x^2 - 8x + 15$ **f** $x^2 - 5x + 6$

End points

You should be able to ...   ... so try these questions

A Substitute in formulas

A1 When a stone is thrown straight up with a speed of u m/s, the formula:
$$h = ut - 5t^2$$
gives its approximate height, h metres, after t seconds.

A stone is thrown upwards with a speed of 60 m/s.
What is its height after:
a 2 seconds   **b** 5 seconds   **c** 10 seconds?

A2 The formula for the volume (V) of a cone is:
$$V = \tfrac{1}{3}\pi r^2 h,$$
where r is the radius of the base and h is the height.

A cone has a base of radius 2.5 cm and a height of 8 cm.
Calculate its volume in cm^3.

B Rearrange formulas

B1 A car hire company uses this formula to calculate the cost in pounds, C, of hiring a car for n days:
$$C = 30n + 20$$
a Make n the subject of the formula.
b With £470, for how many days could you hire a car?

B2 Asif uses this formula to calculate the cost of running his car for a week:
$$C = 10 + \tfrac{1}{5}m,$$
where C is the cost in pounds and m is the number of miles he drives.

a Make m the subject of the formula.
b Asif wants the cost of running his car to be £30 or less per week. What is the maximum number of miles he can drive in a week?

B3 Make k the subject of each formula:
a $h = 5k^2$ **b** $m = \dfrac{n+k}{5}$ **c** $A = k^2 + 9$

C Multiply out brackets

C1 Which of these expressions is equivalent to $(t+5)(t-3)$?
A $t^2 + 8t + 15$ **B** $t^2 + 8t - 15$ **C** $t^2 + 2t - 15$

C2 For each of these, multiply out the brackets and simplify.
a $(a+1)(a+8)$ **b** $(b+4)^2$ **c** $(5c+2)(c+3)$
d $(d+2)(d-1)$ **e** $(2e+5)(3e-10)$ **f** $(f-7)(3f-2)$

D Factorise expressions

D1 Which pair of expressions multiply to give $k^2 + 5k - 14$?
$k+2$ $k-7$ $k-2$ $k+14$ $k+7$ $k-1$

D2 Factorise these expressions.
a $x^2 + 12x + 11$ **b** $x^2 + 9x + 14$ **c** $x^2 + 4x - 5$
d $x^2 + x - 6$ **e** $x^2 - x - 20$ **f** $x^2 - 5x + 6$

Starting points
You need to know about ...

... so try these questions.

A Finding the median of a frequency distribution

- You can always find the median of ungrouped data by:
  - listing the data in order
  - finding the middle value (or the middle pair of values).

 1996 Olympic Games – Pole Vault Final
Best height cleared by each finalist

Height (metres)	5.60	5.70	5.80	5.86	5.92	Total
Frequency	4	3	1	3	3	14

5.60 5.60 5.60 5.60 5.70 5.70 | 5.70 5.80 | 5.86 5.86 5.86 5.92 5.92 5.92

The median is halfway between the middle pair, so
median height = **5.75 m**

- For a distribution with a large total frequency, using cumulative frequencies is quicker than listing the data.

1996 Olympic Games – Pole Vault Final
Heights cleared by the 14 finalists

Height (metres)	5.40	5.60	5.70	5.80	5.86	5.92	Total
Frequency	6	10	5	4	6	3	34
Cumulative Frequency	6	16	21	25	31	34	

The middle pair (the 17th and 18th) are both 5.70, so median height = **5.70 m**

B Calculating the mean of a frequency distribution

- To calculate the mean of ungrouped data:
  - multiply each value by its frequency
  - calculate the total of all the values

**1996 Olympic Games
Pole Vault Final**
Heights cleared by finalists

Height (metres)	Frequency		Total at each height
5.40	6	5.40 × 6	32.4
5.60	10	5.60 × 10	56
5.70	5	5.70 × 5	28.5
5.80	4	5.80 × 4	23.2
5.86	6	5.86 × 6	35.16
5.92	3	5.92 × 3	17.76
Totals	34		193.02

- divide the total of all the values by the total frequency.

$$\text{Mean height} = \frac{193.02}{34} = 5.68\,\text{m (to 3 sf).}$$

**1996 Olympic Games
Men's High Jump Final**

Height (metres)	Frequency	
	Best height cleared	All heights cleared
2.15	–	3
2.20	–	9
2.25	4	12
2.29	3	8
2.32	4	6
2.35	1	3
2.37	1	1
2.39	1	1
Totals	14	43

A1 For the best-height distribution, find the median height cleared by listing the data.

A2 For the all-heights distribution, use cumulative frequencies to find the median height cleared.

**1996 Olympic Games
Women's High Jump Final**

Height (metres)	Frequency	
	Best height cleared	All heights cleared
1.80	–	8
1.85	–	14
1.90	–	13
1.93	5	14
1.96	4	9
1.99	2	5
2.01	1	3
2.03	1	2
2.05	1	1
Totals	14	69

B1 For the best-height distribution, calculate the mean height cleared.

B2 For the all-heights distribution, calculate the mean height cleared.

C Measures of spread

♦ The range is the simplest measure of how spread out a set of data is.

1996 Olympic Games – Pole Vault Final
Best height cleared by each finalist

Height (metres)	5.60	5.70	5.80	5.86	5.92	Total
Frequency	4	3	1	3	3	14

$$\text{Range} = \text{Highest value} - \text{Lowest value}$$
$$= 5.92 - 5.60$$
$$= \mathbf{0.32\,m}$$

♦ The interquartile range measures the spread of the middle 50% of the distribution by ignoring the lowest 25% and the highest 25%.

5.60 5.60 5.60 5|60 5.70 5.70 5.70 | 5.80 5.86 5.86 5|86 5.92 5.92 5.92

$$\text{Interquartile range} = \text{Upper quartile} - \text{Lower quartile}$$
$$= 5.86 - 5.60$$
$$= \mathbf{0.26\,m}$$

D Comparing sets of data

♦ You can compare sets of data using two types of value:
an average, and a measure of spread.

1996 Olympic Games – Pole Vault Finals
Best heights cleared by finalists

	1992	1996
Median	5.625 m	5.75 m
Interquartile range	0.35 m	0.26 m

On average, finalists jumped 12.5 cm higher in 1996 than in 1992.
The finalists were more closely matched in 1996 because the best heights cleared were less spread out than in 1992.

E Using grouped data

♦ Data which is collected in groups, or grouped to make it easier to present, is called a **grouped frequency distribution**.

1996 Olympic Games – Great Britain's Athletics Team

Age	18 – 22	23 – 27	28 – 32	33 – 37	38 – 42	Total
Frequency	9	37	27	5	4	82

♦ Each group of data is a **class**: the size of a class is the **class interval**.

The 18 – 22 class has a class interval of 5 years.

♦ You can show grouped data on a **grouped frequency diagram**.

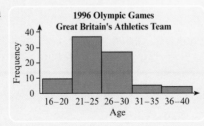

1996 Olympic Games
Great Britain's Athletics Team

C1 Use the data for the high jump finals on page 197 to calculate the range of the best heights cleared for:
a men **b** women.

C2 Calculate the interquartile range of the best heights cleared for:
a men **b** women.

1992 Olympic Games
High Jump Finals
Best heights cleared by finalists

Median – men	2.295 m
Mean – women	1.91 m
Interquartile range	
– men	0.06 m
– women	0.085 m

D1 Use your answers to Questions **A1**, **B1**, and **C2** to compare the best heights cleared in 1992 and 1996 by:
a men **b** women.

1996 Olympic Games
Great Britain's Athletics Team

Women		Men	
Age	Frequency	Age	Frequency
18 – 23	8	18 – 21	3
24 – 29	13	22 – 25	17
30 – 35	10	26 – 29	14
36 – 41	3	30 – 33	8
Total	34	34 – 37	5
		38 – 41	1
		Total	48

E1 Give the class interval for:
a women **b** men.

E2 Draw a grouped frequency diagram to show the ages of:
a women **b** men.

Histograms and frequency polygons

- A grouped frequency diagram is also called a **histogram**.
- The class with the highest frequency is called the **modal class**.
- A **frequency polygon** is a set of straight lines joining the middle points on the top of each bar of a histogram.

The frequency is the number of golfers.

153 golfers played in the 1st and 2nd rounds. These scores are for the top 77 golfers after the 2nd round. Only these 77 golfers played in the 3rd and 4th rounds.

- You can compare frequency distributions on the same diagram by plotting the frequency polygon for each distribution.

The middle scores of each of the classes are 65, 68, 71, 74, 77, 80.

These can be called the **mid-class values**.

The frequencies are plotted against the middle scores.

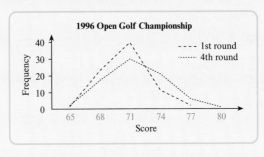

Exercise 16.1
Histograms and frequency polygons

1 Use the histograms to give the modal class for:
   a   the 1st round scores   b   the 4th round scores

2 Golfers aim for as low a score as possible in a round.
   a   Do you think the golfers did better in the 1st round or the 4th round?
   b   Use the frequency polygons to explain your answer.

3 These are the ages of the 153 golfers who played in the 1996 Championship.

Age	17–27	28–38	39–49	50–60	Total
Frequency					
Qualifiers	18	34	22	3	77
Non-qualifiers	14	52	9	1	76

Qualifiers are those golfers who played in all 4 rounds. Non-qualifiers only played in the first 2 rounds.

   a   List the eleven different ages in the 17 – 27 class.
   b   Which age is the mid-class value?
   c   List the mid-class values for each class in the age data.

4 a   Copy these axes on to squared paper.
   b   Label your horizontal axis.
   c   Draw frequency polygons to compare the ages of the qualifiers and non-qualifiers.

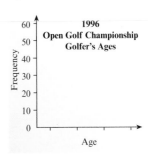

5 Do you think frequency polygons would give a good comparison if there were 97 qualifiers and 56 non-qualifiers? Give reasons for your answer.

Thinking ahead to ...
estimating the range

1996 Open Golf Championship
4th round scores

Score	64–66	67–69	70–72	73–75	76–78	79–81
Frequency	2	17	30	21	6	1

A List the three possible scores which could be:

   a the lowest score   **b** the highest score.

B List the five possible values for the range of the 4th round scores.

C Which single value do you think is the best one to use for the range? Why?

Estimating the range and the total

You cannot calculate the exact range of a set of grouped data because:
- the lowest value could be any value in the first class
- the highest value could be any value in the last class.

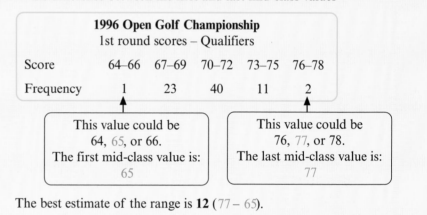

- The best estimate of the range is given by:
  - the difference between the first and last mid-class values

1996 Open Golf Championship
1st round scores – Qualifiers

Score	64–66	67–69	70–72	73–75	76–78
Frequency	1	23	40	11	2

This value could be 64, 65, or 66.
The first mid-class value is: 65

This value could be 76, 77, or 78.
The last mid-class value is: 77

The best estimate of the range is **12** (77 – 65).

Exercise 16.2
Estimating the range and the total

1996 Open Golf Championship
1st round scores – Non-qualifiers

Score	67 – 70	71 – 74	75 – 78	79 – 82
Frequency	4	45	23	4

1996 Open Golf Championship
2nd round scores – Non-qualifiers

Score	67 – 71	72 – 76	77 – 81	82 – 86
Frequency	11	53	11	1

1 For the 2nd round scores:

   a give the class interval

   b list the mid-class values

   c estimate the range of the scores.

The mid-class values here are not integers.

2 Repeat Question **1** for the 1st round scores.

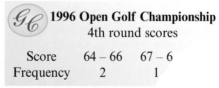

1996 Open Golf Championship
4th round scores

Score	64 – 66	67 – 6
Frequency	2	1

3 **a** List the five possible totals of the scores in the 64 – 66 class.

   b Multiply the mid-class value by the frequency.

   c Why is this the best estimate of the total of the scores for the class?

The **decathlon** is held over two days and consists of 10 events.

Day 1	Day 2
100 m	110 m hurdles
Long jump	Discus
Shot	Pole vault
High jump	Javelin
400 m	1500 m

1996 Olympic Games – Decathlon (Day 2)
Points scored in each of the 5 events by the top 10 decathletes

Points	400 – 499	500 – 599	600 – 699	700 – 799	800 – 899	900 – 999	1000 – 1099	Total
Frequency	1	0	8	10	17	10	4	50

◆ To estimate the total of a grouped frequency distribution:
   ❖ write the data in vertical columns [A]
   ❖ find the mid-class value for each class [B]
   ❖ estimate the total for each class [C] (Frequency × Mid-class value)
   ❖ add up the estimated class totals [D]

The **exact** mid-class value of the 400 – 499 class is 449.5
You can use the simpler value of 450 because you are only calculating an **estimate** of the total points score.

	[A]		[B]	[C]
	Points	Frequency	Mid-class value	Estimated class total
	400 – 499	1	450	450
	500 – 599	0	550	0
	600 – 699	8	650	5200
	700 – 799	10	750	7500
	800 – 899	17	850	14450
	900 – 999	10	950	9500
	1000 – 1099	4	1050	4200
	Totals	50		**41300** [D]

Exercise 16.3
Estimating the total

1

1996 Olympic Games – Decathlon (Day 1)
Points scored in each of the 5 events by the top 10 decathletes

Points	700 – 799	800 – 899	900 – 999	1000 – 1099	Total
Frequency	8	23	16	3	50

Calculate an estimate of the total points scored on day 1.

Alex Kruger (GB) retired on day 1 of the decathlon with a knee injury.

2

1996 Olympic Games – Decathlon
Total points scored by each decathlete

Points	6500 – 6999	7000 – 7499	7500 – 7999	8000 – 8499	8500 – 8999	Total
Frequency	1	1	7	16	6	31

Calculate an estimate of the total points scored by the decathletes.

3 How many points do you think each decathlete scored on average?

4

The throws in the class 68 – are greater than, or equal to, 68 m but less than 70 m.

1996 Olympic Games – Discus Finals

Distance (metres)		56 –	58 –	60 –	62 –	64 –	66 –	68 –	Total
Frequency (of throws)	Women	2	5	10	13	13	4	2	49
	Men	2	3	8	16	13	1	2	45

Use mid-class values:
57, 59, 61, 63, 65, 67, 69.

Calculate an estimate of the total distance thrown by:
a women   **b** men

Estimating the mean

When comparing sets of data, you can only use the total of each set when the sets have the same total frequency.

When the total frequencies are different, you should compare the means of the sets.

1996 Olympic Games – Women's Discus Final

Distance (metres)	56 –	58 –	60 –	62 –	64 –	66 –	68 –	Total
Frequency	2	5	10	13	13	4	2	49

◆ To estimate the mean of a grouped frequency distribution:
  ❖ calculate an estimate of the total of the data

Distance (metres)	Frequency	Mid-class value	Estimated class total
56 –	2	57	114
58 –	5	59	295
60 –	10	61	610
62 –	13	63	819
64 –	13	65	845
66 –	4	67	268
68 –	2	69	138
Totals	49		3089

  ❖ divide the estimate of the total by the total frequency.

Estimate of mean distance = $\dfrac{3089}{49}$ = **63.0 m** (to 3 sf)

Exercise 16.4
Estimating the mean

1

1996 Olympic Games – Men's Discus Final

Distance (metres)	56 –	58 –	60 –	62 –	64 –	66 –	68 –	Total
Frequency	2	3	8	16	13	1	2	45

Calculate an estimate of the mean distance thrown in the men's discus final.

2 Do you think the women or the men threw better in their final? Give reasons for your answer.

3

1996 Olympic Games – Women's Shot Final

Distance (metres)	16.0 –	17.0 –	18.0 –	19.0 –	20.0 –	Total
Frequency	1	4	23	11	2	41

The 16.0 – class has a mid-class value of 16.5

Calculate an estimate of the mean distance thrown in the women's shot final.

4

1996 Olympic Games – Men's Shot Final

Distance (metres)	19.0 –	19.5 –	20.0 –	20.5 –	21.0 –	21.5 –	Total
Frequency	5	11	17	8	0	1	42

Calculate an estimate of the mean distance thrown in the men's shot final.

5 Use your answers to Questions **3** and **4** to compare the women and men.

6 **a** Investigate the effect of different sizes of class interval on the estimate of the mean.
  b Does your investigation support the statement:
  "The smaller the class interval, the better the estimate of the mean"?

Make up your own data and group it in different ways.

Testing a hypothesis

The reaction time is the length of time between the starter's gun firing and the rear foot leaving the starting block.

s is the abbreviation for seconds.

♦ A statement which can be tested by analysing data is a **hypothesis**.

For example, the following data can be used to test the hypothesis: "Athletes' reaction times are faster in finals than in semifinals"

Men's 100 m Final

	Reaction time (s)
Bailey	0.174
Fredericks	0.143
Boldon	0.164
Mitchell	0.145
Marsh	0.147
Ezinwa	0.157
Green	0.169
Christie	DISQ

Men's 200 m Final

	Reaction time (s)
Johnson	0.161
Fredericks	0.200
Boldon	0.208
Thompson	0.202
Williams	0.182
Garcia	0.229
Stevens	0.151
Marsh	0.167

110 m Hurdles Final

	Reaction time (s)
Johnson	0.170
Crear	0.124
Schwarthoff	0.164
Jackson	0.133
Valle	0.179
Swift	0.151
Vander-Kuyp	0.167
Batte	0.160

Linford Christie (GB), the 100 m Gold Medal winner in 1992, was disqualified after a second false start when his recorded reaction time was 0.086 s.

Scientists believe a reaction time under one-tenth (0.100) of a second is impossible.

Women's 100 m Final

	Reaction time (s)
Devers	0.166
Ottey	0.166
Torrence	0.151
Sturrup	0.176
Trandenkova	0.151
Voronova	0.133
Onyali	0.174
Pintusevych	0.176

Women's 200 m Final

	Reaction time (s)
Perec	0.174
Ottey	0.194
Onyali	0.231
Miller	0.172
Malchugina	0.198
Sturrup	0.165
Cuthbert	0.175
Guidry	0.207

100 m Hurdles Final

	Reaction time (s)
Engquist	0.132
Bukovec	0.164
Girard-Leno	0.133
Devers	0.189
Rose	0.179
Freeman	0.181
Shekhodanova	0.175
Goode	0.160

1996 Olympic Games – Reaction Times
Semifinals – 100 m, 200 m, 100 m/110 m Hurdles

Reaction time (s)	0.120–	0.140–	0.160–	0.180–	0.200–	0.220–	0.240–	0.260–	Total
Frequency	7	24	30	22	4	3	3	1	94

Exercise 16.5
Testing a hypothesis

1 Group the data for the six finals in the same way as the semifinals data.

2 a Calculate an estimate of the range of the reaction times for:
    i the semifinals   ii the finals.
  b Calculate an estimate of the mean reaction time for:
    i the semifinals   ii the finals.

3 Do you think the hypothesis is true or false? Why?

There were exactly twice as many semifinalists as finalists.

4 a Copy your grouped frequency distribution from Question **1**, and double each of the frequencies.
  b Draw a frequency polygon to show this new distribution.
  c On the same diagram, draw a frequency polygon for the semifinalists.
  d Do you think your frequency polygons give a fair comparison of the reaction times in the finals and semifinals?
    Explain your answer.

Thinking ahead to ...
measuring and accuracy

A Which of these numbers could be rounded to 12.7?

12.73   12.76   12.68   12.749   12.75

B A number has been rounded to 1 dp to give 9.3.
Give three possible values for the number:

a to 2 dp   **b** to 3 dp.

Measuring and accuracy

♦ Data which results from measuring, such as heights, distances, weights and times, can be given to different degrees of accuracy.
For instance, times are often given to:
   the nearest one-tenth (0.1) of a second, or
   the nearest one-hundredth (0.01) of a second, or
   the nearest one-thousandth (0.001) of a second.

♦ The **limits of accuracy** of a measurement are the values between which the exact measurement must lie.
For instance, the limits of accuracy of a time measured as 9.83 seconds are:
   9.825 seconds and **9.835** seconds.

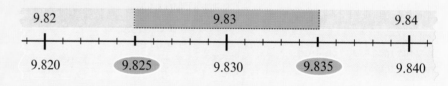

Exercise 16.6
Measuring and accuracy

1 Draw a diagram to show the limits of accuracy of:

a 9.84 seconds   **b** 7.12 metres   **c** 0.82 metres   **d** 0.174 seconds

2 Give the limits of accuracy of these measurements.

a 12.38 seconds   **b** 9.2 metres   **c** 7.3 seconds   **d** 7.30 seconds

♦ Times and distances in athletics events are not measured to the **nearest** unit.
All times are rounded up to the **next** one-hundredth of a second.
For instance, the limits of accuracy of a time given as 9.83 seconds are:
   9.820 seconds and **9.830** seconds.

Exercise 16.7
Measuring in athletics

1 Gail Devers and Merlene Ottey were given the same time in the final of the women's 100 m.
Give the limits of accuracy of their time.

2 Jackie Joyner-Kersee jumped 7.00 metres in the women's long jump final.
Give the limits of accuracy of her distance.

All distances are rounded down to the next centimetre.

Women's 100 m Final	
	Time (s)
Devers	10.94
Ottey	10.94
Torrence	10.96
Sturrup	11.00

3 Explain why it is appropriate in athletics events to round times up to the next unit, and distances down to the next unit.

Drawing a cumulative frequency curve

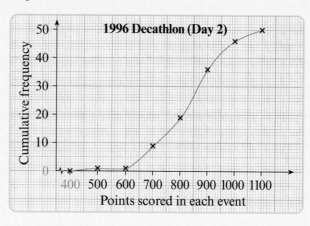

1996 Olympic Games – Decathlon (Day 2)
Points scored in each of the 5 events by the top 10 decathletes

Points	400 – 499	500 – 599	600 – 699	700 – 799	800 – 899	900 – 999	1000 – 1099	Total
Frequency	1	0	8	10	17	10	4	50

- ◆ To draw a cumulative frequency curve:
  - ❖ construct a cumulative frequency table

Points	<400	<500	<600	<700	<800	<900	<1000	<1100
Cumulative frequency	0	1	1	9	19	36	46	50

> If you include a cumulative frequency of 0 in your table then you have a point to start the curve from: (400, 0)

- ❖ plot the cumulative frequencies on a graph
- ❖ join the points with a smooth curve.

Exercise 16.8
Drawing cumulative
frequency curves

1

1996 Olympic Games – Decathlon (Day 1)
Points scored in each of the 5 events by the top 10 decathletes

Points	700 – 799	800 – 899	900 – 999	1000 – 1099	Total
Frequency	8	23	16	3	50

a Copy and complete the cumulative frequency table below.

Points	<700	<800	<900	<1000	<1100
Cumulative frequency	0				

b Use your table to draw a cumulative frequency curve.

> Steve Backley (GB) won the javelin silver medal with the very first throw of the final.

2

1996 Olympic Games – Men's Javelin Final

Distance (metres)	76 –	78 –	80 –	82 –	84 –	86 –	88 –	Total
Frequency		2	4	14	13	8	6	1	48

a Copy and complete the cumulative frequency table below.

Distance (metres)	<76	<78	<80	<82	<84	<86	<88	<90
Cumulative frequency	0	2	6					

b Draw a cumulative frequency curve for the men's javelin final.

3 Using your answers to Question **2**, can you think of a way to find the median distance thrown in the final? Explain your method.

Estimating the median and the interquartile range

There were 48 throws in the final, so the **exact** median distance is halfway between the 24th and 25th longest.

It is impossible to find these distances from the table, so you can only **estimate** the median.

♦ A cumulative frequency table shows which class the median is in.

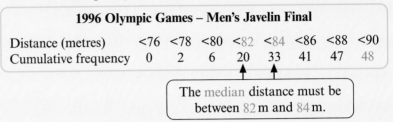

1996 Olympic Games – Men's Javelin Final

Distance (metres)	<76	<78	<80	<82	<84	<86	<88	<90
Cumulative frequency	0	2	6	20	33	41	47	48

The median distance must be between 82 m and 84 m.

As you are only estimating distances within the classes, you can divide the 48 throws into four quarters, using the **12th**, **24th**, and **36th** longest (cumulative frequencies 12, 24, and 36).

♦ To estimate median and quartiles from a cumulative frequency curve:
  ❖ divide the cumulative frequency into four quarters
  ❖ go across to the curve, then go down and read off each value.

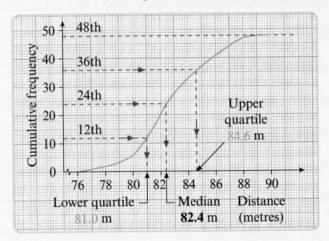

Estimate of median distance = **82.4 m**

Estimate of interquartile range = 84.6 − 81.0
                                              = **3.6 m**

Exercise 16.9
Estimating the median and interquartile range

1 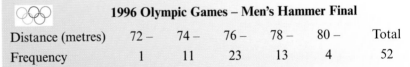 **1996 Olympic Games – Men's Hammer Final**

Distance (metres)	72 –	74 –	76 –	78 –	80 –	Total
Frequency	1	11	23	13	4	52

a Copy and complete the cumulative frequency table below.

Distance (metres)	<72	<74	<76	<78	<80	<82
Cumulative frequency	0	1	12			

b Draw a cumulative frequency curve for the men's hammer final.

2 Use your cumulative frequency curve to estimate:

  a the median distance thrown   **b** the interquartile range.

3 Compare the distances thrown in the men's hammer final and the men's javelin final.

4 **a** From page 205, copy the cumulative frequency table and the cumulative frequency curve for the decathlon (day 2).
  b Estimate the median points score.
  c Estimate the interquartile range of the scores.

Use cumulative frequencies 12.5, 25, and 37.5 to divide the data into four quarters.

> Use cumulative frequencies 12.5, 25, and 37.5 to divide the data into four quarters.

5 Use your answers to Exercise 16.8, Question **1** to estimate:
  a the median points score on day 1 of the decathlon
  b the interquartile range of the scores.

6 Compare the points scored on days 1 and 2 of the decathlon.

7

	1996 Olympic Games – Women's Javelin Final						
Distance (metres)	56 –	58 –	60 –	62 –	64 –	66 –	Total
Frequency	7	11	10	10	7	1	46

  a Make a cumulative frequency table for the women's javelin final.
  b Draw a cumulative frequency curve.

8 **a** Decide how to divide the data into four quarters.
  b Estimate the median distance thrown and the interquartile range.

Estimating cumulative frequencies

♦ You can estimate cumulative frequencies from a cumulative frequency curve.

Example Estimate how many throws were:
  a less than 81.5 m   **b** greater than 85 m.

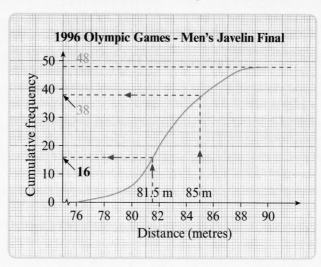

  a Estimated number of throws less than 81.5 m = **16**

  b Estimated number of throws greater than 85 m = 48 – 38
                                                   = **10**

Exercise 16.10
Estimating cumulative
frequencies

1 Use your cumulative frequency curve from Exercise 16.9, Question **1** to estimate how many throws were less than 75 m.

2 The winning throw in the 1976 men's hammer final was 77.52 m. Estimate how many throws were greater than this in 1996.

3

> Jonathan Edwards (GB) won the silver medal in the triple jump.

	1996 Olympic Games – Men's Triple Jump Final						
Distance (metres)	15.5 –	16.0 –	16.5 –	17.0 –	17.5 –	18.0 –	Total
Frequency	1	7	14	6	2	1	31

  a Draw a cumulative frequency curve for the men's triple jump final.
  b Estimate how many jumps were greater than 16.8 m.

End points

You should be able to ... **... so try these questions**

A Use histograms and
frequency polygons

1996 Olympic Games – Reaction Times
Semifinals & Finals – 100 m, 200 m, 100 m/110 m Hurdles

Reaction time (s)	0.12–	0.14–	0.16–	0.18–	0.20–	0.22–	0.24–	0.26–	Total
Frequency Men	7	22	23	10	3	2	2	1	70
Women	5	10	30	17	5	3	1	0	71

A1 Draw a histogram to show the reaction times for:
a men **b** women.

A2 Give the modal class for:
a men **b** women.

A3 **a** Draw frequency polygons for reaction times of men and women.
b List the differences between the two distributions.

1996 Olympic Games – Long Jump Finals

Distance (metres)	6.2 –	6.4 –	6.6 –	6.8 –	7.0 –	Total
Women's Frequency	3	6	9	14	3	35

Distance (metres)	6.4 –	6.8 –	7.2 –	7.6 –	8.0 –	8.4 –	Total
Men's Frequency	1	1	3	17	15	1	38

B Estimate the median and
the interquartile range

B1 **a** Make a cumulative frequency table for the men's long jump final.
b Draw a cumulative frequency curve.
c Use your cumulative frequency curve to estimate:
i the median distance jumped **ii** the interquartile range.

C Calculate estimates of the
mean and the range

C1 Estimate the range of the distances jumped in:
a the women's final **b** the men's final.

C2 Calculate an estimate of the mean distance jumped in:
a the women's final **b** the men's final.

D Compare grouped
frequency distributions

D1 Compare the distances jumped in the women's and men's finals.

E Estimate cumulative frequencies

E1 ### 1996 Olympic Games – Women's Triple Jump Final

Distance (metres)	13.5 –	14.0 –	14.5 –	15.0 –	Total
Frequency	15	21	10	1	47

a Draw a cumulative frequency curve for the women's triple jump final.
b Use your curve to estimate how many jumps were:
i less than 13.8 m **ii** greater than 14.4 m

Some points to remember

♦ You cannot find the modal value of a set of data when it is grouped,
but you can identify the modal class (the class with the highest frequency).

♦ You cannot find **exact** values of the mean, the median, the range and the interquartile range,
of grouped data, but you can calculate an **estimate** of each.

♦ When you estimate the mean of grouped data, usually the smaller the class interval the closer
the estimate is to the exact mean.

Starting points
You need to know about ...

... so try these questions

A Writing fractions as decimals and percentages

♦ To write a fraction as a decimal:
  ❖ divide the numerator by the denominator.

$$\tfrac{3}{8} = 3 \div 8 = 0.375 = 37.5\%$$ $$\tfrac{5}{6} = 5 \div 6 = 0.83... = 83.\dot{3}\%$$

$$\tfrac{7}{4} = 7 \div 4 = 1.75 = 175\%$$ $$\tfrac{5}{3} = 5 \div 3 = 1.6... = 166.\dot{6}\%$$

B Calculating a percentage of a given amount

♦ To calculate 50% of an amount simply:
calculate half the amount by dividing by 2 (50% = $\tfrac{1}{2}$)
To calculate 25% of an amount simply:
calculate a quarter of the amount by dividing by 4.
Some other percentages can be calculated in a similar way.

To calculate 65% of an amount is not as easy.
This is one way: calculate 1%, and then use it to find 65%.

Example   Find 65% of 420 kg:

100%	420
Divide both sides by 100:	
1%	4.20
Multiply both sides by 65:	
65%	273

So 65% of 420 kg is 273 kg.

C Interpreting a calculator display in calculations with money

Interpreting a calculator display correctly is important, particularly when you are dealing with units of money.

For example, when you calculate 24% of £15 the calculator may display the answer as:

| 3.6 |

The calculation is in pounds so the answer is: **£3.60**
(£3.60 is 24% of £15)
When you calculate 24% of £1.50 the calculator displays the answer as:

| 0.36 |

The calculation is in pounds so the answer is: **£0.36**
(£0.36 is 24% of £1.50)
But an amount of money is not usually written as £0.36.
It is more likely that the amount is given as 36 pence.
So 24% of £1.50 is 36 pence.

A1 Write each of these as a decimal and as a percentage:

a $\tfrac{3}{4}$ b $\tfrac{5}{8}$ c $\tfrac{8}{5}$ d $\tfrac{5}{4}$

e $\tfrac{6}{5}$ f $\tfrac{13}{20}$ g $\tfrac{8}{32}$ h $\tfrac{9}{6}$

i $\tfrac{7}{16}$ j $\tfrac{16}{7}$ k $\tfrac{9}{8}$ l $\tfrac{18}{10}$

B1 Calculate:
a 50% of 650 miles
b 75% of £400
c 10% of 20 marks
d 72% of 3450
e 25% of 40 marks
f 36% of 475 kg
g 58% of £415
h 12% of 3 kg
i 7% of £2.50
j 4.5% of 360 metres
k 38% of £4.50
l 15% of 12 cm
m 25% of £25
n 80% of 3 miles.

C1 In each of these calculations interpret your calculator display to give the answer in the units asked for.
a Calculate 16% of £85
   (answer in pounds).
b Calculate 14% of 4 cm
   (answer in millimetres).
c Find 44% of 3.5 kg
   (answer in grams).
d Find 9% of £2.27
   (answer in pence).
e What is 78% of 65 mm:
   i in millimetres
   ii in centimetres?
f What is 12.5% of 72 pence:
   i in pence
   ii in pounds?
g Give 35% of 4 tonnes in:
   i tonnes   ii kilograms.

Writing one number as a percentage of another

When you compare two numbers, you can think of:
one number as a percentage of the other.

For instance, with the numbers 18 and 36 one comparison is:
18 is half of 36, or 18 is 50% of 36.

So 18 as a percentage of 36 is 50%.

When you compare numbers you might have to approximate one number as a percentage of the other.

Example

With the numbers 17 and 60, 17 is a little more than one quarter of 60.
So 17 as a percentage of 60 is a little more than 25%.

> You can also compare the numbers the other way round, e.g.
>
> 36 as a percentage of 18
>
> As 36 is twice 18:
> **36 as a percentage of 18 is 200%**

Exercise 17.1
Comparing numbers

1 What is 35 as a percentage of 70?

2 Give 64 as a percentage of 16.

3 Is 22 as a percentage of 28 a little more, or a little less than 75%?
Explain your answer.

4 A number p as a percentage of 80 is 10%.
   i What is the number p?
   ii Explain how you calculated your answer.

5 Roughly, what is 15 as a percentage of 32?

6 Two numbers k and j are chosen so that this rule is true:

   k as a percentage of j is 75%

   a Jo chooses the value 12 for k. What is the value of j?
   b Rashid chooses the value 28 for j. What is the value of k?
   c List four values you choose for k, and for each give the value of j that makes the rule true.

7 Ian chooses a whole number n and describes it in this way:
   n as a percentage of 40 is a little more than 20% but not as much as 25%.
   a What is the number chosen by Ian?
   b Explain how you calculated Ian's number.

8 This table shows the amount Jim spent each month on food. For each month give the amount spent on travel as a percentage of the total amount Jim spent.

	Amount spent on travel	Amount spent on food	Total amount spent
Oct	£6	£5	£24
Nov	£8	£20	£32
Dec	£12	£15	£60
Jan	£12	£16	£48
Feb	£12	£2	£16
Mar	£2	£5	£20

9 For the amount spent on food as a percentage of the total spent:
   a In which months was this exactly 25%?
   b In which month was it a little more than 30%?
   c What was it in November?

With the two numbers 18 and 36:
to find 18 as a percentage of 36, think of the comparison in this way:

- ◆ 18 is half of 36   or $18 \div 36 = 0.5$
- ◆ 18 is 50% of 36   or $0.5 \times 100 = 50\%$

This can be a single calculation:

$$(18 \div 36) \times 100 = 50\%$$
So 18 as a percentage of 36 is 50%

This method can be used to give any number as a percentage of another.
With any two numbers p and t:

You can **calculate p as a percentage of t in this way**: $(p \div t) \times \mathbf{100}$

Example

Jenny and Bruce walked from John O'Groats to Land's End for charity.
John O'Groats to Land's End is 868 miles.
By the end of day 4 they had walked 113 miles.
What percentage of the total distance is this?

To calculate 113 as a percentage of 868

$$(113 \div 868) \times 100 = 13.018 \ldots$$

By the end of day 4, they had travelled 13.0% (1 dp) of the total distance.

Exercise 17.2
Calculating one number as a percentage of another

1 Calculate, giving your answer correct to 2 dp:

  a 16 as a percentage of 36   **b** 52 as a percentage of 80
  c 14 as a percentage of 48   **d** 85 as a percentage of 184
  e 12 as a percentage of 15   **f** 1.5 as a percentage of 12
  g 0.75 as a percentage of 20   **h** 16 as a percentage of 12
  i 35 as a percentage of 21   **j** 15 as a percentage of 8.

2 A driving school uses this as part of their advertising:

> **70% of our students pass their test first time !**

In July 1997, they had 55 people who took their test for the first time, and 38 of them passed the test.

  a What percentage of those people who took their test for the first time in July 1997, passed the test?
  b How accurate is the advertising for the driving school?
     Explain your answer.

3 A sports club was sent a bill for repairs to its video camera.
The bill was for a total of £65.70, and only £9.20 of this was for parts.

What is the charge for parts as a percentage of the total bill?
Give your answer correct to the nearest whole number.

4 An old stadium had seating for 23 500 spectators.
The stadium was rebuilt, with seating in the new stadium for 40 000.

  a Give the seating of the new stadium as a percentage of the old seating.
     Give your answer correct to the nearest whole number.
  b Is your answer about what you expected?
     Give reasons for your answer.

Thinking ahead to ...
percentage changes

Often percentages are used to describe
a change in an amount.
For example, in supermarkets special offers
can be shown as:

Extra 15% FREE !

For the customer:

A How much extra is free?
Is it more or less than a quarter of the
amount for the normal price?

B What fraction would you use to
describe the extra free amount?

C How many ml of the product are in the special offer pack?

Percentage changes

When you increase an
amount by a percentage, you
will end up with **more than**
the **100%** you started with.

For example:
with an increase of 25%
there is the 100% you start
with, plus the 25% increase.

$$100\% + 25\% = 125\%$$

As a percentage of the start
value, the end value is 125%.

When a value increases by a percentage, the final value can be calculated in
different ways. Two methods are shown here.

Example

Toothpaste is sold in tubes containing 150 ml.
In a special offer, 12% extra toothpaste is put in the tube at the same price.
How much toothpaste is in the special offer tube?

Method 1
❖ Calculate 12% of 150 ml.
❖ Add the extra amount to the 150 ml.

So 150 ÷ 100   gives 1%
     150 ÷ 100 × 12 gives 12%
     So 12% of 150 is 18

The special offer tube contains **168 ml** of toothpaste   (168 = 150 + 18)

Method 2
Think of the toothpaste in this way:

   100% of the contents is 150 ml

The special offer tube has 12%
extra, so it must contain:

      112% of 150 ml

112 % as a fraction is $\frac{112}{100}$

112 % as a decimal is 1.12

Calculate 112% of 150:
      $150 \times 1.12 = 168$

The special offer tube contains
168 ml of toothpaste.

Exercise 17.3
Increasing a value by
a certain percentage

1 In a special offer, the 440 grams of coffee in a jar is to be increased by 10%.
a What percentage of the 440 grams of coffee are in the special offer jar?
b Calculate the amount of coffee in the special offer jar.

2 **a** Increase 350 kg by 18%   **b** Increase 447 km by 16%
c Increase 4.50 metres by 22%   **d** Increase £35 000 by 8%

3 In 1992 in the USA there were a total of 143 081 443 registered cars.
By the year 2010 it is estimated that this total will increase by 44%.
Estimate the number of registered cars in the USA in 2010.

4 A crisp manufacturer sells 25 gram bags of crisps. They decide to increase the
weight of crisps in a bag by 4%. Give the new weight of crisps per bag.

When you decrease an amount by a percentage, you will end up with **less than** the **100%** you started with.

Example

With a decrease of 25% there is the 100% you start with, minus the 25% decrease.

$$100\% - 25\% = 75\%$$

As a percentage of the start value, the end value is 75%.

You can also decrease an amount by a percentage using methods 1 and 2.

For example:
A fast food store decided to decrease the weight of packaging for their regular meals, which weighed 40 grams, by 18%.
Calculate the weight of the new packaging.

Method 1
- Calculate 18% of 40 grams.
- **Take** this weight from the 40 grams.

So 40 ÷ 100   gives 1%
    40 ÷ 100 × 18   gives 18%
So 18% of 40 is 7.2

The new regular meal packaging weighs **32.8 grams**
    (32.8 = 40 − 7.2)

Method 2
Think of the packaging in this way:

  100% of the contents weighs 40 g

The new packaging weighs 18% less, so it must weigh:

    82% of 40 grams

82% as a fraction is $\frac{82}{100}$

82% as a decimal is 0.82

Calculate 82% of 40:

    40 × 0.82 = 32.8

The new regular meal packaging weighs **32.8 grams**.

Exercise 17.4
Decreasing a value by a certain percentage

1　**a**　Decrease 380 kg by 18%.   **b**　Decrease 416 km by 27%.
    c　Decrease 22 metres by 4%.   **d**　Decrease £338 000 by 14%.
    e　Decrease £25.50 by 28%.   **f**　Decrease 28 600 tonnes by 42%.
    g　Decrease 5 300 000 by 11%.   **h**　Decrease 1.6 cm by 25%.

2　Anya grows strawberries for supermarkets.
Last year she used a total of 1560 kilograms of fertilizer.
Next year, she wants to decrease the amount of fertilizer used by 6%.

How much fertilizer would you expect to be used next year?
Give your answer correct to the nearest kilogram.

3　The car ferry *Vista* was built to carry a maximum of 1210 cars.
New safety rules mean that the number of cars must be reduced by 7%.

    a　What is the maximum number of cars for the *Vista* with the new rules?
    b　Explain the degree of accuracy you used, and why.

4　Before a bypass was built, an estimated 41 000 cars a day passed through the town of Ashington.
The bypass was supposed to reduce the cars in Ashington by 35%.

    a　Estimate how many cars passed through Ashington, per day, after the bypass had been built.
    b　How many fewer cars per day is this?

5　Last year the fishing boat *Emma K* landed 9210 kg of shell fish.
This year they expect shell fish landings to be reduced by 17%.

How much shell fish does the *Emma K* expect to land this year?

6　In a sale items were reduced by 20%. Before the sale a kettle cost £24.50

    a　What was the sale price of the kettle?
    b　How much was saved by someone who bought the kettle in the sale?

Looking ahead to ...
percentages and VAT

VAT is short for:
Value-added tax.

VAT is a tax added to the price of goods or services. It was introduced on: 1 April 1973 at a standard rate of 10%.

On 18 June 1979 the standard rate was increased to 15%.

On 1 April 1994 the standard rate was increased to 17.5%.

Shopkeepers, traders, and customers have had to calculate VAT since 1973.

When it was first introduced at 10%, one quick method was: "Divide by 10 and add it on."

When VAT was increased to 15%, a quick method was: "Divide by 10, half the answer, and add both amounts on."

A What quick method can you think of to calculate VAT at 17.5%?

B In 1995 Ria fitted a stair carpet and charged £200 + VAT at 17.5%. What was the total charge to fit the carpet?

C Peter bought a cycle tyre and was charged £12.50 + VAT at 17.5%.
  i What did he pay in total for the tyre?
  ii Explain any rounding you did when calculating the total.

Percentages and VAT

To calculate the total price of goods or services including VAT is the same as: increasing the cost price by the percentage VAT.

Example A garden shed is advertised for: **£114.99 + VAT at 17.5%**
Calculate the total charge for the shed.

117% as a decimal is 1.17.
118% as a decimal is 1.18.

117.5% is half-way between 117% and 118%.

As a decimal, 117.5% must be half-way between 1.170 and 1.180

which is 1.175.

Think of the total charge (cost price + VAT) for the shed in this way:

100% of the cost price + **17.5%** of the price (VAT)

The total charge for the shed is: **117.5%** of its cost price

117.5% as a decimal is 1.175

Calculate 117.5% of £114.99:
$$114.99 \times 1.175 = 135.113 \ldots$$

The total charge for the shed (including VAT) is:

£135.11 (to the nearest penny)

These examples are with VAT at 17.5%.

In all questions that involve VAT you must use the standard rate of VAT at the time.

If you are unsure, ask for the rate of VAT.

Or: you can calculate 17.5% of £144.99 and add this to £114.99

To calculate 17.5% of £114.99
$$114.99 \times 0.175 = 20.123 \ldots$$

The total charge (including VAT) is: £114.99 + £20.123 ...

£135.11 (to the nearest penny)

Exercise 17.5
Calculating prices that include VAT

1 The cost of these items is given without VAT (ex VAT). Calculate the charge, including VAT, for each item.

a camera £16	**b** trainers £44.25	**c** bike £185
d toaster £19.40	**e** pen 72 pence	**f** TV £368.42
g fridge £262	**h** mower £24.55	**i** CD £9.35

2 Jenny was told that repairs to her car would be £245. When she paid she found that the £245 did not include VAT.

  a How much did she pay, including VAT?
  b How much VAT was added to her bill?

Percentages and interest

From the *Oxford Mathematics Study Dictionary*.

Interest The interest is the amount of extra money paid in return for having the use of someone else's money.

When you borrow, or save money with a Bank, Building Society, The Post Office, a Credit Union, or a finance company, interest is *charged* or *paid*.

> Interest is: *charged* on money you borrow and *paid* on money you save.

per annum is a term that means each year.

> Interest is: *charged* or *paid* pa (per annum) and *charged* or *paid* at a fixed rate e.g. 6% pa.

You borrow £350 for one year at 9%. How much do you pay back in total?

At the end of a year you will pay back:

100% of the £350 + 9% interest
You will pay back a total of
109% of £350

Calculate 109% of £350:
$$350 \times 1.09 = 381.5$$

You will pay back a total of **£381.50**

You save £120 for one year at 4%. How much in total will you have?

At the end of a year you will have:

100% of your £120 + 4% interest
You will have a total of
104% of your £120

Calculate 104% of £120:
$$120 \times 1.04 = 124.8$$

You will have a total of **£124.80**

Exercise 17.6
Calculating interest paid for one year

1 To buy a TV, Ewan borrows £340 for one year at a rate of interest of 14% pa. How much, in total, does Ewan pay back for his loan?

2 To buy a new bike for £275, Jess decides to use £120 of her savings and to borrow the rest of the money for a year with an interest rate of 17% pa.
   a How much money will Jess have to borrow to buy the bike?
   b How much will she pay back in total for her loan?
   c In total, how much will she have paid for the bike?

3 Marie won £2500 in a competition.
   She decided to save the money, for a year, at an interest rate of 4.5% pa.
   a At the end of the year, with interest, how much will Marie have in total?
   b How much interest was she paid?

4 A hockey club was given a grant of £84 250. They did not spend the money straight away, but decided to save it for a year at 6.8% pa interest.
   By waiting a year, how much was the grant now worth in total?

Simple interest

Simple interest is a type of interest not often used these days.

◆ Simple interest is fixed to the sum of money you actually borrow or save.

◆ When you borrow a sum of money:
   simple interest is *charged* for each year on the actual sum borrowed.

◆ When you save a sum of money:
   simple interest is *paid* for each year on the actual money saved.

This is known as the: simple interest formula.

The formula can be given in different forms.

If you use the formula in a different form, make sure you know how to use it to calculate the interest.

The amount of interest added to a loan, or added to a sum of money that is saved can be calculated using this formula:

$$I = P \times R \times T$$

In words, the formula is:

$$\textbf{\textit{I}}\text{nterest} = \textbf{\textit{P}}\text{rincipal} \times \textbf{\textit{R}}\text{ate} \times \textbf{\textit{T}}\text{ime}$$

Principal is the amount of money you borrow or save.
Rate is the interest rate pa **as a decimal**.
Time is for how long, usually in years.

> ### Example
>
> Calculate the interest charged on a loan of £750, for 4 years at 7% pa.
> Use the formula
>
> $$I = P \times R \times T \text{ with } P = 750, R = 0.07 \ (7\% = \tfrac{7}{100} = 0.07), T = 4$$
>
> $$I = 750 \times 0.07 \times 4$$
> $$I = 210$$
> **The interest charged on this loan is £210.**
>
> If the £750 had been saved for 4 years at 7% pa:
> **The interest paid on the savings would have been £210.**

Exercise 17.7
Calculating simple interest

1 Calculate the simple interest charged, or paid for each of these:

   a £450 borrowed for 6 years with interest at 12% pa

   b £280 saved for 8 years with a rate of interest of 3% pa

   c £1500 saved for 15 years at 6% pa. interest

   d £6000 borrowed for 10 years at an interest rate of 17% pa

   e £25 borrowed for 20 years with interest at 18% pa.

2 To buy new kit a band borrows £3500 over 10 years at 17% interest pa.

   a Calculate the amount of interest paid on the loan.

   b At the end of the loan, how much in total will have been paid for the kit?

3 Scot forgot about the £150 he had saved at an interest rate of 4.5% pa.
He found it had been earning interest for twelve years.
How much were these savings worth in total at the end of twelve years?

4 A new bridge will cost an estimated £44 million, and take six years to build.
If, at the start, all £44 million is borrowed at a simple interest rate of 8.5%, estimate the total cost of the bridge.

Compound interest

Like simple interest, compound interest is either charged or paid, but not just on the original sum borrowed or saved. For example, £100 saved for 2 years at 4% can be thought of in this way:

♦ At the end of year 1, the total is £104 (£100 + £4 interest)

♦ At the end of year 2, the total is £108.16 (£104 + £4.16 interest)

In short, compound interest includes interest on interest already *paid* or *charged*.

Compound interest is used by banks, building societies, and shops.

By working year-by-year, you can calculate compound interest and see that it builds to a greater total than simple interest over the same time span.

Example   Calculate the interest on £480 saved for 3 years at 7%

♦ Interest paid at the end of year 1 is: £33.60 (£480 × 0.07)
Interest for year 2 will be calculated on £513.60 (£480 + £33.60)

♦ Interest paid at the end of year 2 is: £35.95 (£513.60 × 0.07)
Interest for year 3 will be calculated on £549.55 (£513.60 + £35.95)

♦ Interest paid at the end of year 3 is: £38.47 (£549.55 × 0.07)

The total interest paid is: £33.60 + £35.90 + £38.47 = **£107.97**

> Round the answers to each calculation to the nearest penny.

Exercise 17.8
Calculating compound interest

1 Calculate the total interest paid on these savings at compound interest:

   a £350 for 3 years at 9% pa   **b** £1400 for 4 years at 3% pa
   c £3600 for 5 years at 6% pa   **d** £12 250 for 3 years at 4% pa
   e £4050 for 2 years at 12% pa   **f** £35 250 for 2 years at 12% pa

2 Shelly won £5000, and put it in a savings scheme for five years.
The savings scheme pays interest at 8% pa compound.

   a Calculate the total interest paid on this saving.
   b At the end of five years what was the total in Shelly's saving scheme?
   c   **i** What would the total be if the only rounding was done at the end?
       ii What do you think the banks do with the rounding problem?

Reverse percentages

Calculating the original value of something, before an increase or decrease took place, is called 'calculating a reverse percentage'.

Example   The total price of a bike (including VAT at 17.5%) is £146.85
Calculate the cost price of the bike without VAT.

Total price of bike = 100% of cost price + 17.5% of cost price
146.85 = 117.5% of cost price
146.85 ÷ 117.5 × 100 = 100% of cost price
124.978... = Cost price

The price of the bike without VAT is £124.98 (to the nearest penny)

> When you divide by 117.5, you are calculating 1%.
>
> You then multiply by 100% to calculate the 100%.
>
> This is for VAT at 17.5%
>
> Check on the current rate of VAT to find the number to divide by to calculate 1%.

Exercise 17.9
Calculating reverse percentages

1 These prices include VAT, calculate each price without VAT.
Give your answers correct to the nearest penny.

   a CD player £135.50   **b** camera £34.99   **c** ring £74.99
   d trainers £65.80   **e** TV £186.75   **f** phone £14.49
   g calculator £49.99   **h** PC £799.98   **i** tent £98.99

2 Ella bought a pair of boots for £45 in a sale that made an offer '20% off!'.

   a What was the non-sale price of the boots?
   b How much did Ella save buying the boots in the sale?

3 When Mike sold his bike for £35, he said he made a profit of 35%.
To the nearest pound, how much did Mike pay for the bike?

4 A 600 gram box of cereal is said to hold '35% more than the regular box'.
How many grams of cereal are in the regular box?

Buying on credit

Here the deposit is an amount you must pay in cash.

The deposit paid can be an amount of money (£30), or a percentage of the full price, e.g. 20% deposit.

There are rules for buying on credit. These can be changed by governments, and it may be possible to buy on credit with no deposit.

Buying something on credit, is where you buy something and pay only a deposit. The rest of the price is paid off with a loan.

The loan plus interest on the loan is paid off in a number of equal *instalments*. Usually, instalments can be paid over a number of weeks or months.

Example

This advert is for a colour television.

only £179.99

CREDIT PLAN: **You pay £20 deposit the balance at 23% compound interest in 24 equal instalments (2 years)**

Calculate the monthly instalment for this credit plan.

The amount of the loan is £159.99 (£179.99 – £20 deposit)
- Interest on loan for year 1 is £36.80 (£159.99 × 0.23)
  Interest for year 2 will be calculated on £196.79
- Interest on loan for year 2 is £45.26 (£196.79 × 0.23)
  The total of the loan is: Amount + Total interest
  $$= £159.99 + £36.80 + £45.26$$
  $$= £242.05$$
There will be 24 instalments, so each instalment = £242.05 ÷ 24
  $$= £10.085 ...$$
The monthly instalment will be £10.09 (to the nearest penny)

Exercise 17.10
Buying on credit

The number of instalments is often linked to the number of months in a year.

For example:

24 instalments
is a loan for 2 years

36 instalments
is a loan for 3 years

and so on.

1   Copy and complete the Credit table.

Credit table		Interest rate 23% pa compound			
Price	Deposit	Amount of loan	Total interest	No. of instalments	Each instalment
£59.99	£10			12	
£245	£25			24	
£55.65	None			12	
£1250	None			36	
£355.99	£35			48	
£875	£25			12	
£249.99	£65			24	
£89.95	£0			24	
£105.50	£10			24	
£1500	£150			36	

2   Eric bought a camcorder advertised for £469.99.
He paid no deposit, was charged interest at 26% pa compound, and had the loan over 3 years (36 equal instalments).
  a   Calculate the total interest Eric will pay on this loan.
  b   Calculate the monthly instalment on this loan.

End points
You should be able to ...   ... so try these questions

A Write one number as a percentage of another

A1 What is 12 as a percentage of 48?

A2 Give 60 as a percentage of 20.

A3 Correct to 2 dp, what is 18 as a percentage of 64?

A4 In a 456-page book, 35 of the pages have pictures on them.
Give the number of pages with pictures as a percentage of the total number of pages in the book, correct to 1 dp.

B Increase a value by a certain percentage

B1 Increase 480 km by 16%.

B2 A CJ regular size cola is 380 ml.
CJ decide to increase the size of their regular cola by 12%.
To the nearest ml, give the size of the new regular cola.

C Decrease a value by a certain percentage

C1 Decrease £55.80 by 6%. Give your answer to the nearest penny.

C2 In 1992, there were a total of 42 154 breakdowns on a motorway section.
In 1993 the total number of breakdowns fell by an estimated 7%.
Estimate the number of breakdowns in 1993 on this motorway section.

D Work with VAT

D1 What is the standard rate of VAT today?

D2 The cost of these items is given without VAT (ex. VAT)
a a camping stove £34.75   **b** a body-board £158.40
Calculate the cost, to the nearest penny, of each item including VAT.

E Calculate reverse percentages

E1 The price of a TV is £259.99 including VAT.
Calculate the cost of the TV 'ex.VAT' (without VAT).

F Calculate simple interest

F1 Calculate the interest paid on £480 saved for six years, at a simple interest rate of 4%.

F2 £500 was borrowed at a simple interest rate of 9% over 4 years.
a Calculate the total interest paid on this loan.
b How much was paid back on the loan in total?

G Calculate compound interest

G1 Calculate the total interest paid on these savings at compound interest:
a £680 for 3 years at 6%   **b** £2575 for 4 years at 3%

Some points to remember

- When you work with a calculator it is easier if you think of, and use, percentages as decimals.
- Check that your answer to a calculation is of the right size, and to a sensible degree of accuracy.
- When you are calculating interest, paid or charged, make sure you know whether it is at a rate of simple interest, or compound interest.

Starting points

You need to know about ...

... so try these questions

A The equation of a straight line

♦ You can use the coordinates of points on a line to find the equation of the line.

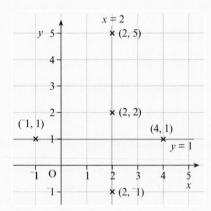

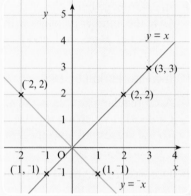

A1

A1

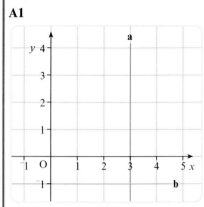

Write down the equation of the lines **a** and **b**.

B Reflections

♦ To describe a reflection you must give the mirror line. On a grid you can give the equation of the mirror line.

Example

B is the image of A after a reflection in $y = {}^-x$.

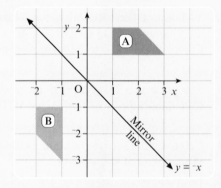

B1　**a**　Copy this diagram.

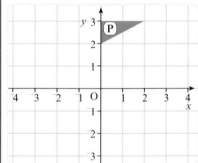

b Draw the image of P after a reflection in:
　i $y = x$　　**ii** $x = {}^-1$

C Rotations

♦ To describe a rotation you must give:
　❖ the angle and direction of rotation
　❖ the centre of rotation.

♦ On a grid you can give the coordinates of the centre.

Example

❖ C is the image of A after a rotation of $^+90°$ (90° anticlockwise) about (4, 1).
❖ D is the image of A after a rotation of $^-90°$ (90° clockwise) about $({}^-1, 2)$.

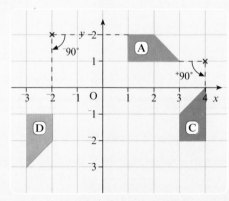

C1

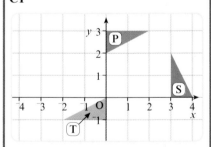

a Triangle S is the image of P after a rotation about (3, 3). What is the angle of rotation?

b Triangle T is the image of P after a rotation of 180°. Give the coordinates of the centre of rotation.

D Translations

♦ A translation only changes the position of a shape.

♦ On a grid you can use a vector to describe a translation.

Example

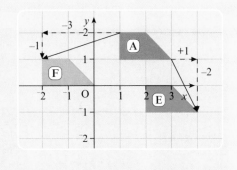

❖ A is translated on to E by the vector $\begin{pmatrix} 1 \\ 2 \end{pmatrix}$.

❖ A is translated on to F by the vector $\begin{pmatrix} -3 \\ 1 \end{pmatrix}$.

E Enlargements

♦ If the scale factor (SF) of an enlargement is **greater than 1**:
the image is **larger** than the object.

♦ If the scale factor of an enlargement is **less than 1**:
the image is **smaller** than the object.

♦ If one shape is an enlargement of another:
the two shapes are **similar**.

Example

G is an enlargement of A with centre (4, ⁻1) and SF 2.

H is an enlargement of A with centre (⁻1, 0) and SF $\frac{1}{2}$.

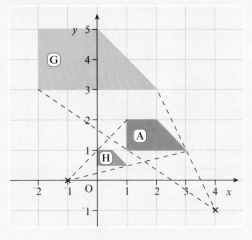

F Tessellations

♦ In a tessellation the shapes fit together with no gaps and no overlaps. A tessellation can be continued in any direction.

Example   Tessellation 1 is made by rotating and translating tile A.

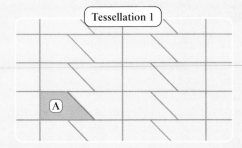

Tessellation 1

In this tessellation all the tiles are the same shape and exactly the same size so they are **congruent**.

D1 These translations map P on to U and V.

Object	Translation	Image
P	$\begin{pmatrix} 2 \\ 0 \end{pmatrix}$	U
P	$\begin{pmatrix} -1 \\ -3 \end{pmatrix}$	V

On your diagram, from Question **B1**, draw and label the image of P after each of these translations.

E1 Copy this diagram and enlarge triangle P with:
   a SF 2 and centre (⁻1, 4)
   b SF $\frac{1}{2}$ and centre (0, 5).

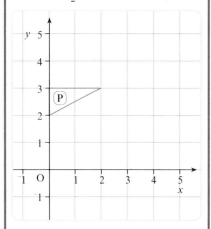

F1 Draw a different tessellation of tile A, from tessellation 1.

F2 In tessellation 2 which tiles are congruent to P?

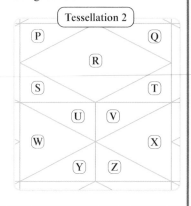

Tessellation 2

Identifying transformations

Exercise 18.1
Identifying single
transformations

The Moors used tessellations of tiles to decorate walls and floors.
These are patterns used at the Alhambra Palace in Spain.

The Moors are Muslims of
mixed Berber and Arab
descent who live in North
West Africa.

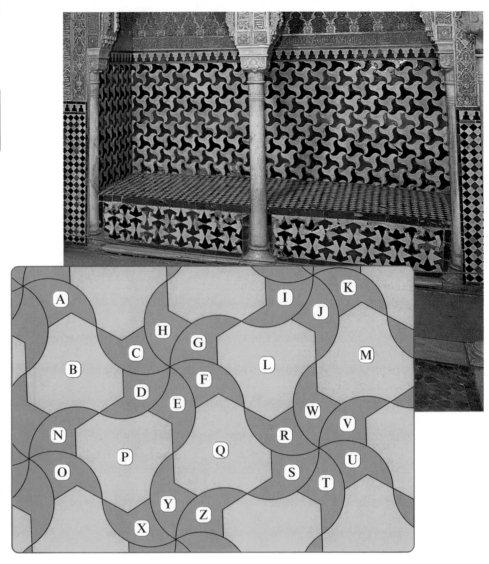

1   This is a tessellation made from
   tiles of two different shapes.

   a   **i**   How many lines of symmetry has tile A?
      ii How many lines of symmetry has tile B?
   b   What is the order of rotational symmetry for:
      i tile A   **ii**   tile B?

When a shape is transformed
the object is said to map
on to the image.

2   Each complete tile on the tessellation is labelled.

   a   What type of transformation will map tile C on to tile H?
   b   Give two different types of transformation that will
      map tile B on to tile M.
   c   Tile C maps on to tile U by a rotation of 180° clockwise.
      Which other tiles are also an image of tile C
      after this rotation?
   d   Which tiles are an image of tile G after a translation?
   e   List all the tiles that are an image of tile D after a rotation:
      i of 60° clockwise   **ii**   of 60° anticlockwise.

Single transformations

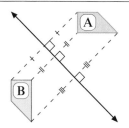

When an object is reflected in a mirror line:

* lines joining corresponding points on the object and image are perpendicular to the mirror line

* the object and image are the same distance from the mirror line.

♦ To describe a **reflection** fully you need to give the mirror line.

Example

A reflection can map triangle 1 on to triangles 3, 4 or 5.
* A reflection in the line GC maps triangle 1 on to triangle 3.
* A reflection in the line HD maps triangle 1 on to triangle 4.
* A reflection in the line HB maps triangle 1 on to triangle 5.

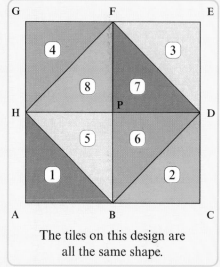

The tiles on this design are all the same shape.

♦ To describe a **rotation** fully you need to give:
* the angle and direction of rotation
* the centre of rotation.

Example

A rotation of 90° anticlockwise ($^+$90°) can map triangle 1 on to triangle 2 or 8.
* A rotation of 90° anticlockwise about the point P maps triangle 1 on to triangle 2.
* A rotation of 90° anticlockwise about the point H maps triangle 1 on to triangle 8.

Exercise 18.2
Describing transformations

A rotation of 90° anticlockwise ($^+$90°) and a rotation of 270° clockwise ($^-$270°) about the same point both map an object on to the same image.

A rotation of 180° anticlockwise ($^+$180°) and a rotation of 180° clockwise ($^-$180°) about the same point both map an object on to the same image.

1 Use the triangles in square ACEG above to answer these questions.

a Using a rotation of 90° clockwise ($^-$90°) about the point P, what is the image of
  i triangle 5   **ii** triangle 2   **iii** triangle 4?

b A rotation maps triangle 2 on to triangle 5.
  What is:
  i the centre of rotation
  ii the angle of rotation?

c Describe fully a rotation that maps:
  i triangle 7 on to triangle 2
  ii triangle 3 on to triangle 1.

d What is the mirror line for a reflection that maps:
  i triangle 2 on to triangle 6
  ii triangle 2 on to triangle 3?

e Which triangle, after a rotation of $^+$90° about the point P, is the image of triangle 6?

f Which triangle, after a reflection in the line FB, is the image of triangle 3?

g What transformation maps triangle 7 on to triangle 4?

h Describe two transformations that map triangle 4 on to triangle 2.

i What transformation can map triangle 8 on to itself?

Exercise 18.3
Describing transformations

This tessellation uses tiles of two different shapes.

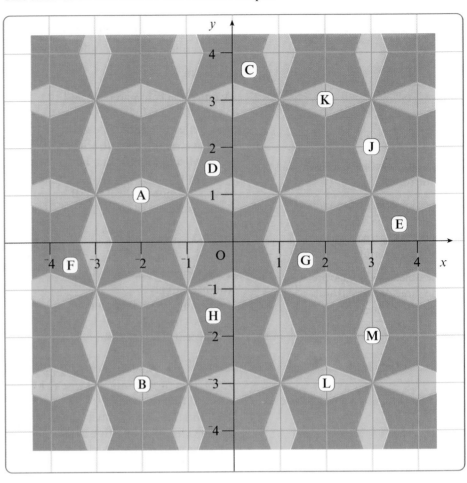

1   You can use vectors and coordinates to describe
transformations on a grid.

   a   What vector translates tile A on to tile B?
   b   Tile A is mapped on to tile B by a rotation of 180°.
What are the coordinates of the centre of rotation?
   c   What is the equation of the mirror line for the reflection
which maps tile A on to tile B?

2   Six of the kites are labelled, C to H.

   a   **i**   Match kites C to H in three pairs so that:

in each pair one kite is a reflection of the other.

   ii   In a table like this show
the equation of the
mirror line for each pair.

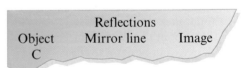

	Reflections	
Object	Mirror line	Image
C		

   b   **i**   Sort kites C to H into three pairs so that:

in each pair one kite is a translation of the other.

   ii   Make a table to show the vector for each translation.

You could trace the object
and try different centres of
rotation.

c **i** Sort kites C to H into three pairs so that:

in each pair one kite is a rotation of the other.

ii Make a table and describe each rotation fully.

3 **a** Describe two transformations that map tile J on to tile B.
b Explain why tile J cannot be a translation of tile B.
c Describe three transformations that map tile J on to itself.

4 This is part of a transformation table
for tiles K, L and M.

> For a translation give the vector.
>
> For a reflection give the equation of the mirror line.
>
> For a rotation give the angle, and the coordinates of the centre.

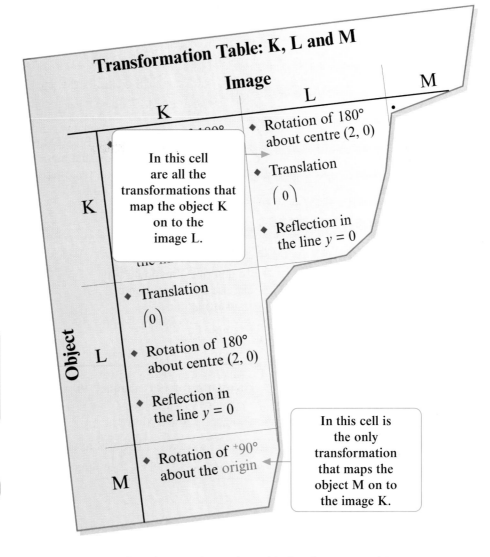

Transformation Table: K, L and M

Image

In this cell are all the transformations that map the object K on to the image L.

Object K on to image L:
- Rotation of 180° about centre (2, 0)
- Translation $\begin{pmatrix} 0 \\ \end{pmatrix}$
- Reflection in the line $y = 0$

Object L:
- Translation $\begin{pmatrix} 0 \\ \end{pmatrix}$
- Rotation of 180° about centre (2, 0)
- Reflection in the line $y = 0$

Object M:
- Rotation of $^+90°$ about the origin

In this cell is the only transformation that maps the object M on to the image K.

> A rotation of $^+90°$ is a rotation of 90° anticlockwise.
>
> A rotation of $^-90°$ is a rotation of 90° clockwise.

> The origin is the point (0, 0).

a **i** Complete the transformation table for tiles K, L and M.
ii Describe any patterns that you notice.
b Describe fully a reflection that maps:
  i tile D on to itself
  ii tile G on to itself.
c Make a transformation table for tiles C, E and F.

Exercise 18.4
Drawing transformations

1 a Draw triangle A on axes with
$^-5 \leqslant x \leqslant {}^+5$ and $^-5 \leqslant y \leqslant {}^+5$.

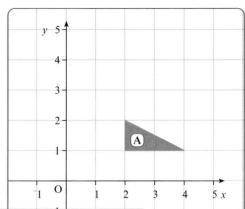

b These transformations map
triangle A on to B, C, D and E.

Object	Transformation	Image
A	Reflection in the line $y = x$	B
A	Reflection in the line $x = 1$	C
A	Rotation of 180° about the origin	D
A	Rotation of $^-$90° about the point (1, 0)	E

Draw and label the images B, C, D and E.
c Describe a transformation that maps B on to C.
d Describe a transformation that maps:
  i D on to E   ii E on to C.

Combined transformations

♦ To describe a mapping you
can use a combination of
transformations.

Example

To map F on to G you can use:

a rotation of –90° about (1, 0)

followed by

a translation $\begin{pmatrix} ^-4 \\ 2 \end{pmatrix}$

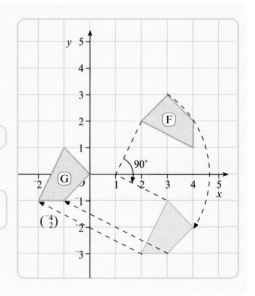

Exercise 18.5
Combined transformations

1 H is the image of F after:

a translation $\begin{pmatrix} ^-4 \\ 2 \end{pmatrix}$

followed by

a rotation of –90° about (1, 0)

a Draw and label F and its image H.
b Compare G and H and comment on any differences.

Use axes with:
$^-5 \leqslant x \leqslant {}^+6$ and
$^-5 \leqslant y \leqslant {}^+5$

2 These transformations map the quadrilateral F on to J and K.

Transformations			
Object	First	Second	Image
F	Rotate 180° about (2, 1)	Rotate ⁺90° about (2, 1)	J
F	Rotate ⁺90° about (2, 1)	Rotate 180° about (2, 1)	K

> Use the same axes as you drew for Question **1**.

a Draw and label the images J and K.
b Compare J and K and comment on any differences.

3

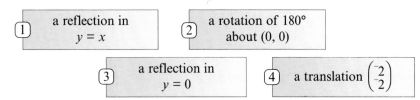

① a reflection in $y = x$

② a rotation of 180° about (0, 0)

③ a reflection in $y = 0$

④ a translation $\begin{pmatrix} ^-2 \\ 2 \end{pmatrix}$

> A pair of transformations are commutative if the image of an object is the same whichever transformation you use first.

Sort the transformations 1 to 4 into two pairs so that:

in each pair the transformations are commutative.

Draw diagrams to explain your answers.

◆ Combined transformations can be equivalent to a single transformation.

Example

A rotation of ⁻90° about (0, 3) maps F on to G.
So

a rotation of ⁻90° about (1, 0)

followed by

a translation $\begin{pmatrix} ^-4 \\ 2 \end{pmatrix}$

is **equivalent to
the single transformation**

a rotation of ⁻90° about (0, 3)

Exercise 18.6
Equivalent transformations

1 These transformations map the quadrilateral F on to L, M and N.

Transformations			
Object	First	Second	Image
F	Reflect in y = 1	Reflect in y = x	L
F	Rotate 180° about (1, 1)	Translate $\begin{pmatrix} 0 \\ 2 \end{pmatrix}$	M
F	Reflect in y = ⁻1	Rotate ⁻90° about (1, ⁻1)	N

> Use axes with:
> $^-5 \leqslant x \leqslant {}^+5$ and
> $^-5 \leqslant y \leqslant {}^+5$

a On a new diagram draw and label the images L, M and N.
b What single transformation maps F on to:
   i L   **ii** M   **iii** N?

Exercise 18.7
Tessellations from
transformations

This is part of a tessellation. Each tile is a transformation of tile P.

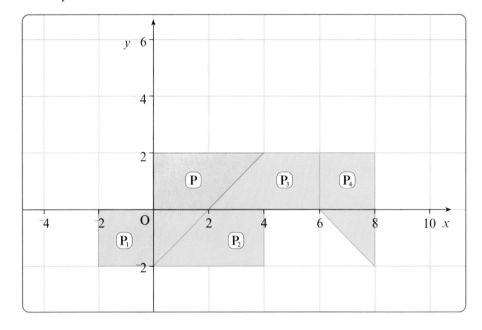

1 **a** Draw these tiles on axes with $^-4 \leq x \leq 10$ and $^-4 \leq y \leq 8$.
  b Describe a single transformation that maps P on to:
   i P_1 **ii** P_2 **iii** P_3

2 In this table each pair of transformations maps tile P on to P_4.
  a For each mapping describe the second transformation fully.

	Object	Image	Transformations	
			First	Second
i	P	P_4	Rotate $^-90°$ about (2, 0)	
ii	P	P_4	Rotate 180° about (1, 4)	
iii	P	P_4	Reflect in y = x	

  b Describe another pair of transformations that maps P on to P_4.

3 These transformations map tile P on to P_5, P_6 and P_7.

Object	Transformations		Image
	First	Second	
P	Rotate $^-90°$ about (2, $^-2$)	Reflect in x = 5	P_5
P	Reflect in y = x	Translate $\begin{pmatrix} ^-2 \\ 0 \end{pmatrix}$	P_6
P	Rotate $^+90°$ about (0, 2)	Reflect in x = 1	P_7

  a On your diagram draw the images P_5, P_6 and P_7.
  b Describe a pair of transformations that map P_5 on to P.
  c Draw four more tiles to continue the tessellation.

Enlargements

Exercise 18.8
Enlargements

1 This is part of a tessellation of tiles arranged in the shape of a Greek cross.

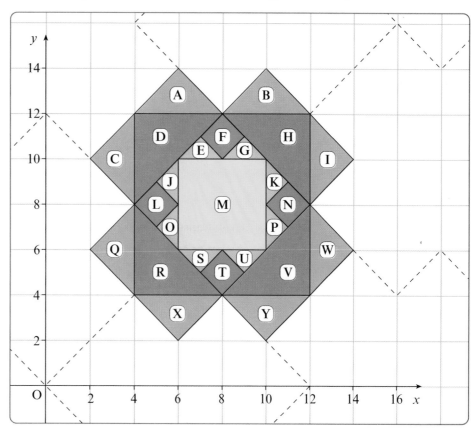

> You could put tracing paper over your drawing for each question.

> If you draw lines through corresponding points on the object and image, they will meet at the centre of enlargement.

a Copy the diagram and label the tiles A to Y.

b What is the image of E after an enlargement with centre (4, 8) and SF 2?

c Find the scale factor and centre for each of these enlargements.

Object	Image	SF	Centre
S	Y		
Y	S		
X	S		
X	U		

d Explain why tile T will not map on to M with just an enlargement.

e This table gives a pair of transformations for three mappings. Describe fully the second transformation for each of these mappings.

> For an enlargement give the scale factor and the coordinates of the centre.
>
> For a translation give the vector.
>
> For a reflection give the equation of the mirror line.
>
> For a rotation give the angle of rotation and the coordinates of the centre.

	Object	Image	Transformations First	Second
i	G	W	Enlarge SF 2 with centre (8, 8)	
ii	Q	E	Rotate ¯90° about (6, 6)	
iii	A	S	Enlarge SF $\frac{1}{2}$ with centre (4, 8)	

Exercise 18.9
Drawing enlargements

1 Draw the triangle A on axes with:
$$^-6 \leqslant x \leqslant 10$$
$$^-6 \leqslant y \leqslant 10.$$

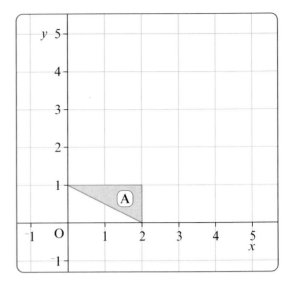

The distance from the centre to a point on the object multiplied by the scale factor gives the distance from the centre to the corresponding point on the image.

2 These transformations map the triangle A on to B_1, B_2, B_3 and B_4.

Object	First transformation	Second transformation	Image
A	Enlarge SF 2 with centre (0, 0)	Translate $\begin{pmatrix} 1 \\ 2 \end{pmatrix}$	B_1
A	Rotate $^-90°$ about (2, 0)	Enlarge SF 2 with centre ($^-1$, 0)	B_2
A	Enlarge SF 2 with centre ($^-1$, 0)	Translate $\begin{pmatrix} 4 \\ 4 \end{pmatrix}$	B_3
A	Rotate $^+90°$ about (0, 1)	Enlarge SF 2 with centre ($^-3$, $^-2$)	B_4

a On your diagram draw and label the images B_1, B_2, B_3 and B_4.
b Describe a single transformation that will map B_1:
   i on to B_2 **ii** on to B_3 **iii** on to B_4.
c What single transformation maps A:
   i on to B_1 **ii** on to B_3.

3 In this table each pair of transformations maps B_2 on to A.
For each mapping describe the second transformation fully.

Object	Image	First transformation	Second transformation
a B_2	A	Rotate $^+90°$ about (5, 0)	
b B_2	A	Rotate $^+90°$ about (5, 2)	

4   Each tile in this pattern is also a transformation of A.

    a   Copy this pattern on axes with:
$$^-6 \leqslant x \leqslant 10$$
$$^-6 \leqslant y \leqslant 10$$

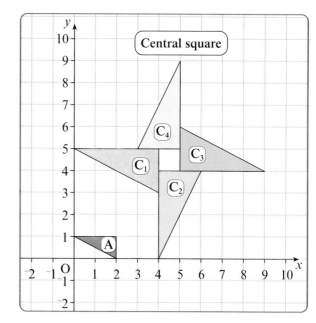

For Question **4a** and **5a** use axes with:
$$^-4 \leqslant x \leqslant 10$$
$$^-4 \leqslant y \leqslant 10$$

For each mapping you do not need more than two transformations.

    b   In a table show what transformations map A on to each triangle in this pattern.

    c   **i**   Make another pattern using four triangles.
        ii   In a table to show what transformations map A on to each triangle in your pattern.
        iii   Pass your table to a partner and ask them to draw your pattern.

5   In this pattern each hexagon is an enlargement of E_1.
The consecutive enlargements touch but do not overlap.

A six-sided polygon is a hexagon.

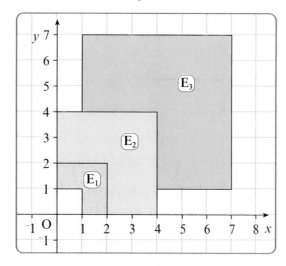

    a   Draw E_1, E_2 and E_3.
    b   Give the coordinates of the centre for the:
        i   enlargement SF 2
        ii   enlargement SF 3.
    c   **i**   Continue the pattern by drawing an enlargement scale factor 4. Label the hexagon E_4.
        ii   What are the coordinates of the centre of enlargement?
    d   Describe fully the transformation that maps E_4 on to:
        i E_1 **ii** E_2.

End points
You should be able to ...   ... try these questions

A Use single transformations

A1 A, B, C and D are congruent equilateral triangles.

Which triangles can A map on to after:
a a translation
b a rotation
c a reflection?

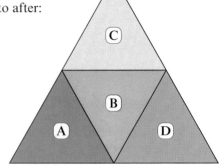

A2 a Draw the hexagon E on axes with:
$$^-4 \leqslant x \leqslant 8$$
$$^-6 \leqslant y \leqslant 6$$

b These transformations map E on to F, G and H.

Object	Transformation	Image
E	Rotate 180° about the origin	F
E	Reflect in x = 0	G
E	Translate $\begin{pmatrix} 2 \\ -2 \end{pmatrix}$	H

Draw and label the images F, G and H.

c Describe a transformation that maps:
  i F on to E
  ii G on to E
  iii H on to E.
d Describe fully a transformation that maps:
  i F on to G
  ii H on to F.

A3 On a new diagram, on axes with:
$$^-6 \leqslant x \leqslant 8 \text{ and } ^-4 \leqslant y \leqslant 4$$
draw an enlargement of E:
a SF 3 with centre (2, 4)
b SF $\frac{1}{2}$ with centre ($^-$3, 1).

B   Use combined transformations

B1   These transformations map the hexagon E, from Question **A2**, on to J, K and L.

	Object	First transformation	Second transformation	Image
	E	Reflect in $y = {}^-1$	Reflect in $x = 0$	K
	E	Reflect in $y = {}^-x$	Reflect in $y = 0$	L
	E	Rotate 180° about $(0, 0)$	Rotate 180° about $(0, {}^-2)$	M

a   On a new diagram, on axes with ${}^-6 \leqslant x \leqslant 6$ and ${}^-6 \leqslant y \leqslant 6$, draw and label E and the images K, L and M.

b   What single transformation maps E on to:
   i K   **ii** L   **iii** M?

c   These transformations map K on to L, M and E.
Describe the second transformation fully.

	Object	Image	First transformation	Second transformation
i	K	L	Rotate ${}^-90°$ about $({}^-1, {}^-3)$	
ii	K	M	Reflect in $x = 0$	
iii	K	E	Translate $\begin{pmatrix} 2 \\ 2 \end{pmatrix}$	

d   What single transformation maps K on to:
   i L   **ii** M   **iii** E.

Some points to remember

♦   Transformations on a grid

Transformation	Describe by giving:		Object and image are:
Enlargement	the coordinates of the centre the scale factor		similar
Reflection	the equation of the mirror line		congruent
Rotation	the coordinates of the centre the angle of rotation		congruent
Translation	the vector		congruent

Southampton Evening Chronicle *Monday 15 April 1912*

TRAGEDY AT SEA

IT IS WITH great regret that we bring you the news that last night at 10:40 pm the 'unsinkable liner' the Titanic hit an iceberg on her way to New York. The Titanic later sank at 2:20 am with the loss of many lives. It was the liner's maiden voyage and on board were 331 first class passengers, 273 second class 712 third class and a full crew – only 32.2 % of those on board survived. Each first-class passenger had paid £870 for the privilege of making the voyage in this luxury floating palace. To reassure the passengers the orchestra was still playing as the liner was going down and many passengers were so sure the ship could not sink that they refused to board the lifeboats.

The captain had been given repeated warnings of icebergs ahead but chose to steam on at 22.5 knots. It was calm weather with good visibility but the lookouts had not been issued with binoculars. The iceberg is thought to have had a height of about 100 feet showing above the water and a weight of about 500 000 tons. The sea water temperature was only 28° Fahrenheit and this took its toll on those jumping over-board. It is thought that the capacity of the lifeboats was insufficient for the number of people on board.

Survivors were picked up by the liner Carpathia which had heard the SOS when it was 58 miles away. The Carpathia steamed at a staggering 17.5 knots to reach the sinking Titanic. The ship's engineer said this was 25% faster than her usual speed.

HOW FAIR WAS THE RESCUE?

Reports coming in give the final casualty figures from the Titanic. There was not enough lifeboat space for all on board because the Titanic was considered to be the first unsinkable ship. The owners White Star admit that lifeboats could only hold 33% of the full capacity of the liner and 53% of those on board on that fateful night. Breaking the survival figure down by class we find 203 first-class, 118 second-class and 178 third-class passengers were rescued. Nearly a quarter of all crew were saved. Analysis of these figures is taking place to see if all people on board had an equal chance of being rescued.

Strange BUT *true*

Fourteen years before the disaster, and before the Titanic had been built, a story was published which described the sinking of an enormous ship called the Titan after it had hit an iceberg on its maiden voyage.

The comparisons between ships is even more amazing.

	Titan (Fiction 1898)	Titanic (True 1912)
Flag	British	British
Month of sailing	April	April
Displacement (tons)	70 000	66 000
Propellers	3	3
Max. speed	24 knots	24 knots
Length	800 feet	882 feet
Watertight bulkheads	19	15
No. of lifeboats	24	20
No. on board (inc crew)	2000	2208
What happened?	Starboard hull split by iceberg	Starboard hull split by iceberg
Full capacity	3000	

Distances at sea are measured in nautical miles and ships' speeds are given in knots. 1 nautical mile is 1852 metres. 1 knot is a speed of 1 nautical mile/hour.

1 In 24-hour time give the time that:
 a the Titanic hit an iceberg
 b the Titanic sank.

2 How long did it take the Titanic to sink after hitting the iceberg?

3 **a** Calculate the number of crew on board the Titanic on her maiden voyage.
 b Calculate approximately how many people died.

4 If all those who survived were in lifeboats, what was the mean number of people per boat?

5 How much money in total was taken in fares for the first class passengers?

6 In 1912 the price of a small house was about £200. In 1996 the same house would cost about £68 000. If fares on a cruise liner increased in the same ratio, what would have been the first class ticket price in 1996?

7 About $\frac{7}{8}$ of an iceberg's height is below water level. Estimate the total height of the iceberg that the Titanic hit.

8 **a** What was the Carpathia's usual speed?
 b At 17.5 knots, how long would it take the Carpathia to steam the 58 nautical miles to the Titanic?
 c The Carpathia received the SOS message at 12:30 am. Approximately how long after the Titanic sank did she arrive at the scene?

9 You can convert a temperature from degrees Celsius (°C) to degrees Fahrenheit (°F) with this formula:

$$F = \frac{9}{5}C + 32$$

 a Make C the subject of the formula.
 b Calculate a water temperature of 28 °F in degrees Celsius.

10 **a** How many people could the lifeboats have held in total?
 b Use your answer to part **a** to calculate an approximate value for the full capacity of the Titanic.

11 Calculate the relative frequency of survival for:
 a first-class passengers
 b second-class passengers
 c third-class passengers.

12 Calculate the total percentage of the passengers aboard who were rescued.
 (About 25% of the crew were rescued.)

13 What is the displacement of the Titanic to 1 sf?

14 The richest person on the boat was Colonel J.J. Astor who was thought to be worth £30 million. Write this number in standard form.

The drive shafts of the Titanic were 201 feet long and fell $3\frac{1}{2}$ feet over their length.

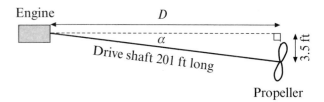

15 Calculate the angle α that a driveshaft made with the horizontal to the nearest degree.

16 Calculate the horizontal distance D to 2 dp.

The Titanic had cranes, known as derricks, for lifting the cargo on to the ship.
This diagram shows a derrick in one position.
The tower and part of the cable are vertical.

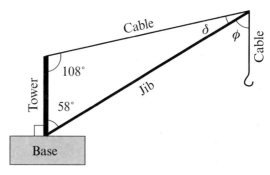

17 What is the angle ϕ? Give your reasons.

18 Calculate the value of angle δ. Give your reasons.

At the enquiry after the sinking, White Star, the owners, said that in the previous ten years they had carried 2 179 594 passengers with the loss of only 2 lives.

19 Give the number of passengers carried to:
 a 1 sf **b** 3 sf
 c 4 sf **d** 5 sf

20 In the ten years between 1981 and 1990 about 1.2×10^7 people from the UK crossed the Atlantic by plane. With the same death rate as White Star gave, roughly how many people would have died in that time?

Banananananananananananananananananananana
On 30 April 1988 in Selinsgrove Pennsylvania USA a banana split was made which was 7.32 km long.

On 31 May 1682 there was a cloudburst in Oxford which gave 24 inches of water in less than a quarter of an hour.

A slight shower!

Jo's always on hand
In 1900 Johann Hurlinger of Austria walked 871 miles from Vienna to Paris on his hands. His average speed was 1.58 mph and he walked for 10 hours each day.

OH! WHAT A LITTLE ONE-WHEEL
In March 1994 in Las Vegas Peter Rosendahl of Sweden rode a unicycle 20 centimetre high for a distance of 3.6 metres. The wheel diameter was only 2.5 cm.

Up the pole!
Mellissa Sanders lived in a hut at the top of a pole in Indianapolis USA for two years starting on 10 October 1986. Her hut measured 1.8 metres wide by 2.1 metres deep.

Stacks of cards!
In 1995 Brian Berg of Spirit Lake Iowa USA built a tower of playing cards with 83 stories. The tower was 4.88 metres high. In 1978 James Warnock of Canada held the previous record with 60 stories.

Number types
On 14 October 1993 Mikhail Shestov set a record when he had typed the numbers 1 to 795 on a PC by the time 5 minutes was up. He had made no errors.

Unique cycle on unicycle
Takayuki Koike of Japan road 100 miles on a unicycle in a record time of 6 hours, 44 minutes and 21 seconds on 9 August 1987.

Rail Trick
The Katoomba Scenic Railway in New South Wales in Australia is the steepest railway in the world. Its gradient is 1 in 0.8 but it is only 310 metres long. The ride takes about 1 minute 40 seconds and carries about 420000 passengers a year.

The circumference of the Earth at the equator is 40 075 km and its mass is 5 880 000 000 000 000 000 000 tons.

Weight watchers

Piece on earth
A jigsaw with 1500 wooden pieces was made for the photograph on the cover of the BEEB magazine. The jigsaw was assembled in 1985 by students from schools in Canterbury. It measured 22.31 metres by 13.79 metres.

Tall stories
The tallest man in the world was Robert Wadlow from Alton Illinois in the USA who was 8 feet 11.1 inches tall. The tallest man in Scotland was Angus Macaskill from the Western Isles who was 7 feet 9 inches tall. The highest mountain in the USA is Mount McKinley at 20 320 feet and the highest one in Scotland is Ben Nevis at 4408 feet.

Can beans be hasbeens?
Baked beans were first introduced into the UK in 1928. By 1992 they were selling at the rate of 55.8 million cans per year.

The swift hare and the XJ tortoise
In 1992 the Jaguar XJ220 set the land speed record for a road car of 217 miles per hour.
The spine-tailed swift has been recorded as flying at 220 miles per hour. Will this mean that Brands Hatch is converted for spine-tailed swift racing?

Can can or cannot
A square based pyramid tower of 4900 cans was built by 5 adults and 5 children at Dunhurst School, Petersfield on 30 May 1994 in a time of 25 minutes 54 seconds.

Barmy salami
A salami is usually about 9cm in diameter and about 35cm long, but at Flekkefjord in Norway in July 1992 a giant salami was made which had a circumference of 63.4 cm and was 20.95 metres long.

AMAZING FACTS
p9

1 Calculate the height of James Warnock's tower of cards in 1978.

2 Give the weight of the Earth in standard form.

3 Give the circumference of the Earth to:
a 4 significant figures
b 3 significant figures.

4 Calculate the diameter of the Earth at the equator.

5 For Peter Rosendahl's mini unicycle give:
a the height of the bike in metres
b the distance he travelled in millimetres
c the circumference of the wheel in centimetres.

6 How many days was it between when Mellissa Sanders came down from her pole hut and Mikhail Shestov set his number typing record?

7 Convert the height of water that fell on Oxford in less than a quarter of an hour to metres.

8 What was the area of the Canterbury jigsaw?

9 If the Canterbury jigsaw had been out in the Oxford rain, what volume of water would have landed on it?

10 What was the average speed of Takayuki Koike's unicycle ride:
a in miles per hour **b** in kilometres per hour?

11 How long would it take Takayuki Koike to unicycle along the length of the Selinsgrove banana split if he always unicycles at the same average speed?

12 How many of the giant banana splits would fit end to end round the equator? Give your answer in standard form to a suitable degree of accuracy.

13 A salami is shaped roughly like a cylinder. Use this to calculate the approximate volume of a normal salami.

14 **a** Calculate the diameter of the Flekkefjord salami in centimetres.
b Calculate the volume of the Flekkefjord salami in cm^3.
c The density of salami is about 1.01 g/cm^3. Calculate the mass (weight) of the giant salami in kg.

15 If the capacity of Mellissa Sanders's hut on a pole was 6.62 metres^3, what was the height of her hut in metres? Give your answer to 3 sf.

16 Give the ratio of the length of the giant salami to the length of the giant banana split in the form $1:n$, to the nearest whole number.

17 **a** What was Robert Wadlow's height in:
i inches (to the nearest inch)
ii centimetres (to 1 dp)
iii metres (to 2 dp)?
b What is the ratio tallest man : highest mountain in the form $1:n$ for:
i the USA **ii** Scotland?

18 For the numbers 1 to 12, fifteen digits are used.
a How many digits are in the numbers 1 to 100?
b How many digits had Mikhail Shestov typed in by the time five minutes was up?
c What was Mikhail Shestov's typing speed in digits per second (to nearest whole number)?

19 For how many days was Johann Hurlinger walking on his hands when he travelled between Paris and Vienna?

20 **a** At what angle does the Katoomba Scenic Railway climb?
b How many metres does the railway rise over its entire length?
c What is the average speed of the train:
i to the nearest metre per second
ii in km per hour?

21 The spine-tailed swift and the Jaguar XJ220 race together at their maximum speeds over a course of 240 miles. How long will the swift have to wait for the Jaguar at the finish line?

22 A baked bean can has a diameter of 7.4 cm and a height of 10.5 cm.
a What is the volume of one can of beans in cm^3?
b What was the total volume of the cans in the Petersfield tower in m^3?

23 The pyramid of cans in Petersfield had one can on the top layer and each can in the stack rested on four cans below.
a How many cans were in:
i the second layer down from the top
ii the third layer down?
b There were 24 layers in the tower. How many cans were on the bottom layer?

24 Imagine that as baked bean cans are bought in the UK they are emptied then lined up end to end round the equator. After roughly how long would they encircle the Earth?

25 Land's End to John O'Groats is 886 miles.
a How many giant salamis long is this?
b If the giant salami was rolled along this distance how many rotations would it make?

26 How many times does a banana split go into a basin plant? Hint: think of a bananagram!

Starting points
You need to know about ...

... so try these questions

A Relative frequency

Relative frequency is a way of estimating a probability.
It can still be used in equally likely situations but is the **only** way when outcomes are not equally likely. It is found by experiment, by survey, or by looking at data already collected.

Example This data shows the colour of cars passing a factory gate one morning.

Colour	Frequency
Red	68
Black	14
Yellow	2
Green	34
Blue	52
Grey	35
Other	23
TOTAL	228

The relative frequency of red cars is $\frac{68}{228} = 0.30$ (to 2 dp).

This probability is an estimate and can be used to predict the number of red cars passing the gate on a different morning.

B Tree diagrams

A tree diagram has branches showing different events.
This is a tree diagram for spinning a coin then rolling a 1 to 6 dice.
The only square numbers on the dice are 1 and 4.

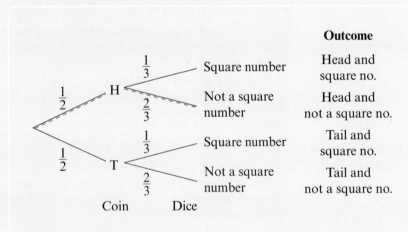

To find the probability of a particular outcome you can multiply the probabilities on the branches that lead to it.

Example To find the probability of a head and a non-square number you multiply the probabilities along the dotted branches.

Probability of a head and non-square no. is $\frac{1}{2} \times \frac{2}{3} = \frac{2}{6}$

A1 What is the relative frequency of blue cars in the survey? Give your answer to 2 dp.

A2 What is the relative frequency of cars which are:
 a not blue
 b either yellow or green
 c neither green nor red
 d either black, grey or blue?

B1 What is the probability of a head and a square number?

B2 What is the probability of a tail and a non-square number?

B3 A red 1 to 6 dice and a blue 1 to 6 dice are rolled.
 a Draw a tree diagram to show the probability of a triangle number on the red dice and an even or odd number on the blue one.
 b What is the probability of getting a non-triangle number on the red with an even number on the blue dice?

Thinking ahead to ...
experimental probability

> Theoretical probability is based on the analysis of equally likely outcomes.
>
> It is usually given as a fraction.

From the number of items you can calculate the theoretical probability of picking any one item at random when each item is equally likely.

Example   In this bag there are known to be 3 red cubes, 5 blue cubes and 1 yellow cube.

The probability of picking a particular cube is equally likely as picking any other cube.

So the probability of picking a red cube at random is $\frac{3}{9}$ (or $\frac{1}{3}$).

A   From this bag what is the probability of picking:

   a   a blue cube   **b**   a yellow cube

   c   a cube which is not blue   **d**   a cube which is not blue and not yellow?

Probability based on experiment

> Relative frequency is usually given as a decimal or a percentage.

You might not know the number, or colour, of cubes in a bag.

The probability of a particular colour can be estimated by doing an experiment to find the relative frequency.

In this experiment a cube is picked at random, its colour recorded, and the cube replaced.

These results are from an experiment:

Colour	Frequency
Red	53
Blue	15
Yellow	67
Total	135

The relative frequency of picking red is $\frac{53}{135}$ = 0.39 (to 2 sf).

This means that it is likely that about 39% of the bag's contents are red.

Exercise 19.1
Relative frequency

1   From the bag above what is the relative frequency of picking:

   a   a blue cube   **b**   a yellow cube?

2   What is the relative frequency of not picking blue?

3   Suppose that you know that the total number of cubes in the bag is 20. Estimate the number of:

   a   red cubes   **b**   blue cubes   **c**   yellow cubes.

4   In another experiment, red, green and blue cubes were in a bag. Cubes were picked out at random, examined and replaced. The relative frequency of red was 0.62 and of blue it was 0.21

   a   What was the relative frequency of green?

   b   Why is it impossible to know how many cubes were in the bag?

Finding relative frequency

> ♦ Traffic police need to know the probability of an accident at different road junctions, so that they can suggest changes.
> ♦ A railway company needs to know how likely trains are to arrive on time, so it can change its timetable.
> ♦ A fairground attendant needs to know your chances of getting a ping-pong ball into a glass jar, so he can make a profit.
>
> In these cases **relative frequency** and not **theoretical probability** is used. Relative frequency can be found either from data that is recorded or by doing an experiment (**experimental probability**).

> You will need three Multilink cubes and special dice for Exercise 19.2.

Exercise 19.2
Relative frequency experiments

1   When a Multilink L-shape is dropped it can come to rest in three positions.

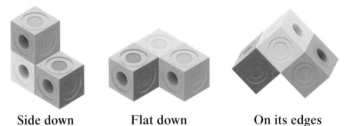

Side down   Flat down   On its edges

a   Make a frequency table like this to record how the shape lands.

Position	Tally	Frequency
Side down		
Flat down		
On its edge		

b   Drop an L-shape fifty times and record the outcomes in your table.
c   Calculate the relative frequency of the shape landing:
    i side down   **ii** flat down   **iii** on its edge.
d   What should the answers to parts **i**, **ii** and **iii** add up to?
e   If your L-shape is dropped 231 times how many times would you expect it to land side down?

For Questions **2** to **5** you need three dice with faces marked like this:

> Dice A has faces 1, 1, 5, 5, 5, 5
> Dice B has faces 3, 3, 3, 4, 4, 4
> Dice C has faces 2, 2, 2, 2, 6, 6

2   a   Roll dice A and B together thirty times and record which dice wins each time.
    b   What is the relative frequency of dice A winning?

3   a   Roll dice B and C together thirty times and record which one wins.
    b   What is the relative frequency of B winning?

> Some experiments in probability do not work out quite as you would expect them to.

4   a   If dice A and C were rolled together, which dice do you think would win most often?
    b   Do an experiment and record your results.
    c   What is the relative frequency of A winning?
    d   Was the result of your experiment what you expected?

5   Roll all three dice together and find the relative frequency that each wins.

Using a relative frequency tree diagram

This diagram shows the relative frequencies of cars leaving a roundabout when they have approached it in the direction of a red arrow.

From this data you can estimate the probability that a car coming from Danbury will take the road to Baldon.

These relative frequencies were found from a survey.

Assume motorists always take the shortest route and that they do not travel on the same road twice.

A tree diagram can help to organise the data.

Example Calculate an estimate of the probability that a car coming from Danbury will take the road to Baldon.

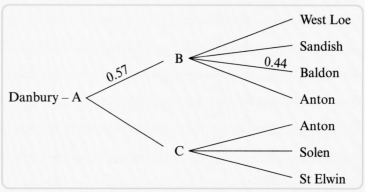

You can multiply the probabilities when you move along the branches of a tree diagram

An estimate of the probability is 0.57 × 0.44 = 0.25 (to 2 dp)

So about 1 car in 4 coming from Danbury takes the Baldon road.

Exercise 19.3
Relative frequency
and tree diagrams

1 Calculate an estimate of the probability that a car approaching roundabout C will take the road to St Elwin.
Explain how you worked this out.

2 Copy the tree diagram and fill in all the probabilities.

3 Estimate the probability that a car from Danbury will take:
   a the Sandish road   b the West Loe road
   c the Solen road   d the St Elwin road.

4 Estimate the probability that a car will go from Danbury:
   a to Anton via roundabout B
   b to Anton via roundabout C
   c to Anton by either route.

5 On Wednesday 342 cars approached roundabout A from Danbury.
   Estimate the number of these cars that took the road to:
   a roundabout B   b roundabout C   c Baldon
   d Solen   e Sandish   f Anton.

Deciding how to find probability

A If outcomes are equally likely, you can calculate the **theoretical probability**.

> The probability of throwing an even number with a fair dice is $\frac{3}{6}$ since there are six equally likely outcomes and three of them are even numbers. This is a **theoretical probability**.

B Sometimes you can only estimate a probability by doing a survey to see how often something happens, or by using data which already exists.

> To find the probability that a shopper will buy your brand of coffee you will need to count how many buy coffee (say 126) and of these how many buy your brand (say 45).
> So the probability that they buy your brand is $\frac{45}{126} = 0.36$
> This is the **relative frequency**.

C Sometimes you can do an experiment to find a probability.

> To find the probability that an elastic band will break when a weight is hung from it you could test 100 bands and find the number that break (say 17).
> So the experimental probability that a band breaks is $\frac{17}{100} = 0.17$
> Again this is the **relative frequency**.

1 kg

D Sometimes there is not enough data to estimate a probability.

> There is not enough data to find the probability that a Chinese tennis player will win at Wimbledon in the next ten years.

Exercise 19.4
Probability decisions

1 For each of these situations say whether A, B, C or D best applies to it.

   a The probability of winning the jackpot on the National Lottery with one ticket.

   b The probability that this dice will land this way up.

   c The probability that a train from London to Glasgow will arrive on time.

   d The probability that a train from London to Glasgow will have a driver over 40.

   e The probability that there is life on another planet.

   f The probability that the next car which passes the school gates will be red.

g The probability that the next earthquake in San Francisco will happen on a Thursday.

h The probability that there will be an earthquake in San Francisco before the year 2010.

i The probability that this spinner will stop on 3.

j The probability that you will live at the same address in 20 years time.

2 a What is wrong with this statement?

> You can calculate the probability that a person, chosen at random, is born in July.
> There are twelve months so the probability is $\frac{1}{12}$.

b Describe fully how you would find the probability that a person, chosen at random, was born in July.

3 Which of the following methods would a weather forecaster use to answer the question 'Will it snow on Christmas Day this year?'? Explain why.

a Carry out an experiment to find the relative frequency.
b Survey people's opinions and find the relative frequency.
c Look at past records to decide on the relative frequency.
d Use equally likely outcomes to calculate the theoretical probability.

4 Maria will open a new restaurant next week. She wants to find the probability that a person, chosen at random, is vegetarian.
Describe what is wrong with each of these surveys.

a She asks the first four people she meets on Friday if they are vegetarian.
b She interviews people who are leaving a butcher's shop.
c She asks every man she sees who has sandals and a beard.
d She asks all the members of her family.
e She asks one hundred babies who are under six months of age.

5 Andy had to answer this question 'What is the probability that a person chosen at random plays soccer?'. This is his answer:

> I asked twenty people and they all said they played soccer. So the probability is 1.

a Why must Andy's probability be incorrect?
b Give four reasons why Andy might have obtained the results he did.
c How would you do a reliable survey to decide on this probability?

6 The theoretical probability of getting a 5 with a fair 1 to 6 dice is $\frac{1}{6}$.

In an experiment you throw a dice to find the relative frequency of 5's. How true is it that the more throws you have, the closer the relative frequency comes to the theoretical probability?

When can you add probabilities?

Exercise 19.5
Adding probabilities

This shows the set of males with criminal records in the town of Humbleton.

Alf | Brian | Colin | Derek

Edwin | Fred | Graeme | Harry

Ian | Jim | Ken | Liam

Mick | Nick | Owen | Pete

Give your probabilities as fractions and do not cancel them down.

1 What is the probability that a male criminal in Humbleton has:

   a a beard   **b** a necklace .

   c a beard or a necklace?

2 Compare your answers for the probabilities in Question **1**.
What link can you find between them?

3 What is the probability that a male criminal in Humbleton has:

   a an earring   **b** a moustache?

4 **a** Predict the probability of a criminal having
either an earring or a moustache.

   b Use the full set above to find the probability that a criminal has
either an earring or a moustache.

   c Why do you think your prediction may not be the
same as the true answer?

5 What is the probability that a criminal, chosen at random, has:

   a a hat   **b** a beard   **c** a beard or a hat?

You can use diagrams to help you see why you can sometimes add probabilities, but at other times you must not.

Look at those criminals who have
- ◆ **dark hair**
- ◆ **earrings**.

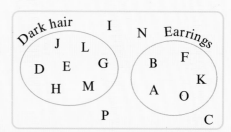

All those with dark hair are in the red loop and all those with an earring are in the blue loop.

From this you can see that the probability of having dark hair is $\frac{7}{16}$

and of having an earring is $\frac{5}{16}$

The probability of having either is $\frac{12}{16}$ (which is $\frac{7}{16} + \frac{5}{16}$)

But now look at those with
- ◆ **a beard**
- ◆ **a moustache**.

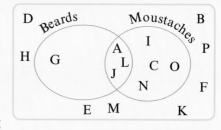

This time the loops overlap because Alf, Liam and Jim have both beards and moustaches.

The probability of having a beard is $\frac{4}{16}$

and of having a moustache is $\frac{7}{16}$.

The probability of having either is $\frac{8}{16}$ (which is **not** $\frac{4}{16} + \frac{7}{16}$).

This shows that:

you can only add probabilities when the sets do not overlap.

Diagrams like these are known as **Venn diagrams** after the mathematician John Venn, who invented them in 1881 for his work on logic.

Exercise 19.6 Probability and Venn diagrams

1 **a** Draw a Venn diagram to show the criminals with a necklace and those with fair hair.
   b Can you add the separate probabilities to find the probability that a criminal has either a necklace or fair hair? Explain your answer.

2 Use your diagram to decide the probability that a criminal has:
   a **either** a necklace **or** fair hair
   b **both** a necklace **and** fair hair
   c **neither** a necklace **nor** fair hair
   d a necklace but not fair hair
   e fair hair but not a necklace.

3 Draw Venn diagrams to help you decide on the probabilities of having:
   a either a hat or an earing
   b either a necklace or dark hair
   c either glasses or fair hair
   d neither glasses nor dark hair.

4 For each of these, say if you can add the separate probabilities to find the probabilities. Explain your reasons.
   a a girl playing hockey in a school or a girl playing basketball
   b a boy playing basketball in a school or a girl playing hockey
   c a driver or a passenger
   d a bus driver or a tall woman
   e a dancer or a mechanic.

Outcomes from a biased dice

> A biased dice is one where each outcome is not equally likely.

This table shows the probabilities of getting each number on a biased 0–9 dice.

Outcome	0	1	2	3	4	5	6	7	8	9
Probability	0.13	0.21	0.05	0.10	0.01	0.25	0.13	0.07	0	0.05

Other probabilities can be found from these probabilities.

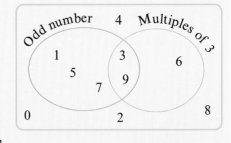

Example What is the probability of getting a number less than 4 in one roll of the dice?

There are four numbers (0, 1, 2, and 3) less than 4.
There is no overlap between them (you can't get a 3 and a 1 in the same roll).
So you can add the probabilities for 0, 1, 2 and 3.

So the probability of a number less than 4 is 0.13 + 0.21 + 0.05 + 0.1 = 0.49

> Note that 0 is counted as the first even number.

A What is the probability, with this dice, of getting:

a a number greater than 6

b an even number

c a prime number

d a number which is not prime

e a number which is a multiple of 3 **and** an even number.

You must be careful with some probabilities where there is an overlap.

Example What is the probability of getting either a multiple of 3 or an odd number?

> Here you can get a multiple of 3 **and** an odd number in the same roll of the dice.

The numbers 3 and 9 come in both sets but must only be counted once.

So the probabilities to add are those for
1,   5,   7,   3,   9 and 6.

0.21 + 0.25 + 0.07 + 0.1 + 0.05 + 0.13

So the probability of a multiple of three or an odd number is 0.81

Exercise 19.7
Outcomes from a biased dice

1 Use the Venn diagram to calculate the probability of getting in one roll:

a a multiple of three **and** an odd number

b a number which is **neither** a multiple of 3 **nor** an odd number

c a number which **is not** a multiple of 3 but **is** an odd number.

2 Use a Venn diagram to find the probability of getting a number greater than 5 or an even number.

3 **a** Why can you add all the probabilities when you find the probability that in one roll you get a number less than 5 or a number greater than 7?

b Calculate this probability.

c What is the probability of **not** getting a number less than 5 **nor** a number greater than 7?

End points

You should be able to ...   ... so try these questions

A Calculate and use relative frequency

A1 Estimate the probability that a tree chosen at random, will be:
a an ash   **b** a hornbeam.

A2 Estimate the probability that a tree is not an oak.

Tree survey of Dudley Wood	
Species of tree	Frequency
Oak	26
Ash	18
Lime	12
Hornbeam	7
Beech	25
Other	18

B Use relative frequency with tree diagrams

B1 The probability that Maria remembers her chain saw is 0.7, the probability that Pete remembers the petrol is 0.6
a Finish the tree diagram to show all the probabilities and outcomes.
b What is the probability that they remember both the saw and the petrol? Is this above or below an even chance?

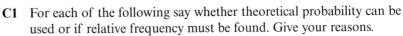

C Decide when you can use theoretical probability and when relative frequency must be used

C1 For each of the following say whether theoretical probability can be used or if relative frequency must be found. Give your reasons.
a The probability that in any book a page chosen at random will be even.
b The probability that it will rain on 1 May.
c The probability that you open any book at random and see a photograph.

D Decide when you can find a probability by adding the separate probabilities

D1 **a** In the Dudley Wood survey estimate the probability that a tree is either an oak or a lime.
b Why is it possible to add the probabilities in this case?

D2 In the apple tree survey why is it not possible to add the probabilities to find the probability of a tree having either canker or deer damage?

Apple tree survey of 100 trees	
Condition	Number of trees
Aphid attack	43
Damage by deer	24
Powdery mildew	58
Canker	15
Healthy	41

Some points to remember

♦ You can only calculate theoretical probability where outcomes are equally likely.

♦ Before you add separate probabilities check that there is no overlap between the sets. A Venn diagram can sometimes help you decide this.

Starting points
You need to know about ...

... so try these questions

A Using the inequality signs > and <

♦ These signs can be used with inequalities:

> stands for **is greater than ...**
< stands for **is less than ...**

$x > 5$ means x can have any value greater than 5 but **not 5** itself.
Here there are an infinite number of values for x.
This includes non-integer values, such as 15.23 or $8\frac{3}{4}$

♦ Inequality signs can also be used to order numbers.

For example: $^-23 < ^-4.23 < 1.5 < 37 < 100$
This can also be written as $100 > 37 > 1.5 > ^-4.23 > ^-23$
(Note. $^-23$ is less than $^-4.23$, but 23 is greater than 4.23)

♦ A range of values can be shown as an inequality.

$^-4 < p < 2$ means p has any value greater than $^-4$ but less than 2.
The numbers $^-4$ and 2 are **not** included.
$^-4 < p < 2$ can also be written as $2 > p > ^-4$

♦ Sometimes you are only interested in the integer values.

The integer values of x described by the inequality $^-3 < x < 5$ are $^-2, ^-1, 0, 1, 2, 3$ and 4.

B Sketching linear graphs

♦ Equations of straight line graphs can be expressed in the form

$y = mx + c$ where m is the **gradient** of the graph and
   c is the **y-intercept**
For example:
   $y = \frac{1}{2}x + 1$ $y = 8 - 2x$

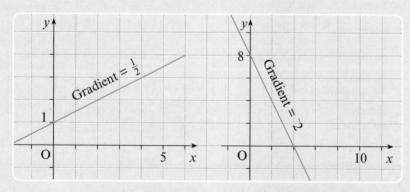

Gradient is $\frac{1}{2}$ Gradient is $^-2$
y- intercept is 1 y-intercept is 8

A1 Replace the ☐ with either > or < to make each of these correct.
a 34 ☐ 12   b 2 ☐ 15
c $^-12$ ☐ $^-56$ d 5 ☐ $^-2$
e $^-2$ ☐ 0   f $^-17$ ☐ $^-5$

A2 Order this set of numbers:
   9, 56, $^-24$, 5, $^-4$, 28, $^-30$
a using the sign >
b using the sign <

A3 Which of these numbers is not a possible value for d, where $d < 5$?

12, $^-35$, 3.217, $^-2$, 5, 4.99, 6.2

A4 What are the integer values of t, where:
a $^-6 < t < 3$
b $^-1 > t > ^-5$?

A5 Explain why there are no integer values for x where:
$^-2 < x < ^-1$?

B1 Sketch the graphs of:
a $y = 2x - 2$
b $y = 12 - x$
c $y = 3x$
d $y = ^-4$

Inequalities

> Often a quantity must be kept within a range of values.
> For instance, the speed on a motorway must stay between 30 mph and 70 mph.

> means **is greater than**

< means **is less than**

≥ means **is greater than or equal to**

≤ means **is less than or equal to**

The legal speed can be shown in shorthand like this:

$$30 < S < 70 \quad \text{where } S \text{ is the speed in mph.}$$

This is called an **inequality**.

This inequality can also be written as $70 > S > 30$

Since you can also drive at speeds equal to 30 mph and 70 mph this is more accurately shown as:

$$30 \leqslant S \leqslant 70 \quad \text{or} \quad 70 \geqslant S \geqslant 30$$

So all speeds **on or between** 30 mph and 70 mph are legal.

> Sometimes numbers at either end of a range are not included.

> **Example** A firm charges £3.00 each if you buy one switch,
> £2.50 each if you buy between 1 and 10 switches,
> and £1.75 each if you buy 10 or more.

For the £2.50 switches this can be written as:

$$1 < N < 10 \quad \text{where } N \text{ is the number of switches (1 and 10 are not included).}$$

Exercise 20.1
Writing ranges as inequalities

1 For tomatoes a greenhouse temperature from 45 °F to 80 °F is recommended.
Let T stand for the temperature in °F.
Write the recommended temperature range as an inequality.

2 Write these page ranges as inequalities.

You sometimes need to choose letters to stand for the variables, such as page number or age.

  a Pages 17 to 52 of a book are in colour.
  b Pages after 10 and before 64 have photographs.
  c The contents finish on page 4, followed by the features pages then the index which starts on page 164. Give the range for the features pages.

3 These are labels for two different drugs.

FERMATOL

For safety reasons this drug must not be used by people older than 65 or younger than 5.

Hypaticain

For safety reasons this drug must not used by the over 65's or by children 5 years and under.

  a Write the safe age range for Fermatol as an inequality.
  b Write the safe age range for Hypaticain as an inequality.
  c What is the difference between the safe age range for each drug?

Remember that ⁻18 is greater than ⁻25.

4 A freezer cabinet must be kept between ⁻25 °C and ⁻18 °C.
Write this temperature range as an inequality.

Inequalities with integer solutions

> An integer is a whole number. It can be positive, negative or zero.

◆ For speeds on a motorway where $30 \leqslant S \leqslant 70$ there is an infinite number of values for S between 30 mph and 70 mph.

◆ The floors with executive suites in a hotel are given by $3 \leqslant F < 8$, where F is the floor number.
In this case there can only be integer values, since floor 3.6 cannot exist.

◆ The inequality $3 \leqslant F < 8$ can be shown on a number line like this:

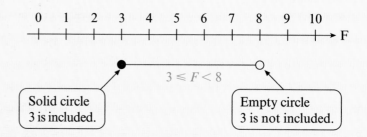

Solid circle 3 is included. $3 \leqslant F < 8$ Empty circle 3 is not included.

The integer values which **satisfy** this inequality are 3, 4, 5, 6, 7

Exercise 20.2
Integer solutions to inequalities

1 Which of the following inequalities can only have integer solutions?
A the level in a fuel tank given by $5 \leqslant h \leqslant 45$, where h is the height in cm
B the cost of sweets given by $32 \leqslant c \leqslant 42$, where c is the cost in pence
C the flats in a block given by $7 \leqslant h \leqslant 12$, where h is the flat number
D the weight of a lorry given by $12 \leqslant w \leqslant 42$ where w is the weight in tonnes
E the length of a car given by $300 \leqslant c \leqslant 450$, where c is the length in cm

2 a Show the inequality $1 < x < 5$ on a number line.
  b What integer values for x satisfy the inequality?

3 a Show the inequality $^-1 \leqslant p < 4$ on a number line.
  b What integer values for p satisfy the inequality?

4 For each of these, what integer values of n satisfy the inequality?
  a $4 < n \leqslant 9$ b $^-2 \leqslant n \leqslant 3$
  c $71 > n \geqslant 68$ d $^-4 \geqslant n > ^-12$
  e $^-3 \leqslant n < 7$ f $2163 < n < 2167$

5 Which one of these inequalities describe a different set of integer values from the others?
  $^-4 \leqslant h < 6$, $^-5 < h < 6$, $^-4 \leqslant h \leqslant 5$, $^-4 < h < 6$, $^-5 < h \leqslant 5$

> Two different inequalities can describe the same set of integers. For example:
>
> $^-1 < x \leqslant 5$
>
> $^-2 \ ^-1 \ 0 \ 1 \ 2 \ 3 \ 4 \ 5 \ 6$
>
> $0 \leqslant x < 6$
>
> Both of these ranges describe the integers 0, 1, 2, 3, 4, 5.

6 Write two different inequalities in g which are satified by these integers:
  $^-3, \ ^-2, \ ^-1, 0, 1$

7 For each pair of inequalities, what integer values satisfy both?
  a $5 \leqslant k < 8$, $6 \leqslant k \leqslant 9$
  b $17 > k > 12$, $14 \geqslant k > 7$
  c $^-3 \leqslant k < 5$ $7 \geqslant k > ^-3$

8 One set of integers satisfies all three of these inequalities.
  Write an inequality in f for this set of integers.
  $^-5 < f \leqslant 8$, $^-24 \leqslant f < 7$ $^-3 \leqslant f \leqslant 7$

Inequalities and regions

Rules which have to be met are called conditions.

♦ Two inequalities can give a region on a graph.

For example, on airline flights there are limits on the luggage you can take.

For hold luggage, the condition on the weight W can be shown on a number line:

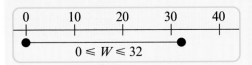

$$0 \leqslant W \leqslant 32$$

and the dimensions D as:

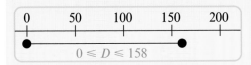

$$0 \leqslant D \leqslant 158$$

These can both be shown on one sketch graph.

The lines $W = 32$ and $D = 158$ split the graph into four regions.

The shaded region matches both conditions.

virgin atlantic

Hold luggage
Two pieces allowed, each to have:
maximum weight 32 kg
maximum dimension 158 cm

Hand luggage
One item only, to have:
maximum weight 6 kg
maximum dimension 114 cm

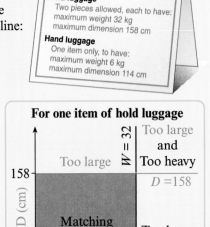

For one item of hold luggage

Exercise 20.3
Regions on graphs

1 These are some bags taken on the airline above.

Bag **A** $W = 24\,\text{kg}$, $D = 175\,\text{cm}$ Bag **B** $W = 5.3\,\text{kg}$, $D = 109\,\text{cm}$
Bag **C** $W = 28\,\text{kg}$, $D = 142\,\text{cm}$ Bag **D** $W = 5.3\,\text{kg}$, $D = 123\,\text{cm}$
Bag **E** $W = 35\,\text{kg}$, $D = 136\,\text{cm}$ Bag **F** $W = 7\,\text{kg}$, $D = 99\,\text{cm}$

a Which of these bags could not be hold luggage? Explain your answer.
b Draw a sketch graph to show the matching region for hand luggage. Label each region.
c Which bags could be taken as hand luggage?

2 This is an extract from a letter to recruit pilots for Jumbo jets.

highly successful career with us flying 747 aircraft. Applicants
should have at least 2000 hours flying experience and be aged
between 28 and 50. Please send a letter of application giving
your full CV to Mark Southgate at Flight Operations
Recruitment to arrive before 15 March.

This sketch graph shows the limits of the regions described in the letter.

a Copy the sketch graph.
b Label each region.
c Shade in the region that satisfies all the conditions in the letter.

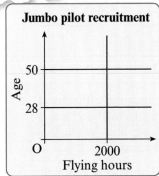

3 These extracts are from notices or notes.

A *Rona Kennedy's exercise bike programme*
You should cycle a distance of between 10 and 20 miles
or for at least 15 minutes before breakfast each day.

B **PEUGEOT 405 SERVICE NOTE**
Your first service should take place within 6000 miles
or 6 months, whichever is the sooner.

C *Sungrow Vegetarian Restaurant*
Our party rates apply to groups of between 8 and 20 people.
Meal prices range from £6 to £12 a head.

D *JENNY'S 15TH BIRTHDAY*
Bike with 14 or more gears. Must cost less than £400.

E **Offkit flea spray**
Use only on cats older than 12 weeks
and heavier than 2 kilograms.

F **Kansas Car Hire**
Prices range from £36 to £62 per day.
Maximum five people per vehicle.

G **Mike's Supplies**
Dave, we need a scaffold tower next week. It needs to be 15
foot or more tall but must not cost more than £50 per day.
Thanks, Mike

H **Sandford Superstore**
We are looking for keen sales staff between the ages of 25 and 35
with at least four years experience of vegetarian beef sales.

It is often difficult to tell if
the signs > and <,
or ≥ and ≤ fit a situation.

For example, does
'prices up to £40' include
a price of exactly £40?
It should not, but probably
does.

Assume for these extracts
that they all mean ≥ and ≤.

a For extracts A, B and C
  i decide what axes you need and sketch a graph
  ii shade the region which meets all the conditions
  iii label the other regions on each graph.
b For extracts D to H sketch a graph and shade the matching region.
  Do not label the other regions.

4 Sketch a graph which **could** describe suitable applicants for
the job of a Victorian chimney sweep's assistant.
You will need to decide on what axes to use and the
inequalities which apply.

In the early 19th Century
young boys were sent up
chimneys with a hand
brush to clean them by
unscrupulous chimney
sweeps.

The practice was made
illegal by parliament in 1833.

Shading regions on graphs

♦ An inequality such as $x > 4$ or $^-5 < y < 2$ can be shown as a region on a graph.

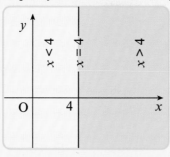

Region shaded ☐ is $x > 4$

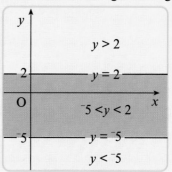

Region shaded ▨ is $^-5 < y < 2$

♦ The conditions satisfied by both inequalities can also be shown on one graph.

Example

Show the region where $x > 4$ and $^-5 < y < 2$.

In this case the shaded region is where the region for $x > 4$ overlaps with the region for $^-5 < y < 2$.

This is the part shaded ▨

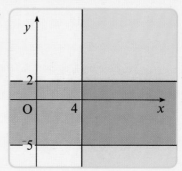

Exercise 20.4
Sketching regions

1 Sketch graphs to show these regions:

 a $x < 5$ **b** $y > ^-3$ **c** $3 < y < 7$
 d $0 < x < 4$ **e** $x < ^-2$ **f** $^-4 < y < ^-1$

2 Write an inequality for each shaded region on these graphs.

a
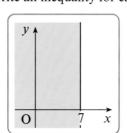

b
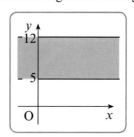

c
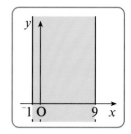

3 Sketch graphs to show the region where

 a $y > 5$ and $x > 3$ **b** $y < ^-1$ and $x > 4$
 c $^-1 < y < 5$ and $x > 2$ **d** $y > 3$ and $2 < x < 8$
 e $0 < x < 5$ and $1 < y < 6$ **f** $^-2 < y < 6$ and $^-5 < x < 0$

4 Give the inequalities which describe the shaded region on this sketch graph.

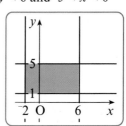

Regions with sloping lines

Exercise 20.5
Regions with sloping lines

This poster is for a stall at a fair.

B stands for the score on the Blue 0 to 9 dice and R for the score on the Red dice.

To calculate the probability of winning a prize a sample-space diagram can be drawn to show all the outcomes.

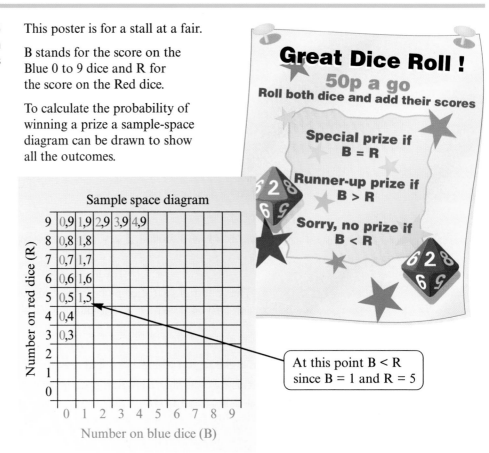

Sample space diagram

At this point B < R since B = 1 and R = 5

1 a Copy and complete the sample-space diagram to show all the outcomes for the two dice.
   b Circle in red all the outcomes where B > R.
   c Circle in blue all outcomes where B < R.
   d Cross out all outcomes where B = R.

2 Describe the position in the sample space diagram of the outcomes where B = R.

3 In this inequality which of these signs is covered up : >, <, ⩾, ⩽ or = ?

4 What is the probability that a player gets:
   a a special prize
   b no prize
   c a prize of some sort?

5 a Draw some x and y axes from ⁻2 to 8.
   b Draw the graph of $y = x$.
   c Shade in and label the region of your graph where $x > y$.
   d Label the region where $y > x$.
   e In which region is the point (⁻6, ⁻4): $x > y$ or $y > x$?

6 By sketching a graph and shading, show the region where $y > x + 3$.

These are the rules at another stall.

7 **a** Draw a sample space diagram for rolling two 0 to 9 dice.
   b Circle in red the outcomes where B + R > 13.
   c Circle in blue the outcomes where B + R < 13.
   d Cross through the outcomes where B + R = 13.
   e Describe the position of the outcomes where B + R = 13.

8 How will the regions be different if the rules are changed to:
B + R = 15, B + R > 15 and B + R < 15?

> You may find it easier to rewrite the equation in the form $y = \ldots$ to plot the graph of $y + x = 8$.

9 **a** Draw some x and y axes from 0 to 12.
   b Draw the graph of $y + x = 8$.
   c Shade and label the region on your graph where $x + y > 8$.
   d Label the region where $x + y < 8$.

10 A small business has two partners who earn £b per day from their contract and three employees who are paid £a per day.
The business must make a profit of more than £180 per day.
The profit will also be (2 lots of b – 3 lots of a).
So the inequality used for the profit is **$2b - 3a > 180$**.

This is a sketch graph of $2b - 3a = 180$.

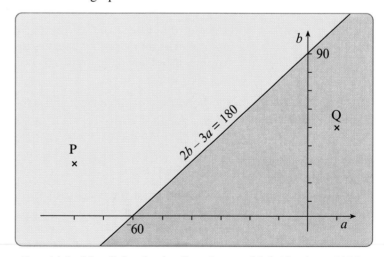

   a On which side of the sloping line do you think $2b - 3a > 180$?
   b What are the coordinates of points P and Q?
   c What is the value of $2b - 3a$:
       i at point P   **ii** at point Q?
   d Have you changed your mind about which side of the line $2b - 3a > 180$?
   Explain your reasons.

Solving inequalities

♦ An inequality can have an unknown on both sides – for instance:

> **Danfield Nurseries**
> We sold 5 trays of roses and 3 single rose plants on Monday.
> On Tuesday we sold 3 trays and 13 single rose plants.
> We sold more rose plants on Monday than on Tuesday.

> How many rose plants are on a tray?

As an inequality this can be written as $5x + 3 > 3x + 13$ where x is the number of rose plants on a tray.

♦ To solve an inequality you can treat it like an equation.

Example 1

Solve this inequality	$5x + 3 > 3x + 13$
Subtract $3x$ from both sides	$2x + 3 > 13$
Subtract 3 from both sides	$2x > 10$
Divide both sides by 2	$x > 5$

So the number of rose plants on a tray must be greater than 5, i.e. at least 6.

Example 2

Solve this inequality	$3x - 8 \leqslant 5x - 2$
Subtract $3x$ from both sides	$^-8 \leqslant 2x - 2$
Add 2 to both sides	$^-6 \leqslant 2x$
Divide both sides by 2	$^-3 \leqslant x$
So	$x \geqslant {}^-3$

So x can have any values greater than or equal to $^-3$.

The only difference from solving an equation is that if you multiply or divide both sides of an inequality by a negative number the inequality signs will reverse. You can avoid having to do this by keeping the coefficient of x positive.

> When you rearrange an inequality try to keep the number in front of the variable positive. (i.e. try to keep the coefficient of x positive).
>
> For example to solve
> $$3x - 8 \leqslant 5x - 2$$
>
> Subtract $3x$ from both sides. Do not subtract $5x$ or you will get $^-2x - 8 \leqslant {}^-2$ and will have the problem of dividing through by $^-2$ and changing the sign.

Exercise 20.6
Solving inequalities

1 Solve each of these inequalities to find the possible values of x.

a $2x > 8$ b $5x \leqslant 20$
c $7x \geqslant {}^-28$ d $5x \geqslant 12$
e $20x \leqslant 10$ f $20 > 4x$
g $150 \leqslant 10x$ h $x^2 < 64$

> Note: For $x^2 < 64$ there are two values between which x must lie. For example $p^2 < 36$ has a range of values $^-6 < p < 6$ because $\sqrt{36}$ has two solutions 6 and $^-6$.

2 Solve each of these inequalities.

a $3y + 6 < 27$ b $13 \geqslant s + 5$
c $5p - 3 \geqslant 27$ d $10 < 2b + 3$
e $6a + 50 \leqslant 2$ f $5x - 2 > 38$
g $2t + 12 \leqslant 5t$ h $4a - 6 \geqslant 22$
i $13 - 4d > 33$ j $3a + 7 \leqslant {}^-32$

3 Solve each of these inequalities.

a $2a - 5 \geqslant a + 6$ b $7k + 4 < 2k - 6$
c $3x + 7 > x - 11$ d $4n - 9 \geqslant 2n - 2$
e $3q + 5 < 1 - 2q$ f $2(2k - 1) > 6$
g $7h + 3 > 13h + 15$ h $2(3c - 2) < 11$

> Where there are brackets, multiply them out first.

End points

You should be able to ...   ... so try these questions

A   Find integer values which satisfy an inequality

A1   For each of these, what integer values of g satisfy the inequality?
  a $^-2 < g < 0$ **b** $^-5 \leqslant g < 4$
  c $7 \geqslant g \geqslant 4$ **d** $^-56 \geqslant g > ^-60$
  e $^-77 < g \leqslant ^-72$ **f** $^-3 < g < 4$

B   Draw a region to illustrate an inequality

B1   Sketch a graph for Bargain Exhausts.
  a   Shade in the region that matches these conditions.
  b   Label the other regions.

B2   Sketch a graph to show the region where $^-1 < x < 3$.

B3   Sketch and shade the region on a graph to show where $^-1 < x < 2$ and $y > 3$.

B4   Write inequalities for the shaded regions in graphs **a** and **b**.

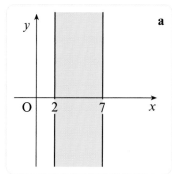
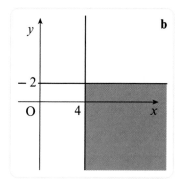

B5   Sketch the graph of $y = 2x - 3$
  Shade in the region of your graph where $y < 2x - 3$.

C   Solve an inequality to find the range of values for x

C1   Solve these inequalities.
  a $5x \leqslant 30$ **b** $12 < 4f$
  c $4a + 5 \geqslant 53$ **d** $5k + 28 > 3$
  e $3(4s - 2) \leqslant 42$ **f** $7d - 10 > 5 - 3d$

Some points to remember

♦ Always check carefully to see if $\geqslant$ rather than $>$, or $\leqslant$ rather than $<$, is used.

♦ When you solve an inequality you can treat it like an equation except that:
  ❖ if you multiply or divide both sides by a negative value you must reverse the signs.

Starting points
You need to know about ...

... so try these questions

A Names of common solids

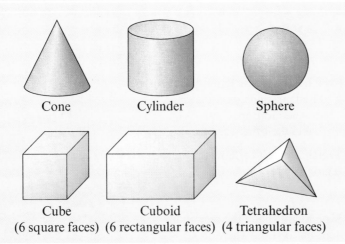

Cone Cylinder Sphere

Cube Cuboid Tetrahedron
(6 square faces) (6 rectangular faces) (4 triangular faces)

B Prisms and pyramids

♦ A **prism** is a solid with a uniform cross-section.

This cross-section is the same all through the solid so it is called a **uniform cross-section**.

♦ The mathematical name for a prism usually depends on the shape of its uniform cross-section.

Example

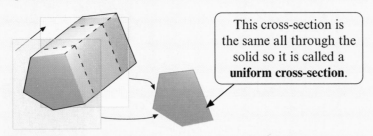

Triangular prism Pentagonal prism

♦ For a **pyramid**, all faces except one meet at a common vertex.

♦ The mathematical name for a pyramid usually depends on the shape of its base.

Example

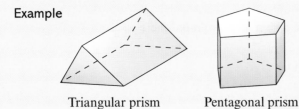

Hexagonal pyramid Square pyramid

A1 For each object, name the solid that most closely matches its shape.
 a sugar lump
 b tennis ball
 c pound coin
 d matchbox
 e can of beans

A2 Name four objects that are in the shape of a cuboid.

A3 Why do you think that containers are usually in the shape of cuboids or cylinders?

B1

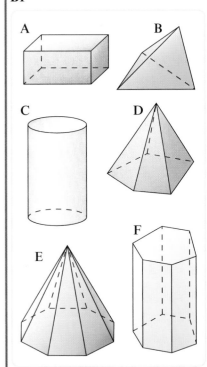

A B C D E F

 a Each of the solids is either a prism or a pyramid. Make a list of:
  i the prisms
  ii the pyramids.

 b Give a mathematical name for each solid.

C Faces, edges and vertices

♦ On a solid: ❖ a flat surface is called a **face**
  ❖ an **edge** is where two faces meet
  ❖ a **vertex** is where two or more edges meet.

Example

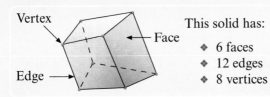

This solid has:
❖ 6 faces
❖ 12 edges
❖ 8 vertices

D Area and volume

♦ Area of a rectangle = Length × Width

♦ Area of a triangle = $\dfrac{\text{Base} \times \text{Height}}{2}$

♦ Area of a circle = πr^2

♦ Area of a trapezium = $\dfrac{c(a + b)}{2}$

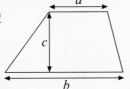

♦ Length, width and height are called the **dimensions** of a cuboid.

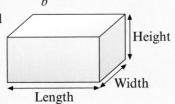

♦ Volume of a cuboid = Length × Width × Height

Example

Volume of this cuboid
= 4 × 3 × 2
= 24 cm³.

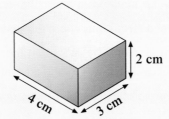

E Nets

♦ A **net** is a flat shape that can be folded up to make a solid.
For example:
A net of a cube

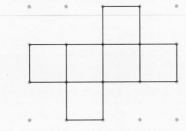

C1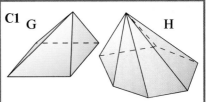

For each pyramid G and H, find the number of:
a faces   **b** edges
c vertices.

D1 Calculate the area of a circle with a radius of 4.5 cm, correct to the nearest cm².

D2 Find the area of this trapezium.

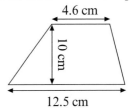

D3 Estimate the volume of these objects in cm³.
a a sugar lump
b an apple

D4 Estimate the volume of air inside a car in m³.

D5 Calculate the volume of this cuboid in cm³.

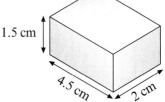

D6 Sketch three different cuboids with a volume of 72 cm³. Show the dimensions clearly on each sketch.

E1 Draw three different nets for a cube where the length of each edge is 4 cm.

E2 Draw a net for a cuboid with:
❖ a length of 5 cm
❖ a width of 3 cm
❖ a height of 2.5 cm.

259

Planes of symmetry

Some solids have **plane symmetry**.
For example, this solid has plane symmetry.

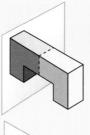

In the mirror, look at half of the solid like this and you see the other half.

So the mirror shows the position of a **plane of symmetry**.

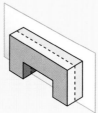

This mirror shows the position of another **plane of symmetry**.

Exercise 21.1
Properties of solids

1 Each of these solids is made from four cubes.

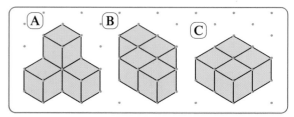

  a Which of these solids are prisms?
  b How many planes of symmetry has solid B?
  c Which solid has exactly 3 planes of symmetry?

2 Draw a prism made from four cubes that has 2 planes of symmetry.

3 Draw all the solids made from four cubes that have 5 planes of symmetry.

4 Draw a solid made from four cubes that has no planes of symmetry.

5 Draw a solid made from five cubes that has:
  a 2 planes of symmetry   **b** 0 planes of symmetry.

6 Each of these prisms has a regular polygon as a uniform cross-section.

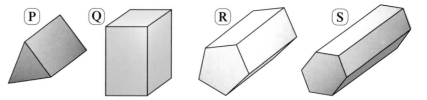

Make a table to show the number of faces, edges, vertices and planes of symmetry for each prism.

7 The uniform cross-section of a prism is a regular polygon with 100 sides. How many faces, edges, vertices and planes of symmetry does it have?

8 The uniform cross-section of a prism is a regular polygon with n sides. How many faces, edges, vertices and planes of symmetry does it have?

9 Each of these nets A to D is for a prism or a pyramid.

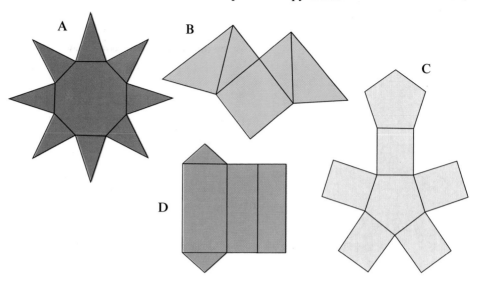

A

B

C

D

a Which of the nets is for:
  i a prism **ii** a pyramid?
b Give the mathematical name for each prism or pyramid.

10 Each of the diagrams X, Y and Z is part of a net for a pyramid.

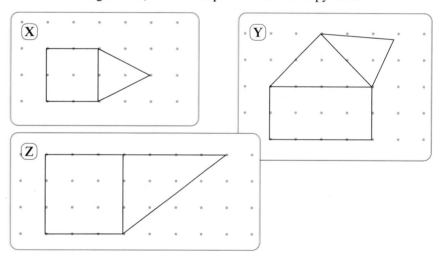

X

Y

Z

You could cut out your nets and check that each makes a pyramid.

a Copy and complete each diagram to make the net of a pyramid.
b How many planes of symmetry would each pyramid have?

For a regular tetrahedron, all faces are equilateral triangles.

11 This net gives a regular tetrahedron. Each edge is 2 cm in length.

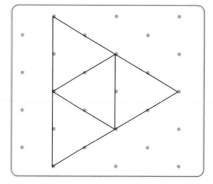

a Draw all the different nets you can find that would give this tetrahedron.
b How many planes of symmetry has a regular tetrahedron?

Volume of a prism

> The depth of a prism is sometimes called the length or height.

Volume of a prism = Area of a uniform cross-section × Depth

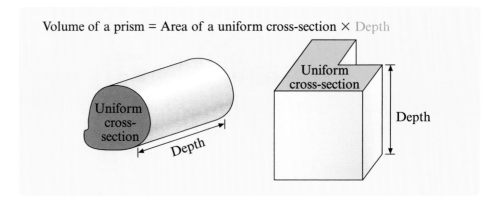

Exercise 21.2
Volume of a prism

1 These drawings show wooden prisms from a child's game.

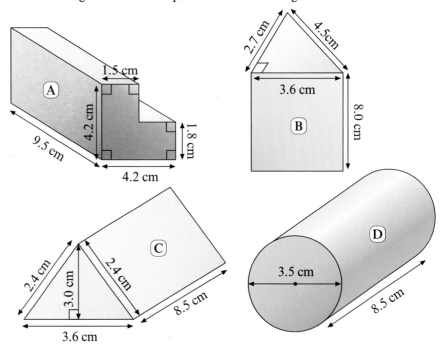

For each prism:

a Describe the shape of a uniform cross-section.
b Calculate the area of this cross-section, correct to 2 dp.
c Find the volume of the solid, to the nearest cm³.

> In calculations with decimals:
> ◆ give your answer to the degree of accuracy asked for e.g. 1 dp or 2 sf
>
> or
>
> ◆ give your answer to the same degree of accuracy used in the question.

2 This sketch shows part of a net for a prism.

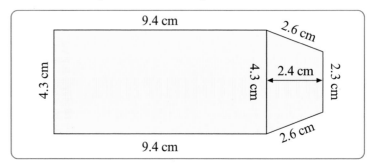

> Capacity is the volume of space inside a container.

a Draw a complete sketch of a net for this prism.
b What is the capacity of the box that can be made from the net?

3   This toy is made from a clear plastic cuboid filled with blue liquid.
     The depth of liquid is 3.5 cm.

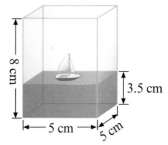

a Calculate the volume of blue liquid in the cuboid.
b The toy is placed on its side.
      What is the depth of blue liquid correct to the nearest 0.1 cm?

4   A box for drawing pins is to be designed in the shape of a cuboid.
     It is to have a capacity of 64 cm³.

     This sketch shows one possible box.

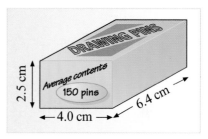

a Show that the capacity of this box is 64 cm³.
b How many faces does it have?
c Calculate the surface area of the box.
d Sketch three more cuboids with a capacity of 64 cm³.
e Find the surface area of each of your cuboids.
f For all possible cuboids with a capacity of 64 cm³, find the dimensions
      of the one with the smallest surface area.

> To find the surface area of
> a solid, calculate the area
> of each face and find the
> total of these areas.

5   For all possible cuboids with a capacity of 100 cm³, find the dimensions of
     the one with the smallest surface area.

6   This competition appeared in a puzzle magazine.

> ## WIN A BOX OF POUND COINS !!
>
> ● A cuboid shaped box is full of pound coins.
>
> ● The areas of the three different rectangular faces
>   are 120 cm², 96 cm² and 80 cm².
>
> ● Each edge measures a whole number of centimetres.
>
> ### FIND THE VOLUME OF THE BOX AND WIN THE MONEY !

a Find the volume of the box described in the competition.
b A pound coin has a diameter of 2.2 cm and a thickness of 0.3 cm.
      Estimate how much money is in the box.

7   Tracy usually makes a fruit cake in a 20 cm square cake tin.
     The finished cake has a depth of 8 cm.

     She makes the same cake in a round cake tin with diameter 24 cm.
     What do you think the depth of this cake will be?

Exercise 21.3
Maximising volume
of cylinders

1 This collecting box is in the shape of a cylinder.
The diameter of the base is 9.3 cm
and its capacity is 1120 cm³.

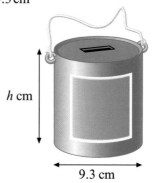

h cm

9.3 cm

Calculate h correct to 1 dp.

2 A designer in a plastics company is sent this letter.

> **World Nature Fund – fighting for the environment**
>
> 18 Westbury Road
> LONDON
> W2 4ZP
>
> Peterfield Plastics
> Unit 381
> Cupar Trading Estate
> SOUTH KILBRIDE   22 August 1996
> Lanarkshire
>
> Dear Ms Barnes,
>
> Our charity has been given a large number of plastic sheets.
> Each sheet measures 500 mm by 200 mm.
>
> We would like to use these sheets of plastic to make collecting
> boxes. Our collectors have found that a cylinder is the easiest
> shape to handle. Of course, we would like the boxes to have the
> maximum possible volume.
>
> Could you please provide us with your proposed design as soon
> as possible, including the dimensions of the collecting box.
>
> I look forward to your ideas.
>
> Yours sincerely,
>
> N Green
>
> Vita A Green.

a Design a suitable collecting box for the charity.
b What is the diameter and height of your box?
c Write a short report to explain how you decided on these dimensions.
d For your design, what percentage of each sheet of plastic is not used?

> The sum of two numbers is
> found by adding:
> for example,
> the sum of 2 and 5 is 7.

3 **a** Sketch two cylinders where the sum of the radius and height is 12 cm.
b Find the volume of each of your cylinders.
c When the sum of the radius and height is 12 cm, what do you think
is the maximum possible volume?

4 Choose a different value for the sum of the radius and height of a cylinder
and investigate the maximum possible volume.

Exercise 21.4
Volume problems

A new park is planned.
It is to have a children's play area and an open-air swimming pool.

1   This is the design for a sandpit to be
dug in the children's play area.

It is in the shape of a cylinder
with radius 2.6 m and depth 0.8 m.

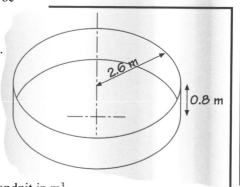

a Calculate the capacity of the sandpit in m³.
b The sandpit is to be filled with sand to a depth of 0.6 m.
Calculate the volume of sand needed.
c The weight of 1 m³ of the sand is about 1.2 tonnes.
Find the weight of sand needed for the sandpit.

2   This is a plan of the space
to be used for swings.

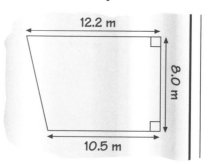

The space is to be dug to a depth of 0.3 m and filled with bark chippings.

a Calculate the volume of bark chippings needed.
b Forestry Products sell bark chippings in bags.
Each bag costs £5.12 and contains 0.07 m³ of chippings.
  i How many bags of chippings should be bought?
  ii What is the cost of these bags of chippings?

3   The diagram shows the uniform cross-section of the
open-air swimming pool.

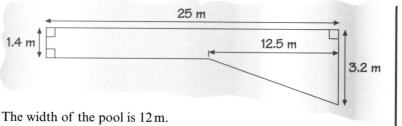

The width of the pool is 12 m.
The depth of water in the shallow end is to be 1 m.

a Calculate the area of the cross-section.
b What is the capacity of the swimming pool?
c Calculate the volume of water in the pool.
d The amount of chlorine added to the water in this pool is
1 cubic centimetre (cm³) per cubic metre (m³) of water.
How much chlorine will be added to the water in this pool?

♦ For liquids, volume or capacity is often measured in litres (l) or millilitres (ml).

   1 litre = 1000 millilitres
   1 millilitre is equivalent in volume to $1\,cm^3$.

♦ Mass (often called weight) is measured in kilograms (kg) or grams (g).

   1 kilogram = 1000 grams
   1 ml of water weighs 1 gram.

♦ Density can be measured in grams per cubic centimetre (g/cm^3).

$$\text{Density} = \frac{\text{Mass in grams}}{\text{Volume in } cm^3}$$

Exercise 21.5
Capacity, volume
and density

1 Write down one choice from each bracket to complete the sentence.
  a The volume of an orange is about ($30\,cm^3$, $300\,cm^3$, $3000\,cm^3$).
  b The capacity of a wine glass is about (75 litres, 7.5 litres, 75 millilitres).
  c The weight of an apple is about (17 grams, 170 grams, 1.7 kilograms).

2 Estimate the capacity of a tea cup in millilitres.

3

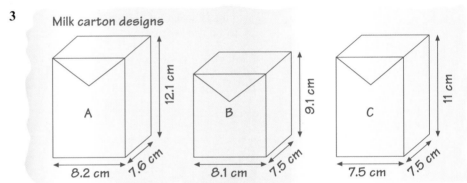

Milk carton designs

A dairy plans to sell cartons containing 550 ml of milk.
Which of these three cartons do you think the dairy should use?
Explain your decision.

4 Find the capacity of this carton in litres.

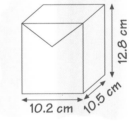

5 A storage tank on a milk lorry is a cylinder of radius 1.2 m and length 4.8 m.
Calculate the capacity of the tank in:
  a cm^3 **b** litres.

6 Each of these pieces of cheese is in the shape of a prism.

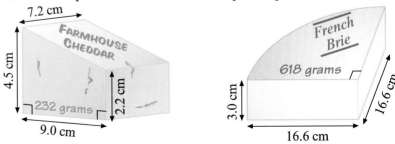

Find the volume and density of each piece of cheese.

7   Each of these containers is marked with the weight of its contents.

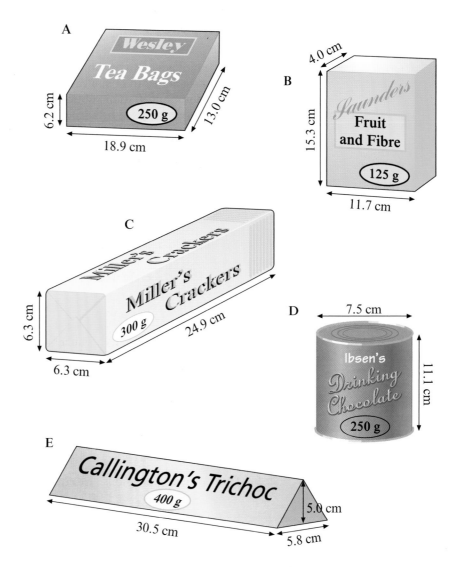

Calculate the capacity of each container in cm³ correct to 2 sf.

8   This table shows the capacity and weight for five more containers.
    Each contains one of the five food products above but is a different size.

Container	Capacity (cm³)	Weight (g)
P	640	200
Q	2700	500
R	770	125
S	230	200
T	930	500

What do you think is in each container?
Explain how you made your decision.

Formulas for length, area and volume

When you calculate with length, area and volume:

- a length added to or subtracted from a length gives a length
- an area added to or subtracted from an area gives an area
- a volume added to or subtracted from a volume gives a volume
- a length multiplied by a length gives an area
- a length multiplied by a length multiplied by a length gives a volume
- the square root of an area gives a length
- to add, subtract, multiply or divide by a number that is not a length does not change whether an expression gives a length, area or volume.

For example, if the letters a, b and c represent lengths:

$3a + b$ represents a **length**: the lengths $3a$ and b add to give a length

$\frac{1}{2}a(b - c)$ represents an **area**: the expression $(b - c)$ is a length; the lengths $(b - c)$ and a multiply to give an area

$5a(b^2 + 3c^2)$ represents a **volume**: the areas b^2 and $3c^2$ add to give an area; the length a and the area $(b^2 + 3c^2)$ multiply to give a volume.

Exercise 21.6
Formulas for length, area and volume

1   In the following expressions, l and w each represent a length. For each expression, decide if it represents a length, area or volume.

   a $4(l + w)$ **b** $4lw^2$ **c** $lw + w^2$

2   One of these expressions gives the volume of the prism.

$\frac{1}{2}(x + y + z + l)$ $x^2 + yz - l^2$ $2zx + zl$

$\frac{1}{2}lz(x + y)$ $\frac{1}{4}l(x + y + z)$

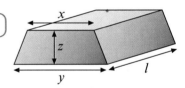

   a   Which is the correct expression for the volume of the prism?
   b   Give reasons for your answer.

3   One of these expressions gives the perimeter of this shape and one gives the area.

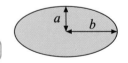

$\pi a^2 b$ πab $\pi b^2 a^2$ $\pi(a + b)$ $\pi b^2(a + 4)$

Which is the correct expression for:

   a   the perimeter   **b**   the area?

| π is a number, not a length. |

4   In the following expressions, r and h each represent a length. For each expression, decide if it represents a length, area or volume. Give reasons for each answer.

   a $\frac{1}{4}rh$ **b** $\sqrt{r^2 + h^2}$ **c** $3(r + h) + \pi h$

   d $r^2(r + h)$ **e** $\frac{4}{3}\pi r^3$ **f** $\pi r(r + h)$

5   The letters x, y and z represent lengths. Explain why $xy + xyz + y(x - z)$ cannot represent a length, area or volume.

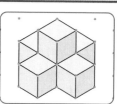

End points

You should be able to ...

... so try these questions

A Describe properties of solids

A1 This solid is made from six cubes.

How many planes of symmetry has this solid?

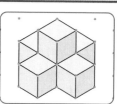

A2 This is a drawing of a hexagonal prism.

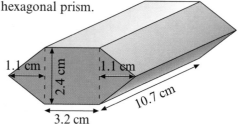

How many faces, edges and vertices does the prism have?

B Find the volume of prisms

B1 Calculate the volume of the prism correct to the nearest cm³.

C Use units for volume, capacity and density

C1 This tank is in the shape of a cylinder with radius 0.8 m and height 3.2 m.

Calculate the capacity of the tank to the nearest:
a cm³   **b** litre.

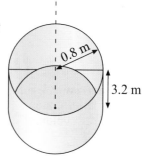

C2 A gold bar with a mass of 3180 grams is in the shape of a cuboid that measures 6.4 cm by 2.5 cm by 10.3 cm.

Calculate the density of the gold in g/cm³ correct to 1 dp.

D Decide if a formula could be for length, area or volume

D1 One of these expressions gives the surface area of this cone and one gives its volume.

$\pi(2l + r)$ $\frac{1}{3}\pi r^2 h$ $2\pi r + l$

$\pi r(l + r)$ $\pi r^2 + 3l$

Which is the correct expression for:
a the surface area   **b** the volume?

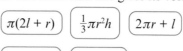

Some points to remember

* Volume of a prism = Area of a uniform cross-section × Depth

* Density = $\dfrac{\text{Mass in grams}}{\text{Volume in cm}^3}$

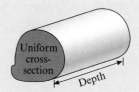

Starting points
You need to know about ...

A Multiplying out brackets

- You can multiply out brackets using a table.

For example: Multiply out $(a - 5)(a + 3)$

- $(a - 5)(a + 3) = (a - 5) \times (a + 3)$

- Work in a table:

$\times$	a	-5
a	a^2	^-5a
$+3$	$3a$	$^-15$

- The total is: $a^2 - 5a + 3a - 15$
  which simplifies to: $a^2 - 2a - 15$

- So $(a - 5)(a + 3) = a^2 - 2a - 15$ for any value of a

A1 For each of these, multiply out the brackets, and simplify.
  a $(c - 4)(c + 7)$
  b $(a + 3)(a + 5)$
  c $(y + 5)(y - 8)$
  d $(h + 1)(h - 6)$
  e $(t - 5)(t + 5)$
  f $(y - 3)(y - 3)$
  g $(p + 5)^2$
  h $(k - 6)(k - 5)$

B Factorising expressions

- When you factorise an expression you write it as a multiplication of its factors.

  For example: $a^2 - 2a - 15$ factorises to give $(a - 5)(a + 3)$

- To factorise $c^2 + 5c - 14$

  ❖ think of a table that gives a total of $c^2 + 5c - 14$ and fill the parts you are sure of

$\times$	c	☐
c	c^2	☐
☐	☐	-14

  ❖ try values that multiplied give $^-14$ in the correct positions in the table

  as $7 \times 2 = 14$ then $^-7 \times 2 = ^-14$ or $7 \times ^-2 = ^-14$
           $14 \times 1 = 14$ then $14 \times ^-1 = ^-14$ or $^-14 \times 1 = ^-14$

Try $^-7$ and $^+2$

$\times$	c	$^-7$
c	c^2	^-7c
$^+2$	$2c$	$^-14$

The total for this table is: $c^2 - 5c - 14$
which is **not** what you want.

Try $^+7$ and $^-2$

$\times$	c	$^+7$
c	c^2	^+7c
$^-2$	^-2c	$^-14$

The total for this table is: $c^2 + 5c - 14$
which **is** what you want.

There is no need to try other multiplications that give $^-14$.

$$c^2 + 5c - 14 \textbf{ factorises to give } (c + 7)(c - 2)$$

B1 Factorise these expressions.
  a $n^2 + 4n - 5$
  b $y^2 - 3y - 10$
  c $k^2 - 7k + 6$
  d $h^2 + 9h + 20$
  e $w^2 - 9w + 20$
  f $v^2 + 3v - 28$
  g $d^2 - 7d + 10$
  h $a^2 + 12a - 13$

B2 Factorise these expressions.
  a $p^2 + 6p + 9$
  b $m^2 - 10m + 25$
  c $s^2 - 4s + 4$
  d $g^2 + 8g + 16$

Solving quadratic equations by factorising

A quadratic equation is:
* an equation with one variable (only one letter, e.g. n)
* an equation where the highest power of the variable is 2 (e.g. n^2)

$$n^2 + 3n - 4 = 0 \qquad 3(a^2 + 1) = 0 \qquad 2v^2 + 3v - 40 = 0$$

are all examples of quadratic equations.

An equation is solved when you find a value, or values for the variable that satisfy the equation.

One way to solve a quadratic equation is to factorise it.

Example To solve $n^2 + 3n - 4 = 0$

$\qquad n^2 + 3n - 4$ factorises to give: $(n + 4)(n - 1)$

So $\qquad\qquad\qquad (n + 4)(n - 1) = 0$

That means: either $(n + 4) = 0$ ... (as $0 \times (n - 1) = 0$)

$\qquad\qquad\qquad$ or $(n - 1) = 0$ ... (as $(n - 4) \times 0 = 0$)

For $(n + 4) = 0$ n must have a value of $^-4$

For $(n - 1) = 0$ n must have a value of $^+1$

So $n^2 + 3n - 4 = 0$ has two values for n that satisfy it.
The values of n are: $n = ^-4$ or $n = ^+1$

The quadratic equation $n^2 + 3n - 4 = 0$ has two solutions $n = ^-4$ or $n = ^+1$.
All quadratic equations have no more than two solutions.

One way to think of a value that will satisfy an equation, is to think of a value for the variable that makes the equation true.

The value of p that satisfies the equation
$$3p = 12$$
is 4

The solution to the equation
is $p = 4$
and
$p = 4$ satisfies $3p = 12$

Exercise 22.1
Solving quadratic equations by factorising

1 Factorise and solve these quadratic equations.

a $n^2 + 13n - 14 = 0$ b $n^2 - 5n - 14 = 0$ c $n^2 - 13n - 14 = 0$
d $b^2 + 2b - 15 = 0$ e $b^2 + 14b - 15 = 0$ f $b^2 - 2b - 15 = 0$
g $a^2 + 7a - 30 = 0$ h $a^2 + 13a + 30 = 0$ i $a^2 + a - 30 = 0$
j $x^2 + 4x - 5 = 0$ k $x^2 + 6x + 5 = 0$ l $x^2 - 6x + 5 = 0$
m $y^2 - 8y + 15 = 0$ n $y^2 - 16y + 15 = 0$ o $y^2 - 14y - 15 = 0$
p $k^2 + 2k - 63 = 0$ q $k^2 - 16k + 63 = 0$ r $k^2 + 62k - 63 = 0$

2 Match each quadratic equation with a pair of factors from List A, and solve the equation.

a $d^2 + 3d - 10 = 0$
b $d^2 - 5d - 6 = 0$
c $d^2 + 3d - 40 = 0$
d $d^2 - 8d - 33 = 0$
e $d^2 - 14d - 33 = 0$

$\qquad\qquad$ List A
$(d + 8)(d - 5) \qquad (d - 11)(d + 3)$
$(d - 2)(d + 5) \qquad (d - 11)(d - 3)$
$(d + 4)(d - 10) \qquad (d + 1)(d - 6)$

Factorising can be used to solve a quadratic equation when one side is equal to 0.

So, you might need to rearrange an equation before you factorise.

To solve $x^2 + 4x = 5$
rearrange to $x^2 + 4x - 5 = 0$
Now factorise and find the solution or solutions.

3 a Factorise $x^2 - 8x + 16$.
$\qquad$ b Explain why $x = ^+4$ is the only solution to $x^2 - 8x + 16 = 0$.

4 For each of these equations:
* rearrange * factorise * find two solutions

a $c^2 + 5c = 6$ b $y^2 = 7 - 6y$ c $p^2 + 9 = 6p$
d $x^2 = 3x + 10$ e $w^2 = 4w - 4$ f $b^2 + 14 = 15b$
g $k^2 - 3k = 70$ h $v^2 + 6v = ^-9$ i $t^2 = 3t + 28$
j $y^2 - 7y = 18$ k $g^2 - 8g = ^-16$ l $a^2 = 21 - 4a$
m $p^2 - 4 = 3p$ n $w^2 = 2w + 24$ o $u^2 + 10 = ^-7u$

Solving quadratic equations by trial and improvement

There is no need to rearrange the equation because you are not going to factorise.

The trial-and-improvement method can be used to solve quadratic equations.
- ◆ You might use this method if you find an equation difficult to factorise.
- ◆ You must remember that you are looking for no more than two solutions.

Example   To solve $h^2 + 4h = 21$

$$h^2 + 4h = 21$$

Try $h = 1$ $1 \times 1 + 4 \times 1 = 5 \neq 21$ ($\neq$ means **does not** equal)
Try $h = 2$ $2 \times 2 + 4 \times 2 = 12 \neq 21$
Try $h = 3$ $3 \times 3 + 4 \times 3 = 21$ ... (both sides are equal to 21)

So, one value of h that satisfies the equation is $h = 3$

For the other value:
Try $h = 4$ $4 \times 4 + 4 \times 4 = 32 \neq 21$
Try $h = 5$ $5 \times 5 + 4 \times 5 = 45 \neq 21$
Try $h = 6$ $6 \times 6 + 4 \times 6 = 60 \neq 21$

The values 32, 45, and 60 are moving away from the 21, so trying $h = 7$, $h = 8$, $h = 9$ will not help to find the other solution.

Try negative values for h:
Try $h = {}^-1$ ${}^-1 \times {}^-1 + 4 \times {}^-1 = {}^-3 \neq 21$ $(1 + {}^-4 = {}^-3)$
Try $h = {}^-2$ ${}^-2 \times {}^-2 + 4 \times {}^-2 = {}^-4 \neq 21$
Try $h = {}^-3$ ${}^-3 \times {}^-3 + 4 \times {}^-3 = {}^-3 \neq 21$
Try $h = {}^-4$ ${}^-4 \times {}^-4 + 4 \times {}^-4 = 0 \neq 21$
Try $h = {}^-5$ ${}^-5 \times {}^-5 + 4 \times {}^-5 = 5 \neq 21$
Try $h = {}^-6$ ${}^-6 \times {}^-6 + 4 \times {}^-6 = 12 \neq 21$
Try $h = {}^-7$ ${}^-7 \times {}^-7 + 4 \times {}^-7 = 21$

So, the other value of h that satisfies the equation is $h = {}^-7$

The quadratic equation $h^2 + 4h = 21$ has two solutions: $h = 3$, and $h = {}^-7$

You can, of course, try any value you like for h.
You must remember that trial and improvement is not like guessing one value, and then another, and so on.

Be systematic with the values you try. It might take a little longer than a lucky guess, but in the end you will find the solution or solutions.

Exercise 22.2
Solving quadratic equations by trial and improvement

1   Solve these quadratic equations by trial and improvement.
   a $y^2 + 2y = 3$ b $k^2 + 2k = 8$ c $n^2 - 7n = {}^-12$
   d $v^2 + 4v = {}^-4$ e $p^2 - 3p = 4$ f $a^2 - 3a = 4$
   g $a^2 + 3a = 4$ h $b^2 - b = 6$ i $b^2 + b = 6$

2   a   Which of these equations have one solution of $p = 4$?
      i $p^2 + 3p = 28$ ii $p^2 - 2p = 8$ iii $p^2 + 3p = 4$ iv $p^2 - 9p = {}^-8$
   b   Explain your answer.
   c   Solve each of the equations.

3   a   Solve each of these quadratic equations.
      i $x^2 - 4 = 0$ ii $x^2 - 25 = 0$ iii $x^2 - 36 = 0$ iv $x^2 - 100 = 0$
   b   A quadratic equation has two solutions: $x = 3$ and $x = {}^-3$.
      Write the equation you think has these solutions.

4   Solve each of these equations by trial and improvement.
   a $x^2 + 4x + 3 = 0$ b $x^2 + 2x - 3 = 0$ c $x^2 - 2x - 8 = 0$
   d $x^2 + 2x + 1 = 0$ e $x^2 + x - 2 = 0$ f $x^2 - x - 2 = 0$

Quadratic graphs

The equation tells you that the graph is quadratic.

When you draw up a table of values you may be able to see symmetry in the y-coordinate values.

When you plot the points you should see that they lie in a curve, known as a **parabola**.

When you join the points you must draw a smooth freehand curve.

Do not use a ruler to join the points.

This is the part of the graph of $y = x^2$ for values of x between $^-4$ and $^+4$.

This graph of $y = x^2$:

♦ is a smooth curve

♦ is symmetrical about the y-axis

♦ passes through the origin $(0, 0)$.

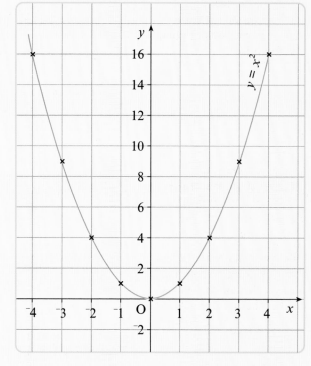

This symmetry can also be seen in the table of values for the graph.

x	$^-4$	$^-3$	$^-2$	$^-1$	0	1	2	3	4
x^2	16	9	4	1	0	1	4	9	16
y	16	9	4	1	0	1	4	9	16

Symmetry in the y-coordinate values

Exercise 22.3
Drawing quadratic graphs

1   To draw a graph of $y = x^2$ for values of x between $^-5$ and $^+5$:

   a   Draw up a table of values with values of x between $^-5$ and $^+5$.

   b   From your table:
      what are the largest, and smallest values you will need on the y-axis?

   c   Draw a pair of axes for your graph.

   d   From your table of values, plot points on the graph.

   e   Join the points with a smooth curve.

   f   Label the graph with its equation.

2   This is part of the table of values for the graph of $y = x^2 + 1$.

   a   Copy and complete the table of values.

   b   Draw the graph of $y = x^2 + 1$.

x	$^-4$	$^-3$	$^-2$	$^-1$	0	1	2	3	4
x^2	16	9							
$^+1$	$^+1$								
y	17								

   c   Compare your graphs of $y = x^2$ and $y = x^2 + 1$.
      How are they the same? How are they different?

When you sketch a graph you only show the shape of the graph and any other information you know – for example, information the equation gives you.

You do not plot points on the graph, nor do any measurements on axes have to be accurate.

Sketching a graph is not the same as drawing a graph.

3 This is a sketch of the graph of $y = x^2$.

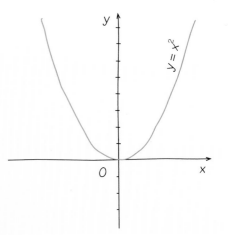

a Make a copy of this sketch
b On your copy, sketch and label these graphs:
   i $y = x^2 + 2$
   ii $y = x^2 + 3$
   iii $y = x^2 + 6$
   iv $y = x^2 - 1$
   v $y = x^2 - 3$

4 Misha sketched graph W, but did not label the graph with its equation.

She had been asked to sketch these graphs:
$$y = x^2$$
$$y = x^2 + 1.5$$
$$y = x^2 - 2.5$$

a Which equation matches graph W?
b Explain your answer.
c Sketch and label all the graphs Misha was asked to sketch.

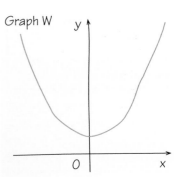

Graph W

5 Draw a pair of axes with:
values of x from $^-3$ to $^+3$, and values of y from $^-4$ to $^+20$.

a Copy and complete this table of values for the graph of $y = x^2 + x$.

x	$^-3$	$^-2$	$^-1$	0	1	2	3
x^2	9	4	1	0	1		
^+x	$^-3$	$^-2$	$^-1$	0			
y	6	2					

b From your table of values:
  i Plot points on the graph
  ii Draw and label the graph of $y = x^2 + x$.

This $^-6$ is calculated from the ^+2x in the equation.

That is:
$^+2 \times$ (the x-coordinate)
  i.e. $^+2 \times {}^-3 = {}^-6$
     $^+2 \times {}^-2 = {}^-4$
and so on.

6 **a** Copy and complete this table of values, with x from $^-3$ to $^+3$.
b On the same axes you used for Question **5** draw and label the graph of $y = x^2 + 2x$.
c Complete a table of values for the graph of $y = x^2 + 3x$ (x from $^-3$ to $^+3$).
d On the same axes, draw and label the graph of $y = x^2 + 3x$.
e Compare your graphs of $y = x^2 + x$, $y = x^2 + 2x$ and $y = x^2 + 3x$. Explain how the graphs differ.

x	$^-3$	$^-2$	
x^2	9	4	
^+2x	$^-6$	$^-4$	
y	3	0	

$x = 0$ is the equation of the y-axis.

$y = 0$ is the equation of the x-axis.

7 The line $x = 0$ is the line of symmetry for the graph of $y = x^2$.
Give the equation of the line of symmetry for each of these graphs:
  a $y = x^2 + 1$ **b** $y = x^2 + 2x$ **c** $y = x^2 - 2$ **d** $y = x^2 + 3x$

8   **a**   Copy and complete this table of values for the graph of $y = x^2 + 2x - 3$.

x	⁻4	⁻3	⁻2	⁻1	0	1	2	3
x^2	16	☐	4	1	☐	1	☐	9
$+2x$	–8	–6	☐	–2	0	2	4	☐
–3	–3	–3	–3	–3	–3	☐	–3	–3
y	5	0	⁻3	⁻4	⁻3	☐	5	☐

b   Explain any symmetry you can find in your table of values.
c   Draw axes with:
values of x from ⁻4 to ⁺3, and values of y from ⁻5 to ⁺25.
d   **i**   Plot the points from your table of values.
ii   Draw and label the graph of $y = x^2 + 2x - 3$.

9   **a**   Copy and complete this table of values for the graph of $y = x^2 - 2x - 3$
for values of x from ⁻4 to ⁺3.

x	⁻4	⁻3	⁻2	⁻1	0	1
x^2	16	9	4	1	0	1
$-2x$	+8	+6	+4	+2	0	–2
–3	–3	–3	–3			
y	21	12				

> The value of $-2x$ is
> calculated by : ⁻2 × (the
> value of x)
>
> So ⁻2 × ⁻4 = ⁺8
> ⁻2 × ⁻3 = ⁺6
> so on.

b   On the same axes as Question **8**, draw the graph of $y = x^2 - 2x - 3$.
c   Compare your graphs of $y = x^2 + 2x - 3$ and $y = x^2 - 2x - 3$
i   How are your graphs the same?
ii   How are your graphs different?

10   **a**   Draw up a table of values for the graph of $y = x^2 + 3x - 4$
with values of x from ⁻4 to ⁺4.
b   Draw a pair of axes with:
values of x from ⁻4 to ⁺4, and values of y from ⁻10 to ⁺25.
c   On your axes, draw a graph of $y = x^2 - 3x - 4$.
d   Give the coordinates of the points where your graph crosses the x-axis.

11   **a**   Draw up a table of values for the graph of $y = x^2 - 3x - 4$
with values of x from ⁻4 to ⁺4.
b   Draw a graph of $y = x^2 - 3x - 4$.
c   Give the coordinates of the points where your graph crosses the x-axis.

12   **a**   Draw up a table of values for the graph of $y = x^2 - 3x - 10$
with values of x from ⁻5 to ⁺5.
b   From your table of values predict where the graph of $y = x^2 - 3x - 10$
will cross the x-axis.
Explain your prediction.
c   Draw a pair of axes with:
values of x from ⁻5 to ⁺5, and values of y from ⁻10 to ⁺30.
d   Draw the graph of $y = x^2 - 3x - 10$.

13   **a**   Draw up a table of values for the graph of $y = x^2 + 2x - 8$,
with values of x from ⁻5 to ⁺5.
b   Draw the graph of $y = x^2 + 2x - 8$.
c   Give the coordinates where $y = x^2 + 2x - 8$ crosses the x-axis.

Solving quadratic equations graphically

This is the graph of $y = x^2 + 5x - 6$, for values of x from $^-8$ to $^+6$.

We can use the graph to solve the equation $x^2 + 5x - 6 = 0$.

The graph of $y = x^2 + 5x - 6$ crosses the graph of $y = 0$ where:
$$x = ^-6 \quad \text{and} \quad \text{where} \quad x = 1$$

At $x = ^-6$, and $x = 1$ the two equations must be equal.
So, we can write:
$$x^2 + 5x - 6 = 0$$

From the graphs, the values of x that satisfy the equation are:
$$x = ^-6 \text{ or } x = 1$$

> $y = 0$ is the equation of the x-axis.

> You can be sure of these solutions, as the values of x from the graph are both integer values.

The graph of $y = x^2 + 5x - 6$ can be used to solve many more equations.

Example From the graph solve $x^2 + 5x - 6 = 5$.
The graph of $y = x^2 + 5x - 6$ crosses the graph of $y = 5$
so we can say: $x^2 + 5x - 6 = 5$
The two equations are equal where $x \approx ^-6.6$ and where $x \approx 1.6$

The solutions for $x^2 + 5x - 6 = 5$ are: $x \approx ^-6.6$ and $x \approx 1.6$

Example From the graph solve $x^2 + 5x - 6 = ^-8$.
The graph of $y = x^2 + 5x - 6$ crosses the graph of $y = ^-8$
so we can say: $x^2 + 5x - 6 = ^-8$

The solutions for $x^2 + 5x - 6 = ^-8$ are: $x \approx ^-4.6$ and $x \approx ^-0.4$

> These values of x, from the graph are not integer values. The values are not exact, they are a good approximation. They answer the question, from the graph.
>
> For more accurate solutions, use the values from the graph as a starting point for the trial-and-improvement method.

Exercise 22.4
Solving quadratic
equations graphically

1 The graph of $y = x^2 + 5x - 6$ can also be used to solve the equation:

$$x^2 + 5x - 6 = 10$$

a What other graph would you draw on the axes to solve $x^2 + 5x - 6 = 10$?
b Explain how you would use the two graphs to solve the equation.
c From the graph on page 276, solve $x^2 + 5x - 6 = 10$.

2 The graph on page 276 can be used to solve these equations:

$$x^2 + 5x - 6 = 0$$
$$x^2 + 5x - 6 = 5$$
$$x^2 + 5x - 6 = {}^-8$$
$$x^2 + 5x - 6 = 10$$

a Give two other equations you think can be solved from the same graph.
b Explain how you would solve your equations.

3 Asif used the same graph to solve $x^2 + 5x - 6 = 22$,
but he could only find one solution.

a Explain why.
b Give the solution you think Asif did find from the graph.
c Is the other solution greater or less than $x = {}^-8$?
Explain your answer.

4 Draw the graph of $y = x^2 - 5x + 6$ for values of x from $^-2$ to $^+6$.

a Use your graph to solve $x^2 - 5x + 6 = 0$.
b On your axes draw and label the graph of $y = 4$.
c Use your graphs to solve $x^2 - 5x + 6 = 4$.
d From your graph solve $x^2 - 5x + 6 = 10$.

5 Draw the graph of $y = x^2 - 4x - 5$ for values of x from $^-3$ to $^+7$.

a Use your graph to solve:
  i $x^2 - 4x - 5 = 0$ ii $x^2 - 4x - 5 = 11$.
b From your graph solve the equation $x^2 - 4x - 5 = {}^-9$.
c Explain why $x^2 - 4x - 5 = {}^-9$ only has one solution.

> If an equation can be made by just rearranging another equation, then:
>
> the two equations are the same, and they will have the same solution or solutions.

6 a Show how each of these equations can be made by rearranging:

$$x^2 - 4x + 3 = 0$$

  i $x^2 + 3 = 4x$
  ii $x^2 = 4x - 3$
  iii $3 = 4x - x^2$

b For values of x from $^-3$ to $^+5$ draw the graph of $y = x^2 - 4x + 3$.
From your graph solve $x^2 - 4x + 3 = 0$.

c i For values of x from $^-3$ to $^+5$ draw the graph of $y = x^2 + 3$.
  ii On your axes draw and label the graph of $y = 4x$.
  iii Use your graph to show why the solutions of $x^2 + 3 = 4x$ are:
  $x = 1$ and $x = 3$.

7 To solve the equation $x^2 + 4 = 5x$:

a Rearrange the equation so that one side is equal to 0.
b For values of x from $^-2$ to $^+5$ draw a graph that will help solve
the equation.
c From your graph, solve the equation $x^2 + 4 = 5x$.

8 With values of x from $^-4$ to $^+4$:

a On the same axes draw the graphs of $y = x^2 - 2x - 3$ and $y = x + 1$.
b Use your graphs to solve the equation $x^2 - 2x - 3 = x + 1$.

Graphs of higher-order equations

A quadratic equation, or expression, is said to be 'of order 2'.

This is because the highest power of the variable is 2, as in:
$$3a^2 + 4a \qquad p^2 + 3p - 4 = 0$$

So an equation or expression of higher order than a quadratic has a highest power of the variable greater than 2, as in:
$$2a^3 + a \qquad a^3 + a^2 - 1 \qquad y^5 + y = 12 \qquad k^4 = 20$$

Example Draw the graph of $y = x^3 + 2$ for values of x from $^-3$ to $^+3$.

For the y-coordinate, substitute the values of x in the equation.

When $x = ^-3$ $y = (^-3)^3 + 2 = ^-27 + 2 = ^-25 \dots (^-3, ^-25)$
When $x = ^-2$ $y = (^-2)^3 + 2 = ^-8 + 2 = ^-6 \dots (^-2, ^-6)$
When $x = ^-1$ $y = (^-1)^3 + 2 = ^-1 + 2 = 1 \dots (^-1, 1)$
When $x = 0$ $y = (0)^3 + 2 = 0 + 2 = 2 \dots (0, 2)$
When $x = 1$ $y = (1)^3 + 2 = 1 + 2 = 3 \dots (1, 3)$
When $x = 2$ $y = (2)^3 + 2 = 8 + 2 = 10 \dots (2, 10)$
When $x = 3$ $y = (3)^3 + 2 = 27 + 2 = 29 \dots (3, 29)$

The graph of $y = x^3 + 2$ for values of x from $^-3$ to $^+3$ is:

> $(^-3)^3$ is:
> $$^-3 \times ^-3 \times ^-3 = ^-27$$

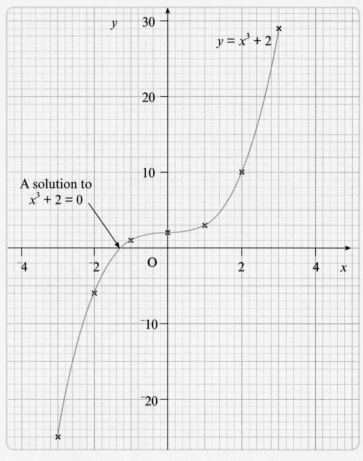

- This graph is a smooth curve.
- This graph will help you find a solution to the equation $x^3 + 2 = 0$:
  from the graph $x \approx ^-1.3$ (remember this is not exact).

The equation $x^3 + 2 = 0$ can be described as a cubic equation.

> In a cubic equation the highest power of the variable is 3.

Exercise 22.5
Drawing graphs of
higher-order equations

1 a Draw the graph of $y = x^3 + 4$ for values of x from $^-3$ to $^+3$.
   b From your graph, give a solution to $x^3 + 4 = 0$.

2 a Draw the graph of $y = x^3 - 2$ for values of x from $^-3$ to $^+3$.
   b From your graph, give a solution to $x^3 - 2 = 0$.

3 Iain sketched four cubic graphs.
This is a copy of his sketch of these graphs:

$$y = x^3 + 6$$
$$y = x^3$$
$$y = x^3 - 5$$
$$y = x^3 + 10$$

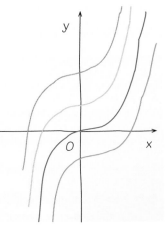

   a Make a copy of Iain's sketch.
   b Label each graph with the equation that best matches the sketch.

4 a Draw the graph of $y = x^3 + x$
     for values of x from $^-3$ to $^+3$.
   b On the same axes draw the graph of $y = 1$.
   c Use your graphs to find a solution to the equation $x^3 + x = 1$.
   d Give a solution to the equation $x^3 + x - 1 = 0$.
     Explain how you were able to give a solution.

Solving higher-order equations by trial and improvement

Example   Find a value of x that satisfies the equation $x^4 = 20$ correct to 3 sf.

For	x^4		$= 20$
Try $x = 2$	$(2)^4$	$= 16$	$\neq 20$
Try $x = 3$	$(3)^4$	$= 81$	$\neq 20$
Try $x = 2.5$	$(2.5)^4$	$= 39.062.. $	$\neq 20$
Try $x = 2.4$	$(2.4)^4$	$= 33.177.. $	$\neq 20$
Try $x = 2.3$	$(2.3)^4$	$= 27.984.. $	$\neq 20$
Try $x = 2.2$	$(2.2)^4$	$= 23.425.. $	$\neq 20$
Try $x = 2.1$	$(2.1)^4$	$= 19.448.. $	$\neq 20$
Try $x = 2.11$	$(2.11)^4$	$= 19.821.. $	$\neq 20$
Try $x = 2.12$	$(2.12)^4$	$= 20.199.. $	$\neq 20$
Try $x = 2.115$	$(2.115)^4$	$= 20.009.. $	$\neq 20$

Here $x = 2.11$ is too small
2.12 is too large, so we try
2.115 which is half-way
between 2.11 and 2.12

The value of x must be between 2.11 and 2.115
So $x = 2.11$ (to 3 sf).

Exercise 22.6
Solving higher-order
equations by trial and
improvement

1 Find a value of x that satisfies the equation $x^3 = 18$ correct to 3 sf.

2 Find a value of x that satisfies the equation $x^3 = 40$ correct to 3 sf.

3 Find a value of x that satisfies the equation $x^3 + 2 = 21$ correct to 3 sf.

End points

You should be able to ...   ... so try these questions

A Describe a quadratic equation

A1 In words describe what makes an equation quadratic.

A2 Give three different examples of quadratic equations.

B Factorise and solve quadratic equations

B1 **a** Factorise and solve $x^2 + 3x - 10 = 0$
 b Factorise and solve $x^2 + 9x + 20 = 0$
 c Factorise and solve $x^2 - 10x + 16 = 0$
 d Factorise and solve $x^2 - 6x + 9 = 0$

C Rearrange quadratic equations

C1 Rearrange these quadratic equations so that one side is equal to 0.
 a $x^2 + 5x = 24$
 b $p^2 - 2 = 3p$
 c $2 = 5c - c^2$
 d $y^2 = 2 + 6y$

D Solve quadratic equations by trial and improvement

D1 Use trial-and-improvement methods to solve these equations.
 a $v^2 - 3v = 4$
 b $b^2 + 4 = 4b$
 c $p^2 + 5p + 6 = 0$
 d $w^2 - 49 = 0$

E Draw up a table of values for a quadratic graph

E1 For the graph of $y = x^2 + 2$, draw up a table of values. Use values of x from $^-4$ to $^+4$.

E2 Explain any symmetry you find in your table of values.

F Draw a quadratic graph from a table of values

F1 Draw the graph of $y = x^2 + 2x - 3$. Use values of x from $^-4$ to $^+3$ in your table of values.

G Use and draw sketch graphs of quadratics

G1 This is the sketch of a quadratic graph. Explain why this cannot be a sketch of $y = x^2 + 1$.

Give a possible equation for the graph.

G2 Sketch a pair of axes. On these axes sketch, and label these graphs:
 $y = x^2 + 5$
 $y = x^2 - 4$
 $y = x^2$

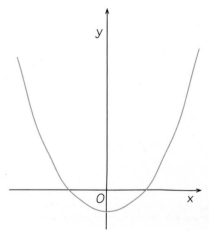

H Solve quadratic equations graphically

x	¯8	¯7	¯6	¯5	¯4	¯3	¯2	¯1	0	1	2	3	4	5	6
y	27	16	7	0	¯5	¯8	¯9	¯8	¯5	0	7	16	27	40	55

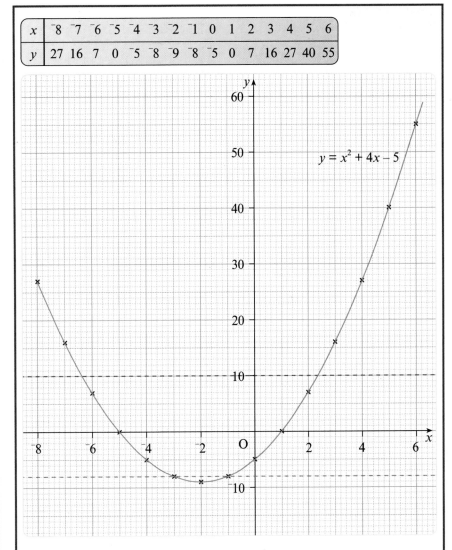

This is the graph of $y = x^2 + 4x - 5$ for values of x from ¯8 to ⁺6.

H1 Use the graph above to solve the equation $x^2 + 4x - 5 = 0$.

H2 Use the graph above to solve $x^2 + 4x - 5 = 10$.
Explain how you used the graph.

H3 From the graph above, $x = ¯3$ or $x = ¯1$ is the solution to an equation.
What equation is this?

H4 Use the graph to explain why $x^2 + 4x - 5 = ¯9$ only has one solution.

I Sketch graphs of higher-order equations

I1 Sketch the graph of $y = x^3$.

Some points to remember

- Quadratic graphs are smooth curves, and points should not be joined using a ruler.
- When you solve a quadratic equation, you should expect to find no more than two solutions.

Starting points

You need to know about ...

... so try these questions

A Investigations using data

◆ The reason for carrying out an investigation using data is to either test a **hypothesis** or answer a **question**.

The start of an investigation into sleep could be:

Hypothesis – most people sleep at least 7 hours a night

Question – how long do people sleep at night?

◆ You can carry out an investigation in four stages:

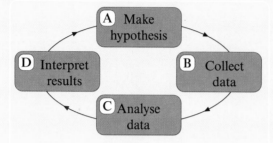

A, make a hypothesis (or ask a question)

B, collect the data you need

C, analyse the data you have collected

D, use the results of your analysis to decide whether the hypothesis is true or false.

◆ Stage D may give you an idea for a follow-up investigation.

For example, the start of a follow-up into sleep could be:

Hypothesis – people need more sleep in the winter

Question – is there a link between sleep and time of year?

B Collecting data

◆ A **data collection sheet** is any form or table used to collect data.

To the BDA,
10 Queen Anne Street, London W1M 0BD
Tel: 0171-323 1531

A charity helping people with diabetes and supporting diabetes research.

I enclose a cheque/postal order* payable to the BDA £ _____

Debit my Access/Visa* card
by the amount of   £ _____
Card number ☐☐☐☐☐☐☐☐☐☐☐☐☐
Expiry data ☐☐☐☐

Please send me more information and membership details

Name _____
Address _____

Signature _____

*Delete which is inapplicable   Reg. Charity no. 215199

Body Matters			
Name	Length of thumb (cm)	Length of foot (cm)	Height (cm)
Sam			
Wasim			
Liz			
Shane			
Des			
Linda			
Dean			
Nisha			

◆ A **questionnaire** collects data by asking questions.

Sleep Questionnaire

1 What is your name? _____

2 How old are you? _____ years

3 What time do you usually go to bed? _____

◆ A data collection sheet or questionnaire is also called a **survey**.

A1 a Make your own hypothesis about sleep.

b Decide what data you need to collect to test your hypothesis.

B1 Design a data collection sheet to use for a traffic survey.

C Types of question

◆ You can use different types of questions on a questionnaire:

❖ multi-choice questions

> **7** What do you sleep on?
> *Please tick one box only*   ☐ Back   ☐ Front   ☐ Side

❖ multi-choice questions with a scale

> **8** How heavy a sleeper are you?   HEAVY ⟶ LIGHT
> *Please tick one box only*   Very   Fairly   Average   Fairly   Very
> ☐ ☐ ☐ ☐ ☐

❖ branching questions

> **9** Do you suffer from regular sleepless nights?
> *Please tick one box only*   ☐ Yes   ☐ No
> *If your answer is NO then go to Question 12*

❖ questions with more than one answer.

> **12** What helps you get a good night's sleep?   ☐ A hot drink just before bed
> *Put a 1 in the box for the most helpful,*   ☐ Eating just before bed
> *a 2 for the next most helpful,*   ☐ Exercise during the evening
> *and so on*   ☐ Relaxation breathing
> ☐ Other *(please state)*
> _____

D Using a scatter diagram

◆ You can use a scatter diagram to investigate if there is a link between two sets of data.

Question – does the time taken to get to sleep depend on the amount of light in the room?

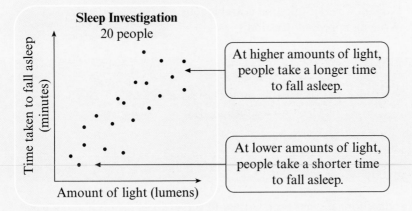

Sleep Investigation
20 people

Time taken to fall asleep (minutes)

Amount of light (lumens)

At higher amounts of light, people take a longer time to fall asleep.

At lower amounts of light, people take a shorter time to fall asleep.

The time taken to fall asleep does depend on the amount of light: as the amount of light increases, the time taken to fall asleep also increases.

C1 Design a questionnaire about sleep which includes different types of question.

D1

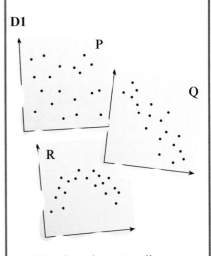

P

Q

R

Match each scatter diagram to each pair of sets of data.

a   Time taken to   against   Time since
      get to sleep   drank coffee

b   Amount   against   Room
      of sleep   temperature

c   Amount   against   Height of bed
      of sleep   off floor

Designing and criticising questions

♦ When you create a questionnaire, your questions must be carefully designed to:
 ❖ make them easy to answer
 ❖ make sure the answers give you the data you need.

Poor question		**Improved question**
How much sleep did you get last night? ☐ Less than average ☐ About average ☐ More than average	This question is **not clear**: the words used need to be more exact. (Different people are likely to have different ideas of what is meant by 'average'.)	How much sleep did you get last night? ☐ Less than 8 hours ☐ About 8 hours ☐ More than 8 hours
Do you agree that we need at least 8 hours sleep each night?	This is a **leading** question: it leads people into giving a certain answer. (The question seems to expect the answer 'Yes'.)	Do you think we need at least 8 hours sleep each night? ☐ Yes ☐ No ☐ Not sure
What do you sleep on?	This question is **ambiguous**: it could have more than one meaning. (The question is meant to be about sleeping position, but could be answered 'a bed'!)	What do you sleep on? ☐ Back ☐ Front ☐ Side

Exercise 23.1
Designing and criticising questions

1 a Explain why this question is not clear.
   b Write an improved question.

> When do you usually go to bed?
> ☐ Early ☐ Late

2 a Explain why this is a leading question.
   b Write an improved question.

> You get a worse night's sleep on a soft bed, don't you?

3 a Explain why this question is ambiguous.
   b Write an improved question.

> Where do you sleep best?

4

> ### *Leisure Centre Survey*
>
> 1 Do you agree that the town needs a new leisure centre? ☐ Yes ☐ No
> 2 Would you be a frequent user of the centre? ☐ Yes ☐ No
> 3 Would you use the courts? ☐ Yes ☐ No
> 4 How much would you be prepared to pay to use the pool? ☐ Less than £1.50
>   ☐ More than £2.50

This questionnaire has been written to survey local people about a new leisure centre.

a Criticise each of the questions.
b Write an improved question for each one.

◆ A survey asks people to give an opinion about something, or asks about facts which are easy to remember.

Example

> **TV Survey**
>
> 1 What is your favourite TV channel? ☐ BBC1 ☐ BBC2 ☐ ITV
>
> ☐ Channel 4 ☐ Channel 5
>
> 2 Did you watch TV last night? ☐ Yes ☐ No

◆ The data needed for some investigations can only be collected:

❖ over a period of time

> How much time do you spend in a week watching each TV channel?

❖ by designing an experiment.

> People take longer to get to sleep the more light there is in the room.

The data collection sheet used for these types of investigation can be called an **observation sheet**.

Exercise 23.2
Experiments

> To design your experiment:
> ❖ decide what data you need
> ❖ decide how to collect it
> ❖ design an observation sheet.

1 Design an observation sheet to collect data on how much time people spend in a week watching each TV channel.

2 Design an experiment to test this hypothesis.

3 **a** Carry out your experiment.
b Analyse the data you collect.

> **Body Matters**
> Your waist is roughly two times the distance around your neck.

4 Do you think the hypothesis is true or false? Explain why.

5 Design an experiment to answer this question.

6 **a** Carry out your experiment.
b Analyse the data you collect.
c Interpret your results to answer the question.

> **Body Matters**
> How many times do people blink in a day?

7 Design an experiment to test this hypothesis.

8 **a** Carry out your experiment.
b Analyse the data you collect.

> **Body Matters**
> Taller people do not have as good a sense of balance as shorter people.

9 Do you think the hypothesis is true or false? Explain why.

Correlation

◆ You can describe the link between two sets of data using the term **correlation**.

Sleep Experiment 1
Does the length of time you take
to fall asleep depend on how light
the room is?

These results show **positive** correlation:
an increase in one set of data tends
to be matched by an increase in the
other set.

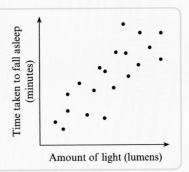

The result of experiment 2
may not be what you expect.
It happens because sleep is
part of your daily rhythm
of sleeping and waking.

Going to bed late means that
you will soon reach your time
for waking, and vice versa.

A daily rhythm, like this
sleep/wake example, is
called a **circadian rhythm**.

Sleep Experiment 2
Does the length of time you
sleep depend on the length of time
since you last slept?

These results show **negative** correlation:
an increase in one set of data tends to be
matched by an decrease in the other set.

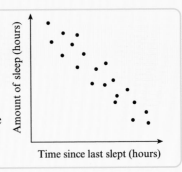

Exercise 23.3
Correlation

1

Mean semi-detached house prices in towns near London – 2nd Quarter 1996												
Distance from London (miles)	44	66	41	75	86	47	68	36	62	77	57	53
Mean house price (£000's)	93	78	98	72	63	97	71	104	86	64	78	88

  a Draw these axes: horizontal 0 to 90, vertical 50 to 130.
  b Plot the house price data on your diagram.
  c Is the correlation positive or negative?

2

A negative number of
dioptres shows short-
sightedness; a positive
number of dioptres shows
long-sightedness.

Eye Tests for 10 people										
Pressure in eye (mmHg)	12.1	11.7	15.2	19.1	11.2	18.9	15.9	17.3	13.0	16.6
Refractive power of lens (dioptres)	3.6	‾3.9	5.1	10.4	‾6.4	3.0	‾6.9	6.5	‾8.4	0.8

  a Draw these axes: horizontal 10 to 20, vertical ‾12 to 12
  b Plot the eye test data on your diagram.
  c Is the correlation positive or negative?

This is called drawing a line
by eye or **by inspection**.

3 For each of your scatter diagrams, draw a line
through the middle of the plots, like this:

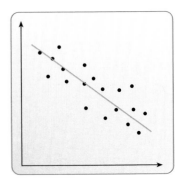

4 Which scatter diagram did you find it
easier to draw the line on? Explain why.

Using a line of best fit

◆ A line drawn through the middle of the plots on a scatter diagram is called a **line of best fit**. The stronger the correlation, the easier it is to draw this line.

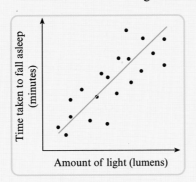

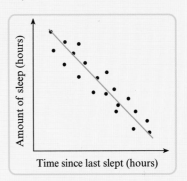

This is **moderate** positive correlation because the plots are well scattered around the line of best fit.

This is **strong** negative correlation because the plots are quite close to the line of best fit.

◆ When it is not possible to draw a line of best fit, there is no link between the two sets of data: there is **no correlation**.

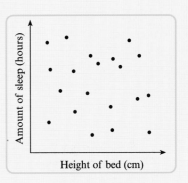

Exercise 23.4
Describing correlation

1 Use this scatter diagram to describe the correlation between income and percentage of income given to charity.

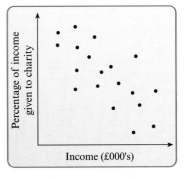

2 Use your scatter diagram from Exercise 23.3 Question **1** to describe the correlation between distance of town from London and mean house price.

3 Use your scatter diagram from Exercise 23.3 Question **2** to describe the correlation between pressure in eye and refractive power of lens.

4 Design an experiment to answer this question:
'Is there any correlation between your fathom and your height?'

Your fathom is the distance between the ends of your fingers when your arms are stretched as wide as possible. This distance is roughly six feet for an adult.

5 **a** Carry out your experiment.
  b Plot the data you collect on a scatter diagram.
  c Draw a line of best fit.
  d Use your scatter diagram to describe any correlation.

Estimating values from a line of best fit

♦ It is possible to estimate values from a line of best fit.

Example

a Estimate the height of a person with head circumference 56 cm.
b Estimate the head circumference of a person 195 cm tall.

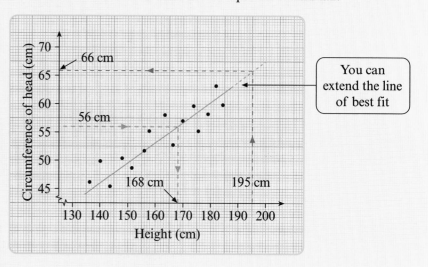

a Estimated height of person with head circumference 56 cm = **168 cm**
b Estimated head circumference of person 195 cm tall = **66 cm**

Exercise 23.5
Estimating values

Use your scatter diagram from Exercise 23.3 Question **1** for Questions **1** to **3**.

1 Estimate the distance from London of a town with a mean house price of:
    a £90 000   **b** £65 000

2 Estimate the mean house price for a town:
    a 70 miles from London   **b** 55 miles from London

3 Extend your line of best fit to estimate:
    a the distance from London of a town with a mean house price of £120 000
    b the mean house price for a town 25 miles from London.

4

Natural Births – Length of Pregnancy & Weight of Baby									
Length of pregnancy (days) 271	287	283	274	271	279	263	276	283	270
Weight of baby (kg) 2.5	4.2	3.8	3.3	4.5	3.4	2.9	4.1	4.3	3.5

This data has been collected to test the hypothesis:
'A longer pregnancy leads to a heavier baby.'
Plot this data on a scatter diagram.

5 **a** Draw a line of best fit on your scatter diagram.
    b Describe the correlation between length of pregnancy and weight of baby.
    c Use your line of best fit to estimate:
      i the length of pregnancy for a baby that weighs 3.5 kg
      ii the weight of a baby with a length of pregnancy of 280 days.

6 Do you think it would make sense to extend this line of best fit? Why?

Misleading diagrams

♦ Diagrams which present data can be misleading in several ways, including:
  ❖ when the vertical axis does not start at 0

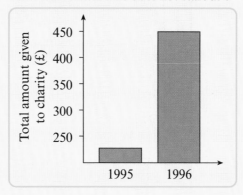

The vertical axis starts at £200.

This gives the impression that the amount given in 1996 was 10 times the amount given in 1995, not 2 times.

  ❖ when enlargements of a shape are used.

The 1996 note is 2 times the height *and* 2 times the width of the 1995 note.

This gives the impression that the amount given in 1996 was 4 times the amount given in 1995.

Exercise 23.6
Misleading diagrams

1 Draw a misleading diagram to show this revenue data by using:

   a a vertical scale which does not start at 0
   b enlargements of a shape.

𝒲𝒟 Wilton Dale Films	1994	1996
Revenue (£m)	6.1	18.3

2 Draw a misleading diagram to show this data for number of visitors.

𝒲𝒟 Wilton Dale Theme Parks	1994	1995	1996
Number of visitors (000's)	24	36	72

3

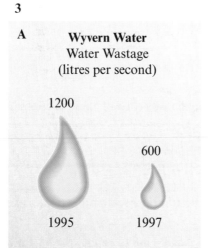

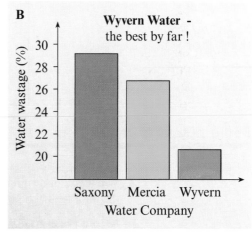

Explain why each of these diagrams is misleading.

End points

You should be able to ...   ... so try these questions

A Design and criticise questions for a questionnaire

A1

Bypass Survey

1 Are you a local?   ☐ Yes   ☐ No
2 What do you think of the traffic in the village? _____
3 Do you agree that the village needs a bypass?   ☐ Yes   ☐ No

a Criticise each of these questions.
b Write an improved question for each one.

B Design experiments

B1 Design an experiment to answer this question.

Body Matters
How long can people hold their breath for?

Petrol Cars – Size of Engine & Petrol Consumption												
Size of engine (litres)	1.6	2.6	1.2	4.0	2.5	1.1	3.2	4.0	3.2	1.8	2.4	3.5
Petrol consumption (mpg)	45	37	40	22	43	48	29	29	33	39	32	25

C Use a scatter diagram and line of best fit to describe correlation

C1
a Draw axes: horizontal 0 to 6.0, vertical 0 to 50
b Plot the petrol car data on your diagram.
c Draw a line of best fit.
d Describe any correlation between size of engine and petrol consumption.

D Estimate values from a line of best fit

D1 Use your scatter diagram to estimate:
a the petrol consumption of a car with a 3.0 litre engine.
b the engine size of a car with petrol consumption of 40 mpg.

D2 Extend your line of best fit to estimate:
a the petrol consumption of a car with a 5.0 litre engine.
b the engine size of a car with petrol consumption of 20 mpg.

E Recognise when diagrams used to present data are misleading

E1 **A**

Flame Gas – blazing the way!

Amount of gas supplied (millions of therms)
60, 58, 56, 54, 52, 50
Western GasOil Flame
Gas Company

B

Flame Gas
Amount of gas supplied (therms)

24m   60m
1996   1997

Explain why each of these diagrams is misleading.

Some points to remember

◆ When you draw a line of best fit on a scatter diagram, make sure the line goes through the middle of the points.

◆ In some cases, it does not make sense to extend the line of best fit on a scatter diagram.

Starting points
You need to know about ...

... so try these questions

A Bearings

- All bearings are:
  - measured clockwise from North
  - written using three figures.

Example

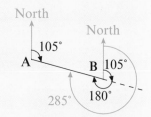

The bearing of B from A is 105°.
The bearing of A from B is 285°.

- You can fix a position by:
  - giving a bearing and distance from one point
  - giving a bearing from two different points.

Example

The point B is on a bearing of 105° from A and is 10 km from A.

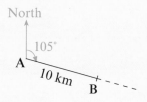

Example

The point C is on a bearing of 078° from A and on a bearing of 320° from B.

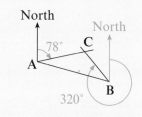

B Pythagoras' rule

- In any right-angled triangle, the area of the square on the hypotenuse is equal to the sum of the area of the squares on the other two sides.

  AB is the hypotenuse, so $AB^2 = AC^2 + BC^2$

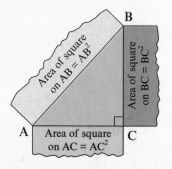

C Trigonometric ratios

- The trigonometric ratios can be used to calculate sides or angles in right-angled triangles.

- Each trig ratio can be written in different ways.

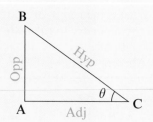

$$\sin \theta = \frac{\text{Opp}}{\text{Hyp}} \qquad \cos \theta = \frac{\text{Adj}}{\text{Hyp}} \qquad \tan \theta = \frac{\text{Opp}}{\text{Adj}}$$

$$\text{Opp} = \text{Hyp} \times \sin \theta \qquad \text{Adj} = \text{Hyp} \times \cos \theta \qquad \text{Opp} = \text{Adj} \times \tan \theta$$

A1 This diagram shows some towns on a radar screen positioned at H.

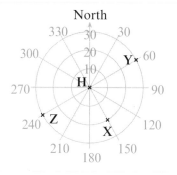

a What is the bearing of:
  i Y from H
  ii H from Y
  iii Z from Y?

b Estimate the bearing of X from Y.

c The rings on the screen are 10 km apart. Point P is due North of X and on a bearing of 030° from H. How far from H is P?

B1 a i From the radar screen above sketch the triangle XHY.
  ii What is the angle $X\hat{H}Y$?
  iii What is the distance HX?
  iv What is the distance HY?

b Calculate the distance XY to the nearest 0.1 km.

C1 Using triangle XHY above calculate the angle $H\hat{X}Y$ to the nearest degree.

C2

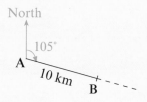

Calculate, to the nearest km:
a TH   b TZ

291

Using trigonometry and Pythagoras' rule

Exercise 24.1
Using trigonometry and
Pythagoras' rule

Accuracy
For this exercise round
your answers to 3 sf.

1 This is Mike's plan for his garden.

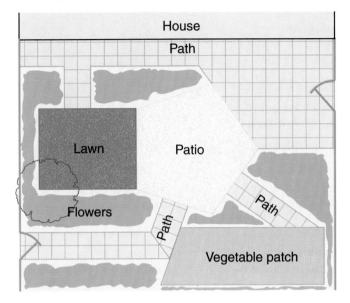

This is a sketch of the vegetable patch.

a What is a mathematical
name for the shape PQRS?
b In ΔPTS:
i what is the length of TS?
ii use Pythagoras' rule to
calculate the length of PS.

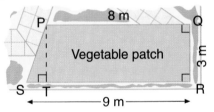

Use the full calculator value
and round your answer at
the end of each question.

c Mike puts netting round the
edge of the vegetable patch.
What length of netting does he need?
d Calculate the area of the vegetable patch.
e A box of fertiliser costs 48 pence and treats 10 square metres.
What would it cost to fertilise the vegetable patch?

2 The patio is a regular pentagon. Each side is 3 metres long.

a What type of triangle is AFE?
b What is the size of angle:
i α   ii β?
c What is the size of FÂM?
d i Draw and label a sketch
of ΔBFA.
ii What is the length of AM?
e Use trigonometry to calculate
the length of:
i AF   ii FM
f Calculate the area of ΔBFA
in square metres.
g What is the total area of
the patio?
h Mike covers the patio in
chippings 7 cm deep.
The chippings cost £14 per cubic metre.
What is the total cost of chippings for his patio, to the nearest 10 pence?

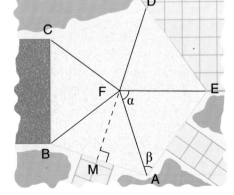

3 On the plan the lawn is a rectangle 3 metres by 5 metres.
The diagonals HB and GC are the same length.

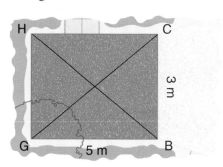

a Use Pythagoras' rule to calculate the length of the diagonal GC.

b When Mike laid the lawn he found that GC was longer than HB. Which of these statements is true?

A $\boxed{C\hat{B}G > 90°}$ B $\boxed{C\hat{B}G = 90°}$ C $\boxed{C\hat{B}G < 90°}$

Exercise 24.2
Choosing trigonometry or
Pythagoras' rule

Accuracy
For this exercise round
your answers to 2 dp.

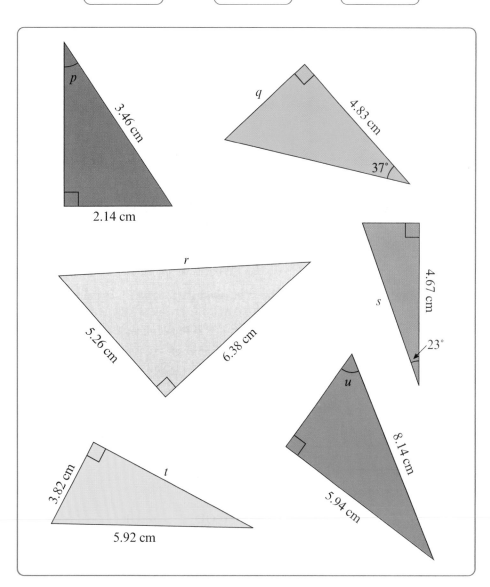

1 For each triangle:
  a calculate the angle or side marked with a letter.
  b say whether you used trigonometry or Pythagoras' rule and explain why.

♦ In any **right-angled triangle** you can use Pythagoras' rule and trigonometry.

- ❖ To find **an angle** when
  you know **two sides** → use **trigonometry**

- ❖ To find **a side** when
  you know an **angle** and **a side** → use **trigonometry**

- ❖ To find **a side** when
  you know **two sides** → use **Pythagoras' rule**

Exercise 24.3
Areas and perimeters

Accuracy
For this exercise round
your answers to 3 sf.

1 This is part of a calculation to find the area of ΔABC.

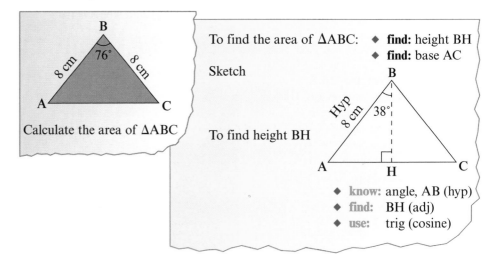

Calculate the area of ΔABC

To find the area of ΔABC: ♦ **find:** height BH
  ♦ **find:** base AC

Sketch

To find height BH

♦ **know:** angle, AB (hyp)
♦ **find:** BH (adj)
♦ **use:** trig (cosine)

a Calculate the height BH.
b Calculate the length of AC.
c Calculate the area of ΔABC.
d What is the perimeter of ΔABC?

2 The quadrilateral OABC is made from two right-angled triangles. AB and BC are 4 cm long, and OB is 8 cm.

a In ΔOAB calculate:
  i the angle AÔB   **ii** OA
b In ΔOBC calculate:
  i the angle CÔB   **ii** OC
c What is the perimeter of OABC?
d Calculate the area of OABC.

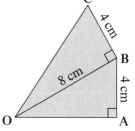

3 If this pattern of triangles is continued the points ABCDE … make a spiral.

a Calculate the lengths:
  i OD   **ii** OE
b Calculate the angles:
  i DÔC   **ii** EÔD
c As the pattern continues:
  i what happens to the length of lines from O?
  ii what happens at O to the angles in the triangles?

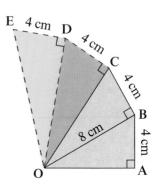

Angles of elevation and depression

♦ From a point A the **angle of elevation** of a point B is the angle between the horizontal and the line of sight from A to B.

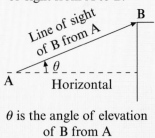

θ is the angle of elevation of B from A

♦ From a point A the **angle of depression** of a point C is the angle between the horizontal and the line of sight from A to C.

β is the angle of depression of C from A

Exercise 24.4
Angles of elevation and depression

Accuracy
For this exercise round your answers to 2 dp.

1 Jan uses a theodolite, at T, to measure the distance and the angle of elevation or depression to points A and B.

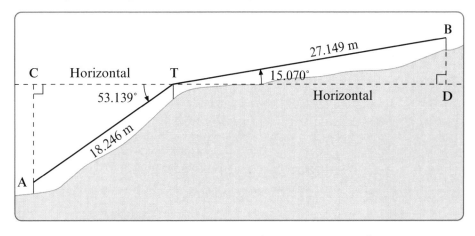

a The angle of depression from T to A is 53.139° and the distance from T to A is 18.246 metres. The point C is vertically above A.
  i Calculate the vertical height AC.
  ii Calculate the horizontal distance CT.

b The angle of elevation from T to B is 15.070° and the distance from T to B is 27.149 metres. The point D is vertically below B.
  i Calculate the vertical height BD.
  ii Calculate the horizontal distance DT.

c On this sketch AE shows the vertical height between A and B, and EB the horizontal distance between A and B. Calculate:
  i the vertical height AE
  ii the horizontal distance EB
  iii the distance AB.

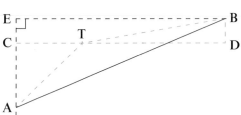

Bearings

Exercise 24.5
Using scale drawings

1 This sketch shows the position of three landmarks A, B and C.

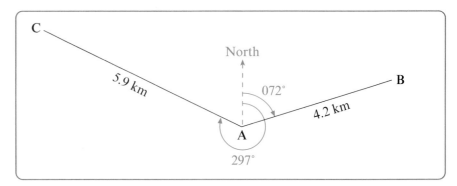

The bearing of B from A is 072° and the distance AB is 4.2 km.
The bearing of C from A is 297° and the distance AC is 5.9 km.

a Make a scale drawing to show the relative position of these landmarks.
b Calculate the bearing of A from B.
c **i** Measure the bearing of C from B.
  ii What is the bearing of B from C?
d Use your drawing to find the distance between B and C.

> Check that any north lines you draw on a diagram are parallel.

2 This sketch shows the position P, Q and R of three buoys.

a Make a scale drawing to show the relative positions of the buoys.
b What is the bearing of Q from R?
c **i** Use your drawing to find the distance between P and R.
  ii How accurate do you think your answer is?

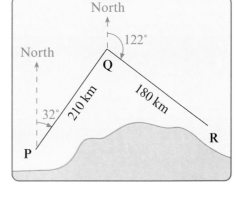

> You can measure each distance and angle from your scale drawing but it is more accurate to calculate them.

d In △PQR:
  i What is the angle PQ̂R?
  ii Calculate the distance between P and R.
e **i** Calculate the angle QP̂R.
  ii What is the bearing of R from P?

Accuracy
For Questions **2d** to **3d**
❖ round each angle to the nearest degree
❖ round each distance to the nearest km.

3 On this sketch TP shows how far P is south of Q, and TQ shows how far P is west of Q.

a Calculate how far P is:
  i south of Q
  ii west of Q.
b In △QUR what is the angle RQ̂U?
c Calculate how far R is:
  i south of Q
  ii east of Q.
d How far is P south of R?

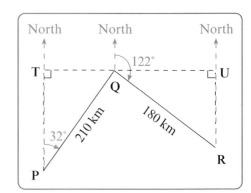

Exercise 24.6
Calculating bearings
and distances

Accuracy
For this exercise
❖ round each distance
to the nearest 0.01 km
❖ round each angle
to the nearest degree.

1 This diagram shows the relative positions of three schools:
Shaw, Castle and Greys.

  a **i** How far north of Castle is Shaw?
     ii How far east of Castle is Shaw?
  b Calculate:
     i the distance of Castle from Shaw
     ii the bearing of Shaw from Castle.
  c **i** How far south of Castle is Greys?
     ii How far east of Castle is Greys?
  d Calculate:
     i the distance from Castle to Greys
     ii the bearing of Greys from Castle.

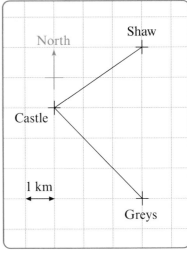

2 There is a lighthouse at Alington, Bandon and Colton.
Bandon is 78 km from Alington on a bearing of 320°.
Colton is due north of Alington and due east of Bandon.

  a Draw a sketch to show the relative positions of these lighthouses.
  b What is the bearing:
     i of Alington from Bandon
     ii of Colton from Bandon
     iii of Alington to Colton?
  c Calculate the distance from:
     i Alington to Colton
     ii Bandon to Colton.

3 This diagram shows the route taken by a boat which starts at P.
The boat sails on a bearing of 143°
for 24 km to a buoy at Q, then sails
due south for 18 km to a buoy at R.
The point S is due north of Q and
due east of P.

  a Calculate the distance:
     i PS   **ii** SQ
  b How far is R south of P?
  c Use your answers to
    Questions **3a** and **3b**:
     i to calculate the distance
      between P and R
     ii to calculate the bearing of
      R from P.
  d What is the bearing of P from R?

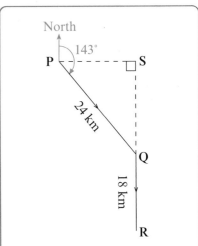

4 Another boat starts at P and sails 8 km
due east, then 17 km due north to a buoy at T.

  a Sketch a diagram to show the route taken by this boat.
  b Calculate:
     i the bearing of T from P
     ii the distance from P to T.

Solving problems

Exercise 24.7
Solving problems

> **Accuracy**
> For this exercise round your answers to 4 sf.

1 This is a sketch of the cross-section of a roof.

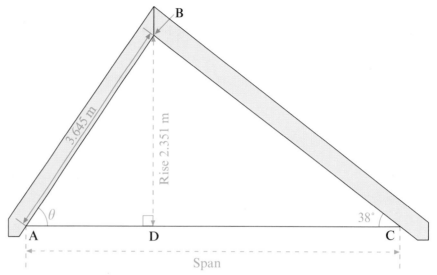

The pitch of the rafter BC is 38°. The rise of the roof is 2.351 metres. The length AB is 3.645 metres.

a For the rafter AB calculate the pitch, θ.
b Calculate the distance AD in metres.
c Calculate the length of BC.
d Calculate the distance DC.
e What is the span of the roof?

2 This diagram shows the cross-section of another roof with a dormer window. The pitch of the roof at E is 47° and the distance EH is 2.449 m.

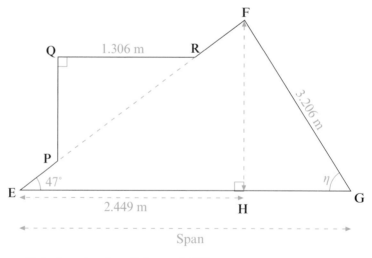

a Calculate the rise of the roof, FH.
b Calculate the distance GH.
c What is the span of the roof?
d For the rafter FG, calculate the pitch, η.
e What is the angle $Q\hat{R}P$?
f Calculate the height of the window, PQ.

End points

You should be able to ...

... so try these questions

A Use Pythagoras' rule and trigonometry

For each of these questions give your answers correct to 1 dp.

A1

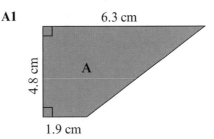

6.3 cm

4.8 cm

A

1.9 cm

4.5 cm

B

32.8°

Calculate the area and perimeter of shapes A and B.

B Use angles of elevation and depression

B1 This sketch shows a point A at the top of a vertical cliff 200 metres above sea level.
The boats at C and D are due west of A.

a The angle of depression from A to D is 38°.
  i What is the angle ADB?
  ii Calculate the distance DB in metres.
b The distance CB is 163 metres.
  i What is the distance between the two boats?
  ii Calculate the angle of depression of C from A.

A

38°

200 m

D   C   B

C Use bearings and distances

C1 A boat sailed 15 km due west from P, and then sailed 17 km on a bearing of 207° to R.
a What is the bearing of Q from R?
b Calculate these distances in kilometres:
  i TR   ii QT   iii TP
c Calculate the distance RP.
d Calculate the bearing:
  i of P from R
  ii of R from P.

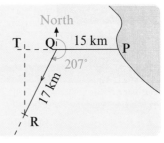

North

T   Q   15 km   P

207°

17 km

R

Some points to remember

♦ Pythagoras' rule and trigonometric ratios can be used in any **right-angled triangle**.
It may help to draw and label a sketch of each triangle you use.

♦ Measured answers from scale drawings will not be as accurate as ones you calculate.

♦ **Angles of elevation** and **angles of depression** are measured from the horizontal.

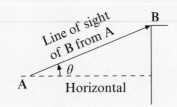

B

Line of sight of B from A

θ

A   Horizontal

θ is the angle of elevation of B from A.

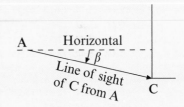

A   Horizontal

β

Line of sight of C from A

C

β is the angle of depression of C from A.

Eurotunnel

The first tunnel-boring machine (TBM) started work for Eurotunnel on the UK side in December 1987 and on the French side in January 1988. Each TBM bored about 4.4 metres per hour.

The two railway tunnels and the smaller service tunnel are each 50 km long with 38 km under the Channel, 3km on land in France and 9km on land in the UK.

The lining rings for the railway tunnels are 40 cm thick and 1.6 metres long. For the service tunnel the rings are 32 cm thick and 1.4 metres long. The ventilation system replaces 145 m³ of air per second.

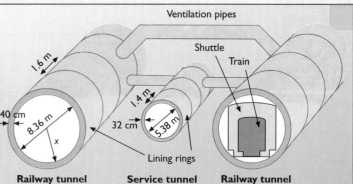

Railway tunnel **Service tunnel** **Railway tunnel**

In Eurotunnel
- Shuttles carry vehicles with their passengers between Folkstone to Calais
- Eurostar trains carry passengers between Waterloo and Paris and Brussels

Eurostar trains fact file

Each train on Eurostar consist of 2 engines, 2 buffet cars and 16 carriages:

- 6 first-class (2 smoking, 4 no-smoking)
- 10 second-class (4 smoking, 6 no-smoking)

These give a total of 794 seats (210 first-class, 584 second-class) and an additional 52 folding seats.

Each train is 394 metres long, 2.8 metres wide and weighs 752 tonnes.

Its maximum speed is 300 km/h on high-speed lines, 220 km/h on standard track and 160 km/h in the tunnel.

 Check-in closes 20 minutes before departure.

Le Shuttle

The maximum speed for any shuttle is 140 km/h.

Passenger-vehicle shuttles

These carry passengers who remain with their car, coach, caravans, minibus, motorcycle or bicycle. Each shuttle can transport 120 cars and 12 coaches. The average journey time is about 35 minutes, of which 26 minutes are spent in the tunnel. At peak times there are up to 4 departures, and one departure per hour at off-peak night times.

Freight shuttles

These transport Heavy Goods Vehicles (HGV's). Their drivers are carried in a club car at the front of each shuttle, which carry up to 28 HGV's. At peak times there are up to 3 departures, and one departure per hour at off-peak night times. The average journey time from motorway to motorway is 80 minutes.

TIMETABLE

Eurostar trains	SUNDAYS						July to September	
London to Paris								
London Waterloo	08:10	10:10	11:57	12:53	13:57	15:10	16:23	16:53
Ashford	09:23	-	-	13:53	-	-	17:24	17:54
Calais-Frethun	-	14:29	-	-	17:56	-	-	-
Lille Europe	-	-	-	-	-	-	19:26	-
Paris Nord	12:23	14:17	15:56	16:53	17:56	19:23	20:29	20:56
Paris to London								
Paris Nord	08:07	10:19	11:43	13:04	15:19	16:07	17:10	18:18
Lille Europe	-	-	12:44	-	-	-	-	-
Calais-Frethun	09:34	-	-	14:31	-	17:34	-	-
Ashford	09:10	-	-	14:07	-	17:11	18:11	-
London Waterloo	10:30	12:30	13:47	15:26	17:13	18:13	19:13	20:13
London to Brussels								
London Waterloo	09:14	12:14	14:10	17:27	18:27	19:27		
Ashford	10:27	13:27	-	-	19:28	20:27		
Lille Europe	12:30	15:29	17:21	-	21:31	-		
Brussels Midi	13:44	16:44	18:34	21:38	22:45	23:43		
Brussels to London								
Brussels Midi	08:27	10:31	12:31	15:28	17:22	19:27		
Lille Europe	09:40	11:45	13:45	16:42	18:36	20:39		
Ashford	09:41	-	-	16:41	18:37	20:41		
London Waterloo	10:47	12:47	14:47	17:43	19:39	21:43		

Traffic in Eurotunnel 1995

	Passenger-vehicle shuttles	Freight shuttles	Eurostar trains	Freight trains
Jan/Feb	101 324 cars	40 328 lorries	728	733
Mar	72 618 cars	22 580 lorries	506	432
Apr	96 735 cars	22 648 lorries	542	404
May	80 995 cars	28 267 lorries	595	465
Jun	100 534 cars	32 657 lorries	730	596
Jul	112 060 cars 2402 coaches	7126 lorries	851	644
Aug	145 861 cars 2728 coaches	36 517 lorries	844	425
Sep	105 914 cars 3033 coaches	38 136 lorries	862	515
Oct	120 368 cars 3794 coaches	42 630 lorries	983	523
Nov	129 286 cars 5120 coaches	48 263 lorries	897	464
Dec	156 999 cars 6306 coaches	41 770 lorries	659	88

1   On which side of the Channel did they first start digging the tunnel?

2   What is the radius of the hole they bored for:
    a   the service tunnel
    b   a railway tunnel?

3   In which month in 1995 did Le Shuttle carry the greatest number of lorries?

4   How many minutes does the 08:10 take from London to Ashford on a Sunday?

5   Is the journey time from London to Paris the same for every train? Explain your answer.

6   How many minutes of each shuttle journey are not spent in the tunnel?

7   What is the difference between the maximum speed of a Eurostar train and a Shuttle in the tunnel?

8   If Amin reaches Waterloo at 3:50 pm on a Sunday, what is the first Eurostar train he can catch to Brussels?

9   a   What is the last train Pia could catch from Waterloo to arrive in Paris by 6:00 pm?
    b   Which stations does this train stop at?

10 Which is the first train from Paris that stops at Lille?

11 What is the time of the first train from Lille to London on a Sunday?

12 a   What is the latest time that Ethel can arrive at Waterloo to catch the 14:10 to Brussels?
    b   At what time should she arrive in Brussels?

13 What is the destination of the first Eurostar train that stops at Calais on a Sunday?

14 a   Calculate the volume of material that was removed (spoil) when they bored the service tunnel. Give your answer in m³ correct to 3 sf.
    b   Rewrite your answer in standard index form.

15 a   What total volume of spoil was removed to make the two railway tunnels?

    b   The total spoil from all the excavations was 8 million m³. What percentage of the spoil was from the two railway tunnels?

16 a   What is the thickness of the lining ring for a railway tunnel in metres?
    b   What is the value of x, the internal radius of a railway tunnel?
    c   Calculate the capacity of a railway tunnel.

17 How many lining rings were used in:
    a   one railway tunnel?
    b   the service tunnel?

18 How many minutes would it take the ventilation system to replace all the air in the two railway tunnels?

19 In what month were coaches carried on Le Shuttle for the first time?

20 How many coaches were carried in total in 1995?

21 a   Draw a graph to show the number of coaches carried during 1995.
    b   Sketch a graph to show the number of coaches you think were carried each month in 1996.

22 a   What was the highest number of cars carried in one month in 1995? Write your answer in standard form correct to 2 sf.
    b   Calculate the mean number of cars carried per week.

23 Calculate the mean number of lorries carried per month.

24 If the average number of passengers on a Eurostar train was 635, estimate the total number of passengers carried on Eurostar trains in 1995. Give your answer in standard form to 2 sf.

25 What is the average number of seats in a first-class carriage?

26 Do you think that every second-class carriage has the same number of seats? Explain your answer.

27 What is the average number of seats per carriage on a Eurostar train?

28 a   What is the maximum speed of a shuttle?
    b   What is the average speed of a shuttle in the tunnel?

29 What is the ratio of first-class to second-class seats in its simplest form?

30 Write the length of a Eurostar train as a percentage of the length of the tunnel.

31 If the average speed of a Eurostar train in the tunnel is 158 km/h, calculate how long it takes to go through the tunnel.

32 What percentage of Eurotunnel is on:
    a   French land?   b   UK land?

33 Estimate the number of passenger-vehicle shuttles used during September. Explain your answer.

Decorum Design

DDC is the favourite shop for trade and private buyers who want a new look for bathrooms, kitchens and bedrooms. Here are some of our items but come to the shop to see our full range.

■ WALLPAPER – rolls

width 53 cm, length 10 metres.

FLORAL DESIGN £5.49 per roll.

£4.97 each for 12 rolls or more

ANTIQUE EMBOSSED £7.99 per roll

WALLPAPER PASTE £4.99 – covers 10 sq metres

TRY OUR ANTIQUE EMBOSSED PAPERS TO COVER THAT TATTY WALL

ALL PAINT PRICES REDUCED BY 20% FOR NEXT THREE WEEKS

■ EMULSION PAINTS – Top quality own brand

BRILLIANT WHITE	1 litre	£3.42
	2 (1/2) litre	£8.45
	5 litre	£16.99
PASTEL SHADES	2 (1/2) litre	£11.99
	5 litre	£19.49

A litre tin will cover about 8 m² with a single coat.

Two coats needed over very dark surfaces.

When calculating how much paint to order, do not subtract the area of doors and windows.

■ WALL TILES – imported Italian and French

JARDIN RANGE – Box of 10 tiles £1.79

ASSISI RANGE – Box of 10 tiles £1.99

JARDIN   ASSISI

For those who have not caught up with metric units yet.

1 foot = 0.3048 metres   1 inch = 25.4 millimetres

All prices include VAT at 17.5%

TILE-FIX CEMENT – £7.99 a tub, covers 4 sq. metres

FORRET – Box of 10 wall tiles £2.14

BENETIA – Box of 10 tiles £2.14

FORRE

BENETIA

■ FLOOR TILES

QUARRY TILES – terracotta, 120mm x 120 mm, 31p each

CERAMIC REGULAR SHAPED TILES – choice of patterns

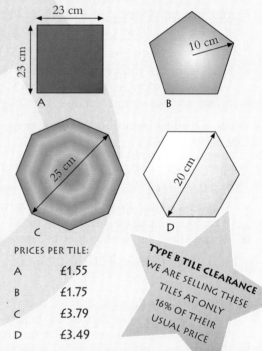

PRICES PER TILE:

A	£1.55
B	£1.75
C	£3.79
D	£3.49

TYPE B TILE CLEARANCE WE ARE SELLING THESE TILES AT ONLY 16% OF THEIR USUAL PRICE

We also sell small square tiles to fit with our type C tile. Pack of ten £5.75

TILE CEMENT – 12 kg bag – £17.89 – enough for 10 square metres of floor.

COLOURED GROUT £7.69 per tub – enough for 15 square metres of floor.

When calculating what to order, allow one complete tile for every part of a tile you need.

■ DESIGN SERVICE

We offer a free design service for bathrooms and kitchens. Just give us your plans to a scale of 1:50 and we will calculate how much paint, wallpaper or tiling you need.

1 What is the cost of a $2\frac{1}{2}$ litre can of pastel shade paint if you buy it within the next 3 weeks?

2 How much does it cost for 9 rolls of floral design wallpaper?

3 Spencer has decided to tile the wall above a bath with Jardin style tiles. He wants to cover an area 2 m by 60 cm.
  a How many tiles will he need to buy?
  b What will this cost him (including tile-fix)?

4 Sally decides to paper a wall in her bedroom with antique embossed paper. The wall is 3.1 metres long by 2.3 metres high.
  a How many widths of antique paper are needed for the length of wall?
  b How many rolls should she buy?
  c What is the total cost of paper and paste?

5 **a** Give a mathematical reason why the type B wall tiles are being sold off so cheaply.
  b What is the reduced price of one type B tile?

6 Mike uses Decorum's design service to calculate the number of quarry tiles he should buy for a floor which is 3.82 metres by 4.15 metres.
  a Make a scale drawing of the floor to the correct scale.
  b Calculate the number of tiles he needs.
  c Decorum add 5 % for tiles that might break. How many should Mike buy?

7 Kate's bedroom is cuboidal in shape.
It is 2.84 metres long by 2.32 metres wide and 2.28 metres high.
She wishes to paint all walls and the ceiling in brilliant white.
  a Calculate the total area she wants to paint.
  b Her room is dark blue now. What size tins of paint should she buy? Give your reasons.

8 For type D tiles:
  a What is the mathematical name of the shape?
  b What is the size of an internal angle?
  c Why does the shape tessellate?
  d What is the length of a side?

9 Steve's floor is 3.95 metres by 2.37 metres and he wants to tile it with type A tiles. He works out that the area of the floor is 9.36 m² and that the area of one tile is 0.0529 m².
He says the number of tiles he needs is 9.36 ÷ 0.0529 = 177 tiles.
  a What is wrong with Steve's method?
  b How many tiles does he really need?
  c What is the cost including grout and cement?

10 This is a scale drawing (scale 1:50) of a wall.
  a What is its true length in metres?
  b What is its true height?

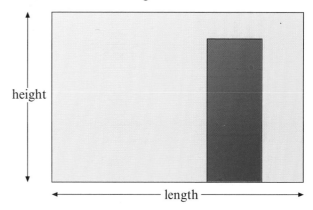

11 Which size tin of brilliant white paint is the best value for money? Explain your answer.

12 Shirley and Arthur measure their kitchen floor as 13 ft 6 inches by 11 ft 10 inches.
  a Give these measurements in metres to the nearest centimetre?
  b How much will they have to pay for tile cement and grout if they tile the floor?

13 Decorum are thinking of selling smaller bags of tile cement. They have chosen a 5 kg size as most useful. If they price it at the same unit cost as the 12 kg bag at what price will they sell it? Give your answer to the nearest penny.

14 An area 1.28 metres high by 2.32 metres wide is to be tiled with either Forret or Benetia tiles.
Which tiles would it be cheaper to use and why?

15 **a** What is the mathematical name of the shape of the type C floor tile?
  b Calculate the size of an internal angle of this shape.
  c Type C shapes will tessellate with squares. Calculate the dimensions of these squares.

16 Type C tiles will also tessellate with isosceles triangles. Draw and cut out an accurate scale model of a type C tile. Use this as a template to show how these will tessellate with triangles.

17 Pragna runs her own business and can claim back the VAT she pays. She buys a 5 litre tin of pastel paint for £19.49 which includes VAT.
  a What is the cost of this tin without VAT?
  b How much VAT can she claim back?

18 Type B tiles would be of more use if the shop also sold another different shaped tile. Draw what you think this tile shape could be.

Number bites

1 Which of these calculations give a negative answer?

$$\boxed{\text{A } ^-4 \times ^-3} \quad \boxed{\text{B } 1.5 \times ^-8} \quad \boxed{\text{C } 8 \div ^-2.4}$$

$$\boxed{\text{D } ^-9 \div 3.7} \quad \boxed{\text{E } 5.1 \times ^-1.1} \quad \boxed{\text{F } ^-8 \div ^-7}$$

$$\boxed{\text{G } ^-2.4 \times ^-3.8} \quad \boxed{\text{H } 4.4 \div ^-1.9}$$

2 Copy and complete these calculations.

a $^-6 \times 3 = \square$ b $^-4 \times ^-2 = \square$ c $^-14 \div 7 = \square$
d $\square \div 6 = ^-3$ e $\square \times ^-4 = ^-20$ f $^-5 \times \square = 35$
g $10 \div ^-2 = \square$ h $8 \times ^-3 = \square$ i $^-15 \div ^-3 = \square$
j $\square \times 7 = ^-28$ k $\square \div ^-2 = 8$ l $^-36 \div \square = ^-4$

3 Find the values of each of these square roots to 2 dp.

a $\sqrt{73}$ b $\sqrt{94.36}$ c $\sqrt{6464}$ d $\sqrt{13.1044}$

4 Find the value of:

a 8^3 b 2.7^3 c 0.5^3 d $^-4^3$ e $^-1.8^3$ f $^-0.3^3$

g $\sqrt[3]{27000}$ h $\sqrt[3]{729}$ i $\sqrt[3]{1}$ j $\sqrt[3]{1.728}$

5 Find the reciprocal of:

a 2 b 10 c 0.4 d 0.6 e $0.\dot{3}$
f 0.16 g 0.01 h 5 i 12 j $0.\dot{2}$
k 11 l $0.\dot{2}\dot{7}$

6 Write as a fraction the reciprocal of:

a $\frac{2}{3}$ b $\frac{4}{5}$ c $\frac{11}{6}$ d $\frac{13}{8}$

e $1\frac{1}{3}$ f $2\frac{2}{5}$ g 1.4 h 1.6

7

5^{-3}		5^{-1}	5^0		5^2	
	$\frac{1}{25}$			5		125

Copy and complete this powers of 5 table.

8 Make a powers of 6 table from 6^{-3} to 6^3.

9 $\boxed{7^0 = 0 \; ✗}$

Explain why this is wrong.

10 Write these as fractions.

a 4^{-1} b 2^{-3} c 3^{-2} d 6^{-2} e 10^{-3} f 10^{-4}
g 6^0 h 7^{-2} i 8^{-2} j 4^{-3} k 3^{-4} l 10^0

11 Calculate:

a 297×3^{-2} b 400×2^{-5} c 63×4^{-1}
d 2.7×10^{-2} e $13 \div 2^{-3}$ f $7.2 \div 5^{-2}$
g $0.9 \div 3^{-4}$ h $62 \div 10^{-2}$

12 Write these as decimals.

a 5^{-1} b 2^{-2} c 8^{-1} d 10^{-2} e 4^{-3}
f 3^{-2} g 8^{-2} h 5^{-3} i 10^{-3} j 100^{-1}
k 6^{-2} l 10^{-5}

13 Write these numbers in standard form.

a $6\,170\,000$ b $92\,000\,000\,000$ c $307\,000$
d $0.000\,025$ e $0.000\,002\,603$ f $0.000\,0001$

14 Write these as ordinary numbers.

a 4.5×10^8 b 3.606×10^{12} c 1.24×10^{-9}
d 7×10^7 e 5.1×10^{-11} f 6.1047×10^{-6}

15 Give the answer to each of these in standard form.

a $75 \times (1.74 \times 10^9)$ b $144 \times (8.6 \times 10^{-6})$
c $(6.09 \times 10^{-7}) \div 7$ d $(4.446 \times 10^{12}) \div 52$
e $(3.2 \times 10^8) \times (5.95 \times 10^{-2})$
f $(2.92 \times 10^{-6}) \div (4 \times 10^7)$
g $(4.7 \times 10^{14}) + (3 \times 10^{15})$ h $(4.5 \times 10^9) - (4 \times 10^8)$

16 Give the answer to these using index notation.

a $4^{-7} \times 4^3$ b $3^8 \times 3^{-2}$ c $5^6 \div 5^2$ d $2^5 \div 2^{-3}$
e $5^0 \times 5^7$ f $7^{-4} \times 7^{-2}$ g $4^{-6} \div 4^3$ h $6^{-3} \div 6^{-8}$

17 Copy and complete these calculations.

a $3^8 \times 3^\square = 3^6$ b $6^\square \div 6^3 = 6^2$
c $2^{-4} \div 2^\square = 2^{-7}$ d $8^\square \times 8^{-3} = 8^2$
e $3^\square \div 3^{-7} = 3^5$ f $7^{-5} \times 7^\square = 7^{-8}$

18 Without using a calculator, give the answer to these in standard form.

a $(6 \times 10^7) \div (3 \times 10^4)$ b $(5 \times 10^{-2}) \times (8 \times 10^6)$
c $(2 \times 10^{-3}) \times (3.5 \times 10^{-5})$ d $(4 \times 10^{-2}) \div (8 \times 10^4)$

19

$$\boxed{p = \tfrac{1}{3}} \quad \boxed{q = \tfrac{3}{4}} \quad \boxed{r = \tfrac{2}{5}} \quad \boxed{s = \tfrac{5}{6}}$$

$$\boxed{w = 1\tfrac{2}{3}} \quad \boxed{x = 2\tfrac{1}{2}} \quad \boxed{y = 1\tfrac{4}{5}} \quad \boxed{z = 3\tfrac{1}{6}}$$

Evaluate:

a $p+r$ b $r+s$ c $q+s$ d $r-p$ e $q-r$
f $s-p$ g $w+z$ h $s+w$ i $x+y$ j $y-w$

20 Evaluate:

a pr b pq c rs d $\dfrac{r}{q}$ e $\dfrac{p}{s}$ f $\dfrac{s}{q}$

g ry h sw i xy j $\dfrac{q}{x}$ k $\dfrac{z}{w}$ l $\dfrac{z}{s}$

21 Evaluate:

a $3q$ b $8s$ c $12p$ d $\dfrac{20}{s}$ e $\dfrac{12}{q}$ f $\dfrac{3}{r}$

g $2w$ h $12z$ i $4y$ j $\dfrac{5}{w}$ k $\dfrac{36}{y}$ l $\dfrac{16}{x}$

22 Find the LCM of:

a 4 and 9 b 6 and 8 c 16 and 120
d 126 and 300 e 14, 20 and 175

23 Find the HCF of:

a 45 and 81 b 42 and 154 c 90 and 175
d 72 and 132 e 84, 105 and 175

Sequences

1   Each diagram shows the first three patterns in a sequence.

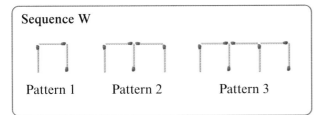

Sequence W

Pattern 1   Pattern 2   Pattern 3

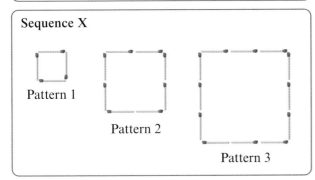

Sequence X

Pattern 1

Pattern 2

Pattern 3

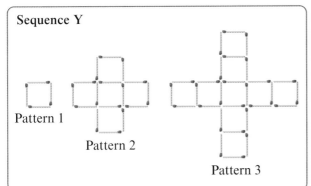

Sequence Y

Pattern 1

Pattern 2

Pattern 3

For each sequence:

a   Draw the 4th pattern.

b   Find a rule for the number of matches (*m*)
in the *n*th pattern.
Write it in the form *m* = … .

c   Show how you found your rule.

d   Use your rule to calculate the number of
matches in the 10th pattern.

2   Copy and complete each mapping diagram.

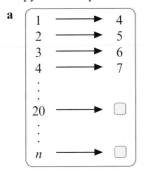

a

1	→	4
2	→	5
3	→	6
4	→	7
⋮		
20	→	☐
⋮		
n	→	☐

b

1	→	1
2	→	3
3	→	5
4	→	7
⋮		
40	→	☐
⋮		
t	→	☐

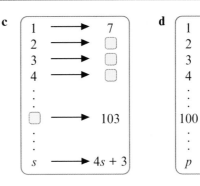

c

1	→	7
2	→	☐
3	→	☐
4	→	☐
⋮		
☐	→	103
⋮		
s	→	4*s* + 3

d

1	→	11
2	→	20
3	→	29
4	→	38
⋮		
100	→	☐
⋮		
p	→	☐

3   These are the first three patterns in a sequence.

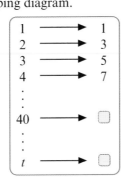

Sequence Z

Pattern 1

Pattern 2

Pattern 3

a   Find a rule for the number of matches in
the *n*th pattern in the form *n* ⟶ … .

b   Show how you found your rule.

4   Copy and complete
this mapping diagram.

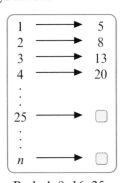

1	→	5
2	→	8
3	→	13
4	→	20
⋮		
25	→	☐
⋮		
n	→	☐

5   A 1, 4, 7, 10, 13, …   B 1, 4, 9, 16, 25, …
C 7, 13, 19, 25, 31, …   D 3, 12, 27, 48, 75, …
E 7, 12, 17, 22, 27, …   F 2, 6, 10, 14, 18, …
G 11, 14, 19, 26, 35, … H 9, 17, 25, 33, 41, …

For each of the sequences A to H:

a   Find an expression for the *n*th term.

b   Use your expression to find the 30th term.

6   Multiply out the brackets from:

a   5(*p* + 2)   **b**   8(*n* − 3)   **c**   4(*c* + 5)
d   2(3*r* + 1)   **e**   5(7 + *x*)   **f**   7(2*s* − 3)
g   3(1 − 5*t*)   **h**   2(3*m* − 6)   **i**   20(5*k* − 1)
j   8(4 − *z*)   **k**   10(5 − 2*t*)   **l**   4(*a* + *b*)
m   3(2*g* + *h*)   **n**   5(*x* − *y*)   **o**   7(3*c* − 2*d*)

Properties of shapes

1

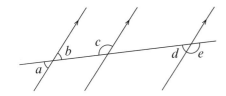

   a If $a = 47°$, calculate angles b to e.
   b If $a = 51.5°$, calculate the angles b to e.
   c If $e = 169°$, calculate angles a to d.

2 These polygons are drawn on a grid of parallel lines. The diagonals of PQRS are marked in red.

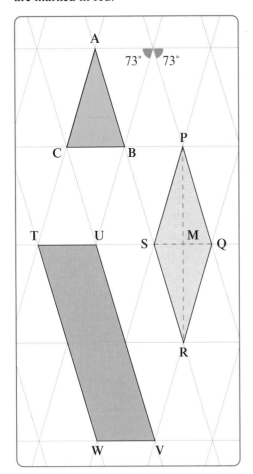

   a Work out each interior angle of $\triangle ABC$.
   b What type of triangle is ABC?
   c Work out each interior angle of:
      i PQRS   **ii** TUVW.
   d Explain why PQRS is a rhombus.
   e Explain why TUVW cannot be a rhombus.
   f The diagonals of PQRS intersect at M. Work out each of these angles:
      i $P\hat{M}Q$ **ii** $P\hat{Q}M$ **iii** $M\hat{Q}R$
      iv $Q\hat{R}M$ **v** $S\hat{R}M$

3 These quadrilaterals are on an isometric grid.

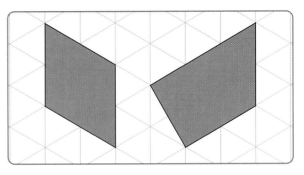

   a Show how each of these quadrilaterals will tessellate on its own.
   b Show how they will tessellate together.

4 Calculate the angles a to m in the diagram below.

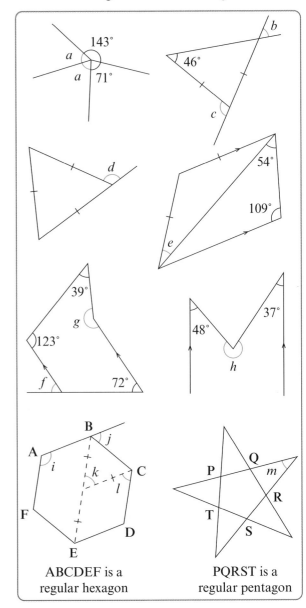

ABCDEF is a regular hexagon

PQRST is a regular pentagon

Linear graphs

1 Give the gradient of each of these lines.

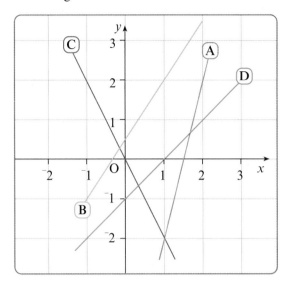

2 On a grid, draw lines with each of these gradients.

a 3   **b** $\frac{1}{2}$ **c** $^-2$ **d** $\frac{3}{4}$

e 1   **f** $\frac{-1}{2}$ **g** $\frac{2}{3}$ **h** 4

i $\frac{1}{4}$ **j** $\frac{-2}{3}$ **k** $\frac{1}{5}$ **l** 5

3 Each of these is the equation of a linear graph:

$y = 2x + 1$ $y = 3x - 2$ $y = x - 2$
$y = 2x - 3$ $y = x + 2$ $y = x$

For each equation:

a Draw up a table of values.
Use values of x from $^-1$ to 4.
b List the coordinates of points on the line.
c Draw the graph of the equation.

4 For each of these lines give the gradient and the y-intercept.

a $y = 4x - 3$ **b** $y = 1 + 2x$ **c** $y = 2 - 3x$
d $y = x$ **e** $y = ^-x$ **f** $y = 2 + 5x$
g $y = ^-1 - 2x$ **h** $y = x + 1$ **i** $y = 1.5x + 2$
j $y = 0.5 + x$ **k** $y = 3 - 0.5x$ **l** $y = 1$
m $y = \frac{1}{2}x$ **n** $y = \frac{3}{4}x - 1$ **o** $y = x - \frac{3}{5}$
p $y = 1.6 - x$ **q** $y = x + 1.2$ **r** $y = ^-3x$

5 Here is a description of five different lines.

Line A: has a gradient of 2 and a y-intercept of $^-8$
Line B: gradient 3, y-intercept 4
Line C: gradient $\frac{3}{4}$, y-intercept $^-1$
Line D: y-intercept 3, gradient $^-5$
Line E: gradient $^-7$

Give an equation for each of these lines.

6 Rewrite each of these equations to read $y = ...$

a $2y = 4x - 8$ **b** $3y = 6x + 9$
c $5y = 10x - 15$ **d** $4y = 2 + 8x$
e $3y = 2x + 6$ **f** $2y = 5x + 7$
g $4y = 3x + 1$ **h** $3y = 6x - 3$
i $5y = 6x + 2$ **j** $4y = 1 + x$
k $2y = x$ **l** $3y = ^-2x$
m $8y = 4 + 6x$ **n** $2y = 5 - 3x$
o $3y = 1 - 2x$ **p** $2 - 2x = 2y$

7 Write three different equations that can be rewritten as $y = 3 - 5x$.

8 Write three different equations that can be rewritten as $y = x + 0.5$

9 For each of these equations draw a graph.

a $y = 2x$ **b** $y = 3x - 5$ **c** $y = \frac{1}{2}x$
d $2y = 3x - 4$ **e** $4y = 5x$ **f** $3y = 3x$
g $2y = 4 - 3x$ **h** $2y = 6$ **i** $5y = x$
j $5y = ^-x$ **k** $3y = 4x + 6$ **l** $y = 0.25x$

10

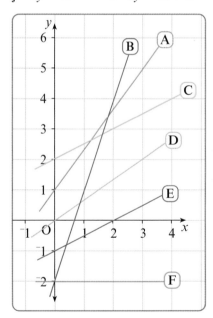

Give an equation for each of the lines A to F.

11 Without drawing a graph, which of these lines is drawn through the point $(3, 2)$?

a $y = x - 1$ **b** $3y = 7x - 15$
c $y = 2$ **d** $3y = x + 3$
e $3y = 2x$ **f** $y = 2x - 4$
g $3y = 12 - 2x$ **h** $y = 5 - 2x$

12 Without drawing a graph, give the equation of three different lines that are drawn through the point $(1, 3)$.

Comparing data

1

CHILDREN IN CARE Expenditure (1994–95)	£m
Child Care	18.5
Fundraising	7.0
Administration	3.0
Other costs	1.5

CHILD SAFETY Expenditure (1994–95)	%
Child Care	65
Fundraising	20
Administration	10
Other costs	5

Draw a pie chart for each charity to show how their money is spent.

2

Chris

Ring score	6	7	8	9	10
Frequency	1	4	2	1	4

Dani

Ring score	3	4	5	6	7	8	9
Frequency	2	1	0	3	4	2	3

Sam

Ring score	1	2	3	4	5	6
Frequency	4	3	1	0	3	5

Find the median score for each archer by listing the data.

3

Bella

Ring score	2	3	4	5	6	7	8	Total
Frequency	3	4	7	6	11	6	6	43

Emily

Ring score	5	6	7	8	9	Total
Frequency	12	19	17	9	7	64

Gavin

Ring score	3	4	5	6	7	8	9	10
Frequency	4	2	5	7	8	11	9	6

For each distribution:

a construct a cumulative frequency table

b find the median score.

4 Calculate the mean score for each archer. Give your answers to 1 dp.

5

Asif

Ring score	3	4	5	6	7	8	9
Frequency	1	3	2	2	3	4	1

Suki

Ring score	4	5	6	7	8
Frequency	3	6	2	1	3

Compare these two distributions using the mode and the range.

6

Kurt

Ring score	3	4	5	6	7	8	9
Frequency	1	5	3	1	1	2	4

Jean

Ring score	4	5	6	7	8	9
Frequency	5	8	15	13	10	9

Compare these distributions using the median and the range.

7

Ring score	3	4	5	6	7	8	9	10
Frequency	1	7	10	10	5	4	1	2

Sally

Gavin

Ring score	2	3	4	5	6	7	8	9
Frequency	1	2	3	7	14	13	6	7

Compare these distributions using the mean and the range.

8

Peggy

Ring score	2	3	4	5	6	7	8
Frequency	1	0	2	3	5	4	1

Toby

Ring score	3	4	5	6	7	8	9
Frequency	2	4	5	4	6	0	1

Ring score	2	3	4	5	6	7	8	9
Frequency	2	1	3	2	3	6	4	3

Sue

For each distribution of scores:

a find the lower and upper quartiles

b calculate the interquartile range.

9

	Number of chips								
Restaurant	34	35	36	37	38	39	40	41	Total
P	8	10	14	9	6	5	4	4	60
Q	8	7	5	9	12	11	8	0	60
R	0	3	5	10	12	14	10	6	60

For each restaurant:

a find the median number of chips

b find the lower and upper quartiles

c draw a box-and-whisker plot.

Working in 2-D

1 Calculate the area of each shape below.

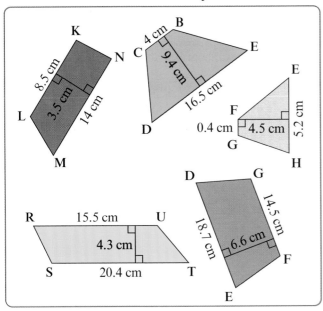

2 This is a sketch and a net of a magazine file.

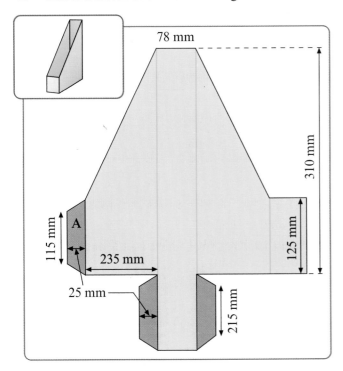

a Calculate the area of glue tab A.
b Calculate the total area of the net.

The net is cut from a rectangle of card which measures 550 mm by 575 mm.

c Calculate the area of card wasted when the net is cut out.

3 Calculate the diameter of a circle that has the same perimeter as a 9 cm by 7 cm rectangle.

4 Calculate the perimeter and area of:
a a circle of diameter 6.5 cm
b a circle of radius 4.8 cm
c a semicircle of diameter 12.4 cm.

5 Calculate the area of the shaded part.

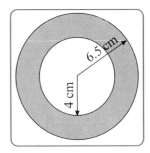

6 The design of this logo uses three shapes.

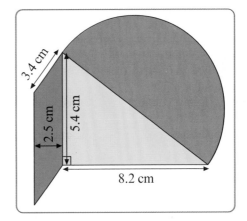

a Name the three shapes used in this logo.
b Calculate the total area of the logo.
c Calculate the perimeter of the logo.

7 This diagram shows a plastic sail for a toy boat.

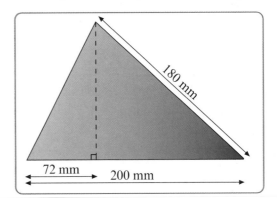

a Calculate the height of the plastic sail.
b Calculate the area of a sail.

Sails are cut from a roll of plastic 205 mm wide and 50 metres long.

c How many sails can be cut from one roll?
d Calculate the area of waste from one roll.

Solving equations

1 Simplify each of these expressions.

    a $7k + 8k - 9k$ **b** $2l + 3m + 4l - 2m$

    c $4n - 3p + n - 4p$ **d** $3q + 5q - 4q + 6r$

    e $5s - 7t - 4s + 7t$ **f** $6 + 5u + 3 + 7v$

    g $8w - 7x - 2w + 9x$ **h** $10 - 5y + 1 + 2y$

    i $3z + 5 + 6 - 8z - 9 + 10z$

2 Some expressions are arranged in a square.

$4g + h$	$3g - h$	$5g$
$5g - h$	$4g$	$3g + h$
$3g$	$5g + 2h$	$4g - h$

    a Find the value of each expression in the square when $g = 7$ and $h = 3$.

    b Draw the square with these values.

    c Is it a magic square?

    d For each row, column and diagonal, find the total of the three expressions.

    e Describe how you could change one expression to make this square into a magic square.

3 Solve these equations.

    a $7x + 1 = 3x + 21$ **b** $3x - 2 = x + 7$

    c $5(x + 1) = 24$ **d** $4(x + 3) + 9 = 13$

    e $3x - 2 = 2(x + 1)$ **f** $4x + 5 = 2x - 1$

    g $6x - 8 = 10 - 3x$ **h** $13 - 4x = 2x + 4$

    i $11 - x = 3(x - 1)$ **j** $2x + 11 = 4 - 5x$

    k $21 - 3x = 15 - 2x$ **l** $3x - 10 = 10 - x$

    m $4x + 23 = 2(4 - x)$ **n** $4(x - 1) = 2(x + 7)$

    o $3(5 - 2x) = 7(x + 4)$ **p** $5(10 - x) = 4(3x + 4)$

4

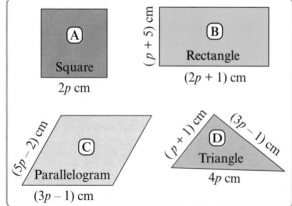

    a Find the perimeter of each shape when $p = 7$.

    b For each shape, write an expression for the perimeter in terms of p.

    c Find a value of p that gives shape D a perimeter of 24 cm.

    d Which value of p gives shape C a perimeter of 34 cm?

    e Find a value of p that gives shape B a perimeter of 21 cm.

    f Find a value of p so that the perimeters of shapes A and B are equal.

    g Find a value of p so that the perimeters of shapes A and C are equal.

    h Find a value of p so that the perimeters of shapes B and C are equal.

    i Explain why the perimeters of shapes A and D are equal for any value of p.

5 For each puzzle A and B, write an equation and solve it to find the number.

A   I think of a number, double it and subtract 3. I get the same answer if I subtract my number from 12. What is my number?

B   I think of a number, add 1 and multiply by 2. I get the same answer if I subtract 5 and multiply by 3. What is my number?

6 For each pair of equations:

    a On one set of axes, draw a graph for each equation.

    b Use your graphs to find values for x and y that fit both equations.

    A $y = x - 6$ **B** $y = 2x$
        $x + y = 8$ $y = 4x - 3$

    C $y = 2x + 9$ **D** $y = 6x - 10$
        $y = 3 - x$ $y - x = 4$

7 For each pair of equations, use algebra to find the values of x and y.

    A $4x + y = 9$ **B** $3x + y = 37$
        $2x + y = 6$ $2x + 5y = 29$

    C $3x + 5y = 20$ **D** $5x + 4y = 5$
        $2x + 3y = 14$ $2x + 6y = 13$

    E $3x + y = 18$ **F** $2x - 3y = 3$
        $11x - y = 10$ $6x + y = 29$

    G $3x - y = 16$ **H** $3x - 2y = 1$
        $x + 2y = 3$ $2x + 5y = 7$

    I $5x - 2y = 10$ **J** $2x - y = 7$
        $4x - 2y = 7$ $9x - 3y = 24$

Estimation and approximation

1 Round each number to the degree of accuracy given:

a	5.674	(2 dp)
b	12.652	(1 dp)
c	2143	(nearest ten)
d	534.687	(2 dp)
e	34.648	(nearest whole number)
f	2639.2	(nearest thousand)
g	13 468.284 52	(2 dp)
h	0.0666	(2 dp)
i	63.68	(nearest ten)
j	59.999	(1 dp)
k	8502	(nearest thousand)
l	68.499 99	(nearest whole number)
m	56.289 64	(3 dp)

2 Round each of these to the number of significant figures given.

a	56.83	(3 sf)
b	16 389	(3 sf)
c	2.456	(2 sf)
d	45.923	(1 sf)
e	15.777 77	(4 sf)
f	725 184	(2 sf)
g	94.56	(1 sf)
h	93 747 656	(5 sf)
i	564.23	(4 sf)
j	196.5	(1 sf)
k	6.7849	(2 sf)
l	15.682	(4 sf)
m	673 492.35	(4 sf)
n	0.035 62	(2 sf)
o	0.027 95	(3 sf)
p	3.0004	(3 sf)

3 By approximating each number to 1 sf work out approximate answers to each of these.

a	84.3 × 452.53
b	4.876 × 37.71
c	5683.2 × 9.372
d	458.12 × 518
e	734.6 ÷ 2.316
f	56.8243 ÷ 7.8931
g	41 952 + 77 442
h	34.6296 + 87.3
i	6834 − 1939.453
j	45.95 × 2.943 56
k	74.68 × 4.87
l	7468 × 0.487
m	7.468 × 48.7

4 Work out approximate answers then calculate each of these exactly.

a	56.6 × 21.5
b	4924 × 3.7
c	246.3 × 9.67
d	54.27 × 21.6
e	17.63 × 1839
f	3.45 × 0.054
g	0.42 × 264
h	38.6 × 25.002

5 For each of these rectangles, estimate its area then calculate the area using the measurements given.

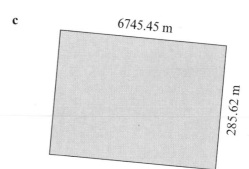

a 384.56 m, 25.83 m

b 15.26 m, 9.78 m

c 6745.45 m, 285.62 m

Probability A

1 With a 1 to 6 dice what is the probability that you score:

   a 5   **b** an even number

   c a multiple of 3   **d** a prime number?

2 For this wheel, what is the probability that the pointer stops on:

   a B   **b** A

   c either A or D

   d C   **e** not C

   f N   **g** A or B

3 For the wheel give an event which has a probability of $\frac{3}{5}$.

4

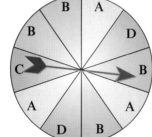

Draw a sample space diagram to show the outcomes when rolling a 1 to 4 dice and a 1 to 8 dice together.

5 From your sample space diagram, give the probability of getting:

   a at least one 3

   b at least one 6

   c a total of 7 by adding the scores

   d a 5 and a 2

   e a 3 and a 4

   f two prime numbers

   g two non-prime numbers

   h a total which is less than 6

   i a total which is greater than 6

   j a total which is a multiple of 3

   k two numbers the same

   l two numbers which are different.

6 A cube dice has three red faces and three blue faces. Draw a tree diagram to show three rolls of the dice.

7 From your tree diagram give the probability in three rolls of getting:

   a three reds

   b exactly two of one colour

   c at least two blues

   d no blues

   e all colours the same

   f no colours the same.

8 This tree diagram is for two spinners. The outcomes are not all equally likely.

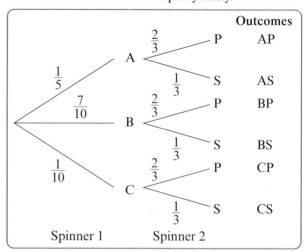

By multiplying probabilities give the probability of:

   a B and P   **b** C and S

   c A and P   **d** B and S

   e A and S   **f** C and P

9 Four CD's P to S are stacked in random order.

   a List all the different arrangements that are possible.

   b Give the probability that the CD at the bottom is red.

   c What is the probability that the top and bottom CD's are blue?

   d What is the probability that there is a blue CD at the top?

   e Give the probability that the two blue CD's are next to each other.

10 Five mugs are hanging from hooks. A pair of mugs are chosen at random.

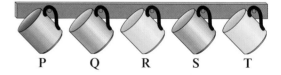

   a List every pair it is possible to pick.

   b What is the probability of picking:

      i a pair of the same colour

      ii a pair where only one mug is red

      iii a pair of yellow mugs?

Using algebra A

1 The dimensions of this trapezium are in centimetres.

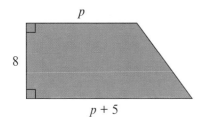

p

8

p + 5

a Write an expression for the area of the trapezium.
b What is the area when $p = 6.4$?
c What value of *p* gives an area of 54 cm^2?

2 This shape is cut from a rectangle.

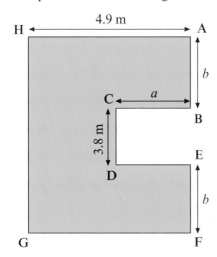

4.9 m
H   A
b
C   a
B
3.8 m
E
D
b
G   F

The length of AB is *b* metres and BC is *a* metres.
a Write an expression for the length of GH.
b Write an expression for the perimeter of this shape in terms of *a* and *b*.
c What is the perimeter if $a = 1.8$ and $b = 4.1$?

3 Find three pairs of equivalent expressions.

A $2(2a + 4)$ **B** $4a + 4$ **C** $2a + 6$

D $4(a + 2)$ **E** $2a + 8$ **F** $2(a + 2)$

G $2a + 5$ **H** $2(a + 3)$ **I** $4(a + 1)$

4 Multiply out these brackets.

a $3(a + 6)$ **b** $5(6 + z)$ **c** $3(n - 4)$
d $3(2n + 4)$ **e** $x(x + 2)$ **f** $4p(p - 3)$
g $3b(3 + b)$ **h** $a(2a - 8)$ **i** $4p(3p - 4)$

5 The length of a rectangle is 8 cm greater than its width.

a If the rectangle is *w* centimetres wide, write an expression for the length of the rectangle.
b Write an expression for the perimeter of the rectangle in terms of *w*.
c What value of *w* gives a perimeter of 72 cm?

6 The length of a rectangle is three times its width. The perimeter is 80 cm. What is the area?

7 Multiply these terms.

a $8p \times 6q$ **b** $9y \times y$ **c** $mn \times mn$
d $pq \times 4p$ **e** $8m \times mn$ **f** $9b \times 2a^2$
g $a^3 \times g^3$ **h** $4p \times 5p^2$ **i** $7a^3 \times 4b$

8 Multiply out these.

a $6(4a - 3b)$ **b** $p(n - p)$ **c** $s(s + t)$
d $6m(n - m)$ **e** $5x(x + y)$ **f** $u(4u + 3)$
g $p(5q + 3r)$ **h** $3n(4m + 7n)$ **i** $9a(3b + a)$

9 Which of these expressions is equivalent to $4a(2ab + 3a) + a(5b - a) + 4b(2a^2 + 5a)$?

A $35a^2b + 11a^2$

B $12a^2b + 14ab + 7a^2$

C $41ab + 10a$

D $16a^2b + 11a^2 + 25ab$

10 Simplify these.

a $8n + 4m - 6n + 3m$ **b** $12a^2 - a + 9a^2$
c $b^3 - b^3 + 2b$ **d** $8x - 4xy - 2y + 6xy$
e $p + 8q - 5q + 3p$ **f** $8p^2 + 3pq + 5q^2 - pq$
g $4m^2 + mn - 6n + nm$ **h** $x + 2xy + x - 4xy$

11 Multiply out these brackets and simplify.

a $6(7a - 2b) + 7(2a + b)$
b $9(3x + y) + 4(y - 2x)$
c $x(6x - 2) + 2x(5x + 3)$
d $8x(2y + 3x) + x(6x - 3y)$

12 Write an expression for the width of rectangles A and B.

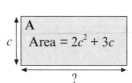
c **A** Area = $2c^2 + 3c$?

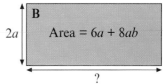
2*a* **B** Area = $6a + 8ab$?

13 Factorise these fully.

a $7p + 3pq$ **b** $m + 3mn$ **c** $8pq + 4q$
d $3y - 12xy$ **e** $2b^2 + 10b$ **f** $18ab + 24bc$
g $x^2y - 2xy$ **h** $9a^2b + 6ab^2$ **i** $12m^2n - 9mn$

Constructions and Loci

1 Construct these triangles accurately. Show all your construction lines.

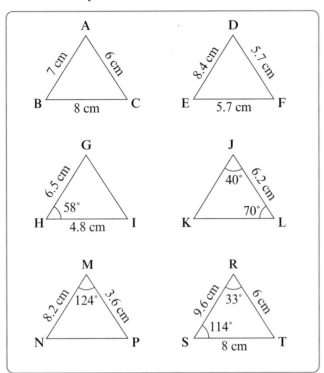

2 Copy each line full size and contruct a perpendicular bisector of it.

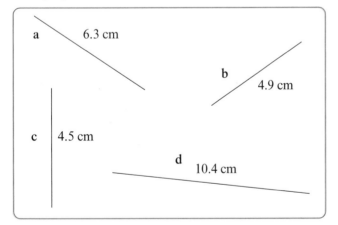

a 6.3 cm

b 4.9 cm

c 4.5 cm

d 10.4 cm

3 Draw each angle accurately and construct its bisector.

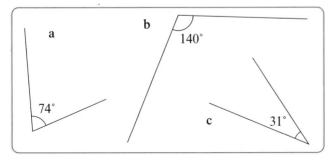

a 74°

b 140°

c 31°

4 Draw each of the following shapes full size and show the locus of points 2 cm from each one.

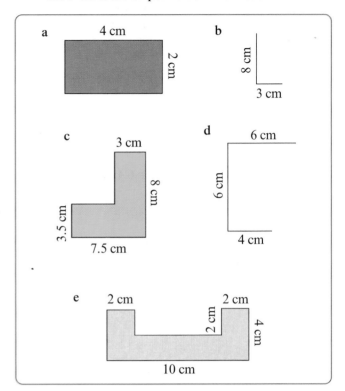

a 4 cm, 2 cm

b 8 cm, 3 cm

c 3 cm, 8 cm, 3.5 cm, 7.5 cm

d 6 cm, 6 cm, 4 cm

e 2 cm, 2 cm, 2 cm, 4 cm, 10 cm

5 A field for the village fete is shaped as a triangle with these dimensions.

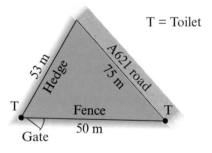

T = Toilet

53 m Hedge, A621 road 75 m, Fence 50 m, Gate

Colonel Briggs Shilton has set out these conditions for the position of the drinks tent.

> **Condition 1** – The tent must be equidistant from the hedge and the fence.
> **Condition 2** – The distance from each toilet to the tent must be equal.

a Construct a scale drawing of the field to a scale of 1 to 1000.
b Find by construction the position of the tent.
c Why is this position not a sensible one?
d Give some different conditions which you think puts the tent in a better position.

Ratio

1 Green dyes are a mix of blue and yellow dyes.

Copy the table below and calculate the missing amounts.

Dye	Blue	:	Yellow
Grass	1	:	3
Lime	3	:	7
Pea	5	:	9

Dye	Blue	Yellow	Total
Grass	120 ml		
Lime	450 ml		
Pea		360 ml	
Lime		175 ml	
Pea	600 ml		
Grass		510 ml	
Lime	645 ml		
Pea		495 ml	
Grass	720 ml		
Lime			1200 ml
Grass			860 ml
Pea			700 ml
Grass			1280 ml
Lime			890 ml
Pea			1050 ml

2 Share each of these amounts in the given ratio.

a £84 2:5   b £248 5:3   c 195 g 9:4
d £120 2:1:3   e 200 g 3:4:1   f 360 ml 2:3:4
g 420 g 2:3:2 h £495 1:1:7   i 99 cm 4:5:2
j 2 m 5:2:1   k 1.4 kg 1:2:4 l 2.7 cm 1:6:2

3 This recipe makes 25 biscuits.

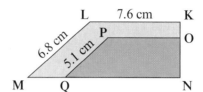

Chocolate Biscuits
50 g icing sugar • 225 g margarine
100 g plain chocolate • 225 g flour

Calculate how much of each ingredient is needed to make:
a 45 biscuits   b 10 biscuits

4
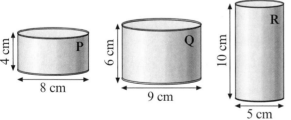

For each tin, give the ratio of height to diameter:
a in its simplest terms   b as a fraction
c as a decimal   d as a percentage.

5
A 2 : 5   B 3 : 1   C 4 : 3   D 1 : 3   E 3 : 5

These are the ratios of men to women in five self-defence classes.
What fraction of each class are men?

6
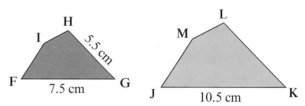

Shape JKLM is an enlargement of shape FGHI.
a Calculate the scale factor of the enlargement.
b Find the length LK.

7
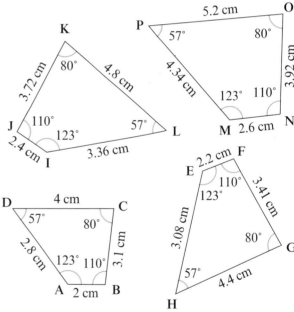

NOPQ is an enlargement of NKLM.
a Calculate the scale factor of the enlargement.
b Find the length PO.

8

Which of these trapeziums are similar to ABCD?

9
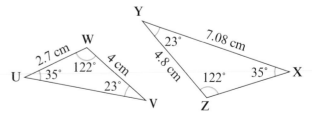

a Explain why triangles UVW and XYZ are similar.
b Give the corresponding length to WV.
c Find the length XZ.
d Find the length UV.

Distance, speed and time

1 A chairlift travels at a constant speed
of 2.6 metres per second.
What distance does one of the chairs travel in:

a 2 seconds **b** 5 seconds
c 9.3 seconds **d** 1 minute
e 3 minutes and 38 seconds?

2 At a constant speed, a plane takes 2 hours
to travel 1208 miles.
Find the plane's speed in miles per hour.

3 An escalator is 32.8 metres long and travels at a
speed of 0.75 m/s.
How long does it take to travel to the top of this
escalator?

4 It takes 20 seconds to go up an escalator that is
14 m long. What is its speed in m/s?

5 Write these speeds in metres per second, to 1 dp.

a 129 metres per minute
b 2 kilometres per second
c 432 metres per hour
d 20 kilometres per hour

6 Write these speeds in kilometres per hour, to 1 dp.

a 2 kilometres per minute
b 40 000 metres per hour
c 65 100 metres per hour
d 6 metres per second

7 Write these speeds in miles per minute.

a 60 mph **b** 30 mph
c 90 mph **d** 45 mph
e 25 mph **f** 42 mph

8 Write these speeds in miles per hour.

a 0.6 miles per minute
b 1.2 miles per minute
c 0.45 miles per minute
d 0.1 miles per second

9 How far does a plane travel in 3 h 20 min at a
constant speed of 960 kilometres per hour?

10 How far can a car travel at a constant speed of
51 mph in:

a 1 h 30 min **b** 45 min
c 20 min **d** 55 min
e 2 h 25 min **f** 3 h 45 min?

11 Calculate the time taken in hours and minutes, to
the nearest minute, to travel 60 km at a speed of:

a 120 km/h **b** 30 km/h
c 75 km/h **d** 9 km/h
e 55 km/h **f** 49 km/h
g 50 km/h **h** 150 km/h.

12 This sketch graph shows two different journeys
from Bristol to Glasgow.

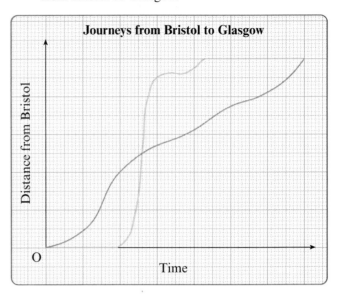

Journeys from Bristol to Glasgow

Distance from Bristol

Time

O

Which line do you think shows a plane journey?
Explain your answer.

13 Calculate the average speed
(in mph or km/h to 2 dp) of a car which travels:

a 90 km in 2 h
b 115 km in 3 h
c 40 miles in 50 min
d 50 km in 35 min
e 70 miles in 1 h 20 min
f 100 km in 1 h 12 min
g 400 miles in 7 h 30 min
h 500 metres in 1 min.

14 Mandy left Glasgow at 10:00 am and
cycled 28 miles at a speed of 10 mph.
Amin left Glasgow at 10:20 am and travelled along
the same route at a speed of 12 mph.

a Show both their journeys on one graph.
b About what time did Amin pass Mandy?

15 Andy left Taunton at 3:00 pm and took
45 minutes to drive 50 miles to Bristol. He stayed
there for 2 h 30 min. He then returned along the
same route and arrived home at 7:05 pm.

a Draw a graph to show Andy's complete journey.
b At what time did he begin his return journey to
Taunton?
c Calculate his average speed for the journey to
Bristol.
d What was his average speed on the return
journey?

Trigonometry

1 Find angle θ to the nearest degree when:

   a $\sin \theta = \frac{5}{6}$ **b** $\cos \theta = \frac{3}{8}$

   c $\tan \theta = \frac{9}{5}$ **d** $\sin \theta = \frac{11}{15}$

   e $\tan \theta = \frac{3}{13}$ **f** $\cos \theta = \frac{5}{8}$

2 In each of these triangles calculate the angle θ to the nearest degree.

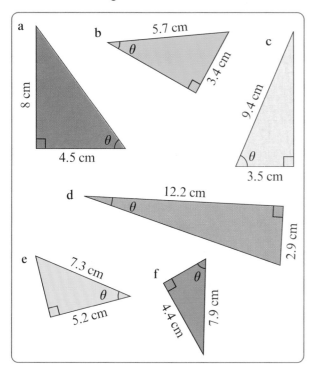

3 In each of these triangles calculate the length marked with a letter, to the nearest millimetre.

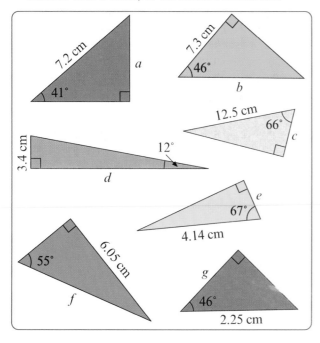

4 In this question give each answer correct to 3 sf.

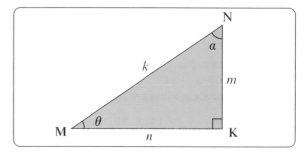

In $\triangle$NKM:

  a calculate θ when:
    i $n = 4.60\,cm$ and $k = 10.60\,cm$
    ii $m = 8.40\,cm$ and $n = 4.62\,cm$
    iii $k = 5.65\,cm$ and $m = 3.00\,cm$

  b calculate a when:
    i $n = 6.62\,cm$ and $k = 10.60\,cm$
    ii $m = 15.00\,cm$ and $n = 10.50\,cm$

  c calculate m when:
    i $\theta = 55°$ and $k = 3.58\,cm$
    ii $a = 16°$ and $n = 41.50\,cm$
    ii $\theta = 38°$ and $k = 4.05\,cm$

  d calculate k when:
    i $a = 25°$ and $m = 19.00\,cm$
    ii $\theta = 61$ and $n = 2.40\,cm$

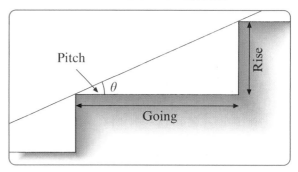

5 Calculate the pitch θ for each of these stairs, correct to 2 dp.

Stair	Rise (mm)	Going (mm)
A	160	310
B	173	294
C	153	319

6 For safety the pitch θ of these stairs must be between 32° and 22°.

  a For a going of 303 mm what is the maximum rise, to the nearest mm?

  b For a rise of 175 mm what is the maximum going, to the nearest mm?

Using algebra B

1 A formula for making tea in a pot for p people is:

$$t = p + 1$$

where t is the number of spoons of tea.

a Find the number of spoons of tea needed for 5 people.

b Rearrange the formula to make p the subject.

c Calculate p when $t = 3$.

2 A formula for the perimeter of a square (P) of edge length x is:

$$P = 4x$$

a Make x the subject of the formula.

b Find the edge length of a square that has a perimeter of 41 cm.

3 A cook book gives this formula for the time in minutes (T) to cook a turkey that weighs W pounds:

$$T = 20W + 20$$

a How long would it take to cook a turkey that weighs 12.5 pounds?

b Make W the subject of the formula.

c What is the weight of the largest turkey that is cooked in 2 hours?

4 A formula for converting litres (l) to pints (p) is:

$$p = \tfrac{7}{4}l$$

a Use the formula to convert 5 litres to pints.

b Make l the subject of the formula.

c Convert 8.5 pints to litres, correct to 2 dp.

5 The formula for the area of a rectangle (A) with length l and width w is:

$$A = lw$$

a Make w the subject of the formula.

b Find the width of a rectangle 10 cm in length with an area of 62 cm².

6 The formula for the perimeter of a rectangle (P) with length l and width w is:

$$P = 2l + 2w$$

a Make w the subject of the formula.

b Find the width of a rectangle 10 cm in length with a perimeter of 28.4 cm.

7 Make k the subject of these formulas:

a $V = 4k - 25$ **b** $y = 3(k - 1)$

c $j = \dfrac{k}{7}$ **d** $w = \tfrac{3}{4}k$

e $2v + k = 5$ **f** $k - b = 7$

g $d = \tfrac{2}{5}k + 1$ **h** $h = \dfrac{k + 3}{8}$

i $p = w + k$ **j** $q = 20 - 5k$

k $v = 13 - \tfrac{1}{3}k$ **l** $v = s + tk$

m $h = \dfrac{k + a}{b}$ **n** $h = 2gk$

o $2y + 5k = 3$ **p** $3k - 2h = 9$

8 Make p the subject of these formulas:

a $A = p^2$ **b** $v = 5p^2$

c $g = p^2 + 1$ **d** $q = 3p^2 - 5$

e $j = \tfrac{1}{4}p^2$ **f** $F = \tfrac{2}{3}p^2$

g $p^2 + z = 2$ **h** $K = 2\pi p^2$

i $A = 2p^2 + 1$ **j** $H = 3p^2 - 8$

9

A $\boxed{y = (x + 2)(x + 4)}$ B $\boxed{y = (x + 3)(x - 1)}$

C $\boxed{y = 2x^2 + 3x - 5}$ D $\boxed{y = x^2 - x - 2}$

For each formula, find the value of y when:

a $x = 6$ **b** $x = 3$ **c** $x = 1.5$

10 For each formula in x, y and z, find the value of x when $y = 5$ and $z = 2$.

a $x = 3yz + y$ **b** $x = 4z(y - 3)$

c $x = \sqrt{y^2 + 12z}$ **d** $x = 2y^2 - 3z^2$

e $x = (5z + y)^2$ **f** $x = 2z^3 - y$

g $x = \dfrac{y + 3z}{2y}$ **h** $x = \dfrac{1}{y} + \dfrac{1}{z}$

11 For each of these multiply out the brackets and simplify:

a $(n + 2)(n + 5)$ **b** $(f + 1)(f + 10)$

c $(w + 2)(w + 6)$ **d** $(2n + 1)(n + 3)$

e $(4d + 7)(d + 3)$ **f** $(2y + 9)(2y + 5)$

g $(x - 3)(x + 6)$ **h** $(v + 3)(v - 2)$

i $(b + 3)(b - 5)$ **j** $(m - 7)(m - 1)$

k $(h - 1)(h - 5)$ **l** $(t - 3)(t - 7)$

m $(2p + 1)(3p - 1)$ **n** $(5x + 6)(3x - 2)$

o $(6y + 3)(2y - 5)$ **p** $(3g - 7)(4g - 5)$

12 $\boxed{x + 1}$ $\boxed{x + 2}$ $\boxed{x + 3}$ $\boxed{x + 6}$ $\boxed{x + 4}$ $\boxed{x + 12}$

Which pair of expressions multiply to give:

a $x^2 + 7x + 12$ **b** $x^2 + 8x + 12$

c $x^2 + 7x + 6$ **d** $x^2 + 5x + 6$

e $x^2 + 13x + 12$ **f** $x^2 + 6x + 8$?

13 Factorise:

a $x^2 + 12x + 11$ **b** $x^2 + 8x + 15$

c $x^2 + 4x + 4$ **d** $x^2 + 9x + 20$

e $x^2 + 3x - 4$ **f** $x^2 + 2x - 15$

g $x^2 + 4x - 12$ **h** $x^2 - x - 6$

i $x^2 - 11x + 10$ **j** $x^2 - 2x - 8$

k $x^2 - 3x + 2$ **l** $x^2 - 4x + 4$

Grouped data

1996 Olympic Games
Reaction Times
Sprint Hurdles
(Semi-Finals & Finals)

Reaction time (s)	Frequency Men	Women
0.120 –	1	1
0.130 –	4	2
0.140 –	1	2
0.150 –	4	2
0.160 –	5	5
0.170 –	4	7
0.180 –	2	5
0.190 –	3	0
Totals	24	24

Use Table A for Questions 1 to 12

1 Draw a histogram to show the reaction times for:

   a men   **b** women.

2 Give the modal class for:

   a men   **b** women.

3 Draw frequency polygons to compare the reaction times of men and women.

4 Calculate an estimate of the range of the times for:

   a men   **b** women.

5 Calculate an estimate of the mean reaction time for:

   a men   **b** women.

6 For these two distributions, the totals of the reaction times are just as useful for comparison as the means. Explain why.

7 Draw a cumulative frequency curve for:

   a men   **b** women.

8 Estimate how many reactions times were less than 0.135 s for:

   a men   **b** women.

9 Estimate how many reactions times were greater than 0.175 s for:

   a men   **b** women.

10 Estimate the median reaction time for:

   a men   **b** women.

11 Calculate an estimate of the interquartile range for:

   a men   **b** women.

12 Use your answers to Questions **4**, **5**, **10**, and **11** to compare the two distributions.

1996 Olympic Games
GB Athletics Team

Age	Frequency Track	Field
18 – 22	7	2
23 – 27	27	10
28 – 32	20	7
33 – 37	3	2
38 – 42	2	2
Totals	59	23

Use Table B for Questions 13 to 15

13 Draw a histogram to show the distribution of:

   a track athletes   **b** field athletes.

14 Explain why drawing frequency polygons on the same diagram would not give a good comparison of the ages of track athletes and field athletes.

15 Calculate an estimate of the mean age of:

   a track athletes   **b** field athletes.

1996 Olympic Games – Men's 20 km walk

Time (min)	80 –	84 –	88 –	92 –	96 –	100 –	Total
Frequency	18	21	9	2	1	1	52

1996 Olympic Games – Men's 50 km walk

Time (min)	220 –	230 –	240 –	250 –	260 –	Total
Frequency	8	13	9	4	2	36

1996 Olympic Games – Women's 10 km walk

Time (min)	41–	42–	43–	44–	45–	46–	47–	48–	Total
Frequency	1	4	7	3	12	5	4	2	38

Use Tables C, D and E for Questions 16 to 18.

16 For each distribution:

   a draw a histogram
   b calculate an estimate of the range of the times
   c calculate an estimate of the mean time
   d draw a cumulative frequency curve
   e estimate the median time
   f calculate an estimate of the interquartile range.

17 For the men's 20 km walk, estimate how many times were:

   a under 86 minutes   **b** under 90 minutes
   c over 87 minutes   **d** over 84.5 minutes.

18 For the women's 10 km walk, estimate how many times were:

   a under 42.5 minutes   **b** under 43.8 minutes
   c over 45.7 minutes   **d** over 46.8 minutes

Working with percentages

1 Calculate, giving answers correct to 2 dp:

    a 38 as a percentage of 60

    b £14 as a percentage of £55

    c 68 as a percentage of 24

    d 1550 as a percentage of 2500

    e 3500 km as a percentage of 75 000 km

    f 12.5 kg as a percentage of 40 kg

    g £125.50 as a percentage of £150

    h 132 miles as a percentage of 868 miles

    i £9.38 as a percentage of £56.45

    j 15 650 km as a percentage of 1.5 million km.

2 Give answers to each of these correct to 2 dp.

    a Increase 25 kg by 18%

    b Increase 1400 km by 65%

    c Increase 3560 miles by 4%

    d Increase 1350 yards by 35%

    e Increase £25 645 by 6%

    f Increase 137 500 tonnes by 5.5%

    g Increase 0.7 cm by 50%

    h Increase 42 mm by 12.5%

    i Increase £35.99 by 7%

    j Increase 365 ml by 15%.

3 Give your answers to these correct to 2 dp.

    a Decrease 485 ml by 12%

    b Decrease £45.75 by 20%

    c Decrease 65 mm by 65%

    d Decrease 0.8 cm by 8%

    e Decrease 15 875 tonnes by 75%

    f Decrease £15 944 by 34%

    g Decrease 1760 yards by 28%

    h Decrease 5682 miles by 56%

    i Decrease 3600 km by 35.5%

    j Decrease 48 kg by 48%.

4 The price of each item is given ex. VAT. Calculate the price including VAT at today's standard rate.

    a crash helmet £185.85

    b cycle tyre £11.69

    c fishing rod £44.86

    d steam iron £21.75

    e microwave oven £268.55

    f VCR £159.99

    g personal CD player £135.38

    h CD £9.24

    i phone £49.99

    j multi-media PC £1499.

5 A printer is advertised for £132 + VAT. Calculate the total price of the printer.

6 Callum sees the same model TV advertised by two shops in this way:

TV World	£199.99 inc. VAT
Price busters	£169.99 ex.VAT

    a From which shop would you advise Callum to buy the TV?

    b Give reasons for your answer to part **a**.

7 Calculate the simple interest charged or paid on each of these:

    a £675 borrowed for 5 years at 12% pa

    b £12 400 borrowed for 2 years at 17% pa

    c £170 saved for 4 years at 3% pa

    d £65 saved for 9 years at 4% pa

    e £1500 borrowed for 3 years at 18% pa

    f £4600 borrowed for 4 years at 12.5% pa

    g £25 saved for 3 years at 5% pa

    h £150 saved for 6 years at 4.5% pa

    i £200 borrowed for 2 years at 22.9% pa

    j £175 borrowed for 3 years at 18% pa.

8 Calculate the compound interest charged or paid on each of these:

    a £500 saved for 3 years at 6% pa

    b £1400 borrowed for 2 years at 19% pa

    c £250 saved for 2 years at 7.5% pa

    d £105 saved for 4 years at 3%

    e £12 500 borrowed for 3 years at 16%

    f £32 saved for 3 years at 4%

    g £750 borrowed for 3 years at 21%

    h £3675 borrowed for 2 years at 17%

    i £125 saved for 3 years at 8%

    j £500 saved for 3 years at 4.5%.

9 These prices include VAT. Calculate each price ex. VAT.

    a freezer £299.99   **b** CD £12.99

    c camera £44.99   **d** phone £9.99

    e climbing boots £75   **f** tent £89.95

    g kettle £26.99   **h** PC £129.99

    i calculator £18.99   **j** TV £139.99

10 Jo bought a ski jacket in a 15% off sale for £85.45.

    a What was the pre-sale price of the jacket?

    b How much did she save in the sale?

11 In 1995 a ferry company made a profit of £3 600 000.
This was 14% more than the profit for 1994.

Calculate the profit made in 1994.

Transformations

1 Draw the pentagon A on axes with:
$^-4 \leqslant x \leqslant 10$ and
$^-6 \leqslant y \leqslant 8$.

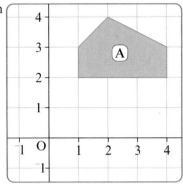

2 Draw the image of A after:

   a an enlargement SF 2 with centre (6, 5)

   b an enlargement SF $\frac{1}{2}$ with centre (7, $^-4$).

3 These transformations map A on to B, C, D, E and F.

Object	Transformation	Image
A	Rotate $^+90°$ about (0, 0)	B
A	Rotate $^-90°$ about (1, 1)	C
A	Reflect in x = 5	D
A	Rotate $^+90°$ about (6, 2)	E
A	Reflect in y = ^-x	F

   a On a new diagram, on axes with:
$^-6 \leqslant x \leqslant 10$ and $^-6 \leqslant y \leqslant 6$
draw and label the images B, C, D, E and F.

   b Describe fully the transformation that maps:
    i C on to A   **ii** D on to A.

   c For each of these mappings which pentagon is the image of B?

	Object	Transformation	Image
i	B	Rotate 180° about (0, 1)	
ii	B	Reflect in y = 0	
iii	B	Translate $\begin{pmatrix} 8 \\ ^-4 \end{pmatrix}$	

   d Describe fully the transformation that maps C on to E.

4

	Transformations		
Object	First	Second	Image
A	Rotate $^+90°$ about (0, 1)	Reflect in y = 0	G
A	Reflect in y = 0	Rotate $^+90°$ about (0, 1)	H

   a On a new diagram draw the images G and H.

   b Compare G and H and comment on any differences.

   c In this table each pair of transformations maps G on to H. Describe the second transformation fully.

	Object	Image	First transformation	Second transforma
i	G	H	Translate $\begin{pmatrix} 6 \\ 0 \end{pmatrix}$	
ii	G	H	Rotate $^-90°$ about (1, $^-2$)	
iii	G	H	Rotate 180° about (0, $^-1$)	

   d What single transformation maps G on to H?

5 These transformations map A on to J, K and L.

	Transformations		
Object	First	Second	Image
A	Enlarge SF 2 with centre (0, 1)	Reflect in y = 1	J
A	Reflect in x = 1	Enlarge SF 2 with centre (5, 0)	K
A	Enlarge SF 2 with centre (5, 0)	Reflect in x = 4	L

   a On a new diagram, on axes with:
$^-10 \leqslant x \leqslant 12$ and $^-10 \leqslant y \leqslant 10$
draw the images J, K and L

   b What single transformation maps
    i J on to K   **ii** L on to K?

Probability B

In an experiment a Multilink cube was dropped on to a hard surface and its resting position was recorded.

Peg

Position	Frequency
Peg up	7
Peg to side	51
Peg down	5
Peg tilting	2

1 Give the relative frequency to 2 dp of the cube coming to rest:

  a peg down
  b peg to side
  c peg tilting
  d peg up.

2 Why should all the unrounded answers to Questions **1a** to **1d** add up to 1?

3 What is the relative frequency of a cube resting:

  a without the peg down
  b with either a peg up or a peg down
  c with neither a peg to the side nor a peg up?

4 From the results do you think that each face of the cube is equally likely to be on the top. Explain your answer.

5 The same Multilink cube is dropped 150 times on the same surface. Estimate the number of times it will come to rest:

  a peg down
  b peg to the side
  c peg tilting.

6 Do an experiment yourself to find the relative frequency of different positions a Multilink cube can come to rest.

  a Compare your relative frequencies with the results of the experiment above.
  b How could you improve the accuracy of your experiment to find the relative frequencies?

7 The probability that Mike is late for work on a Monday is 0.4 and on a Tuesday it is 0.2

  a Draw a tree diagram to show the outcomes and probabilities.
  b Estimate the probability that Mike is late on Monday and Tuesday.
  c Estimate the probability that Mike is late on neither day.
  d Estimate the probability that he is late at least once in the two days.

8 Would you use theoretical probability or relative frequency to find the probability that:

  a a person in the UK is right- or left-handed
  b the next volcanic eruption occurs in May
  c the next person you meet in school is female
  d the next wine gum in the tube is black
  e a toothpaste tube will leak before it is finished
  f if you visited a foreign country at random you would be expected to drive on the left
  g your toast lands jam side down on the floor if you drop it
  h it rains when you have no waterproofs?

A biased spinner has seven sides. On the sides are the numbers 7, 15, 24, 25, 29, 30, 36.

The probability of the spinner landing on each number is given in this table.

Number	7	15	24	25	29	30	36
Probability	0.04	0.15	0.19	0.14	0.14	0.13	0.21

9 **a** What is the probability of the spinner landing on a number less than 20?
  b Why can you add the probabilities in this case?

10 **a** Complete the Venn diagram to show multiples of 3 and multiples of 5 for the spinner.

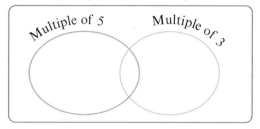

  b Why can you not add probabilities in this case?

11 From your Venn diagram calculate the probability of getting in one spin:

  a a multiple of 5 and a multiple of 3
  b either a multiple of 3 or a multiple of 5
  c neither a multiple of 3 nor a multiple of 5
  d a multiple of 3 but not a multiple of 5.

12 Use a Venn diagram to find the probability of getting either a square number or an even number.

Inequalities

1 Copy each of these and insert > or < in place of the box to make it correct.

  a 9 ☐ ⁻4   **b** ⁻8 ☐ ⁻3
  c 4 ☐ ⁻2   **d** ⁻2 ☐ 2
  e ⁻5.6 ☐ ⁻4.23   **f** ⁻8 ☐ ⁻11

2 Which of these numbers is not a possible value for t, where $t \leqslant ⁻7$?
  ⁻8, 4, 71, ⁻3.2, ⁻7.003, ⁻28.6, ⁻7, ⁻0.33

3 What are the integer values for k where:

  a $9 > k \geqslant 4$ **b** $⁻3 \leqslant k \leqslant ⁻1$
  c $⁻5 \leqslant k < 1$ **d** $⁻4 \geqslant k > ⁻7$
  e $⁻56 < k < ⁻57$ **f** $24 \leqslant k \leqslant 24$
  g $⁻14 \geqslant k > ⁻16$ **h** $6 > k > 0$

4 Write two other inequalities in h which describe the same integer values as $⁻2 < h < 2$.

5 Explain why these two inequalities are different types of inequality from each other.

> • This chair is suitable for people with weights given by $5 \leqslant w \leqslant 15$, where w is their weight in stones.

> • The waiters in a restaurant are given by $5 \leqslant w \leqslant 15$ where w is the number of waiters.

6 This diagram shows the inequality $⁻2 < x \leqslant 3$.

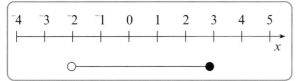

Draw similar diagrams to show these inequalities:

  a $7 \leqslant x \leqslant 10$ **b** $⁻4 \leqslant x < 1$
  c $⁻5 < x < ⁻2$ **d** $0 < x \leqslant 4$

7 Solve the following inequalities.

  a $3x \geqslant 27$ **b** $6t < ⁻42$
  c $42 \geqslant 4p$ **d** $k^2 \leqslant 121$
  e $1 + 3w < 7$ **f** $5q + 7 > 53.5$
  g $19 \leqslant 3t - 5$ **h** $7 - 2h \geqslant 3$
  i $4(3f - 2) < 28$ **j** $c^2 - 5 < 76$
  k $36 \leqslant 3(2g + 3)$ **l** $3x + 5 > x - 1$
  m $3j - 2 < 2j + 17$ **n** $5d + 20 \geqslant 6 - 2d$
  o $24 - 8v > 6 - 4v$ **p** $2(x + 3) \leqslant x - 7$
  q $5 - 3s > 5 + 3s$ **r** $9u + 6 \leqslant 7u$

8 The conditions on x are given by the inequality $⁻4 \leqslant x < 3$.
  What is:

  a the smallest possible value of x^2
  b the largest possible value of x^2?

9 Sketch graphs to show the regions which satisfy the following conditions.

> **Ⓐ**   ***Anita Southgate Floral Blinds***
> Blinds fit windows between 1 metre and 2 metres wide and up to 1 metre 20 cm high.

> **Ⓑ**   **ANTOK SUPPLY SERVICES**
> Drivers should be between 21 and 55 with a clean driving licence. We need drivers who have had experience of working with at least four previous companies.

> **Ⓒ**   ***Clarkson Hi Fi Sale***
> Each rack holds up to 45 compact discs. We have different models with prices from £12.

> **Ⓓ**   **Opus 4123R Fax Machine**
> Will take fax rolls up to 214 millimetres wide and up to 50 metres long.

> **Ⓔ**   **REGENT CAR SALES**
> Our new models will do up to 50 miles per gallon at speeds between 50 and 60 miles per hour.

10 Sketch graphs and shade the regions which satisfy the following conditions.

  a $x > 4$ **b** $⁻3 < y < 4$
  c $y < 6$ **d** $4 > x > 1$
  e $x < 4$ and $y > 6$
  f $⁻1 < x < 2$ and $y < ⁻2$
  g $0 < x < 4$ and $0 > y > ⁻4$
  h $y > x - 2$
  i $x + y < 6$
  j $y < 2x + 2$

11 What two inequalities define the shaded region on this sketch?

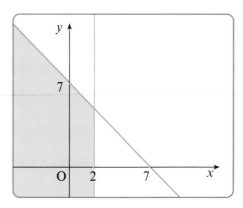

Working in 3-D

1 Each of these solids is made from three cubes.

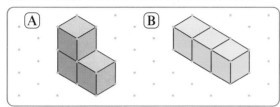

How many planes of symmetry has each solid?

2 **a** Draw a solid made from five cubes with 1 plane of symmetry.

   b Draw a solid made from six cubes with 3 planes of symmetry.

3 How many planes of symmetry has:

   a a cuboid with no square faces

   b a cube?

4

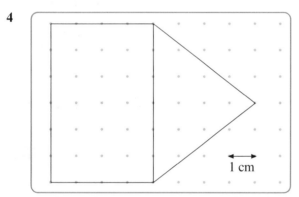

1 cm

   a Copy and complete this diagram to make the net of a prism.

   b What is the capacity of the box that can be made from the net?

   c What is the surface area of the box that can be made from the net?

5 Solids X and Y are prisms.

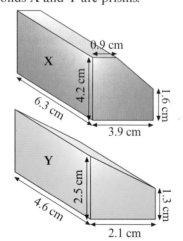

Calculate the volume of each solid.

6 Each prism P and Q has a volume of 1000 cm³.

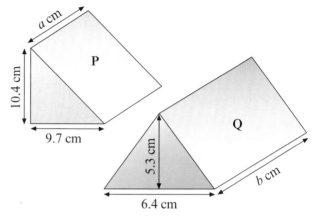

Find the values of *a* and *b* correct to 1 dp.

7 Each of these containers is in the shape of a cylinder.

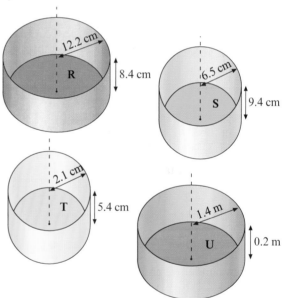

Find the capacity of each container, to 1 dp:

   a in ml   **b** in litres.

8 In the following expressions, *r*, *h* and *l* each represent a length.
Decide if each expression represents:
a length, area, volume or none of these.
Give reasons for each answer.

   a $4h$ **b** h^2

   c rh **d** rhl

   e $2(h + l)$ **f** pr^2

   g $hl + r$ **h** $\frac{1}{3}rh^2$

   i $\sqrt{h^2 + l^2}$ **j** $prh - 3l^2$

   k $r^3 + h^2 + rl$ **l** $h^3 + rl^2$

   m $5(rh + hl + rl)$ **n** $prh(h + l)$

   o $2h(r - l)$ **p** $\frac{4}{3}p(r + h)$

Quadratics

1 Factorise and solve these quadratic equations:

   a $c^2 + 5c + 6 = 0$ **b** $g^2 + g - 20 = 0$

   c $h^2 - 6h - 16 = 0$ **d** $t^2 + 3t - 54 = 0$

   e $p^2 - 4p - 45 = 0$ **f** $k^2 + 3k - 40 = 0$

   g $x^2 - 7x + 10 = 0$ **h** $v^2 + 9v - 36 = 0$

   i $d^2 + 8d + 15 = 0$ **j** $h^2 - 9h + 18 = 0$

   k $n^2 + 6n - 72 = 0$ **l** $y^2 - 7y - 30 = 0$

   m $a^2 + 5a - 36 = 0$ **n** $x^2 + 8x - 48 = 0$

   o $u^2 - 12u + 27 = 0$ **p** $c^2 + 18c + 77 = 0$

   q $g^2 - g - 72 = 0$ **r** $y^2 + y - 42 = 0$

   s $k^2 + 15k + 56 = 0$ **t** $x^2 - 7x - 60 = 0$

2 Solve these equations by trial and improvement:

   a $k^2 + 4k - 5 = 0$ **b** $h^2 - 2h = 3$

   c $w^2 + 3w = 10$ **d** $p^2 + 4p = 5$

   e $d^2 = 4$ **f** $a^2 + a = 6$

   g $x^2 - 3 = 2x$ **h** $y^2 + y = 2$

   i $d^2 - 5 = 4d$ **j** $x^2 + 2x = 8$

   k $x^2 - 1 = 0$ **l** $v^2 + 1 = 2v$

3 **a** Draw up a table of values for the graph of:

$$y = x^2 - 4x$$

     with values of x from $^-2$ to $^+5$.

   b From your table of values, draw and label the graph.

4 On a pair of axes **sketch**, and label these graphs:

   a $y = x^2$ **b** $y = x^2 + 2$ **c** $y = x^2 - 3$

5 **a** Draw up a table of values for the graph of:

$$y = x^2 - 5x + 4$$

     with values of x from $^-5$ to 0.

   b From your table of values, draw and label the graph.

6 **a** Draw up a table of values for the graph of:

$$y = x^2 + 2x - 8$$

     with values of x from $^-5$ to $^+3$.

   b From your table of values draw and label the graph.

   c Use your graph to solve the equation:

$$x^2 + 2x - 8 = 0$$

     Explain your answers.

7 **a** With values of x from $^-4$ to $^+3$, draw up a table of values for the graph of:

$$y = x^2 + 3x - 18$$

   b Use your graph to solve the equaton:

$$x^2 + 3x - 18 = 0$$

8 **a** Draw the graph of $y = x^2 - 6x + 5$ for values of x from $^-6$ to $^+1$.

   b Use your graph to solve the equation:

$$x^2 - 6x + 5 = 0$$

   c On the same axes draw a graph of:

$$y = 2$$

   d Use your graphs to solve the equation:

$$x^2 - 6x + 5 = 2$$

     Give reasons for your answer.

9 **a** Draw the graph of $y = x^2 + 4x - 21$ for values of x from $^-8$ to $^+4$.

   b Use your graph to solve the equation:

$$x^2 + 4x - 21 = 0$$

   c On the same axes draw a graph of $y = ^-5$.

   d Use your graphs to solve the equation:

$$x^2 + 4x - 21 = ^-5$$

   e **i** Explain how you would solve the equation:

$$x^2 + 4x - 21 = 4$$

      ii Solve the equation: $x^2 + 4x - 21 = 4$

10 Show how each of these equations can be made by rearranging $x^2 + 8x - 20 = 0$.

   a $x^2 - 20 = ^-8x$ **b** $20 = x^2 + 8x$

   c $x^2 = 20 - 8x$

11 Show how each of these equations can be made by rearranging $x^2 - 7x = 60$.

   a $x^2 - 60 = 7x$ **b** $x^2 = 7x + 60$

   c $x^2 - 7x - 60 = 0$

12 Rearrange the equation $x^2 - 55 = 6x$ to make three other quadratic equations.

13 Make three other quadratic equations by rearranging $60 - 11x = x^2$.

14 With values of x from $^-4$ to $^+3$:

   a Draw the graph of $y = x^2 + 3$.

   b On the same axes draw a graph of $y = 2x + 4$.

   c Use your graphs to solve the equation:

$$x^2 + 3 = 2x + 4$$

   d Either by drawing another graph or using these graphs solve the equation:

$$x^2 - 2x - 1 = 0$$

15 Sketch the graph of $y = x^3 + 1$.

16 For values of x from $^-3$ to $^+3$ draw a graph of $y = x^3 + 2x$.

17 Use trial and improvement to solve the equation:

$$x^5 = 20$$

(Give your answer correct to 3 sf.)

Processing data

1

> ### Town Centre Survey
> 1 Do you come into the town centre often? ☐ Yes ☐ No
> 2 Do you agree that the town centre should be pedestrianised? ☐ Yes ☐ No
> 3 What do you think about buses? _____

  a Criticise each of these questions.
  b Write an improved question for each one.

2

> ### Body Matters
> Right-handed people are more likely to have a stronger left eye than right eye.

Design an experiment to test this hypothesis.

3   **a** Carry out your experiment.
     b Analyse the data you collect.

4   **a** Do you think the hypothesis is true or false?
     b Explain why.

5

> ### Body Matters
> Do right-handed people fold their arms differently to left-handed people?

Design an experiment to answer this question.

6   **a** Carry out your experiment.
     b Analyse the data you collect.
     c Interpret your results to answer the question.

7

Motorbikes – Size of Engine & Price

Engine size (cc)	250	900	600	125	650	900	500	750
Price (£)	4500	8100	6700	2400	5100	6700	3400	9200

  a Draw axes: horizontal 0 to 1200
               vertical 0 to 12000
  b Plot the motorbike data on your diagram.
  c Draw a line of best fit.
  d Describe any correlation between size of engine and price.

8 Estimate the price of a motorbike with engine size:
  a 800 cc   **b** 450 cc

9 Estimate the engine size of a motorbike costing:
  a £4000   **b** £6500

10 Extend the line of best fit on your scatter diagram to estimate:
  a the price of a motorbike with a 1000 cc engine
  b the engine size of a motorbike costing £10000.

11

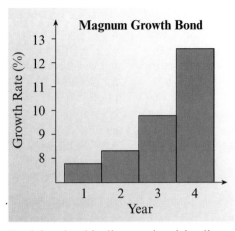

Explain why this diagram is misleading.

12

Vector Videos
Total Sales (000's)

Explain why this diagram is misleading.

13

> 𝒲𝒟 **Wilton Dale Theme Parks**
>
> | | 1994 | 1996 |
> |---|---|---|
> | Number of injuries | 21 | 14 |

Draw a misleading diagram to show this injury data by using:

  a a vertical scale which does not start at 0
  b enlargements of a shape.

14

> 𝒲𝒟 **Wilton Dale Theme Parks**
>
> | | 1994 | 1996 |
> |---|---|---|
> | Number of rides | 6 | 15 |

Draw a misleading diagram to show this data.

15

> 𝒲𝒟 **Wilton Dale Films**
>
> | | 1994 | 1995 | 1996 |
> |---|---|---|---|
> | Number of films made | 10 | 12 | 18 |

Draw a misleading diagram to show this data.

Trigonometry and Pythagoras' rule

1

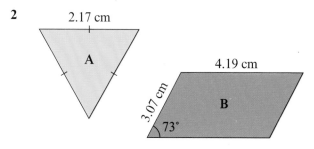

For each triangle calculate the side or angle marked with a letter, correct to 3 sf.

2

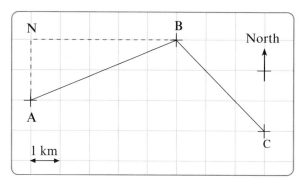

Calculate the area and perimeter of shapes A and B, correct to 2 dp.

3 This diagram shows the top of a building T and a person at G.
The horizontal distance GB is 5.19 m.
The point E is 1.82 m above the ground.
The angle of elevation from E to T is 39°.

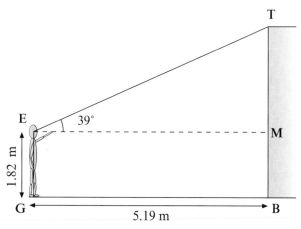

a Calculate, to the nearest 0.01 m:
  i the vertical height MT
  ii the total height TB.
b Calculate the angle of depression from E to B to the nearest degree.

4 This diagram shows the position of three markers A, B and C on an orienteering map.
N is a point due north of A and due west of B.

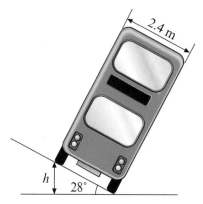

a How far is A:
  i west of B   **ii** south of B?
b In △ ABN, calculate:
  i AB in km to 2 dp
  ii NB̂A to the nearest degree.
c Calculate to the nearest degree the bearing of:
  i A from B   **ii** B from A
d Calculate the distance BC in km to 2 dp.
e Calculate the bearing of:
  i C from B   **ii** B from C
f Calculate the distance between A and C.

5 Double-decker buses are tested for stability for angles up to 28° from the horizontal.

a Calculate the height h in metres, for a double-decker when it is tipped to the maximum test angle, correct to 1 dp.

b For a single-decker bus the test angle is larger. A single decker bus 2.8 metres wide is tested and the height h is 1.31 metres.
What is the test angle, correct to 1 dp?

Formula sheet

In the GCSE examination you will be given a formula sheet like this one.
You should use it as an aid to memory, and it will be useful to become familiar with the information on the sheet.
The formula sheet is the same for all Examining Groups.

Area of triangle $= \frac{1}{2} \times$ Base $\times$ Height

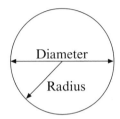

Circumference of circle $= \pi \times$ Diameter
$= 2 \times \pi \times$ Radius
Area of circle $= \pi \times$ (Radius)^2

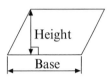

Area of parallelogram $=$ Base $\times$ Height

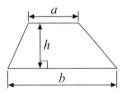

Area of trapezium $= \frac{1}{2}(a + b)h$

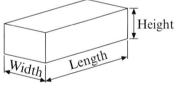

Volume of cuboid $=$ Length $\times$ Width $\times$ Height

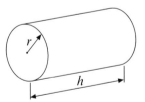

Volume of a cylinder $= \pi r^2 h$

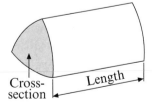

Volume of prism $=$ Area of cross-section $\times$ Length

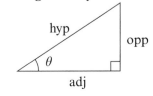

Pythagoras' theorem
$a^2 + b^2 = c^2$

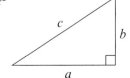

Trigonometry

$\sin \theta = \dfrac{\text{opp}}{\text{hyp}}$

$\cos \theta = \dfrac{\text{adj}}{\text{hyp}}$

$\tan \theta = \dfrac{\text{opp}}{\text{adj}}$

Number

N1

Units, conversions, and compound measures

N1.1 Given that 1 mile = 5280 feet:
Convert a speed of 50 mph to a speed in feet per second.

N1.2 A milk tank holds 25 000 litres when full.
The contents of the tank are emptied into a bottling plant.
To completely empty the tank, from full, takes 15 minutes 24 seconds.

a Calculate how many litres per second flow from the tank.
Give your answer to 2 dp.

b How many litres per minute is this?
Give your answer correct to the nearest litre.

N1.3 When Joel went to New York, the exchange rate was:

$$£1 = \$1.55$$

He changed £425 to US dollars.
The smallest amount the bank can give is a $1 note.

a How many dollars did he have in total?

In New York Joel saw a camera for sale at $85.
He had seen the same model camera for sale in his local shop for £54.99.

b **i** Which camera is cheaper?
ii Explain your answer, and the degree of accuracy you used.

N1.4 Given that 8 kilometres = 5 miles:

The speed limit on UK motorways is 70 mph.

a What is this speed in kph?

In France coaches are limited to 110 kph.

b What is this speed in mph?

N1.5 Deon spent £10 on petrol.
She noticed that the pump showed 16.8 litres.

a What was the price per litre for the petrol (to 2 dp)?

Given that 1 gallon = 4.55 litres:

b How many gallons did Deon buy for her £10?
Give your answer correct to 2 dp.

Deon travelled 127 miles on the £10 worth of petrol.

c Calculate her petrol cost per mile. Give your answer to
the nearest penny.

d To the nearest mile, how many miles per gallon is this?

N1.6 Lennie is making a bookshelf.
The cutting list says that he needs a piece of wood $42\frac{1}{2}$ inches long.

His tape measure is metric, and he knows that 2.54 cm = 1 inch

To the nearest millimetre, how long is the piece of wood he needs?

N1.7 In a French supermarket Sylvie bought 400 g of pasta for 9.50 FF.

a At this price, what would she pay for 1 kg of the pasta?

When Sylvie bought the 400 g of pasta the exchange rate
was £1 = 7.60 FF.

b Explain why the 400 g of pasta would cost £1.25 in sterling.

N2
Degrees of accuracy

N2.1 'Iso-cool' deodorant is sold in two sizes:

Regular, which contains 80 ml
Large, which contains 155 ml.

The contents of the regular size is measured to the nearest 10 ml.

a What is the smallest amount it can contain when unopened?

The contents of the large size is measured to the nearest 5 ml.

b What is the smallest amount it can contain when unopened?

N2.2 George always measures in imperial units.
He uses a tape marked in tenths of an inch.
He measures the width of a table as 27 inches (to the nearest inch).

a **i** What is the widest the table could be?
 ii What is the narrowest the table could be?

b George wants to convert his measurements to millimetres:
 i what is the widest the table could be?
 ii what is the smallest the width of the table could be?

> You are expected to
> know that:
> 1 inch = 25.4 millimetres.

N2.3 Sanjay used a pedometer to help him calculate how far he walked on a sponsored walk.
He calculated that he walked a distance of 17 014 metres.

a **i** Round the distance Sanjay walked to a sensible degree of accuracy.
 ii Give your reasons for choosing the degree of accuracy.

b How far would you say Sanjay had walked in miles?
 Sanjay misread his answer: it should have been 17 041 metres.

c Would you change any of your answers? Give your reasons.

> You are expected to
> know that:
> 1 mile = 1.6 kilometres.

N2.4 The distance between two railway stations A and B is given as:

160 km (to the nearest kilometre).

a **i** What is the furthest apart the stations could be?
 ii What is the shortest possible distance between A and B?

b What is the distance between A and B given to 1 sf?
c What is this distance in miles?

N2.5 A digital temperature display is correct to 1 dp.

The display shows 12.4 °C

Which of these temperatures could not be the
temperature correct to 3 dp?

12.449 °C 12.300 °C 12.380 °C 12.350 °C 12.406 °C

N2.6 For a school trip 148 students pay £19.50 each.

Without using a calculator:

a **i** Estimate the total amount paid by students.
 ii Show your working and explain any rounding you use.

b **i** Is your estimate more, or less, than the actual total?
 ii Explain how you decided.

c Calculate, without a calculator the exact total paid by students.
 You must show all your working.

> You must show enough
> working to convince
> someone that you did not
> use a calculator.

N3
Types of number

N3.1 **a** List all the factors of 12.
  b **i** What are the prime factors of 12?
      ii Write 12 as a product of primes.
  c Which of these numbers is a multiple of 12?
        16   288   300   432   612   724

12 is not a square number.

  d Which square number is nearest to 12?
  e What is the value of 12^2?

> Remember:
> 1 is a factor of all numbers.

N3.2 **a** List all the whole numbers less than 20 that have exactly two factors.
  b What mathematical name do we give numbers with exactly two factors?
  c List the whole numbers, less than 20, that have exactly 4 factors.

N3.3 A number n is:
        ◆ larger than 10
        ◆ smaller than 50
        ◆ a square number.
  and also ◆ a triangular number.

  a Find the value of n.
  b List all the factors of n.
  c Write n as a product of prime numbers.
  d Explain why 4500 is a multiple of n.

N3.4 Sofka says that:

  "if you double any number and then add 1,
  the answer must be an odd number".

  a **i** Do you agree with Sofka?
      ii Explain your answer.
  b **i** Are all prime numbers odd numbers?
      ii Explain your answer.

N3.5 The value of 3^n is 729.
  a **i** What is the value of n?
      ii What is the value of n^3?
  b **i** Is 729 a square number?
      ii Explain your answer.
      iii What is $\sqrt{729}$?
  c Write 729 in standard form.

N3.6 The winning numbers for the Lottery were given in this way:
  The numbers possible are from 1 to 49.

  1st Number   ◆ a square number between 20 and 30
  2nd Number   ◆ the ninth triangular number
  3rd Number   ◆ a multiple of 7, and a multiple of 5
  4th Number   ◆ the number of prime numbers between 10 and 20
  5th Number   ◆ the square root of 1369
  6th Number   ◆ the sixth multiple of 3
  Bonus Number ◆ 2 to the power of 3

  a What are the six winning numbers?
  b List all the factors of the Bonus Number.
  c Which of the winning numbers is prime?
  d **i** Find the sum of the six winning numbers.
      ii Write this sum in standard form.

> Remember:
> sum is another word
> for total.

N4
Fractions, decimals and
percentages

N4.1 In a test of memory, four students were given fifteen seconds to read from a list of numbers.

- Claire read out $\frac{3}{4}$ of the numbers
- Rob read out $\frac{3}{5}$ of the numbers
- Joel read out $\frac{5}{8}$ of the numbers
- Nicole read out $\frac{7}{10}$ of the numbers

a **i** Which student read out most numbers?
ii Which student read out fewest numbers?
You must show, and explain, all your working.

There were 40 numbers in the list.

b How many numbers did Joel read out?
c How many more numbers did Claire read out than Rob?

N4.2 **a** Write $\frac{3}{8}$ as a decimal.

b Is $\frac{3}{8}$ larger or smaller than 0.4? Explain your answer.

c List these numbers in order, starting with the smallest.
$\frac{1}{2}$ 0.6 $\frac{1}{5}$ $\frac{3}{8}$ 0.085

d Which is larger: 0.805 or 0.85? Explain your answer.

N4.3 Ian packs and labels pizzas.
He starts his shift with a sheet of 1000 labels.
After working for an hour he has used 150 labels.

a **i** What fraction of the labels had Ian used after an hour?
ii Write this fraction in its lowest terms.

During the second hour Ian used $\frac{1}{5}$ of the labels that were left over.

b How many labels did Ian use in the second hour?

During the third hour Ian used $\frac{1}{2}$ of the labels that he had left.

c How many pizzas did Ian pack in the first three hours of his shift?

N4.4

JETSTREAM **THE HOLIDAY AIRLINE**

Report for the year 1996

1996 was another year in which Jetstream increased its number of flights.

There were a total of 2448 flights:

$\frac{3}{8}$ of all flights were to Malaga

$\frac{1}{6}$ of all flights were to Orlando

$\frac{1}{4}$ of all flights were to Corfu

$\frac{1}{12}$ of all flights were to Faro

All other flights were to Malta

a How many Jetstream flights were there to each destination?
b What fraction of the flights were to Malta?

Jetstream say in their brochure:

"Over 35% of all our flights are to Malaga"

c Are Jetstream right to claim this? Explain your answer.
d Roughly 15% of all Jetstream flights were to which destination?
Explain your answer.

N4.5 Lisa works at the checkout of a supermarket.
This shows the hours she worked in the week before her holidays.

Mon	$5\frac{1}{2}$
Tues	$4\frac{3}{4}$
Wed	5
Thurs	$5\frac{3}{4}$
Fri	$4\frac{1}{2}$

a How many hours, in total, did Lisa work in the week?

Lisa is paid £3.85 per hour.

b How much did Lisa earn in total for the week's work?
Give your answer to the nearest penny.

After her holiday Lisa's pay was increased to £3.90 per hour.

c Roughly, what is this pay rise as a percentage?

N4.6 Pure gold is 24-carat gold.
In an 18-carat gold ring, only $\frac{18}{24}$ of the weight is pure gold.
What percentage of the weight is pure gold?

N4.7 The diagram shows a hole drilled in a steel sheet
for a pipe.
The hole must be larger than the
pipe to give a gap of $\frac{1}{16}$ inch.

a What is the radius of the pipe?
b What is the diameter of the
hole drilled in the steel sheet?

Hole in sheet must
have $\frac{1}{16}$ inch gap
around the pipe.

pipe
diameter
$\frac{3}{4}$ inch

N4.8 This diagram shows how the total price of a pair of trainers is made up.

£3	£2	£30	£13
Cost to make	Transport	Profit	Advertising

a What is the total price of a pair of these trainers?
b What fraction of the total price is what it costs to make the trainers?
c Approximately what percentage of the price goes to advertising?
d **i** What fraction of the price does profit represent?
     ii What percentage of the total price is profit?

N4.9 In 1994 Tessa needed a new engine in her car.
Her local garage said it would charge £385 + VAT.
(In 1994 the rate of VAT was 17.5%.)

How much would Tessa have to pay the garage, in total, for the engine?
(Give your answer to the nearest penny.)

N4.10 The same model of camcorder was advertised in two shops in this way:

Spotlight Price £289.99 (inc VAT)   Camdeals Price £249.99 + VAT
(VAT was charged at $17\frac{1}{2}$%)

In which shop was the camcorder cheaper: Spotlight or Camdeals?
Explain your answer.

N4.11   A sports stadium has seating for 60 000 people.
For the semifinals of a tournament the seats are priced in this way:

20% of the seats £22.50
28% of the seats £18
17% of the seats £12.50
30% of the seats £8.50
the remaining seats .... NO CHARGE

a   **i** For what percentage of the seats is no charge made?
      ii How many seats is this?
b How many seats are to be sold for £12.50?

Every seat in the stadium was full for the semifinal.

c How much, in total, was taken from ticket sales?

N4.12   A motorbike costs £9650 new.
The secondhand price guide describes how the value drops each year:

At the end of the first year the bike loses 16% of its value

At the end of year 2 it loses 9% of its value at the start of that year

At the end of year 3 it loses 7% of its value at the start of that year

At the end of three years Tony says the bike has lost 32% of £9650.

a Do you agree with Tony?
Explain your answer.
b At the end of three years, calculate what the value of the bike will be according to the price guide.

N4.13   A hockey club won £2400 on the lottery.
The winnings were invested in a savings scheme for 3 years, at a compound interest rate of $7\frac{1}{2}\%$ p.a.

a Calculate the total interest earned over the three years.
Give your answer to the nearest penny.

With this money and profits from a jumble sale, the club decides to invest £3650 in a scheme at a compound interest rate fixed at 6.8% p.a.

b After how many years will their investment grow to at least £5000?
Explain your answer, and show your calculations.

N4.14   Rick's car broke down on the motorway and the total bill for towing and repairs came to £435. Rick paid with his new credit card.

Rick decides that he will not use the card again until the £435 is paid off, and that he will pay £35 at the end of each month off his credit card bill.

The credit card company charges interest at 2% per month on the money that Rick owes them on the first day of the month.

a At the start of month 2, how much will Rick owe on his credit card?
b   **i** After how many months will Rick owe roughly £235?
       Explain your answer.
     ii To the nearest penny, how much will Rick owe after this time?

N4.15   Jan bought a CD player just before the sales.
Jade bought exactly the same model CD player in the sale with 20% off.
Jade paid £124. What did Jan pay?

N5
Indices and standard form

In general you will not gain marks by simply copying your calculator display.

You must interpret the display and write it as a number in standard form.

N5.1 Calculate the value of:
$$(25.8 \times 10^{-3}) \times (1.5 \times 10^{5})$$
Give your answer in standard form.

N5.2 The Moon is said to have a mass of 7.343×10^{19} tonnes.
The Earth is said have a mass 81 times greater than the mass of the Moon.
Calculate the mass of the Earth.
Your answer should be in standard form.

N5.3 The approximate surface area of the Earth is given as:
$$1.971 \times 10^{8} \text{ square miles}$$
Water covers about 1.395×10^{8} square miles of the Earth's surface.
Approximately what area of the Earth's surface is not covered by water?
Your answer should be in standard form.

N5.4 If $k = 6.75 \times 10^{-2}$, and $w = 2.15 \times 10^{-3}$, give the value in standard form, of:
a $2k$ **b** $\frac{1}{2}w$ **c** kw **d** w^2 **e** $k + w$

N5.5 What is the value of $\sqrt{16 \times 10^{-4}}$?

N5.6 The area of the Earth's surface is given as 5.1×10^{10} km².
Land covers roughly 30% of the Earth's surface.

a Roughly what area (in km²) of the Earth's surface is not land?

The Pacific Ocean covers approximately 165 250 000 km².

b In standard form write the area of the Earth's surface covered by the Pacific Ocean.

The ten largest oceans and seas in the world cover a total area of about 352 100 000 km².

c **i** Write this total area in standard form.
ii Roughly what fraction of this total is made up by the Pacific Ocean? Show your calculations.

N5.7 The area of Australia is given as about 7.618×10^{6} km².
This area is about 35 times the size of the UK.
Give the approximate area of the UK in standard form.

N5.8 It is estimated that by 2050, India will have overtaken China as the most populous country in the world.

Population estimates for 2050 are given as: India 1.591×10^{9}
China 1 554 875 000

In 2050, roughly how many more people will live in India than in China?

N5.9 United Nations estimates show that in the 1980's the population of the world increased from 4.45×10^{9} to 5.292×10^{9}.

a How many people does this increase represent?
Give your answer in standard form.
b Roughly, what is this increase as a percentage?

N5.10 In 1991 UK manufacturers of sweets and chocolate spent £8.834×10^{7} on advertising. Advertising for tea was about a quarter of this amount.

Roughly how much was spent in the UK in 1991 on advertising tea?

N6
Ratio

N6.1 The weights of two tins of baked beans are in the ratio 15 : 25.

    a Write this ratio in its simplest terms.

    The smaller tin contains 225 grams of beans.

    b Calculate the weight of beans in the larger tin.

    c Calculate the weight of beans in the smaller tin, as a percentage of the weight of beans in the larger tin.

N6.2 A salad dressing is made from three ingredients:
olive oil (V), malt vinegar (M), and raspberry wine vinegar (R), in the ratio:

$$
\begin{array}{ccccc}
V & : & M & : & R \\
5 & : & 2 & : & 1
\end{array}
$$

    a How much malt vinegar, is needed to mix with 350 ml of olive oil.

    Rick is making 2 litres of this salad dressing.

    b How much of each ingredient does he need?

> Check that your answers give a total of 2 litres.

N6.3 The plan of a sports hall is drawn to a scale of 1 : 250.

    On the plan the length of the weights room is 9 cm.

    a In metres, what is the actual length of the weights room?

    The fitness gym is 18 metres wide.

    b What measurement represents this width on the plan?

    c Roughly, what is this actual width in feet?

N6.4 A Victorian field microscope enlarges lengths in the ratio 2 : 7.
A woodlouse, 1.2 cm long, is looked at under this microscope.

    How long will the woodlouse appear through the microscope?

N6.5 This is a recipe for 25 sultana scones:

    500 g   S.R. flour
      25 g   baking powder
    250 g   butter
      25 g   caster sugar
    125 g   sultanas
    cold milk to mix.

    This recipe is changed to make just 5 scones.

    a What weight of sultanas was used for just 5 scones?

    This recipe is changed to make 480 scones.

    b Give the weight of each ingredient, in kg, for this recipe.

N6.6 Students at Aselbury College organise a sponsored swim for charity.
They decide to donate the proceeds to charities in this ratio:

    Famine aid : Disaster aid : Medical research : The homeless
        4   :   3   :   2   :   5

    After the event they donated £147.21 to Disaster aid.

    a How much did they donate to Medical research?
    b What was the total raised by the sponsored swim?

    The ratio of males to females who swam was 2 : 3.

    c What fraction of those who swam were female?
    d To the nearest pound, how much was raised by the female swimmers?

N7
Whole number arithmetic

N7.1 Calculate the exact value of 473×54 without using a calculator. You must show all your working.

N7.2 One week the lottery jackpot prize was:
nine million three hundred and twenty thousand and forty pounds.

a If this is written as a number, how many digits are there?
b Write the jackpot prize: **i** as a number **ii** to 3 sf.

N7.3 At the start of her holiday, Ann's car had done 36 405 miles in total.
At the end of her holiday the total was 37 512 miles.

How many miles did Ann travel in total during her holiday?

N7.4 Put brackets in these statements to make them correct.

a $12 + 9 \div 3 \times 2 = 30$
b $12 + 9 \div 3 \times 2 = 14$
c $12 + 9 \div 3 \times 2 = 3.5$

N7.5 In 1991–92 the average daily sale of *The Sun* was 3.64 million copies.
Write this many copies as a number.

N7.6 The cities of Oslo (Norway) and Calcutta (India) have very different climates. The temperature was taken at the same time, on the same day, in both cities. In Calcutta the temperature was 34 °C, the temperature in Oslo was 50 °C colder.

What was the temperature in Oslo?

N7.7 There are many measures of length. We often use miles to measure distance, but we could use yards, chains, or furlongs.

1 mile = 1760 yards   1 mile = 8 furlongs   1 chain = 22 yards

Do not use a calculator for the following calculations and show all your working to show that you have not used a calculator.

a How many yards are there in a furlong?
b How many yards are there in 3 miles and 5 furlongs?
A road race is over 9900 yards.
c How many miles and furlongs is this?
d How many chains are there in:
    i 3 furlongs   **ii** 7 miles
A horse race is a distance of 4500 yards.
e **i** Is this longer or shorter than a $2\frac{1}{2}$ mile race?
    ii What is the difference between the two distances, in yards?

N7.8 Gita screen-prints T-shirts.
To buy and print a T-shirt costs 80 pence. She sells each one for £6.
Last year Gita bought and sold about 10 000 T-shirts.

Show how you calculate the following without using a calculator.

a How much in total does it cost Gita to buy and print 300 T-shirts?
b Roughly how much profit did she make in total last year?

N7.9 The average price of a ticket in a 75 000 seat stadium is £14.

a Show, without using a calculator, how ticket sales can total one million and fifty thousand pounds.

The stadium needs total ticket sales to rise to one and a half million pounds.

b Without a calculator, calculate the average price of a ticket for this.

N8
Distance, speed and time

N8.1 The distance from Leeds to Great Yarmouth is 187 miles.
Patrice calculated that his average speed for the journey was 55 mph.
How long did the journey take him:

a in hours **b** in minutes?

N8.2 A train travels 374 km between two stations at an average speed of 136 kph.

a How many minutes does the journey take?

In the timetable for the next year the same journey will take 21 minutes less.

b What will be the average speed for this journey?

N8.3 At the Regent Cinema the main film starts at 19:55.
The film lasts for 1 hour 52 minutes.
At what time will the film end?

N8.4 The graph shows a swimming race between Ejaz and Nick.

a Who won the race?
b How far did they swim?
c How long was the pool? Explain your answer.
d At what time did Nick first overtake Ejaz?
e At the turn, how far ahead, in time, was Nick?
f Who swam faster out of the turn? Explain how you decided.
g Who had the better start to the race? Explain why.
h Describe the race.

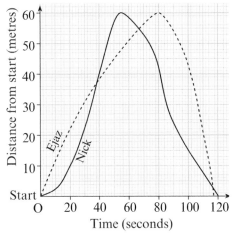

N8.5 The graph shows the journey of a bus and a taxi between Barnsley and Retford.

Barnsley to Retford is a distance of 60 km.

a When did the taxi pass the bus for the first time?
b At 18 45 how far from Retford was:
  i the bus
  ii the taxi?
c What was the average speed of the taxi between Barnsley and Retford?

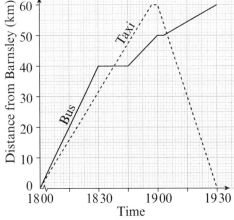

d Describe the journey of the bus, in terms of distances, speeds and times.
e How long did the taxi spend in Retford before returning to Barnsley?

The taxi driver sets a target to average 50 mph over a journey.

f For the return trip, was he on target? Explain your answer.

N8.6 Carla travelled 245 km, at an average speed of 58 kph.
She wrote on a postcard to her brother that the journey took about 4 hours.

a Do you think 4 hours is a good estimate of the journey time?
Explain your answer, showing any calculations you did.

b **i** Calculate the journey time, correct to 1 dp.
ii What was the journey time, to the nearest quarter of an hour?

N8.7 **a** **i** Which train has the shortest journey time between Exeter and London?
ii What is the journey time?

b What is the longest journey time?

c How long does it take the 0837 from Exeter to travel to Taunton?

Exeter to London Paddington is a distance of 193 miles.

d Find the average speed of the 0756 from Exeter to London Paddington. Give your answer correct to 2 sf.

Mondays to Fridays		
Exeter St Davids Depart	Taunton Depart	London Paddington Arrive
0600	0628	0835
0620	0648	0920
0659	0726	0930
0756	0820	1002
0837	0904	1110
0950	1024	1225
1131	1158	1350

Colin calculates that the average speed of the 0600 from Exeter to London must be less than 90 mph.

e Explain whether you agree or disagree with Colin.
Show all your calculations, and do not use a calculator.

N8.8 The 1996 Atlanta Olympic Marathon was won by Josia Thugwane of South Africa in a time of 2 hours 12 minutes and 36 seconds (2:12:36).
The Olympic Marathon is run over:

26 miles and 385 yards, which is 42.195 km.

a Give the marathon distance, in kilometres, correct to 1 dp.
b Show that Josia's average speed over the course was about $19\frac{1}{4}$ kph.
Explain your calculations.

N9
Miscellaneous

N9.1 Morag either runs or cycles to work. When she compares her average running speed with her average cycling speed, she finds the two average speeds are in the ratio:

1 : 2.5

It takes Morag 45 minutes to run to work.

a How long would you expect Morag to spend cycling to work?

Morag says that the journey to work is almost exactly 6 km.

b Using this distance, calculate her average cycling speed (in kph).

N9.2 The rainfall at an airport was measured (in mm) each day for a week.
The records were given in this way:
Mon. 4.2 Tue. 3.5 Wed. 0.4 Thurs. 2.1 Fri. 0 Sat. 0 Sun. 1.2

a Calculate the average daily rainfall:
i in millimetres **ii** in inches.

The runways have a total surface area of 4.2 km².

b Calculate the total volume of rain that fell on the runways over the week:
i in litres **ii** in gallons.

c In litres per hour, what was the average amount of rain that fell on the runways over the week?

You should know that:

1 gallon ≈ 4.546 litres.

Algebra

A1
Formulas

A1.1 One formula used to calculate velocity (v) is: $v = u + ft$

    a Calculate the value of v when $u = 0$, $f = 8$ and $t = 12$

    b Calculate the value of v when $u = 3.5$, $f = 15.6$ and $t = \frac{1}{4}$

    c **i** Rearrange the formula to express t in terms of v, u, and f.

       ii Calculate t when $u = 6.2$, $v = 30.7$ and $f = 5$.

A1.2 Tradewinds is a mail-order firm that sells T-shirts for £6.99 each.
To every order they add £3.50 for postage and packing.

    a Write down a formula for the total cost, £C, of an order for n T-shirts.

    b Show how you use your formula to calculate the total cost for an order of 5 T-shirts.

A1.3 Trolleycraft's new supermarket trolley has 8 wheels.
Jenny uses Trolleycraft's formula to work out how many wheels to order:

$$w = 8t + 3600$$

where w is the total number of wheels to order and t is the number of trolleys they expect to sell.
Trolleycraft expect to sell 15 000 of these new trolleys.

    a Calculate the total number of wheels Jenny should order.

Jenny was on holiday, Gary used the formula and ordered 28 200 wheels.

    b How many trolleys did Gary expect to sell?

A1.4 The power used by a light bulb can be calculated with this formula: $P = IR^2$

where R is the resistance (in ohms) and I is the current (in amps)

    a Calculate the value of P (watts) when $I = 8$ and $R = 60$.

    b Rearrange the formula to express I in terms of R and P.

A1.5 The formula for the volume (V) of a cone is: $V = \frac{1}{3}\pi r^2 h$

where r is the radius of the base and h the perpendicular height.

    a Calculate the volume of a cone where $r = 4$ cm and $h = 12.5$ cm.

    b **i** Rearrange the formula to express r in terms of V and h.

       ii Calculate the value of r, to 1 dp, when $V = 50$ and $h = 25$.

A1.6 The diagram shows how boards in a fence are nailed together – with some nails just for decoration!
A single board needs 5 nails, two boards need 8 nails, three boards need 11 nails, and so on.

    a How many nails are needed for a fence of 15 boards?

    b **i** If b is the number of boards, and n the number of nails, write a formula for the total number of nails for any number of boards.

       ii Use your formula to calculate the number of nails needed for a fence with 1484 boards.

A1.7 Eco-hire use this formula to calculate the cost (£C) of car hire:

$$C = 12.50 + 0.18k + 35d$$

where k is the distance travelled in km and d is the number of days hire.
What is the total cost of 4 days hire when 1152 km was travelled?

A2
Solving linear and simultaneous linear equations

A2.1 Solve these equations:

a $5x + 3 = 12 - 2x$ **b** $3(x - 4) = 45 - 4x$ **c** $\frac{1}{2}x = 3.5$

d $5(y + 2) = 3(6 - y)$ **e** $6a - 30 = a$ **f** $4(1 - c) = 10$

A2.2 Pia is 5 years older than Sean.
If Pia is n years old, write an expression in n for Sean's age.

A2.3 A hockey club has d members. Two-fifths of its members are injured.

a Write an expression for the number of members who are not injured.

b 18 members have injuries, how many members are there in total?

> An expression in n, is an expression that uses the letter n.
>
> For example: $n + 2$,
> and $3n - 7$

A2.4 A picnic mug costs 8 pence and a plate costs 7 pence.

a Sally bought n mugs. Write an expression for the total cost in pence.

b She bought two more plates than mugs.

  i Write an expression for the number of plates she bought.

  ii Write an expression for the total cost of the plates bought.

Nick bought k mugs, and three more plates than mugs.
In total he paid 81 pence.

c Write an equation in k, for the mugs and plates Nick bought.

d Solve your equation to find:

  i the number of mugs he bought

  ii the number of plates he bought.

A2.5 At the heritage tram centre, adult tickets are £6.
The charge for children is £3.50.
On 28 July 1990, n adult tickets were sold.
The number of child tickets sold was 228 more than the number for adults.

a Write an expression in n, for the number of tickets sold at £3.50.

b Write an expression in n, for the total paid for adult tickets.

c Write an expression in n, for the total paid for tickets on 28 July 1990.

The total for ticket sales on 28 July 1990 was £24 947.00

d Write an equation in n, for the total ticket sales.

e Solve your equation to find:

  i the number of adult tickets sold on 28 July 1990

  ii the number of tickets sold at £3.50 on that day.

> As you are told that the total for the ticket sales was:
> £24 947.00
> you can check your answer.

A2.6 **a**   **i** Rewrite the equation $5x + 8y = 31$, to express x in terms of y.

  ii Solve your equation to find the value for x when $y = 7$

b Solve the equation $5(p - 3) = 8(p - 6)$

A2.7 I start with a number, k.
I double my number.

a Write an expression, in k, for the number I now have.

I start with k, treble it and subtract 5.

b Write an expression, in k, for the number I now have.

With one starting number k, when I double it, it gives exactly the same answer as trebling it and subtracting 5.

c   **i** Show this as an equation in k.

  ii Solve your equation to find this starting number.

A2.8 Liam and Neil have ages that total 33 years. Liam is 5 years older than Neil.

a If Neil is j years old, write an equation in j for their total ages.

b Solve your equation to find each of their ages.

A2.9 The plan shows a walkway around a tank at the sea-life centre.
Every edge of the walkway has a rail (but not over the way in or the way out !).

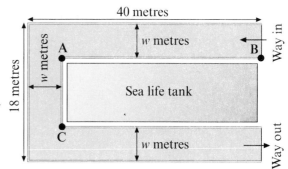

a Write an expression, in w, for the distance AB on the plan.
b Write an expression, in w, for the distance AC.
c What is the total length of rail used for the outside edge of the walkway?
d Write an expression, in w, for the total length of rail used for the inside edge of the walkway.
e Write an expression, in w, for the total length of rail used for the walkway.

The total length of the inside and outside rails is 184 metres.

f   **i** Write an equation in w, for the total length of rail used.
      ii Solve your equation and find the width (w) of the walkway.

A2.10 Wasim is a fencing contractor.
He has the contract for a post-and-rail fence around a car park.

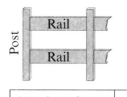

This table shows the number of rails needed for the number of posts used.

Number of posts	1	2	3	4
Number of rails	0	2	4	

a How many rails are needed with ten posts?

If x is the number of posts and y is the number of rails Wasim uses:

b Write down a formula that links x and y.
c Write your formula to express x in terms of y.

Wasim ordered 158 posts at the start of the job.

d How many rails should he have ordered for this number of posts?

The shape of the car park was changed and Wasim needed an extra 66 rails.

e How many extra posts did he need?

A2.11 Solve the simultaneous equations:

a $2x - y = 3$
    $3x + y = 5$

b $3w + 2t = 7$
    $2w + 2t = 5$

c $a - 3b = {}^-5$
    $4a + 2b = 8$

d $2p - t = 10$
    $5p + 2t = 7$

e $3y + 2a = 7$
    $4a + y = 9$

f $v + 5w = 95$
    $12v - 8w = 120$

A2.12 Jim has a part-time job stacking shelves in a supermarket.
In his pay packet last week he had £10 notes, £5 notes and £1 coins.
There were 4 fewer £5 notes than £10 notes.
There were 8 more £1 coins than £5 notes.

Jim had n £10 notes in his wage packet.

a Write an expression for the number of £5 notes in the packet.
b Jim had £96. How many £10 notes, £5 notes and £1 coins were there?

A2.13   **a**   Copy and complete these mappings.

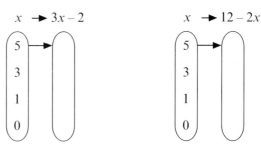

$x \rightarrow 3x - 2$

$x \rightarrow 12 - 2x$

> The solution to:
> $12 - 2x = 3x - 2$
> will be the value of x where
> the two graphs cross.

Draw a pair of axes with x from 0 to 6, and y from ⁻3 to 14.

b   On your axes draw the graphs of: $x \rightarrow 3x - 2$, and $x \rightarrow 12 - 2x$.

c   From your graph, estimate the solution to the equation $12 - 2x = 3x - 2$.

A2.14   On the axes are the graphs of two mappings.

The graphs are the straight lines P and K.

a   For each line, copy and complete the mapping:

$x \longrightarrow$

0
2
4
6
8

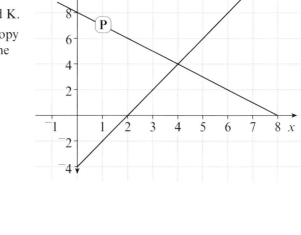

b   **i** Which one of these equations can be solved from the graph?

$2x - 4 = 2x + 8$ $x - 2 = x + 8$ $2x - 4 = 8 - x$

ii Explain why.

iii Use the graph to solve that equation for x.

A2.15   A train from York to Scarborough had five coaches.
As the train left York, in the first coach there were 57 passengers, and there were p passengers in each of the other coaches.

a   Write an expression for the total number of passengers on the train.

The conductor counted 301 passengers a few minutes after leaving York.

b   Write an equation in p, and solve it, to give the number of passengers in each coach.

c   Factorise completely:

i $9y^2 - 12y$ **ii** $4a^2 + 24a$ **iii** $125h + 50h^2$

d   Solve the simultaneous equations:

$$3p - t = 6$$
$$4p + 4t = 16$$

A3
Quadratic and
higher-order equations

A3.1 Anna wants to solve the equation $x^2 + 4x = 20$, correct to 1 dp.

First she tries $x = 4.0$, and finds the value of $x^2 + 4x$ to be 32.

Try other values of x to find a solution to the equation $x^2 + 4x = 20$.
You must show all your working, and give your solution correct to 1 dp.

A3.2 A number, w, is the solution to the equation $w^3 = 40$.

a Between which two consecutive integer values must w lie?

b Use trial and improvement to find a value for w, correct to 1 dp.

A3.3 A number p is the solution to the equation $p^2 - 2p = 18$.

a Show that the solution to the equation lies between:
$$p = 5 \quad \text{and} \quad p = 6$$

b Use trial and improvement to find a solution to the
equation $p^2 - 2p = 18$.
Give the value for p correct to 1 dp.

A3.4 Connor enters puzzle competitions to win prizes.
This is the latest puzzle.

> Two integers, both less than 100, are squared.
> When the squares are subtracted the answer is 1331.

Connor starts his working by writing this:
If the two numbers are k and m, then $k^2 - m^2 = 1331$.

He then uses trial and improvement. This is the start of his work:

Trial	k	m	k^2	m^2	$k^2 - m^2$	1331?
1	60	50	3600	2500	1100	Too small
2	62	50	3844	2500	1344	Too big

Rhian looked at trial 1 of Connor's work, and said that 50 and 60 could
not possibly be correct, because of their last digits.

a Explain how, by just looking at the last digits, $60^2 - 50^2$ cannot be 1331.

b Either by continuing Connor's trials, or by another method of your
own, find values for k and m such that:
$$k^2 - m^2 = 1331$$

If you use a method of your own, you must show all your working.

A3.5 Use trial and improvement to solve the equation:
$$x^2 - 5x = 32$$

Give your answer correct to 1 dp.

A3.6 Given that:
> y is a decimal number to 1 dp, and
> $y^5 = 1307$ correct to the nearest whole number.

Find a suitable value for y, making sure you show all your working.

A3.7 **a** Find a value for c that solves the equation $c^3 - 4c = 105$.

b Explain the method you use and show any stages in your work.

c Find a solution to the equation $c^3 - 4c = 0$.

A4
Linear and
quadratic graphs

A4.1 **a** On a pair of axes plot the points given in the table.

x	⁻4	⁻3	1
y	5	3	⁻5

b Draw a straight-line graph through the points.
c What is the gradient of the straight line ?
d Write down the values of y when $x = ⁻2$, $x = ⁻1$, and $x = 0$.
e On the same axes draw the graph of $y = 3x - 1$.

A4.2 When Gita keyed in the equation
$y = \frac{3}{4}x + 2$ her calculator displayed
this graph.

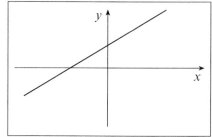

When Ian keyed in $4y = 3x + 8$, the graph looked the same as for Gita.

a Show that Gita and Ian's equations are equivalent.
b What is the gradient of the graph of $y + 3x = 4$?
c Sketch the graph of $y = 3x - 4$.

A4.3 A standard and a longlife light bulb were both tested.
The standard bulb lasted for x days.
The longlife bulb lasted for y days.

a The combined life of the two bulbs was 16 days.
Explain why $x + y = 16$.
b The longlife bulb lasted 5 days longer than the standard bulb.
Write down a different equation that connects x and y.
c Draw the graph of $x + y = 16$.
d On the same axes draw the graph for your equation in part **b**.
e Use your graphs to find the life of each type of bulb.

A4.4 **a** On a pair of axes draw the graph of $y = 3x + 5$.
Use values of x from ⁻3 to 3.
b On the same axes draw the graph of $y = 1 - x$.
c Use your graphs to solve the simultaneous equations:

$$y = 3x + 5$$
$$y = 1 - x$$

A4.5 **a** On a pair of axes draw the graph of $y = 4 - x$.
Use values of x from ⁻2 to 5.
b On the same axes draw the graph of the equation $y = 2x - 2$.
c Use your graphs to solve the simultaneous equations:

$$y = 4 - x$$
$$y = 2x - 2$$

A4.6 **a** Complete the table for the equation $4y + x = 4$.
b Repeat the table for the equation $4y = x + 8$.
c On the same axes draw graphs for each equation.
d Solve the simultaneous equations:
$$4y = x + 8$$
$$4y + x = 4$$

x	⁻4	0	4
y			

A4.7 This is a sketch of a graph of the equation $4y = x + 1$.

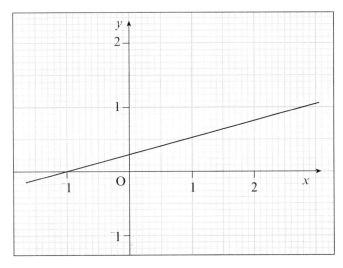

   a Draw a graph of the equation $4y = x + 1$.
   b On the same grid draw the graph of $y = ^-1 - x$.
   c Use these graphs to solve the simultaneous equations:

$$y = ^-1 - x \quad \text{and} \quad 4y = x + 1$$

A4.8 **a** On one pair of axes draw graphs of $2y = 3x - 4$ and $y = 5 - x$.
   Use values of x from $^-2$ to 4.
   b Use your graphs to solve the following pair of simultaneous equations:

$$2y = 3x - 4$$
$$\text{and} \quad y = 5 - x$$

   c Give the gradient of a line parallel to the line $2y = 3x - 4$.
   d Solve the equation $2x + 1 = ^-1.8$.

A4.9 This graph shows the charge for video repairs.

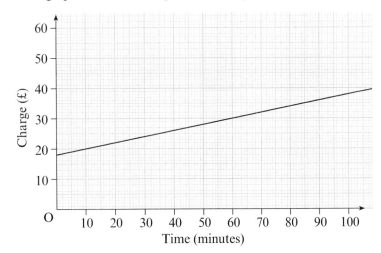

   a What is the charge for a repair which takes 45 minutes?
   b What is the gradient of the straight-line graph?
   c What does the gradient of the line tell you about the charge?
   d Write down the equation of the line.
   e Ella decides that the most she can spend on repairing her video is £50.
   What is the maximum time that can be taken for this repair?

A4.10 For the equation $y = x^2$:

a Draw up and complete this table of values.

x	0	1	2	3	4	5
y						

b Draw a pair of axes with:
values of x from 0 to 6, and values of y from 0 to 30.

> Your graph should be a smooth curve.

c Draw a graph of $y = x^2$ on these axes.
d Use your graph to find an approximate value of x when $y = 12$.
e Use trial and improvement to find a value of x for which $x^2 = 14$. Give your answer correct to 2 decimal places.

A4.11 a Draw up and complete this table of values for the mapping $y = x^2 - 2$.

x	‾3	‾2	‾1	0	1	2	3
$y = x^2 - 2$							

b Draw a pair of axes with values of: x from ‾3 to 3, and y from ‾3 to 8.
c Draw a graph of the mapping $y = x^2 - 2$.
d From your graph give the two values of x when $y = 1$.

A4.12 a Draw up and complete this table of values for the equation $y = 2x^2$.

x	‾3	‾2	‾1	0	1	2	3
$y = 2x^2$			2				

b Draw a pair of axes with values of x from ‾3 to 3, and y from 0 to 20.
c Draw a graph of $y = 2x^2$.
d Draw up a table of values for the equation $y = 4x + 5$. Use values of x from ‾1 to 3.
e On the same axes draw the graph of $y = 4x + 5$.
f From your graph give values for x where the line and the curve meet.

A4.13 A designer is told that an arch-shape:

♦ has the equation $y = 8 - \dfrac{x^2}{2}$

and ♦ has the y-axis as a line of symmetry.

a Draw up and complete this table of values for the equation.

x	0	1	2	3	4
y			6		

b Draw a pair of axes with values of x from ‾4 to 4, and y from 0 to 10.
c On your axes, draw a graph to show the complete arch-shape.
d Use your curve to estimate the value of y when $x = 2.5$.
e From your graph find two values of x where $8 - \dfrac{x^2}{2} = 4$.

A4.14 y and x are both positive values, and they are linked by the equation:

$$y = \sqrt{x}$$

a Copy and complete this table. Give values of y correct to 2 dp.

x	0	2	4	6	8	10	12	14	16
y	0	1.41	2						

b i Draw a pair of axes with the x-axis from 0 to 16, and the y-axis from 0 to 4.
ii On the axes draw the graph of $y = \sqrt{x}$.
c Use your graph to find the value of $\sqrt{5}$.

A5
Inequalities and
regions

A5.1 The school hockey team is planning a dance show to raise money for kit.

Ticket sales must raise at least £420.

The Dance Show
tickets: £3
(before the day of the show)

At the door
tickets: £4

The inequality for this is:
$$3b + 4d \geqslant 420$$

b is the number of tickets sold before the show.
d is the number of tickets sold at the door.

a Before the show 46 tickets are sold.
What is the minimum number of tickets the team must sell at the door?

This is a sketch of the line $3b + 4d = 420$.

b Copy the sketch and shade the region which shows $3b + 4d \geqslant 420$.

The dance show will be in the sports hall.
Safety rules allow an audience of only 150.

c Write an inequality with b and d to match the safety rules.
d What is the maximum number of tickets that can be sold at the door?
(46 tickets have been sold, and the safety rules must not be broken.)
e What is the range of possible values for d?

A5.2 Write down all the whole number values of x, such that:
a $^-4 \leqslant x < 5$ **b** $^-1 < x \leqslant 1$ **c** $3 \leqslant x < 4$

A5.3 Solve the inequalities:
a $2x - 3 > 13$ **b** $2(2x + 1) < 14$ **c** $4(x - 3) < 10$
d $x^2 < 196$ **e** $9x + 4 > 15x + 16$ **f** $5x + 3 < 41.5$
g $x^2 < 1$ **h** $x - 3 \leqslant 14$ **i** $3 < x + 1 \leqslant 10$

A5.4 **a** Draw a pair of axes with values of x from 0 to 5, and y from 0 to 5.
b Draw and label the line $y = 2$.
c Draw and label the line $x = 4$.
d Draw and label the line $x + y = 5$.
e Shade the single region which satisfies all these inequalities:
$$y > 2 \qquad 0 < x < 4 \qquad x + y > 5$$

A5.5 **a** p is an integer such that $^-6 \leqslant p < 1$.
  i List all the possible values of p.
  ii What is the smallest possible value of p^3?
b Rachel plays snooker every week. She always scores at least 50, but has never managed to score more than 107.
Use s for Rachel's score, and write the information as two inequalities.

A5.6 **a** Solve each of these inequalities:
$$7x - 3 \leqslant 3x + 6 \qquad 2(3x + 1) > 8$$
b What whole number values of x satisfy both the inequalities?

Remember:
square root ($\sqrt{}$) can be
positive or negative.
For example, $\sqrt{4} = ^+2$ or $^-2$.

A5.7 **a** List all the integers which satisfy: $^-1.5 < n \leqslant 2.5$
b List all the integers which satisfy: $50 < n^2 \leqslant 100$
c List all the integers which satisfy: $4 \leqslant 0.5n < 9$

A6
Manipulation

A6.1 Given that $v = \frac{1}{2}$, $w = \frac{3}{4}$, $x = 3$ and $y = ^{-}2$ evaluate:

    a vw **b** wx **c** $v + w$ **d** $\dfrac{v + w}{x}$ **e** $x + vy$

A6.2 Multiply out:

    a $5x(2x - 3)$ **b** $4(3x^2 + 1)$ **c** $3y(x - 2)$ **d** $a(a^2 - 2a + 3)$

A6.3 Expand and simplify:

    a $(x + 3)(x + 2)$ **b** $(y + 1)(y - 2)$ **c** $(2x + 1)(2x + 1)$
    d $(5w + 2)(2w + 5)$ **e** $(c - 2)(c - 2)$ **f** $(x + 2)(2x - 3)$

A6.4 Use the formula $v = \dfrac{1}{r} + \dfrac{1}{t}$ to:

    a calculate v when $r = 5$ and $t = 3$
    b give the value of v as a decimal when $r = 2$ and $t = 4$.

A6.5 For the formula $v = u + ft$:

    a calculate the value of v if $u = 12.5$, $f = 32$ and $t = 24.75$
    b rearrange the formula so that u is the subject
    c **i** make t the subject of the formula
        ii calculate the value of t, when $f = 32$, $v = 252$ and $u = 248$.

A6.6 **a** Evaluate the formula $s = \frac{1}{2}ft^2$:

        i when $f = 32$ and $t = 5$ **ii** when $f = 32$ and $t = \frac{1}{2}$.

    b Make f the subject of the formula.
    c Make t the subject of the formula.
    d **i** Calculate a value for t when, $s = 256$, and $f = 32$.
        ii Ikbal said that when t is calculated from this formula, it always has
          two values. Do you agree? Explain your answer.

A6.7 Factorise each of these expressions completely:

    a $vx + vy$ **b** $2x - 4y$ **c** $p^2 + p$ **d** $3t - kt + t^2$
    e $3ax^2 - 6ax$ **f** $h^2 + ht$ **g** $a^2b - b^2a$ **h** $6a^2 + 2a^2b$

A6.8 Factorise each of these expressions:

    a $a^2 - 3a$ **b** $t^2 + 4t + 3$ **c** $m^2 - 4m - 45$ **d** $p^2 - 13p + 36$
    e $h^2 + 6h - 16$ **f** $x^2 - x - 72$ **g** $n^2 + 21n$ **h** $b^2 + 15b - 16$

A6.9 To calculate the focal length of a lens this formula is used: $\dfrac{1}{f} = \dfrac{1}{v} + \dfrac{1}{u}$

    where f is the focal length, v is the distance from image to lens, and u is
    the distance from object to lens.

    a Calculate the exact value of f when $v = 2$ and $u = 5$.
    b Calculate f when $u = 1$ and $v = 2$.

A6.10 This logo is four rectangles (equal in size)
around a square.

    a Write and simplify an expression for
        the perimeter of the logo.
    b Multiply out $4w(w + 4)$.
    c Expand and simplify $(2w + 4)(2w + 4)$.
    d What is the area of the square in the logo?

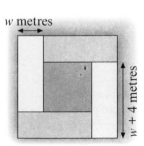

w metres

$w + 4$ metres

A7

Networks and flowcharts

A7.1 The network diagram shows six post-boxes. Letters are collected from the boxes in this way: the first box visited must be C, then the others in any order. At the end the van must return to C.

a John always visits the boxes in this order:

C to B to A to F to D to E to C.

How far does John travel?

b Sue takes a shorter route that starts and ends at C.

i Suggest a shorter route that Sue might take.

ii How long is Sue's route?

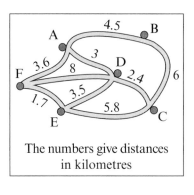

The numbers give distances in kilometres

A7.2 **a** Patrick inputs 13 and another number. The output is ODD.

Give a possible second input number.

b Ria inputs 24 and another number. She says the output cannot be ODD. Do you agree? Explain your answer.

c The output is EVEN. What can you say about the inputs?

The first two parts of the flowchart are changed so that the ouput can never be ODD. The first change is: Input one odd and one even number.

d What change do you suggest for the second part?

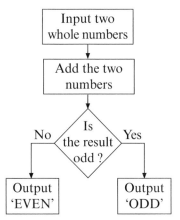

A7.3 This flowchart can be used to find the cube root of 40.

Draw up, and complete the table of values from the flowchart.

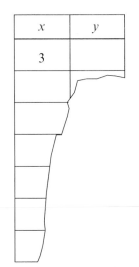

x	y
3	

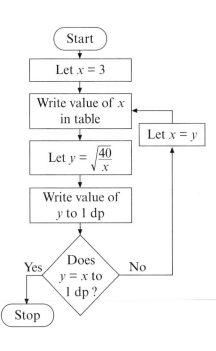

A7.4 This flowchart is being used to find an approximate solution to the equation:

$$x^4 = 50$$

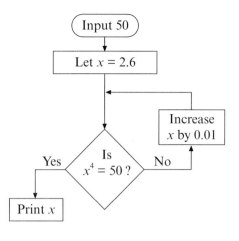

a Draw up a table showing your use of the flowchart to solve the equation:

x	x^4
2.6	45.69 …
2.61	

b Give an approximate solution to the equation $x^4 = 50$.

c If you used the flowchart to solve $x^4 = 30$, what would you choose as a good start value for x? Give a reason for your answer.

A8

Number patterns and sequences

A8.1 A computer design is built up in this way:

on line 1   a single star is printed
on line 2   three stars are printed
and so on …

a How many stars will be printed on line 8?
b After line 10 is printed, how many stars will have been printed in total?

Let p be the number of rows, and a the number of stars printed in a line.

c **i** Write a formula for the number of stars in a line.
   ii Use your formula to find the number of stars in line 375.
d **i** Write a formula for the total number of stars in the pattern.
   ii Use your formula to calculate the total number of stars after line 212 is printed.

> When you are looking for rules, or writing formulas, it often helps to look at differences in sequences.

A8.2 Jo is planning a design for paving slabs in a shopping centre.
Work on the scheme will start on Day 1. The numbers on the plan shows the day each slab is to be put in place. So:

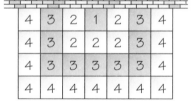

on day 1   1 slab is placed
on day 2   5 slabs are placed
on day 3   9 slabs are placed.

This pattern continues to build up.

a Copy and complete this table, up to day 7.
b Predict the number of slabs placed on day 10.

Day number, d	1	2	3	4	5	6
Number of slabs, n	1	5	9			

c **i** Write a formula in n and d, that can be used to calculate the number of slabs placed on any day.
   ii With your formula, calculate how many slabs are placed on day 41.

A8.3 Matches are arranged to make house shapes.

a How many matches are in the 3-house shape?

b Predict the number of matches in the 6-house shape.

Let n be the number of houses, and w be the number of matches.

c **i** Write a formula for the number of matches in any house shape.

ii Use your formula to find the number of matches in a 44-house shape.

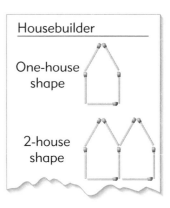

Housebuilder

One-house shape

2-house shape

A8.4 This is part of a sequence (P) of whole numbers.

$$\dots , 2 , 4 , 8 , 16 , a , b , c , \dots$$

a **i** In sequence P, what are the values of a, b, and c?

ii Explain how you decided on values for a, b, and c.

b For the complete sequence P, are all numbers even? Explain your answer.

c Write an expression for the nth term of sequence P.

This is part of another whole number sequence (R).

$$0 , 1 , 3 , 7 , 15 , \dots , \dots , \dots ,$$

d **i** What are the next two terms of sequence R?

ii What link can you find between sequence P and sequence R?

e Write an expression for the nth term of sequence R.

f Calculate the 150th term of sequence R.

A8.5 When Forth CD opened, on the first Friday, every fourth customer was given a free CD.

a Which of these were given a free CD?

Jenny	Raj	Ranjit	Dave	Iqubal	Mel
50th	72nd	104th	138th	216th	550th

Every 150th customer was given a free personal CD player.

b Which was the first customer to have a free CD and CD player?

A8.6 The nth term of a sequence is given by the expression:

$$n(n + 1)$$

a List the first five terms of the sequence.

Tony says that every number in the sequence is an even number.

b Do you agree with Tony? Explain your answer.

A8.7 Square tiles are put together to make a pattern of L-shapes. The first pattern uses 5 tiles, the second pattern uses 7 tiles, and so on.

a Draw a table to show the number of tiles used in the first nine patterns.

b Write a formula for the number of tiles in any pattern.

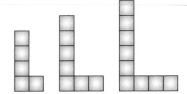

A9
Miscellaneous questions

A9.1 Triangle ABC has sides of: w cm, $(w + 2)$ cm, and $(w - 3)$ cm.

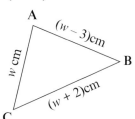

a Write and simplify an expression for the perimeter of ABC.

ABC has a perimeter of 41 cm.

b Write down an equation for the perimeter of ABC.

c Solve your equation, and find the length of each side of the triangle.

A9.2 The diagram shows how a rectangle of paper k cm wide, is cut into rectangles of different size.

Rectangle C is half the area of the paper.
Rectangle A has half the area of rectangle C.
Rectangle B has half the area of rectangle A.

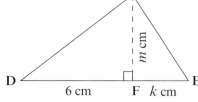

> Write expressions in terms of j and k.
> Do not introduce any other letters.

Write expressions for:

a the length of rectangle A   **b** the length of rectangle B

c the width of rectangle B   **d** the area of rectangle C

e the area of rectangle A   **f** the area of rectangle B.

A9.3 **a** For triangle CDE, write an expression for the length of:

   i DE   **ii** CE

Misha and Greg work out a formula for the area (A) of triangle CDE.

Misha gives $A = \dfrac{m(6 + k)}{2}$

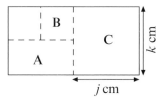

and Greg gives $A = 0.5\,km + 3\,m$.

b Which formula is correct? Explain your answer.

A9.4 The diagram shows a kite shape with one line of symmetry. Let A be its area.

Kim and Patrick both write a formula for the area of the kite.

Kim writes:

   $A = 3x^2 - [ab + b(3x - a)]$

Patrick writes:

   $A = 3x(x - b)$

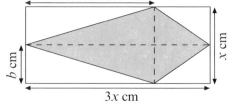

a Show that these two formulas are equivalent.

b Find the area of the kite shape if $x = 8.4$ cm, $a = 5.6$ cm, and $b = 4.2$ cm.

A9.5 The diagram shows a square of side $2d$, and an equilateral triangle of side $3d - 1$.

a Write and simplify expressions for:

   i the perimeter of the square

   ii the perimeter of the triangle.

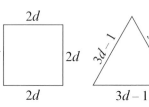

The two shapes have the same perimeter.

b Write and solve an equation to give the dimensions of each shape.

A9.6 You are taking part in a quiz.
You don't have a calculator, and you don't have anything to write with.
The first question in the arithmetic round is: "Work out **0.4 × 700**"

a i Explain a method you would use to work out the answer.
  ii What is 0.4×700?

b Factorise $na + nb$

c The second question in the round is:
"Work out **(0.4 × 560) + (0.4 × 140)**"
  i Explain how your answers to parts **a** and **b** can help with the second question.
  ii What is $(0.4 \times 260) + (0.4 \times 140)$?

A9.7 Salma chooses a whole number.
All she will say about it is that n represents the number.

a Explain why $2(n - 1)$ must be an even number.

b Write an expression for the number that is:
  i one more than Salma's number
  ii one less than Salma's number.

c Explain why when Salma calculates:

  n + **one more than** n + **one less than** n

the answer must be a multiple of three.

> The numbers 12, 13, and 14 are consecutive.

A9.8 Two consecutive numbers are chosen so that:
  $(3 \times \text{first number}) + (4 \times \text{second number}) = 172$

a The first number is n, write an equation that links 172 and the numbers.

b Solve your equation to find the two numbers.

c What are the common factors of the two numbers?

d What is the LCM of the two numbers?

e Multiply the two numbers, and give the answer in standard form.

A9.9 a Factorise $ay - by$

b Explain how this factorisation can help you calculate the value of:
  0.9×999

without using a calculator, or writing anything down.

c Write the answer to 0.9×999 in standard form.

A9.10 You think of a whole number n, and tell Sian and Mina.

  Sian doubles your number and adds 3.
  Mina subtracts 4 from your number.

a Write an expression for:
  i Sian's number
  ii Mina's number.

Sian and Mina multiply their numbers.

b Write and simplify an expression for the answer to the multiplication.

A9.11 Two groups of people went to the cinema:

Group A. Two adults and five children. Their tickets cost £26 in total.
Group B. Four adults and three children. Their tickets cost £31 in total.

The charge for an adult is £p, and the charge for a child is £m.

a Write an equation in p and m, for:
  i the total paid by group A   ii the total paid by group B.

b Solve your simultaneous equations to find the charge for:
  i an adult ticket   ii a child's ticket.

Shape, space and measures

S1
Angles and polygons

S1.1

Regular polygons					
A	B	C	D	E	F

a Name each regular polygon in the table.
b For polygons A, B and C, give the sum of the interior angles.
c For polygons D, E and F give the size of one interior angle.
d i A regular heptagon has how many sides?
   ii Calculate the size of one interior angle of a regular heptagon.
e Calculate the size of an exterior angle of polygon F.
f Which of these polygons are shapes that will tessellate?
Explain your answer.

S1.2 The diagram shows part of the roof frame of a building.
AR = RC = RT = PT = DP = AP
Angle ADT = 55°
Angle ABT = 38°

a What type of triangle is ΔARP?

b Calculate angle PTR.
Explain your working.

Sketch a diagram to work on. Label any angle or distance you know, or have calculated on your sketch.

When you are asked to explain or give reasons, it is important to do so clearly. In this way you will gain the maximum number of marks.

c Calculate angle CAS. Give reasons for your answer.

An identical frame is placed so that the quadrilateral ABWD is formed.

d What is the mathematical name of the quadrilateral:
  i ABWD
  ii ACWD
  iii PRCD?

e How many lines of symmetry has the shape:
  i ABWD
  ii ACWD
  iii PRCD?

f i What is the mathematical name for the shape PDXYCR?
  ii Is PDXYCR a regular shape? Explain your answer.

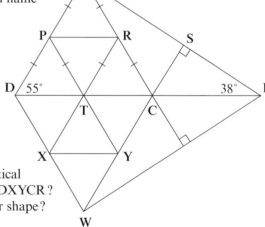

S1.3 A quadrilateral has angles of 54°, 37°, 40°, and k°.
Calculate the value of k.

S1.4 ABCDEFGHI, is a regular polygon.
K is the centre of the polygon.

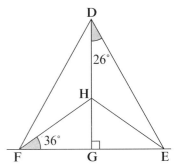

a Calculate the value of y and the value of x.
Explain your calculations.

b What can you say about the angles KGE and GEK?
Give reasons for your statement.

c Calculate the size of angle GKE.
Explain your working.

GHIA and KGFE are both quadrilaterals.

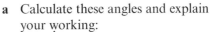

d Is GHIA congruent to KGFE?
Explain your answer.

e **i** What is the sum of the interior angles of GHIA?
ii Calculate the size of angle AGH.

S1.5 The diagram shows a mast DG.
Wires from the mast are fixed at E and F.

FG = GE, and angle DGE = 90°.

a Calculate these angles and explain your working:
  i GĤF
  ii HÊG
  iii DÊH

b Give two reasons why angle FHD = 126°.

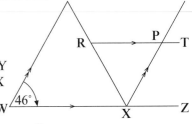

S1.6 **a** A design is to be made of a tessellation of regular hexagons of side 4 cm.
Explain what it means for a shape to tessellate.

b Name a different polygon that will tessellate with a regular hexagon.
Explain your answer with a sketch.

c Name a regular polygon that will not tessellate.
Give reasons for your answer.

S1.7 Triangle A is right-angled and isosceles.

a **i** Sketch a possible triangle A.
ii Show how you can arrange 4 copies of triangle A as a square.

You have 20 copies of triangle A.

b What is the smallest number of copies you need to make a square?
Sketch your arrangement of triangles.

Asa used all 20 triangles and arranged them in two squares.

c Show how he might have done this.

S1.8 In this diagram:

RT is parallel to WZ, and WV is parallel to XY.
VW = WX, and angle WVX is 46°.

a For each angle, calculate its size, and explain your working.
  i WVX   **ii** YXZ   **iii** VXY
  iv XPR   **v** YPT   **vi** TPX

b Explain why angle XRP is 67°.

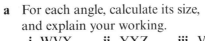

c Is triangle PRX equilateral? Give reasons for your answer.

S2
Angles in circles

S2.1 The diagram shows a circle, centre A.
Angle BDC = 28°, and BD = 12.5 cm.

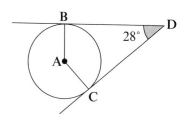

a What is the length of CD?
b What is the size of angle:
  i BDA
  ii DCA?
c Calculate the length of AD,
  correct to the nearest millimetre.

S2.2 In the diagram, AP is a diameter of the circle.
B, C, D, E, and F are points on the
circumference of the circle.

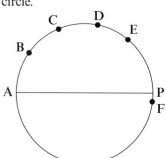

a Without measuring, give the size of
  angle ABP.
  Explain your answer.
b Give one other angle equal in size
  to angle ABP.
  Give reasons for your answer.
c What is the size of angle PFA?
  Explain your answer.
d Must AP be a fixed distance?
  Explain your answer.

S2.3 P is the centre of the circle, and AF is a diameter.
Angle ABP is a right angle.

a Are PB and CF parallel?
  Explain your answer.

If angle APB = 62°:

b What is the size of angle PFC?
  Explain your answer.

If the radius of the circle is 6.5 cm, and AC = 12 cm:

c Calculate the length of CF.
d Give the size of angle FDA, and explain your reasons.

S2.4 a i Draw a straight line 4 cm long. Label the line AB.
    ii Draw a circle with AB as its diameter.
    iii Mark a point C on the circumference so that angle CBA = 60°.
    iv Mark three other points, D, E, and F, on the circumference
      so that ADCBEF is a regular hexagon.
  b Calculate the size of one interior angle of ABCDEF.
    Show and explain your calculations.

S2.5 a i Draw a circle of radius 5 cm.
    ii Mark and label points K, L, and M on the circumference so that:
      triangle KLM is right-angled, with KM as the hypotenuse.
    iii What other mathematical term is given to the line KM?

AB is the perpendicular bisector of KL, and
CD is the perpendicular bisector of LM.

  b What can you say about where AB and CD intersect?
    Explain your answer.

Build up your diagram
so that it shows all the
information you are
given in the question.

When you explain you must
give mathematical reasons.

S3
Fixing position

S3.1 ABCD is a rectangle.
A is at (3, 5), B is at (3, 3), and C is at (¯3, 3).

a Give the coordinates of D.
b Give the coordinates of the point where the diagonals of ABCD intersect.
c Give the coordinates of the mid-point of CD.

S3.2 a i Copy this grid.
ii Join the points A(3, 0), and B(0, 3) with a straight line.

PQRS is a square, with AB as a line of symmetry. P is (1, 2), and Q is (3, 2).

b Give the coordinates of:
i R   ii S.
c On your grid:
i Draw two other squares with AB as a line of symmetry.
ii Give the coordinates of the vertices of each square.

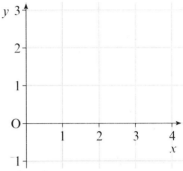

S3.3 On the grid the line AB is one side of a square ABCD.

a List the coordinates of A B, C and D.
b Give the coordinates of the point where the diagonals of ABCD intersect.

A second square DEFG is drawn by joining the mid-points of the sides of ABCD.

c Give the coordinates of the vertices of the square DEFG.
d What is the area of DEFG?
e Give the coordinates of the point of intersection of the diagonals of DEFG.

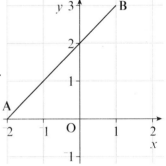

S3.4 The diagram represents a cuboid drawn on a 3-D grid.
The coordinates (x, y, z) of:
A are: (4, 0, 0)
C are: (0, 5, 3).
a Give the coordinates of:
i B   ii D
b Give the coordinates of the mid-point of the line BD.
c Give the coordinates of the mid-point of the line DC.
d i Explain how you calculate the volume of this cuboid.
ii If this cuboid is drawn on a one centimetre 3-D grid: Calculate the volume of the cuboid.

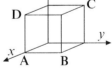

S3.5 Two points A and B are plotted on a 3-D grid marked in centimetres.
A is the point (3, ¯2, 5), and B is the point (3, ¯2, 8).

a Describe the position of B from A.
b What is the length AB?

S3.6 The direction of A from B is south-east.
What is the direction of B from A?

S3.7 Three towns, A, B and C are located so that:
A is due south of B, A is south-west of C, and
A and C are the same distance from B.
What is the direction of C from B?

S4
Length, area and volume

S4.1 The diagram shows a wire frame for a plastic refuse sack. The frame is made of three circles of wire and four straight wires welded together.

The top circle has a diameter of 45 cm, the middle circle a diameter of 40 cm, the bottom circle a diameter of 35 cm. The straight wires are 75 cm long.

a Calculate the circumference of the top wire circle.
b Give the radius of the middle wire circle.
c Calculate the total length of wire used in the frame.

S4.2 Kim designed this logo for a beekeeping society.

The logo is based on an equilateral triangle with two semicircles.

The triangle has a side of 5 cm.

a Name the other shape used in the logo.
b **i** Calculate the height of the triangle.
   ii Find the area of the triangle.
c Calculate the area of one semicircle.
d Calculate the total area of the logo.
e Give the perimeter of the logo to 2 sf.

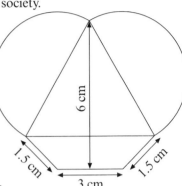

S4.3 A washer is made by cutting a circle of metal from the centre of a metal disc.

a Calculate the area of metal cut from the centre of the metal disc.
b Calculate the shaded area of the washer.

Discs are cut from the centre of a strip of metal 25 metres long and 20 mm wide.

c **i** What is the largest number of discs that can be cut from one 25 metre strip?
   ii Calculate the total area of waste when washers are made from this strip.

8 mm

16 mm

S4.4 The diagram shows the parallelogram shape of the car park planned for a school.

a Calculate the perpendicular distance from S to TV.
b What will be the area of the car park?

The planners say that the angle at V must be 65°.

c By how much will this increase the area of the car park? (The car park will still be a parallelogram.)

R — 150 metres — S

80 metres

50°

V — T

S4.5 The diagram shows the top of a tissue box. A hole has been cut to remove a tissue.

a What shape is the hole?
b Find the area of the top, after the hole is cut.

140 mm
80 mm
50 mm
60 mm
120 mm

S4.6 Milk is transported by road in tankers.
The storage tank is a cylinder of
radius 1.4 metres and length 7.75 metres.

    a Give these measurements in centimetres.
    b Calculate the volume, in cm³ of the tank.
    c Write your answer to part **b** in standard form.
    d What is the volume of the storage tank in litres.
        (Give your answer to the nearest litre.)

> Make sure you give your
> answer in the units asked
> for in the question.

S4.7 The diagram shows a water tank.
The cross-section ABCD is
a trapezium.

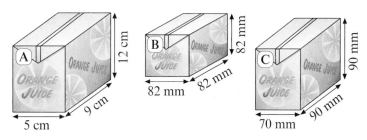

    a Calculate the area of
       the cross-section ABCD.
    b What is the volume of the tank?
    c Will the tank hold 1500 litres of water?
       Explain your answer, and show your working.

> This type of question can be
> confusing because different
> units of measure are used.
>
> One way to avoid confusion
> is to decide on the units you
> will work in, and change all
> the dimensions to those units,
> **before** you start to calculate.

S4.8 The diagrams show three cartons.

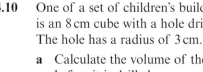

A supermarket brand of orange juice will be sold in 550 ml cartons.

Which of these cartons do you think it is best to use?
Explain your answer and show all your working.

S4.9 The diagram shows a plastic door wedge.

The wedge is made from
23 750 mm³ of plastic.

Calculate the distance w.

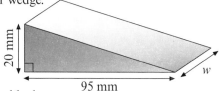

S4.10 One of a set of children's building blocks
is an 8 cm cube with a hole drilled through it.
The hole has a radius of 3 cm.

    a Calculate the volume of the block
       before it is drilled.
    b What is the volume of the block
       after the hole has been drilled?

The outside of the drilled block is to be painted.

    c Calculate the area to be painted on each block.

A litre of the paint to be used will cover 4 m².

    d How many cm² will a litre of this paint cover?
    e How many drilled blocks can be painted with 1 litre of this paint?

S4.11 In each of the expressions below, k and p both represent a length.
For each expression say if it represents an area, a length, or a volume.

a $3k$ **b** $2kp$ **c** $k^2(k + p)$ **d** $\frac{1}{k} \times p^3$

e Explain your answer to part **c**.

S4.12 All of the letters h, j, k, l and m represent lengths.
The letters are used in this set of expressions:

$$jk, \quad 0.75\pi h^2, \quad \pi k, \quad \tfrac{1}{2}\pi\,km, \quad \tfrac{1}{3}\pi m^2 l, \quad \sqrt{k^2 + h^2}$$

a Which of these expressions may represent area?
b Explain how you decide if an expression represents area.
c Which of the expressions represent a volume?
d Explain how you decide if an expression represents volume.

S4.13 This diagram shows a magazine storage box.
The letters represent lengths in centimetres.

This formula was given for the volume of the box.

$$V = \frac{c(b + e)}{2}$$

Explain why this formula cannot be for volume.

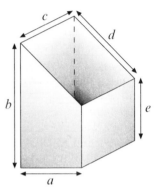

S4.14 The diagram shows a cross-section of a building used as a velodrome.
The letters represent distances in metres.

An architect wants to estimate the area (A) of the cross-section.

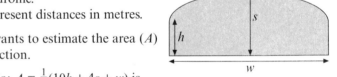

a The formula: $A = \frac{1}{5}(10h + 4s + w)$ is suggested for this calculation.
Explain why this cannot be a formula for area.

b Three other formulas are suggested. They are:

$$A = \tfrac{1}{5} \times 10hsw \qquad A = \tfrac{1}{5}w(10h + 4s) \qquad A = \tfrac{1}{5}(w + 10h)$$

Which of these formulas might be a formula for area?
Explain your answer.

S4.15 Alex is a designer who works for a packaging company.
A supermarket asked for a box that was like a squashed cylinder.

The final design Alex decided on had lengths in centimetres labelled as:

$$b \qquad h \qquad \text{and} \qquad s$$

These expressions represent quantities that are part of Alex's design:

$$\pi bh \qquad \pi(b + s) \qquad \pi bhs \qquad \pi h(b + s)$$

a Which of these expressions might represent area?
b Which expression might be for volume?
Explain how you decided.

S5
Construction, loci and
scale drawing

S5.1 The diagram shows the position of two ships A and B.
Use a scale of 1 cm = 1 km.

a On a grid mark the position of
A and B.

The ships hear a mayday call from
a yacht.

A helicopter spots the yacht and
estimates that ship A is closest
to the yacht.

The coastguard estimates that:
the yacht is less than 3 km from A, and
the yacht is less than 3.5 km from B.

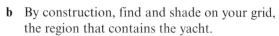

b By construction, find and shade on your grid,
the region that contains the yacht.

S5.2 On a grid mark the points P(2, 1) and R(5, 4).

a On your grid mark any two points A and B, that are the same
distance from both P and R.

b Draw the locus of points that are the same distance from both P and R.

S5.3 The diagram shows two grooves in a stage floor, AB and CB, 6 metres long.
A screen PR, 5 metres long, slides in the grooves.
When fully in use, the ends P and R are in groove AB.
For storage, P and R are in groove BC.

a Construct an accurate diagram of the grooves.
Use a scale of 1 : 200.

b On your diagram draw the position of the screen,
when the end R is 3.5 m from A.

c On your diagram show the position of
the screen when it is at the same angle
to each groove.

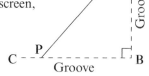

S5.4 AB and AC are straight lines that meet at A.
A circle with centre P touches both straight lines.

a Draw an accurate diagram showing the circle
and the two straight lines.

b Draw another circle that touches the
lines AB and AC, and label its centre D.

c Draw the locus of the centres of circles
that touch the lines AB and AC.

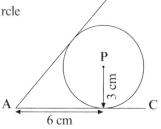

S5.5 The diagram shows a wheel of radius 1 cm that travels
for 8 cm horizontally and then up a slope
at an angle of elevation of 40°.
P is the centre of the wheel.

Draw the locus of the point P, as the
wheel moves horizontally and then
up the slope.

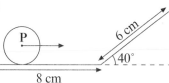

When questions ask for
construction, make sure
that you:
♦ leave all your
construction lines visible
♦ do any drawing in pencil,
so that mistakes can be
erased
♦ do not erase any line,
unless you have something
to replace it with.

S5.6 The diagram shows a side view of a stepladder.
There are hinges at T, L, R and P.
LP and PR are safety stays.

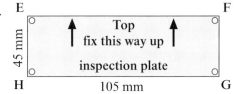

a Make a scale drawing that shows the
position of T, L, P and R.
Use a scale of 1 : 50.

b Draw the locus of P as the ladder is
opened and closed. Each leg moves
by an equal amount.

When the ladder is fully open, LPR is horizontal.

c On a scale drawing show the position of T, L, P, and R
when the ladder is fully open.

d When the ladder is fully open:
   i what is the angle at T?   **ii** how far below T is the hinge at P?

Scales can be given in
different forms.
For example:
1 cm = 1 metre, or 1 : 100
Make sure you know how
to interpret a scale.

S5.7 Paula works on aircraft engines.
She is making this rectangular
inspection plate EFGH.

a Make an accurate drawing
of rectangle EFGH.

E   F
Top
fix this way up
inspection plate
45 mm
H   105 mm   G

Paula has to mark the centre of a hole to be drilled in the plate.
These are the instructions she is given:

The centre of the hole must be:

    ◆ the same distance from edges EF and GH
    ◆ exactly 75 mm from the corner at G.

b Construct the locus of points the same distance from EF and GH.
c Construct the locus of points exactly 75 mm from G.
d Mark the centre of the hole to be drilled, and label it C.

S5.8 The diagram shows two towns:
Westbridge (W) and Dillton (D).

A local radio station has a digital
beacon, with a maximum range
of 75 km, located at R.

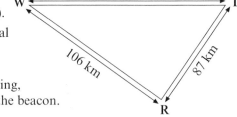

a Draw an accurate scale drawing,
showing the two towns and the beacon.
Use a scale of 1 cm = 10 km.

b On your drawing show the locus of the maximum beacon range.

A booster beacon (B) is going to be built so that it is exactly the same
distance from W and D, and exactly 60 km from R.

c Show on your diagram where B must be built.
d What will be the distance BW (in km)?

When no scale is given for
the question you must:

◆ decide on a suitable scale

◆ mark the scale you have
used on your diagram.

S5.9 A gardener decides to plant three beech trees, so that each one is
15 metres away from the other two.
Draw a diagram of the position of the three trees.
Use a scale of 1 cm = 3 m.

S5.10 A rotating water sprinkler, centre C, is centrally placed on a lawn 8 metre
square. Water is sprinkled between 1.5 m and 3.5 m from the sprinkler.
On a scale drawing show the area of lawn not watered.

S6
Maps and bearings

S6.1

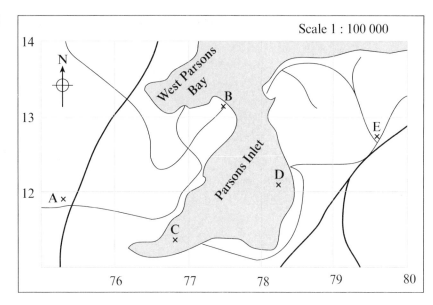

Scale 1 : 100 000

There are five locations marked A, B, C, D and E on the map.

a Give a four-figure map reference of the square containing location E.

b Give a six-figure map reference for location D.

c **i** Estimate the distance between location A and location D.
   ii Explain how you decided on your estimate.

Ejaz estimates the bearing of D from A as 100°.

d **i** Do you think this is a reasonable estimate?
   ii Give reasons for your answer.

Sean gives the bearing of A from C as 248°. Ejaz says that is impossible.

e Explain why Ejaz is correct.

Sonya rowed, in a straight line, from C to D.

f Estimate how far Sonya rowed.

S6.2 Some Ordnance Survey maps use a scale of 1:50 000.
A distance is measured on the map as 4.6 cm.

a What is this as a distance on the ground?

Mustafa calculates that, in a straight line, two radio masts are 32.5 km apart.

b On a map to this scale, how long is the straight line joining the mast?

S6.3 A coastguard lookout (L) fixes the position of two boats in this way:
   Provider (P) bearing 315° at a distance of 3500 metres
   Salama (S) bearing 240° at a distance of 5000 metres.

Use a scale of 1 cm = 1 km.

a Draw a scale drawing to show the location of L, P, and S.
b What is the bearing of:
   i P to L   **ii** P to S   **iii** S to P?
c **i** What is the distance PS?
   ii To what degree of accuracy is your answer given?

When a question does not give a scale for drawing, you must decide on a sensible scale to use.

Show the scale you are using on your drawing.

S6.4 A walker stops at a stile and notices that a pylon is due north of him.
From the stile the walker sets a bearing of 072° and walks 500 metres.
He stops and sees that the pylon is due west of him.

a Show this data on a scale drawing.
b How far due north of the stile is the pylon?

S7
Nets and polyhedra

S7.1

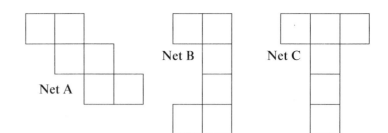

Net A   Net B   Net C

a **i** Which of these is not the net of a cube?
ii Give a reason for your answer.
b How many vertices has a cube?
c How many edges has a cube?

S7.2 **a** Sketch two possible nets for a regular tetrahedron.
b How many faces has a regular tetrahedron?
c **i** How many faces meet at a vertex of a regular tetrahedron?
ii Make a sketch to show your answer.

S7.3 The diagram shows a triangular prism.

a What is the mathematical term for the shape of the base of the prism?
b How many faces has a triangular prism?
c Draw an accurate net of the prism on centimetre square paper.
d Calculate the area of the triangular cross-section of the prism.

The net of this prism is cut from a rectangle of card 16 cm × 13 cm.

e Calculate the area of wasted card. (The net has no glue tabs.)

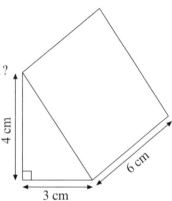

4 cm   6 cm   3 cm

S7.4 In the diagram:
BCDE is a square of side 4.0 cm and AP = 5.0 cm.

a Give the mathematical name of the 3-D shape ABCDE.
b Give the precise mathematical name of the shape ACD.
c The shape ABCDE has:
i how many faces?
ii how many vertices?
d Draw an accurate net of ABCDE.
e What is the distance AC (to 1 dp)?

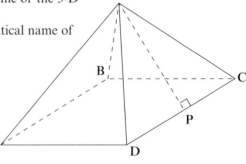

S7.5 **a** What precise mathematical name is given to this regular 3-D mathematical shape?
b How many vertices has this shape?
c **i** How many faces has this shape?
ii What shape are the faces?
d How many edges has the shape?
e Sketch a net of the shape.

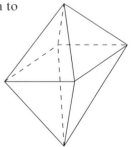

S8
Pythagoras and
trigonometry

S8.1 In triangle ABC calculate:

  a the length of AC
  b the length of BC
  c angle ABC
  d angle CAD.

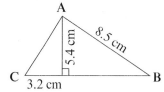

S8.2 Triangle RST has a right angle at S.
RS = 2.3 cm and RT = 10.8 cm.

  a Calculate the length of TS.
  b Calculate angles SRT and RTS.

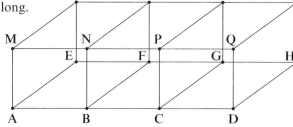

S8.3 This frame is made with 28 rods, each 18 cm long.

Cables joining the points are fixed along the frame.

  a What is the shortest length of cable needed to join D to J?
    (Remember that the cable is fixed along the frame.)
  b List all the routes from D to J that are the shortest distance.
  c Find the shortest length of cable joining A to Q, along the frame.
  d As a straight line, calculate the shortest distance from A to Q.

Coordinates are used for each point on the frame.
For example: F is (0, 0, 0)   B is (18, 0, 0)   and H is (0, 36, 0)

  e Complete these coordinates for P: (*, 18, *)
  f Give the coordinates of Q.
  g Give the coordinates of M.

> When problems involve trigonometry, draw a diagram of the triangle, label the sides opp, adj, hyp.
> This will help you decide which trig ratio to use.

S8.4 When an aircraft takes off it climbs to its cruising height in two stages.
This diagram shows that for the first part of the climb, a ground distance of 15 miles was covered.

1 mile is 5280 feet

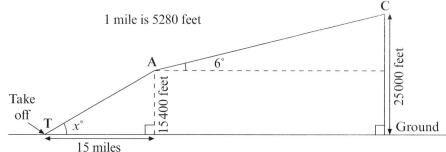

  a **i** At first the aircraft climbs at $x°$ to the horizontal.
      Calculate the value of x.
    ii Give your answer correct to the nearest degree.
  b **i** For the second part, the climb is at 6° to the horizontal.
      Calculate the ground distance covered for this part of the climb.
    ii Give your answer correct to the nearest 50 feet.
  c Give the total ground distance covered for the whole climb.

> For each part of the question you can work in feet, or in miles, but not both.
>
> For part **b** work in feet, for part **c** work in miles.

S8.5 The diagram shows a bracket used for shelves in a shop. To the nearest millimetre the bracket is: 195 mm high.

a Calculate the length PK.
b Calculate angle KJP.
c How long is PL?
d Find the length of ML.
e Calculate angle PLM.

As the height of the bracket is given to the nearest mm, it is sensible to give your answers to the nearest mm.

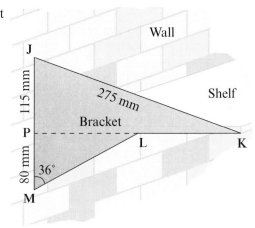

S8.6 An aircraft takes off from point P on a runway. It passes over the end of the runway E, at a height of 350 feet.

The angle of elevation of the aircraft from P is 6°.

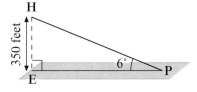

a What is the distance PE?

A second aircraft also takes off at point P on the runway, but passes over point E at a height of 420 feet.

b i Calculate the angle of elevation of this aircraft from P.
  ii Give this angle of elevation to the nearest degree.

S8.7 The diagram shows a ladder placed between two sets of racks in a factory. The ladder fixing is in the floor at P and reaches point B on one set of racks and point D on the other set.

a Calculate the height of B above the floor.
b Find the distance PA.
c Calculate the distance PC.
d What is the height of D above the floor?
e Calculate angle BPD, the angle that the ladder turns through.

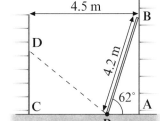

S8.8 The diagram shows a lift bridge. The angle between a tower and the bridge is 35°.

Both parts of the bridge move by exactly the same amount.

a Calculate the length AB.
b Find the distance AC.

When the distance AC is 5.2 metres:

c Calculate the angle between a tower and the bridge.

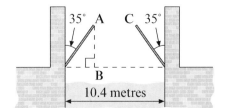

S8.9 A, B and C are towns on an island.

    a Calculate the shortest distance between A and C.
Give your answer to 1 dp.

    b To the nearest kilometre, calculate the shortest distance between B and C.

Town D is 30 km west of B and 20 km south of A.

    c Is the shortest distance from D to C more or less than 25 km? Explain your answer.

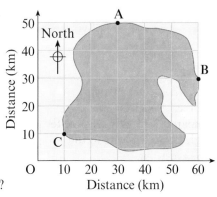

S8.10 Alison demolishes factory chimneys with explosives. She uses a device to measure the angle of elevation of the chimney top.

The device, 1.40 metres high, is set up on level ground 18.00 metres from the chimney base.

The angle of elevation is measured as 63°.

    a Calculate the height of the chimney correct to 2 dp.

Dave says that the nearest building is no more than 90 feet from the chimney.

    b Do you think the chimney can be demolished safely with explosives or must it be taken down, brick by brick? Explain your answer.

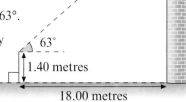

S8.11 A camera, on a tower fixed to a harbour wall is 15.6 metres above the water level at W.

An object is spotted in the water at P. The angle of depression from the camera C to P is 44°.

    a Calculate the distance PW.

A buoy is fixed at Y, 125 metres from W.

    b Calculate the angle of depression from C to the buoy at Y.
Give your answer to the nearest degree.

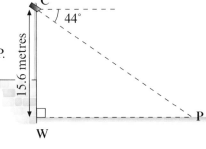

S8.12 The diagram shows the fishing boat Predator (P) and two lights A and B marking wrecks.
A is 550 metres north of B.

From P: the bearing of A is 046°, and
          the bearing of B is 136°.

    a Calculate:
      i angle BPA   **ii** angle PBA.

    b Calculate the distance:
      i PA   **ii** PB.

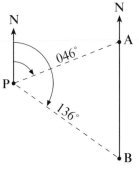

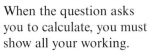

When the question asks you to calculate, you must show all your working.

Scale drawing is not accurate enough, and will not gain the marks for the question.

S9
Symmetry

S9.1 The diagram shows part of a shape. AB and CD are lines of symmetry of the complete shape.

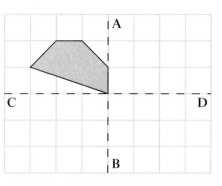

   a Copy the grid, with the lines of symmetry labelled.
   b On your grid, draw the complete shape.
   c What order of rotational symmetry has the complete shape?

S9.2
   a What order of rotational symmetry has this shape?
   b How many lines of symmetry has this shape?
   c Draw a quadrilateral that has:
      i no lines of symmetry
      ii exactly two lines of symmetry
      iii exactly four lines of symmetry.
      For each shape you draw, show any lines of symmetry.

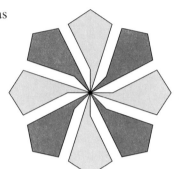

S9.3
   a Hexagon A has six lines of symmetry.
      i Sketch hexagon A, and show the six lines of symmetry.
      ii What is the mathematical term that describes this type of hexagon?
   b Sketch a hexagon that has only two lines of symmetry.
      Show any angles that are equal, and any sides that are equal in length.

S9.4 The diagram shows the start of a shape.
   a On a grid complete the shape so that it has both:
      ◆ no line symmetry, and
      ◆ an order of rotational symmetry of 2.
   b Darren completed the shape so that on a grid it had both:
      ◆ one line of symmetry, and
      ◆ no rotational symmetry.
      Draw a shape Darren might have drawn.
   c Swapna completed the shape so that on a grid it had both:
      ◆ one line of symmetry, and
      ◆ rotational symmetry of order 2.
      Show a shape that Swapna could have drawn.

S9.5 Starting with only these three squares shaded:
   a What is the smallest number of squares you need to shade to make a design with one line of symmetry?
      On a grid, sketch your design.

   Starting with the three shaded squares:

   b With as few extra shaded squares as possible, a design that has exactly two lines of symmetry is made.
      i How many extra squares do you think need to be shaded?
      ii Sketch your design and show clearly the two lines of symmetry.

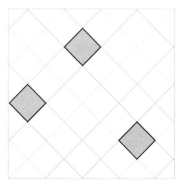

S10
Transformations
and vectors

S10.1 Copy this grid, and the triangle ABC.

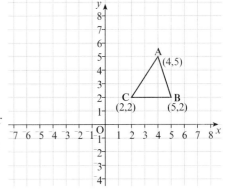

a Rotate ABC 180° about O. Label the image A'B'C'

b Rotate triangle ABC 90° clockwise about (2, ⁻1). Label the image A''B''C''

c Draw the image of ABC, after a translation with vector $\begin{pmatrix} 7 \\ 5 \end{pmatrix}$

Label the image A'''B'''C'''.

S10.2 Copy the grid and triangle ABC as for Question **S10.1**.

a Triangle ABC is reflected in the line $y = x$. Draw the reflection of ABC and label it A'B'C'.

b With B as the centre of enlargement, enlarge ABC by a scale factor of ⁺2. Label the image A''B''C''.

S10.3 A helicopter flew 40 km west and 15 km south from its base to rescue a climber. The helicopter then flew 10 km east and 35 km north, to a hospital.

a Write a vector to describe the flight to the rescue site.

Use a scale of 1 cm = 10 km:

b On a grid draw a diagram to represent the flight to the rescue site, and the flight from the rescue site to the hospital.

c State the vector that represents the direct journey from the helicopter base to the hospital.

The helicopter flies directly back to base from the hospital.

d Give a single vector that represents this journey.

S10.4 a Enlarge shape A so that every line of the shape is twice as long.

b What is the area of shape A before enlargement?

c Describe the effect this enlargement has on the area of the shape?

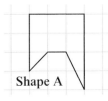

If shape A were enlarged by an SF of ⁺3:

d What would be the area of the image?

e Describe the lengths in the image.

Shape A

S10.5 a What single transformation will move the shape from position A to position B?

The point (2, 1) is marked on the grid.

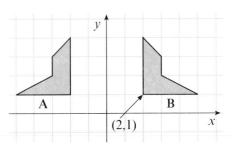

b The shape can be moved from position A to position B by combining two different transformations.

Give the two different transformations.

S11
Similarity and congruence

S11.1 Duncan is in a boat, and he can see the North Ronaldsay lighthouse. He knows that the lighthouse is 42 metres tall.

Holding a pencil 18 cm long at arms length, Duncan finds his view of the lighthouse is just blocked.

Duncan estimates the distance between his eye and the pencil to be 0.8 m.

a Roughly how far is Duncan from the lighthouse?
b Explain how you calculated the distance, giving mathematical reasons.

S11.2 Triangle A′B′C′ is an enlargement of triangle ABC with SF $^+2$.

a **i** Are triangles ABC and A′B′C′ congruent or similar?
ii Explain the difference between congruent and similar.
b A″B″C″ is an enlargement of ABC.
Are ABC and A″B″C″ congruent or similar?
Give reasons for your answer.

S11.3 In the diagram:

AT = 14 cm   BT = 6 cm   BC = 10 cm

Calculate the length of RT.
Explain your calculation.

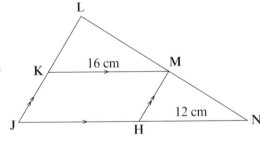

S11.4 In the diagram:

KM is parallel to JN
LJ is parallel to MH
KM = 16 cm, HN = 12 cm
and LN = 28 cm.

a List any pairs of similar triangles in the diagram.
b Calculate the length of LM.

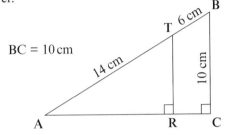

S11.5 Triangles NRC and WVY are similar.

a What is the size of angle RNC?
Give reasons for your answer.

Dave calculates the distance VY to be 11.5 cm.

b Explain why Dave must be wrong.
c Calculate the distance VY.

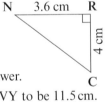
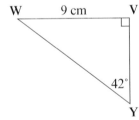

S11.6 The diagram shows a stepladder used in a library. M and N are mid-points of the sides AR and AP.

a Explain why triangle ARP is similar to triangle AMN.
b Calculate the length of RP.
Explain your working.
c Is triangle ARP an enlargement of △AMN?
Explain your answer.

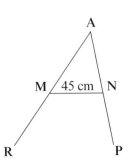

S12
Miscellaneous

S12.1 The diagram shows a rectangle of paper with two folds, AB and CD.
The two folds cross at the point P so that:
AP = 10 cm and PB = 20 cm.

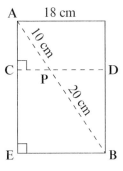

a Use Pythagoras' theorem to calculate the distance AE.
b Use similar triangles to calculate the distance CP.
c Calculate the distance AC.
d Calculate the size of angle ABE.
e Explain why angle ABE and angle APC are equal.

S12.2

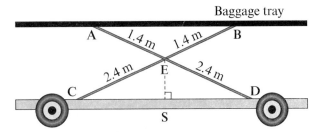

Baggage tray

The diagram shows a baggage tray lift used for loading aircraft.
As the angle at E changes, the legs AD and BC move up or down.

a Complete the following statements:
   i As the angle at E becomes smaller the baggage tray moves _____ .
   ii As the angle at E becomes larger the baggage tray moves _____ .
b What is the mathematical name given to triangle AEB?

The baggage tray is at its full height when angle CED = 35°.

c At its full height what is the size of angle EDC?

A safety rod is fixed between E and S when the tray is at full height.
S is the mid-point of CD and angle ESD = 90°.

d Calculate the length of ES.
e Use Pythagoras' theorem to calculate the distance SD.
f Use similar triangles to calculate the distance AB.
g When the tray is at full height, what is the perpendicular distance between the tray and CD?

> It might help to draw a diagram of your own.
> On your diagram you can mark distances and angles that you know or have calculated.

S12.3 Draw a pair of axes with:
       the x-axis from 0 to 12
       the y-axis from 0 to 10.

a i Plot and label the following points:
     A (0,0)   B (4, 10)   C (8, 10)   D (12, 0)
    ii Join A to B, B to C, and C to D with straight lines.
b Draw straight lines to join:
    i points A and C
    ii points B and D.
Label the point where BD crosses AC as P.
From your diagram:

c List two triangles that are similar.
d List two triangles that are congruent.
e Calculate the area of triangle APD.
f Calculate the size of angle APD.

Handling data

D1
Probability

D1.1 When 50 000 copies of a paperback book were printed, 200 copies were found to have mistakes.
Unfortunately all 50 000 copies were sent out to bookshops.
What is the the probability that the first book sold will have mistakes?

D1.2 In a board game two fair 1 to 6 dice are thrown.
The numbers on the dice are added to give the player's score.
  a List all the possible outcomes when these two dice are thrown.
  b What is the probability that the player will score 10 with one throw?
  c **i** Is any score more likely than any other scores with a throw ?
  ii Explain your answer using probabilities.

  If a player rolls a 'double', e.g. two 2's, two 3's, the other player misses a go.

  d What is the probability that a player will **not** roll a 'double'?
  e What is the probability that a player will, with two throws of the dice:
  i throw a double, followed by a double
  ii throw a score of 9, followed by a double
  iii throw a double, followed by a score less than 5 ?

D1.3 Javed collected data on the faxes received by a company.
Every fax was for one of the following departments: UK Sales, Export Sales, Production.

UK Sales received half of all faxes.
Export Sales received one third of all faxes.
Production received all the other faxes.

Yesterday, two faxes were received before 7 am.

  a Calculate the probability that:
  i the first fax was for UK Sales
  ii the first fax was for Production
  iii both faxes were for Export Sales.
  b Calculate the probability that both faxes are:
  either for Production or for Export Sales.

D1.4 A games company made spinners to be given away by a petrol company.
The spinners were 5-sided, showing scores of 0, 1, 2, 3 and 4.
There was a fault in manufacture, and all the spinners were biased in the same way.
This table shows probabilities for the spinners:

Score	0	1	2	3	4
Probability	0.2	0.3	0.1	0.1	

  a **i** What is the probability of scoring 4?
  ii Give reasons for your answer.
  b **i** Describe how the spinners are biased.
  ii Make a table to show scores and probabilities for an unbiased spinner. Explain the probabilities in your table.

A biased spinner is spun 200 times.

  c Roughly how many times would you expect a score of 1?

A biased spinner is spun 2000 times.

  d Can you say exactly how many times it will show a score of 3?
  Give reasons for your answer.

D1.5 Hannah can travel to work in two different ways: by train or by bus. She has found that both ways have problems.

Bus: The journey takes 25 minutes, but there is a probability of 0.4 that the bus will be 10 minutes late.

Train: The journey takes 17 minutes, but there is a probability of 0.7 that the train will be 12 minutes late.

Hannah has calculated the probability that she takes the train to be 0.25.

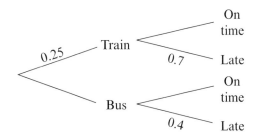

a Copy and complete the tree diagram to show all the missing probabilities.

b Calculate the probability that Hannah will take the bus and that it will be late.

c Calculate the probability that Hannah will take about half an hour to travel to work.

D1.6 In a survey of VDU operators the following probabilities were found:

The operator is female   0.6
The operator wears glasses   0.3
The operator is left-handed   0.1

a What is the probability that an operator is female and left-handed?

b Give the probability of an operator being male.

c What is the probability that an operator will be male, left-handed and someone who wears glasses?

D2
Interpreting data

D2.1 In a survey Ella asked three groups of 100 people this question:

"Do you think we should build more canals?"

These are the results:

Set A Yes 3   **Set B** Yes 88   **Set C** Yes 44
    No 97   No 12   No 56

The three groups of people she asked were:

◆ The Road Transport Federation
◆ People leaving a cinema
◆ The Canal Heritage Society.

a Match each set of results to a group of 100 people.

b Explain how you decided on your match.

c Which group do you think best shows public opinion? Give reasons for your answer.

D2.2 Imagine you want to find out the most popular flavour of crisps that are bought, and that you can ask 50 people.

a Design a data collection sheet for this information.

b Fill in your data collection sheet as if you had carried out the survey. (Invent replies for all 50 people asked.)

c Explain what the results of your survey show, and how this might help when ordering crisps for the school shop.

D2.3 In a hockey tournament, points are awarded as follows:

Win 3 points
Draw 1 point
Lose 0 points

These are some of the results from the tournament:

	Played	Win	Draw	Lose	Points
St Gregory A	8	4	1	3	
Milford	10	6		2	
Ashton	7		4		10
Pelbridge	11	7			22

Copy and complete the table.

D2.4 In a soft drinks survey, students in years 10 and 11 were asked to comment on the soft drink they choose most often. These are the results.

		Orange juice	Milk	Fizzy drinks		
				Lemonade	Cola	Water
Year 10	F	15	7	21	40	15
	M	.25	15	17	35	9
Year 11	F	21	9	18	34	22
	M	18	12	19	37	16

Lyn says that males (M) prefer fizzy drinks, and females (F) choose drinks that are not fizzy.

Does the data in the table support Lyn's view?
Explain your answer. Make sure you refer to years 10 and 11.

D2.5 A paper ran the following headline about teenagers and what they eat.

> **Has fruit had its chips?**
> 92 out of every 100 teenagers eat no fruit each
> day, but over half of them eat chips every day.

Is this true in your school?
List four questions you might ask to test this headline in your school.

D2.6 In a housing survey Ria and Mel wrote different questions to collect the same data.
Mel asked: "What type of house do you live in?"
Ria asked: Tick the box that describes the type of house you live in

Flat ☐ Semi-detached ☐ Detached ☐ Terrace ☐

a For each question:
  i give one advantage   **ii** give one disadvantage.
b How might you improve Ria's question?
  Give reasons for your answer.

If, in the survey, you wanted to know the ages of the people questioned:

c **i** Give an example of two different types of question you could use.
  ii Which of the questions do you think is better? Explain why.

D3
Drawing and interpreting
graphs and charts

D3.1 The pie chart shows the results of a survey.
In a college, 1800 students were asked how
they travelled in on the first day of term.

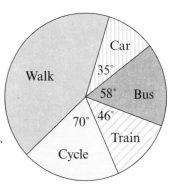

a How many of the students travelled
to college by train?

b How many students walked to college?

In another survey on student housing a
total of 1950 students were asked questions.

c Would it be easy to draw a pie chart to
show this data?
Explain your answer.

D3.2 The table shows the results of a survey into how students spend their
money each month on average.

Rent	Electricity	Gas	Food	Clothes	Books
£12	£7	£4	£8	£3	£2

Show this data as a pie chart.
You must show any calculations you do, and draw accurately.

D3.3 The table shows the results of a survey into
the viewing choices of teenagers in one
region of the country.

a Draw and label a pie chart to show
this information.

For the survey 15 644 teenagers took part.

b How many teenagers said they
chose Channel 4?

BBC 1	6%
BBC 2	4%
ITV	25%
Channel 4	44%
Satellite	21%

D3.4 Jenny sells ice-cream on a beach.
The table shows the number of boxes of
each flavour she orders for one week.

a Show this information as a pie chart.

This diagram shows the data in the table.

A   B   C   D   E

Vanilla	150
Strawberry	180
Choc Chip	60
Almond	0
Lemon	80
Lime	70

b Match each part of the diagram to a flavour from the table.

D3.5 This sales graph was printed in a
paper with the headline:

Sales rocket between '93 and '96

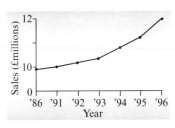

a Do you agree with the headline?
Explain your answer.

The graph has been drawn to mislead.

b Explain any misleading parts of the graph.

D3.6 A supermarket conducted a survey into how far shoppers travel to the store. They asked 100 male, and 100 female shoppers – these are the results.

Distance (d km) to store	$0 < d \leq 2$	$2 < d \leq 4$	$4 < d \leq 6$	$6 < d \leq 8$
Male shoppers	14	22	18	46
Female shoppers	18	24	30	28

The frequency polygon for the male shoppers is shown below.

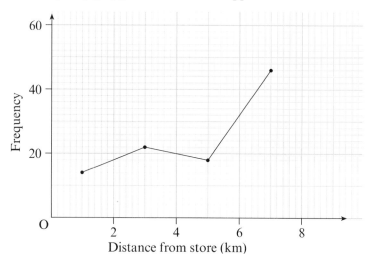

a **i** Copy the frequency polygon diagram.
  ii On the same diagram draw the frequency polygon for female shoppers.
b Describe any similarities or differences between the two frequency polygons.

D4
Scatter diagrams and correlation

D4.1 Scatter graphs A, B, and C describe different situations.

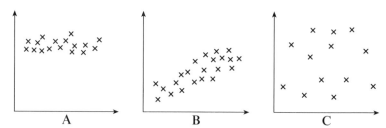

For each of these, say which graph might describe the situation.
You might possibly state 'none of these'.

a The size of feet against age at which the driving test was passed.
b Height against age for children in a junior band.
c Height against boot size for members of a rugby club.
d Age against number of visits to a cinema in one year.
e The age of adults compared with their height.
f The number of tickets sold against how many days until a pop concert.

Give reasons for your answers.

D4.2 A taxi driver recorded the time (*t* minutes), and distance (*d* km) for her twelve fares one day.

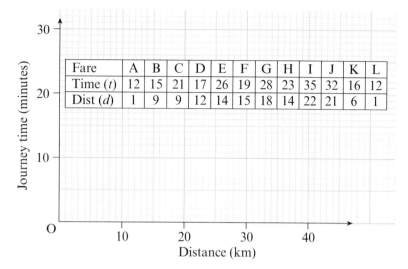

Fare	A	B	C	D	E	F	G	H	I	J	K	L
Time (*t*)	12	15	21	17	26	19	28	23	35	32	16	12
Dist (*d*)	1	9	9	12	14	15	18	14	22	21	6	1

a **i** Copy the axes as above.
   ii Draw a scatter diagram to show the information in the table.

b Describe the correlation shown by the scatter diagram.

c Add a line of best fit to your scatter diagram.

Her next fare is a journey of 18 km.

d From your diagram estimate how long this fare will take.
   Give reasons for your answer.

D4.3 This scatter graph shows the petrol consumption of cars, against engine size.

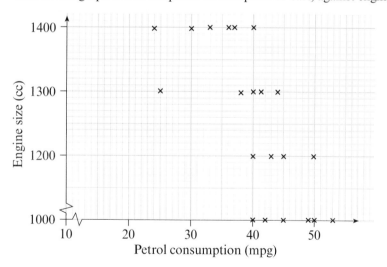

a Describe how petrol consumption (mpg) changes with engine size.

b What type of correlation does the graph show?

A new car is made with a 1250 cc size engine.

c Estimate the petrol consumption of this engine.
   Explain how you decided on your estimate.

D4.4 The graph shows the results for a group of students who are studying French and Mathematics.

In each test there were a possible 30 marks.

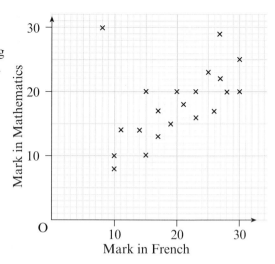

a Describe, in a sentence, what the graph tells you about the results.
b What correlation does the graph show?

Make a copy of the graph.

c On your copy of the graph, add a line of best fit (by inspection).

Iain is an average member of the group. He gained 18 marks in the French test, but was absent for the Mathematics test.

d Estimate what mark Iain might have gained in Mathematics. Give reasons to support your estimate.

Sofka is very good at Mathematics, but has only been studying French for a few months.

e Put a circle around the cross on your graph that could represent Sofka.

D4.5 Carlos carried out a survey of children between 7 and 15 years old. As part of the survey, age, height, weight, and shoe size were recorded.

a Sketch scatter graphs to show the most likely result of plotting:
   i age against shoe size
   ii height against weight
   iii shoe size against weight.

Carlos also collected data on fitness and drew a scatter diagram of height against fitness.

b **i** What correlation would you expect the graph to show?
   ii Give reasons for your answer.
   iii Sketch a possible scatter diagram for this type of data.

D4.6 As part of Jan's work she collects data on the value of cars. The data is for two groups of cars:

   Group A, from new to 5 years old
   Group B, from 30 to 80 years old.

She sketches scatter graphs for the data in each group.

a Sketch a scatter graph that could show Group A.
b Sketch a possible scatter diagram for Group B.
c Explain any differences you think your two sketch graphs show.

D5
Averages and range

D5.1

Temperature (°C)	22	23	24	25	26	27	28	29	30	31
Number of days	4	3	4	2	6	3	5	1	2	1

The table shows the temperature at each midday, on a beach in August.

a What is the modal temperature?

b Find the median temperature.

c State the range for this distribution of temperatures.

d Calculate the mean temperature.
Give your answer correct to 1 dp.

D5.2 Kim conducted an experiment to find out how good adults were at estimating time.
She asked a group of 65 adults to estimate one minute, while she timed their estimate accurately. These are the results:

Time in seconds	51	52	53	54	55	56	57	58	59	60
Frequency	9	11	0	14	12	7	8	4	0	0

a Calculate the median estimate.

b Calculate the mean estimate.
Give your answer correct to the nearest second.

Kim repeated this experiment with a group of 14-year-olds.
This time she found:

♦ the median estimate was 54 seconds
♦ the range of estimates was 18 seconds

Compare the results of the two groups.

c Which group do you think is better at estimating one minute?
You must give reasons for your answer.

D5.3 A seed company makes this claim on every packet of tomato seeds.

Average contents   30 seeds

As a result of complaints, Rashid was asked to provide data on the number of tomato seeds in a packet. These are his results for 100 packets:

Number of seeds	≤24	25	26	27	28	29	30	31	32	33	34	≥35
Frequency	0	5	4	15	33	1	0	0	7	1	34	0

a What is the range of this distribution?

b What is the median number of tomato seeds in a packet?

c Do you think the claim on the packet of tomato seeds is true?
Explain your answer.

The company decides to alter its claim of an average of 30 seeds.

d What claim do you suggest they print on packets of tomato seeds?
Give reasons for your answer.

A customer wants 240 tomato seeds.

e How many packets do you suggest she buys?
Explain your answer.

f   **i** Are your chances of being correct more or less than 'evens'.
ii Explain your answer.

D5.4 The table shows the results of a survey (in 1990) to find out how many CDs teenagers buy in a year.

Number of CDs	Frequency (f)	Mid-point (x)	fx
1 to 5	3		
6 to 10	8		
11 to 15	12		
16 to 20	10		
21 to 25	6		
26 to 30	1		

a What is the modal class for this distribution?

b Copy and complete the table.

c **i** Calculate an estimate of the mean number of CDs bought in a year by teenagers.

 ii Explain why an exact value for the mean cannot be calculated.

The survey was repeated in 1995, but the number of CDs were grouped in this way: 1 to 10, 11 to 20, and 21 to 30.

An estimate was calculated for the mean number of CDs bought.

d Which estimated mean is likely to be more accurate, the 1990 or 1995? Give reasons for your answer.

D5.5 A manufacturer of fuses tests them until they fail. This table shows the failure times, to the nearest hour.

Failure time	Frequency of fuses	Mid-point
1 to 10	0	5
11 to 20	16	
21 to 30	12	
31 to 40	41	
41 to 50	8	
51 to 60	13	

a Give the class which contains the median failure time.

b Calculate an estimate of the mean failure time. Give your answer to the nearest minute.

c **i** Give a reason why the mean failure time is not the best average to use when comparing these fuses with a set made by another company.

 ii What might be a better average to use? Explain your answer.

D5.6 A group of 75 students were asked how much they spent on food each day. The results are shown in this frequency table.

Amount spent	Frequency
£0.01 to £1	2
£1.01 to £2	17
£2.01 to £3	23
£3.01 to £4	18
£4.01 to £5	9
£5.01 to £6	6

a Which is the modal class?

b Calculate an estimate of the mean amount spent each day by students on food.

c Give the class in which the median amount students spent on food lies.

d **i** Copy and complete this headline with the value you think best.

 On average, students spend _____ a day on food.

 ii Give reasons for your answer.

D6
Cumulative frequency

D6.1 Alison and James are professional snooker players. They practised daily before their last tournament and recorded the scores for 80 breaks.

This table shows Alison's break scores.

Break score (x)	$70 < x \leqslant 80$	$80 < x \leqslant 90$	$90 < x \leqslant 100$	$100 < x \leqslant 110$	$110 < x \leqslant 120$
Frequency	8	34	25	9	4

> **Remember:** cumulative frequency is shown along the vertical axis of a cumulative frequency graph.

a Draw a cumulative frequency graph to show Alison's break scores.
b **i** Explain how you can use your graph to find Alison's median score.
   ii What is Alison's median break score?
c Give the interquartile range of her scores.

For his 80 break scores, James had a median score of 94, and an interquartile range of 14.

d Who was the more consistent player, Alison or James?
   Give reasons for your answer.

D6.2 A consumer group tested a sample of eighty *Super Cell* batteries.
The life of a battery in a torch was recorded, in hours, in this table.

Life (hours)	450–	500–	550–	600–	650–	700–	750–	800–	850–
Frequency	5	7	14	28	0	14	11	7	2

a Draw up a cumulative frequency table for this data.
b Draw a cumulative frequency graph for the test results.
c Use your graph to estimate the number of *Super Cell* batteries which lasted more than 620 hours.
d Find the interquartile range for the data.
e Show on your graph the median life of a *Super Cell* battery.

In a second test eighty *Mega Power* batteries were tested.
The median life for a *Mega Power* battery was 560 hours, and the interquartile range of the *Mega Power* test data was 130 hours.

f Comment on the two types of battery tested.

D6.3 A survey asked people how many telephone calls they made in a week.
These are the results.

Number of calls	0 – 10	11 – 20	21 – 30	31 – 40	41 – 50	51 – 60	61 – 70	71 – 80
Number of people	8	15	26	21	4	2	0	9

a Draw a cumulative frequency table for the data.
b Draw a cumulative frequency graph to show the results of the survey.
c From your graph, estimate the median number of telephone calls made.

This headline was printed in a newspaper.

Survey shows we're hooked!

80% of people make more than 35 telephone calls a week

d Does this survey data support this headline?
   Give reasons for your answer.

D7
Miscellaneous

D7.1 Barry grows strawberries. He picks the crop during the month of June. The bar chart shows the strawberries he picked last year.

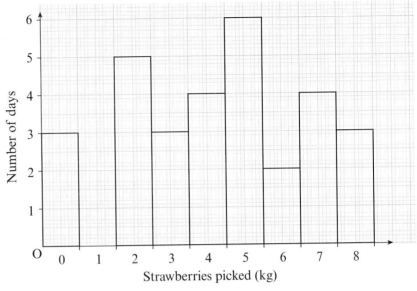

a On how many days did Barry pick no strawberries?
b In total, what weight of strawberries did Barry pick in June?
c What was the modal weight of strawberries Barry picked?
d Calculate the mean weight of strawberries picked per day in June.

Barry says that this data is typical for the month of June.

e Find the probability that Barry will pick at least 3 kg of strawberries on the 18th of June next year.

D7.2 Jake made a spinner to use in a game. He tested the spinner 150 times.

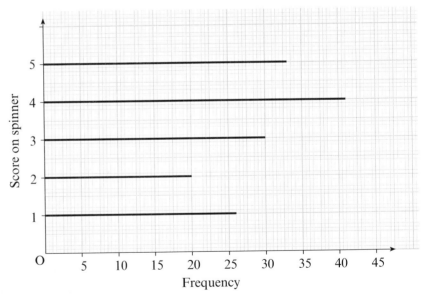

a Which score appears to be:
   i the easiest to spin   ii the most difficult to spin?
b Do you think the spinner is fair?
   Explain your answer.
c Estimate the probability that in a single spin you will score 2.

D7.3

Pupils spend hours every day watching television!

Jenny became fed up with headlines like this. She decided on a survey in her school. The question she asked was:

"*How many minutes did you spend watching TV last night?*"

These are the results:

45	75	100	120	80	55
180	145	90	90	5	135
60	25	120	180	150	25
90	60	75	150	145	0
120	135	45	60	60	0
180	75	90	120	150	30
150	0	60	90	105	0

a Draw a frequency table with a class interval of 30 minutes for this data. The first class should be:

0 minutes up to, but not including, 30 minutes.

b What is the modal class for this data?

c In which class is the median?

d Draw a cumulative frequency curve for this data.

e Estimate the number of pupils who watched TV for at least an hour.

f **i** With this data if you were asked the question:

"On average how long did these students spend watching TV?" what would be your answer?

ii Explain why you chose a particular average.

Jenny thinks the pupil group she asked are typical.

g If you asked a pupil at random, estimate the probability that they watched at least two hours TV last night.

D7.4 The pie chart shows the results of a survey into when people last visited a dentist.

In the report written with this pie chart was the comment:

"… only 4200 of those in the survey had been to the dentist this year …"

a How many people in total, are represented by this pie chart? Explain how you calculated this total.

b How many of those in the survey never visit the dentist?

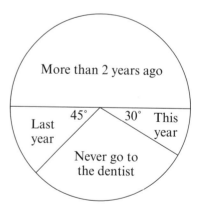

A television documentary about this report claimed that:

"… The report shows that three-quarters of those in the survey haven't been to the dentist in the last two years …"

c **i** With this data, is this a sensible claim to make?

ii Give reasons for your answer.

d **i** Would you choose a pie chart, or a different diagram for this data?

ii Give reasons for your answer.

Using and applying mathematics

U1
Opposite corners

This investigation is about squares drawn on centimetre square dotty grid paper with each corner on a dot.

For this pair of dots …

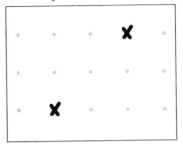

… a square can be drawn with the dots as opposite corners.

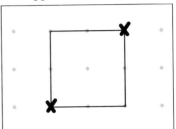

1 a Draw a square with this pair of dots as opposite corners.

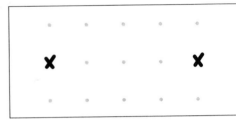

b Which of these pairs of dots can be the opposite corners of a square ?

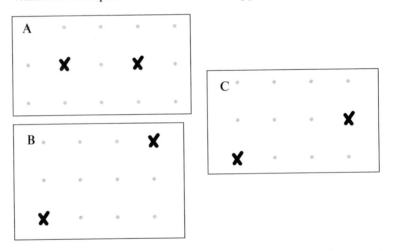

c Investigate to find a rule for when a pair of dots can be the opposite corners of a square.

2 a Find the area of this square.

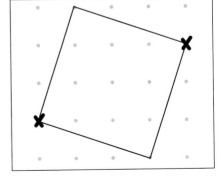

b Find a rule to calculate the area of any square given the position of the dots on opposite corners.

U2
Last one in ?

Kate designs a new game for a school fete.

Any number of players can take part in each game.

At the beginning of each game, a circle of chairs is made, one chair for each player.

The chairs are numbered 1, 2, 3, 4, 5, ...

Each player sits on a chair.

This diagram shows a circle of chairs for 15 players:

Kate begins at chair 1.

To each player in turn she says, 'Stay, Go, Stay, Go ... ' and so on round the circle.

For 'Stay', the player stays on the chair; for 'Go', the player leaves.

This continues round and round the circle until only one player is left on a chair.

That person wins the game.

1   In a game where 15 players take part, which chair is the winning chair ?

2   Find a rule that gives the winning chair for any number of players.

U3
Number strips

For this pair of numbers on a strip of five squares ...

... the blank squares are filled so that each number is the sum of the two numbers on its left.

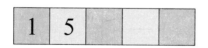

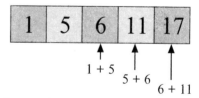

1   On a strip of five squares:
  a   Find the number in the last square, if the numbers in the first two squares are 6 and 3.
  b   Try different pairs of numbers in the first two squares.
      Find a rule to calculate the last number from the first two numbers.
      without calculating the numbers in between.
  c   Investigate rules for longer strips.

2   **a**   Find all the numbers in a strip of five squares with 5 as the first number and 16 as the last number.
  b   Investigate methods to complete a strip when you know the first and last number.

SECTION 1

Starting points

A1 a $^-2$ b $^-7$ c 4 d 10 e $^-4$ f 5

A2 a $^-2$ b $^-2$ c 9 d $^-9$ e $^-3$ f 2 g $^-4$ h $^-5$ i 4 j $^-6$

B1 a 5, 10, 15, 20, 25, 30, 35, etc. b 8, 16, 24, 32, 40, 48, 56, etc.
c 12, 24, 36, 48, 60, 72, 84, etc.

B2 a 40, 80, 120, etc. b 24, 48, 72, etc.

B3 a 1, 2, 3, 4, 6, 8, 12, 24 b 1, 2, 3, 5, 6, 10, 15, 30
c 1, 5, 25 d 1, 17

B4 a 1, 2, 3, 6 b 1, 5 **B6** 2, 3, 5, 7, 11, 13, 17, 19

C1 a 5^2 b 2^5 **C2** a 64 b 81 c 2.25 d 1.610 51

D1 a 2, 3, 7 b 2, 7, 11 **D2** a $2^3 \times 3 \times 5$ b $2 \times 5^2 \times 7$

E2 a $1\frac{1}{3}$ b $2\frac{1}{6}$ c $5\frac{3}{4}$ **E3** a $\frac{7}{5}$ b $\frac{10}{3}$ c $\frac{5}{1}$ d $\frac{37}{13}$ e $\frac{11}{1}$

F1 a $\frac{4}{10}, \frac{6}{15}, \frac{8}{20}$, etc. b $\frac{1}{3}, \frac{2}{6}, \frac{3}{9}$, etc. c $\frac{2}{3}, \frac{10}{15}, \frac{40}{60}$, etc.

G1 a 0.4375 b 0.5 c 0.63 d 0.4259

H1 a £1100 b 92 litres c 112.5

Exercise 1.1

1 A, B, D, F, H, I

2 a $3 \times ^-5 = ^-15$ b $^-2 \times 6 = ^-12$ c $5 \times ^-4 = ^-20$ d $^-3 \times ^-6 = 18$
e $^-12 \div ^-3 = 4$ f $^-8 \div 4 = ^-2$ g $24 \div ^-6 = ^-4$ h $^-40 \div ^-5 = ^-8$

3 a $4 \times ^-7 = ^-28$ b $^-15 \div ^-5 = 3$ c $^-4 \times 8 = ^-32$ d $^-3 \times ^-6 = 18$
e $^-35 \div ^-7 = 5$ f $36 \div ^-6 = ^-6$ g $^-3 \times ^-12 = 36$ h $14 \div 7 = 2$

4 a 9.43 b $^-9.43$ c $^-9.43$ d $^-7.2$ e 7.2 f $^-7.2$

5 An odd number of negatives give a negative answer;
an even number of negatives give a positive answer.

Exercise 1.2

4 a 6.93 b 8.49 c 6.25 d 5.18 e 30 f 0.1
$^-6.93$ $^-8.49$ $^-6.25$ $^-5.18$ $^-30$ $^-0.1$

Exercise 1.3

2 a 729 b 27 000 c 42.875 d $^-729$ e $^-1.331$ f 0.064

4 a 7 b 2.5 c 20 d $^-5$ e 0.7

6 b 3 or $^-3$

Exercise 1.4

1 a 0.25 b 10 c 0.4 d 0.3 e 1.5 f 1.2

2 a $\frac{5}{3}$ b $\frac{4}{7}$ c $\frac{2}{3}$ d $\frac{3}{10}$ e $\frac{5}{6}$

Exercise 1.5

1

2^{-4}	2^{-3}	2^{-2}	2^{-1}	2^0	2^1	2^2	2^3	2^4
$\frac{1}{16}$	$\frac{1}{8}$	$\frac{1}{4}$	$\frac{1}{2}$	1	2	4	8	16

2

4^{-3}	4^{-2}	4^{-1}	4^0	4^1	4^2	4^3
$\frac{1}{64}$	$\frac{1}{16}$	$\frac{1}{4}$	1	4	16	64

3 a $\frac{1}{5}$ b $\frac{1}{243}$ c $\frac{1}{64}$ d $\frac{1}{49}$ e $\frac{1}{100}$ f $\frac{1}{1}$

Exercise 1.6

1 a 42 b 16.25 c 6.24 d 0.0132 e 756 f 1587.5
g 12.24 h 470

2 a 0.125 b 0.25 c 0.04 d 0.01

3 a 42 b 16.25 c 6.24 d 0.0132

4 a 0.1 b 0.001 c 0.0001 d 0.000 01

Exercise 1.7

1 a 3.8×10^5 b 4.51×10^7 c 9.2×10^{-4} d 2.62×10^{-5}

2 a 94 200 b 0.0025 c 741 400 000 d 0.000 000 627

3 b P 1.3×10^5 Q 5.7×10^3 R 6.42×10^{-3} S 5.8×10^{-5}

5 a 8.76×10^6 b 1.7×10^5 c 1.98×10^4 d $7.884 62 \times 10^{13}$
e 7.68×10^{-15} f 3.972×10^4

Exercise 1.8

1 a 3^7 b 4^2 c 2^3 d 7^{-6} e 6^{-2}
f 7^{-6} g 5^0 h 2^5 i 6^{-1} j 7^{-3}

2 a $2^3 \times 2^4 = 2^7$ b $4^5 \times 4^{-2} = 4^3$ c $3^5 \div 3^3 = 3^2$ d $7^7 \times 7^{-3} = 7^4$
e $8^4 \div 8^6 = 8^{-2}$ f $5^4 \div 5^2 = 5^2$ g $2^{-6} \times 2^5 = 2^{-1}$ h $3^4 \div 3^1 = 3^3$

3 a 3^8 b 5^9 c 4^{-10} d 4^{-10} e 2^{-16} f 7^0

4 a $2^3 \times 2^2 = 32$ b $3^6 \times 3^{-3} = 27$ c $2^8 \div 2^2 = 64$ d $4^2 \div 4^{-1} = 64$
e $(3^2)^2 = 81$ f $(5^3)^1 = 125$ g $(2^{-3})^1 = 0.125$ h $(5^{-1})^2 = 0.04$

Exercise 1.9

1 a 2.4×10^4 b 2×10^{-6} c 2×10^3 d 6×10^{-11}

Exercise 1.10

1 a 36 b 420 c 420 d 3150 e 630 f 1890 g 14 850

2 45, 90, 315, 630

Exercise 1.11

1 a $\frac{5}{6}$ b $\frac{13}{20}$ c $\frac{1}{6}$ d $\frac{11}{20}$ e $\frac{29}{35}$ f $\frac{9}{12}$ or $\frac{3}{4}$ g $\frac{3}{6}$ or $\frac{1}{2}$

2 a $1\frac{1}{6}$ b $1\frac{1}{20}$ c $1\frac{1}{12}$

3 a $2\frac{3}{10}$ b $1\frac{3}{10}$ c $3\frac{5}{6}$ d $\frac{9}{10}$ e $3\frac{23}{34}$ f $\frac{23}{28}$

Thinking ahead

A a 8 b 8 c 12.8 d 12.8

Exercise 1.12

1 a $\frac{5}{12}$ b $\frac{1}{2}$ c $\frac{12}{35}$ d $\frac{3}{7}$ e $\frac{2}{5}$ f $\frac{7}{9}$ g $\frac{8}{15}$ h $\frac{5}{12}$

2 a $2\frac{2}{5}$ b 6 c 12 d $10\frac{1}{2}$ e 21 f $31\frac{1}{2}$ g $4\frac{2}{7}$ h $4\frac{3}{13}$

3 a $4\frac{1}{2}$ b $2\frac{11}{12}$ c $2\frac{4}{7}$ d $7\frac{1}{3}$ e 1 f $1\frac{1}{9}$ g 6 h $\frac{20}{33}$

Exercise 1.13

1 a 36 b 15 c 77 d 3

End points

A1 a $^-7 \times ^-2 = ^-14$ b $^-3 \times ^-5 = 15$ c $^-12 \div 4 = ^-3$ d $20 \div ^-5 = ^-4$
e $6 \times ^-3 = ^-18$ f $^-16 \div ^-2 = 8$ g $^-4 \times ^-9 = 36$ h $^-21 \div 7 = ^-3$

B1 a 1.2 b 35.937 c 6 d $^-1.5$

B2 a 0.125 b 5 c 1.8 d $2\frac{1}{2}$ e $\frac{4}{5}$

C1

3^{-4}	3^{-3}	3^{-2}	3^{-1}	3^0	3^1	3^2	3^3	3^4
$\frac{1}{81}$	$\frac{1}{27}$	$\frac{1}{9}$	$\frac{1}{3}$	1	3	9	27	81

C2 a $\frac{1}{6}$ b $\frac{1}{16}$ c $\frac{1}{10}$ d $\frac{4}{4}$

C3 a 17 b 1184 c 0.1 d 56.25

D1 a 7.062×10^7 b 3.75×10^{-6}

D2 a 0.000 000 069 b 10 300 000 000

D3 a 9.984×10^{14} b 9.4×10^{-8} c 4.8×10^{27}

D4 a 4.2×10^{-3} b 2×10^4 **E1** a 2^2 b 3^{-9} c 5^{10} d 4^{-6}

E2 a $3^4 \times 3^6 = 3^{10}$ b $4^3 \div 4^{-4} = 4^7$ c $7^{-2} \times 7^7 = 7^5$ d $(6^{-2})^0 = 6^0$

F1 a $\frac{13}{15}$ b $\frac{13}{30}$ c $\frac{5}{8}$ d $3\frac{37}{42}$ **F2** a $\frac{3}{10}$ b $\frac{1}{4}$ c 6 d $1\frac{3}{7}$

G1 a 84 b 360 **G2** a 7 b 35

SECTION 2

Starting points

A1 a 21 b 3 c 0 d 18 **A2** a 19 b 36 c 4 d 12

B2 Examples: 1, 9, 25, 49, 81, ... **B3** 1, 3, 6, 10, 15, 21

B4 5, 25, 125, 625 **B5** 34 **B6** ..., 29, 47, 76, 123

C1 a 33, 39 b 30, 41 **C2** 31

C3 a ..., 31, 42, 55 b ..., 32, 38, 44 c ..., 47, 65, 86 d ..., 57, 83, 114

D1 b i 16 ii 26
c

Pattern number (n)	Number of matches (m)
1	6
2	11
3	16
4	21
5	26

d $m = 5n + 1$

Exercise 2.1

1

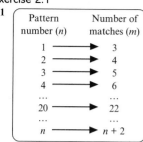

Pattern number (n)	Number of matches (m)
1	3
2	4
3	5
4	6
...	...
20	22
...	...
n	$n + 2$

2 a

Pattern number (n)	Number of matches (m)
1	4
2	8
3	12
4	16
5	20
6	24

2 b $n \rightarrow 4n$ **c** 400 matches

Thinking ahead
A 301 matches

Exercise 2.2

1 a $m = 2n + 1$ **b** 17 matches
2 a $m = 4n + 1$ **b** 161 matches   **c** Pattern 32
3 a $m = 6n - 2$ **b** 598 matches   **4 b** $m = 4n + 2$

5 a

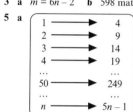

1	4
2	9
3	14
4	19
...	...
50	249
...	...
n	$5n - 1$

b

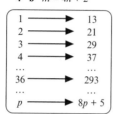

1	13
2	21
3	29
4	37
...	...
36	293
...	...
p	$8p + 5$

c

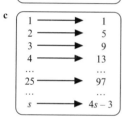

1	1
2	5
3	9
4	13
...	...
25	97
...	...
s	$4s - 3$

Thinking ahead
A a 19, 21   **b** 29   **c** 105

Exercise 2.3

1 A a $3n + 3$ **b** 153   **B a** $5n - 4$ **b** 246
C a $10n + 3$ **b** 503   **D a** $8n - 6$ **b** 394
2 b $3n + 2$ **3** $n + 7$ **4** $^-2n + 22$

Thinking ahead
A a

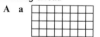

b 800 small squares

Exercise 2.4

1 a n^2 **b** $n^2 + n$ **c** n^2
2 $(n^2 + n) \div 2$, $n(n + 1) \div 2$ or equivalent

Thinking ahead
A 402 triangles

Exercise 2.5

1 a $3n^2$ **b** 1200
2 a 35   **b**

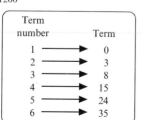

Term number	Term
1	0
2	3
3	8
4	15
5	24
6	35

c $n^2 - 1$

3 A a 39, 52   **b** $n^2 + 3$ **B a** 144, 196   **b** $(2n)^2$ or $4n^2$
C a 41, 48   **b** $7n - 1$ **D a** 41, 54   **b** $n^2 + 5$

Exercise 2.6

1 a 5th number   40 $= 5 \times 8$ **b** 10th number   130 $= 10 \times 13$
2 a 5th triangle number $15 = \dfrac{5 \times 6}{3}$ **b** 78   **c** $\dfrac{n(n + 1)}{2}$
3 a 5th power $32 = 2 \times 2 \times 2 \times 2 \times 2 = 2^5$ **b** 256   **c** 2^n

Exercise 2.7

1 a

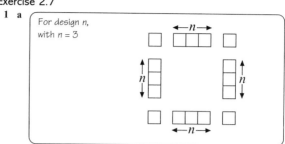

For design n, with $n = 3$

b

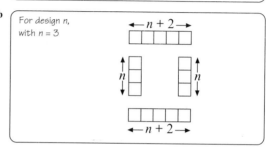

For design n, with $n = 3$

c i $4(50+1)$
$= 4 \times 51$
$= 204$

ii $4 \times 50 + 4$
$= 200 + 4$
$= 204$

iii $2(50 + 2) + 2 \times 50$
$= 2 \times 52 + 2 \times 50$
$= 104 + 100$
$= 204$

d Design 80   **2 a** $2(n + 2) + 2$ or $2n + 6$ or equivalent

Thinking ahead
A A and F, B and E, C and G, D and H

Exercise 2.8

1 16   **2** 0
3 $2(a + 4)$ and $2a + 8$
$2(a + 2)$ and $2a + 4$
$4(2a - 3)$ and $8a - 12$
$2(a - 6)$ and $2a - 12$
4 b $12 + 3x$
5 $5(2n - 1) = 5 \times (2n - 1) = (5 \times 2n) - (5 \times 1) = 10n - 5$
6 a $4n + 4$ **b** $5m - 15$ **c** $6c - 54$ **d** $6p + 4$
e $16s - 40$ **f** $12 + 4t$ **g** $15 - 3k$ **h** $14n - 10$
i $60f - 390$ **j** $900 + 540h$ **k** $30 - 70q$ **l** $10y + 15z$
7 $2(n + 4) + 2n$
$= 2n + 8 + 2n$
$= 4n + 8$
8 a $8p + 10$ **b** $5q - 4$ **c** $19r + 30$ **d** $6s + 2t$

End points

A1 a $m = 2n + 3$ **b** 203 matches

B1 a

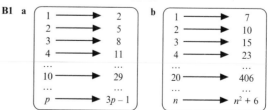

1	2
2	5
3	8
4	11
...	...
10	29
...	...
p	$3p - 1$

b

1	7
2	10
3	15
4	23
...	...
20	406
...	...
n	$n^2 + 6$

C1 A a $3n + 4$ **b** 64   **B a** $5n - 3$ **b** 97
C a $n^2 + 1$ **b** 401   **D a** $n + 5$ **b** 25
E a $3n + 6$ **b** 66   **F a** $5n^2$ **b** 1000

D1 a $4n + 20$ **b** $7x - 14$ **c** $15k - 5$ **d** $12 + 30t$

SECTION 3

Starting points

A1 **a** **i** reflex   **ii** acute   **iii** right   **b** **i** equilateral   **ii** right-angled
  c Triangles BFD, ABD, ADE

B1 **a** 60°   **b** 300°   **c** 45°

B2 **a** $a = 35°$ $b = 72.5°$

C1 $d = 116°$ $e = 116°$ $f = 64°$ $g = 64°$

D1 **1** trapezium   **2** rectangle, square   **3** square, rhombus
  4 rectangle, square, parallelogram, rhombus

E1 1080°   **E2** 142°   **E3** 129°   **E4** **a** 1800°   **b** 150°

Exercise 3.1

1 **b** $a = 74°$, $b = 53°$, $c = 53°$, $d = 74°$, $e = 53°$, $f = 53°$

2 $a = 62°$, $b = 120°$, $c = 117°$

Exercise 3.2

1 **a** Any five pairs from: a, c and e **b**, d and f g, i and k h, j and l

  b Any three pairs from: b with i or k c with h
                 d with k e with j or h
                 h with c or e i with b
                 j with e k with d or b

2 $a = 72°$ $b = 135°$ $c = 45°$

3 **d** **i** 65°   **ii** 54°   **iii** 61°   **iv** 54°   **v** 126°   **vi** 61°

4 $a = 42°$, $b = 77°$, $c = 61°$, $p = 72°$, $q = 72°$, $r = 72°$, $x = 68.5°$,
  $y = 68.5°$, $z = 68.5°$

5 **a** **i** 52°   **ii** 52°   **iii** 52°   **iv** 64°   **b** AB and DC are parallel
  c trapezium

Exercise 3.3

1 **b** As the parallelogram is stretched: ◆ $\hat{ABC}$ does not change
                        ◆ $\hat{ABD}$ becomes larger
                        ◆ $\hat{CBD}$ becomes smaller

  c $\hat{AMB}$ becomes smaller   **d** **i** obtuse   **ii** right   **ii** acute

2 **a** statement 3   **b** statements 1, 2 and 3

3 **a** $\hat{ABC} = 120°$, $\hat{BCD} = 90°$, $\hat{CDA} = 60°$, $\hat{DAB} = 90°$
  b **i** $\hat{BCA}$, $\hat{CDM}$, $\hat{ADM}$ **ii** $\hat{ACD}$, $\hat{ADC}$, $\hat{ABD}$, $\hat{CBD}$
  c right angle   **d** 2 from AD, CD and AC   AB, BC   AM, MC
  e No   **f** BD

Exercise 3.4

1 **b** A triangle or right-angled triangle   **B** quadrilateral or trapezium
  C hexagon   D pentagon
  E hexagon or regular hexagon
  F triangle or equilateral triangle   G pentagon
  H triangle or equilateral triangle   I hexagon

  c **i** A 90°, 60°, 30°   B 120°, 120°, 60°, 60°
    C 60°, 120°, 90°, 90°, 60°, 300°   D 120°, 120°, 120°, 90°, 90°
    E 120°, 120°, 120°, 120°, 120°, 120°
    F 60°, 60°, 60°   G 60°, 120°, 90°, 30°, 240°
    H 60°, 60°, 60°   I 120° 120°, 60°, 300°, 30°, 90°

2 **a** polygons A, G and I   **b** cards 2, 5 and 6
  c **i** card 2, irregular   **ii** card 6, only one obtuse angle
  d card 1   **e** 19 different 7-dot polygons

Exercise 3.5

1 **a** **i** polygons B and I   **ii** cells d and g
  b **ii** 8 cells
    iii cell f: a regular polygon will always have at least one line
     of symmetry

Exercise 3.6

2 **a** 144°   **b** 360° is not a multiple of 144°

3 360° is not a multiple of 135°   **4** **a** Yes   **b** No

Exercise 3.7

1 **a** polygon J : 2   polygon K : 2   polygon L : 1
  b **i** Polygon K is a rhombus, polygon L is a rhombus
    ii $a = 108°$, $b = 36°$, $c = 72$, $d = 144°$, $e = 108°$

2 **a** **i** parallelogram   **ii** heptagon
  b $a = 135°$, $b = 45°$, $c = 135°$, $d = 75°$, $e = 285°$, $f = 75°$, $g = 105°$

Exercise 3.8

1 **a** $a = 56°$, $b = 42°$, $c = 69°$, $d = 104°$, $e = 89°$

2 **b** 30°   **c** 150°   **3** $e = 40°$, $f = 140°$, $g = 70°$, $h = 40°$

Exercise 3.9

1 **b** **ii** Exterior angle at B is 67.5°   Exterior angle at D is 157.5°

2 **a** **i** $\hat{AFC} = 45°$ $\hat{FAC} = 67.5°$ $\hat{ACF} = 67.5°$
    ii Exterior angle at A is 112.5°   Exterior angle at C is 112.5°
    Exterior angle at F is 135°
  b 5 different triangles   **c** 45°, 67.5°, 90°, 112.5°, 135°, 157.5°

End points

A1 $a = 42°$, $b = 67°$, $c = 109°$

B1 **a** **i** polygon C   **ii** polygons B and E
  b A rhombus   B right-angled triangle   C isosceles triangle
  D rectangle   E kite

D1

Polygon	a Interior angles	b Exterior angles
B	120°	60°
	30°	150°
	30°	150°
E	90°	90°
	120°	60°
	90°	90°
	60°	120°

D2 45°

SECTION 4

Starting points

A1 **e** $(-1, 2)$

A2 **a** $(0, 2)$ **b** No – they are parallel   **c** All coordinates $(0, *)$

A3 **a** horizontal   **b** vertical   **c** vertical
  d horizontal   **e** horizontal   **f** vertical

B1 **a**

x	-2	-1	0	1	2	3
y	-7	-4	-1	2	5	8

  b

x	-2	-1	0	1	2	3
y	0	1	2	3	4	5

  c

x	-2	-1	0	1	2	3
y	-2	-1	0	1	2	3

  d

x	-2	-1	0	1	2	3
y	-5	-4	-3	-2	-1	0

  e

x	-2	-1	0	1	2	3
y	-2	-0.5	1	2.5	4	5.5

B3 **a** yes   **b** no   **c** yes   **d** yes   **e** no   **f** no   **g** yes   **h** no

Exercise 4.1

1 **a** 30 pence   **b** 10 pence   **2** **a** more than 25 pence   **b** 26 pence

3 34 pence   **4** 20 seconds at Low call   **5** Low call charge

6 26 pence   **7** 100 seconds

8 **c** Peak charge   **d** Peak, Infotel, Low call, Weekend
  e The steeper the graph, the greater the charge per minute

9 16 pence   **10** **a** $c = t \div 2$ **b** 45 pence

Exercise 4.2

1 line **a** 3   line **b** 2   line **c** 1   line **d** 2   line **e** 2   line **f** 1
  line **g** 3   line **h** 1

3 The steeper the graph, the larger the value of its gradient.

Exercise 4.3

1 a i line **a** $\frac{3}{2}$, line **b** $\frac{4}{3}$, line **c** $\frac{4}{5}$, line **d** $\frac{5}{4}$, line **e** $\frac{3}{2}$, line **f** $\frac{5}{2}$, line **g** $\frac{1}{2}$
  ii line **a** 1.5, line **b** 1.3, line **c** 0.8, line **d** 1.25, line **e** 1.5,
  line **f** 2.5, line **g** 0.5

b Lines **f, a/e, b, d, c, g,** **2** They have the same gradient.

Exercise 4.4

1 a Lines **a, c, e, f, h**
  b line **a i** ⁻$\frac{1}{2}$ **ii** ⁻0.5 line **b i** $\frac{5}{2}$ **ii** 2.5
  line **c i** ⁻$\frac{3}{2}$ **ii** ⁻1.5 line **d i** $\frac{3}{2}$ **ii** 1.5
  line **e i** ⁻$\frac{3}{4}$ **ii** ⁻0.75 line **f i** ⁻$\frac{1}{2}$ **ii** ⁻0.5
  line **g i** $\frac{1}{2}$ **ii** 0.5 line **h i** ⁻1 **ii** ⁻1

3 positive **4** line A   **5** line G
6 line F
  line F gradient $\frac{1}{4}$, line H gradient $\frac{1}{7}$
7 ⁻1 or ⁻$\frac{2}{2}$ **8** line C: ⁻$\frac{6}{5}$ = ⁻1.2 **9** No, gradient of line E is ⁻$\frac{3}{2}$
10 No, gradient of line D is $\frac{2}{3}$ **11 e** (3, 3) **f** ⁻5 or ⁻$\frac{10}{2}$ **g** (⁻1, 4)

Exercise 4.5

1 a Multiply x values by 3 and then add 2
b

x	⁻2	⁻1	0	1	2	3
y	⁻4	⁻1	⁻2	5	8	11

c (⁻2, ⁻4), (⁻1, ⁻1), (0, ⁻2), (1, 5), (2, 8), (3, 11)

2 a Multiply x values by 2, then subtract 3
b

x	⁻1	0	1	2	3
y	⁻5	⁻3	⁻1	1	3

3 a

x	⁻2	⁻1	0	1	2	3
y	⁻3	⁻1	1	3	5	7

4 graph through (⁻2, ⁻9), (⁻1, ⁻5), (0, ⁻1), (1, 3), (2, 7) **5 b** (2, 3)

Exercise 4.6

1 a 2 **b** ⁻5 **2 a** 3 **b** ⁻1 **3** lines **b** and **c**
4

Line	Gradient	y-intercept
a	3	⁻2
b	1	2
c	4	0
d	5	⁻4
e	2	3
f	3	⁻$\frac{1}{2}$
g	5	1
h	$\frac{1}{2}$	0
i	⁻5	5
j	1	0
k	1	⁻2
l	⁻4	0

5

Line	Equation
K	$y = 3x + 5$
M	$y = \frac{1}{2}x - 1$
P	$y = 1.5 + 2x$
R	$y = 2 - 3x$
T	$y = x$

Exercise 4.7

2 c $y = x + 2$ and $y = 3x$ **d** $y = x + 2$
3 a gradient ⁻3, y-intercept 2

Exercise 4.8

1 a 2 or $\frac{4}{2}$ **b** ⁻4 **c** $y = 2x - 4$ **2 a** ⁻3 **b** $y = 3x - 3$
3

Line	Equation
C	$y = 3x + 1$
D	$y = 2x + 3$
E	$y = ⁻3x + 1$
	or $y = 1 - 3x$

Exercise 4.9

1 a 4 **b** $y = 2x - 5$ **2 a** 2 **b** $y = \frac{3}{2}x + 2$
3 a $y = 2x + 4$ **b** $y = \frac{4}{3}x - 3$ **c** $y = x - 2$ **d** $y = \frac{3}{5}x$
  e $y = \frac{2}{5}x + 1$ **f** $y = 3x - 2$ **g** $y = 1.5 - 2x$ **h** $y = \frac{1}{4}x$
  i $y = 1 - x$ **j** $y = 2 + 2x$ **k** $y = \frac{1}{5}x + \frac{1}{5}$ **l** $\frac{2}{3}x = y$
4 equation **c**

Exercise 4.10

1 a $y = \frac{3}{2}x + 1$ **b** $\frac{3}{2}$ **c** 1 **2 a** $\frac{2}{3}$ **b** ⁻1
4 c (4, 2) **6** yes $(2 \times 3) = (5 \times 2) - 4$

Exercise 4.11

1 a (2.5, 3) **b** $5y = 2x + 10$ and $y = 2x - 2$
2 b (2, 3) **3 c** (1.2, 2.2)

End Points

A1 a a line that slopes upwards from left to right
  b a line that slopes downwards from left to right
  c a measure of the slope of the line

B1 The gradient of line D is 1. **B2 a** $\frac{3}{2}$ **b** 1.5

B3 line B $\frac{2}{3}$ line C ⁻1

C1

x	⁻1	0	1	2	3
y	⁻7	⁻4	⁻1	2	5

D1 $y = \frac{3}{4}x + 1.5$ **E1** gradient 2 y-intercept ⁻5
F1 $3y = 2x - 6$ and $y = 2x - 2$

Section 5

Starting points

B1

Number of children in car	Tally	Frequency
0	⊮⊮⊮⊮ ⊮⊮⊮⊮ |	11
1	⊮⊮⊮⊮ ||	7
2	||||	4
3	|	1
4	|	1

B2

Colour of car	Frequency
Red	5
Blue	6
Green	2
White	3
Silver	2
Black	4
Brown	2

D1

Red	Blue	Green	White	Silver	Black	Brown
21%	25%	8%	13%	8%	17%	8%

E1 a 15 and 42 **b** 39.5 **c** 42.5 **d** 69
E2 a 25 **b** 38 **c** 48.8 (to 1 dp) **d** 93
F1 blue **F2 a** 0 **b** 3
G1 a £340 **b** £340 **c** £314.89 (to 2 dp)
  d i The modal wage and median wage are not misleading averages.
    ii The mean wage *is* a misleading average because only 6 of the
    9 wages are greater than it; the very small wage of £112 is the
    reason for this.

H1 a 54% **b** 35% **c** 11% **H2 a** 39% **b** 33% **c** 28%

Exercise 5.1

1 Caring For Children **a** £72m **b** 5° **c** 306°, 32°, 8°, 14°
  Child Action **a** £48m **b** 7.5° **c** 252°, 66°, 18°, 24°
  Caring In Crisis **a** 100% **b** 3.6° **c** 252°, 54°, 36°, 18°

2 a Caring For Children 85%, 9%, 2%, 4%
  Child Action 70%, 18%, 5%, 7%

Thinking ahead

A a 7 **b** 4

Exercise 5.2

1 a 2 arrows   **b** 5 5 5 5 6 6 7 8 8 9   **c** 6

2 a 15 arrows   **b** 5 5 5 6 6 7 7 7 7 9 9 9 10 10 10   **c** 7

3 b 5

Thinking ahead

A 24

Exercise 5.3

1 Jodie   **a** 84   **b** 16   **c** 5.3 (to 1 dp)
Geeta   **a** 156   **b** 20   **c** 7.8

2 b 7.4

Exercise 5.4

1 a Javed 6 Lisa 5.5   **b** Javed 6 Lisa 3
c Javed's scores are higher on average, but Lisa is more consistent.

2 a Amy 5.76 Paul 5.65   **b** Amy 4 Paul 5
c Amy's scores are higher on average, and she is also more consistent.

3 a Viv's scores are higher on average, and they are equally consistent.

Exercise 5.5

1 William   **a** 2 4 4 4 5 5 6 6 6 6 7 7 7 8 8   **b** 7, 4.5   **c** 2.5
Bryony   **a** 4 4 5 5 5 5 6 6 6 7 7 7 9 9   **b** 7, 5   **c** 2
Daniel   **a** 2 3 4 4 5 5 5 6 6 6 6 6 7 7 7 9 9 9 10 10   **b** 8, 5   **c** 3

2

	Sheera	Dave
Range	8	6
Interquartile range	2	3.5

Sheera is the more consistent archer: although the range of her scores is larger than Dave's, because of her few extreme scores, the interquartile range of her scores is smaller.

Thinking ahead

A a 5   **b** 7   **c** 7

Exercise 5.6

1

Ring score	Cumulative frequency
≤5	2
≤6	7
≤7	19
≤8	26
≤9	31

2

Ring score	2	3	4	5	6	7	8
Frequency	3	7	12	19	13	9	4
Cumulative frequency	3	10	22	41	54	63	67

3 a 15   **b** 36   **c** 64

4

Age	Cumulative frequency
10 and under	8
11 and under	15
12 and under	25
13 and under	36
14 and under	44
15 and under	53
16 and under	64

5

Distance to target in metres	Cumulative number of arrows hitting target
≤10	20
≤15	39
≤20	56
≤25	72
≤30	87
≤35	100
≤40	111

6

	Ring score									
	≤1	≤2	≤3	≤4	≤5	≤6	≤7	≤8	≤9	≤10
April	4	11	18	26	31	37	39	42	47	48
May	6	11	15	24	29	32	40	42	44	48
June	3	9	15	19	24	28	36	40	42	48

7 Jade is improving as an archer because her cumulative frequencies for each score have fallen between April and June.

Thinking ahead

A a 5 5 5 5 5 5 5 6 6 6 6 6 6 6 7 7 7 7
7 7 7 7 7 8 8 8 8 8 8 8 8 8 8
8 8 8 8 8 9 9 9 9 9 9 9 9 9 9 9 9
b 8

Exercise 5.7

1 Lee   **b** between the 20th and 21st largest   **c** 5
Faith   **b** the 23rd largest   **c** 6
Aqib   **b** the 20th largest   **c** 7
Tegan   **b** between the 24th and 25th largest   **c** 4.5

Thinking ahead

A b i X 38 Y 36 Z 38   **ii** X 3.5 Y 4 Z 2.5

End points

A1 Total spent £14.4m   360° ÷ 14.4 = 25°   230°, 85°, 25°, 20°

B1 a 2 4 4 4 5 5 5 5 <u>5</u> 6 6 6 6 6 6 7 7   5.5   **b ii** 5

C1 a 5.3 (to 1 dp)   **b** 4.6 (to 1 dp)

D1

	Manoj	Pat
Mean	5.3	4.6
Range	5	7

Manoj's scores are higher on average, and he is also more consistent.

D2

	Kim	Stuart
Mode	7	6
Range	6	7

Kim's scores are higher on average, and she is also more consistent.

E1 a 3.5   **b** 2

SECTION 6

Starting points

A1 23.2 cm   **A2** 57.5 cm   **A3** 44.4 cm

A4 a 16.3 cm   **b** 2.2 cm   **c** 15.1 cm

B1 121.6 cm²   **B2** 56.3 cm²   **B3** 15.1 cm²   **B4** 58.1 cm²

C1 a 128.6 cm²   **b** 53 cm²   **D1** $p = 4.1$ cm $e = 9.7$ cm

Exercise 6.1

1 a 102.5 cm²   **b** 5.6 cm²   **2 a** 109.2 cm²   **b** 327.6 cm²

3 b trapezium   **c** 12 816.1 cm²   **4 b** 677 cm²   **c** 2708.1 cm²

5 a 65.9 cm   **b** 2866.7 cm²

6 a 9731.3 cm²   **b** 19 462.5 cm²   **c** 432.5 cm   **d** 519 cm

7 no – nearer $\frac{1}{3}$ of a square metre   **8 a** 384 cm²   **b** 384 cm²

9 a 1920 cm²   **b** 8448 cm²   **10** 6528 cm²   **11** 08-28, 08-38, 08-58

13 3188 cm²   **14** 3652 cm²

Exercise 6.2

1 a triangle   **b** 61.4 cm²   **2** 52.4 cm²

3 a 18 mm   **b** 1017.9 mm²   **4** 180 mm   **5** 3010.6 mm²

6 120 424 mm²   **7** 183.7 cm²   **8** less   **9** 85.4 cm

10 a 154 mm   **b** 136 mm   **11** 504 mm²   **12** 928 mm²

13 16 288 mm²   **14** 4656 mm²   **15** about $\frac{1}{5}$ **16** 18 mm

17 $\frac{1}{4}$ **18** 254.5 mm²   **19** 763.4 mm²   **20** 278.1 mm²

21 a 176.7 mm² blue, 176.7 mm² yellow, 128.7 mm² green
b between $\frac{1}{2}$ and $\frac{3}{5}$

Exercise 6.3

1 **a** $2.9\,\text{cm}$ **b** $4.7\,\text{cm}$ **c** $13.0\,\text{cm}^2$ **2** $30.0\,\text{cm}^2$

3 **a** $6.5\,\text{cm}$ **b** $21.5\,\text{cm}^2$ **4 a** $9.5\,\text{cm}^2$ **b** $21.6\,\text{cm}^2$

5 $10.4\,\text{cm}$ **6** $62.4\,\text{cm}^2$ **7** $8.6\,\text{cm}^2$ **8** $49.8\,\text{cm}^2$

9 $262.6\,\text{cm}^2$ **10** $413.4\,\text{cm}^2$ **11** $73.4\,\text{cm}$

Exercise 6.4

1 **a** 99 metres **b** 33 metres **2** 94.5 metres **3** $23.2\,\text{cm}$

4 6240 tins **5** $398.2\,\text{m}$

Exercise 6.5

3 **a** trapezium **b** rectangle **c** rectangle

5 $25\,\text{mm}$, area of $1500\,\text{mm}^2$ **8 a** 18 **b** 33

End points

A1 KLMN $27.1\,\text{cm}^2$

CDEF $29.4\,\text{cm}^2$

DEFG $46.3\,\text{cm}^2$

B1 **a** $109\,\text{cm}^2$ **b** $147\,\text{cm}^2$ **B2** RST $41.4\,\text{cm}^2$ **C1** $15.1\,\text{m}$

SKILLS BREAK 1A

1 Year by year: present year – 1957

2 $9\frac{1}{2}$ hours or 9 hours and 30 minutes.

3 £2.70 or 270p **4** It was malnourished.

5 $12.3\,\text{kg}$ **6** over $1000\,\text{kg}$ **7** $0.55\,\text{kg}$ **8** 50%

9 7319 pups **10** Year by year: present year – 1975 **11** 35 minutes

12 about $\frac{1}{3}$ **13** about 55% **14** about 8 seals **15** $\frac{1}{3}$

16 about 4% **17** 2 males **18** 2 females **19** $0.83\,\text{kg}$

20 $770\,\text{g}$ **21** $14.5\,\text{kg}$ **22** Tony **23** 24%

24 **a** $19\,\text{kg}$ **b** $18.5\,\text{kg}$ **c** $11.7\,\text{kg}$

25 Bill $23\,\text{kg}$ **26** Bill $65\,000\,\text{g}$
Ben $17\,\text{kg}$ Ben $56\,000\,\text{g}$
Mandy $12\,\text{kg}$ Mandy $66\,000\,\text{g}$
Tony $24\,\text{kg}$ Tony $98\,000\,\text{g}$
Rory $19\,\text{kg}$ Rory $85\,000\,\text{g}$

27 about $140\,\text{kg}$ **28** Outer Hebrides

29 Inner Hebrides 2100 **30** Inner Hebrides 2000
Outer Hebrides 9500 Outer Hebrides $10\,000$
Orkney 7000 Orkney 7000
Isle of May 900 Isle of May 1000
Farne Islands 900 Farne Islands 1000

32 about $80\,000$ grey seals

33 **a** $40\,\text{km}$ **b** 1 hour 45 minutes
c 3 minutes **d** $\frac{1}{3}\,\text{km}$ or $0.33\,\text{km}$ or $333\,\text{m}$

34 about $24\,000$ people **35** 45 minutes

36 **a** $\frac{1}{6}$ **b** $\frac{1}{6}$ **37 a** 46p **b** £1.44 **c** 81p

SKILLS BREAK 1B

1 about 16 miles **2** 4 square miles **3** about 33 square miles

4 about 17 square miles **5** right **6** Silchurch

7 **a** Robridge **b** $286°$

8 **a** 382593 **b** 343583 **c** $362589,\ 378593$
d 354585 **e** 422580

10 **a** $48\,\text{km}$ **b** $88\,\text{km}$ **c** $128\,\text{km}$ **d** $40\,\text{km}$
e $192\,\text{km}$ **f** $456\,\text{km}$

11 **a** 34 miles **b** 60 miles **c** 25 miles **d** 75 miles
e 147 miles **f** 234 miles

12 $\frac{5}{8}$ **13** $16\,\text{km}$ **14** 43 minutes

15 **a** 105 minutes **b** 150 minutes **16** 125 minutes

17 13 minutes **18 a** 153 days **b** 398 trips

19 **a** $15\,625$ adults **b** 9375 children **20** no **21** 163.4

22 about 5470 **23** yes

---

24 Adult £5.80
Child £3.20
Sen Cit £3.70

26 £1847.50 **27** £10.32 **29** $5000\,\text{lb}$ or 2.23 tons

30 500 gallons of water **31** 58.73 tons **32** $p + n = 8$

33 **a** $27p + 37n = W$ **b** $27p + 37n + 58.73 = W$

SECTION 7

Starting points

A1 **a** 17 **b** 6 **c** 24 **d** $^-3$ **A2 a** 13 **b** 7 **c** 49 **d** $^-11$

B1 C: $8x + 3y$

B2 **a** $9t$ **b** $10s + 9k$ **c** $3c + 8b$ **d** $11x + 2$ **e** $7v + 16$

C1 **a** $6x + 30$ **b** $3 + 3n$ **c** $4b - 20$ **d** $70 - 7t$ **e** $8n + 12$
f $15 + 12y$ **g** $8p - 22$ **h** $9 - 27w$

D1 C: $x = 6$

D2 **a** $z = 1.5$ **b** $y = 3$ **c** $x = ^-2$ **d** $w = 4$ **e** $v = 8$
f $t = ^-1$ **g** $s = 2$

E1 A $(1, 4)$, C $(3, 14)$, D $(^-1, ^-6)$

E2 **a**

x	$^-2$	$^-1$	0	1	2
y	1	3	5	7	9

b

x	$^-2$	$^-1$	0	1	2
y	8	7	6	5	4

Thinking ahead

A P and U   R and T   Q and S

Exercise 7.1

1 **a** A and H   B and D   C and G   F and I
b A: 54   B: 106   C: 26   D: 106   E: 10   F: 46   G: 26
H: 54   I: 46

2 **a** $8t$ **b** $5x$ **c** $3 + 5h$ **d** a **e** $1 - 5y$ **f** $6 - 3f$

3 **a i** $3x - y = 13$ $x - 2y = 1$ $2x = 10$ $x = 5$ $2x - y = 8$
$3x - 2y = 11$ $2x - 2y = 6$ $3x = 15$ $x - y = 3$

b

13	1	10
5	8	11
6	15	3

Yes, it is a magic square.

c The total is $6x - 3y$ for each row, column and diagonal.
d The total of the three expressions is always the same, so the square will be magic for any totals of x and y.

Exercise 7.2

1 **a** $z = 1$ **b** $y = 3$ **c** $x = 9$ **d** $w = 12$ **e** $v = 4$
f $u = 1.2$ **g** $t = 5$ **h** $s = 8$ **i** $r = 2$ **j** $q = 1.8$
k $p = 2$ **l** $n = 1.5$ **m** $m = 4$ **n** $l = 3.6$ **o** $k = 2.5$
p $j = 10$ **q** $h = 5$ **r** $g = 3.5$

2 **a** $z = ^-5$ **b** $y = ^-1$ **c** $x = ^-2$ **d** $w = ^-3$ **e** $v = ^-4$
f $u = ^-6$ **g** $t = ^-0.5$ **h** $s = ^-1.2$ **i** $r = ^-3.5$

3 **a** $z = 0.3\dot{3}$ or $\frac{1}{3}$ **b** $y = 0.8\dot{3}$ or $\frac{5}{6}$ **c** $x = 3.5$
d $w = 5$ **e** $v = 2$ **f** $u = 0.4$

Exercise 7.3

1 **a** $5\,\text{cm}, 10\,\text{cm}, 11\,\text{cm}$ **b** $20\,\text{cm}$ **c** $6x - 4$ **d** $x = 18$

2 **a** 50 metres **b** $8p$ **c** $4p + 10$ **d** $20, 25$ **e** $p = 2.5$

3 $t = 1$

4 **a** $x = 11$
b

22	9	32
31	21	11
10	33	20

c $x = 20$ **d** $x = 13$ **e** $8x - 4 = 4(2x - 1)$

ANSWERS

Exercise 7.4

1 D

2 A $3n + 5 = 13 - n$ $n = 2$ B $4(n - 2) = 5(n - 3)$ $n = 7$
   C $3(n - 1) = 4(8 - n)$ $n = 5$ D $(10 - 6n) = (7 - 3n)$ $n = 1$
   E $(2n - 11) = 15 - 2n$ $n = 6.5$

3 **b** $n = 7$

Exercise 7.5

1 **a** 56p   **b** 6p

c

Cost of biscuit	10p	20p	30p	40p
Cost of coffee	66p	46p	26p	6p

f 40p

g **i**

Cost of biscuit	10p	20p	30p	40p
Cost of coffee	50p	40p	20p	10p

h (26, 34)   **2** **a** 80p   **b** 64p

Exercise 7.6

1 **a** Rita $t + 2b = 70$
     Simon $3t + b = 130$

b Rita

t	0	10	20	30	40
b	35	30	25	20	15

Simon

t	0	10	20	30	40
b	130	100	70	40	10

d tea 38p, biscuit 16p

2 **a** equation 1 $b = 2$, equation 2 $b = {}^-3$

b $a + b = 6$

a	0	1	2	3	4	5
b	6	5	4	3	2	1

$3a + b = 9$

a	0	1	2	3	4	5
b	9	6	3	0	${}^-3$	${}^-6$

d $a = 1.5$ $b = 4.5$

3 **a** equation 1, $y = 2$; equation 2, $y = 1$

b $y = x + 4$

x	${}^-4$	${}^-2$	0	2	4
y	0	2	4	6	8

$y = 2x + 5$

x	${}^-4$	${}^-2$	0	2	4
y	${}^-3$	1	5	9	13

d $x = {}^-1$ $y = 3$

4 **c** A $x = 3$ $y = {}^-2$
     B $x = {}^-2.5$ $y = 1$
     C $x = 1.8$ $y = 3.6$

Exercise 7.7

1 A and C

2 **a** £3.04   **b** £1.24   **c** £4.00   **d** 96p   **e** 28p   **f** 68p

3 **a** The twins are 120 cm, and the woman is 160 cm.

4 **a** pear: 3   banana: 6   apple: 5   orange: 2

Thinking ahead

A **a** **i** $3p + 6q = 33$ **ii** $2p + 4q = 22$ **iii** $4p + 6q = 34$
     iv $2p + 2q = 12$ **v** $p + q = 6$
   b $p = 1$ $q = 5$

Exercise 7.8

1 **a** $x = 6$ $y = 9$ **b** $x = 8$ $y = 1$ **c** $x = 1.5$ $y = 3.5$

2 B

---

3 **a** $6m + 9n = 84$ **b** $6m + 8n = 78$ **c** $n = 6$ **d** $m = 5$

4 **a** $v = 2$ $w = 12$ **b** $v = {}^-1$ $w = {}_{\cdot}3$ **c** $v = 2.5$ $w = {}^-0.5$

Exercise 7.9

1 **a** $a = 10$ $b = 2$ **b** $a = 2$ $b = 5$ **c** $a = 5.5$ $b = 1.5$
   d $a = {}^-2$ $b = 8$ **e** $a = 3$ $b = 1$ **f** $a = 6$ $b = {}^-3$

2 **a** $m = 5$ **b** $n = 10$ **3** $p = 3$ $q = 1$

4 **a** $25m - 10n = 140$ **b** $14m - 10n = 74$ **c** $m = 6$ **d** $n = 1$

5 **a** $x = 4$ $y = 2$ **b** $x = 3$ $y = 5$ **c** $x = 2$ $y = 1$
   d $x = 2.5$ $y = 1.5$ **e** $x = 5$ $y = {}^-1$ **f** $x = 7$ $y = {}^-4$

Exercise 7.10

1

2 **a** Check that the magic total is 88.   **c** Yes, it is a magic pentagram.

4 **a** $8x + 16y$ **5** values that fit $8x + 16y = 48$

6 values that fit $2x + 4y = 100$

7 **a** $2x + 10y = 18$ **b** $2x + 4y = 12$ **c** $x = 2$ $y = 1$

8 **a** $3x + 9y = 18$ $2x + 4y = 10$ **b** $x = 3$ $y = 1$

9 **a** $x + 3y = 14$ **b** $2x - 6y = 4$ **c** $x = 8$ $y = 2$

10 **b** magic total = 88

11 $x = 10$ $y = 2$, magic total = 112   **12** $x = 5$ $y = 1$, magic total = 56

Exercise 7.11

1 Susan is 38, her brother 35.

2 **a** $2x + 5y = 256$ $x + y = 89$ **b** 26 large and 63 small

3 **a** $4n$ **b** $n - 8$ **c** $4n - 8$ **d** $12(n - 8) = 4n - 8$
   e Pia is 11 years old.

4 257 20p coins   123 10p coins   **5** $m = 4$ $c = {}^-2$

End points

A1 **a** $2k + 9m$ **b** $2p + 8$

B1 **a** $z = 6.5$ **b** $y = 3$ **c** $x = 1.5$ **d** $w = 1$ **e** $v = {}^-3$ **f** $t = 1.5$

B2 **a** $3x + 2$ **b** $3x + 2 = 26$ $x = 8$, $x + 8 = 16$, $x - 6 = 2$

B3 $n = 2.5$

C1 **a**

$y = 2x - 3$

x	${}^-4$	${}^-2$	0	2	4
y	${}^-11$	${}^-7$	${}^-3$	1	5

$y = 4x - 4$

x	${}^-4$	${}^-2$	0	2	4
y	${}^-20$	${}^-12$	${}^-4$	4	12

c $x = 0.5$ $y = {}^-2$

D1 **a** $m = 1.5$ $n = 0.25$ **b** $m = {}^-2$ $n = 3$ **c** $m = 12$ $n = 2$

D2 **c** 83 20p coins and 57 50p coins

SECTION 8

Starting points

A1 **a** 2000   **b** 2200   **c** 2180   **d** 2176

A2 **a** 45.64   **b** 45.6

A3 **a** 34.60   **b** 3   **c** 38.5   **d** 3500

A4 **c, d, e, f**

B1 **a** 177.753   **b** 43.463   **c** 3.984   **d** 3442.8895

B2 **a** 27.98   **b** 11.17   **c** 149.86   **d** 232.236

B3 Numbers are not in correct columns.

B4 Lower numbers were not always subtracted from top ones.

Exercise 8.1

1 **a** round up   **b** don't round   **c** round up   **d** don't round
   e round down

3 **a** round down to 95 cm   **b** round down to 67 000
   c round up to 80   **d** round up to 16 m

Exercise 8.2

1 a 10:43 – 11:00 am, 71 934 – 72 000, 63 479.6 – 63 500,
1452.56 – 1450 m², 56 – 60 min, 492 – 500
b 10.84 s, 100 m, 2003   **c** 19.6
4 a 10 243   **b** 24.6

Exercise 8.3

2 a 70 000   **b** 72 000   **c** 71 900   **d** 71 930
3 a 1450   **b** 21 700   **c** 143   **d** 2 130 000   **e** 150 000
5

45 000	2400	300 000	15
45 300	2400	303 000	14.8
45 290	2395	302 600	14.82

6 If 54.2 and 26.8 are slightly inaccurate, then the area will be very inaccurate.
8 3 sf, 4 sf , 5 sf or 6 sf

Exercise 8.4

1 0.008 cm
2 The last two zeros imply that these values are zero – they are not.
3

0.03	0.025	0.0254
0.009	0.0091	0.00914
0.04	0.039	0.0394
0.6	0.62	0.621
0.002	0.0018	0.00176
0.06	0.061	0.0610
0.03	0.028	0.0283
0.005	0.0045	0.00454

4 Japan   **5** It would appear that many had the same area.
6 a 244 020 km²   **b** 460 km²   **c** 370 000 km²
d 9 561 000 km²   **e** 2 km²
7 Bangladesh and Congo

Exercise 8.5

1 estimates: **a** 6000   **b** 24 000   **c** 4 000 000   **d** 25 000
e 750   **f** 100   **g** 250   **h** 30 000
2 a estimate £18 000   **b** because both numbers will round up.
3 about 100 people per km²
5 a too large   **b** too large   **c** right size   **d** too small
e too small   **f** too large   **g** right size   **h** too small
7 When all numbers are about the same order of magnitude (same size)

Thinking ahead

A 9.234, smaller   **B** 12 666.67 (2dp), larger
C a gets smaller   **b** gets larger

Exercise 8.6

1 a 17 784   **b** 17.784   **2** estimate 0.1, exact 0.1035
3 a 7500, 8657.5   **b** 21, 17.5741   **c** 0.18, 0.201 526
d 1000, 1360   **e** 9000, 8796.245   **f** 72, 70.8167
4 a 0.6 m², 70 m²   **b** 0.822 m², 97.350 42 m²
5 a estimates: C 40 m   D 50 000 m
6 estimates: A 36 000 cm²   B 20 000 cm²   C 84 cm²
7 0.5 cm

Exercise 8.7

1 a It has shrunk. In 1971 the length increased.
b

1925	286	273
1957	142	144
1963	118	112
1971	114	120
1994	93	98

d Method 1. Rounding is done at the end.

Exercise 8.8

1 a 3.34 m, 1.63 m, 12.44 m   **b** 67.725 848 m³   **c** 0.01 735 243 m³
2 72 m³, error = 4.291 504 43 m³   **3** to 1 decimal place (to nearest mm)

4 a 3.65 cm   **b** 3.75 cm   **5** 5.95 cm and 6.05 cm
6 a 289.928 625 cm³   **b** 305.146 875 cm³   **c** 15.218 25 cm³

End points

A2 a round up   **b** round down
B1 a 346   **b** 345.68   **c** 300
B2 a 34.7   **b** 1.97   **c** 195 000   **d** 0.003 19   **e** 144   **f** 6.99
C1 a estimate 10 m³   **b** 8.90 m³

SECTION 9

Starting points

A1 a $\frac{1}{4}$ **b** $\frac{1}{3}$ **c** $\frac{1}{12}$ **d** $\frac{1}{6}$ **e** $\frac{1}{12}$
A2 a $\frac{5}{12}$ **b** $\frac{1}{3}$ **c** $\frac{2}{3}$ **d** $\frac{1}{6}$ **e** 1   **f** 0
A4 a $\frac{1}{6}$ **b** $\frac{1}{2}$ **c** $\frac{1}{3}$ **B1** $\frac{1}{5}$
C1 a $\frac{3}{16}$ **b** $\frac{5}{16}$ **c** $\frac{2}{7}$ **d** $\frac{3}{32}$
D2 a $\frac{1}{16}$ **b** $\frac{1}{8}$ **E2** $\frac{1}{8}$

Exercise 9.1

1 a $\frac{1}{18}$ **b** $\frac{1}{36}$ **c** $\frac{1}{6}$ **d** $\frac{1}{6}$ **e** $\frac{5}{6}$ **f** $\frac{1}{12}$ **g** $\frac{5}{18}$ **h** $\frac{1}{4}$ **i** $\frac{5}{12}$
3 a $\frac{1}{10}$ **b** $\frac{3}{20}$ **c** $\frac{1}{4}$ (0 is considered to be an even number)

Exercise 9.2

1 a $\frac{2}{9}$ **b** $\frac{7}{27}$ **c** $\frac{2}{9}$ **d** $\frac{2}{3}$ **e** $\frac{19}{27}$ **f** $\frac{1}{27}$ **g** $\frac{1}{9}$ **h** $\frac{2}{3}$
3 a $\frac{1}{8}$ **b** $\frac{1}{4}$ **c** $\frac{7}{8}$ **d** $\frac{3}{4}$ **e** 0   **f** $\frac{3}{8}$

Exercise 9.3

1 a list of 24 arrangements   **c** $\frac{1}{24}$
2 NOT, NTO, ONT, OTN, TON, TNO   **3** 2 ways
4 a

No. of letters	1	2	3	4
No. of arrangements	1	2	6	24

b $a = 2, b = 3, c = 4, d = 5, e = 6$ **c** 120, 720
5 b 27 (i.e. 3^3)

Exercise 9.4

1 a AB, AC, AD, AE, BC, BD, BE, CD, CE, DE   **c** 10 handshakes
2 b 15 handshakes
3 a

No. of people	1	2	3	4	5	6
No. of handshakes	0	1	3	6	10	15

c 21 handshakes
4 a S1P, S1Z1, S1S2, S1Z2, PZ1, PS2, PZ2, Z1S2, Z1Z2, S2Z2
b $\frac{1}{10}$ **c** $\frac{1}{5}$ **d** $\frac{9}{10}$ **e** $\frac{7}{10}$
5 $\frac{3}{14}$

Exercise 9.5

1 about 7 times   **2 a** 0.23 (2 dp)   **b** 2   **c** 0.77 (i.e. 1 − 0.23)
3 a 0.25 (2 dp)   **b** 0.75 (2 dp)   **c** about 150
4 0.26 (2 dp)   **5** 0.49   **6 a** 0.04   **b** 605   **c** 43

End points

A2 a $\frac{1}{4}$ **b** $\frac{1}{12}$ **c** $\frac{1}{12}$ **d** 0   **A4 a** $\frac{1}{8}$ **b** $\frac{3}{4}$ **c** $\frac{1}{4}$ **d** $\frac{3}{8}$
B1 a 24 ways   **b** $\frac{1}{2}$ **C1** 6 ways   **C2** $\frac{1}{2}$ **D1** 0.36 (2 dp)

SECTION 10

Starting points

A1 a $3a + 12$ **b** $2b - 12$ **c** $6c + 15$ **d** $8d - 8$
e $32 - 8e$ **f** $15 + 30f$
B1 a $5a + 4b - 6$ **b** $4p + 6q - 10$ **B2 a** $8a + 10$ **b** $14a + 10$
C1 a $p = 3$ **b** $q = 10$ **c** $t = 0.75$ **d** $x = 18.75$ **e** $x = {}^-4.5$
D1 A and E   B and F   C and D
E1 a 31.28   **b** 12.6   **c** 4.12   **d** 27.92   **e** 29.76   **f** 45.08

Exercise 10.1

1 a i 16.3 m   **ii** 3.4 m   **iii** 11.9 m   **b** 54.1 m
c Length: 10.5 m   Width: 8.2 m   **d** 26.9 m   **e** 107.87 m²
f 306.27 m²

2 a 27.9 m   **b** 19.4 m   **c** 21.4 m²   **d** 86.12 m²

Exercise 10.2

1 b i $13.4 + w$ **ii** $16.2 - 2w$ **d i** $32.4 - 2w$ **ii** 28.4 m
e ii $8.1(16.2 - 2w) = 131.22 - 16.2w$ **f** $w = 2.7$

2 a i $46 + p$ **ii** $24 - p$ **iii** $9.6(14.4 - p) = 138.24 - 9.6p$ **iv** $24p$
b 48 m   **c** 6.4 m

Exercise 10.3

1 a $2a + 8$ **b** $3b - 15$ **c** $8c + 12$ **d** $d^2 + 7d$
e $6e - e^2$ **f** $4f + f^2$ **g** $2p^2 + 9p$ **h** $4r^2 - 2r$

2 A $a(a + 5), a^2 + 5a$ **B** $b(b - 2), b^2 - 2b$ **C** $c(c - 6), c^2 - 6c$
D $d(12 - d), 12d - d^2$ **E** $4(e + 8), 4e + 32$ **F** $7(8 - f), 56 - 7f$

3 P $5(2p + 2), 10p + 10$ **Q** $4(3q - 2), 12q - 8$ **R** $r(2r + 2), 2r^2 + 2r$

4 A $2a$ **B** b **C** c

5 D $d + 3$ **E** $e + 2$ **F** $5 + f$ **G** $2g + 3$

6 a $4x + 12 = 4(x + 3)$ **b** $6p - 4 = 2(3p - 2)$ **c** $2a + 8 = 2(a + 4)$
d $10 - 5q = 5(2 - q)$ **e** $b^2 - 6b = b(b - 6)$ **f** $y^2 + 4y = y(y + 4)$
g $2r^2 + 3r = r(2r + 3)$ **h** $3d^2 - 5d = d(3d - 5)$ **i** $3t^2 + 4t = t(3t + 4)$
j $6s^2 + 7s = s(6s + 7)$

Exercise 10.4

1 a $a + 8$ **b** $4a + 16$ **c** 209 cm²   **2 a** $5d$ **b** 23.2 cm

3 225 m²   **4** 84.5 cm²

Exercise 10.5

1 a $6ab$ **b** $3pq$ **c** $20xy$ **d** $30pq$ **e** $2x^2$ **f** a^2b
g $2xy^2$ **h** $6a^2b$ **i** $6p^2q$ **j** a^5 **k** $6b^3$ **l** $10c^3b$

2 A and **E** $((2b^2)^3$ and $8b^6)$ **B** and **F** $(6b^5$ and $3b^2 \times 2b^3)$
C and **H** $(3b^2 \times 2b^4$ and $6b^6)$ **G** and **I** $(6(b^4)^2$ and $6b^8)$

3 a $ab + 4a$ **b** $xy + xz$ **c** $2mn + 3mp$ **d** $6xy + 4xz$
e $ac + c^2$ **f** $p^2 - pq$ **g** $3bc + 3b^2$ **h** $4a^2 - 4ab$
i $3p^2 - 4p$ **j** $2ab - 4ac$ **k** $6a^2 + 8ab$ **l** $8pq - 12p^2$
m $6p^2q + 4pq^2$ **n** $4x^2y - 8xy^2$ **o** $3abx^2 - 3aby^2$

4 a $9a + 22b$ **b** $2x^2 + x$ **c** $4a + 5ab$ **d** Not possible
e $11a + 2b$ **f** $6x^2 + 4xy$ **g** $4p^2 + 6q$ **h** $6a$

5 a $9a + 26b$ **b** $10x + 5y$ **c** $2x^2 + x$ **d** $10x^2 + 3xy$
e $2a^2b$ **f** $3a^2b + 3ab + 2ab^2 - 2b^2$

6 a $6a^2 + 6ab + 12b^2$ **b** $16x^2y + 20xy^2 - 6xy$ **c** $8p^2q - 7pq^2$
d $14m^2n - 8mn^2 - 12m^3$

Exercise 10.6

1 A left circle 24   right circle 18   total 42
B left square 14   left circle 70   right circle 30

2 C $15c + 24$ **D** $3a^2 + 12a$ **E** $6pq + 8p^2$ **F** $2ab^2 + 4a^2b$

3 G left square x right square y total $ax + ay$
H left square c right square 4   total $2c^2 + 8c$
I left square $3b$ right square $2a$ total $3ab + 2a^2$
J left square $2x^2$ right square $3x$ total $4x^2 + 6x$
K left square $2b$ right square 3   total $4b^2 + 6b$
L left square $2a$ right square $3b$ right circle $15b$

Exercise 10.7

1 a $2(x + 7)$ **b** $3(a + 5)$ **c** $6(p - 4)$ **d** $2(4x - 5y)$
e $x(5 + y)$ **f** $p(q + 7)$ **g** $2d(3 + 2e)$ **h** $c(5 + a)$
i $3a(2b + 3)$ **j** $2a(1 - 4b)$ **k** $3a(a + 4)$ **l** $5y(3x + 4z)$
m $ab(a + b)$ **n** $3cd(4c - 5d)$ **o** $5y(5x^2 + 3z)$

2 M left square $2a$ right square 6   right circle $6a$
N left square $2x$ right square y left circle $6x^2$
O top square b left square b left circle b^2
P top square $2p$ right square $4p$ right circle $8p^2$

3 a b **b** top square b left square 5   right square a

4 R top square c left square c right square 8   right circle $8c$
S top square 2   left square $2d$ right square $3b$ left circle $4d$

5 Any two from:

- top square $4p$ left square p right square $2q$
- top square $2p$ left square $2p$ right square $4q$
- top square p left square $4p$ right square $8q$
- top square 4   left square p^2 right square $2pq$
- top square 2   left square $2p^2$ right square $4pq$
- top square 1   left square $4p^2$ right square $8pq$

6 a $5(x + 2y + 4)$ **b** $3(2a - 3b + 4c)$ **c** $x(2x + 3 + y)$
d $7(2x - 4y + 3z)$ **e** $2x(x + 4y + 3)$ **f** $ab(6b + 2a + 5)$

End points

A1 a $20f - 16$ **b** $m^2 + mn$ **c** $2pr - 2p^2$
d $a^2b + ab^2$ **e** $2m^2n + 3mn^2$ **f** $6xy^2 - 10x^2y$

A2 a $22b + 16$ **b** $26b + 14$ **c** $10ab^2 + 4a^2b$ **d** $3x^2y + 19xy + 7xy^2$

B1 a i $p - 8.4$ **ii** $p - 6.1$ **b i** $4p$ **ii** 14 cm

B2 a $a + 5$ cm   **b** $4a + 10$ cm
c $a(a + 5) = a^2 + 5a$ **d** 11.5   **e** 51.51 cm²

C1 a $4(2p + q)$ **b** $6(a - 2b)$ **c** $a(a + b)$ **d** $m(7 + 3n)$
e $2y(4x + 5)$ **f** $2a(2b + 3a)$ **g** $xy(3y - 5x)$ **h** $2pq(2 - 3p)$
i $h(2g^2 - 5h)$

SECTION 11

Starting points

A1 a AI or AK or KI or AJ   **b** EB   **c** EF or EB or EC
d triangle ECB   **e** triangle GIA   **f** triangle HIJ
g AK or BC (or FC)   **h** GD   **i** FC   **B1** F

Exercise 11.1

2 Rydon and Barton   **3** Rydon only   **7** just over 20 miles

Exercise 11.2

2 isosceles

3 a right-angled   **b** scalene   **c** equilateral   **d** scalene

4 It is an impossible triangle since $6 + 3 < 10$.

6 Two possible answers: R to U is just over 50 miles or about 105 miles.

Exercise 11.3

3 b and **c** are congruent (LMN and PQR)

Thinking ahead

A A, C and H

Exercise 11.4

2 60°, 30°

Thinking ahead

E b The locus cuts the line AB in half at right angles.

Exercise 11.5

1 c The distances are always equal.

3 c All three bisectors meet at one point.

4 e The bisectors all intersect at the centre of the circle.

Exercise 11.6

1 a 2 cm   **b** 20 metres

2 The distance from tap to tree will be about 35 metres.

Exercise 11.7

4 c External corners are smooth curves, internal corners are right angles.

Exercise 11.8

1 d The locus is a circle with diameter AB.

2 e Angle RCS is a right angle   **f** It is a right-angled triangle.

3 BGC, BGA, EGC, EGA, ECB, EAB

4 a RS = 28.6 metres   **b** RU = 20.2 metres

End points

B1 Both bisectors have the same gradient.

C2 The three bisectors intersect at a point.

SECTION 12

Starting points

A1 **a** 3 : 1 **b** 1 : 3

B1 **a** 4 : 1 **b** 2 : 5 : 4 **c** 9 : 12
12 : 3 1 : 2½ : 2 3 : 4
6 : 8

B2 2 : 5 1 : 3 : 2 10 : 20
10 : 25 3 : 9 : 6 2½ : 5
1 : 2½

B3 **a** 3 : 2 **b** 2 : 3 **c** 2 : 4 : 1 **d** 10 : 1 **e** 4 : 3 : 6

C1 **a** 0.625 **b** 1.8 **c** 0.58\dot{3} **d** 1.3\dot{6}

C2 **a** 61.\dot{1}% **b** 50% **c** 70.8\dot{3}% **d** 87.5%

D1 **a** 1, 3, 4, 7, 11, 18, 29, 47, ... **b** 2, 2, 4, 6, 10, 16, 26, 42, ...
c 1, 5, 6, 11, 17, 28, 45, 73, ... **d** 3, 6, 9, 15, 24, 39, 63, 102, ...

E1 **a** GI **b** H **c** G and I **d** GH

F3 JKL and PQR are similar

Exercise 12.1

1 **a** 480 ml **b** 1200 ml **2** **a** 315 ml **b** 525 ml

3 **a** 50 ml **b** 175 ml **4** **a** 250 kg **b i** 2 : 1 : 9 **ii** 2400 kg

5 **a** 800 cm (8 m) **b** 9 cm **6** **a** 16 cm **b** 225 cm (2.25 m)

7 **a** 6.3 cm **b** 1 : 5000

Exercise 12.2

1 Sarah 20, Denzil 15 **2** sweets £3, comics £6, videos £9

3 Amy £75, Ben £45, Zoe £30 **4** **a** 75 min **b** 90 min

Exercise 12.3

1 345 g caster sugar 450 ml water 75 g cocoa 1800 ml chilled milk

2 **a** 60 g **b** 75 ml
c 300 g white sugar 100 ml milk 100 ml water 50 g butter 20 g cocoa

3 **a** 7 drops **b** 2 egg whites

Exercise 12.4

1 **a** 2 : 1 **b** $\frac{2}{1}$ **2** 2 : 3 and $\frac{2}{3}$ **3** **a** $\frac{5}{3}$ **b** $\frac{3}{5}$

4 **a** $\frac{1}{5}$ **b** $\frac{4}{5}$

5 **a** $\frac{2}{3}$

b The fraction $\frac{2}{5}$ has no meaning here because totalling the number of parts, height plus diameter, to give 5 does not mean anything

Exercise 12.5

1 P $\frac{1}{4}$, 0.25, 25% Q $\frac{2}{5}$, 0.4, 40% R $\frac{2}{3}$, 0.\dot{6}, 66.\dot{6}%

S $\frac{3}{2}$, 1.5, 150% T $\frac{7}{3}$, 2.\dot{3}, 233.\dot{3}%

3–7

Photo	Width	Height	Ratio
A	1	1	1.0000
B	2	1	2.0000
C	3	2	1.5000
D	5	3	1.6667
E	8	5	1.6000
F	13	8	1.6250
G	21	13	1.6154
H	34	21	1.6190
I	55	34	1.6176
J	89	55	1.6182
K	144	89	1.6180
L	233	144	1.6181
M	377	233	1.6180
N	610	377	1.6180
O	987	610	1.6180

Exercise 12.6

1 **a** 1.4 **b** 7 cm **2** **a** 2.5 **b** 12.75 cm

3 **a** 0.75 **b** 8.1 cm

Exercise 12.7

1 **a i** 1.6 **ii** 1.6 **iii** 1.6 **iv** 1.6
b DEFG and WXYZ are not similar because, although all ratios of lengths of corresponding sides are equal, all corresponding angles are not equal.

2 HIJK and STUV are not similar because, although all corresponding angles are equal, all ratios of lengths of corresponding sides are not equal.

3 MNOP: all corresponding angles are equal and all ratios of lengths of corresponding sides are equal.

4 **a** EFGH and MNOP ABCD and IJKL QRST and UVWX
b 2 or 0.5 1.5 or 0.\dot{6} 1.\dot{3} or 0.75

5 QRST and UVWX

6 **a i** 0.6 **ii** 0.6 **iii** 0.6
b Yes: triangles PQR and XYZ are similar.
d Different-sized triangles with the same angles can be cut out and placed on top of each other to show they must be similar.

Exercise 12.8

1 **a** 4.56 cm **b** 4.2 cm

2 **a i** ST **ii** FD
b US has been multiplied by the ratio greater than 1 instead of the ratio less than 1.

3 12.3 cm

4 **a** 1.6 cm
b The angle at J is equal to the angle at M, so JK and MN must be at the same angle to LM, and are therefore parallel to each other.

End points

A1 **a** 450 ml **b** 630 ml **B1** Amy £160, Ben £128, Zoe £112

C1 **a i** 375 g **ii** 3 tablespoons **b** 10 eggs

D1 **a** 3 : 4 **b** $\frac{3}{4}$ **c** 0.75 **d** 75% **D2** $\frac{2}{5}$

E1 EFGH and NOPQ **F1** 4.5 cm

SKILLS BREAK 2A

1 Large £1.27 Super £1.69 Major £2.54 Professional £4.24

2 5 litre 19.8 p/l 8 litre 16.1 p/l 10 litre 16.9 p/l
12 litre 16.6 p/l 8 litre best buy

3 12 litre

5 1 gallon £4.99/gallon 1.5 gallon £4.33/gallon
2 gallon £4.00/gallon 2.5 gallon £4.00/gallon 2 or 2.5 gallon

6 5 kg **7** **a** 313 grams **b** less than 7.5 kg

8 **a** 0.98 kg **b** 2.2 lb **9** **a** 33 grams

10 **a** 66 **b** 10 grams **c i** $\frac{1}{100}$ **ii** 0.01 **iii** 1%

12 £3563.20 **13** **a** 24.75 m² **b** 15 pence **14** 4752 cm²

16 **a** 180 metres, 3×50 metres + 1×30 metres, 6×30 metres

17 2.4 m²

18 **a** rectangle **b** 5.5 metres × 1.9 metres **19** 6.3 m²

20 25 m² **22** 76°

23 **a** rectangle **b** 3.1 metres **c** 17.7 m²

24 **a** £180 **b** £14.40 **c** £10.80

25 Super Hover £24 Mowhog £26.67 Mastermow £33.33

SKILLS BREAK 2B

1 12 lines of symmetry **2** 12 **3** 41 metres (to nearest metre)

4 133 metres² (to nearest m²) **5** **a** octagon **b** 45° **c** 135°

6 695 cm² **7** 4 planes of symmetry **8** 1080 tonnes

9 46 metres **10** about 17 cm **11** about 370 steps

12 **a** 1.01×10^4 tonnes **b** 2.5×10^6 rivets

13 **a** 1650 **b** 1700 **c** 2000 **14** 0.05% (c)

15 **a** 225° **b** 045° **16** £7.43

17 **a** 308 million Francs **b** About £41 million

18 **a** 2200 000 **b** 2190 000 **c** 2189 000 **d** 2188 900

19 In French 0.42, in English 0.38

20

	French	English
Range	14	12
Mean	5	4.9
Median	5	4
Mode	2	4

Different answers are possible but must be justified.

21 **a** EP, EV, EM, PV, PM, VM **b** $\frac{1}{2}$ **c** $\frac{1}{6}$

d **i** $\frac{1}{3}$ **ii** $\frac{1}{2}$ **e** Profit

22 **a** £851 **b** adult £99, child £89 **c** £277

SECTION 13

Starting points

A1 **a** 5000 m **b** 0.34 m **A2** **a** 4800 m **b** 1.5 m **c** 1.8 m

A3 **a** 4 cm **b** 400 000 cm **c** 390 cm **d** 17 or 18 cm

A4 **a** 5.13 km **b** 11.36 km **A5** 12.5 miles

B1 **a** 15.4 pounds **b** 8.4 pounds

B2 **a** 7.3 kg **b** 2.3 kg **c** 3.5 kg **d** 2.0 kg

B3 2.2 pounds in 1 kilogram

B4 **a**

Gallons	1	2	3	4	5	6	7	8
Litres	4.55	9.1	13.65	18.2	22.75	27.3	31.85	36.4

c **i** 11.4 litres **ii** 3.3 gallons

C1 **a** 9:30 am **b** 2:21 pm **C2** **a** 02:23 **b** 17:25

C3 75 minutes **C4** 6h 40 min **D1** 13:00

D2 06:25   08:25   09:55   11:45   13:45   17:00
4h 40min 4h 45min 4h 45min 4h 50min 4h 55min 4h 45min

D3 the 13:45 bus **D4** 17:15 **D5** about 3 hours

D6 about 9:45 pm

Exercise 13.1

1 **a** **i** 5.1 m **ii** 25.5 m **iii** 11.5 m **b** **i** 153 m **ii** 9180 m
c **i** 413 seconds **ii** 6 min 53 seconds

2 **b**

Alperton	30 seconds
The Angel	80 seconds
Chancery Lane	15 seconds
Kentish Town	67 seconds

c 2.02 pm (and 23 seconds)

Exercise 13.2

1 604.6 mph **2** **b** 608.2 mph

3 **a** 10.33 miles per min **b** 103.3 miles

4 **a** 6.72 miles per min **b** 17.9 minutes

5 **a** 35.6 minutes **b** 3487.5 miles

Exercise 13.3

1 **b** about 175 metres **c** about 2.7 seconds **d** 120 metres
f **i** yellow car 20 m/s, black car 10 m/s **ii** red car
iii It is the steepest line.
g **i** about 3.5 seconds

2 **a**

red car	140 metres
black car	100 metres
blue car	115 metres
yellow car	90 metres

b the black car **c** **i** about 2 seconds **ii** about 3.3 seconds
d

red car	0 m/s
black car	40 m/s
blue car	30 m/s
yellow car	20 m/s

e It had stopped (possibly broken down).

3 **b** 90 metres

Exercise 13.4

1 **a** 30 miles **b** 50 minutes **c** 18 miles
d **i** 9 minutes **ii** 21 minutes
e 11 miles
f 1 E 2 B 3 A 4 C 5 D

Exercise 13.5

1 **a** 0.2 miles per minute **b** 12 mph

2 **a** 0.875 miles per minute **b** 52.5 mph

3 58.9 mph **4** 1:40 pm **5** 16 miles

6 **a** **i** 20 minutes **ii** 33 mph
b 0755   25 mph
1000   29 mph
c 45 miles **d** 13:46

Exercise 13.6

1 **a** 1500 metres **b** student A **c** 10 minutes
d A: 1500 m B: 1200 m C: 700 m D: 0 m
e 100 m/min (or 6000 m/h or 6 km/h)
f **i** A: Sharon B: Jane C: Lorna D: Jason
ii 500 metres
iii Walked: she travelled at about the same speed as Jane.
g **i** (m/min) **ii** (m/h) **iii** (km/h)

	(m/min)	(m/h)	(km/h)
A	150	9000	9
B	100	6000	6
C	60	3600	3.6
D	300	18 000	18

2 **a** **i** 13:45 **ii** 20 minutes
b **i** 1400 and 1416 **ii** 1 mile per min (or 60 mph)
c The motorbike and car passed each other, going in
opposite directions.
e   car   motorbike
i 30 miles   60 miles
ii 18 mph   33 mph

Exercise 13.7

1 **a** **ii** 11.1 km/h
b **ii** about 3:15 pm (3:16 by calculation)
iii about 2:45 pm (2:47 by calculation)

2 **a** **ii** 9 mph **iii** 9.2 mph
b **i** 10 miles **iii** 12.8 mph **c** **ii** 20 mph

Exercise 13.8

1 **a** A about 5.6 gallons B about 3.5 gallons
b about 35 miles **c** 2 times **d** about 6.4 gallons
e A 3 gallons B 2.9 gallons or 3 gallons
f **i** A about 9.2 gallons B about 12.6 gallons
ii A 43.5 mpg (to 1 dp) B 31.7 mpg (to 1 dp)

2 **a** 0.89 cars per household (2 dp) **b** about 55 cars per km of road
c No

3 **a** 0.45 cars per household (2 dp)
b The number of cars per household almost doubled between
1963 and 1993.

End points

A1 225.25 metres **A2** 4 min 49 seconds **A3** 45.6 mph

A4 about 16:32

B1 **a** 2.5 miles **b** 26 minutes **c** 2 times **d** about 10.3 mph
e **i** 20:40 and 21:08 **ii** steepest part of the graph
f 50 minutes **g** 60 mph **h** **i** about 21:26 **ii** 15.5 km or 16 km

C1 **b** 7.7 mph **D1** 3000 people **D2** 0.51 litres/second

D3 £1.95 per person

SECTION 14

Starting points

A1 **a** GI **b** GÎH **c** GÎH and IĜH **d** GH

B1 A and C, B and E. **B2** **a** XZ **b** GF

C1 **a** 0.42 **b** 0.12 or 0.13 **c** 0.30 **d** 2.22

Thinking ahead

A **b** 0.55 **c** It is the same as for triangle ABC.

B **a** triangle ABC: 1.83
triangle PQR: 1.83
b The ratios are the same.

Exercise 14.1

1 a i $\dfrac{BC}{AC}$ and $\dfrac{DE}{EF}$

   ii The value is 1.18 (to 2 dp) each time.

b i $\dfrac{AC}{BC}$ and $\dfrac{EF}{DE}$

   ii The value is 0.85 (to 2 dp) each time.

c $\dfrac{AB}{AC}$, $\dfrac{FD}{EF}$, and $\dfrac{HI}{GI}$ (≈ 0.82)

   $\dfrac{AC}{AB}$, $\dfrac{EF}{FD}$ and $\dfrac{GI}{HI}$ (≈ 1.22)

   $\dfrac{GH}{HI}$, $\dfrac{ED}{DF}$ and $\dfrac{BC}{AB}$ (≈ 1.44)

   $\dfrac{HI}{GH}$, $\dfrac{DF}{ED}$ and $\dfrac{AB}{BC}$ (≈ 0.69)

2 a There are three pairs of equal angles.

b $\dfrac{KL}{LJ} = \dfrac{MO}{NO} \approx 1.67$

   $\dfrac{KL}{KJ} = \dfrac{MO}{MN} = 1.25$

   $\dfrac{KJ}{JL} = \dfrac{MN}{NO} \approx 1.33$

   $\dfrac{LJ}{KL} = \dfrac{NO}{MO} = 0.6$

   $\dfrac{KJ}{KL} = \dfrac{MN}{MO} = 0.8$

   $\dfrac{JL}{KJ} = \dfrac{NO}{MN} = 0.75$

3 6 pairs of corresponding ratios

Exercise 14.2

1 The first line is: 40 23 46 0.87 1.74 0.50 0.58 1.15 2.00

3 The ratios are about the same each time:
approximately 0.87, 1.73, 0.50, 0.58, 1.15, 2.00

Exercise 14.3

1 b $\sin 30° = 0.5$ $\cos 30° = 0.87$ (to 2dp) $\tan 30° = 0.58$ (to 2dp)

d $\sin 30° = \dfrac{\text{opp}}{\text{hyp}}$ $\cos 30° = \dfrac{\text{adj}}{\text{hyp}}$ $\tan 30° = \dfrac{\text{opp}}{\text{adj}}$

Exercise 14.4

1 b

Triangle	$\sin\theta$	$\cos\theta$	$\tan\theta$
A	0.96	0.28	3.43
B	0.80	0.60	1.33
C	0.38	0.92	0.42
D	0.60	0.80	0.75
E	0.96	0.28	3.43
F	0.92	0.38	2.40

Exercise 14.5

2 a 21° **b** 46° **c** 69°   **3 a** 21° **b** 65° **c** 59°

4 28°   **5** $a = 42°, b = 56°, c = 46°$

6 $a = 37°, b = 52°, c = 30°, d = 41°, e = 61°,$
$f = 60°, g = 38°, h = 44°, i = 60°, j = 51°$

7 a Wayne's value of 1.252427184 ...   **b** It is greater than 1.

Exercise 14.6

2 EF = 3.9 cm, HG = 5.7 cm, JK = 3.5 cm, MN = 20.7 cm

3 b 7.5 cm   **4** AB = 6.9 cm, DE = 6.5 cm, GI = 7.1 cm,

5 JK = 3.1 cm, NO = 8.1 cm, PR = 11.5 cm

Thinking ahead

A a less than 5.6 cm   **C** 5.40 cm

Exercise 14.7

1 b A 3.79 cm B 4.32 cm C 9.46 cm D 42.1°
   E 10.15 cm F 45.0°

2 $a = 42°, b = 1.33$ cm, $c = 13.2$ cm, $d = 31.3°, e = 72.4°$

Exercise 14.8

1 a 75.52° **b** 4.84 m

2 a i 76° **ii** 1.09 m **b** 1.39 m

3

c	d	
	min	max
4 m	0.97 m	1.23 m
6 m	1.46 m	1.85 m
8 m	1.94 m	2.47 m

4 a i rise = 140 mm **ii** going = 112 mm **b** 51.34°

5 a 0.420 m **b** 8.03 m **c** 8.83 m **d** 8.01 m **e** 10.41 m

6 a 2.86°

   b A $\theta = 3.33°$ (unsafe) **B** $\theta = 2.01°$ (safe)
     C $\theta = 1.51°$ (safe) D $\theta = 1.06°$ (safe)

7 2.80° **8** maximum: 32.73° minimum: 21.66°

End points

A1 ABC and ONM   **B1** $\alpha = 48.59°, \beta = 35.54°, \theta = 59.74°$

C1 AB ≈ 10.7 cm   EF ≈ 3.75 m   GI ≈ 6.63 cm

SECTION 15

Starting points

A1 48 cm²   **A2 a** 19 **b** 2.5 **c** 49 **d** 20

B1 a 12 **b** 39   **C1 a** $n = 20$ **b** $n = 2$

C2 a $7n + 9 = 65$ **b** 8

D1 a $5x + 8$ **b** $9a + 2b$ **c** $5x^2 + 2x$ **d** $6a + 5a^2 - 7$
   e $3t^2$ **f** $10cd$ **g** $12k^2$ **h** $7w^2$

Thinking ahead

A a 3 hours 20 minutes **b** 3 pounds

Exercise 15.1

1 a £10.25 **b** $n = \dfrac{c - 50}{15}$ **c** 129 words **d** 63 words

2 a $t = 5d$ **b** 7.5 seconds

3 a 720° **b** $n = \dfrac{s}{180} + 2$ **c** 20 sides **d** n is not an integer

4 a 58 pills **b** 3 **c** $d = \dfrac{100 - n}{3}$ **d** 30 days

5 a 550 ice-creams **b** $x = \dfrac{800 - n}{5}$ **c** 60 pence

   d $n < 0$ so no ice-creams are sold according to the formula.

6 a 94 miles **b** 600 mph **c** $t \rightarrow \boxed{\times s} \rightarrow d$ **d** $t \leftarrow \boxed{\div s} \leftarrow d$
   e 2.5 hours

7 a $p = t - 1$ **b** $p = \dfrac{s}{7}$ **c** $p = \dfrac{y + 2}{5}$ **d** $p = 10 - v$

   e $p = \dfrac{12 - h}{9}$ **f** $p = r - q$ **g** $p = \dfrac{t}{q}$ **h** $p = \dfrac{x - f}{2}$

   i $p = \dfrac{k + m}{l}$ **j** $p = 9g$ **k** $p = mn$ **l** $p = 2s + 2$

Exercise 15.2

1 a 17.6 pounds **b** $k = \dfrac{5p}{11}$ **c** 1.36 kg

2 a $h = \dfrac{2A}{b}$ **b** 80 cm

3 a 20 °C **b** $F \rightarrow -32 \rightarrow \boxed{\times 5} \rightarrow \boxed{\div 9} \rightarrow C$

   c $F = \dfrac{9C}{12} + 32$ **d** 75.2 °F

4 a $y = \dfrac{4z}{3}$ **b** $y = \dfrac{3m}{x}$ **c** $y = 2d - 8$ **d** $y = \dfrac{7}{4}(k + h)$

5 a 36.14 km/h **b** $d = \dfrac{5st}{18}$ **c** $t = \dfrac{18d}{5s}$

6 a ⁻24 °C **b** $h = 300(G - T)$ **c** 15 000 metres

Exercise 15.3

1 a 403.44 cm² **b** $x = \sqrt{\dfrac{s}{6}}$ **c** 4.47 cm

2 a 7.07 cm² **b** $B : r = \sqrt{\dfrac{A}{\pi}}$ **c** 7.98 cm

3 a 207 metres **b** $t = \sqrt{\dfrac{10d}{49}}$ **c** 9.51 seconds

4 a $k = \sqrt{m-1}$ **b** $k = \sqrt{\dfrac{m-1}{3}}$ **c** $k = \sqrt{m-n}$

5 a $A = 314.16\,\text{cm}^2$ **b** $r = \sqrt{\dfrac{A}{4\pi}}$
$V = 523.60\,\text{cm}^3$
$r = \sqrt[3]{\dfrac{3v}{4\pi}}$

c $r = 3.99\,\text{cm}$ **d** $r = 2.88\,\text{cm}$

6 a $x = \sqrt{\dfrac{5y+1}{7}}$ **b** $x = \sqrt{\dfrac{3A}{2\pi}}$ **c** $x = \sqrt{\dfrac{r^3}{k}}$

Exercise 15.4

1 82.5 km **2 a** 121.5 cm³ **b** 64 **c** 2

3 a

	A	B	C	D
i	42	42	42	42
ii	16	20	20	12
iii	6	12	12	0
iv	10.75	15.75	15.75	5.75

4 87.29 m/s **5 a** 31.11 m/s **b** 21.14 m/s

Exercise 15.5

1

	1	2	3	4
a	1500	180	150	18

b 1848 cm²

2 a

	20 cm	7 cm
10	200 cm²	70 cm²
4	80 cm²	28 cm²

b 378 cm²

3 a

×	40	+5
60	240	300
+1	40	5

so 45 × 61 = 2745

b

×	20	+5
20	400	100
+7	140	35

so 25 × 27 = 675

c

×	30	+2
80	240	160
+4	120	8

so 32 × 84 = 2688

Thinking ahead

A a 1 n^2 **2** $3n$ **3** $2n$ **4** 6 **b** $n^2 + 5n + 6$

Exercise 15.6

1 a $a^2 + 4a + 3$ **b** $b^2 + 6b + 8$ **c** $c^2 + 13c + 40$
d $d^2 + 14d + 45$ **e** $e^2 + 8e + 7$ **f** $f^2 + 13f + 22$

2 a i $x^2 + 2x + 1$ **ii** $x^2 + 4x + 4$ **iii** $x^2 + 6x + 9$

3 a D

4

×	2x	+4
3x	6x²	12x
+1	2x	4

so $(2x + 4)(3x + 1) = 6x^2 + 14x + 4$

5 B

6 a $2a^2 + 9a + 4$ **b** $3b^2 + 14b + 15$ **c** $6c^2 + 25c + 14$
d $12d^2 + 25d + 12$ **e** $4e^2 + 12e + 9$ **f** $25f^2 + 10f + 1$

7 a Jo $5 \times (5 + 3) = 5 \times 8 = 40$
Liz $(5 + 1)(5 + 2) - 2 = 6 \times 7 - 2 = 40$
b Jo $n(n + 3) = n^2 + 3n$
Liz $(n + 1)(n + 2) - 2$
$= n^2 + 3n + 2 - 2$
$= n^2 + 3n$

8 A $y = 4x^2 + 8x$ B $y = 4x^2 + 8x + 3 - 3$
$= 4x^2 + 8x$

Exercise 15.7

1 A

2 A and I B and F
C and H D and G

3 a $a^2 + 2a - 3$ **b** $b^2 - 2b - 8$ **c** $c^2 - 13c + 40$
d $2d^2 + 13d - 45$ **e** $6e^2 - 11e - 7$ **f** $10f^2 - 32f + 22$

4 A **5** C

6 a $2z^2 + 3tz + t^2$ **b** $6k^2 + 17mk + 5m^2$ **c** $2c^2 + 17cd + 21d^2$
d $6p^2 + 13pq - 5q^2$ **e** $5f^2 - 8fg + 3g^2$ **f** $49w^2 - v^2$

Thinking ahead

A $(x + 2)(x + 6)$

B a

×	p	−2
p	p²	−2p
+7	7p	−14

b $(p - 2)(p + 7) = p^2 + 5p - 14$

Exercise 15.8

1 a $x^2 + 8x + 7 = (x + 7)(x + 1)$ **b** $x^2 + 3x + 2 = (x + 2)(x + 1)$
c $x^2 + 4x + 3 = (x + 3)(x + 1)$ **d** $x^2 + 8x + 12 = (x + 2)(x + 6)$
e $x^2 + 6x + 9 = (x + 3)(x + 3)$ **f** $x^2 + 13x + 36 = (x + 4)(x + 9)$
$= (x + 3)^2$

2 a $x^2 + 6x + 8 = (x + 4)(x + 2)$ **b** $x^2 + 6x + 5 = (x + 5)(x + 1)$
c $x^2 + 7x + 10 = (x + 5)(x + 2)$ **d** $x^2 - 11x + 10 = (x - 1)(x - 10)$
e $x^2 + 7x + 12 = (x + 4)(x + 3)$ **f** $x^2 - 10x - 11 = (x + 1)(x - 11)$

3 a $(x + 1)(x - 4)$ **b** $(x - 2)(x - 4)$

4 a $x^2 + 2x - 3 = (x + 3)(x - 1)$ **b** $x^2 + 3x - 10 = (x + 5)(x - 2)$
c $x^2 - 4x - 5 = (x - 5)(x + 1)$ **d** $x^2 - 3x - 28 = (x - 7)(x + 4)$
e $x^2 - 8x + 15 = (x - 5)(x - 3)$ **f** $x^2 - 5x + 6 = (x - 2)(x - 3)$

End points

A1 a 100 m **b** 175 m **c** 100 m **A2** 52.36 cm³

B1 a $n = \dfrac{c - 20}{30}$ **b** 15 days **B2 a** $m = 5(c - 10)$ **b** 100 miles

B3 a $k = \sqrt{\dfrac{h}{5}}$ **b** $k = 5m - n$ **c** $\sqrt{A - 9}$ **C1** C

C2 a $a^2 + 9a + 8$ **b** $b^2 + 8b + 16$ **c** $5c^2 + 17c + 6$
d $d^2 + d - 2$ **e** $6e^2 - 5e - 50$ **f** $3f^2 - 23f + 14$

D1 $(k - 2)(k + 7)$

D2 a $(x + 11)(x + 1)$ **b** $(x + 2)(x + 7)$ **c** $(x + 5)(x - 1)$
d $(x + 3)(x - 2)$ **e** $(x - 5)(x + 4)$ **f** $(x - 2)(x - 3)$

SECTION 16

Starting points

A1 2.305 metres **A2** 2.25 metres

B1 1.97 metres (to 3 sf) **B2** 1.91 metres (to 3 sf)

C1 a 0.14 metres **b** 0.12 metres

C2 a 0.07 metres **b** 0.06 metres

D1 a On average, the men jumped 1 cm higher in 1996; but the finalists were slightly more closely matched in 1992.
b In 1996, the women jumped 6 cm higher on average, and the finalists were more closely matched than in 1992.

E1 a 6 years **b** 4 years

Exercise 16.1

1 a 70 – 72 **b** 70 – 72

2 a The golfers did better in the 1st round.
b In the 1st round, the frequencies were greater at the lower scores, and less at the higher scores.

3 a 17, 18, 19, 20, 21, 22, 23, 24, 25, 26, 27 **b** 22 **c** 22, 33, 44, 55

5 a No – the frequencies need to be about the same for the frequency polygons to give a good comparison.

Thinking ahead

A a 64, 65, 66 **b** 79, 80, 81 **B** 13, 14, 15, 16, 17

Exercise 16.2

1 **a** 5 **b** 69, 74, 79, 84 **c** 15

2 **a** 4 **b** 68.5, 72.5, 76.5, 80.5 **c** 12

3 **a** 128, 129, 130, 131, 132 **b** 130 **c** It is the middle one.

Exercise 16.3

1 43 900 points

2 252 750 points **3** The mean number of points is 8153 (to 4 sf).

4 **a** 3089 m **b** 2837 m

Exercise 16.4

1 63.0 m (to 3 sf)

2 The women and men threw as well as each other.
The mean distances thrown by the women and the men were the same.

3 18.7 m (to 3 sf) **4** 20.1 m (to 3 sf)

5 On average, the men threw the shot 1.4 m further than the women.

Exercise 16.5

1

Reaction time (s)	Frequency
0.120 –	5
0.140 –	8
0.160 –	23
0.180 –	5
0.200 –	4
0.220 –	2
Total	47

2 **a i** 0.140 s **ii** 0.100 s **b i** 0.174 s **ii** 0.170 s

3 The hypothesis is probably false.
The mean reaction time in the finals was only four-thousandths of a second faster than in the semifinals.
The range of the times, however, was much smaller in the finals, the four slowest times all being in the semifinals.

Thinking ahead

A 12.73, 12.68, 12.749, 12.75
(12.75 can be rounded to 12.7 if you decide to round mid-points down.)

Exercise 16.6

2 **a** 12.375 s and 12.385 s **b** 9.15 m and 9.25 m
c 7.25 s and 7.35 s **d** 7.295 s and 7.305 s

Exercise 16.7

1 10.930 and 10.940 **2** 7.00 m and 7.01 m

3 It would be unfair to round a time of 9.832 s down to 9.83 s, because the rounded time would be faster than the time actually run; similarly, it would be unfair to round a distance of 6.138 m up to 6.14 m, because the rounded distance would be longer.

Exercise 16.8

1 **a**

Points	Cumulative frequency
< 700	0
< 800	8
< 900	31
< 1000	47
< 1100	50

2 **a**

Distance (metres)	Cumulative frequency
< 76	0
< 78	2
< 80	6
< 82	20
< 84	33
< 86	41
< 88	47
< 90	48

Exercise 16.9

1 **a**

Distance (metres)	Cumulative frequency
< 72	0
< 74	1
< 76	12
< 78	35
< 80	48
< 82	52

2 **a** about 77.3 m **b** about 2.2 m (78.4 – 76.2)

3 On average, the javelin finalists threw 5.1 m further; but the hammer finalists threw more consistently.

4 **b** about 840 points **c** about 180 points (920 – 740)

5 **b** about 880 points **c** about 115 points (935 – 820)

6 On average, the decathletes scored 40 points more in each event on day 1; the decathletes were also more consistent on day 1.

7 **a**

Distance (metres)	Cumulative frequency
< 56	0
< 58	7
< 60	18
< 62	28
< 64	38
< 66	45
< 68	46

8 **b** Median: about 60.8 m
Interquartile range: about 4.4 m (63.2 – 58.8)

Exercise 16.10

1 about 5 throws **2** about 22 throws (52 – 30)

3 **b** about 15 jumps (31 – 16)

End points

A2 **a** 0.16 – **b** 0.16 –

A3 **b** The women recorded more reaction times than men in the middle of the spread of times, while the men recorded more times than the women at the ends.

B1 **a**

Distance (metres)	Cumulative frequency
< 6.4	0
< 6.8	1
< 7.2	2
< 7.6	5
< 8.0	22
< 8.4	37
< 8.8	38

c i about 7.93 m **ii** about 0.45 m (8.17 – 7.72)

C1 **a** 0.8 m **b** 2.0 m **C2 a** 6.75 m (to 3 sf) **b** 7.89 m (to 3 sf)

D1 On average, the men jumped 1.14 m longer than the women; the women were much more closely matched than the men.

E1 **b i** about 8 jumps **ii** about 15 jumps (47 – 32)

SECTION 17

Starting points

A1 **a** 0.75, 75% **b** 0.625, 62.5% **c** 1.6, 160% **d** 1.25, 125%
e 1.2, 120% **f** 0.65, 65% **g** 0.25, 25% **h** 1.5, 150%
i 0.4735, 47.35% **j** 2.285..., 228.6% (1 dp) **k** 1.125, 112.5%
l 1.8, 180%

B1 **a** 325 miles **b** £300 **c** 2 marks **d** 2848
e 10 marks **f** 171 kg **g** £240.70 **h** 0.36 kg
i 17.5 pence **j** 16.6 metres **k** £1.71 **l** 1.8 cm
m £6.25 **n** 2.4 miles

C1 **a** £13.60 **b** 5.6 mm **c** 1540 grams **d** 20.43 pence
e i 50.7 mm **ii** 5.07 mm **f i** 9 pence **ii** £0.09
g i 1.4 tonnes **ii** 1400 kg

Exercise 17.1

1 50% **2** 400% **3** more **4** 8 **5** 50%

6 **a** 16 **b** 21 **7 a** 9

8 Oct 25% Nov 25% Dec 20% Jan 25% Feb 75% Mar 10%

9 **a** Dec **b** Jan **c** 62.5%

Exercise 17.2

1 **a** 44% **b** 65% **c** 29.17% **d** 46.20% **e** 80%
f 12.5% **g** 3.75% **h** 133.33% **i** 166.67% **j** 187.5%

2 **a** 69.10% **3** 14% **4 a** 170%

Thinking ahead

A less than a quarter **B** $\frac{15}{100}$ or $\frac{3}{20}$ **C** 345 ml

Exercise 17.3

1 a 110% **b** 484 grams

2 a 413 kg **b** 518.52 km **c** 5.49 metres **d** £37 800
 e £36.30 **f** 30 186 tonnes **g** 3 815 000 litres **h** 0.69 cm

3 206 037 278 **4** 26 grams

Exercise 17.4

1 a 311.6 kg **b** 303.68 km **c** 21.12 metres **d** £290 680

2 1466 kg **3 a** 1125 cars **4 a** 26 650 cars **b** 14 350 cars

5 7644.3 kg **6 a** £19.60 **b** £4.90

Thinking ahead

B £235 **C a** £14.69

Exercise 17.5

1 a £18.80 **b** £51.99 **c** £217.38 **d** £22.80 **e** 85 pence
 f £432.89 **g** £307.85 **h** £28.85 **i** £10.99

2 a £287.88 **b** £42.88

Exercise 17.6

1 £387.60 **2 a** £155 **b** £181.35 **c** £301.35

3 a £2612.50 **b** £112.50 **4** £89 979

Exercise 17.7

1 a £324 **b** £67.20 **c** £1350 **d** £10 200 **e** £90

2 a £5950 **b** £9450 **3** £231 **4** £66 440 000

Exercise 17.8

1 a £103.26 **b** £175.71 **c** £1217.61 **d** £1529.58
 e £1030.32 **f** £8967.60

2 a £2346.64 **b** £7346.64 **c i** £7346.6404

Exercise 17.9

1 a £115.32 **b** £29.78 **c** £63.82 **d** £56 **e** £158.94
 f £12.33 **g** £42.54 **h** £680.83 **i** £84.25

2 a £56.25 **b** £11.25 **3** £26 **4** £444

Exercise 17.10

1

Amount of loan	Total interest	Each instalment
£49.99	£11.50	£5.13
£220	£112.84	£13.87
£55.65	£13	£5.73
£1250	£1076.08	£64.62
£320.99	£276.33	£12.45
£850	£195.50	£18.13
£184.99	£94.88	£11.67
£89.95	£46.14	£5.67
£95.50	£48.98	£6.02
£1350	£1162.17	£69.79

2 a £470.17 **b** £26.12

End points

A1 25% **A2** 300% **A3** 28.13% **A4** 7.7%

B1 556.8 km **B2** 426 ml **C1** £52.45 **C2** 39 200

D1 The current rate of VAT is 17.5% (update as necessary).

D2 a £40.83 **b** £186.12 **E1** £221.27

F1 £115.20 **F2 a** £180 **b** £680 **G1 a** £129.89 **b** £323.19

SECTION 18

Starting points

A1 a $x = 3$ **b** $y = \bar{1}$ **C1 a** $^+90°$ **b** (0, 1)

F2 Q, S, T, U, V, Y, Z

Exercise 18.1

1 a i 0 **ii** 3 **b i** 1 **ii** 3

2 a a rotation
 b any two from: rotation, translation and reflection
 c A and F **d** N, V and Z **e i** C, X and R **ii** E, T and J

Exercise 18.2

1 a i triangle 8 **ii** triangle 1 **iii** triangle 3
 b i B **ii** $^+90°$
 c i a rotation of $^+90°$ about the point D
  ii a rotation of 180° about the point P
 d i BD **ii** HD or PD **e** triangle 7 **f** triangle 4
 g a rotation of $^-90°$ about the point F
 h a rotation of 180° about the point P and a reflection in AE
 i a reflection in GP

Exercise 18.3

1 a $\begin{pmatrix} 0 \\ 4 \end{pmatrix}$ **b** $(\bar{2}, \bar{1})$ **c** $y = \bar{1}$

2 a **i** **ii**

Pairs	Object	Mirror line	Image
C and E	C	$y = x$	E
	E	$y = x$	C
D and H	D	$y = 0$	H
	H	$y = 0$	D
F and G	F	$x = \bar{1}$	G
	G	$x = \bar{1}$	F

b **i** **ii**

Pairs	Object	Vector	Image
C and F	C	$\begin{pmatrix} \bar{4} \\ \bar{4} \end{pmatrix}$	F
	F	$\begin{pmatrix} 4 \\ 4 \end{pmatrix}$	C
D and G	D	$\begin{pmatrix} 2 \\ 2 \end{pmatrix}$	G
	G	$\begin{pmatrix} \bar{2} \\ \bar{2} \end{pmatrix}$	D
E and H	E	$\begin{pmatrix} 4 \\ 2 \end{pmatrix}$	H
	H	$\begin{pmatrix} \bar{4} \\ \bar{2} \end{pmatrix}$	E

c **i** **ii**

Pairs	Object	Rotation	Image
C and E	C	180°, (2, 2)	E
	E	180°, (2, 2)	C
D and H	D	$^-90°$, $(\bar{2}, 0)$	H
	H	$^+90°$, $(\bar{2}, 0)$	D
F and G	F	$^-90°$, $(\bar{1}, \bar{3})$	G
	G	$^+90°$, $(\bar{1}, \bar{3})$	F

3 a reflection in $y = -x$ and a rotation of $^+90°$ about $(3, \bar{3})$
 b J and B are in a different orientation
 c reflection in $y = 2$
  reflection in $x = 3$
  rotation of 180° about (3, 2)

4 a i **Image**

		K	L	M
Object	**K**	Reflection $x = 2$ Reflection $y = 3$ Rotation 180°, (2, 3)	(as shown)	Rotation $^-90°$, (0, 0)
	L	Translation $\begin{pmatrix} 0 \\ 6 \end{pmatrix}$ Rotation 180°, (2, 0) Reflection $y = 0$	Reflection $x = ^-2$ Reflection $y = ^-3$ Rotation 180°, (2, $^-3$)	Rotation $^-90°$, (3, $^-3$) Rotation $^+90°$, (2, $^-2$) Reflection $y = ^-x$
	M	(as shown)	Rotation $^+90°$, (3, $^-3$) Rotation $^-90°$, (2, $^-2$) Reflection $y = ^-x$	Reflection $x = 3$ Reflection $y = ^-2$ Rotation 180°, (3, $^-2$)

b i reflection in $y = x + 2$ **ii** reflection in $y = x - 2$

c **Image**

		C	E	F
Object	**C**	Reflection $y = x + 4$	Reflection $y = x$ Rotation 180°, (2, 2)	Reflection $y = ^-x$ Translation $\begin{pmatrix} ^-4 \\ ^-4 \end{pmatrix}$
	E	Reflection $y = x$ Rotation 180°, (2, 2)	Reflection $y = x + 4$	Rotation 180°, (0, 0)
	F	Reflection $y = ^-x$ Translation $\begin{pmatrix} 4 \\ 4 \end{pmatrix}$	Rotation 180°, (0, 0)	Reflection $y + x = ^-4$

Exercise 18.4

1 c rotation of $^+90°$ about (1, 1)
   d i rotation of $^+90°$ about (0, 1)   **ii** reflection in $y = x - 1$

Exercise 18.5

1 b G and H are in the same orientation but in different positions.

2 b J and K are exactly the same

3 2 and 3 are commutative
   1 and 4 are commutative

Exercise 18.6

1 b i rotation of $^+90°$ about (1, 1)
   ii rotation of 180° about (1, 2)
   iii reflection in $y = ^-x$

Exercise 18.7

1 b i translation $\begin{pmatrix} ^-2 \\ 2 \end{pmatrix}$
   ii rotation of 180° about (2, 0)   **iii** rotation of 180° about (3, 1)

2 a i reflection in $x = 5$ **ii** reflection in $y = x$
   iii rotation 180° about (4, 1)

Exercise 18.8

1 b B

c

Object	Image	SF	Centre
S	Y	2	(4, 8)
Y	S	$\frac{1}{2}$	(4, 8)
X	S	$\frac{1}{2}$	(8, 8)
X	U	$\frac{1}{2}$	(12, 8)

d T and M are in different orientations.
e i rotation of $^-90°$ about (8, 8)   **ii** enlargement SF $\frac{1}{2}$ centre (8, 12)
   iii rotation of 180° about (6, 8)

Exercise 18.9

2 b i rotation of $^-90°$ about (4, 1)
   ii translation $\begin{pmatrix} 4 \\ 2 \end{pmatrix}$ or rotation of 180° about (5, 4)
   iii rotation of $^+90°$ about (2, 5)
c i enlargement SF 2 centre ($^-1$, $^-2$)   **ii** enlargement SF 2 centre ($^-5$, $^-4$)

3 a enlargement SF $\frac{1}{2}$ centre ($^-1$, 0)
   enlargement SF $\frac{1}{2}$ centre ($^-3$, $^-2$)

5 b i (0, 0)   **ii** ($^-0.5$, $^-0.5$)   **c ii** ($^-1$, $^-1$)
   d i enlargement SF $\frac{1}{4}$ centre ($^-1$, $^-1$)
   ii enlargement SF $\frac{1}{2}$ centre ($^-3$, $^-3$)

End points

A1 a C and D   **b** B, C and D   **c** B, C and D

A2 c i rotation of 180° about (0, 0)   **ii** reflection in $x = 0$
   iii translation of $\begin{pmatrix} 2 \\ 2 \end{pmatrix}$
   d i reflection in $y = 0$ **ii** rotation of 180° about (1, $^-1$)

B1 b i rotation of 180° about (0, $^-1$)   **ii** rotation of $^+90°$ about (0, 0)
   iii translation of $\begin{pmatrix} 0 \\ ^-4 \end{pmatrix}$
   c i translation of $\begin{pmatrix} 0 \\ ^-4 \end{pmatrix}$
   ii reflection in $y = ^-3$ **iii** rotation of 180° about (1, 0)
   d i rotation of $^-90°$ about (1, $^-1$)   **ii** rotation of 180° about (0, $^-3$)
   iii rotation of 180° about (0, $^-1$)

SKILLS BREAK 3A

1 a 22 40 hours   **b** 02 20 hours   **2** 3 h 40 min

3 a 892 crew   **b** 1497 people   **4** about 35.6 people/boat

5 £293 190   **6** £295 800   **7** 800 ft

8 a 14 knots   **b** 3 h 19 min   **c** 1 h 29 min

9 a $C = \dfrac{5(F - 32)}{9}$ **b** $^-2.2$ °C   **10 a** 1170   **b** 3545

11 a 0.61   **b** 0.43   **c** 0.25   **12** 38% (2 sf)   **13** 70 000 tons

14 £3 × 10^7 **15** 1°   **16** 200.97 ft   **17** 58°: alternate angles

18 14°: angles in a triangle

19 a 2 000 000   **b** 2 180 000   **c** 2 180 000   **d** 2 179 600

20 11 people

SKILLS BREAK 3B

1 3.53 metres (to nearest cm)   **2** 5.88 × 10^{21}

3 a 40 080 km   **b** 40 100   **4** 12 756 km

5 a 0.2 m   **b** 3600 mm   **c** 7.9 cm   **6** 1830 days   **7** 0.61 m

8 308 m² (to nearest m²)   **9** approximately 188 m³

10 a 14.8 mph   **b** 23.9 km/h   **11** about 18 minutes

12 5.5 × 10^3 **13** 2230 cm³ (to 3sf)

14 a 20.2 cm (to 3sf)   **b** 670 000 (to 3sf)   **c** 677 kg (3sf)

15 1.75 m   **16** 1:349

17 a i 107 inches   **ii** 271.8 cm   **iii** 0.27 m   **b i** 1:2278   **ii** 1:569

18 a 192 digits   **b** 2274 digits   **c** 8 digits/min   **19** 56 days

20 a about 51° **b** 242 m **c i** 3.1 m/s **ii** about 11 km/h

21 just under 1 minute (54 seconds)

22 a 452 cm³ (nearest cm³) **b** 2.21 m³

23 a 4 cans **b** 9 cans **c** 576 cans **24** 6.8 years

25 a 68 000 salamis (to 3sf) **b** 2 250 000 rotations

26 Once

SECTION 19

Starting points
A1 0.23 **A2 a** 0.77 **b** 0.16 **c** 0.55 **d** 0.44

B1 $\frac{1}{6}$ **B2** $\frac{1}{3}$ **B3 b** $\frac{1}{4}$

Thinking ahead
A a $\frac{5}{9}$ **b** $\frac{1}{9}$ **c** $\frac{4}{9}$ **d** $\frac{3}{9} = \frac{1}{3}$

Exercise 19.1
1 a 0.11 **b** 0.50 (to 2 dp)

2 0.89 (to 2 dp) **3 a** 8 red **b** 2 blue **c** 10 yellow

4 a 0.17
b The relative frequency only gives the probability, not the number.

Exercise 19.2
1 d 1 **2 b** A usually beats B: probability about 0.7

3 b B usually beats C: probability about 0.7

4 c C usually beats A: unexpected
Probability of A winning is about 0.4.

5 Probabilities: A wins, about 0.33; B wins, about 0.37; C wins, about 0.30

Exercise 19.3
1 0.4: probabilities at a roundabout must total 1

3 a 0.11 (to 2 dp) **b** 0.09 **c** 0.15 **d** 0.17

4 a 0.12 **b** 0.10 **c** 0.22

5 a 195 **b** 147 **c** 86 **d** 53 **e** 39 **f** 75 or 76

Exercise 19.4
1 a A **b** C **c** B **d** either A (if data on ages known) or B **e** D
f B **g** A **h** B or D **i** A **j** D

2 a Other factors may affect the probability – such as climate, hardship, war etc.

3 method **c**

4 a sample too small **b** biased to meat eaters
c biased to vegetarians (possibly !)
d sample too small, liable to be similar to each other
e difficulty understanding and explaining, some milk only

5 a We all know someone who does not play soccer.
b answers such as 'asked in a soccer changing room', 'asked only young males'

6 The probability is that the relative frequency will approach the theoretical value. There is no certainty however.

Exercise 19.5
1 a $\frac{4}{16}$ **b** $\frac{7}{16}$ **c** $\frac{11}{16}$ **3 a** $\frac{5}{16}$ **b** $\frac{7}{16}$

4 b $\frac{10}{16}$ **c** Two have both earrings and moustaches.

5 a $\frac{4}{16}$ **b** $\frac{4}{16}$ **c** $\frac{6}{16}$

Exercise 19.6
1 b No: some necklace wearers also have fair hair.

2 a $\frac{11}{16}$ **b** $\frac{5}{16}$ **c** $\frac{5}{16}$ **d** $\frac{2}{16}$ **e** $\frac{4}{16}$

3 a $\frac{7}{16}$ **b** $\frac{12}{16}$ **c** $\frac{11}{16}$ **d** $\frac{9}{16}$

4 a Can't add: some girls may play both.
b Can add: girls cannot be boys.
c Can add: drivers are never passengers.
d Can't add: some bus drivers could also be tall women.
e Can't add: some dancers could also be mechanics.

Thinking ahead
A a 0.12 **b** 0.32 **c** 0.47 **d** 0.53 **e** 0.13

Exercise 19.7
1 a 0.15 **b** 0.19 **c** 0.53 **2** 0.44

3 a The sets do not overlap. **b** 0.55 **c** 0.45

End points
A1 a 0.17 (to 2 dp) **b** 0.07 **A2** 0.75

B1 b 0.42: below an even chance

C1 a theoretical probability: probably equal numbers of odd and even pages
b relative frequency: from records
c relative frequency: from an experiment

D1 a 0.36 (to 2 dp) **b** A tree can't be an oak and a lime at the same time.

D2 The sets may overlap – an apple tree may have both canker and deer damage

SECTION 20

Starting points
A1 a 34 > 12 **b** 2 < 15 **c** ⁻12 > ⁻56 **d** 5 > ⁻2
e ⁻2 < 0 **f** ⁻17 < ⁻5

A2 a 56 > 28 > 9 > 5 > ⁻4 > ⁻24 > ⁻30 **b** ⁻30 < ⁻24 < ⁻4 < 5 < 9 < 28 < 56

A3 12, 5, 6.2 **A4 a** ⁻5, ⁻4, ⁻3, ⁻2, ⁻1, 0, 1, 2 **b** ⁻2, ⁻3, ⁻4

A5 ⁻2 and ⁻1 are not included and there are no other integers between ⁻1 and ⁻2.

Exercise 20.1
1 45 ≤ T ≤ 80

2 a 17 ≤ p ≤ 52 **b** 10 < p < 64 or 11 ≤ p ≤ 63
c 4 < p < 164 or 5 ≤ p ≤ 163

3 a 5 ≤ a ≤ 65 **b** 5 < a ≤ 65
c a child who is 5 can use Fermatol but not Hypaticain

4 ⁻25 < T < ⁻18

Exercise 20.2
1 B and C **2** 2, 3, 4 **3** ⁻1, 0, 1, 2, 3

4 a 5, 6, 7, 8, 9 **b** ⁻2, ⁻1, 0, 1, 2, 3 **c** 70, 69, 68
d ⁻4, ⁻5, ⁻6, ⁻7, ⁻8, ⁻9, ⁻10, ⁻11 **e** ⁻3, ⁻2, ⁻1, 0, 1, 2, 3, 4, 5, 6
f 2164, 2165, 2166

5 ⁻4 < h < 6 **7 a** 6, 7 **b** 13, 14 **c** ⁻2, ⁻1, 0, 1, 2, 3, 4

8 ⁻3 ≤ f < 7

Exercise 20.3
1 a A and E **b** B only

Exercise 20.4
2 a x < 7 **b** 5 < y < 12 **c** ⁻1 < x < 9

4 ⁻2 < x < 6 and 1 < y < 5

Exercise 20.5
2 diagonal line from bottom left to top right **3** ≤

4 a $\frac{10}{100} = \frac{1}{10}$ **b** $\frac{45}{100} = \frac{9}{20}$ **c** $\frac{55}{100} = \frac{11}{20}$ **5 e** y > x

8 The diagonal line separating the regions moves to the right.

10 b P (⁻80, 30), Q (10, 50)
c i At P 2b – 3a is 300. **ii** At Q 2b – 3a is 70.
d 2b – 3a > 180 is true on the left-hand side of the line.

Exercise 20.6
1 a x > 4 **b** x ≤ 4 **c** x ≥ ⁻4 **d** x ≥ 2.4 **e** x ≤ 0.5
f x < 5 **g** x ≥ 15 **h** ⁻8 < x < 8

2 a y < 7 **b** s ≤ 8 **c** p ≥ 6 **d** b > 3.5 **e** a ≤ ⁻8
f x > 8 **g** t ≥ 4 **h** a ≥ 7 **i** d < ⁻5 **j** a ≤ ⁻13

3 a a ≥ 11 **b** k < ⁻2 **c** x > ⁻9 **d** n ≥ 3.5 **e** q < ⁻0.8
f k > 2 **g** h < ⁻2 **h** c < 2.5

End points
A1 a ⁻1 **b** ⁻5, ⁻4, ⁻3, ⁻2, ⁻1, 0, 1, 2, 3 **c** 7, 6, 5, 4 **d** ⁻56, ⁻57, ⁻58, ⁻59
e ⁻76, ⁻75, ⁻74, ⁻73, ⁻72 **f** ⁻2, ⁻1, 0 1, 2, 3

B4 a 2 < x < 7 **b** x > 4 and y < 2

C1 a x ≤ 6 **b** f > 3 **c** a ≥ 12 **d** k > ⁻5 **e** s ≤ 4 **f** d > 1.5

SECTION 21

Starting points

A1 **a** cube **b** sphere **c** cylinder **d** cuboid **e** cylinder

B1 **a** **i** A, C, F **ii** B, D, E

b A: cuboid (rectangular prism)
B: tetrahedron (triangular pyramid)
C: cylinder (circular prism)
D: pentagonal pyramid
E: octagonal pyramid
F: hexagonal prism

C1

	G	H
a	5	7
b	8	12
c	5	7

D1 $64 \, cm^2$ **D2** $85.5 \, cm^2$

D3 **a** about $4 \, cm^3$ **b** about 110 to $270 \, cm^3$ for an average size apple

D4 about $3 \, m^3$ **D5** $13.5 \, cm^3$

Exercise 21.1

1 **a** B and C **b** 1 **c** A

6

	Faces	Edges	Vertices
P	5	9	6
Q	6	12	8
R	7	15	10
S	8	18	12

7 102, 300, 200 **8** $n + 2$, $3n$, $2n$

9 **a** **i** C and D **ii** A and B

b A octagonal pyramid, B square pyramid, C pentagonal prism, D triangular prism

10 **b** X: 4 Y: 2 Z: 1 **11** 6

Exercise 21.2

1

	A	B	C	D
a	hexagon	right-angled triangle	isosceles triangle	circle
b	$11.16 \, cm^2$	$4.86 \, cm^2$	$5.4 \, cm^2$	$9.62 \, cm^2$
c	$106 \, cm^3$	$39 \, cm^3$	$46 \, cm^3$	$82 \, cm^3$

2 **b** $74.4 \, cm^3$ **3** **a** $87.5 \, cm^3$ **b** $2.2 \, cm$

4 **a** $4 \times 6.4 \times 2.5 = 63 \, cm^3$ **b** 6 **c** $103.2 \, cm^2$
f 4 cm by 4 cm by 4 cm

5 to 2 dp, 4.64 cm by 4.64 cm by 4.64 cm

6 **a** $8 \times 12 \times 10 = 960 \, cm^3$ **b** about £600 **7** about 7 cm

Exercise 21.3

1 16.5 cm **3** **c** $804.2 \, cm^3$ to 1 dp (radius, 8 cm; height, 4 cm)

4 For a sum of x, $h = \frac{1}{3}x$ and $r = \frac{2}{3}x$ gives maximum volume

Exercise 21.4

1 **a** $17.0 \, m^3$ **b** $12.7 \, m^3$ **c** 15.3 or 15.2 tonnes

2 **a** $27.6 \, m^3$ **b** **i** 395 **ii** £2022.40

3 **a** $46.25 \, m^2$ **b** $555 \, m^3$ **c** $435 \, m^3$ **d** $435 \, cm^3$

Exercise 21.5

1 **a** $300 \, cm^3$ **b** 75 millilitres **c** 170 grams

2 about 100 ml

3 The capacity of B is closest to 550 ml, but C would help to avoid spillage on opening.

4 1.37 litres **5** **a** $21\,714\,688.4 \, cm^3$ **b** 21 714.7 litres

6

	Volume	Density
Cheddar:	$217.1 \, cm^3$	$1.1 \, g/cm^3$
Brie:	$649.3 \, cm^3$	$1.0 \, g/cm^3$

7 A: $1500 \, cm^3$ B: $720 \, cm^3$ C: $990 \, cm^3$ D: $490 \, cm^3$ E: $440 \, cm^3$

8 P: Crackers Q: Fruit and Fibre R: Tea Bags S: Trichoc
T: Drinking Chocolate

Exercise 21.6

1 **a** length **b** volume **c** area **2** **a** $\frac{1}{2}lz(x + y)$

3 **a** $\pi(a + b)$ **b** πab

4 **a** area **b** length **c** length **d** volume **e** volume **f** area

5 xy and $y(x - z)$ represent areas but xyz represents a volume. An area added to a volume is not a length, area or volume.

End points

A1 4 **A2** 8 faces, 18 edges, 12 vertices **B1** $110 \, cm^3$

C1 **a** $6\,433\,982 \, cm^3$ **b** 6434 litres **C2** $19.3 \, g/cm^3$

D1 **a** $\pi r(l + r)$ **b** $\frac{1}{3}\pi r^2 h$

SECTION 22

Starting points

A1 **a** $c^2 + 3c - 28$ **b** $a^2 + 8a + 15$ **c** $y^2 - 3y - 40$
d $h^2 - 5h - 6$ **e** $t^2 - 25$ **f** $y^2 - 6y + 9$
g $p^2 + 10p + 25$ **h** $k^2 - 11k + 30$

B1 **a** $(n + 5)(n - 1)$ **b** $(y - 5)(y + 2)$ **c** $(k - 6)(k - 1)$
d $(h + 5)(h + 4)$ **e** $(w - 5)(w - 4)$ **f** $(v + 7)(v - 4)$
g $(d - 5)(d - 2)$ **h** $(a + 13)(a - 1)$

B2 **a** $(p + 3)(p + 3)$ **b** $(m - 5)(m - 5)$
c $(s - 2)(s - 2)$ **d** $(g + 4)(g + 4)$

Exercise 22.1

1 **a** $n = {}^-14$ or $n = 1$ **b** $n = 7$ or $n = {}^-2$ **c** $n = 14$ or $n = {}^-1$
d $b = {}^-5$ or $b = 3$ **e** $b = {}^-15$ or $b = 1$ **f** $b = 5$ or $b = {}^-3$
g $a = {}^-10$ or $a = 3$ **h** $a = {}^-10$ or $a = {}^-3$ **i** $a = {}^-6$ or $a = 5$
j $x = {}^-5$ or $x = 1$ **k** $x = {}^-5$ or $x = {}^-1$ **l** $x = 5$ or $x = 1$
m $y = 5$ or $y = 3$ **n** $y = 15$ or $y = 1$ **o** $y = 15$ or $y = {}^-1$
p $k = {}^-9$ or $k = 7$ **q** $k = 9$ or $k = 7$ **r** $k = {}^-63$ or $k = 1$

2 **a** $d^2 + 3d - 10 = 0$ with factors $(d - 2)$, $(d + 5)$; $d = 2$ or $d = {}^-5$
b $d^2 - 5d - 6 = 0$ with factors $(d + 1)$, $(d - 6)$; $d = {}^-1$ or $d = 6$
c $d^2 + 3d - 40 = 0$ with factors $(d + 8)$, $(d - 5)$; $d = {}^-8$ or $d = 5$
d $d^2 - 8d - 33 = 0$ with factors $(d - 11)$, $(d + 3)$; $d = 11$ or $d = {}^-3$
e $d^2 - 14d + 33 = 0$ with factors $(d - 3)$, $(d - 11)$; $d = 3$ or $d = 11$

3 **a** $(x - 4)(x - 4)$

4 **a** $c = {}^-6$ or $c = 1$ **b** $y = {}^-7$ or $y = 1$ **c** $p = 3$
d $x = 5$ or $x = {}^-2$ **e** $w = 2$ **f** $b = 1$ or $b = 14$
g $k = 10$ or $k = {}^-7$ **h** $v = {}^-3$ **i** $t = 7$ or $t = {}^-4$
j $y = 9$ or $y = {}^-2$ **k** $g = {}^-4$ **l** $a = 3$ or $a = {}^-7$
m $p = 4$ or $p = {}^-1$ **n** $w = 6$ or $w = {}^-4$ **o** $u = {}^-5$ or $u = {}^-2$

Exercise 22.2

1 **a** $y = 1$ or $y = {}^-3$ **b** $k = {}^-4$ or $k = 2$ **c** $n = {}^-4$ or $n = {}^-3$
d $v = {}^-2$ **e** $p = 4$ or $p = {}^-1$ **f** $a = 4$ or $a = {}^-1$
g $a = 1$ or $a = {}^-4$ **h** $b = 3$ or $b = {}^-2$ **i** $b = 2$ or $b = {}^-3$

2 **a** **i** and **ii**
c **i** $p = 4$ or $p = {}^-7$ **ii** $p = 4$ or $p = {}^-2$
iii $p = 1$ or $p = {}^-4$ **iv** $p = 8$ or $p = 1$

3 **a** **i** $x = 2$ or $x = {}^-2$ **ii** $x = 5$ or $x = {}^-5$
iii $x = 6$ or $x = {}^-6$ **iv** $x = 10$ or $x = {}^-10$
b $x^2 - 9 = 0$

4 **a** $x = {}^-3$ or $x = {}^-1$ **b** $x = {}^-3$ or $x = 1$ **c** $x = 4$ or $x = {}^-2$
d $x = {}^-1$ **e** $x = {}^-2$ or $x = 1$ **f** $x = 2$ or $x = {}^-1$

Exercise 22.3

7 **a** $x = 0$ **b** $x = {}^-1$ **c** $x = 0$ **d** $x = {}^-1.5$

8 **b** symmetry in the values of y

10 **d** $({}^-4, 0)$ and $(1, 0)$ **11** **c** $({}^-1, 0)$ and $(4, 0)$

13 **c** $({}^-4, 0)$ and $(2, 0)$

Exercise 22.4

1 **a** $y = 1$ **c** $x = 2.2$ or $x = {}^-7.2$ **3** **b** $x = 3.4$ **c** less than ${}^-8$

4 **a** $x = 3$ or $x = 2$ **ii** $x = 0.4$ or $x = 4.6$ **d** $x = {}^-0.7$ or $x = 5.7$

5 **a** **i** $x = {}^-1$ or $x = 5$ **ii** $x = {}^-2.5$ or $x = 6.5$ **b** $x = 2$

6 **b** $x = 1$ or $x = 3$ **7** **c** $x = 4$ or $x = 1$ **8** **b** $x = 4$ or $x = {}^-1$

Exercise 22.5

1 **b** $x = {}^-1.6$ **2** **b** $x = 1.3$ **4** **c** $x = 0.7$ **d** $x = 0.7$

Exercise 22.6

1 $x = 2.6$ **2** $x = 3.4$ **3** $x = 2.7$

End points

B1   **a** $x = 2$ or $x = ^-5$ **b** $x = ^-5$ or $x = ^-4$ **c** $x = 8$ or $x = 2$
    d $x = 3$

C1   **a** $x^2 + 5x - 24 = 0$ **b** $p^2 - 3p - 2 = 0$ **c** $c^2 - 5c + 2 = 0$
    d $y^2 - 6y - 2 = 0$

D1   **a** $v = 4$ or $v = ^-1$ **b** $b = 2$ **c** $p = ^-3$ or $p = ^-2$
    d $w = ^-7$ or $w = 7$

H1 $x = 1$ or $x = ^-5$ **H2** $x = ^-6.4$ or $x = 2.4$ **H3** $x^2 + 4x - 5 = ^-8$

SECTION 23

Starting points

D1   **a**   matches with Q   **b**   matches with R   **c**   matches with P

Exercise 23.1

1   **a**   Different people are likely to have different ideas of what is meant by 'early' and 'late'.

2   **a**   The question leads people into giving the answer 'Yes'.

3   **a**   The question could be answered in several different ways, e.g. 'on the sofa', 'in Australia', etc.

4   **a**   Question 1 is a leading question; it leads people into giving the answer 'Yes'.
Question 2 is not clear; different people are likely to have different ideas of what is meant by 'frequent'.
Question 3 is ambiguous; the courts could be tennis, or squash, or badminton, etc.
Question 4 has a poor list of choices, i.e. there is no box to tick to answer £2.

Exercise 23.3

1   **c**   negative   **2**   **c**   positive

Exercise 23.4

1   moderate negative correlation: i.e., people with higher incomes give a smaller percentage of their income to charity than people with lower incomes.

2   strong negative correlation: i.e., house prices decrease the further towns are away from London.

3   moderate positive correlation: i.e. the greater the pressure in the eye, the higher the refractive power of the lens.

Exercise 23.5

1   **a**   about 49 miles   **b**   about 79 miles

2   **a**   about £73 000   **b**   about £85 000

3   **a**   about 14 miles   **b**   about £110 000

5   **b**   Moderate positive correlation: i.e., the longer the pregnancy, the heavier the baby is.
    c   **i**   about 273 days   **ii**   about 3.9 kg

6   No: doctors do not allow a pregnancy to continue after about 41 weeks, because of the risk to the mother's health.

Exercise 23.6

3   A: The water wastage in 1997 is half the wastage in 1995, but the diagram gives the impression the wastage is a quarter because the height *and* the width of the 1995 water drop have been halved.
    B: The vertical axis does not start at 0, which gives the impression that the water wastage of Mercia and Saxony is about 3 to 4 times that of Wyvern.

End points

A1   **a**   Question 1 is not clear; different people are likely to have different ideas of what is meant by 'local'.
Question 2 is ambiguous; it could refer to the *amount* of traffic, or the *type* of traffic, etc.
Question 3 is leading; it leads people into giving the answer 'Yes'.

C1   **d**   Strong negative correlation: i.e. the larger the size of engine, the lower the number of miles to the gallon.

D1   **a**   about 32 mpg   **b**   about 1.9 litres

D2   **a**   about 18 mpg   **b**   about 4.7 litres

E1   A: the vertical axis does not start at 0 which gives the impression that the amount of gas supplied by Flame is about 6 times that of Western and 2.5 times that of GasOil.
    B: the amount of gas supplied in 1997 is 2.5 times the amount supplied in 1996 but the diagram gives the impression it is much more than this because the height and the width of the 1996 flame have been increased 2.5 times.

SECTION 24

Starting points

A1   **a**   **i**   060°   **ii**   240°   **iii**   240°   **b**   about 205°   **c**   20 km

B1   **a**   **i**   90°   **ii**   20 km   **iii**   30 km   **b**   36.1 km

C1   56°   **C2**   **a**   26 km   **b**   15 km

Exercise 24.1

1   **a**   trapezium   **b**   **i**   1 m   **ii**   3.16 m   **c**   23.2 m   **d**   25.5 m^2
    e   £1.22 with some left over or £1.44 for 3 boxes

2   **a**   isosceles   **b**   **i**   72°   **ii**   54°   **c**   54°   **d**   **ii**   1.5 m
    e   **i**   2.55 m   **ii**   2.06 m   **f**   3.10 m^2 **g**   15.5 m^2 **h**   £15.20

3   **a**   5.83 m   **b**   A

Exercise 24.2

1

	a	b	Know	Find
$p = 38.21°$	Trig	two sides	an angle
$q = 3.64$ cm	Trig	a side and an angle	a side
$r = 8.27$ cm	Pyth	two sides	a side
$s = 5.07$ cm	Trig	a side and an angle	a side
$t = 4.52$ cm	Pyth	two sides	a side
$u = 46.86°$	Trig	two sides	an angle

Exercise 24.3

1   **a**   6.30 cm   **b**   9.85 cm   **c**   31.0 cm^2 **d**   25.9 cm

2   **a**   **i**   30°   **ii**   6.93 cm   **b**   **i**   26.6°   **ii**   8.94 cm
    c   23.9 cm   **d**   29.9 cm^2

3   **a**   **i**   9.80 cm (or 9.79 cm)   **ii**   10.6 cm
    b   **i**   24.1°   **ii**   22.2°
    c   **i**   The lengths increase.   **ii**   The angles decrease in size.

Exercise 24.4

1   **a**   **i**   14.60 m   **ii**   10.95 m   **b**   **i**   7.06 m   **ii**   26.22 m
    c   **i**   21.66 m   **ii**   37.16 m   **iii**   43.01 m

Exercise 24.5

1   **b**   252°   **c**   **i**   278°   **ii**   098°   **d**   9.4 km

2   **b**   302°   **d**   **i**   90°   **ii**   277 km   **e**   **i**   41°   **ii**   073°

3   **a**   **i**   178 km   **ii**   111.3 km   **b**   32°   **c**   **i**   95 km   **ii**   153 km
    d   83 km

Exercise 24.6

1   **a**   **i**   2 km   **ii**   3 km   **b**   **i**   3.61 km   **ii**   056°
    c   **i**   3 km   **ii**   3 km   **d**   **i**   4.24 km   **ii**   135°

2   **b**   **i**   140°   **ii**   090°   **iii**   180°   **c**   **i**   59.75 km   **ii**   50.14 km

3   **a**   **i**   14.44 km   **ii**   19.17 km   **b**   37.17 km
    c   **i**   39.88 km   **ii**   159°   **d**   339°

4   **b**   **i**   025°   **ii**   18.79 km

Exercise 24.7

1   **a**   40.2°   **b**   2.785 m   **c**   3.819 m   **d**   3.009 m
    e   5.795 m (or 5.794 m)

2   **a**   2.626 m   **b**   1.839 m   **c**   4.288 m   **d**   55.00° (or 54.99°)
    e   47°   **f**   1.401 m

End points

A1   A   19.7 cm^2, 19.5 cm   B   6.0 cm^2 11.6 cm

B1   **a**   **i**   38°   **ii**   256 m   **b**   **i**   93 m   **ii**   50.8°

C1   **a**   27°   **b**   **i**   15.1 km   **ii**   7.7 km   **iii**   22.7 km
    c   27.3 km   **d**   **i**   56°   **ii**   236°

SKILLS BREAK 4A

1 UK   **2 a** 2.69 m   **b** 4.18 m   **3** November   **4** 73 minutes

5 no   **6** 9 minutes   **7** 160 km/h   **8** 17:27

9 a 13:57   **b** Calais-Frethun and Paris   **10** 11:43   **11** 09:40

12 a 13:50   **b** 18:34   **13** London

14 a 1 140 000 m³   **b** 1.14 × 10⁶ m³

15 a 5 490 000 m³ (to 3 sf)   **b** 68.6 %

16 a 0.4 m   **b** 3.78 m   **c** 2 240 000 m³   **17 a** 31 250   **b** 35 715

18 516 minutes   **19** July   **20** 23 383 coaches

22 a 1.6 × 10⁵   **b** 23 513   **23** 30 077 lorries

24 December, 5.3 × 10⁶ people   **25** 35 seats

27 50 seats (53 if folding seats are included)

28 a 140 km/h   **b** 115 km/h

29 105 : 292 (approximately 7 : 20 ≈ 1 : 2.8)   **30** 0.8 %

31 19.0 minutes   **32 a** 6 %   **b** 18 %

SKILLS BREAK 4B

1 £9.59 to nearest penny   **2** £49.41   **3 a** 56 tiles   **b** £18.73

4 a 6 widths   **b** 2 rolls   **c** £20.97

5 a They do not tessellate.   **b** 28p   **6 b** 1120 tiles   **c** 1176 tiles

7 a 30.1 m² (to 3 sf)   **b** 1 tin of 5 litres and 1 tin of $2\frac{1}{2}$ litres

8 a Hexagon   **b** 120°   **c** 120° divides exactly into 360°   **d** 10 cm

9 a Neither dimension is an exact multiple of the tile size.
b 198 tiles (if no spares)   **c** £306.90 + £17.89 + £7.69 = £332.48

10 about 3.4 metres wide by 2.2 metres high

11 the $2\frac{1}{2}$ litre tin, which is £3.38 per litre

12 a 4.11 m by 3.60 m   **b** £43.47   **13** £7.45

14 Forret tiles are cheaper since only 160, rather than 170 tiles, need to be bought.

15 a octagon   **b** 135°   **c** 9.6 cm by 9.6 cm (to 1 dp)

17 a £16.59   **b** £2.90

IN FOCUS 1

1 B, C, D, E, H

2 a 6 × ⁻3 = ⁻18   **b** ⁻4 × ⁻2 = 8   **c** ⁻14 ÷ 7 = ⁻2   **d** ⁻18 ÷ 6 = ⁻3
e ⁻5 × ⁻4 = ⁻20   **f** ⁻5 × ⁻7 = 35   **g** 10 ÷ ⁻2 = ⁻5   **h** 8 × ⁻3 = ⁻24
i ⁻15 ÷ ⁻3 = 5   **j** ⁻4 × 7 = ⁻28   **k** ⁻16 ÷ ⁻2 = 8   **l** ⁻36 ÷ 9 = ⁻4

3 a 8.54   **b** 9.71   **c** 80.40   **d** 3.62

4 a 512   **b** 19.683   **c** 0.125   **d** ⁻64   **e** ⁻5.832
f ⁻0.027   **g** 30   **h** 9   **i** ⁻1   **j** ⁻1.2

5 a 0.5   **b** 0.1   **c** 2.5   **d** 1.6   **e** 3   **f** 6
g 100   **h** 0.2   **i** 0.083   **j** 4.5   **k** 0.09   **l** 3.6

6 a $\frac{3}{2}$ **b** $\frac{5}{4}$ **c** $\frac{6}{11}$ **d** $\frac{8}{13}$ **e** $\frac{3}{4}$ **f** $\frac{5}{12}$ **g** $\frac{5}{7}$ **h** $\frac{3}{5}$

7

5^{-3}	5^{-2}	5^{-1}	5^{0}	5^{1}	5^{2}	5^{3}
$\frac{1}{125}$	$\frac{1}{12}$	$\frac{1}{5}$	1	5	25	125

8

6^{-3}	6^{-2}	6^{-1}	6^{0}	6^{1}	6^{2}	6^{3}
$\frac{1}{216}$	$\frac{1}{36}$	$\frac{1}{6}$	1	6	36	216

9 $7^{0} = 1$

10 a $\frac{1}{4}$ **b** $\frac{1}{8}$ **c** $\frac{1}{9}$ **d** $\frac{1}{36}$ **e** $\frac{1}{1000}$ **f** $\frac{1}{10\,000}$
g 1   **h** $\frac{1}{49}$ **i** $\frac{1}{64}$ **j** $\frac{1}{64}$ **k** $\frac{1}{81}$ **l** $\frac{10}{10}$

11 a 33   **b** 12.5   **c** 15.75   **d** 0.027   **e** 104   **f** 180
g 72.9   **h** 6200

12 a 0.2   **b** 0.25   **c** 0.125   **d** 0.01   **e** 0.015 625   **f** 0.1
g 0.015 625   **h** 0.008   **i** 0.001   **j** 0.01   **k** 0.027   **l** 0.000 01

13 a 6.17 × 10⁶   **b** 9.2 × 10¹⁰   **c** 3.07 × 10⁵
d 2.5 × 10⁻⁵   **e** 2.603 × 10⁻⁶   **f** 1 × 10⁻⁵

14 a 450 000 000   **b** 3 606 000 000 000   **c** 0.000 000 001 24
d 70 000 000   **e** 0.000 000 000 051   **f** 0.000 006 104 7

15 a 1.305 × 10¹¹   **b** 1.2384 × 10⁻³   **c** 8.7 × 10⁻⁸   **d** 8.55 × 10¹⁰
e 1.904 × 10⁷   **f** 7.3 × 10⁻¹⁴   **g** 3.47 × 10¹⁵   **h** 4.1 × 10⁹

16 a 4⁻⁴   **b** 3⁶   **c** 5⁴   **d** 2⁸   **e** 5⁷   **f** 7⁻⁶   **g** 4⁻⁹   **h** 6⁵

17 a 3⁸ × 3⁻² = 3⁶   **b** 6⁵ ÷ 6³ = 6²   **c** 2⁻⁴ ÷ 2³ = 2⁻⁷
d 8⁵ × 8⁻³ = 8²   **e** 3⁻² ÷ 3⁻⁷ = 3⁵   **f** 7⁻⁵ × 7⁻³ = 7⁻⁸

18 a 2 × 10³   **b** 4 × 10⁵   **c** 7 × 10⁻⁸   **d** 5 × 10⁻⁷

19 a $\frac{11}{15}$ **b** $1\frac{7}{30}$ **c** $1\frac{7}{12}$ **d** $\frac{1}{15}$ **e** $\frac{7}{20}$ **f** $\frac{1}{2}$
g $4\frac{5}{6}$ **h** $2\frac{1}{2}$ **i** $4\frac{3}{10}$ **j** $\frac{2}{15}$

20 a $\frac{2}{15}$ **b** $\frac{1}{4}$ **c** $\frac{1}{3}$ **d** $\frac{8}{15}$ **e** $\frac{2}{5}$ **f** $1\frac{1}{9}$
g $\frac{18}{25}$ **h** $1\frac{7}{18}$ **i** $4\frac{1}{2}$ **j** $\frac{3}{10}$ **k** $1\frac{9}{10}$ **l** $3\frac{4}{5}$

21 a $2\frac{1}{4}$ **b** $6\frac{2}{3}$ **c** 4   **d** 24   **e** 16   **f** $7\frac{1}{2}$
g $3\frac{1}{3}$ **h** 38   **i** $7\frac{1}{5}$ **j** 3   **k** 20   **l** $6\frac{2}{5}$

22 a 36   **b** 24   **c** 240   **d** 6300   **e** 700

23 a 9   **b** 14   **c** 15   **d** 12   **e** 7

IN FOCUS 2

1

Sequence W	Sequence X	Sequence Y
b $m = 2n + 1$	$m = 4n$	$m = 12n - 8$
d 21 matches	40 matches	112 matches

2 a 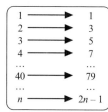   **b**

c   **d**

3 a $n \rightarrow 4n^2$

4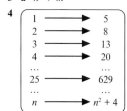

5 A $3n - 2$ 88   B n^2 900
C $6n + 1$ 181   D $3n^2$ 5400
E $5n + 2$ 152   F $4n - 2$ 118
G $n^2 + 10$ 910   H $8n + 1$ 241

6 a $5p + 10$ **b** $8n + 24$ **c** $4c + 20$ **d** $6r + 2$
e $35 + 5x$ **f** $14t - 21$ **g** $3 - 15t$ **h** $6m - 12$
i $100k + 20$ **j** $32 - 8z$ **k** $50 - 10t$ **l** $4a + 4b$
m $6g + 3h$ **n** $5x - 5y$ **o** $21c - 14d$

IN FOCUS 3

1 a $b = 47°$ $c = 133°$ $d = 47°$ $e = 133°$
b $b = 51.5°$ $c = 128.5°$ $d = 51.5°$ $e = 128.5°$
c $a = 11°$ $b = 11°$ $c = 169°$ $d = 11°$

2 a 73°, 73° and 34°   **b** isosceles
c i 146° and 34°   **ii** 73° and 107°
f i 90°   **ii** 73°   **iii** 73°   **iv** 17°   **v** 17°

4 $a = 73°$ $b = 46°$ $c = 92°$ $d = 120°$ $e = 17°$
$f = 72°$ $g = 198°$ $h = 275°$ $i = 120°$ $j = 60°$
$k = 60°$ $l = 60°$ $m = 36°$

IN FOCUS 4

1

Line	Gradient
A	4
B	$\frac{3}{2}$
C	⁻2
D	1

3 a $y = 2x + 1$

x	⁻1	0	1	2	3	4
y	⁻1	1	3	5	7	9

$y = 3x - 2$

x	⁻1	0	1	2	3	4
y	⁻5	⁻2	1	4	7	10

$y = x - 2$

x	⁻1	0	1	2	3	4
y	⁻3	⁻2	⁻1	0	1	2

$y = 2x - 3$

x	⁻1	0	1	2	3	4
y	⁻5	⁻3	⁻1	1	3	5

$y = x + 2$

x	⁻1	0	1	2	3	4
y	1	2	3	4	5	6

$y = x$

x	⁻1	0	1	2	3	4
y	⁻1	0	1	2	3	4

b $y = 2x + 1$ (⁻1, ⁻1), (0, 1), (1, 3), (2, 5), (3, 7), (4, 9)
$y = 3x - 2$ (⁻1, ⁻5), (0, ⁻2), (1, 1), (2, 4), (3, 7), (4, 10)
$y = x - 2$ (⁻1, ⁻3), (0, ⁻2), (1, ⁻1), (2, 0), (3, 1), (4, 2)
$y = 2x - 3$ (⁻1, ⁻5), (0, ⁻3), (1, ⁻1), (2, 1), (3, 3), (4, 5)
$y = x + 2$ (⁻1, 1), (0, 2), (1, 3), (2, 4), (3, 5), (4, 6)
$y = x$ (⁻1, ⁻1), (0, 0), (1, 1), (2, 2), (3, 3), (4, 4)

4

Line	Gradient	y-intercept
a	4	⁻3
b	2	1
c	⁻3	2
d	1	0
e	⁻1	0
f	5	2
g	⁻2	⁻1
h	1	1
i	1.5	2
j	1	0.5
k	⁻0.5	3
l	0	1
m	$\frac{1}{2}$	0
n	$\frac{3}{4}$	⁻1
o	1	⁻$\frac{3}{5}$
p	⁻1	1.6
q	1	1.2
r	⁻3	0

5

Line	Equation
A	$y = 2x - 8$
B	$y = 3x + 4$
C	$y = \frac{3}{4}x - 1$
D	$y = 3 - 5x$
E	$y = ⁻7x$

6 a $y = 2x - 4$ **b** $y = 2x + 3$ **c** $y = 2x - 3$
d $y = \frac{1}{2} + 2x$ **e** $y = \frac{2}{3}x + 2$ **f** $y = \frac{5}{2}x + \frac{7}{2}$
g $y = \frac{3}{4}x + \frac{1}{4}$ **h** $y = 2x - 1$ **i** $y = \frac{6}{5}x + \frac{2}{5}$
j $y = \frac{1}{4} + \frac{1}{4}x$ **k** $y = \frac{1}{2}x$ **l** $y = \frac{⁻2}{3}x$

m $y = \frac{1}{2} + \frac{3}{4}x$ **n** $y = \frac{5}{2} - \frac{3}{2}x$
o $y = \frac{1}{3} - \frac{2}{3}x$ **p** $1 - x = y$

10

Line	Equation
A	$y = \frac{4}{3}x + 1$
B	$y = 3x - 2$
C	$y = \frac{1}{2}x + 2$
D	$y = \frac{2}{3}x$
E	$y = \frac{1}{2}x - 1$
F	$y = ⁻2$

11 Lines **a**, **b**, **c**, **d**, **e**, **f**, and **g**

IN FOCUS 5

1 Children In Care   Child Safety
Total spent £30m   Total percentage 100%
360° ÷ 30 = 12°   360° ÷ 100 = 3.6°
222°, 84°, 36°, 18°   234°, 72°, 36°, 18°

2 Chris   6 7 7 7 7 8 8 9 10 10 10 10
8
Dani   3 3 4 6 6 6 7 7 7 7 8 8 9 9 9
7
Sam   1 1 1 1 2 2 2 3 5 5 5 6 6 6 6 6
4

3 Bella   3 7 14 20 31 37 43
6
Emily   12 31 48 57 64
7
Gavin   4 6 11 18 26 37 46 52
7.5

4 Bella   5.4 (to 1 dp)
Emily   6.9 (to 1 dp)
Gavin   7.2 (to 1 dp)

5 Asif: mode 8, range 6
Suki: mode 5, range 4
Asif's scores are higher on average, but Suki is more consistent.

6 Kurt: median 5, range 6
Jean: median 7, range 5
Jean's scores are higher on average, and she is also more consistent.

7 Sally   mean 5.9 (to 1 dp) range 7
Gavin   mean 6.4 (to 1 dp) range 7
Gavin's scores are higher on average, and they are equally consistent.

8 Peggy   **a** 5, 7   **b** 2
Toby   **a** 4, 7   **b** 7
Sue   **a** 4.5, 8   **b** 3.5

9 P   **a** 36   **b** 35, 38
Q   **a** 38   **b** 35.5, 39
R   **a** 38.5   **b** 37, 40

IN FOCUS 6

1 KLMN   39.4 cm²   BCDE   96.4 cm²   EFGH   12.6 cm²
RSTU   77.2 cm²   DEFG   109.6 cm²

2 a 3000 mm²   **b** 168 735 mm²   **c** 147 515 mm²   **3** 10.2 cm

4 a perimeter 20.4 cm   area 33.2 cm²
b perimeter 30.2 cm   area 72.4 cm²
c perimeter 31.9 cm   area 60.4 cm²

5 82.5 cm²

6 a right-angled triangle   semicircle   parallelogram
b 111.4 cm²   **c** 35.8 cm

7 a 108 mm   **b** 10 800 mm²   **c** 462   **d** 5 260 400 mm²

IN FOCUS 7

1 a 6k   .   **b** 6l + m   **c** 5n − 7p   **d** 4q + 6r   **e** s
f 9 + 5u + 7v   **g** 6w + 2x   **h** 11 − 3y   **i** 5z + 2

2 a,b

31	18	35
32	28	24
21	41	25

c No: it is not a magic square.

d

Across	$12g$	$12g$	$12g + h$
Down	$12g$	$12g + h$	$12g$
Diagonals	$12g$	$12g$	

e Change $5g + 2h$ to $5g + h$

3 a $x = 5$ **b** $x = 4.5$ **c** $x = 3.8$ **d** $x = ^-2$ **e** $x = 4$
f $x = 3$ **g** $x = 2$ **h** $x = 1.5$ **i** $x = 3.5$ **j** $x = ^-1$
k $x = 6$ **l** $x = 5$ **m** $x = ^-2.5$ **n** $x = 9$ **o** $x = ^-1$
p $x = 2$

4 a A 56 cm   B 54 cm
    C 106 cm   D 56 cm
b A $8p$ B $6p + 12$
    C $16p - 6$ D $8p$
c $p = 3$ **d** $p = 2.5$ **e** $p = 1.5$
f $p = 6$ **g** $p = 0.75$ **h** $p = 1.8$

5 A $2n - 3 = 12 - n$ $n = 5$
    B $2(n + 1) = 3(n - 5)$ $n = 17$

6 b A $x = 7$ $y = 1$ B $x = 1.5$ $y = 3$
    C $x = ^-2$ $y = 5$ D $x = 2.8$ $y = 6.8$

7 A $x = 1.5$ $y = 3$ B $x = 12$ $y = 1$ C $x = 10$ $y = ^-2$
    D $x = ^-1$ $y = 2.5$ E $x = 2$ $y = 12$ F $x = 4.5$ $y = 2$
    G $x = 5$ $y = ^-1$ H $x = 1$ $y = 1$ I $x = 3$ $y = 2.5$
    J $x = 1$ $y = ^-5$

In Focus 8

1 a 5.67 **b** 12.7 **c** 2140 **d** 534.69 **e** 35
f 3000 **g** 13 468.28 **h** 0.07 **i** 60 **j** 60.0
k 9000 **l** 68 **m** 56.290

2 a 56.8 **b** 16 400 **c** 2.5 **d** 50 **e** 15.78
f 730 000 **g** 90 **h** 93 748 000 **i** 564.2 **j** 200
k 6.8 **l** 15.68 **m** 673 500 **n** 0.036
o 0.0280 **p** 3.00

3 a 40 000 **b** 200 **c** 54 000 **d** 250 000 **e** 350
f 7.5 **g** 120 000 **h** 120 **i** 5000 **j** 150
k 350 **l** 3500 **m** 350

4 a 1200, 1216.9 **b** 20 000, 18 218.8 **c** 2000, 2381.721
d 1000, 1172.232 **e** 40 000, 32 421.57 **f** 0.15, 0.1863
g 120, 110.88 **h** 1200, 965.0772

5 a 12 000 m², 9933.1848 m² **b** 200 m², 149.2428 m²
c 2 100 000 m², 1 926 635.429 m²

In Focus 9

1 a $\frac{1}{6}$ **b** $\frac{1}{2}$ **c** $\frac{1}{3}$ **d** $\frac{1}{2}$

2 a $\frac{2}{5}$ **b** $\frac{3}{10}$ **c** $\frac{1}{2}$ **d** $\frac{1}{10}$ **e** $\frac{9}{10}$ **f** 0 **g** $\frac{7}{10}$

3 One possible answer is the probability of B or D.

5 a $\frac{11}{32}$ **b** $\frac{1}{8}$ **c** $\frac{1}{8}$ **d** $\frac{1}{32}$ **e** $\frac{1}{16}$ **f** $\frac{1}{4}$ **g** $\frac{5}{16}$ **h** $\frac{7}{16}$
i $\frac{9}{16}$ **j** $\frac{7}{32}$ **k** $\frac{1}{8}$ **l** $\frac{7}{8}$

7 a $\frac{1}{8}$ **b** $\frac{3}{4}$ **c** $\frac{1}{2}$ **d** $\frac{1}{8}$ **e** $\frac{1}{4}$ **f** 0

8 a $\frac{7}{15}$ **b** $\frac{1}{30}$ **c** $\frac{2}{15}$ **d** $\frac{7}{30}$ **e** $\frac{1}{15}$ **f** $\frac{1}{15}$

9 a 24 arrangements **b** $\frac{1}{4}$ **c** $\frac{1}{6}$ **d** $\frac{1}{2}$ **e** $\frac{1}{2}$

10 a PQ, PR, PS, PT, QR, QS, QT, RS, RT, ST
b i $\frac{1}{5}$ **ii** $\frac{3}{5}$ **iii** $\frac{1}{10}$

In Focus 10

1 a any expression equivalent to $8p + 20$ **b** 71.2 cm² **c** 4.25 cm

2 a $3.8 + 2b$ **b** any expression equivalent to $2a + 4b + 17.4$
c 37.4 metres

3 A and D ($2(2a + 4)$ and $4(a + 2)$) B and I ($4a + 4$ and $4(a + 1)$)
C and H ($2a + 6$ and $2(a + 3)$)

4 a $3a + 18$ **b** $30 + 5z$ **c** $3n - 12$ **d** $6n + 12$
e $x^2 + 2x$ **f** $4p^2 - 12p$ **g** $9b + 3b^2$ **h** $2a^2 - 8a$
i $12p^2 - 16p$

5 a $w + 8$ **b** $4w + 16$ **c** 14 **6** 300 cm²

7 a $48pq$ **b** $9y^2$ **c** m^2n^2 or $(mn)^2$ **d** $4p^2q$
e $8m^2n$ **f** $18a^2b$ **g** a^3g^3 **h** $20p^3$ **i** $28a^3b$

8 a $24a - 18b$ **b** $np - p^2$ **c** $s^2 + st$
d $6mn - 6m^2$ **e** $5x^2 + 5xy$ **f** $4u^2 + 3u$
g $5pq + 3pr$ **h** $12mn + 21n^2$ **i** $27ab + 9a^2$

9 D $16a^2b + 11a^2 + 25ab$

10 a $7m + 2n$ **b** $21a^2 - a$ **c** $2b$
d $8x - 2y + 2xy$ **e** $4p + 3q$ **f** $8p^2 + 2pq + 5q^2$
g $4m^2 - 6n + 2mn$ **h** $2x - 2xy$

11 a $56a - 5b$ **b** $19x + 13y$ **c** $16x^2 + 4x$ **d** $30x^2 + 13xy$

12 A: $2c + 3$ B: $3 + 4b$

13 a $p(7 + 3q)$ **b** $m(1 + 3n)$ **c** $4q(2p + 1)$
d $3y(1 - 4x)$ **e** $2b(b + 5)$ **f** $6b(3a + 4c)$
g $xy(x - 2)$ **h** $3ab(3a + 2b)$ **i** $3mn(4m - 3)$

In Focus 11

5 c The tent is outside the field and across a main road.

In Focus 12

1

Red	Yellow	Total
120 ml	360 ml	480 ml
450 ml	1050 ml	1500 ml
200 ml	360 ml	560 ml
75 ml	175 ml	250 ml
600 ml	1080 ml	1680 ml
170 ml	510 ml	680 ml
645 ml	1505 ml	2150 ml
275 ml	495 ml	770 ml
240 ml	720 ml	960 ml
360 ml	840 ml	1200 ml
215 ml	645 ml	860 ml
250 ml	450 ml	700 ml
320 ml	960 ml	1280 ml
267 ml	623 ml	890 ml
375 ml	675 ml	1050 ml

2 a £24 : £60 **b** £155 : £93 **c** 135 g : 60 g
d £40 : £20 : £60 **e** 75 g : 100 g : 25 g **f** 80 ml : 120 ml : 160 ml
g 120 g : 180 g : 120 g **h** £55 : £55 : £385 **i** 36 cm : 45 cm : 18 cm
j 125 cm : 50 cm : 25 cm **k** 200 g : 400 g : 800 g
l 3 mm : 18 mm : 6 mm

3

	Icing sugar	Margarine	Plain chocolate	Flour
a	90 g	405 g	180 g	405 g
b	20 g	90 g	40 g	95 g

4

	P	Q	R
a	1:2	2:3	2:1
b	$\frac{1}{2}$	$\frac{2}{3}$	$\frac{2}{1}$
c	0.5	0.$\dot{6}$	2
d	50%	66.$\dot{6}$%	200%

5 A $\frac{2}{7}$ B $\frac{3}{4}$ C $\frac{4}{7}$ D $\frac{1}{4}$ E $\frac{3}{8}$

6 a 1.4 **b** 7.7 cm **7 a** 0.75 **b** 5.7 cm

8 EFGH and IJKL

9 a All corresponding angles are equal.
b YZ **c** 3.24 cm **d** 5.9 cm

In Focus 13

1 a 5.2 metres **b** 13 metres **c** 24.18 metres **d** 156 metres
e 566.8 metres

2 604 mph **3** about 44 seconds **4** 0.7 m/s

5 a 2.15 m/s **b** 2000 m/s **c** 0.12 m/s **d** 5.56 m/s

6 a 120 km/h **b** 40 km/h **c** 65.1 km/h **d** 21.6 km/h

7 a 1 mile/min **b** 0.5 miles/min **c** 1.5 miles/min
   d 0.75 miles/min **e** 0.42 miles/min **f** 0.7 miles/min

8 a 36 mph **b** 72 mph **c** 27 mph **d** 360 mph

9 3200 km

10 a 76.5 miles **b** 38.25 miles **c** 17 miles
   d 46.75 miles **e** 123.25 miles **f** 191.25 miles

11 a 30 min **b** 2 hours **c** 48 min
   d 6 hours 40 min **e** 1 hour 5 min **f** 1 hour 13min
   g 1 hour 12 min **h** 24 min

12 blue line

13 a 45 km/h **b** 38.33 km/h **c** 48 mph **d** 85.71 km/h
   e 52.5 mph **f** 83.33 km/h **g** 53.33 mph **h** 30 km/h

14 b midday **15 b** 6:15 pm **c** 66.67 mph **d** 60 mph

IN FOCUS 14

1 a 56° **b** 68° **c** 61° **d** 47° **e** 13° **f** 51°

2 a 61° **b** 37° **c** 68° **d** 13° **e** 45° **f** 34°

3 $a = 4.7$ cm, $b = 10.5$ cm, $c = 5.1$ cm, $d = 16.0$ cm, $e = 1.6$ cm,
   $f = 7.4$ cm, $g = 1.6$ cm

4 a i 64.3° **ii** 61.2° **iii** 32.1°
   b i 38.6° **ii** 35.0°
   c i 2.93 cm **ii** 145 cm **iii** 2.49 cm
   d i 21.0 cm **ii** 4.95 cm

5 A: 27.30°, B: 30.47°, C: 25.62° **6 a** 189 mm **b** 433 mm

IN FOCUS 15

1 a 6 spoons of tea **b** $p = t - 1$ **c** $p = 2$

2 a $x = \dfrac{P}{4}$ **b** 10.25 cm

3 a 270 min (4h 30min) **b** $W = \dfrac{T - 20}{20}$ **c** 5 pounds

4 a 8.75 pints **b** $l = \dfrac{4p}{7}$ **c** 4.86 litres

5 a $w = \dfrac{A}{l}$ **b** 6.2 cm **6 a** $w = \dfrac{p - 21}{2}$ **b** 4.2 cm

7 a $k = \dfrac{V + 25}{4}$ **b** $k = \dfrac{y + 3}{3}$ **c** $k = 7j$ **d** $k = \dfrac{4w}{3}$

   e $k = 5 - 2v$ **f** $k = 7 + b$ **g** $k = \dfrac{5(d - 1)}{2}$ **h** $k = 8h - 3$

   i $k = p - w$ **j** $k = \dfrac{20 - q}{5}$ **k** $k = 3(13 - v)$ **l** $k = \dfrac{v - s}{t}$

   m $k = bh - a$ **n** $k = \dfrac{h}{2g}$ **o** $k = \dfrac{3 - 2y}{5}$ **p** $k = \dfrac{9 + 2h}{3}$

8 a $p = \sqrt{A}$ **b** $p = \sqrt{\dfrac{v}{5}}$ **c** $p = \sqrt{g - 1}$ **d** $p = \sqrt{\dfrac{q + 5}{3}}$

   e $p = \sqrt{4j}$ **f** $p = \sqrt{\dfrac{3F}{2}}$ **g** $p = \sqrt{2 - z}$ **h** $p = \sqrt{\dfrac{K}{2\pi}}$

   i $p = \sqrt{\dfrac{5A - 1}{2}}$ **j** $p = \sqrt{\dfrac{7H + 8}{3}}$

9

	A	B	C	D
a	80	45	85	28
b	35	12	22	4
c	19.25	2.25	4	‾1.25

10 a 35 **b** 16 **c** 7 **d** 38 **e** 225
   f 11 **g** 1.1 **h** 0.7

11 a $n^2 + 7n + 10$ **b** $f^2 + 11f + 10$ **c** $w^2 + 8w + 12$
   d $2n^2 + 7n + 3$ **e** $4d^2 + 19d + 21$ **f** $4y^2 + 28y + 45$
   g $x^2 + 3x - 18$ **h** $v^2 + v - 6$ **i** $b^2 - 2b - 15$
   j $m^2 - 8m + 7$ **k** $h^2 - 6h + 5$ **l** $t^2 - 10t + 21$
   m $6p^2 + p - 1$ **n** $15x^2 + 8x - 12$ **o** $12y^2 - 24y - 15$
   p $12g^2 - 43g + 35$

12 a $(x + 3)(x + 4)$ **b** $(x + 2)(x + 6)$ **c** $(x + 6)(x + 1)$
   d $(x + 3)(x + 2)$ **e** $(x + 12)(x + 1)$ **f** $(x + 2)(x + 4)$

13 a $(x + 11)(x + 1)$ **b** $(x + 3)(x + 5)$ **c** $(x + 2)(x + 2)$ or $(x + 2)^2$
   d $(x + 5)(x + 4)$ **e** $(x - 1)(x + 4)$ **f** $(x + 5)(x - 3)$
   g $(x + 6)(x - 2)$ **h** $(x - 3)(x + 2)$ **i** $(x - 10)(x - 1)$
   j $(x + 2)(x - 4)$ **k** $(x - 1)(x - 2)$ **l** $(x - 2)(x - 2)$ or $(x - 2)^2$

IN FOCUS 16

2 a 0.160– **b** 0.170– **4 a** 0.07 s **b** 0.06 s

5 a 0.163 s (to 3sf) **b** 0.165 s (to 3 sf)

6 The totals are just as useful as the means for comparison because the total frequencies are the same.

8 a 3 times **b** 2 times **9 a** 7 times (24 – 17) **b** 9 times (24 – 15)

10 a about 0.164 s **b** about 0.170 s

11 a about 0.027 s (0.177 – 0.150) **b** about 0.024 s (0.179 – 0.155)

12 The results were very similar for men and for women. On average, the men's reaction times were slightly quicker than the women's. The times for the women were slightly less spread out than for the men.

14 The frequency polygons would not give a good comparison because the numbers of track athletes and field athletes are nowhere near the same.

15 a 27.1 years (to 3 sf) **b** 28.3 years (to 3 sf)

16

	Men's 20 km	Men's 50 km	Women's 10 km
b	20 min	40 min	7 min
c	86.2 min	239 min	45.1 min
e	85.5 min	238 min	45.4 min
f	5.1 min	16.5 min	2.5 min
	(88.0 – 82.9)	(247 – 230.5)	(46.2 – 43.7)

17 a about 29 **b** about 44 **c** about 18 (52 – 34) **d** about 31 (52 – 21)

18 a about 3 **b** about 11 **c** about 15 (38 – 23) **d** about 7 (38 – 31)

IN FOCUS 17

1 a 63.33% **b** 25.45% **c** 283.33% **d** 62% **e** 4.67%
   f 31.25% **g** 83.67% **h** 15.21% **i** 16.62% **j** 1.04%

2 a 29.5 kg **b** 2310 km **c** 3702.4 miles **d** 1822.5 yards
   e £27 183.70 **f** 145 062.5 tonnes **g** 1.05 cm **h** 47.25 mm
   i £38.51 **j** 419.75 ml

3 a 426.8 ml **b** £36.60 **c** 22.75 mm **d** 0.74 cm
   e 3968.75 tonnes **f** £10 523.04 **g** 1267.2 yards
   h 2500.08 miles **i** 2322 km **j** 24.96 kg

4 *With VAT at a standard rate of 17.5%*
   a £218.37 **b** £13.74 **c** £52.71 **d** £25.56 **e** £315.55
   f £187.99 **g** £159.01 **h** £10.86 **i** £58.74 **j** £1761.33

5 £155.10

6 a Pricebusters **b** cheaper by 25p (*both if VAT at 17.5%*)

7 a £405 **b** £4216 **c** £20.40 **d** £23.40 **e** £810
   f £2300 **g** £3.75 **h** £40.50 **i** £91.60 **j** £94.50

8 a £95.51 **b** £582.54 **c** £38.91 **d** £13.18 **e** £7011.20
   f £4 **g** £578.67 **h** £1355.71 **i** £32.46 **j** £70.58

9 *With VAT at a standard rate of 17.5%*
   a £255.31 **b** £11.06 **c** £38.29 **d** £8.50 **e** £63.83
   f £76.55 **g** £22.97 **h** £110.63 **i** £16.16 **j** £119.14

10 a £100.53 **b** £15.08 **11** £3157 895.

IN FOCUS 18

3 b i rotation of ⁺90° about (1, 1). **ii** reflection in $x = 5$
   c i C **ii** F **iii** E **d** rotation of 180° about (4, ‾1).

4 b F and G are in a different orientation and position.
   c i rotation of 180° about (4, 0) **ii** rotation of ‾90° about (3, 0)
   iii translation of $\begin{pmatrix} 2 \\ 2 \end{pmatrix}$

   d rotation of 180° about (1, 0)

5 b i rotation of 180° about (‾0.5, 1.5) **ii** translation $\begin{pmatrix} ‾14 \\ 0 \end{pmatrix}$

IN FOCUS 19

1 a 0.08 **b** 0.78 **c** 0.03 **d** 0.11

2 It is certain that the peg will rest in one of these positions.

3 a 0.92 **b** 0.18 **c** 0.11

4 Each face is not equally likely.

5 a about 12 times **b** about 118 times **c** about 5 times

6 b Do a greater number of trials. **7 b** 0.08 **c** 0.48 **d** 0.52

8 a relative frequency **b** theoretical
c could be either – probably theoretical **d** theoretical
e relative frequency **f** theoretical **g** theoretical
h relative frequency

9 a 0.19 **b** It can't land on 7 and 15 at the same time.

10 The two sets overlap. **11 a** 0.28 **b** 0.82 **c** 0.18 **d** 0.40

12 0.67

IN FOCUS 20

1 a > **b** < **c** > **d** < **e** < **f** >

2 4, 71, $^-$3.2, $^-$0.33

3 a 8, 7, 6, 5, 4 **b** $^-$3, $^-$2, $^-$1 **c** $^-$5, $^-$4, $^-$3, $^-$2, $^-$1, 0
d $^-$4, $^-$5, $^-$6 **e** no values **f** 24 only **g** $^-$14, $^-$15
h 5, 4, 3, 2, 1

4 Any two from $^-$1 ≤ h < 2, $^-$2 < h ≤ 1, $^-$1 ≤ h ≤ 1, 2 > h > $^-$2,
2 > h ≥ $^-$1, 1 ≥ h > $^-$2, 1 ≥ h ≥ $^-$1

5 A person's weight can be a non-integer number of stones but the number of waiters must be integer.

7 a $x \geqslant 9$ **b** $t < ^-7$ **c** $p \leqslant 10.5$ **d** $^-11 \leqslant k \leqslant 11$
e $w < 2$ **f** $q > 9.3$ **g** $t \geqslant 8$ **h** $h \leqslant 2$ **i** $f < 3$
j $^-9 < c < 9$ **k** $g \geqslant 4.5$ **l** $x > ^-3$ **m** $j < 19$ **n** $d \geqslant ^-2$
o $v < 4.5$ **p** $x \leqslant ^-13$ **q** $s < 0$ **r** $u \leqslant ^-3$

8 a 0 **b** 16 **11** $x < 2$ and $x + y < 7$ (or $y < 7 - x$)

IN FOCUS 21

1 A: 2 B: 5 **3 a** 3 **b** 9 **4 b** 48 cm³ **c** 88 cm²

5 X: 78.6 cm³ Y: 18.4 cm³ **6** $a = 19.8$ $b = 59.0$

7

	a	b
R	3927.8 ml	3.9 litres
S	1247.7 ml	1.2 litres
T	219.9 ml	0.2 litres
U	1231 504.3 ml	1231.5 litres

8 a length **b** area **c** area **d** volume
e length **f** area **g** none **h** volume
i length **j** area **k** none **l** volume
m area **n** volume **o** area **p** length

IN FOCUS 22

1 a $c = ^-3$ or $c = ^-2$ **b** $g = ^-5$ or $g = 4$ **c** $h = 8$ or $h = ^-2$
d $t = ^-9$ or $t = 6$ **e** $p = 9$ or $p = ^-5$ **f** $k = ^-8$ or $k = 5$
g $x = 5$ or $x = 2$ **h** $v = ^-12$ or $v = 3$ **i** $d = ^-5$ or d $^-3$
j $h = 6$ or $h = 3$ **k** $n = ^-12$ or $n = 6$ **l** $y = 10$ or $y = ^-3$
m $a = ^-9$ or $a = 4$ **n** $x = ^-12$ or $x = 4$ **o** $u = 9$ or $u = 3$
p $c = ^-11$ or $c = ^-7$ **q** $g = 9$ or $g = ^-8$ **r** $y = ^-7$ or $y = 6$
s $k = ^-7$ or $k = 8$ **t** $x = 12$ or $x = ^-5$

2 a $k = 1$ or $k = ^-5$ **b** $h = 3$ or $h = ^-1$ **c** $w = 2$ or $w = ^-5$
d $p = 1$ or $p = ^-5$ **e** $d = 2$ or $d = ^-2$ **f** $a = 2$ or $a = ^-3$
g $x = 3$ or $x = ^-1$ **h** $y = 1$ or $y = ^-2$ **i** $d = 5$ or $d = ^-1$
j $x = 2$ or $x = ^-4$ **k** $x = 1$ or $x = ^-1$ **l** $v = 1$

6 c $x = 2$ or $x = ^-4$ **7 b** $x = 3$ or $x = ^-6$ **8 b** $x = 5$ or $x = 1$

9 b $x = 3$ or $^-7$ **d** $x = 2.5$ or $x = ^-6.5$ **e ii** $x = 3.4$ or $^-7.4$

14 $x = ^-0.4$ or $x = 2.4$ **17** $x = 1.82$

IN FOCUS 23

1 a Question 1 is not clear; different people are likely to have different ideas of what is meant by 'often'.
Question 2 is leading; it leads people into giving the answer 'Yes'.
Question 3 is ambiguous; it could refer to the *number* of buses on the roads, or the *comfort* of buses, etc.

7 d moderate positive correlation: i.e., the larger the size of engine, the higher the price

8 a about £7200 **b** about £4900

9 a about 320 cc **b** about 690 cc

10 a about £8500 **b** about 1220 cc

11 The vertical axis does not start at 0, which gives the impression that the growth rate in year 4 is about 7 times the rate in year 1.

12 The number of videos sold in 1997 is 1.5 times the number sold in 1996, but the diagram gives the impression it is much more than this because the height *and* the width of the 1996 video have been increased 1.5 times.

IN FOCUS 24

1 $a = 3.04$ cm $b = 30.1°$ $c = 5.73$ cm $d = 6.07$ cm

2 A 2.04 cm² 6.51 cm B 12.30 cm² 14.52 cm

3 a i 4.20 m **ii** 6.02 m **b** 19.32°

4 a i 5 km **ii** 2 km **b i** 5.39 km **ii** 21.80°
c i 248° **ii** 068°
d 4.24 km **e i** 135° **ii** 315° **f** 8.06 km

5 a 1.1 m **b** 34.7°

EXAM-STYLE QUESTIONS

N1.1 $73\frac{1}{3}$ feet per second

N1.2 a 27.06 litres per second (2 dp)
b 1623 litres per minute (nearest litre)

N1.3 a $658 **b i** New York camera

N1.4 a 112 kph **b** 68.75 mph

N1.5 a 59.52p **b** 3.69 gallons (2 dp) **c** 8p (nearest penny)
d 34 miles per gallon

N1.6 1080 mm **N1.7 a** 23.75 FF **b** £1.25

N2.1 a 75 ml **b** 152.5 ml

N2.2 a i $27\frac{5}{10}$ of an inch **ii** $26\frac{5}{10}$ of an inch
b i 699 mm **ii** 673 mm (to nearest mm)

N2.4 a i 160.5 km **ii** 159.5 km **b** 200 km (to 1 sf) **c** 125 miles

N2.5 12.300 °C

N3.1 a 1, 2, 3, 4, 6, 12 **b i** 2, 3 **ii** $2^2 \times 3$ **c** 288, 300, 432, 612
d 9 **e** 144

N3.2 a 2, 3, 5, 7, 11, 13, 17, 19 **b** prime numbers **c** 6, 8, 10, 14, 15

N3.3 a 36 **b** 1, 2, 3, 4, 6, 9, 12, 18, 36 **c** $2^2 \times 3^2$
d $4500 \div 36 = 125$

N3.4 b i No **ii** 2 is an even prime number

N3.5 a i 6 **ii** 216 **b i** yes **ii** $\sqrt{729} = 27$ **iii** 27
c 7.29×10^2

N3.6 a 25, 45, 35, 4, 37, 18, 8 **b** 1, 2, 4, 8 **c** 37
d i 164 **ii** 1.64×10^2

N4.1 a i Claire **ii** Rob **b** 25 **c** 6 words

N4.2 a 0.375 **b** smaller **c** 0.085, $\frac{1}{5}$, $\frac{3}{8}$, $\frac{1}{2}$, 0.6 **d** 0.85

N4.3 a i $\frac{150}{1000}$ **ii** $\frac{3}{20}$ **b** 170 **c** 660

N4.4 a Malaga 918, Orlando 408, Corfu 612, Faro 204, Malta 306
b $\frac{1}{8}$ **c** Yes **d** Orlando

N4.5 a 25.5 hours **b** £98.18 **c** 1%

N4.6 75% **N4.7 a** $\frac{3}{4}$ inch **b** $\frac{13}{16}$ inch

N4.8 a £48 **b** $\frac{1}{16}$ **c** about 25% (27.08%) **d i** $\frac{5}{8}$ **ii** 62.5%

N4.9 £452.38 **N4.10** Spotlight

N4.11 a i 5% **ii** 3000 **b** 10 200 **c** £852 900

N4.12 a Tony is wrong **b** £6860.11

N4.13 **a** £581.51 **b** 5 **N4.14** **a** £408.70 **b** **i** 7 **iii** £239.47

N4.15 £155

N5.1 3.870×10^3 **N5.2** 5.9478×10^{21}

N5.3 5.76×10^7

N5.4 **a** 1.35×10^{-1} **b** 1.075×10^{-3} **c** $1.451\,25 \times 10^{-4}$
d 4.6225×10^{-6} **e** 6.965×10^{-2}

N5.5 4×10^{-2}

N5.6 **a** 3.57×10^{10} **b** 1.6525×10^8
c **i** 3.521×10^8 **ii** roughly $\frac{1}{2}$

N5.7 $2.18 \times 10^5 \, \text{km}^2$ **N5.8** $36\,000\,000$

N5.9 **a** $842\,000\,000$ **b** roughly 19% **N5.10** roughly £22 000 000

N6.1 **a** 3:5 **b** 375 grams **c** 60%

N6.2 **a** 140 ml
b olive oil 1250 ml, malt vinegar 500 ml,
raspberry wine vinegar 250 ml

N6.3 **a** 22.5 m **b** 6 cm **c** about 60 feet **N6.4** 4.2 cm

N6.5 **a** 25 g
b flour 9.6 kg, baking powder 480 grams, butter 4.8 kg,
caster sugar 480 g, sultanas 2.4 kg

N6.6 **a** £98.14 **b** £686.98 **c** $\frac{3}{5}$ **d** £412.19 **N7.1** 25 542

N7.2 **a** 7 **b** **i** £9 323 040 **ii** £9 320 000 **N7.3** 1107 miles

N7.4 **a** $(12 + (9 \div 3)) \times 2 = 30$ **b** $(12 + 9) \div 3 \times 2 = 14$
c $(12 + 9) \div (3 \times 2) = 3.5$

N7.5 3 640 000 **N7.6** $^-16\,°C$

N7.7 **a** 220 yards **b** 6380 yards **c** 5 miles and 5 furlongs
d **i** 30 chains **ii** 560 chains
e **i** 4500 yards is longer than 2.5 miles **ii** 100 yards

N7.8 **a** £240 **b** £52 000

N7.9 **a** $75\,000 \times 14 = 1\,050\,000$ **b** £20

N8.1 **a** 3 hours 24 minutes **b** 204 minutes

N8.2 **a** 165 minutes **b** 156 kph **N8.3** 21:47 hours

N8.4 **a** Ejaz **b** 120 metres **c** 60 metres **d** after about 35 s
e about 15 m **f** Ejaz **g** Ejaz

N8.5 **a** about 18:40 hrs **b** **i** 20 km **ii** about 13 km
c about 30 kph **e** about 10 minutes **f** yes

N8.6 **a** Yes **b** **i** 4.3 hours (1 dp) **ii** 4.25 hours

N8.7 **a** **i** 7:56 from Exeter **ii** 2 hours 6 minutes **b** $^-0620$ train
c 27 minutes **d** 92 miles per hour (to 2 sf)

N8.8 42.2 km (to 1 dp)

N9.1 **a** 18 minutes **b** 20 km per hour

N9.2 **a** **i** 1.6 mm **ii** 0.064 of an inch **b** **i** 4.788×10^7 litres
ii 1.05×10^7 gallons **c** 285 000 litres per hour

A1.1 **a** 96 **b** 7.4 **c** **i** $t = \dfrac{V - u}{f}$ **ii** 4.9

A1.2 **a** $C = £6.99n + £3.50$ **b** £38.45

A1.3 **a** 123 600 wheels **b** 3075 trolleys

A1.4 **a** 28 800 **b** $I = \dfrac{P}{R^2}$

A1.5 **a** 209 cm³ (to 3 sf) **b** **i** $r = \dfrac{\sqrt{3v}}{\pi h}$ **ii** 1.4 cm

A1.6 **a** 47 nails **b** **i** $3b + 2 = n$ **ii** 4454 nails are needed.

A1.7 £359.86

A2.1 **a** $x = 1\frac{2}{7}$ **b** $x = 8\frac{1}{7}$ **c** $x = 7$ **d** $y = 1$ **e** $a = 6$
f $c = ^-1.5$

A2.2 Sean's age $= n - 5$

A2.3 **a** members not injured $= \frac{3}{5} d$ **b** 45 members

A2.4 **a** $8n$ pence **b** **i** $n + 2$ **ii** $7(n + 2) = (7n + 14)$ pence
c $15k + 21 = 81$ pence or equivalent **d** **i** 4 mugs **ii** 7 plates

A2.5 **a** $n + 228$ **b** £6n **c** £6n + £3.50(n + 228) or equivalent
d £6n + £3.50 (n + 228) = £24 947.00 or equivalent
e **i** 2542 **ii** 2770

A2.6 **a** **i** $y = \dfrac{31 - 5x}{8}$ **ii** $x = ^-5$ **b** $p = 11$

A2.7 **a** $2k$ **b** $3k - 5$ **c** **i** $2k = 3k - 5$ **ii** $k = 5$

A2.8 **a** $j + j + 5 = 33$ **b** Liam is 19 and Neil is 14

A2.9 **a** $40 - w$ **b** $18 - 2w$ **c** 98 m **d** $98 - 4w$
e $196 - 4w$ **f** **i** $196 - 4w = 184$ **ii** 3 m

A2.10 **a** 18 rails **b** $2x - 2 = y$ (or equivalent) **c** $x = \frac{y}{2} + 1$
d 314 **e** 33

A2.11 **a** $x = 1.6, y = 0.2$ **b** $w = 2, t = 0.5$ **c** $a = 1, b = 1$
d $p = 3, t = ^-4$ **e** $a = 2, y = 1$ **f** $v = 20, w = 15$

A2.12 **a** $n - 4$
b 7 ten pound notes, 3 five pound notes, and 11 one pound coins.

A2.13 **a** 13, 17, 1, $^-2$ and 2, 6, 10, 12 **c** $x = 2.8, y = 6.4$

A2.14 **a** $^-4$, 0, 4, 8, 12 and 8, 6, 4, 2, 0 **b** **i** $2x - 4 = 8 - x$
iii $x = 4, y = 4$

A2.15 **a** total $= 57 + 4p$
b 57 in the first coach and 61 in each other one
c **i** $3y(3y - 4)$ **ii** $4a(a + 6)$ **iii** $25h (5 + 2h)$
d $p = 2.5, t = 1.5$

A3.1 2.9 or $^-6.9$ **A3.2** **a** $3 < w < 4$ **b** $w = 3.4$ (1 dp)

A3.3 **b** 5.4 or $^-3.4$ **A3.4** **b** $k = 66, m = 55$

A3.5 8.7 (to 1 dp) or $^-3.7$ (to 1 dp) **A3.6** $y = 4.2$ (to 1 dp)

A3.7 **a** $c = 5$ **c** $c = 2$ or $^-2$ or 0

A4.1 **c** gradient $= ^-2$ **d** 1, $^-1$, $^-3$ **A4.2** **b** $^-3$

A4.3 **b** $y = x + 5$ or equivalent
e standard, about $5\frac{1}{2}$ days; longlife, $10\frac{1}{2}$ days

A4.4 **c** $x = ^-1, y = 2$ **A4.5** **c** $x = 2, y = 2$

A4.6 **d** $x = ^-2, y = 1.5$ **A4.7** **c** $x = ^-1, y = 0$

A4.8 **b** about $x = 2.75$ and $y = 2.25$ **c** 1.5 **d** $x = ^-1.4$

A4.9 **a** about £27 **b** $\frac{1}{5}$ **d** $y = \dfrac{x}{5} + £18$ or equivalent
e 160 minutes (2 hours 40 minutes)

A4.10 **d** about 3.5 **e** about 3.75

A4.11 **d** about 1.75 and $^-1.75$ **A4.12** **f** about $^-0.9$ and 2.9

A4.13 **d** about 5 **e** about 3 and $^-3$ **A4.14** **c** about 2.3

A5.1 **a** 94 **c** $b + d \leqslant 150$ **d** 104 (46 previously sold)
e $0 \leqslant d \leqslant 104$

A5.2 **a** $^-4$, $^-3$, $^-2$, $^-1$, 0, 1, 2, 3, 4 **b** 0, 1 **c** 3

A5.3 **a** $x > 8$ **b** $x < 3$ **c** $x < 5.5$ **d** $^-14 < x < 14$
e $x < ^-2$ **f** $x < 7.7$ **g** $^-1 < x < 1$ **h** $x \leqslant 17$
i $2 < x \leqslant 9$

A5.5 **a** **i** $^-6$, $^-5$, $^-4$, $^-3$, $^-2$, $^-1$, 0 **ii** $^-216$ **b** $50 < s, s < 147$

A5.6 **a** $x \leqslant 2.25, x > 1$ **b** 2

A5.7 **a** $^-1, 0, 1, 2$ **b** 8, 9, 10 **c** 8, 9, 10, 11, 12, 13, 14, 15, 16, 17

A6.1 **a** $\frac{3}{8}$ **b** $2\frac{1}{4}$ **c** $1\frac{1}{4}$ **d** $\frac{5}{12}$ **e** 2

A6.2 **a** $10x^2 - 15x$ **b** $12x^2 + 4$ **c** $3xy - 6y$ **d** $a^3 - 2a^2 + 3a$

A6.3 **a** $x^2 + 5x + 6$ **b** $y^2 - y - 2$ **c** $4x^2 + 4x + 1$
d $10w^2 + 29w + 10$ **e** $c^2 - 4c + 4$ **f** $2x^2 + x - 6$

A6.4 **a** $\frac{8}{15}$ **b** 0.75 **A6.5** **a** 804.5 **b** $v - ft = u$
c **i** $\dfrac{v - u}{f} = t$ **ii** 0.125

A6.6 **a** **i** 400 **ii** 4 **b** $f = \dfrac{2s}{t^2}$ **c** $t = \dfrac{\sqrt{2s}}{f}$ **d** **i** ± 4 **ii** yes

A6.7 **a** $v(x + y)$ **b** $2(x - 2y)$ **c** $p(p + 1)$ **d** $t(3 - k + t)$
e $3ax(x - 2)$ **f** $h(h + t)$ **g** $ab(a - b)$ **h** $2a^2(3 + b)$

A6.8 **a** $a(a - 3)$ **b** $(t + 3)(t + 1)$ **c** $(m - 9)(m + 5)$
d $(p - 9)(p - 4)$ **e** $(h - 2)(h + 8)$ **f** $(x + 8)(x - 9)$
g $n(n + 21)$ **h** $(b - 1)(b + 16)$

A6.9 **a** $1\frac{3}{7}$ **b** $\frac{2}{3}$

A6.10 **a** $8w + 16$ **b** $4w^2 + 16w$ **c** $4w^2 + 16w + 16$ **d** $16\,\text{m}^2$

A7.1 **a** 31.4 km **A7.2** **b** It cannot be odd.
c either both even or both odd

A7.3 **a** 3, 3.7 3.7, 3.3 3.3, 3.5 3.5, 3.4 3.4, 3.4

A7.4 **a** 2.6, 45.69... 2.61, 46.40... 2.62, 47.12... 2.63, 7.84...
2.64, 48.57... 2.65, 49.31... 2.66, 50.0641
b $x = 2.66$ **c** 2.3

A8.1 **a** 15 **b** 100 **c i** $a = 2p - 1$ **ii** $a = 749$
d i $a = p^2$ **ii** 44 944

A8.2 **b** 37 slabs **c i** $n = 4d - 3$ **ii** 161

A8.3 **a** 13 **b** 25 **c i** $w = 4n + 1$ **ii** 177 matches

A8.4 **a i** 32, 64, 128 **b** No **c** nth term $= 2^{n-1}$
d 31, 63 **ii** $R = P - 1$ **e** $N = 2^{n-1} - 1$
f $7.136\,2385 \times 10^{44} - 1$

A8.5 **a** Raj, Ranjit, Iqubal **b** 300th customer

A8.6 **a** 0, 2, 6, 12, 20, **b** yes **A8.7** **b** $t = 2p + 3$

A9.1 **a** $(3w - 1)$ cm **b** $3w - 1 = 41$ **c** $w = 14$

A9.2 **a** j **b** $\frac{j}{2}$ **c** $\frac{k}{2}$ **d** $jk\,\text{cm}^2$ **e** $\frac{jk}{2}\,\text{cm}^2$ **f** $\frac{jk}{4}\,\text{cm}^2$

A9.3 **a i** $6\,\text{cm} + k\,\text{cm}$ **ii** $CE = \sqrt{m^2 + k^2}$ **b** $A = \frac{m(6 + k)}{2}$

A9.4 **b** $105.84\,\text{cm}^2$

A9.5 **a i** $4 \times 2d = 8d$ **ii** $3(3d - 1)$
b square side 6 cm and triangle side 8 cm

A9.6 **a ii** 280 **b** $n(a + b)$ **c ii** 160

A9.7 **b i** $n + 1$ **ii** $n - 1$

A9.8 **a** $3n + 4(n + 1) = 172$ or $3n + 4n + 4 = 172$ **b** 24 and 25
c 1 **d** 600 **e** 6×10^2

A9.9 **a** $y(a - b)$ **b** 8.991×10^2

A9.10 **a i** $2n + 3$ **ii** $n - 4$ **b** $2n^2 - 5n - 12$

A9.11 **a i** $2p + 5m = £26$ **ii** $4p + 3m = £31$ **b i** £5.50 **ii** £3

S1.1 **a** A equilateral triangle B square C pentagon
D hexagon E octagon F decagon
b A 180°, B 360°, C 540°, **c** D 120°, E 135°, F 144°
d **i** 7 **ii** 128.57° (2 dp)
f equilateral triangles, squares and hexagons

S1.2 **a** isosceles **b** 70° **c** 70°
d i trapezium **ii** rhombus **iii** trapezium
e i 1 **ii** 2 **iii** 1 **f i** hexagon **ii** no

S1.3 229°

S1.4 **a** $x = 40°$ and $y = 140°$ **b** They are equal. **c** 80°
d no **e i** 360° **ii** angle AGH = 40°

S1.5 **a i** 54° **ii** 36° **iii** 28° **S1.7** **b** 2 copies

S1.8 **a i** 67° **ii** 6° **iii** 67° **iv** 46° **v** 46° **vi** 134°
c no

S2.1 **a** 12.5 cm **b i** 14° **ii** 90° **c** 12.9 cm (to nearest mm)

S2.2 **a** 90° **b** ACP, ADP, AEP or AFP **c** 90° **d** yes

S2.3 **a** yes **b** 62° **c** 5 cm **d** 90° **S2.4** **b** 60°

S2.5 **a iii** diameter **b** intersect at the centre of the circle

S3.1 **a** (‾3,5) **b** (0,4) **c** (‾3,4) **S3.2** **b i** (3,0) **ii** (1,0)

S3.3 **a** A (‾2,0), B(1,3), C(4,0), D(1,‾3) or A(‾2,0), B(1,3), C (‾2,6), D (‾5,3)
b (1,0) or (‾2,3)
c D (‾0.5, 1.5), E (2.5, 1.5), F (2.5, ‾1.5), G (‾0.5, ‾1.5) or
D(‾0.5, 1.5), E (‾0.5, 4.5), F (‾3.5, 4.5), G (‾3.5, 1.5)
d area = 9 square units **e** (1,0) or (‾2,3)

S3.4 **a i** B(4, 5, 0) **ii** D(4, 0, 3) **b** (4, 2.5, 1.5) **c** (2, 2.5, 3)
d ii $60\,\text{cm}^3$

S3.5 **a** B is above A **b** 3 cm **S3.6** north-west

S3.7 east **S4.1** **a** 141 cm (to 3 sf) **b** 20 cm **c** 677 (to 3sf)

S4.2 **a** trapezium **b i** 4.33 cm **ii** $10.83\,\text{cm}^2$
c 9.8 cm (to 1dp) **d** $37.14\,\text{cm}^2$ **e** $21.71\,\text{cm}$

S4.3 **a** $50.27\,\text{mm}^2$ **b** $150.8\,\text{mm}^2$ **c i** 1562 discs **ii** $2644.6\,\text{cm}^2$

S4.4 **a** 61.28 m **b** $9192.53\,\text{m}^2$ **c** $1683\,\text{m}^2$

S4.5 **a** trapezium **b** $13\,300\,\text{mm}^2$

S4.6 **a** radius = 140 cm, length = 775 cm **b** $47\,700\,000\,\text{cm}^3$ (to 3 sf)
c 4.77×10^7 **d** 47 700 litres

S4.7 **a** $0.5775\,\text{m}^2$ **b** $1.47\,\text{m}^3$ **c** no **S4.9** $w = 25\,\text{mm}$

S4.10 **a** $512\,\text{cm}^3$ **b** $286\,\text{cm}^3$ (to 3 sf) **c** $327.5\,\text{cm}^2$
d $40\,000\,\text{cm}^3$ **e** 122 blocks

S4.11 **a** length **b** area **c** volume **d** area

S4.12 jk, $0.75\pi h^2$, $\frac{1}{2}\pi km$ **c** $\frac{1}{3}\pi m^2 l$

S4.14 **b** $A = \frac{1}{5}w(10h + 4s)$ **S4.15** **a** $\pi bh, \pi h(b + s)$ **b** πbhs

S5.6 **d i** 60° **ii** 2.08 cm (to 2 dp) **S5.8** **d** 62 km

S6.1 **a** 7912 **b** 782122 **c i** about 6 km
d i no **f** about 3.3 km

S6.2 **a** 2.3 km **b** 65 cm

S6.3 **b i** 135° **ii** 200° **iii** 020° **c i** about 5.4 km

S6.4 **b** about 150 m **S7.1** **a i** B **b** 8 **c** 12

S7.2 **b** 4 **c i** 3

S7.3 **a** rectangle **b** 5 **d** $6\,\text{cm}^2$ **e** $124\,\text{cm}^2$

S7.4 **a** square-based pyramid **b** equilateral triangle
c i 5 **ii** 5 **e** 5.39 cm (2 dp)

S7.5 **a** octahedron **b** 6 **c i** 8 **ii** triangles **d** 12

S8.1 **a** 6.28 cm **b** 9.76 cm **c** 39.44° **d** 30.7°

S8.2 **a** 10.554 cm **b** SRT = 77.7°, RTS = 12.3°

S8.3 **a** 72 cm
b DCBNJ, DCBFJ, DCPNJ, DCPKJ, DCGFJ, DCGKJ, DQLKJ,
DQPKJ, DQPNJ, DHLKJ, DHGKJ, DHGFJ
c 72 cm
d 56.9 cm (to 1 dp) **e** P (18, 18, 18)
f Q (18, 36, 18) **g** M (18, ‾18, 18)

S8.4 **a i** 11.003 541 **ii** 11° (to nearest degree)
b i 91 337.903 ft **ii** 91 350 ft
c 170 550 ft (or 32.301 136 miles)

S8.5 **a** 250 mm **b** 65.28° **c** 58 mm **d** 99 mm **e** 54°

S8.6 **a** 3330 ft. **b i** 7.2° **ii** 7°

S8.7 **a** 3.71 m **b** 1.97 m **c** 2.53 m **d** 3.35 m **e** 65°

S8.8 **a** 4.26 m **b** 4.43 m **c** 30°

S8.9 **a** 44.7 km **b** 54 km **c** more **S8.10** **a** 36.73 m (to 2 dp)

S8.11 **a** 16.15 m **b** 83°

S8.12 **a i** 90° **ii** 44° **b i** 382 m **ii** 396 m **S9.1** **c** 2

S9.2 **a** 4 **b** none **S9.3** **a ii** regular

S10.3 **a** $\begin{pmatrix} ‾40 \\ ‾15 \end{pmatrix}$ **c** $\begin{pmatrix} 30 \\ 20 \end{pmatrix}$ **d** $\begin{pmatrix} 30 \\ ‾20 \end{pmatrix}$

S10.4 **b** $7.5\,\text{cm}^2$ **c** The area increases by a factor of 4.
d $67.5\,\text{cm}^2$ **e** 3 times the original lengths

S10.5 **a** a reflection in the y-axis
b several answers including: a reflection in $x = 2$ and a
translation $\begin{pmatrix} ‾4 \\ 0 \end{pmatrix}$

S11.1 **a i** 186 m

S11.2 **a i** similar **b** similar **S11.3** RT = 7 cm

S11.4 **a** LKM and LJN , LKM and MHN
b 16 cm

S11.5 **a i** 34° **c** 10 cm **S11.6** **b** 90 cm **c** yes

S12.1 **a** 24 cm **b** 6 cm **c** 8 cm **d** 53.13°

S12.2 **a i** ... up **ii** ... down **b** isosceles **c** 72.5°
d 2.29 m **e** 72 cm **f** 84 cm **g** 3.62 m

S12.3 **d** BPA and CPD **e** 45 square units **f** 77.3°

D1.1 $\frac{1}{250}$

D1.2 **b** $\frac{1}{12}$ **c i** Yes: 7 is more likely. **ii** $P(7) = \frac{6}{36} = \frac{1}{6}$
d $\frac{5}{6}$ **e i** $\frac{1}{36}$ **ii** $\frac{1}{54}$ **iii** $\frac{1}{36}$

D1.3   **a**   **i** $\frac{1}{2}$ **ii** $\frac{1}{6}$ **iii** $\frac{1}{9}$ **b** $\frac{5}{36}$

D1.4   **a**   **i** 0.3   **ii** P(4) = 1 – P(sum of all of the other probabilities)
    b   **i** Spinners are biased in favour of 0, 1 and 4 and against 2 and 3.
    c   roughly 60 times
    d   No: you can only say how many times it is likely to show a score of three.

D1.5   **b** 0.3   **c** 0.175   **D1.6**   **a** 0.06   **b** 0.4   **c** 0.012

D2.1   **a** Set A Road Transport Federation,   Set B Canal Heritage Society, Set C People leaving a cinema

D2.3   From top left to bottom right the missing numbers are: 13, 2, 20, 2, 0, 1 and 0.

D2.4   No: the data does not support Lyn's view.

D3.1   **a** 230 students   **b** 755 students   **D3.3**   **b** 6883 teenagers

D3.4   **b** A matches Lime, B matches Vanilla, C matches Choc-Chip, D matches Strawberry, E matches Lemon.

D3.5   **a** No: the sales axis does not start from 0.
    b The scale of the *x*-axis is not uniform.

D4.1   **a** matches C, **b** matches B, **c** matches B, **d** matches C, **e** matches A **f** matches B

D4.2   **b** positive correlation

D4.3   **a** Petrol consumption (mpg) decreases as engine size increases.
    b negative correlation

D4.4   **a** It shows a likely link between student attainment in Mathematics and French.
    b positive correlation

D4.5   **b**   **i** no correlation   **ii** Fitness does not depend on height.

D5.1   **a** 26 °C   **b** 26 °C   **c** 9 °C   **d** 25.8° (1 dp)

D5.2   **a** 54 seconds   **b** 54 seconds
    c Group 1: it has the same median but a lower range.

D5.3   **a** 9 seeds   **b** 30 seeds
    c It depends which average is taken. Since the mean number of seeds is 30, it can be argued that it is true.
    f There is a greater than evens chance.

D5.4   **a** 11 to 15
    b

Number of CDs	Frequency	Mid-point	*fx*
1 to 5	3	3	9
6 to 10	8	8	64
11 to 15	12	13	156
16 to 20	10	18	180
21 to 25	6	23	138
26 to 30	1	28	28

    c   **i** 14.375 CDs   **ii** The data is only available in groups.
    d The 1990 mean is more likely to be accurate because a smaller class interval is used.

D5.5   **a** 31 to 40   **b** 34 minutes
    c   **i** The extreme values in the distribution distort the mean.
       ii The median might be a better average as the extreme values will be ignored.

D5.6   **a** £2.01–£3   **b** £2.94   **c** £2.01–£3

D6.1   **b**   **ii** about 88   **c** about 4.5
    d Alison: the interquartile range of her scores was smaller.

D6.2   **c** about 46   **d** about 200   **e** about 625
    f Mega Power has a smaller range and the median is higher; it therefore appears to be a better battery.

D6.3   **c** about 27.5
    d No: only about 30% of the people asked made more than 35 calls a week.

D7.1   **a** 3 days   **b** 129 kg   **c** 5 kg   **d** 4.3 kg   **e** $\frac{11}{15}$

D7.2   **a**   **i** 4   **ii** 2   **b** no   **c** about $\frac{2}{15}$

D7.3   **b** from 60 up to but not including 90 minutes
    c from 90 up to but not including 120 minutes
    e about 31 people   **g** $\frac{31}{42}$

D7.4   **a** 50 400   **b** 14 700   **c**   **i** yes